Walt Disney World®, Universal Studios and Orlando

> "When it comes to information on regional history, what to see and do, and shopping, these guides are exhaustive."
>
> —*USAir Magazine*

> "Usable, sophisticated restaurant coverage, with an emphasis on good value."
>
> —Andy Birsh, *Gourmet Magazine* columnist

> "Valuable because of their comprehensiveness."
>
> —*Minneapolis Star-Tribune*

> "Fodor's always delivers high quality...thoughtfully presented...thorough."
>
> —*Houston Post*

> "An excellent choice for those who want everything under one cover."
>
> —*Washington Post*

Fodor's Travel Publications, Inc.
New York • Toronto • London • Sydney • Auckland
http://www.fodors.com/

Fodor's Walt Disney World, Universal Studios and Orlando

Editor: Alison Stern

Contributors: Pam Acheson, Robert Andrews, Robert Blake, Marianne Camas, Catherine Fredman, Barbara Freitag, Andrew Holleran, Mary Meehan, Valerie Meyer, Dee Rivers, Heidi Sarna, Helayne Schiff, Linda K. Schmidt, Mary Ellen Schultz, Marshall Schwartzman, Lindy Shepherd, Dinah Spritzer, Rowland Stiteler

Creative Director: Fabrizio La Rocca

Cartographer: David Lindroth

Cover Photograph: Comstock, Inc.

Text Design: Between the Covers

Copyright

Special Sales

CONTENTS

Contents

Maps

ON THE ROAD WITH FODOR'S

MANY YEARS AGO, I wrote the *Official Guide to Walt Disney World*. After that, I was for many years the book's executive editor, and I followed the field of WDW books as it grew. And grew. And grew. But not until we at Fodor's produced the volume you now hold in your hands have I ever felt that there was a perfect guidebook to the most unusual of vacation kingdoms.

It's the best book for visiting with kids, for instance. If a ride routinely scares toddlers, we say so. I have two of my own, so I know how important that can be. But it's also a great guide for grown-ups on their own—that's how I traveled when I first visited Orlando. And it's also the book for people who can't stand waiting in line; I hate queuing up as much as you do, so we made sure to tell you how to avoid the crowds. I love what Disney does, and I've seen it at very close range and from behind the scenes. Yet we're not in Disney's pocket: The information in this guide originated with the authors and revisers and has not been authorized or endorsed by The Walt Disney Company or any of its affiliates. That way we can always say what we really think. We can also cover all of Orlando's many attractions with equal care, to help you decide how you want to spend your time.

Because this is a Fodor's guide, you'll find great writing. Our descriptions of the various theme-park rides don't merely recite historical facts or repeat what you read in a brochure. We also capture the magic of each attraction or ride, and we tell you enough about it so you can easily plan in advance what you want to see—and what you could miss.

About Our Writers

Our Orlando guidebook is a collaboration of a number of extraordinary writers.

Catherine Fredman's very first visit to Walt Disney World coincided with her 34th birthday, so, of course, she really got into the swing of the fireworks and laser shows. As part of that bang-up trip, she became a human projectile on Splash Mountain, memorized the lyrics of "It's a Small World," and outsmarted the hoardes in getting ol' big ears's autograph. She deftly manages to tickle every sentence's funny bone, a talent so irresistible it keeps her on the move across America for a variety of magazines. She picks up her mail and does her laundry in New York City.

A blizzard can keep some folks from their appointed rounds, but not Orlando-based **Marianne Camas,** especially when the action takes place at Blizzard Beach, Disney's newest water-park attraction. Marianne, now a pro at attaining flotation on the Summit Plummet ride, has been a fervent Disney fan since childhood—a proud possession is her Mickey ear gear in the orginal felt. Long before Disney came to Florida, grade-schooler Marianne pilgrimaged to Disneyland, where she stood in line for the Matterhorn so many times she can still recite the ride's P.A. announcement by heart. When not exploring Mouseville with her five-year-old niece (who's convinced her aunt owns the place), Marianne works as senior editor of AAA's *Car & Travel* magazine.

As one of Fodor's veteran Orlando writers, **Mary Meehan** has fearlessly traveled from the top of the Twilight Zone Tower of Terror to the foot of the Great Wall at Splendid China. Along the way, she has covered our After Dark beat. It's obviously difficult for someone who managed to snub Sylvester Stallone at the opening of Planet Hollywood to reach excitement saturation. After eight years in the newspaper/publishing trenches, she is now spokesperson for Hospice of Central Florida.

Good meals stick to your ribs; great meals stick in your mind. That's the belief of **Rowland Stiteler,** who has served as editor and dining critic of *Orlando* and *Central Florida* magazines. Always trying to beat the buffet blahs, he keeps an eye out for the hottest news in Floridian cuisine, from the newest northern Italian bistro to the coolest recipe for kumquat sorbet. As a rule, he feels many Central Florida restaurants put more emphasis on the sizzle than on the steak, but if you are willing to search it out, good dining—from haute to homey—can be found throughout the Orlando area. Stiteler, a journalist for 25 years, won top honors for best feature story in the 1994 Florida Magazine Association awards competition.

New This Year

This year we've reformatted our guides to make them easier to use. You may notice our fresh graphics, new in 1996. More readable and more helpful than ever? We think so—and we hope you do, too.

Happy Anniversary

In October 1996, Disney began celebrating its 25th anniversary. Special events are planned throughout the year, and one thing is certain—there will be plenty of fireworks, fun, and festivities.

On the Web

Also check out Fodor's Web site (http://www.fodors.com/), where you'll find travel information on major destinations around the world and an ever-changing array of travel-savvy interactive features.

Let Us Do Your Booking

Our writers have scoured Walt Disney World and the outlying areas to come up with a well-balanced list of the best B&Bs, inns, resorts, rental condos, and hotels, both small and large, new and old. But you don't have to beat the bushes for a reservation. Now that we've teamed up with an established hotel-booking service, reserving a room at the property of your choice is easy. It's fast and free, and confirmation is guaranteed. If your first choice is booked, the operators can recommend others. Call 1–800/FODORS–1 or 1–800/363–6771 (0800–89–1030 in Great Britain; 0014–800–12–8271 in Australia; 1–800/55–9101 in Ireland).

How to Use This Book

Organization

Up front is the **Gold Guide.** Its first section, **Important Contacts A to Z,** gives addresses and telephone numbers of organizations and companies that offer destination-related services and detailed information and publications. **Smart Travel Tips A to Z,** the Gold Guide's second section, gives specific information on how to accomplish

what you need to in the Orlando area as well as tips on savvy traveling. Both sections are in alphabetical order by topic.

When it comes to vacations, it's true that getting started is half the fun, but visiting Walt Disney World for the first time can be a lot like trying to solve a gigantic jigsaw puzzle. The countless attractions inspire a thousand questions. Our Disney at-a-glance guide, **Ready, Set, Disney!: Everything You Need to Know About Getting Started at Walt Disney World,** up front in Chapter 1, provides the answers. Now, 11 easy-to-digest topics turn WDW inside out, break down the major and minor parks, outline the main attractions, provide an overview of hotels and restaurants, and otherwise give you the lay of the land. It's part reference guide, part motivator, and after reading it, you'll be set to engineer a totally memorable vacation to the most fun place on earth.

At the end of the book you'll find our **Portrait** section, which includes "The Mouse and the Dynamo" by Andrew Holleran, a fascinating essay on the history of Walt Disney and his theme parks, and suggestions for other texts on the wonderful worlds of Disney.

Icons and Symbols
★ Our special recommendations
✕ Restaurant
🏠 Lodging establishment
⚠ Campgrounds
☺ Rubber duckie (good for kids)
☞ Sends you to another section of the guide for more information
✉ Address
☎ Telephone number
☉ Opening and closing times
💰 Admission prices (those we give apply only to adults; substantially reduced fees are almost always available for children, students, and senior citizens)

Numbers in white and black circles—② and ❷, for example—that appear on the maps, in the margins, and within the tours correspond to one another.

Restaurant and Hotel Price Categories

The restaurants and lodgings we list are the cream of the crop in each price range. Price categories are as follows:

For restaurants:

CATEGORY	COST*
$$$$	over $40
$$$	$30–$40
$$	$20–$30
$	under $20

All prices are per person, excluding drinks, service, and 6% sales tax.

For hotels:

CATEGORY	COST*
$$$$	over $180
$$$	$120–$180
$$	$65–$120
$	under $65

All rates are for two adults traveling with up to two children during high season, plus 10% tax.

Restaurant Reservations and Dress Codes

Reservations are always a good idea; we note only when they're essential or when they are not accepted. Book as far ahead as you can, and reconfirm when you get to town. Unless otherwise noted, the restaurants listed are open daily for lunch and dinner. We mention dress only when men are required to wear a jacket or a jacket and tie. Look for an overview of local habits under Dining in Smart Travel Tips A to Z.

Hotel Facilities

We always list the facilities that are available—but we don't specify whether they cost extra: When pricing accommodations, always ask what's included.

Credit Cards

The following abbreviations are used: **AE,** American Express; **D,** Discover; **DC,** Diners Club; **MC,** MasterCard; and **V,** Visa.

Please Write to Us

You can use this book in the confidence that all prices and opening times are based on information supplied to us at press time; Fodor's cannot accept responsibility for any errors. Time inevitably brings changes, so always confirm information when it matters—especially if you're making a detour to visit a specific place. In addition, when making reservations be sure to mention if you have a disability or are traveling with children, if you prefer a private bath or a certain type of bed, or if you have specific dietary needs or any other concerns.

Were the restaurants we recommended as described? Did our hotel picks exceed your expectations? Did you find a museum we recommended a waste of time? If you have complaints, we'll look into them and revise our entries when the facts warrant it. If you've discovered a special place that we haven't included, we'll pass the information along to our correspondents and have them check it out. So send your feedback, positive *and* negative, to the Walt Disney World Editor at 201 East 50th Street, New York, New York 10022—and have a wonderful trip!

Karen Cure
Editorial Director

JOIN THE CELEBRATION!
Disney's 25th Birthday Bash

OCTOBER 1, 1996, marks the beginning of Walt Disney World's gala 15-month-long celebration of its opening day on October 1, 1971. New attractions will open apace, including a state-of-the-art sports complex and new shops, restaurants, and clubs. And it goes without saying that all of WDW will be decked to the nines. Here are some other key features of the festivities made public at press time:

In the Magic Kingdom

The magic will be its most dazzling in the land of the Cinderella Castle. You can't have a birthday without a cake, so to match the scope of this anniversary, Disney is planning the **world's largest birthday cake**—decorating that famed icon of the Magic Kingdom known as the Cinderella Castle with 25 glowing candles, splashes of candy canes, and red and pink "icing."

Returning visitors will be guests of honor. Throughout the year, Disney will mount a nationwide campaign to seek out everyone who has ever visited WDW. In a special **25th Anniversary Welcome Center,** the Magic Kingdom will welcome past guests with special badges. And every day 1,400 of these Disney goers will play a special part in a huge **25th Anniversary Parade,** an interactive affair with gigantic floats inspired by the *Lion King, Cinderella, the Little Mermaid, Aladdin,* and *Snow White.* Count on goose bumps aplenty. Returning guests will also wave flags alongside a cast of entertainers at daily **Homecoming Rallies** on the stage in front of the Cinderella Castle.

Mickey's Starland becomes a festive fairgrounds where your children are sure to meet their favorite Disney characters. And there's a new roller coaster for youngsters and a Minnie Mouse house next to Mickey's bungalow. As many as 10 characters at a time will greet guests in the county-fair settings of **Mickey's Toontown Fair.**

Epcot Center

Don't miss **IllumiNations 25,** a special anniversary edition of Disney's most popular nighttime spectacle. It's a good guess that this new version, with a finale that brings all the animals and people of the world into a grand Circle of Life sky show to the accompaniment of the lilting theme song from the *Lion King,* is sure to leave you breathless.

And throughout the year there will be special mini festivals: an **International Food & Wine Festival** in September and October; **Holidays Around the World,** including a 25th anniversary version of the nightly candlelight processional in November and December; the **Epcot International Flower and Garden Festival** in April and May; and a summer-long **All-American Musical Salute,** with nightly orchestra concerts in the America Gardens Theatre.

Disney—MGM Studios

Here, Disney's newest animated film inspires a new stage show, *Disney's The Hunchback of Notre Dame: A Musical Adventure.* And on the Backstage Walking Tour, props, sets, and special effects will be on display from the fall 1996 live-action version of the venerable animated favorite *101 Dalmatians.*

Disney's BoardWalk

This all-new nighttime entertainment, shopping, and dining complex, a sort of mini Atlantic City with class, opens October 1. A stylish dance hall ringing with hits from the 1930s through the '90s, complete with sparkling lights, will be featured, along with sports bars, piano bars, and a microbrewery.

25th Anniversary Strategies

Disney's expecting big crowds, as much as double the usual numbers, which are already said to nudge 40 million per year. So plan ahead. Make your reservations early. Give yourself an extra day in the area to take it all in. Get a jump start on the day by starting out with the sun. Be sure to study the strategies sketched in the chapters that follow. Then settle back and relax. It's going to be a wonderful year!

Orlando Area

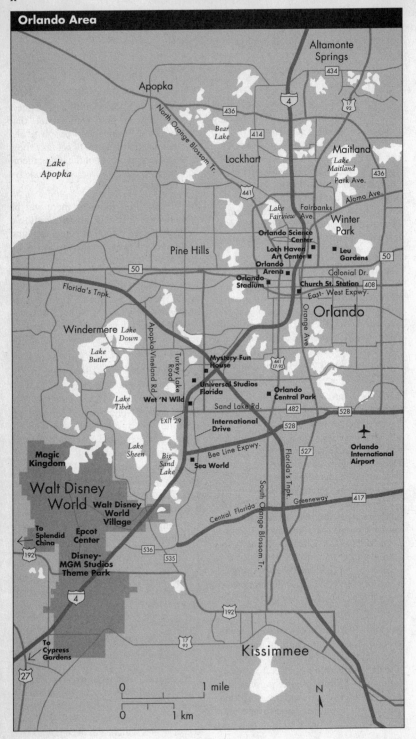

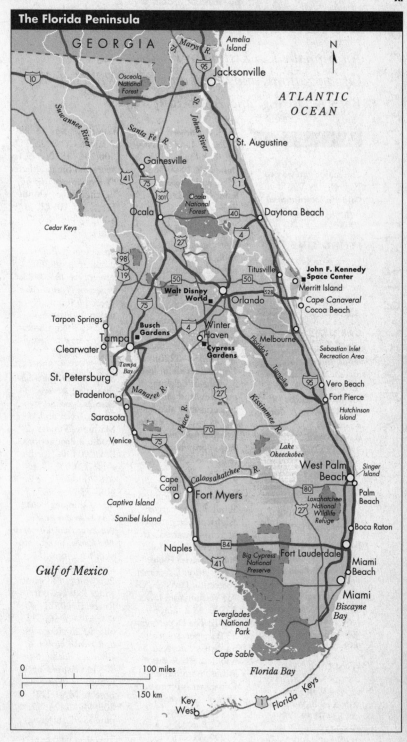

The Florida Peninsula

IMPORTANT CONTACTS A TO Z

An Alphabetical Listing of Publications, Organizations, and Companies that Will Help You Before, During, and After Your Trip

A

AIR TRAVEL

The major gateway to Walt Disney World is **Orlando International Airport** (☎ 407/825–2001).

FLYING TIME

Flying time is 2½ hours from New York, 3½ hours from Chicago, and 5 hours from Los Angeles.

CARRIERS

Carriers serving Orlando International include **America West** (☎ 800/235–9292), **American Airlines** (☎ 800/433–7300), **Continental** (☎ 800/525–0280), **Delta** (☎ 800/221–1212), **Northwest** (☎ 800/225–2525), **TWA** (☎ 800/221–2000), **United Airlines** (☎ 800/241–6522), and **USAir** (☎ 800/428–4322).

For inexpensive, no-frills flights, contact **Carnival Airlines** (☎ 800/824–7386), **Kiwi International** (☎ 800/538–5494), and **Private Jet** (☎ 404/231–7571, 800/546–7571, or 800/949–9400).

FROM THE UNITED KINGDOM➣ Carriers serving Walt Disney World include **American** (☎ 0345/789–789), **British Airways** (☎ 0181/897–4000; outside London, 0345/222–111), **Continental** (☎ 0800/776–464), **Delta** (☎ 0800/414–767), **Northwest** (☎ 01293/561–000), **TWA** (☎ 0800/222–222), **United** (☎ 0800/888–555), and **Virgin Atlantic** (☎ 01293/747–747).

COMPLAINTS

To register complaints about charter and scheduled airlines, contact the U.S. Department of Transportation's **Aviation Consumer Protection Division** (✉ C-75, Washington, DC 20590, ☎ 202/366–2220). Complaints about lost baggage or ticketing problems and safety concerns may also be logged with the **Federal Aviation Administration (FAA) Consumer Hotline** (☎ 800/322–7873).

PUBLICATIONS

For general information about charter carriers, ask for the Department of Transportation's free brochure **"Plane Talk: Public Charter Flights"** (✉ Aviation Consumer Protection Division, C-75, Washington, DC 20590, ☎ 202/366–2220). The Department of Transportation also publishes a 58-page booklet, **"Fly Rights,"** available from the Consumer Information Center (✉ Supt. of Documents, Dept. 136C, Pueblo, CO 81009; $1.75).

For other tips and hints, consult the Consumers Union's monthly **"Consumer Reports Travel Letter"** (✉ Box 53629, Boulder, CO 80322, ☎ 800/234–1970; $39 1st year) and the newsletter **"Travel Smart"** (✉ 40 Beechdale Rd., Dobbs Ferry, NY 10522, ☎ 800/327–3633; $37 per year).

Some worthwhile publications on the subject are ***The Official Frequent Flyer Guidebook,*** by Randy Petersen (✉ Airpress, 4715-C Town Center Dr., Colorado Springs, CO 80916, ☎ 719/597–8899 or 800/487–8893; $14.99 plus $3 shipping); ***Airfare Secrets Exposed,*** by Sharon Tyler and Matthew Wunder (✉ Studio 4 Productions, Box 280400, Northridge, CA 91328, ☎ 818/700–2522 or 800/408–7369; $16.95 plus $2.50 shipping); ***202 Tips Even the Best Business Travelers May Not Know,*** by Christopher McGinnis (✉ Irwin Professional Publishing, 1333 Burr Ridge Pkway., Burr Ridge, IL 60521, ☎ 800/634–3966; $11 plus $3.25 shipping); and ***Travel Rights,*** by Charles Leocha (✉ World Leisure Corporation, 177 Paris St., Boston, MA 02128, ☎ 800/444–2524; $7.95 plus $3.95 shipping).

Travelers who experience motion sickness or ear problems in flight should get the brochures **"Ears, Altitude,** and Airplane Travel" and **"What You Can Do for Dizziness & Motion Sickness"** from the American Academy of Otolaryngology (✉ 1 Prince St., Alexandria, VA 22314, ☎ 703/836–4444, FAX 703/683–5100, TTY 703/519–1585).

By Bus➤ Public buses operate between the airport and the main terminal of the **Tri-County Transit Authority** (1200 W. South St., Orlando, ☎ 407/841–8240), downtown.

By Limousine➤ **Mears Transportation Group** (☎ 407/422–5566) will meet you at the gate, help you with your luggage, and whisk you away, in either an 11-passenger van, a town car, or a limo. Vans run to Walt Disney World and along U.S. 192 every 30 minutes; prices range from $12.50 one-way for adults ($8.50 for children 4–11) to $22 round-trip for adults ($16 children 4–11). Limo rates run around $50–$60 for a town car that will accommodate three or four and $90 for a stretch limo that will seat six. **Town & Country Transportation** (☎ 407/828–3035) charges $30–$40 one-way for up to seven, depending on the hotel.

B

For local contacts in the hometown of a tour operator you may be considering, consult the Council of Better Business Bureaus (✉ 4200 Wilson Blvd., Suite 800, Arlington, VA 22203, ☎ 703/276–0100, FAX 703/525–8277).

Greyhound Lines (555 N. Magruder Ave., Orlando, ☎ 407/292–3422 or 800/231–2222) serves Orlando from most American cities.

FROM THE HOTELS TO THE ATTRACTIONS

Scheduled service and charters linking just about every hotel and major attraction in the area are available from **Gray Line of Orlando** (☎ 407/422–0744), **Mears Transportation Group** (☎ 407/422–5566), **Phoenix Tours** (☎ 407/859–4211), and **Rabbit Bus Lines** (☎ 407/291–2424).

WITHIN ORLANDO

For information on local bus service, contact the **Tri-County Transit Authority Information Office** (1200 W. South St., Orlando, ☎ 407/841–8240).

C

The major car-rental companies represented in Orlando are **Alamo** (☎ 800/327–9633; in the U.K., 0800/272–2000), **Avis** (☎ 800/331–1212; in Canada, 800/879–2847), **Budget** (☎ 800/527–0700; in the U.K., 0800/181181), **Dollar** (☎ 800/800–4000; in the U.K., 0990/565656, where it is known as Eurodollar), **Hertz** (☎ 800/654–3131; in Canada, 800/263–0600; in the U.K., 0345/555888), and **National InterRent** (☎ 800/227–7368; in the U.K., where National is known as Europcar InterRent, 01345/222525). Rates in Orlando begin at $28 a day and $136 a week for an economy car with unlimited mileage. This does not include tax on car rentals, which is 6%.

RENTAL WHOLESALERS

Contact **Auto Europe** (☎ 207/828–2525 or 800/223–5555).

BABY-SITTING

Baby-sitting is widely available; ask at your hotel desk. **Fairy Godmothers** (☎ 407/277–3724) will care for infants and children in your hotel room or will take your youngsters to the theme parks. Walt Disney World's preschool and drop-off day-care facilities in the Lake Buena Vista area, **KinderCare,** will also send baby-sitters to your hotel room (☎ 407/827–5437). The KinderCare center proper accepts children who are potty trained and walking (☎ 407/827–5437; available daily 6 AM–8 PM); you don't have to stay at Disney to use the program. These programs charge between $5 and $10 an hour, depending on the ages and number of children and the type of service provided.

EDUCATIONAL PROGRAMS

Contact **The Disney Institute** ☎ 407/827–1100, **Walt Disney World**'s Wonders Program (☎ 407/354–1855) and Kidventure Program (☎ 407/824–3784), **Sea World** (☎ 407/363–2380), and **Busch Gardens** (☎ 813/987–5555).

FLYING

Look into **"Flying with Baby"** (✉ Third Street Press, Box 261250, Littleton, CO 80163, ☎ 303/595–5959; $4.95 includes shipping), cowritten by a flight attendant. **"Kids and Teens in Flight,"** free from the U.S. Department of Transportation's Aviation Consumer Protection Division (✉ C-75, Washington, DC 20590, ☎ 202/366–2220), offers tips on children flying alone. Every two years the February issue of *Family Travel Times* (☞ Know-How, *below*) details children's services on three dozen airlines. **"Flying Alone, Handy Advice for Kids Traveling Solo"** is available free from the American Automobile Association (AAA) (✉ send stamped, self-addressed, legal-size envelope: Flying Alone, Mail Stop 800, 1000 AAA Dr., Heathrow, FL 32746).

KNOW-HOW

Family Travel Times, published quarterly by Travel with Your Children (✉ TWYCH, 40 5th Ave., New York, NY 10011, ☎ 212/477–5524; $40 per year), covers destinations, types of vacations, and modes of travel.

The *Family Travel Guides* catalog (✉ Carousel Press, Box 6061, Albany, CA 94706, ☎ 510/527–5849; $1 postage) lists

about 200 books and articles on traveling with children. Also check *Take Your Baby and Go! A Guide for Traveling with Babies, Toddlers and Young Children,* by Sheri Andrews, Judy Bordeaux, and Vivian Vasquez (✉ Bear Creek Publications, 2507 Minor Ave. E, Seattle, WA 98102, ☎ 206/322–7604 or 800/326–6566; $5.95 plus $1.50 shipping). The Globe Pequot Press (✉ Box 833, 6 Business Park Rd., Old Saybrook, CT 06475, ☎ 203/395–0440) publishes *100 Best Family Resorts in North America,* by Jane Wilford with Janet Tice ($14.95 plus $3 shipping), and eastern and western editions of *50 Great Family Vacations in North America* by Candyce Stapen ($18.95 plus $3 shipping).

CRUISING

Joint Walt Disney World–cruise packages have become increasingly popular since they debuted a few years ago. Two of the most popular include three- and four-day land packages to Walt Disney World plus cruises to the Bahamas on **Carnival Cruise Lines'** *Fantasy* (Box 526170, Miami, FL 33152-6170, ☎ 305/599–2600 or 800/327–9501); or aboard the Big Red Boats of **Premier Cruise Lines** (400 Challenger Rd., Cape Canaveral, FL 32920, ☎ 407/783–5061).

CUSTOMS

CANADIANS

Contact **Revenue Canada** (✉ 2265 St.

Laurent Blvd. S, Ottawa, Ontario K1G 4K3, ☎ 613/993–0534) for a copy of the free brochure **"I Declare/Je Déclare"** and for details on duty-free limits. For recorded information (within Canada only), call 800/461–9999.

U.K. CITIZENS

HM Customs and Excise (✉ Dorset House, Stamford St., London SE1 9NG, ☎ 0171/202–4227) can answer questions about U.K. customs regulations and publishes a free pamphlet, **"A Guide for Travellers,"** detailing standard procedures and import rules.

D

DISABILITIES AND ACCESSIBILITY

COMPLAINTS

To register complaints under the provisions of the Americans with Disabilities Act, contact the U.S. Department of Justice's **Disability Rights Section** (✉ Box 66738, Washington, DC 20035, ☎ 202/514–0301 or 800/514–0301, FAX 202/307–1198, TTY 202/514–0383 or 800/514–0383). For airline-related problems, contact the U.S. Department of Transportation's **Aviation Consumer Protection Division** (☞ Air Travel, *above*). For complaints about surface transportation, contact the Department of Transportation's **Civil Rights Office** (✉ 400 7th St., SW, Room 10215, Washington DC, 20590 ☎ 202/366–4648).

LODGING

For questions about or reservations at Disney-owned properties, call **WDW Special Request Reservations** (☎ 407/354–1853).

Disney properties that have wheelchair-accessible facilities include the **Yacht Club** ☎ 407/934–7000; **Beach Club** ☎ 407/934–8000; **Dixie Landings** ☎ 407/934–6000; and the **Grand Floridian** ☎ 407/824–3000 (Walt Disney World Central Reservations, ☎ 407/934–7639, TTY 407/939–7670), the **All-Star Sports Resort** (☎ 407/939—5000), and the **All-Star Music Resort** (☎ 407/939—6000).

Other wheelchair-accessible hotels are the **Embassy Suites Resorts** at Lake Buena Vista (☎ 407/239–1144 or 800/362–2779, TTY 800/451–4833), which provides free transportation to the Disney parks, and the one on International Drive South also. (☎ or TTY 407/352–1400 or 800/433–7275); the **Hilton Gateway** on U.S. 192 in Kissimmee (☎ 407/396–4400 or 800/445-8667); the **Hampton Inn** (5621 Windhover Dr., ☎ 407/351–6716 or 800/231–8395); and the two **Motel Six** properties (5731 W. Irlo Bronson Memorial Hwy., Kissimmee 34746, ☎ 407/396–6333; 7455 W. Irlo Bronson Memorial Hwy., Kissimmee 34747, ☎ 407/396–6422).

Hotels with facilities for guests with vision impairments include the **Buena Vista Palace** in Walt Disney World Village (☎ 407/827–2727 or 800/327–2990) and the **Embassy Suites Resorts** at Lake Buena Vista and International Drive (☞ *above*).

See also Chapter 8 for details.

ORGANIZATIONS

The **Disabled Traveler's Helpline of Central Florida** (☎ 800/945–2045, FAX 407/856–5949) can answer questions about the accessibility of many area attractions, hotels, and restaurants. Both Walt Disney World (☎ 407/824–4321) and Universal Studios (☎ 407/363–8000) publish guidebooks for guests with disabilities; allow six weeks for delivery. If you need the information in a hurry, send a large, self-addressed envelope with at least $1 in postage to the **Disabled Travelers Friendship Network** (Box 690801, Orlando, FL 32869–0801), which operates under the wing of the Disabled Traveler's Helpline and is affiliated with **Friends of the Family** (Box 690801, Orlando, FL 32869–0801, ☎ 407/856–7676 or 800/945–2045), which will customize your itinerary, supply tour guides who push wheelchairs, and meet you at the airport.

TRAVELERS WITH HEARING IMPAIRMENTS➤ The **American Academy of Otolaryngology** (⊠ 1 Prince St., Alexandria, VA 22314, ☎ 703/836–4444, FAX 703/683–5100, TTY 703/519–1585) publishes a brochure, "Travel Tips for Hearing Impaired People."

TRAVELERS WITH MOBILITY PROBLEMS➤ Contact the **Information Center for Individuals with Disabilities** (⊠ Box 256, Boston, MA 02117, ☎ 617/450–9888; in MA, 800/462–5015; TTY 617/424–6855); **Mobility International USA** (⊠ Box 10767, Eugene, OR 97440, ☎ and TTY 541/343–1284, FAX 541/343–6812), the U.S. branch of a Belgium-based organization (☞ *below*) with affiliates in 30 countries; **MossRehab Hospital Travel Information Service** (☎ 215/456–9600, TTY 215/456–9602), a telephone information resource for travelers with physical disabilities; the **Society for the Advancement of Travel for the Handicapped** (⊠ 347 5th Ave., Suite 610, New York, NY 10016, ☎ 212/447–7284, FAX 212/725–8253; membership $45); and **Travelin' Talk** (⊠ Box 3534, Clarksville, TN 37043, ☎ 615/552–6670, FAX 615/552–1182) which provides local contacts worldwide for travelers with disabilities.

TRAVELERS WITH VISION IMPAIRMENTS➤ Contact the **American Council of the Blind** (⊠ 1155 15th St. NW, Suite 720, Washington, DC 20005, ☎ 202/467–5081, FAX 202/467–5085) for a list of travelers' resources or the **American Foundation for the Blind** (⊠ 11 Penn Plaza, Suite 300, New York, NY 10001, ☎ 212/502–7600 or 800/232–5463, TTY 212/502–7662), which provides general advice and publishes "Access to Art" ($19.95), a directory of museums that accommodate travelers with vision impairments.

IN THE U.K.

Contact the **Royal Association for Disability and Rehabilitation** (✉ RADAR, 12 City Forum, 250 City Rd., London EC1V 8AF, ☎ 0171/250–3222) or **Mobility International** (✉ rue de Manchester 25, B-1080 Brussels, Belgium, ☎ 00–322–410–6297, FAX 00–322–410–6874), an international travel-information clearing-house for people with disabilities.

MEDICAL SUPPLIES

Undoubtedly the best in town, **Care Medical Equipment** (☎ 407/856–2273 in Orlando, 407/933—1412 in Kissimmee, or 800/741–2282; FAX 407/856–5949) does everything from renting wheelchairs and scooters to supplying oxygen. The organization is particularly effective at coordinating with hometown medical personnel to ensure the appropriate equipment. Prices are reasonable, and reliability is superior.

NURSING SERVICES

Rescare (1801 Lee Rd., Suite 175, Winter Park 32789, ☎ 407/740–5650, FAX 407/740–7178) reliably provides LPNs, home health aides, therapists, and RNs on call around the clock. Prices are reasonable, although professional services are never

cheap. **Careteam** (1085 W. Morse Blvd., Suite A, Winter Park 32789, ☎ 407/628–8845) has a similar setup, with similar prices and reliability.

PUBLICATIONS

Several publications for travelers with disabilities are available from the **Consumer Information Center** (✉ Box 100, Pueblo, CO 81009, ☎ 719/948–3334). Call or write for its free catalog of current titles. The Society for the Advancement of Travel for the Handicapped (☞ Organizations, *above*) publishes the quarterly magazine **"Access to Travel"** ($13 for 1-year subscription).

Fodor's *Great American Vacations for Travelers with Disabilities* (available in bookstores, or ☎ 800/533–6478; $18 plus $4 shipping) details accessible attractions, restaurants, and hotels in U.S. destinations. The 500-page *Travelin' Talk Directory* (✉ Box 3534, Clarksville, TN 37043, ☎ 615/552–6670, FAX 615/552–1182; $35) lists people and organizations who help travelers with disabilities. For travel agents worldwide, consult the *Directory of Travel Agencies for the Disabled* (✉ Twin Peaks Press, Box 129, Vancouver, WA 98666, ☎ 360/694–2462 or 800/637–2256, FAX 360/696–3210; $19.95 plus $3 shipping).

THEME PARKS

Walt Disney World (☎ 407/560–6233; TTY 407/827–5141), **Universal Studios** (☎

407/354–6356; TTY 407/363–8265), and **Sea World** (☎ 407/351–3600; TTY 407/363–2617) make arrangements for guides who know sign language. Advance reservations are necessary; provide two weeks' notice if possible.

TRAVEL AGENCIES & TOUR OPERATORS

The Americans with Disabilities Act requires that all travel firms serve the needs of all travelers. That said, you should note that some agencies and operators specialize in making travel arrangements for individuals and groups with disabilities, among them **Access Adventures** (✉ 206 Chestnut Ridge Rd., Rochester, NY 14624, ☎ 716/889–9096), run by a former physical-rehab counselor.

TRAVELERS WITH MOBILITY PROBLEMS➤ Contact **Hinsdale Travel Service** (✉ 201 E. Ogden Ave., Suite 100, Hinsdale, IL 60521, ☎ 708/325–1335), a travel agency that benefits from the advice of wheelchair traveler Janice Perkins; and **Wheelchair Journeys** (✉ 16979 Redmond Way, Redmond, WA 98052, ☎ 206/885–2210 or 800/313–4751), which can handle arrangements worldwide.

TRAVELERS WITH DEVELOPMENTAL DISABILITIES➤ Contact the nonprofit **New Directions** (✉ 5276 Hollister Ave., Suite 207, Santa Barbara, CA 93111, ☎ 805/967–2841) and **Sprout** (✉ 893 Amsterdam Ave., New York,

NY 10025, ☎ 212/222–9575), which specializes in custom-designed itineraries for groups but also books vacations for individual travelers with developmental disabilities.

TRAVEL GEAR

The **Magellan's** catalog (☎ 800/962–4943, FAX 805/568–5406), includes a section devoted to products designed for travelers with disabilities.

DISCOUNTS AND DEALS

AIRFARES

For the lowest airfares to Orlando, call 800/FLY–4–LESS. Also try 800/FLY–ASAP.

CLUBS

Contact **Entertainment Travel Editions** (⊠ Box 1068, Trumbull, CT 06611, ☎ 800/445–4137; $28–$53, depending on destination), **Great American Traveler** (⊠ Box 27965, Salt Lake City, UT 84127, ☎ 800/548–2812; $49.95 per year), **Moment's Notice Discount Travel Club** (⊠ 7301 New Utrecht Ave., Brooklyn, NY 11204, ☎ 718/234–6295; $25 per year, single or family), **Privilege Card** (⊠ 3391 Peachtree Rd. NE, Suite 110, Atlanta, GA 30326, ☎ 404/262–0222 or 800/236–9732; $74.95 per year), **Travelers Advantage** (⊠ CUC Travel Service, 49 Music Sq. W, Nashville, TN 37203, ☎ 800/548–1116 or 800/648–4037; $49 per year, single or family), or **Worldwide Discount Travel Club** (⊠ 1674 Meridian Ave., Miami Beach, FL 33139, ☎

305/534–2082; $50 per year for family, $40 single).

HOTEL ROOMS

For discounts on hotel rates, contact the **Hotel Reservations Network** (☎ 800/964–6835).

STUDENTS

Members of Hostelling International–American Youth Hostels (☞ Students, *below*) are eligible for discounts on car rentals, admissions to attractions, and other selected travel expenses.

PUBLICATIONS

Consult *The Frugal Globetrotter,* by Bruce Northam (⊠ Fulcrum Publishing, 350 Indiana St., Suite 350, Golden, CO 80401, ☎ 800/992–2908; $16.95 plus $4 shipping). For publications that tell how to find the lowest prices on plane tickets, *see* Air Travel, *above.*

DRIVING

If you want to have your car in Florida without driving it there, board the **Auto-Train** in Lorton, Virginia (☎ 703/690–3355), near Washington, DC. Its southern terminus is Sanford, Florida (☎ 407/323–4800), some 23 miles north of Orlando.

ROAD SERVICE

AAA Emergency Road Service (☎ 407/877–2266 or 800/222–4357). In Walt Disney World, there is a **Car Care Center** (☞ Essential Disney *in* Chapter 2).

To become a member of the AAA, call 800/564–6222. In the United Kingdom, contact the Automobile Association (AA) or the

Royal Automobile Club (RAC).

E

EMERGENCIES

Police or **ambulance** (☎ 911). All of the area's major theme parks have first-aid centers.

DOCTORS

Hospital emergency rooms are open 24 hours a day. The most accessible hospital is the **Orlando Regional Medical Center/Sand Lake Hospital,** in the International Drive area (9400 Turkey Lake Rd., ☎ 407/351–8500).

For minor medical problems, contact **Housemed** (2901 Parkway Blvd., Kissimmee, ☎ 407/396–1195, 407/648–9234 or 407/846–2093), which runs a clinic that's open 9–9 daily and a minor-emergency mobile service that offers hotel-room visits by physicians for minor medical care and dispenses nonnarcotic medication. Closer to Orlando, a block east of Kirkman Road, is **Centra Care** (601 E. Rollins St. ☎ 407/660–8118; open daily 8 AM–midnight). Near WDW, in Lake Buena Vista, the most convenient facility is the **Buena Vista Walk-in Medical Center,** next to the Walt Disney World Village entrance (Rte. 535, ☎ 407/828–3434), open daily 8–8; it also provides free shuttle service from any of the Disney theme park's first-aid stations.

24-HOUR PHARMACIES

Eckerd Drugs (908 Lee Rd., Orlando, ☎ 407/644–6908) is just off

I–4 at the Lee Road exit, and **Walgreen's** (6201 International Dr., ☎ 407/345–8311 or 407/345–8402) is opposite Wet 'n' Wild; **Walgreen's** (4578 S. Kirkman Rd., ☎ 407/293–8458) is just north of Universal Studios.

DENTISTS

Emergency dental referral (☎ 407/847–7474).

G

GAY AND LESBIAN TRAVEL

ORGANIZATIONS

The Genesis Foundation (Box 560213, Orlando, FL 32856, ☎ 407/857–5444, FAX 407/438–3695) has organized an annual Gay Day at Walt Disney World for the past five years. The **International Gay Travel Association** (✉ Box 4974, Key West, FL 33041, ☎ 800/448–8550, FAX 305/296–6633), a consortium of more than 1,000 travel companies, can supply names of gay-friendly travel agents, tour operators, and accommodations.

PUBLICATIONS

The premier international travel magazine for gays and lesbians is **Our World** (✉ 1104 N. Nova Rd., Suite 251, Daytona Beach, FL 32117, ☎ 904/441–5367, FAX 904/441–5604; $35 for 10 issues). The 16-page monthly **"Out & About"** (☎ 212/645–6922 or 800/929–2268, FAX 800/929–2215; $49 for 10 issues and quarterly calendar) covers gay-friendly resorts, hotels, cruise lines, and airlines.

TOUR OPERATORS

Toto Tours (✉ 1326 W. Albion Ave., Suite 3W, Chicago, IL 60626, ☎ 312/274–8686 or 800/565–1241, FAX 312/274–8695) offer group tours to worldwide destinations.

TRAVEL AGENCIES

The largest agencies serving gay travelers are **Advance Travel** (✉ 10700 Northwest Fwy., Suite 160, Houston, TX 77092, ☎ 713/682–2002 or 800/292–0500), **Islanders/Kennedy Travel** (✉ 183 W. 10th St., New York, NY 10014, ☎ 212/242–3222 or 800/988–1181), **Now Voyager** (✉ 4406 18th St., San Francisco, CA 94114, ☎ 415/626–1169 or 800/255–6951), and **Yellowbrick Road** (✉ 1500 W. Balmoral Ave., Chicago, IL 60640, ☎ 312/561–1800 or 800/642–2488). **Skylink Women's Travel** (✉ 2460 W. 3rd St., Suite 215, Santa Rosa, CA 95401, ☎ 707/570–0105 or 800/225–5759) serves lesbian travelers.

I

INSURANCE

IN CANADA

Contact **Mutual of Omaha** (✉ Travel Division, 500 University Ave., Toronto, Ontario M5G 1V8, ☎ 800/465–0267(in Canada) or 416/598–4083).

IN THE U.S.

Travel insurance covering baggage, health, and trip cancellation or interruptions is available from **Access America** (✉ 6600 W. Broad St., Richmond, VA 23230, ☎ 804/285–3300 or 800/334–7525), **Carefree Travel Insurance** (✉ Box 9366, 100 Garden City Plaza, Garden City, NY 11530, ☎ 516/294–0220 or 800/323–3149), **Near Travel Services** (✉ Box 1339, Calumet City, IL 60409, ☎ 708/868–6700 or 800/654–6700), **Tele-Trip** (✉ Mutual of Omaha Plaza, Box 31716, Omaha, NE 68131, ☎ 800/228–9792), **Travel Guard International** (✉ 1145 Clark St., Stevens Point, WI 54481, ☎ 715/345–0505 or 800/826–1300), **Travel Insured International** (✉ Box 280568, East Hartford, CT 06128, ☎ 203/528–7663 or 800/243–3174), and **Wallach & Company** (✉ 107 W. Federal St., Box 480, Middleburg, VA 22117, ☎ 540/687–3166 or 800/237–6615).

IN THE U.K.

The **Association of British Insurers** (✉ 51 Gresham St., London EC2V 7HQ, ☎ 0171/600–3333) gives advice by phone and publishes the free pamphlet **"Holiday Insurance and Motoring Abroad,"** which sets out typical policy provisions and costs.

L

LODGING

For information on hotel consolidators, *see* Discounts, *above.*

APARTMENT & VILLA RENTAL

Among the companies to contact are **Property Rentals International** (✉

1008 Mansfield Crossing Rd., Richmond, VA 23236, ☎ 804/378–6054 or 800/220–3332, FAX 804/379–2073), **Rent-a-Home International** (✉ 7200 34th Ave. NW, Seattle, WA 98117, ☎ 206/789–9377 or 800/488–7368, FAX 206/789–9379, rentahomeinternational@msn.com), and **Vacation Home Rentals Worldwide** (✉ 235 Kensington Ave., Norwood, NJ 07648, ☎ 201/767–9393 or 800/633–3284, FAX 201/767–5510). Members of the travel club **Hideaways International** (✉ 767 Islington St., Portsmouth, NH 03801, ☎ 603/430–4433 or 800/843–4433, FAX 603/430–4444, info@hideaways.com; $99 per year) receive two annual guides plus quarterly newsletters and arrange rentals among themselves.

HOME EXCHANGE

Some of the principal clearinghouses are **HomeLink International/ Vacation Exchange Club** (✉ Box 650, Key West, FL 33041, ☎ 305/294–1448 or 800/638–3841, FAX 305/294–1148; $78 per year), which sends members five annual directories, with a listing in one, plus updates; **Intervac International** (✉ Box 590504, San Francisco, CA 94159, ☎ 415/435–3497, FAX 415/435–7440; $65 per year), which publishes four annual directories; and **Loan-a-Home** (✉ 2 Park La., Apt. 6E, Mount Vernon, NY 10552, ☎ 914/664–7640; $40–$50 per year), which specializes in long-term exchanges.

M

MONEY

ATMS

For specific **Cirrus** locations in the United States and Canada, call 800/424–7787. For U.S. **Plus** locations, call 800/843–7587 and enter the area code and first three digits of the number from which you're calling (or of the calling area in which you want to locate an ATM).

N

NEWSPAPERS: ORLANDO

The leading Orlando region newspaper is the **Orlando Sentinel** (Box 2833, Orlando, FL 32802, ☎ 407/420–5000).

P

PACKING

For strategies on packing light, get a copy of **The Packing Book,** by Judith Gilford (✉ Ten Speed Press, Box 7123, Berkeley, CA 94707, ☎ 510/559–1600 or 800/841–2665, FAX 510/524–4588; $7.95 plus $3.50 shipping).

PASSPORTS AND VISAS

U.K. CITIZENS

For fees, documentation requirements, and to request an emergency passport, call the **London Passport Office** (☎ 0990/210410). For U.S. visa information, call the **U.S. Embassy Visa Information Line** (☎ 01891/200–290; calls cost 49p per minute or 39p per minute cheap rate) or send a self-addressed, stamped envelope to the **U.S.**

Embassy Visa Branch (✉ 5 Upper Grosvenor St., London W1A 2JB). If you live in Northern Ireland, write to the **U.S. Consulate General** (✉ Queen's House, Queen St., Belfast BTI 6EO).

PHOTO HELP

The **Kodak Information Center** (☎ 800/242–2424) answers consumer questions about film and photography. The **Kodak Guide to Shooting Great Travel Pictures** (available in bookstores; or contact Fodor's Travel Publications, ☎ 800/533–6478; $16.50 plus $4 shipping) explains how to take expert travel photographs.

R

RADIO NEWS: ORLANDO

To get plugged into Orlando news, tune in to **WDBO-AM,** 580 on the AM dial.

S

SAFETY

"Trouble-Free Travel," from the AAA, is a booklet of tips for protecting yourself and your belongings when away from home. Send a stamped, self-addressed, legal-size envelope to Trouble-Free Travel (✉ Mail Stop 75, 1000 AAA Dr., Heathrow, FL 32746).

SENIOR CITIZENS

Fairy Godmothers (☎ 407/277–3724) squires older travelers as well as youngsters around the theme parks.

EDUCATIONAL TRAVEL

The nonprofit **Elderhostel** (✉ 75 Federal St.,

THE GOLD GUIDE / IMPORTANT CONTACTS

3rd Floor, Boston, MA 02110, ☎ 617/426–7788), for people 55 and older, has offered inexpensive study programs since 1975. Courses cover everything from marine science to Greek mythology and cowboy poetry. Fees for programs in the United States and Canada, which usually last one week, run about $300, not including transportation.

ORGANIZATIONS

Contact the **American Association of Retired Persons** (✉ AARP, 601 E St. NW, Washington, DC 20049, ☎ 202/434–2277; annual dues $8 per person or couple). Its Purchase Privilege Program secures discounts for members on lodging, car rentals, and sightseeing, and the AARP Motoring Plan (☎ 800/334–3300) furnishes domestic trip-routing information and emergency road-service aid for an annual fee of $39.95 ($59.95 for a premium version). Senior citizen travelers can also join the AAA for emergency road service and other travel benefits (☞ Driving, *above, and* Discounts & Deals *in* Smart Travel Tips A to Z).

Additional sources for discounts on lodgings, car rentals, and other travel expenses, as well as helpful magazines and newsletters, are the **National Council of Senior Citizens** (✉ 1331 F St. NW, Washington, DC 20004, ☎ 202/347–8800; annual membership $12) and Sears's **Mature Outlook** (✉ Box 10448, Des

Moines, IA 50306, ☎ 800/336–6330; annual membership $14.95).

PUBLICATIONS

The 50+ Traveler's Guidebook: Where to Go, Where to Stay, What to Do, by Anita Williams and Merrimac Dillon (✉ St. Martin's Press, 175 5th Ave., New York, NY 10010, ☎ 212/674–5151 or 800/288–2131; $13.95 plus $4 shipping), offers many useful tips. **"The Mature Traveler"** (✉ Box 50400, Reno, NV 89513, ☎ 702/786–7419; $29.95), a monthly newsletter, covers all sorts of travel deals.

SIGHTSEEING

IN THE THEME PARKS

Guided tours are available in all the area's major theme parks (*see* A to Z sections *in* individual theme-park descriptions *in* Chapters 2 and 3).

AROUND ORLANDO

BALLOON RIDES➤ Quick, look up! Any morning in Orlando chances are fair to good that you'll spot a bright-colored hot-air balloon floating through the skies. You don't have to have your own gear to experience these silent, beautiful craft. Several operators offer trips, which usually include a Continental-breakfast picnic with champagne or a gala restaurant meal. They'll take children as well as adults, though most discourage parents from bringing babies and toddlers, who may be frightened by the experience. The cost is about $150 per adult at **Bal-**

loons by Terry (3529 Edgewater Dr., Orlando, ☎ 407/422–3529); **Aerial Adventures,** the Church Street Station Balloon team (also 3529 Edgewater Dr., Orlando, ☎ 407/841–UPUP); and **Rise & Float Balloon Tours** (5767 Major Blvd., opposite Universal Studios at the Mystery Fun House, Orlando, ☎ 407/352–8191), whose hot-air balloon is decorated with two hot-pink flamingos and a giant palm tree.

HELICOPTER RIDES➤ Seven different area tours, ranging from $20 to $399, are available from **Falcon Helicopter Service** (8990 International Dr., Orlando, ☎ 407/354–1400 at the Hyatt Hotel at I–4 and U.S. 192, ☎ 407/396–7222; and at Howard Johnson's, 5071 W. Irlo Bronson Memorial Hwy., Kissimmee, ☎ 407/397–0228).

STUDENTS

GROUPS

A major tour operator specializing in student travel is **Contiki Holidays** (✉ 300 Plaza Alicante, Suite 900, Garden Grove, CA 92640, ☎ 714/740–0808 or 800/266–8454).

HOSTELING

In the United States, contact **Hostelling International–American Youth Hostels** (✉ 733 15th St. NW, Suite 840, Washington, DC 20005, ☎ 202/783–6161 for reservations worldwide or 800/444–6111 for reservations at U.S. hostels using a credit card, FAX 202/783–6171); in Canada, **Hostelling Interna-**

tional–Canada (✉ 205 Catherine St., Suite 400, Ottawa, Ontario K2P 1C3, ☎ 613/237–7884); and in the United Kingdom, the **Youth Hostel Association of England and Wales** (✉ Trevelyan House, 8 St. Stephen's Hill, St. Albans, Hertfordshire AL1 2DY, ☎ 01727/855215 or 01727/845047). Membership (in the U.S., $25; in Canada, C$26.75; in the U.K., £9.30) gives you access to 5,000 hostels in 77 countries that charge $5–$40 per person per night.

I.D. CARDS

To be eligible for discounts on transportation and admissions, get either the **International Student Identity Card,** if you're a bona fide student, or the **GO 25: International Youth Travel Card,** if you're not a student but under age 26. Each includes basic travel-accident and illness coverage, plus a toll-free travel hot line. In the United States, either card costs $18; apply through the Council on International Educational Exchange (☞ Organizations, *below*). In Canada, cards are available for $15 each ($16 by mail) from Travel Cuts (☞ Organizations, *below*), and in the United Kingdom for £5 each at student unions and student travel companies.

ORGANIZATIONS

A major contact is the **Council on International Educational Exchange** (✉ mail orders only: CIEE, 205 E. 42nd St., 16th Floor, New York, NY 10017,

☎ 212/822–2600, info@ciee.org), with walk-in locations in Boston (✉ 729 Boylston St., 02116, ☎ 617/266–1926), Miami (✉ 9100 S. Dadeland Blvd., 33156, ☎ 305/670–9261), Los Angeles (✉ 10904 Lindbrook Dr., 90024, ☎ 310/208–3551), 43 other college towns in the U.S., and in the United Kingdom (✉ 28A Poland St., London W1V 3DB, ☎ 0171/437–7767). Twice per year, it publishes *Student Travels* magazine. The CIEE's Council Travel Service offers domestic air passes for bargain travel within the United States and is the exclusive U.S. agent for several student discount cards.

The **Educational Travel Centre** (✉ 438 N. Frances St., Madison, WI 53703, ☎ 608/256–5551 or 800/747–5551, ℻ 608/256–2042) offers rail passes and low-cost airline tickets, mostly for flights that depart from Chicago.

In Canada, also contact **Travel Cuts** (✉ 187 College St., Toronto, Ontario M5T 1P7, ☎ 416/979–2406 or 800/667–2887).

T
TOUR OPERATORS

Among the companies that sell tours and packages to Orlando, the following are nationally known, have a proven reputation, and offer plenty of options.

GROUP TOURS

Escorted tours to Walt Disney World generally only spend a day or two

at the park as part of a longer Florida itinerary.

DELUXE➤ **Tauck Tours** (✉ Box 5027, 276 Post Rd. W, Westport, CT 06881, ☎ 203/226–6911 or 800/468–2825, ℻ 203/221–6828).

FIRST-CLASS➤ **Mayflower Tours** (✉ Box 490, 1225 Warren Ave., Downers Grove, IL 60515, ☎ 708/960–3793 or 800/323–7604, ℻ 708/960–3575).

PACKAGES

Contact **Adventure Vacations** (✉ 10612 Beaver Dam Rd., Hunt Valley, MD 21030–2205, ☎ 410/785–3500 or 800/638–9040, ℻ 410/584–2771), **American Airlines Fly AAway Vacations** (☎ 800/321–2121), **Continental Vacations** (☎ 800/634–5555), **Delta Dream Vacations** (☎ 800/872–7786), **Globetrotters** (✉ 139 Main St., Cambridge, MA 02142, ☎ 617/621–9911 or 800/333–1234), **United Vacations** (☎ 800/328–6877), and **USAir Vacations** (☎ 800/455–0123). **Funjet Vacations,** based in Milwaukee, Wisconsin, **Gogo Tours,** based in Ramsey, New Jersey, and **Kingdom Tours,** based in Plains, Pennsylvania, sell Walt Disney World packages only through travel agents. For rail packages that combine air, hotel, and tour options, contact **Amtrak's Great American Vacations** (☎ 800/321–8684).

Regional operators specialize in assembling Walt Disney World packages for travelers from their local area.

Arrangements may include charter or scheduled air. Contact **Apple Vacations** (⌧ 25 N.W. Point Blvd., Elk Grove Village, IL 60007, ☎ 708/640–1150 or 800/365–2775), and **Travel Impressions** (⌧ 465 Smith St., Farmingdale, NY 11735, ☎ 516/845–8000 or 800/284–0044, FAX 516/845–8095).

Disney Vacations land-only packages are available through Disney's Central Reserve Office (☎ 407/934–7639). Disney's packages tend to be pricier but include more than those sold by most other operators. Meals, use of sports facilities, tips, and theme park admissions are included in the package price.

Also contact **Amtrak**'s Great American Vacations (☎ 800/321–8684).

FROM THE U.K.➤ Tour operators offering packages to Walt Disney World and the Orlando area are **British Airways Holidays** (⌧ Astral Towers, Betts Way, London Rd., Crawley, West Sussex RH10 2XA, ☎ 01293/723–111), **Jetsave Travel Ltd.** (⌧ Sussex House, London Rd., East Grinstead, West Sussex RH19 1LD, ☎ 01342/312–033), **Key to America** (⌧ 1–3 Station Rd., Ashford, Middlesex TW15 2UW, ☎ 01784/248–777), **Kuoni Travel** (⌧ Kuoni House, Dorking, Surrey RH5 4AZ, ☎ 01306/742–222), and **Premier Holidays** (⌧ Westbrook, Milton Rd., Cambridge CB4 1YQ, ☎ 01223/516–688).

Car rental is included in all Florida holidays.

Travel agencies that offer cheap fares to Orlando and Miami include **Trailfinders** (⌧ 42–50 Earl's Court Rd., London W8 6FT, ☎ 0171/937–5400), **Travel Cuts** (⌧ 295A Regent St., London W1R 7YA, ☎ 0171/637–3161), and **Flightfile** (⌧ 49 Tottenham Court Rd., London W1P 9RE, ☎ 0171/700–2722). ☞ Students, *above*.

ORGANIZATIONS

The **National Tour Association** (⌧ NTA, 546 E. Main St., Lexington, KY 40508, ☎ 606/226–4444 or 800/755–8687) and the **United States Tour Operators Association** (⌧ USTOA, 211 E. 51st St., Suite 12B, New York, NY 10022, ☎ 212/750–7371) can provide lists of members and information on booking tours.

PUBLICATIONS

Contact the USTOA (☞ Organizations, *above*) for its **"Smart Traveler's Planning Kit."** Pamphlets in the kit include the "Worldwide Tour and Vacation Package Finder," "How to Select a Tour or Vacation Package," and information on the organization's consumer protection plan. Also get copy of the Better Business Bureau's **"Tips on Travel Packages"** (⌧ Publication 24-195, 4200 Wilson Blvd., Arlington, VA 22203; $2). The National Tour Association will send you **"On Tour,"** a listing of its member operators, and a personalized

package of information on group travel in North America.

Amtrak (☎ 800/USA–RAIL) operates the *Silver Star* and the *Silver Meteor* to Florida. Both stop in Winter Park (150 Morse Blvd.), Orlando (1400 Sligh Blvd.), and Kissimmee (416 Pleasant St.). ☞ Driving, *above*.

For travel apparel, appliances, personal-care items, and other travel necessities, get a free catalog from **Magellan's** (☎ 800/962–4943, FAX 805/568–5406), **Orvis Travel** (☎ 800/541–3541, FAX 703/343–7053), or **TravelSmith** (☎ 800/950–1600, FAX 415/455–0554).

For names of reputable agencies in your area, contact the **American Society of Travel Agents** (⌧ ASTA, 1101 King St., Suite 200, Alexandria, VA 22314, ☎ 703/739–2782), the **Association of Canadian Travel Agents** (⌧ Suite 201, 1729 Bank St., Ottawa, Ontario K1V 7Z5, ☎ 613/521–0474, FAX 613/521–0805) or the **Association of British Travel Agents** (⌧ 55-57 Newman St., London W1P 4AH, ☎ 0171/637–2444, FAX 0171/637–0713).

DISNEY PARKS AND HOTELS

Contact **Walt Disney World Information** (⌧

Box 10040, Lake Buena Vista, FL 32830, ☎ 407/824–4321, TTY 407/827–5141); for reservations, contact the **Central Reservations Office** (for lodging and entertainment, ☎ 407/934–7639, TTY 407/345–5984; for dining, ☎ 407/939–3463). To be a member of the audience at a show being taped at Disney-MGM Studios, call **Production Information** (☎ 407/560–4651).

OTHER THEME PARKS

Contact **Sea World** (✉ 7007 Sea World Dr., Orlando 32821, ☎ 407/351–3600), **Universal Studios Florida** (✉ 1000 Univeral Studios Plaza, Orlando 32819-8000, ☎ 407/363–8000, TTY 407/363–8265), and **Busch Gardens** (✉ Box 9158, Tampa 333674, ☎ 813/987–5283).

GREATER ORLANDO

Contact the **Orlando/Orange County Conven-**

tion and Visitors Bureau (✉ 8445 International Dr., Orlando, FL 32819, ☎ 407/363–5871). Ask for the free *Discover Orlando* guidebook; it includes the Orlando Magicard, good for discounts on area attractions. For information about the Kissimmee area on U.S. 192, contact the **Kissimmee/St. Cloud Convention and Visitors Bureau** (✉ 1925 E. Irlo Bronson Memorial Hwy., Kissimmee, FL 34744, ☎ 407/847–5000 or 800/327–9159). For information about the tony suburb of Winter Park, contact the **Winter Park Chamber of Commerce** (✉ Box 280, Winter Park, FL 32790, ☎ 407/644–8281).

STATEWIDE

For information on destinations outside the immediate Orlando–Kissimmee area, contact the **Florida Department of Commerce Division of**

Tourism (✉ 126 W. Van Buren St., Tallahassee, FL 32399-2000, ☎ 904/487–1462).

W
WEATHER

For current conditions and forecasts, plus the local time and helpful travel tips, call the **Weather Channel Connection** (☎ 900/932–8437; *95¢* per minute) from a Touch-Tone phone.

The *International Traveler's Weather Guide* (✉ Weather Press, Box 660606, Sacramento, CA 95866, ☎ 916/974–0201 or 800/972–0201; $10.95 includes shipping), written by two meteorologists, provides month-by-month information on temperature, humidity, and precipitation in more than 175 cities worldwide.

SMART TRAVEL TIPS A TO Z

Basic Information on Traveling in Orlando and Savvy Tips to Make Your Trip a Breeze

A

AIR TRAVEL

If time is an issue, **always look for nonstop flights,** which require no change of plane. If possible, **avoid connecting flights,** which stop at least once and can involve a change of plane, even though the flight number remains the same; if the first leg is late, the second waits.

For better service, **fly smaller or regional carriers,** which often have higher passenger satisfaction ratings. Sometimes they have such in-flight amenities as leather seats or greater legroom and they often have better food.

CUTTING COSTS

The Sunday travel section of most newspapers is a good place to look for deals.

MAJOR AIRLINES➤ The least-expensive airfares from the major airlines are priced for round-trip travel and are subject to restrictions. Usually, you must **book in advance and buy the ticket within 24 hours** to get cheaper fares, and you may have to **stay over a Saturday night.** The lowest fare is subject to availability, and only a small percentage of the plane's total seats is sold at that price. It's smart to **call a number of airlines, and when you are quoted a**

good price, book it on the spot—the same fare may not be available on the same flight the next day. Airlines generally allow you to change your return date for a $25 to $50 fee. If you don't use your ticket, you can apply the cost toward the purchase of a new ticket, again for a small charge. However, most low-fare tickets are nonrefundable. To get the lowest airfare, **check different routings.** If your destination has more than one gateway, **compare prices to different airports.**

FROM THE U.K.➤ To save money on flights, **look into an APEX or Super-Pex ticket.** APEX tickets must be booked in advance and have certain restrictions. Super-PEX tickets can be purchased right at the airport.

ALOFT

AIRLINE FOOD➤ If you hate airline food, **ask for special meals when booking.** These can be vegetarian, low-cholesterol, or kosher, for example; commonly prepared to order in smaller quantities than standard fare, they can be tastier.

SMOKING➤ Smoking is not allowed on flights of six hours or less within the continental United States. Smoking is also prohibited on flights within Canada. For U.S. flights longer than six hours or inter-

national flights, **contact your carrier regarding their smoking policy.** Some carriers have prohibited smoking throughout their system; others allow smoking only on certain routes or even certain departures of that route.

AIRPORT TRANSFERS

BY BUS

Public buses operate between the airport and the main terminal of the Tri-County Transit Authority, in downtown Orlando. Though the cost is 75¢, other options are preferable because center-city Orlando is far from most of the hotels used by theme-park vacationers.

BY TAXI

Taxis take only a half hour to get from the airport to most hotels used by WDW visitors; they charge about $25 plus tip to the International Drive area, about $10 more to the U.S. 192 area. Depending on the number of people in your party, this will cost more or less than paying by the head for an airport shuttle.

B

BUS TRAVEL

If you are staying along International Drive, in Kissimmee, or in Orlando proper, you can ride public buses to get around the immediate area. To find out which bus to take, ask your hotel clerk or call the Tri-County Transit Authority Information Office (☎ 407/841–8240) for more information.

FROM THE HOTELS TO THE ATTRACTIONS

Scheduled service and charters linking just about every hotel and major attraction in the area are available. In addition, many hotels run their own shuttles especially for guests; to arrange a ride, all you have to do is ask your hotel's concierge, inquire at the front desk, or phone the operator directly.

When making your plans, remember that the bus schedule may not always coincide with your schedule: Buses may not run to the places you want to see on the days or at the times you prefer, whether that's back to your hotel at midday or out to the theme parks in late afternoon. Some buses also pick up or drop off guests at several hotels, adding to your ride time and delaying your arrival at your destination.

One-way fares are usually $6–$7 per adult, a couple of dollars less for children 4–11, between major hotel areas and the Disney parks. Excursion fares to Busch Gardens and Cypress Gardens, which are more than a half-hour's drive, are $27 per person, including admission as well as round-trip fare.

C

CAMERAS, CAMCORDERS, AND COMPUTERS

IN TRANSIT

Always keep your film, tape, or disks out of the sun; never put these on the dashboard of a car. Carry an extra supply of batteries, and **be prepared to turn on your camera, camcorder, or laptop computer for security personnel** to prove that it's real.

X-RAYS

Always **ask for hand inspection at security.** Such requests are virtually always honored at U.S. airports. Photographic film becomes clouded after successive exposure to airport x-ray machines. Videotape and computer disks are not by X-rays, but **keep your tapes and disks away from metal detectors.**

CAR RENTAL

Although public transportation in Orlando is practically nonexistent and taxis are expensive because of the distances involved, it is by no means absolutely necessary to rent a car when you are in Orlando. If you are staying at a Disney hotel or purchase a multiday passport instead of buying daily admission tickets to the Disney parks, your transportation within Walt Disney World is free. Outside Walt Disney World, just about every lodging is linked by private shuttle to area attractions. However, should you want to visit the major

theme parks outside Walt Disney World, venture off the beaten track, or eat where most tourists don't, then a rental car is essential. Fortunately, Orlando offers some of the lowest rental-car rates in the United States.

CUTTING COSTS

To get the best deal, **book through a travel agent who is willing to shop around.** When pricing cars, **ask where the rental lot is located.** Some off-airport locations offer lower rates— even though their lots are only minutes away from the terminal via complimentary shuttle. You also may want to **price local car-rental companies,** whose rates may be lower still, although service and maintenance standards may not be as high as those of a national firm. Ask your agent to **look for fly-drive packages,** which also save you money, and **ask if local taxes are included** in the rental or fly-drive price. These can be as high as 20% in some destinations. Don't forget to find out about required deposits, cancellation penalties, drop-off charges, and the cost of any required insurance coverage.

Also **ask your travel agent about a company's customer-service record.** How has it responded to late plane arrivals and vehicle mishaps? Are there often lines at the rental counter, and—if you're traveling during a holiday period—does a confirmed reservation guarantee you a car?

INSURANCE

When driving a rented car, you are generally responsible for any damage to or loss of the rental vehicle, as well as any property damage or personal injury that you cause. Before you rent, **see what coverage you already have** under the terms of your personal auto insurance policy and credit cards.

For about $14 a day, rental companies sell protection, known as a collision- or loss- damage waiver (CDW or LDW), that eliminates your liability for damage to the car; it's always optional and should never be automatically added to your bill.

In most states, the renter's personal auto insurance or other liability insurance covers damage to third parties. Only when the damage exceeds the renter's own insurance coverage does the car-rental company pay. If you do not have auto insurance or an umbrella insurance policy that covers damage to third parties, purchasing CDW or LDW is highly recommended.

U.K. CITIZENS

In the United States you must be 21 to rent a car; rates may be higher if you're under 25. You'll pay extra for child seats (about $3 per day), compulsory for children under five, and for additional drivers (about $2 per day). To pick up your reserved car you will need the reservation voucher, a passport, a U.K. driver's license, and a travel policy that covers each driver.

SURCHARGES

Before you pick up a car in one city and leave it in another, **ask about drop-off charges or one-way service fees,** which can be substantial. Note, too, that some rental agencies charge extra if you return the car before the time specified on your contract. To avoid a hefty refueling fee, **fill the tank just before you turn in the car**—but be aware that gas stations near the rental outlet may overcharge.

CHILDREN AND TRAVEL

All the theme parks get high marks from young travelers. Hotel facilities for children range from okay to fabulous. The only problem is that the times when your kids are out of school are the times when every other child in the universe is out of school and every other parent is packing up the car to drive to Orlando as well. Preschoolers can find these crowds overwhelming. So if your children are of varying ages and those in school are good students, consider taking them out so you can visit in the less-congested off-season. Educational programs and the broadening experience of travel itself may persuade your children's teachers to excuse the absence. Teachers may also arrange special study assignments relating to the trip.

If your children cannot afford to miss school, try to take your vacation in late May or early June, as soon as the school year ends.

When traveling with children, **plan ahead** and **involve your youngsters** as you outline your trip. When packing, **include a supply of things to keep them busy** en route (☞ Children & Travel *in* Important Contacts A to Z). On sightseeing days, try to **schedule activities of special interest to your children,** like a trip to a zoo or a playground. If you **plan your itinerary around seasonal festivals,** you'll never lack for things to do. In addition, **check local newspapers for special events** mounted by public libraries, museums, and parks.

BABY-SITTING

Baby-sitting is widely available; **check with your hotel desk.**

At Walt Disney World, there are strong children's facilities and programs at the Contemporary, Dolphin, Grand Floridian, Polynesian Village, Wilderness Lodge, Yacht and Beach Clubs, and Swan; the Polynesian Village's Neverland Club will enchant you and your offspring with its Peter Pan–theme clubhouse and youngsters-only dinner show. Parents also rave about the Sand Castle Club at the Yacht and Beach Clubs. The Hilton, near Disney Village Marketplace, has a Youth Hotel where parents can leave their offspring until midnight for a night on the World; meals are served and there's even a dormitory.

Off-site, many hotels have supervised children's programs. Standouts are: Shamu's Playhouse and other camplike programs at the Stouffer Orlando Resort opposite Sea World; at the Hyatt Regency Grand Cypress near Disney Village, which has a separate teens-only evening program; the Westgate Lakes Resort; and the Holiday Inn at Lake Buena Vista and the Holiday Inn Maingate East. These have trained counselors and planned activities as well as attractive facilities; some even have mascots. The age range varies from 4 or 5 to 15; some accept children as young as 2, however. The Peabody Hotel has an evening program that allows you to drop off your youngsters while you dine in the hotel's restaurants; call ahead. ☞ Chapter 8.

BABY SWAP

Parents with small children under the height limit for major attractions have to take turns waiting in the long lines, right? Wrong. In what's unofficially known as the Baby Swap, both of you queue up, and when it's your turn to board, one stays with the youngsters until the other returns; the waiting partner then rides without waiting again. Universal Studios calls it a Baby Exchange and has Baby Exchange areas at most rides.

CHARACTER MEALS

At special breakfasts, brunches, and dinners offered by many Walt Disney World restaurants, Mickey, Donald, Goofy, Chip 'n' Dale,

and other favorite characters sign autographs and pose for snapshots. Reservations are not always necessary, but these early morning feeding frenzies are wildly popular, so **show up early if you don't like to wait.** Universal Studios has its own character meal, right in the park before official park-opening hours; Woody Woodpecker, the Flintstones, and other favorites are on hand, and you will be strategically positioned to head the stampede to Back to the Future . . . The Ride. Plan your character meal for toward the end of your visit, when your little ones will be used to seeing these large and sometimes frightening figures; they're also a good way to kill the morning on the day you check out. ☞ Chapters 3 and 7.

DINING

Many restaurants in the Orlando area have a special children's menu. And providing that reassuring taste of home, franchised fast-food eateries abound. The McDonald's on International Drive has an elaborate multilevel playground that seems almost bigger than the restaurant.

DRIVING

If you are renting a car, don't forget to **arrange for a car seat when you reserve.** Sometimes they're free.

EDUCATIONAL PROGRAMS

Be sure to reserve ahead for any of these behind-the-scenes tours and programs.

WALT DISNEY WORLD➤ Walt Disney World offers its six-hour Wonders Program courses year-round for those ages 10–15; the cost is $79 per course. Your youngsters can sign up for Wildlife Adventure: Exploring the Environment, which visits Discovery Island and WDW's 7,500-acre conservation preserve, where several rare species have found refuge from encroaching development; Art Magic: Bringing Illusion to Life, which introduces students to animation, costuming, landscaping and set design in movies, stage shows, and theme parks; Showbiz Magic: The Walt Disney World of Entertainment, during which students get to meet the performers and technicians who create the Disney shows and get an understanding of how music, lighting, costumes, and timing all combine to beguile an audience; or Passport: Secret Mission to Other Lands, a scavenger hunt through Epcot Center's World Showcase. In summer there is also a separate four-hour Kidventure Program, which focuses on Discovery Island plants and wildlife and is open to students ages 8–14; it costs $30, including boat transportation.

The newly opened Disney Institute proclaims guests can come here to "make your own magic." Participants stay in special lodgings in Walt Disney Village, near the classroom facilities. Among the 80 classes offered

THE GOLD GUIDE / SMART TRAVEL TIPS

are those in animation, culinary arts, rock climbing, radio and TV production. Guests select three-, four-, or seven-night packages. Rates begin at approximately $582 per person, double occupancy, for a minimum 3-night stay that includes accommodations, programs, baggage handling, a one-day Disney theme park pass, and tax. **Children must be at least 10 years old to participate.**

SEA WORLD➤ Three year-round Sea Safari programs ($5.95 adults, $4.95 children 3–9) offer behind-the-scenes looks at park operations: Backstage Explorations and Animal Lover's Adventure are 90-minute guided tours of park facilities; Animal Training Discoveries consists of a 45-minute chat and demonstration with the park's trainers. For a wide selection of age-specific classes on wildlife and ecology, you'll have to wait for summer, when the calendar is chockablock with programs ranging from one day to one week in length; most cost $15–$60. In addition, the bring-your-own-sleeping-bag Education Sleepovers, offered exclusively to school groups in winter, are open to individual visitors. How about bedding down in the shark exhibit at Terrors of the Deep? Or try Cool Nights with Penguins to see the nightlife of the tuxedoed masses. There's even talk of conducting overseas trips that combine classes at the park with

a few days in Belize or the Bahamas.

BUSCH GARDENS➤ Multiday Zoo Camps keep children learning here from June through October. There's a different program for each age group, from kindergartners through 10th graders, and each program lasts several days ($80–$100 per session). Youngsters can also sign up for classes that last just a few hours ($15–$20), from a hands-on introduction to wildlife for toddlers to a night hike for preteens.

FLYING

As a general rule, infants under two not occupying a seat fly for free. If your children are two or older **ask about special children's fares.** Age limits for these fares vary among carriers. Rules also vary regarding unaccompanied minors, so again, check with your airline.

BAGGAGE➤ In general, the adult baggage allowance applies to children paying half or more of the adult fare.

SAFETY SEATS➤ According to the FAA, it's a good idea to **use safety seats aloft** for children weighing less than 40 pounds. Airline policies vary. U.S. carriers allow FAA-approved models but usually require that you buy a ticket, even if your child would otherwise ride free, since the seats must be strapped into regular seats. However, some airlines may require you to hold your baby during takeoff and landing—defeating the seat's purpose.

FACILITIES➤ When making your reservation, **request for children's meals or freestanding bassinets** if you need them; the latter are available only to those seated at the bulkhead, where there's enough legroom. If you don't need a bassinet, **think twice before requesting bulkhead seats**—the only storage space for in-flight necessities is in inconveniently distant overhead bins.

GAMES

Milton Bradley and Parker Brothers have travel versions of some of their most popular games, including Yahtzee, Trouble, Sorry, and Monopoly. Prices run $5 to $8. Look for them in the travel section of your local toy store.

LODGING

In all but the smallest motels there is little or no charge for children under 18 who share a room with an adult.

PLAYGROUNDS, GAME ROOMS, THEME POOLS

All hotels on Disney property and many others in the area have playgrounds and arcades with video games and pinball machines. The one in Disney's Contemporary Resort is, hands down, the biggest game room in any hotel in the area. Parrot Cay, a little island in the Caribbean Beach Resort's lagoon, is anchored by a winning little playground with soft white sand underfoot. Swimming pools are long on Disney charm, with such special effects as a pirate stronghold and a cannon that lets out periodic booms, the Stormalong Bay area between Disney's Yacht and Beach Club, and the lagoon at Disney's Dixie Landings Resort.

STROLLER RENTALS

Stroller rentals are available in theme parks, but you may want to bring your own, since fees run $5–$6 per day (plus a deposit). Also, you will probably need a stroller in places where you can't rent one—to explore Orlando off the beaten track, to explore Orlando's malls, even just to get around your hotel, if it's big. No one rents double strollers, and the singles available in Walt Disney World are sturdy but unyielding, not optimal for infants.

If you do rent a stroller, there is always the possibility that it will be taken. A word to the wise: although it is tempting, **don't leave packages in strollers.** At the three Disney theme parks, you can arrange to have large packages sent to the gate, where you can pick it up upon leaving. Experienced park visitors suggest either taping a large card with your name to the stroller or leaving some small personal item to mark it, such as a bandanna, a T-shirt, even a clear plastic bag with diapers inside; the theory is that people who wouldn't think twice about purloining theme-park property that they will subsequently return hesitate to make off with something that belongs to a fellow parent. If your stroller does disappear, you can easily pick up a replacement; ask any park staffer for the nearest location.

CUSTOMS AND DUTIES

To speed your clearance through customs, **keep receipts for all your purchases abroad** and **be ready to show the inspector what you've bought.** If you feel that you've been incorrectly or unfairly charged a duty, you can **appeal assessments in dispute.** First ask to see a supervisor. If you are still unsatisfied, **write to the port director** your point of entry, sending your customs receipt and any other appropriate documentation. The address will be listed on your receipt. If you still don't get satisfaction, you can take your case to customs headquarters in Washington.

IN CANADA

If you've been out of Canada for at least seven days, you may bring in C$500 worth of goods duty-free. If you've been away for fewer than seven days but for more than 48 hours, the duty-free allowance drops to C$200; if your trip lasts between 24 and 48 hours, the allowance is C$50. You cannot pool allowances with family members. Goods claimed under the C$500 exemption may follow you by mail; those claimed under the lesser exemptions must accompany you.

Alcohol and tobacco products may be included in the seven-day and 48-hour exemptions but not in the 24-hour exemption. If you meet the age requirements of the province or territory through which you reenter Canada, you may bring in, duty-free, 1.14 liters (40 imperial ounces) of wine or liquor or 24 12-ounce cans or bottles of beer or ale. If you are 16 or older, you may bring in, duty-free, 200 cigarettes, 50 cigars or cigarillos, and 400 tobacco sticks or 400 grams of manufactured tobacco. Alcohol and tobacco must accompany you on your return.

An unlimited number of gifts with a value of up to C$60 each may be mailed to Canada duty-free. These do not affect your duty-free allowance on your return. Label the package "Unsolicited Gift—Value Under $60." Alcohol and tobacco are excluded.

IN THE U.K.

From countries outside the EU, including the United States, you may import, duty-free, 200 cigarettes, 100 cigarillos, 50 cigars, or 250 grams of tobacco; 1 liter of spirits or 2 liters of fortified or sparkling wine or liqueurs; 2 liters of still table wine; 60 milliliters of perfume; 250 milliliters of toilet water; plus £136 worth of other goods, including gifts and souvenirs.

D

DISABILITIES AND ACCESSIBILITY

Central Florida attractions are among the

most accessible destinations in the world for people who have disabilities. The hospitality industry continues to spend millions on barrier-removing renovations. Though some challenges remain, most can be overcome with planning.

When discussing accessibility with an operator or reservationist, ask hard questions. Are there any stairs, inside *or* out? Are there grab bars next to the toilet *and* in the shower/tub? How wide is the doorway to the room? To the bathroom? For the most extensive facilities, meeting the latest legal specifications, **opt for newer facilities,** which more often have been designed with access in mind. Older properties or ships must usually be retrofitted and may offer more limited facilities as a result. Be sure to **discuss your needs before booking.**

The main park-information centers (☞ Chapters 2 and 3) can answer specific questions and dispense general information for guests with disabilities.

LOCAL TRANSPORTATION

Although there are some lift-equipped vans for rent and some shuttle service available, guests need to plan itineraries in advance. The exception is on Disney property: Every other Disney bus on each route is lift-equipped, so there's never more than a 30-minute wait for hotel-to-theme-park trips. Consult transportation companies for more information.

Designated parking is available for guests with disabilities. It's near the turnstile area for most parks. The Magic Kingdom's special lot is near the Transportation and Ticket Center, where ferries depart for the Magic Kingdom and monorails travel there and to Epcot Center. Monorail entrances are level, but the ramp up is quite steep.

LODGING

Hotels and motels here are continually being renovated to comply with the Americans with Disabilities Act. Call the Disabled Traveler's Helpline of Central Florida for up-to-the-minute information.

GUESTS USING WHEEL-CHAIRS➤ Staying at Disney-owned resort hotels is particularly convenient, since the Disney transportation system has dozens of lift-equipped vehicles. Most resorts here in every price range have rooms with roll-in showers or transfer benches in the bathrooms.

You will be comfortable at any number of on-property Disney resorts. Especially worthwhile and convenient is the Grand Floridian, a luxurious monorail resort, and Port Orleans, which has all the advantages of Dixie Landings but a much more intimate feel. One of the most accommodating off-site resorts is the Marriott Orlando World Center; its level of commitment is especially apparent on Sunday mornings, when the Garden Terrace Restaurant hosts one of

the most delicious and hospitable Sunday brunches in central Florida.

GUESTS WITH VISUAL IMPAIRMENTS➤ In most properties, only elevators are braille-equipped, but some have programs to help employees understand how best to assist guests with visual impairments. Particularly outstanding is the Buena Vista Palace on Hotel Plaza Boulevard at Walt Disney World Village; its Australian-themed Outback Restaurant even has a table-side storyteller who paints pictures with words. The Embassy Suites Resorts at Lake Buena Vista and International Drive offer services such as talking alarm clocks and braille or recorded menus.

GUESTS WITH HEARING IMPAIRMENTS➤ Most area properties have purchased the equipment necessary to accommodate guests with hearing impairments. Telecommunications devices for the deaf, flashing or vibrating phones and alarms, and closed captioning are common; an industry-wide effort to teach some employees sign language is under way. The Grosvenor Resort, on Hotel Plaza Boulevard, has excellent facilities but no teletype reservations line.

THEME PARKS

DISCOUNTS➤ Guests with disabilities can **take advantage of a wide variety of discounts:** 50% at Busch Gardens for wheelchair users and the visually or hearing impaired; at least 50% at Cypress Gardens and Sea World for guests with visual or hearing impairments; and 20% at Universal Studios for those with a disability that limits enjoyment of the park.

GUESTS USING WHEELCHAIRS➤ Accessibility in the area is constantly improving for people who use wheelchairs. At Walt Disney World, a new standard of access was set with the opening of the Disney-MGM Studios. All of its restaurants, shops, and attractions, except one thrill ride, can be enjoyed right from a wheelchair. Epcot Center comes in a close second; some of the rides have a tailgate that drops down to provide a level entrance to the ride vehicle. Though the Magic Kingdom, now in its third decade, was designed before architects gave consideration to access issues, renovation plans are under way. Even so, the 18 accessible attractions combine with the live entertainment around the park to provide a most memorable experience. For specific accessibility information, *see* the For Travelers with Disabilities section for each park.

Universal Studios and Sea World are both substantially barrier-free. Universal has retrofitted its major attractions, with the exception of Back to the Future, for wheelchair accessibility. At Sea World, most shows are in stadiums or theaters and have always been barrier-free. Now guests can even take their wheelchairs on the Behind the Scenes tours. Cypress Gardens and Splendid China are accessible by guests with disabilities.

In some attractions, guests who use scooters may be required to transfer to a wheelchair. In others, guests must be able to leave their own wheelchair to board the ride vehicle, and must have a traveling companion assist them, as park staff cannot do so. Attractions with emergency evacuation routes that have narrow walkways or steps require additional mobility. Turbulence on other attractions poses a problem for some guests.

Rest rooms at all of these parks have standard accessible stalls. Yet more spacious facilities are available in First Aid stations.

GUESTS WITH VISUAL IMPAIRMENTS➤ WDW and Universal Studios have produced descriptive cassette tapes that can be borrowed, along with portable tape recorders (deposit required); Sea World has no cassette program but does offer a braille guidebook and a free tour. The other parks have no services for the visually impaired. Service animals, while welcome, must be leashed or in a harness; they may board many rides, but not all—usually not those with loud noises, pyrotechnics, and other intense effects.

GUESTS WITH HEARING IMPAIRMENTS➤ Walt Disney World publishes a special guidebook describing the theme and story of various attractions in the three parks. At Epcot Center, you can rent personal translator units that amplify the sound tracks of seven shows ($4 plus $40 deposit). There and in the Magic Kingdom (and in Disney-MGM Studios by special arrangement), four-hour guided tours in sign language are available. Advance reservations are a must; provide two-weeks' notice if possible ($5 for adults, $3.50 for children 3–9).

Both Universal Studios and Sea World can also provide guides fluent in sign language with advance notice; Universal also has scripts available for all its shows. Busch Gardens, Cypress Gardens, and Splendid China do not offer assistance in sign.

WHEELCHAIRS

Probably the most comfortable course is to bring your wheelchair from home. However, except in theater-style shows, access may be difficult if it's wider than 24½ inches and longer than 32 inches (44 inches for scooters); consult hosts and hostesses at the attraction. Thefts of personal wheelchairs while guests are inside attractions are rare but have been known to occur; take the precautions you would in any public place.

Wheelchair rentals are available from area medical-supply companies that will deliver to your hotel and let you keep the chair for the duration of your vacation. You can also rent by the day in major theme parks ($6 a day for wheelchairs, $25–$30 daily for the limited number of scooters, plus a deposit; *see* Chapters 2 and 3 for specifics).

In Disney parks, since rental locations are relatively close to parking, it may be a good idea to send someone ahead to get the wheelchair and bring it back to the car; at day's end, a Disney host or hostess may escort you to your car and then return the wheelchair for you. Here and at the other major area theme parks, rented wheelchairs that disappear while you're in a ride can be replaced throughout the parks—ask any staffer for the nearest location. Attaching some small personal item to the wheelchair may prevent other guests from taking yours by mistake.

DISCOUNTS AND DEALS

You shouldn't have to pay for a discount. In fact, you may already be eligible for all kinds of savings. Here are some time-honored strategies for getting the best deal.

LOOK IN YOUR WALLET

When you **use your credit card to make travel purchases,** you may get free travel-accident insurance, collision damage insurance, medical or legal assistance, depending on the card and bank that issued it. Visa and MasterCard provide one or more of these services, so **get a copy of your card's travel benefits.** If you are a member of the AAA or an oil-company-sponsored road-assistance plan, always **ask hotel or car-rental reservationists for auto-club discounts.** Some clubs offer additional discounts on tours, cruises, or admission to attractions. And don't forget that auto-club membership entitles you to free maps and trip-planning services.

DIAL FOR DOLLARS

To save money, **look into "1-800" discount reservations services,** which often have lower rates. These services use their buying power to get a better price on hotels, airline tickets, and sometimes even car rentals. When booking a room, always **call the hotel's local toll-free number** (if one is available) rather than the central reservations number—you'll often get a better price. Ask the reservationist about special packages or corporate rates, which are usually available even if you're not traveling on business.

JOIN A CLUB?

Discount clubs can be a legitimate source of savings, but you must use the participating hotels and visit the participating attractions in order to realize any benefits. Remember, too, that you have to pay a fee to join, so **determine if you'll save enough to warrant your membership fee.** Before booking with a club, **make sure the hotel or other supplier isn't offering a better deal.**

DRIVING

If you have arrived by plane, **use the Beeline Expressway (Rte. 528) to get to the hotels from the airport.** Follow the expressway west to International Drive, and exit at Sea World. Or stay on the Beeline to I–4, and head either west to Walt Disney World and U.S. 192/Kissimmee or east to downtown Orlando. Call your hotel for the best route.

The most important artery in the Orlando area is I–4, which links the Atlantic Coast to Florida's Gulf of Mexico. However, the interstate actually runs north and south in the Orlando area. So **think north when I–4 signs say east and think south when the signs say west.**

Two other main roads you're likely to use are International Drive, also known as I–Drive, and U.S. 192, sometimes called the Spacecoast Parkway or Irlo Bronson Memorial Highway. You can get onto International Drive from I–4 Exits 28, 29, and 30B. U.S. 192 cuts across I–4 at Exits 25A and 25B.

G

GAY AND LESBIAN TRAVEL

The Genesis Foundation has organized an annual Gay Day at Walt Disney World for the past five years. In 1995, the event was expanded to include an entire weekend's worth of activities, including a Lesbian and Gay Business Expo at the Orange County Convention Center.

I
INSURANCE

Travel insurance can protect your monetary investment, replace your luggage and its contents, or provide for medical coverage should you fall ill during your trip. Most tour operators, travel agents, and insurance agents sell specialized health-and-accident, flight, trip-cancellation, and luggage insurance as well as comprehensive policies with some or all of these coverages. Comprehensive policies may also reimburse you for delays due to weather—an important consideration if you're traveling during the winter months. Some health-insurance policies do not cover preexisting conditions, but waivers may be available in specific cases. Coverage is sold by the companies listed in Important Contacts A to Z; these companies act as the policy's administrators. The actual insurance is usually underwritten by a well-known name, such as The Travelers or Continental Insurance.

Before you make any purchase, **review your existing health and homeowner's policies** to find out whether they cover expenses incurred while traveling.

BAGGAGE

Airline liability for baggage is limited to $1,250 per person on domestic flights. On international flights, it amounts to $9.07 per pound or $20 per kilogram for checked baggage (roughly $640 per 70-pound bag) and $400 per passenger for unchecked baggage. Insurance for losses exceeding the terms of your airline ticket can be bought directly from the airline at check-in for about $10 per $1,000 of coverage; note that it excludes a rather extensive list of items, shown on your airline ticket.

COMPREHENSIVE

Comprehensive insurance policies include all the coverages described above plus some that may not be available in more specific policies. If you have purchased an expensive vacation, especially one that involves travel abroad, comprehensive insurance is a must; **look for policies that include trip delay insurance,** which will protect you in the event that weather problems cause you to miss your flight, tour, or cruise. A few insurers will also sell you a waiver for preexisting medical conditions. Some of the companies that offer both these features are Access America, Carefree Travel, Travel Insured International, and TravelGuard (☞ Important Contacts A to Z).

FLIGHT

You should **think twice before buying flight insurance.** Often purchased as a last-minute impulse at the airport, it pays a lump sum when a plane crashes, either to a beneficiary if the insured dies or sometimes to a surviving passenger who loses his or her eyesight or a limb. Supplementing the airlines' coverage described in the limits-of-liability paragraphs on your ticket, it's expensive and basically unnecessary. Charging an airline ticket to a major credit card often automatically provides you with coverage that may also extend to travel by bus, train, and ship.

U.K. TRAVELERS

According to the Association of British Insurers, a trade association representing 450 insurance companies, it's wise to **buy extra medical coverage when you visit the United States.** You can buy an annual travel insurance policy valid for most vacations during the year in which it's purchased. If you are pregnant or have a preexisting medical condition make sure you're covered before buying such a policy.

TRIP

Without insurance, you will lose all or most of your money if you cancel your trip regardless of the reason. Especially if your airline ticket, cruise, or package tour is nonrefundable and cannot be changed, it's essential that you **buy trip-cancellation-and-interruption insurance.** When considering how much coverage you need, look for a policy that will cover the cost of your trip plus the nondiscounted price of a one-way airline ticket should you need to return home early. Read the fine print carefully, especially sections that define "family member" and "preexisting medical conditions." Also **consider default or bankruptcy insurance,** which protects you against a supplier's failure to deliver. Be aware, however, that if you buy such a policy from a travel agency, tour operator, airline, or cruise line, it may not cover default by the firm in question.

L

LODGING

APARTMENT & VILLA RENTAL

If you want a home base that's roomy enough for a family and comes with cooking facilities, **consider taking a furnished rental.** This can also save you money, but not always—some rentals are luxury properties (economical only when your party is large). Home-exchange directories list rentals—often second homes owned by prospective house swappers—and some services search for a house or apartment for you (even a castle if that's your fancy) and handle the paperwork. Some send an illustrated catalog; others send photographs only of specific properties, sometimes at a charge; up-front registration fees may apply.

HOME EXCHANGE

If you would like to find a house, an apartment, or some other type of vacation property to exchange for your own while on holiday, **become a member of a home-exchange organization,**

which will send you its updated listings of available exchanges for a year, and will include your own listing in at least one of them. Arrangements for the actual exchange are made by the two parties involved, not by the organization.

M

MONEY

ATMS

CASH ADVANCES➤ Before leaving home, **make sure that your credit cards have been programmed for ATM use.**

O

OPENING AND CLOSING TIMES

Most major attractions, restaurants, hotels, and shops are open for business seven days a week year-round.

DAILY HOURS

Theme-park hours vary from season to season; daily hours are extended mornings and evenings in busy periods. Walt Disney World's Magic Kingdom, for instance, closes at 7 PM in November but stays open until 2 AM on New Year's Eve. Cypress Gardens is open 9:30–5:30 daily year-round.

HOLIDAYS

Some public and private establishments close on holidays—not only the traditional holidays of New Year's Day, Easter, Memorial Day, Fourth of July, Labor Day, Thanksgiving, and Christmas but also for Martin Luther King,

Jr.'s, Birthday (the second Monday in January), Presidents' Day (the third Monday in February), and Columbus Day (the second Monday in October).

P

PACKING FOR ORLANDO

Comfortable walking shoes or sneakers are essential. The entire area is extremely casual, day and night, so men will need a jacket and tie in only a handful of restaurants. For sightseeing and theme-park visits, pack shorts, sundresses, cotton slacks or jeans, T-shirts, and a light sweater as protection against the sometimes glacial air-conditioning. Experienced theme-park visitors also suggest using a waist pouch ("fanny pack") rather than a tote bag or purse. And don't forget your sunglasses!

In winter, be prepared for a range of temperatures: Take clothing that you can layer, including a sweater and warm jacket. For summer, you'll want a sun hat, sunscreen lotion, and a poncho and folding umbrella in case of sudden thunderstorms (a daily occurrence during the summer months).

Bring an extra pair of eyeglasses or contact lenses in your carry-on luggage, and if you have a health problem, **pack enough medication** to last the trip. It's important that you **don't put prescription drugs or valuables in** luggage to be checked, for it could go astray.

LUGGAGE

Toy guns, toy knives, and the like sold in Frontierland and Adventureland should be packed in checked luggage. Security may give you a hard time if you try to carry them on board.

Airline baggage allowances depend on the airline, the route, and the class of your ticket; ask in advance. In general, on domestic flights you are entitled to check two bags. A third piece may be brought on board, but it must fit easily under the seat in front of you or in the overhead compartment. In the United States, the FAA gives airlines broad latitude regarding carry-on allowances, and they tend to tailor them to different aircraft and operational conditions. Charges for excess, oversize, or overweight pieces vary.

SAFEGUARDING YOUR LUGGAGE➤ Before leaving home, **itemize your bags' contents** and their worth, and label them with your name, address, and phone number. (If you use your home address, cover it so that potential thieves can't see it readily.) Inside each bag, **pack a copy of your itinerary.** At check-in, **make sure that each bag is correctly tagged** with the destination airport's three-letter code. If your bags arrive damaged—or fail to arrive at all—file a written report with the airline before leaving the airport.

PASSPORTS
AND VISAS

CANADIANS

No passport is necessary to enter the United States.

U.K. CITIZENS

British citizens need a valid passport to enter the United States. If you are staying for fewer than 90 days and traveling on a vacation, with a return or onward ticket, you probably will not need a visa. However, you will need to fill out the Visa Waiver Form, 1-94W, supplied by the airline.

It is advisable that you **leave one photocopy of your passport's data page** with someone at home and keep another with you, separated from your passport, while traveling. If you lose your passport, promptly call the nearest embassy or consulate and the local police; having the data page information can speed replacement.

PLANNING

Careful planning is key to the most hassle-free visit to the Orlando area. The first step is to **figure out everything you want to see and do in the area.** Will you be staying put in the Orlando area, or do you want to spend some time at the beach? Once you've settled on your sightseeing priorities, you can figure out how long you want to stay, make reservations, and buy tickets.

HOW LONG TO STAY

There are a couple of ways to approach this

question. If your objective is to enjoy the complete Walt Disney World resort experience, five days is a comfortable period to allow; this gives you time to see all of its major and minor parks, to sample the restaurants and entertainment, and to spend some time around the pool. Six days would be better. Figure on an additional day for every other area theme park you want to visit, and then add your travel time to and from home.

If you're coming to the area mostly to go on the rides and see the theme parks, allow one day per theme park. This supposes that you're willing to start out early every day, move quickly, breeze through shops, and hurry through meals. Then add your travel time to and from home.

In either case, **add time for visiting the minor theme parks,** for exploring Orlando off the beaten track, and for shopping in Orlando's flea markets and discount malls. In addition, **add an extra day or two if you're traveling with small children,** who may have limited patience for marathon touring; if you want to linger during your stays; if you're staying off Disney property or using local shuttle transportation rather than your own or a rental car to accommodate the extra time you will spend just getting to and from your destinations; or if you're visiting during a busy period, when long lines will make it nearly impossible to see all the most popular attractions—unless you have a lot of stamina for long days on your feet and are willing to be on the go from early in the morning until park closing. You could easily spend two weeks in the area and still not see it all.

CREATING AN ITINERARY

Once you know what you want to see and do, the first step is to **lay out a day-by-day touring plan,** using the Strategies for Your Visit sections of our theme-parks sections in Chapters 2 and 3 and the italicized Crowds and Strategy information following each review. Don't try to plot your route from hour to hour; instead break the day up into morning, afternoon, and evening sections. Finally, **make a schedule for calling for any reservations** you will need. Put each day's plan on a separate index card, and carry the card with you as you explore.

WHAT TO SEE WHEN➣ First find out the busy days of the week in the parks you want to visit. Usually Friday, Saturday, and Sunday are quietest, except during holiday weeks. Then, beginning with the dates on which you plan to visit, **decide which parks you will see on each day.**

Think creatively. If you're staying on Walt Disney World property in a not-too-busy period and have at least five days, **consider spending afternoons at one of the water parks,** at your hotel swimming pool, or at a spa or sports facility. If you buy a multi-day pass, which is good for unlimited visits to WDW's major parks, you can also **visit two or more theme parks in a single day**—say, combine a visit to the Magic Kingdom in the morning, when the park isn't crowded, with an afternoon in Epcot Center's Future World, that area's least busy time.

MAKING RESERVATIONS➣ Make a list of all the things you want to do that require reservations. Note on the list how far in advance you can book for each. In this book, this information is usually in the italicized information following each review. Then, based on your travel schedule, designate the date on which you should call for the reservations you want. Some reservations can be made as soon as you book your hotel; others will have to wait until you're in the area.

BUYING YOUR TICKETS

If you aren't signing up for an escorted tour or travel package, **buy your WDW tickets as soon as your travel dates are definite.** Prices typically go up two or three times a year, so you may just beat a price hike and save some money. Many local offices of the American Automobile Association (AAA) also sell tickets to WDW; you don't have to be a AAA member to buy these tickets.

The Orlando airport has Universal Studios and Walt Disney World gift shops, where tickets, maps, and information are available. Buying tickets here while waiting for your bags to be unloaded will save time later. Local Disney Stores also sell tickets. If there is one in your city, inquire there. There are several Disney Stores in Orlando-area malls and you can buy your tickets there without waiting in line at the parks.

Before you get your tickets for other Orlando-area attractions, check into various money-saving offers. The Orlando Magicard, available free from the Orlando/Orange County Convention and Visitor's Bureau, entitles you to discounts at restaurants, dinner shows, and sometimes even theme parks—though never WDW. AAA members can often qualify for 10%–20% discounts on non-Disney theme-park tickets; call your branch office for more information. If applicable, also *see* Travelers with Disabilities, *above,* and Senior-Citizen Discounts, *below,* for further discount information.

S

SENIOR CITIZENS

Bear in mind that school vacation times can spell ordeal rather than adventure if you have limited energy or patience. What endurance you have will go farther if you arrive in the theme parks at opening time or even before. Do a little homework about your destination, and have a plan of action. In the morning take in first those attractions that you most want to see. This way you can take it easy when the day warms up. Then relax in the shade, have a nice long lunch, see some shows in air-conditioned theaters, and maybe even go back to your hotel to relax around the pool, read, or nap. Refreshed, you can return to one of the theme parks, when they're open late, or explore Pleasure Island, Church Street Station, or Orlando's other after-dark options. Don't overdo it.

DISCOUNTS

Most hotels and restaurants in the area have senior-citizen discounts. Pick up brochures as you visit places, read the newspapers, especially the *Orlando Sentinel,* and don't be shy about asking for suggestions at your hotel.

To qualify for age-related discounts, **mention your senior-citizen status up front** when booking hotel reservations, not when checking out, and before you're seated in restaurants, not when paying the bill. Note that discounts may be limited to certain menus, days, or hours. When renting a car, **ask about promotional car-rental discounts**—they can net even lower costs than your senior-citizen discount.

STUDENTS ON THE ROAD

To save money, **look into deals available** **through student-oriented travel agencies.** To qualify, you'll need to have a bona fide student ID card. Members of international student groups are also eligible (☞ Students *in* Important Contacts A to Z).

T

TAXIS

Taxi fares start at $2.45 and cost $1.40 for each mile thereafter. Sample fares: To WDW's Magic Kingdom, about $20 from International Drive, $11–$15 from U.S. 192. To Universal Studios, $6–$11 from International Drive, $25–$30 from U.S. 192. To Church Street Station, downtown, $20–$25 from International Drive, $30–$40 from U.S. 192.

For information on getting to or from the airport by taxi, *see* Airport Transfers *in* Air Travel, *above.*

TELEPHONES

LONG-DISTANCE

The long-distance services of AT&T, MCI, and Sprint make calling home relatively convenient and let you avoid hotel surcharges; typically, you dial an 800 number in the United States.

TOUR OPERATORS

A package or tour to Orlando can make your vacation less expensive and more hassle-free. Firms that sell tours and packages reserve airline seats, hotel rooms, and rental cars in bulk and pass some of the savings on to you. In addition, the best operators have local representatives available to help you at your destination.

You can often get a room, in your choice of hotel, for dates that Walt Disney World's own Central Reservations Office says are sold out. When booking your package, ask **whether hotels are on park grounds or outside the park;** you might pay less for a package that includes an off-site hotel, but you'll sacrifice convenience. Finally, **make sure any admission tickets included** in your package are not limited to certain days of the week.

A GOOD DEAL?

The more your package or tour includes, the better you can predict the ultimate cost of your vacation. Make sure you know exactly what is covered, and **beware of hidden costs.** Are taxes, tips, and service charges included? Transfers and baggage handling? Entertainment and excursions? These can add up.

Most packages and tours are rated deluxe, first-class superior, first class, tourist, or budget. The key difference is usually accommodations. If the package or tour you are considering is priced lower than in your wildest dreams, **be skeptical.** Also, **make sure your travel agent knows the accommodations** and other services. Ask about the hotel's location, room size, beds, and whether it has a pool, room service, or programs for children, if you care about these. Has your agent been there in

SMART TRAVEL TIPS / THE GOLD GUIDE

person or sent others you can contact?

BUYER BEWARE

Each year a number of consumers are stranded or lose their money when operators—even very large ones with excellent reputations— go out of business. To avoid becoming one of them, take the time to **check out the operator**—find out how long the company has been in business and ask several agents about its reputation. Next, **don't book unless the firm has a consumer-protection program.** Members of the USTOA and the NTA are required to set aside funds for the sole purpose of covering your payments and travel arrangements in case of default. Nonmember operators may instead carry insurance; look for the details in the operator's brochure— and for the name of an underwriter with a solid reputation. Note: When it comes to tour operators, **don't trust escrow accounts.** Although there are laws governing those of charter-flight operators, no governmental body prevents tour operators from raiding the till.

Next, **contact your local Better Business Bureau and the attorney general's offices** in both your own state and the operator's; have any complaints been filed? Finally, **pay with a major credit card.** Then you can cancel payment, provided that you can document your complaint. Always **consider trip-cancella-**

tion insurance (☞ Insurance, *above*).

BIG vs. SMALL➤ Operators that handle several hundred thousand travelers per year can use their purchasing power to give you a good price. Their high volume may also indicate financial stability. But some small companies provide more personalized service; because they tend to specialize, they may also be more knowledgeable about a given area.

USING AN AGENT

Travel agents are excellent resources. In fact, large operators accept bookings made only through travel agents. But it's good to **collect brochures from several agencies** because some agents' suggestions may be skewed by promotional relationships with tour and package firms that reward them for volume sales. If you have a special interest, **find an agent with expertise in that area;** ASTA can provide leads in the United States. (Don't rely solely on your agent, though; agents may be unaware of small-niche operators, and some special-interest travel companies only sell direct.)

SINGLE TRAVELERS

Prices are usually quoted per person, based on two sharing a room. If traveling solo, you may be required to pay the full double-occupancy rate. Some operators eliminate this surcharge if you agree to be matched up with a

roommate of the same sex, even if one is not found by departure time.

Travel catalogs specialize in useful items that can **save space when packing** and make life on the road more convenient. Compact alarm clocks, travel irons, travel wallets, and personal-care kits are among the most common items you'll find.

U

U.S. GOVERNMENT

The U.S. government can be an excellent source of travel information. Some of this is free and some is available for a nominal charge. When planning your trip, **find out what government materials are available.** For just a couple of dollars, you can get a variety of publications from the Consumer Information Center in Pueblo, Colorado. Free consumer information also is available from individual government agencies, such as the Department of Transportation or the U.S. Customs Service. For specific titles, *see* the appropriate publications entry in Important Contacts A to Z.

W

WEDDINGS

Planning on living happily ever after? Then maybe you should tie the knot at Walt Disney World. The **Fairy Tale Wedding Pavilion** near the Grand Floridian

Beach Resort is the setting for many of the 1,000 weddings that take place at WDW each year. The WDW bride can ride in a Cinderella coach, have rings borne to the altar in a glass slipper, and invite Mickey and Minnie to attend the reception. Call or fax for more information (☎ 407/828–3400; FAX 407/828–3744).

WHEN TO GO

Timing can spell the difference between a good vacation in the theme parks and a great one. During certain periods, the parks are oppressively crowded, with discouraging lines. At other times, you can step right into the major rides and attractions. During busy periods, the parks have longer hours, run all rides at full capacity, and add entertainment and parades such as SpectroMagic in Disney's Magic Kingdom, that you can't see in quiet periods. If you have children, it's more fun to travel when you can count on there being plenty of other children around; if you prefer a more adult experience, you will be happier skipping school vacation periods.

CLOSED FOR REPAIRS?

Before you finalize your travel schedule, call the theme parks you plan to visit in order to find out about any planned maintenance that will close major attractions you want to see.

CROWDS

The most crowded times of the year in all of the Central Florida theme parks are when school is out. The single busiest week is from Christmas through New Year's Day. All of the area's attractions are also packed around Easter. Memorial Day weekend is not only crowded but also hot and humid. Other busy periods are from mid-June through mid-August, Thanksgiving week in November, the week of Presidents' Day in mid-February, and the weeks of college spring break in late March.

Are crowds inescapable, then? Not at all. Particularly from early September until just before Thanksgiving, attendance is very light. Mid-afternoons will still feel busy, but you're not packed in body-to-body as during the most crowded seasons. The least crowded time of all is from just after the Thanksgiving weekend until the beginning of the Christmas holidays. Another excellent time is January and the first week of February. If you must go in summer, late August is best.

Cypress Gardens attracts older travelers, so it is busier during the winter.

CLIMATE

The following are average daily maximum and minimum temperatures for Orlando.

Climate in Orlando

Jan.	70F	21C	May	88F	31C	Sept.	88F	31C
	49	9		67	19		74	23
Feb.	72F	22C	June	90F	32C	Oct.	83F	28C
	54	12		74	23		67	19
Mar.	76F	24C	July	90F	32C	Nov.	76F	24C
	56	13		74	23		58	14
Apr.	81F	27C	Aug.	90F	32C	Dec.	70F	21C
	63	17		74	23		52	11

1 Destination: Walt Disney World®, Universal Studios and Orlando

READY, SET, DISNEY!

Everything You Need to Know About Getting Started at Walt Disney World: Our New Disney-at-a-Glance Guide

AS DUSK FALLS on Walt Disney World, the sky over Cinderella Castle turns a perfect pink. It is the end of your first day in Never-Never-Land, and you've racked up an Indiana Jones-worthy number of accomplishments. Suppressing the urge to squeeze just one more attraction into the day's itinerary, you beckon to your brood—who by now are moving like a trained corps de ballet—and all plunk down onto a bench. Voilà! A flock of doves wheel from the marzipanlike heights of the enchanted castle into the clouds overhead, and you realize—with a deep sigh of contentment—that "Once Upon a Time" is happening this very moment.

Now it can be told: You're in Walt Disney World's "sweet zone"—where only children of all ages who have satisfied their yearning for wonderment can enter. The key to entering this sweet zone is a combination of canny strategizing, patience, and luck—and this special Disney-at-a-Glance guide is here to get you started. Walt Disney World can be tremendous, terrific, and delightful. But many visitors, especially first-time travelers, find WDW, the abbreviation for Walt Disney World, to be like a giant jigsaw puzzle that's blank on both sides. Flummoxed by the breadth of the choices, they don't know where to start. What are the must-dos? The must-sees? Where to stay? Where to eat? The 43-square-mile complex is, after all, double the size of Manhattan. The Magic Kingdom alone has more than 40 major adventures. Then there's Epcot Center—twice the size of the Magic Kingdom—and Disney-MGM Studios and Typhoon Lagoon and Blizzard Beach and Discovery Island—and still more. You can get out of breath just trying to list them all.

For those with what feels like a million questions, this tell-all Disney Digest introduces each park step by step. Use our tips to design a manageable tour around your priorities. Then let the kid inside you take over. But don't pout if you can't fit everything in—you'll have joined the ranks of the average How-come-I-can't-do-it-all? Disney visitor.

Getting Oriented in Walt Disney World

THE BIG PICTURE➤ The sheer scope of this Florida family entertainment capital makes the name Walt Disney World highly appropriate. But don't let its enormity stop you in your tracks. Basically, Disney is just Florida scrub sprinkled with hotel complexes, theme parks, and water parks—several of each genre. What most people imagine to be Walt Disney World, the **Magic Kingdom,** is actually just a small part of it. Similar to California's Disneyland, it's the wellspring of Mickeymania, a paradise for the young at heart, and the most popular individual theme park in the United States, welcoming more than 11 million visitors every year. As much a part of the Disney experience is **Epcot Center.** Designed to promote enthusiasm for the learning process, it's packed with multi-million-dollar, fun-filled, science-inspired rides that are sure to turn on every family's curiosity quotient and ignite every child's Jurassic spark. As you'll find out, Epcot Center covers everything from dinosaurs to nuclear energy and is more like a huge world's fair than an amusement park. The golden age of Hollywood is long gone, but its ghosts linger at **Disney-MGM Studios,** WDW's third theme park, the home of a real-live movie studio and still more astonishing rides, including the Twilight Zone Tower of Terror. Disney also has fabulous water parks: **Blizzard Beach, Typhoon Lagoon,** and **River Country.** Finally, there's **Discovery Island**—a natural habitat for more than 200 species of animals who run the gamut from scary to sweet. You can see why staying at WDW for much less than a week is like getting only half a serving of dessert.

THE FIRST DAY➤ Most people tackle the Magic Kingdom first. Take I-4 to the Magic Kingdom exit and follow the signs to the parking lot; then board the next tram to the Transportation and Ticket Center, a.k.a. the TTC. It's the only place the tram goes. There, you can buy your tickets, pick up an essential park map and entertainment flyer, and catch a paddlewheeler or the monorail to head into the park and start having fun.

The Magic Kingdom Is Aptly Named

Packed with more fantasy per square foot than any other place on earth, the Magic Kingdom fulfills the promise of photographs and much, much more. Kids think they've found heaven on earth, and they may be right. And for adults—so many of whom have grown up with Cinderella, Peter Pan, Dumbo, Davy Crockett, and Pinocchio—it's one of those magical places "so full of echoes, allusions, and half-memories as to be almost metaphysical," according to renowned travel writer Jan Morris.

WAGON WHEEL➤ For the four-year-old self you're about to return to, everything is very neatly organized, although the walkways through the park twist and turn so as to conceal its actual layout—a wagon wheel with hub and spokes. Passing through the park entrance turnstiles, you find yourself in Town Square, which leads to Main Street USA, a boulevard that runs due north, ending at Central Plaza, also known as the Hub. Main Street USA is the first of the Magic Kingdom's seven lands. The landmark Cinderella Castle anchors the Hub and is encircled by the rest of the lands: Adventureland, Frontierland, Liberty Square, Fantasyland, Mickey's Toontown Fair, and Tomorrowland. Rope Drop, as the ceremonial stampede that kicks off each day is called, occurs in the Magic Kingdom at the Central Plaza end of Main Street USA.

MAIN STREET USA➤ Today seems a century away in this pastel-candy-colored valentine to turn-of-the-century America, replete with gingerbread trim and the music of calliopes. Once past the Victorian-style station of the **Walt Disney World Railroad,** you're in Town Square, site of information central, better known as **City Hall.** Follow Main Street up to Central Plaza and Cinderella Castle. (Disneyfact: Did you know that at the top of the Castle is an apartment once intended for Walt Disney and his family?) While strolling, enjoy the antique automobiles oohga-oohga-ing, the barbershop quartets, and the vintage Disney cartoons on view in the **Main Street Cinema.**

ADVENTURELAND➤ Bear left at the Hub, and you'll catch sight of tangled tropical vegetation. Elephant calls, pounding drums, squawking parrots, and other elements of jungle chatter fill the air. This is your chance to stare a gigantic hippo in the eye, to sail between the guns of two warring pirate ships, and to be serenaded by a tiki god statue with blinking red eyes. Adventureland is home to such popular favorites as **Pirates of the Caribbean,** a cruise through the midst of a rowdy pirate battle; the **Swiss Family Robinson Treehouse,** the shipwrecked family's digs, complete with running water; and the "danger-filled" **Jungle Cruise,** where Audio-Animatronic headhunters and hippos immediately target you as "jungle bait." Meet Claude Birdbrain at the **Enchanted Tiki Birds,** one of the first Disney Audio-Animatronic achievements—it's corny but utterly delightful.

FRONTIERLAND➤ Keep to the main footpath, and you'll notice a subtle change in the vegetation. Frontierland lies straight ahead. If you're accustomed to a morning run, you'll love the rope-drop dash to Disney's wettest attraction, **Splash Mountain.** A flume ride peopled by Br'er Rabbit and 67 Audio-Animatronic friends, culminating in a nail-biting 52½-foot drop (the flume world's longest and sharpest), it provides more thrills than almost any other ride in the Magic Kingdom. Make sure you're wearing your Mickey Mouse rain poncho if you sit in the first or last rows! Ready for more? Climb aboard a runaway gold-rush mine train at the **Big Thunder Mountain Railroad;** then take in the sit-back-and-watch pleasures: the **Diamond Horseshoe Jamboree,** and **Country Bear Jamboree.**

LIBERTY SQUARE➤ Disney's answer to Williamsburg lies next along your path. Centered around a 130-year-old live oak tree, hung with 13 lanterns representing the 13 original Colonies, it's made up primarily of Early America–themed shops and eateries; the main draw for Disneyphiles is the **Haunted Mansion**—"Tomb, Sweet Tomb" to such characters as Manny Festation, Clare Voince, and Paul Tergyst. The **Hall of Presidents,** a multimedia tribute to the Constitution, features amazingly lifelike Audio-Animatronic figures of every American president. Nearby, you can cool down with a trip on a romantic side-wheeler, the **Liberty Square Riverboat,** or the Gullywhumper, one of the **Mike Fink Keel Boats.**

FANTASYLAND➤ In "the happiest kingdom on earth," storybook dreams come true with a minimum of high-tech and a full load of fairy-tale charm. Seated in a pirate ship, you soar above moonlit London and a tick-tocking crocodile on **Peter Pan's Flight;** get vertigo on the **Mad Tea Party** whirling teacup ride; experience the mild **Snow White's Adventures;** hop on **Cinderella's Golden Carrousel** and ride through **It's a Small World**—Arnold Schwarzenegger's favorite WDW ride; plop yourself into the jump seat of Mr. J. Thaddeus Toad's runaway Model-T and career along the road to "Nowhere in Particular" on **Mr. Toad's Wild Ride;** and wind up at the "mane" attraction, the **Legend of the Lion King** stage show featuring the music of Elton John. Fantasyland is the place for very young children, who often cite **Dumbo** as their favorite ride.

MICKEY'S TOONTOWN FAIR➤ This tribute to the world's most famous mouse opened in mid-1996 as part of WDW's 25th anniversary celebration. (Repeat visitors will recognize this area as Mickey's Starland, built in 1988 to celebrate the Mickster's 60th birthday.) Playing on the theme of a country fair, you can visit Mickey's country house (be sure to check out the vegetables growing in his backyard garden), Minnie's bungalow, and get wet at Donald's Boat, an interactive fountain with hidden spigots. There's also a kid-sized roller coaster, **Goofy's Barnstormer.** But the real fun here is the chance to get photos with Disney characters, who are always on hand.

TOMORROWLAND➤ Fascinating mostly for its backward look at forward thinking, recently revamped Tomorrowland contains the must-do **Space Mountain,** a two-minute, in-the-dark, roller-coaster ride crammed with scary sights. Hint: Hold on to your eyeglasses. With the addition of the new **Alien Encounter,** this land has become, in the words of Disney Imagineers, "an intergalactic docking bay for extraTERRORestrials." Developed with *Star Wars* producer George Lucas, it makes

use of computer simulations, lasers, and other electronic technology. Robin Williams is the voice of **The Timekeeper,** Tomorrowland's other new attraction.

Excellent Edutainment: Epcot Center

Epcot Center is that rare paradox, an educational theme park—and a very successful one. A subtle blend of the entertaining and the edifying, this enormous park encourages the brain to keep simmering even when the body is enjoying taking a break. The 40-acre World Showcase Lagoon separates its two main segments: **Future World**—anchored by the trademark 17-story silver geosphere known as **Spaceship Earth,** where the focus of activities inside the pavilions is on discovery and the fascination of science; and **World Showcase,** where you can tour a good part of the world, minus jet lag, via exhibition pavilions that represent 11 nations.

FUTURE WORLD➤ This Einstein among theme-park lands is made up of eight captivating attractions. The high-tech introduction in the newly refurbished **Universe of Energy** serves as a counterpoint to your ride in the middle of a dinosaur-ridden primeval landscape where moonlight and erupting volcanoes illuminate a giant sea snake attack—and that's only the beginning. **Wonders of Life, Body Wars** has you zipping platelet-to-platelet through the human circulatory system; *The Making of Me,* a film, shows where babies come from; and Cranium Command, an entertaining movie, takes you inside the "Home of the Flying Endorphins," in which celebrities provide voices for body parts. The **Living Seas** introduces you to the aquatic splendors of a Caribbean coral reef through 18-foot-high aquarium windows; guests with SCUBA open-water certification can really get into the swim of things with Epcot Divequest, as you can scuba in the tank along with the fishies. There's also **Sea Base Alpha,** which is supposed to look like a prototype undersea research facility but is actually just a series of quite interesting exhibits. **The Land** pavilion has a boat ride, the *Lion King* "Circle of Life" presentation, and Food Rocks, starring the likes of the Peach Boys and Chubby Cheddar. In **Journey into Imagination,** Disney bills "Honey, I Shrunk the Audience" as a "4-D" show. In the 100,000-square-foot Innoventions, top corporations roll out new products for techy tykes, teens, gizmoids, preteen prodigies, and their elders; the Sega room alone has more than 130 video games.

WORLD SHOWCASE> With your eyes closed, twirl the globe and aim your finger; it just might land on one of the countries featured in World Showcase, the equivalent of a gerrymandered international dateline, featuring the cultures and cuisines of 11 countries. Each pavilion is staffed by natives of the sponsoring country, but they all speak excellent English, so you can skip the phrase books. Even so, all the globe's citizenry understands "oohs" and "ahs," probably the gist of your vocabulary while touring these parts. Buy a spinning doll at Der Teddybär in Germany or china in the United Kingdom, climb a mountain in Canada, eat tacos in Mexico or couscous in Morocco—while belly dancers gyrate, and see the Eiffel Tower in France, the Piazza San Marco in Italy, and Beijing's Temple of Heaven in China—all in a single day. World Showcase also provides strong evidence of the universality of one common language—food—with some of the finest dining in all of Florida. Note: Book ahead in these restaurants, since they are very popular.

Reel Life: Disney-MGM Studios

With a cast that reads like the credits of the biggest blockbuster ever made—to Walt's name, add George Lucas, Stephen Spielberg, Jim Henson, plus the Duke, Bogie, and Marilyn—this is Disney's attempt to bring Hollywood to Florida. Here, more than a dozen top attractions marry movies to the latest in Disney-ride technology; grace notes are the fully operational film and television production center and nostalgia tours of the "Hollywood that never was and always will be." No need to scope out this sequins-and-sunglasses theme park for your favorite stars; the gimmick here is that you are the celebrity, given the full star treatment, as when a Grace Kelly look-alike asks for your autograph. Fancy yourself the next Clark Gable? Get a screen test at **L.A. Cinema Storage**; then head to **Cover Story** to see that famous face—your own—on the covers of all the big magazines.

Disney-MGM's **amazing rides** are the key to its success: there's that stunt artist's show-case, the Indiana Jones Stunt Spectacular; the Star Wars simulator adventure; Jim Henson's Muppet*Vision 3-D; the Great Movie Ride—the greatest; and the Art of Animation, a behind-the-scenes look at Disney animators animating. (Disneyfact: Did you know that when they began working on *Snow White*, *Pinocchio*, and *Bambi* there were no Dopey, Jiminy Cricket, or Thumper planned?) For those who have always dreamed of hearing "You oughtta be in pictures," there's **Superstar Television**, which presents the opportunity to costar in such TV shows as "I Love Lucy" and "The Golden Girls." Finally, this is home to the 199-foot-tall, 13-story **Twilight Zone Tower of Terror**, housed in WDW's tallest structure. Be sure to ask if everyone's having fun before the free-falling elevator plunges more than 160 feet toward terminal velocity.

The Wetter, the Better!

What could be better than an entire park devoted to water rides? How about three of them? Since the opening of the first of these, **River Country**, Disney has been uniting humans and water in a tumultuously semiamphibious state of cohabitation. **Typhoon Lagoon** came next, followed by **Blizzard Beach**. And they're always jam-packed. The best—or is it the worst?—is the wild, 55 mph, dead-drop to a splashy landing from the Summit Plummet, the fastest water slide on the planet, a feature at Blizzard Beach. This park has no fewer than 19 water slides and "icy" bobsled runs that stay warm and fast—including the Slush Gusher and Teamboat Springs. In Typhoon Lagoon, a doozy known as Keelhaul Falls has you spiraling 400 feet downward, and Humunga Kowabunga sends you careening at 30 mph down a 50-foot-high slide. Then—oh, buoy!—there are Typhoon Lagoon's Jib Jammer, Rudder Buster, and Stern Burner storm slides and River Country's Whoop 'n' Holler Hollow, a pair of water slides down the side of an ersatz mountain.

If you have water babies in your party, look for Typhoon Lagoon's scaled-down Ketchakiddie Creek, Blizzard Beach's Tike's Peak, and its unnamed River Country counterpart. If you're a beach potato type, you'll get a charge out of the parks' amazing creativity. Typhoon Lagoon's centerpiece is Mount Mayday, a lively volcano that periodically tries to dislodge the *Miss Tilly*, a shrimp boat impaled on the top rim, with rip-roaring geysers.

Antarctica with waving palm trees, bikinis, and flip-flops confronts you at Blizzard Beach. The Imagineers envisioned a freak blizzard, whose heavy snowfall turned to melt before a planned ski resort could be completed. Left with the biggest Sno-Kone in the world, they transformed it into a slippery-when-wet water adventure with ski and toboggan runs that are the tallest, fastest, and most exhilarating in the world of water slides. The 90-foot-tall "snowcapped" Mt. Gushmore is the centerpiece.

You can easily get submerged without even leaving your Disney hotel grounds: Almost every major swimming pool has a little something special going for it, even if it's just a water slide. The 790,000-gallon **Stormalong Bay** at the Yacht and Beach Club is a maze of whirlpools and waterfalls. At Port Orleans's **Doubloon Lagoon,** a water slide in the shape of a sea serpent runs the length of the lagoon.

What's New, What's Great

One reason 70% of WDW's guests are repeat visitors is that Disney's Imagineers are constantly devising new state-of-the-art attractions, spending many millions in the process. Just because they've created the theme-park world's eighth wonder of the world today doesn't mean they won't be working on a ninth wonder tomorrow.

Disney's Boardwalk, a re-creation of a 1920s seaside resort, is the latest addition to WDW's multi-use venues. It's a village with a deluxe hotel, shops, and three clubs: ESPN World, with an interactive sports video arcade and restaurant; the Atlantic Dance Hall, a 1930s-style dance hall featuring live music that runs the gamut from Glen Miller to Gloria Estefan; and Jellyrolls, a rollicking singalong club with twin pianos. There's also plenty of imbibing and dining opportunities that run the gamut from pizza and pasta to fresh seafood and specialty beers.

Fantasia Gardens Miniature Golf, lets duffers of all ages take their turns at whacking little round balls. There are two courses: Fantasia Gardens, a state-of-the-art miniature golf course themed after the Disney animated classic, complete with hazards featuring the dancing hip-

pos and Mickey as The Sorcerer's Apprentice; and Fantasia Fairways, a putting course that's designed for older children and adults.

Disney Village Marketplace continues to expand its horizons, adding several restaurants with celebrity caché. The House of Blues, conceived by Dan Aykroyd, a.k.a Elwood Blues in his "Saturday Night Live" days, is a 1,500-seat restaurant/music spot that also houses television and radio facilities. Gloria Estefan is the creator of Lario's, which brings the Latin beat of Miami's South Beach to landlocked Orlando. Wolfgang Puck's Café is the first Florida venture for the famed California-cuisine chef. Rainforest Café is part of an environmentally friendly restaurant chain that has a decor to match its name. Cascading waterfalls, thunder, lightning, and tropical birds compete for your attention along with an eclectic menu. The new, 50,000-square foot **World of Disney** shop is the largest emporium for Disney character merchandise on the planet. **Team Mickey Superstore** is the headquarters for collectible merchandise. And if that's not grandiose enough, the 10-screen Pleasure Island cineplex is expanding to 24 theaters, making it the largest theater complex in the Sunshine State.

At Epcot, the **Universe of Energy** has been re-energized with a more contemporary pre-show. But never fear, the dinosaurs remain the same. By summer 1997, a major transformation to **The World of Motion** will be completed. Gone will be the pleasant little ride that took a lighthearted look at man's experiments in transportation. In its place will be **Test Track,** a high-tech thrill ride in which you, the test driver, will not only get to race around at 60 mph; you'll get to check out your vehicle under the extremes of blazing heat and numbing cold.

The Bus Stops Here: Getting Around WDW

Walt Disney World operates a transportation system that most medium-size cities would envy. More than 110 buses cover about 8.5 million miles a year, shuttling visitors around the World. Add in the monorails and boats, and you have about 200,000 passenger trips per day.

HOW TO GET THERE FROM HERE➤ You don't have to be a rocket scientist to get anywhere in Disney. The transportation system is what urban planners would call multimodal—your kids will call it just plain fun, especially the boats and the monorails. Parking lots are there when you need them. So are Disney staffers, ready and willing to give directions. Many hotels have system maps. If you can't figure it out or find someone to ask, there's a number to call (☎ 407/824–4457). Transportation is free if you're staying in a Disney hotel or carrying a multiday passport; everyone else pays just $2.50.

WDW's fastest and most frequently used mode of transportation is the **monorail**; one loop shuttles between Epcot Center and the TTC, while the other connects the TTC with the Magic Kingdom and the Polynesian, Grand Floridian, and Contemporary resorts. It does not, however, go to the nearby Wilderness Lodge.

Boats ferry guests staying at the Polynesian, Grand Floridian, and Contemporary resorts and the Wilderness Lodge to the Magic Kingdom and take WDW Swan, Dolphin, and Boardwalk guests to Epcot Center and Disney-MGM Studios.

There is a huge network of **buses,** which run every 15 to 20 minutes, picking up and dropping off guests at the theme parks, the water parks, the hotels, and almost every other destination in Walt Disney World.

When the Going Gets Tough . . .

START EARLY➤ As Ben Franklin said, early to bed and early to rise makes you healthy, wealthy, and wise—it also gives you the chance to take WDW's most popular rides without waiting in line. By 10 or 11 AM, the parks are bursting at the seams, and you wait everywhere in busy seasons. How early, you ask? Note that though the Magic Kingdom, Epcot Center, and Disney-MGM officially open at 9 AM, visitors may enter at 8:30, and sometimes even at 8, with some special breakfasts beginning at 7:30. For more information, *see* Opening and Closing Hours *in* Chapter 2.

In summer, it's especially important to arrive early because by noon the heat and humidity become a challenge, and sometime between 3 and 5 PM it is almost guaranteed to rain. Weather dictates one other summer strategy: Do outdoor rides before noon, when the sun is almost sure to shine. Then in the afternoon, you can relax somewhere that's cool and dry—perhaps in a seat to watch "Honey, I Shrunk the Audience."

GO WHERE—AND WHEN—THE CROWDS DON'T➤ To minimize time in line, go against the flow. In a Disney Olympics, the Gold should go to whomever runs past Spaceship Earth at Epcot Center's front door and heads on to the Living Seas or Journey into Imagination. Circle back to Spaceship Earth later. Are we suggesting running up the down escalator at Macy's on Christmas Eve? Yes. Unless, that is, you're one of the first guests through the Epcot Center entrance turnstiles, in which case the advice is different: Claim your Spaceship Earth ride vehicle before someone else beats you to it.

Another way to hang-ten on the tidal wave of tourists: Have lunch at either 11:30 or around 2:30.

STOP THE WORLD, I WANT TO GET OFF➤ Chances are, toward midafternoon, you'll be tired of the whining, the pointing, and the childish behavior—and that's just on the part of the parents. Slow down to .00001 mph and give your unbionic feet a rest. Scattered throughout the parks are green oases made just for time-outs. In Epcot Center there's one just behind the Rose & Crown Pub in the United Kingdom; in the Magic Kingdom, Tom Sawyer's Island is wonderful for the weary.

DON'T SHOP TILL AFTER YOU'VE DROPPED➤ Do all your seeing, riding, and walking before hitting the souvenir shops—you can do that later in the afternoon when lines clog every attraction. If you are staying at a Disney hotel or the Swan or Dolphin, remember that you can have purchases sent right to your hotel concierge or front desk.

Checking In: Should You Be Mickey's Guest?

If you'll be spending most of your time at WDW theme parks, it makes sense to stay on the property. With 13 successful resorts in all but rock-bottom-budget price categories—and more on the way— it's clear that Disney's head honchos are used to winning those little red hotels in "Monopoly." But the reason they're major players in Florida's hotel stakes is because their resorts, in addition to selling sleep, pack as much excitement as the WDW attractions: You can lodge in Polynesian, southwestern, Caribbean, even grand hotel style. Your favorite little leaguers can even bed down in the lee of a multistory baseball bat.

FOR BIG SPENDERS ONLY➤ Still, with more than 20,000 hotel rooms at WDW alone, it's easy to be thrown into a stall at decision time. If you feel you deserve the crème de la crème, there are the showplaces: the turn-of-the-century-style **Grand Floridian**—with a handkerchief-white beach and fine restaurants; the stunning **Wilderness Lodge**, a Honey-I-Blew-Up-the-Log-Cabin-size national park–style hotel where you can "rough it"; the delightful new **BoardWalk Inn and Villas,** with its colorful awnings and breezy balconies; the **Contemporary,** at which latter-day Judy Jetsons arrive in high style aboard the in-house monorail; the gorgeous **Polynesian,** where the only thing missing is a welcoming conch-shell fanfare; the **Yacht Club and Beach Club** resorts, which make boaties feel right at home with their turn-of-the-century New England, nautical nuances; and if you're sweet on suites, the **Villas at the Disney Institute** and the **Old Key West Resort.** The latter is the choice of Disney chairman Michael Eisner and family when in residence.

OPTIONS FOR TIGHTWADS➤ No longer are Disney hotels concentrated in the luxury price category. The moderately priced **Dixie Landings, Caribbean Beach, Port Orleans,** and the new **Coronado Springs** resorts, and, in the economy range, the **All-Star Sports and Music resorts** all offer rooms starting at $69 per night. If you can get by without a lobby, elevators, and bellhops, think about the Ft. Wilderness Campground.

THE ACCESSIBILITY FACTOR➤ If convenient access is high on your list, note that the Contemporary, Polynesian, Grand Floridian, and Wilderness Lodge are closest to the Magic Kingdom, while the Caribbean Beach, the Yacht and Beach Clubs, and the Michael Graves–designed Swan and Dolphin hotels are nearest to Epcot Center. In fact, you can walk there from the Yacht and Beach Clubs. Dixie Landings, Port Orleans, and the Villas at the Disney Institute and Old Key West Resort are 1½ miles west of Epcot Center and Pleasure Island. The economy-priced All-Star Resorts are closest to Blizzard Beach. The two newest on-property resorts are the Board-

walk Resort near Epcot Center and the Coronado Springs Hotel north of Blizzard Beach on World Center Drive.

COMPROMISING POSITIONS➤ A fair compromise in terms of convenience and price can be found at any of the seven hotels that constitute Hotel Plaza, near the Disney Village Marketplace and Typhoon Lagoon. The biggies of the hotel-chain world are here, including Hilton, Travelodge, and Courtyard by Marriott. Note, however, that they do not offer many of the perks you would receive as a guest at a Disney-owned hotel.

WHY STAY ON-SITE?➤ Of course, you can still pay much less off-property, and if money is seriously an object, there's no real choice. But in most cases perks sich as early admission to theme parks, proximity, and guaranteed entry to all parks even when the turnstiles close to outsiders tip the balance in the dollars-versus-distance equation in favor of an on-property base. Benefits like these make it possible for you to see more each day—and even cut your visit short by a night, thereby saving plenty on your vacation bill.

WHEN TO STAY OFF-PROPERTY➤ If you need to save a serious bundle or if you plan to include Univeral Studios, Sea World, and Busch Gardens in your Central Florida itinerary, hotels outside WDW remain a viable choice. Because the local hotel scene is overbuilt, good deals abound—maybe even steals. Decent, safe, pleasant hotel rooms on International Drive and on U.S. 192 in Kissimmee can go for as little as $30 a night. But remember, I-Drive is at least 20 minutes from WDW's gates, and that's when there's no traffic jam. As for transportation, although many hotels offer shuttle buses to and from WDW, you pay per head; if you're traveling with your family, it makes sense to rent a car—something you don't necessarily need if you're staying on Disney property. For other recommendations, *see* Chapter 8.

Tips for Tots—
and Their Parents

Breakfast with Tigger and Pooh. A paw autograph from Goofy. Ten twirls around on Cinderella's Golden Carrousel. It takes a tyke to truly appreciate some experiences at WDW. Here are a few tips on handling the very young and the restless.

QUEUE TACTIC➤ The wait times for major attractions are often posted, so if it's going to be more than 20 minutes to ride Dumbo, the Flying Elephant, send your favorite Mousketeers off with another adult for a power snack while you stand in line. If you suspect that your tot may want to take a second whirl on Cinderella's Golden Carrousel, lurk at the very end of the line while your significant other rides a flashing steed.

CHARACTER BREAKFASTS➤ A must for most tots is breakfast à la Disney, where they can chow down on Mickey Mouse–shape waffles while engaging in a heart-to-heart with Disney characters. Ariel wanna-bes will choose the Under the Sea Breakfast at the Coral Reef restaurant at Epcot Center. Or have Breakfast with Pooh at the Old Key West Resort with Minnie Mouse at the Polynesian's Papeete Bay Verandah, or try the Once Upon a Time Breakfast at King Stefan's Banquet Hall in Cinderella Castle.

KIDS' NIGHT OUT➤ One of the better-thought-out programs for kids is the Polynesian's **Neverland Club.** Youngsters ages 4–12 have a ball, beginning with a crawl out a window that leads into the world of Peter Pan. Then there's a dinner-show meal, with visiting Disney characters and Discovery Island animals, and Disney movies while Papa and Mama Bear enjoy a night out of their own at Pleasure Island. You don't have to be a guest at the hotel to sign up your offspring. Similar programs include **Camp Swan** and **Camp Dolphin** and the **Vacation Station** at the Hilton.

PARADES!➤ Fun for the kiddies comes in the shape of the Magic Kingdom parades, every one of them a winner. The real dazzler is the seasonal **SpectroMagic** parade, which involves Disney characters and lavish floats and costumes outlined with twinkling lights. This parade runs twice nightly during peak season, at 9 and 11 PM and during busy periods at other times of the year; the Cinderella Castle forecourt is one good place from which to watch, although if you want to make a quick exit afterwards, a better choice is Town Square near the WDW railroad station underpass. If SpectroMagic is too late for your youngsters, there's always the 3 PM **Character Parade**—its specific theme changes from time to time; good vantage points

are near the Sleepy Hollow Sandwich Shop and and Diamond Horseshoe Jamboree area. Get there 20 minutes early to stake out a spot. One to three times a day, Disney-MGM Studios' Hollywood Boulevard has its own character parade, usually themed around the most recently released Disney animated film. The current parade features larger-than-lifesize characters from *Toy Story*.

BABY SWAP➤ No, this does not refer to what you feel like doing with your offspring at the whining end of a full, rich Disney day. If a child is too small for a ride that's a must for you, tell an attendant you intend to baby-swap as you approach the boarding area. One parent waits at the starting point with the little tykes while the other enjoys the ride, then they swap positions so the waiting parent can take a turn.

PLACES AND PARAPHERNALIA➤ Keep in mind that the **Baby Services** in each major park has rocking chairs and peace and quiet for nursing mothers, microwaves to heat up baby food, small toilets for toddlers, changing tables, and other thoughtful facilities for families with young children. Changing tables are in all women's rest rooms and some of the men's. Strollers are available for rent in every park; if you bring your own, mark it with a recognizable bit of clothing to prevent it from getting lost or removed when you leave it outside a ride's entrance.

EATS AND TREATS➤ Many times in the course of a long, hot Disney day, kids want to know three things: When can we eat? Where do we eat? What are we eating? Since restaurant lines can be long, keep in mind that Disney security will not wrestle you to the ground if you carry a small backpack stocked with a candy bar and small plastic bottles that you can refill at water fountains. Brave souls have been known to bring in a sandwich and a juice box or two or three; there is no salami detector at the gates.

Beauty and the Feast

Let's eat! This familiar cry may not be prompted entirely by hunger at WDW; here it's not the food but the decor that does the dazzling. You can breakfast in Bora-Bora at **Minnie's Menehune** at the Polynesian, then lunch in the Florida Keys' restaurant called **Olivia's Cafe,** at the Old Key West Resort. In the afternoon, for a positively ducal English-tea-and-clotted-cream service, take a break at the **Grand Floridian.** For dinner, you might virtually munch your way around the world at the 11 ethnic restaurants of Epcot Center—Disney's bona fide dining capital. When the fare is as good as the fettuccine at Italy's **Alfredo di Roma** restaurant with its beautiful faux marble and frescoes, you just might forget you're in Florida.

Rest assured: When you want to eat, there's always food nearby. And you're sure to find something that'll tickle your taste buds among the 6,000 menu items Disney offers at its more than 250 restaurants—from haute to healthy, hamburgers to nouvelle, from the varied fare at the food courts at the Caribbean Beach, Dixie Landings, and Port Orleans resorts to the creamy yogurt treats at Tomorrowland's **Auntie Gravity's Galactic Goodies** and the expensive-but-worth-it dinners at the Grand Floridian's **Victoria and Albert's;** don't forget the **California Grill,** high up in the Contemporary Hotel, the place for viewing fireworks over the Magic King-dom. And no less than *Vogue* magazine raved about the **San Angel Inn** in Epcot Center's Mexico, where stars shimmer in a perpetual midnight sky and a simmering volcano casts a glow over diners.

In Disney-MGM Studios there are two don't-misses at meal time: At the **Prime Time Café,** waitresses act just like Mom—no dessert if you don't eat your meat loaf and your vegetables! They will even spoon-feed you! The **Brown Derby** delivers nonstop Grace Kelly glamor and a pretty fair Cobb salad.

So Much Disney, So Little Time

Those who want to give you the long and short of it usually forget to give you the short. We don't—just turn to our **Blitz Tours** in Chapter 2, which show you how to master Disney: The Challenge—doing an entire Disney park in a single day. Pay attention to our tips, and don't worry if you miss a few attractions. It takes practice to see everything while remaining stress-free. The payoff will come when you make your magical second trip—your first Disneyversary!

WHAT'S WHERE

Universal Studios, Sea World, and Beyond

Universal Studios

With Disney-MGM Studios just down the road, is Universal Studios Florida even worth the visit? The answer is a resounding "yes." Far from being a "me-too" version of Disney, Universal is a theme park with plenty of hip originality and a saucy, sassy personality of its own. It doesn't hesitate to invite comparisons with the competition either; after a stunt man in the Wild, Wild, Wild West Stunt Show falls down a well, he emerges spouting water and shouting, "Look, Ma, I'm Shamu!" Disney-MGM's strolling actors are pablum compared with the Blues Brothers' peeling rubber in the Bluesmobile. And let's face it, even the Muppets are matched by E. T., Tickli Moot Moot, and the other inventions of Steven Spielberg, Universal's genius-on-call.

While Disney has a goodly share of gravity-challengers— especially the free-falling Twilight Zone Tower of Terror ride—and other white-knucklers, Universal is the theme park that reverberates with really bloodcurdling screams—usually your own. Tops for terror is **Jaws**, where 40 feet of teeth come in for the kill and almost wind up in your lap. Then, in a manner of speaking, head for Detonation Unknown and assorted fires, floods, and explosions at **Earthquake, Dynamite Nights Stuntacular,** and **Kongfrontation.** Careen past dinosaur mouths and lava showers in the teeth-loosening **Back to the Future** ride. Not all of Universal's attractions, of course, leave your heart fluttering in the vicinity of your tonsils. E. T. does, after all, go home in **E.T. Adventure**—you feel the wind on your face while pedaling him across the moon and get a photo op in his closet. Then you can rescue Elroy Jetson from intergalatic baddies in the **Funtastic World of Hanna-Barbera** or fire up your Nutrana Wand at **Ghostbusters.** And, on the biggest backlot in the world, see sitcoms filmed and make your own screen debut with Captain Kirk.

In **Terminator 2 3-D,** you can have a close encounter with the T-man himself in what Universal calls a "four-dimensional, interactive spectacular."

Power Rangers may have backed Barney onto the Gymboree set's B-list, but Universal has injected new energy into the vaunted Purple One's life. **A Day in the Park with Barney** includes a boppin' musical revue and a hands-on educational playground. The rest of Universal Studios allows teens to "ride the movies," but Barney makes it possible for tykes to walk through a magical land of primary-color trees and indoor clouds, bringing all their television fantasies into action. Give the kids a break from high-flying karate kicks long enough and they'll love it.

Sea World

Sleek dolphins perform like Mary Lou Retton, and orca whales sail through the air like featherweight Nijinskys at the aptly named 135-acre Sea World. The world's largest zoological park is entirely devoted to mammals, birds, fish, and reptiles that live in the ocean and its tributaries. Every attraction is designed to teach visitors about the marine world and its vulnerability to man's use. Yet the presentations are never pedantic, always enjoyable, and almost always memorable. The park rivals Disney properties for sparkly cleanliness, a smiley staff, and attention to detail.

The highlight is **Shamu Stadium,** where you can see Shamu and his sidekicks, Namu and Kandu, propel their trainers into the air like Saturn missiles. Whales, as you will learn, are right up there with dolphins and chimpanzees as the Einsteins of the animal world. Unlike old dogs, these orcas constantly beg to learn new tricks. Don't forget that these guys like to make a big splash: Wear rain gear if you plan to sit within the first four rows! Everything else goes swimmingly here, too. Friendly denizens await at **Penguin Encounter, Dolphin Community Pool, Sea Lion & Otter Stadium,** and **Wild Arctic,** a part thrill ride, part environmental lesson, part zoo exhibit that features polar bears cavorting among ice floes and boulders in 900,000 gallons of man-made sea water. Their nonstop antics, plus a thermostat set at 50 degrees, make this truly the coolest place in the park. At the other extreme is **Key West,** a tropically themed venue that captures the sultry ambience of the southernmost city in the U.S.

Busch Gardens

Now that you've enjoyed Sea World's seafari, why not head for the safari-in-a-day fun of the African-themed park that is Busch Gardens? Wildlife at its chest-thumping best is the specialty here, befitting Busch Gardens' claim to be one of America's leading legitimate zoos. Going eyeball-to-eyeball with a Western Lowland gorilla will please any budding Jane Goodall. You'll often feel you're on a Tarzan-movie set. Walking around the sights, however, might throw your personal gyroscope into a spin: In Timbuktu you'll find, of all things, a Dolphin Theater, and you experience the Serengeti Plain from a space-age monorail. The mightiest spins come on the roller coaster and the Congo River Rapids ride. Best of all is the 55-foot drop of the Tanganyika Tidal Wave, an outrageous way to test zero gravity.

Cypress Gardens

A botanic garden, amusement park, and water-skiing circus rolled into one, Cypress Gardens is uniquely Floridian. Here flowers bloom in colors so kitschy you'd think you were viewing vintage tinted postcards. A 45-minute drive from Walt Disney World, the park encompasses 233 acres and contains more than 8,000 varieties of plants gathered from 75 countries. Amid all these sylvan glades you discover a bevy of hoop-skirted Southern belles, a mammoth walk-through butterfly conservatory, and the Water Ski Stadiums, home to those amazing aquatic revues. Even the cerise-and-cerulean sunsets look color-coordinated with the cypress-draped canals: for fans, this is Florida at its Technicolor best.

The Space Coast

Exploration of the last remaining frontier—outer space—first became a reality at the Kennedy Space Center, an hour's drive east of Orlando. Here the history of travel was rewritten when astronauts blasted off to the moon. Today the home-launch base of America's Space Shuttle program has become an out-of-this-world tourist attraction. Highlights of a visit to **Spaceport USA** include two-hour bus tours that offer camera stops near Space Shuttle Launch Pads, the massive Vehicle Assembly Building, a 365-foot Saturn V Moon Rocket, and an IMAX movie that will make you feel you're standing on the launch pad during a Space Shuttle take-off. For information on future launch schedules, phone 407/452–2121.

FODOR'S CHOICE

No two people agree on what makes a perfect vacation, but it's fun and helpful to know what others think. Here's a compendium compiled from the must-see lists of hundreds of Florida travelers. These special memories-in-the-making await you at three of the top Orlando attractions—WDW, Universal Studios, and Sea World. For detailed information about each entry, refer to the appropriate chapters in this guidebook.

Walt Disney World: Magic Kingdom

Looking like an illuminated page from a fairy-tale book, **Cinderella Castle** is the fulfillment of every child's dream. Everyone falls under its spell at dusk, when doves are released to circle the Castle's cloud-borne towers.

With the steepest drop of any flume ride in existence, **Splash Mountain** makes you feel like Wily E. Coyote as you head over that final hang-onto-your-hat moment.

Get a paw autograph from Goofy, and feast on Mickey Mouse–shape pancakes at one of the **Disney Character breakfasts.**

Walt Disney believed we are all children at heart, and **It's a Small World** proves it. With hundreds of dancing babies—Dutch moppets in clogs, Russian balalaika players, tiny Tower-of-London guards, Polynesian hip-twitchers—even grumps exit grinning.

Join the magnificent Mr. Toad on his collision course with a runaway train on Fantasyland's **Mr. Toad's Wild Ride.**

The best 10-minute African safari in the world, the **Jungle Cruise** throws hyperactive hippos and hungry headhunters at you every step of the way. Beware of Old Smiley, the crocodile, who's always waiting for a handout—or, as the guide quips, "a foot out."

The portrait busts bespeak the world's greatest "ghost writers" at the **Haunted Mansion,** where ghoulish wit and Victorian decor add up to a delightful scarefest.

Have a heart-to-heart with you-know-who at **Mickey's Toontown Fair** in his dressing room.

"You can fly, you can fly, you can fly" over moonlit London on **Peter Pan's Flight.**

Stake out your place in the fun at Disney's lanai-by-the-lagoon, the **Polynesian Resort.**

At Tomorrowland's **Space Mountain,** you penetrate hyperspace by plummeting through the darkened abyss of the world's largest enclosed roller coaster.

Dine atop the world at the chic **California Grill** in the Contemporary Resort, where you'll enjoy a truly magical view of Cinderella's Castle and have the best seat in the house for the evening fireworks.

Epcot Center

You'll need a chin wrap to keep your mouth closed at Epcot Center's **Spaceship Earth,** where you'll see Roman centurions building roads, Michelangelo painting the Sistine Chapel ceiling, and many other Audio-Animatronic wonders.

The funniest 3-D show in the world, **Honey, I Shrunk the Audience** is the wildest sensation at Epcot Center's Journey into Imagination.

Dine under a perpetually starry purple sky within sight of a glowing volcano at Disney's dreamiest restaurant, Epcot Center's **San Angel Inn.**

Buy some not-to-be-believed **animal crackers** at the Süssigkeiten bakery at World Showcase's Germany pavilion.

Go under the sea at The Living Seas' **EpcotDivequest.**

Disney-MGM Studios

Flout every law of gravitation at the **Twilight Zone Tower of Terror,** a deserted hotel where you'd be better off taking the stairs if there were any. The elevator comes to a dead stop, then plunges so fast your stomach will be relocated close to your screechbox.

Will you be the one chosen to reenact "I Love Lucy"'s famous candy-factory scene at **Superstar Television**?

Take a behind-the-scenes look at the great animated cartoons at **Magic of Disney Animation.** (Disneyfact: Did you know that Disney animators modeled the Tramp from *Lady and the Tramp* on an adorable mutt found at the local pound?)

Other Walt Disney World Delights

Celebrate New Year's Eve every day of the year at midnight on **Pleasure Island.**

Stomp your feet and chow down on all the fixin's at the **Hoop-Dee-Doo Revue,** Disney's most popular dinner show, staged at Fort Wilderness's rustic Pioneer Hall.

Land on your snowy butt after the wild 55-mph plunge on the Summit Plummet water ride at **Blizzard Beach.**

Make real sure your swimsuit is tied on tightly before tackling **Typhoon Lagoon**'s Humunga Kowabunga!

For a true "When You Wish Upon a Star" finale, cap it all off with the best Disney evening extravaganzas: the **IllumiNations** show in Epcot Center or the dazzling **SpectroMagic** parade in the Magic Kingdom.

Universal Studios Florida

You saw Elliot save him in the movies and now it's your turn at **E.T. Adventure.** The little guy even thanks you personally, but how he learns your name is a trade secret Universal won't reveal.

There are plenty of fish in the sea, but only one with Bruce's talents: Play Tooth or Consequences with him at **Jaws.**

Thrill zealots run to **Back to the Future . . . The Ride,** where Doc Brown captains a time-traveling trip covering everything from dinosaurs to the Wright Brothers at Kitty Hawk.

Sea World

Bed down with sharks, eels, and barracudas on the special bring-your-own-sleeping bag Education Sleepovers offered at Sea World's **Terrors of the Deep** aquarium.

Check out that polar-bear paradise, **Wild Arctic**—easily the coolest place in all Florida.

Pet and feed the spooky residents of **Stingray Lagoon.**

Don't forget to pick out a pair of neoprene **Aqua Socks** water shoes decorated in black and white, à la orca, at Fashionations.

FESTIVALS AND SEASONAL EVENTS

Scheduling a vacation to Orlando around one of the area's many festivals and seasonal events can add extra excitement to your trip. Top area events include the Florida Citrus Bowl on New Year's Day, the Walt Disney World Wine Festival in February, the Magic Kingdom's Eastertime Celebration during April, Light Up Orlando in November, and the Walt Disney World Christmas festivities. The following is the annual calendar of special events.

DECEMBER➤ Early in the month, Orlando's Loch Haven Park stages a **Pet Fair & Winterfest** (☎ 407/644-2739). For Christmastime, Cypress Gardens mounts its annual **Poinsettia Festival** (☎ 813/324-2111), featuring 48,000 multicolored blooms. For a **Disney Christmas,** Walt Disney World gears up by decorating Main Street in perfect Victorian style, complete with a magnificent Christmas tree in Town Square, strolling characters, special afternoon parades, and entertainment. Every weekend in December before Christmas, **Mickey's Very Merry Christmas Party** in the Magic Kingdom can really get you into the holiday spirit. Other special holiday events include the **Jolly Holidays Dinner Show,** in the Contemporary's Convention Center, and the **Candle-**

light Processional and **Holidays Around the World** at Epcot. A Nativity Pageant, *Mickey's Christmas Carol* stage show, and appearances by the North Pole's most important citizen take place at Disney Village Marketplace (☎ 407/824-4321). December 31 festivities include the **Citrus Bowl Parade** in Orlando (☎ 407/629-4944), a street party at Church Street Station (☎ 407/422-2434), and a double fireworks display and extra-late hours in Walt Disney World's Magic Kingdom, which usually records some of the biggest crowds of the year for the event.

JANUARY➤ The **Comp USA Florida Citrus Bowl Football Classic** (☎ 407/423-2476) takes place at the Orlando Citrus Bowl on January 1. At the end of the month, **Scottish Highland Games** are played at Orlando's Central Florida Fairgrounds (☎ 407/672-1682).

FEBRUARY➤ Early in the month, the **Walt Disney World Village Wine Festival** (☎ 407/934-6743) showcases the vintages of 60 participating wineries from all over the country, and the **National Championship Rodeo Finals** at the Orlando Arena (☎ 407/849-2020) give cowboys from all over a chance to compete. It's followed at the end of the month by Kissimmee's **Silver Spurs Rodeo** (☎ 407/847-5000), one of the oldest and largest events of its kind in the South, drawing cowboys from all over the United States and Canada. At about the

same time, or early in March, the **Annual Central Florida Fair** is held at Orlando's Central Florida Fairgrounds (☎ 407/295-3247), with shows, rides, exhibits, and entertainment. **Pleasure Island Mardi Gras** (☎ 407/939-7814) is touted as the biggest, most authentic Mardi Gras festival outside New Orleans.

MARCH➤ It's baseball spring-training time, with the **Houston Astros** at Osceola County Stadium in Kissimmee (☎ 407/933-5500) and the **Kansas City Royals** at Baseball City Stadium (☎ 813/424-2424). Cypress Gardens kicks off its **Spring Flower Festival** (☎ 813/324-2111), which runs through May and features extraordinary floral topiaries and a profusion of spring blossoms.

One weekend in early March, the **Kissimmee Bluegrass Festival** showcases bluegrass bands and gospel music at the Silver Springs Arena (☎ 407/856-0246). On March 17, the **St. Patrick's Day Street Party** encourages the "wearin' o' the green" at Church Street Station (☎ 407/422-2434). Midmonth, the **Nestle Invitational,** a regular PGA Tour event, stops at Orlando's Bay Hill Club (☎ 407/876-2888), and the **Winter Park Sidewalk Art Festival** (☎ 407/644-

8281) draws thousands of art enthusiasts to trendy Park Avenue.

APRIL➤ From early April through early May, the **Orlando Shakespeare Festival** pays tribute to the Bard at Orlando's Lake Eola Amphitheater (☎ 407/423–6905). Also early in April, the **Dr. Pepper Annual Surf Festival** (☎ 407/783–5813) draws professional and amateur surfers to Cocoa Beach. On Easter Sunday there are **Easter Sunrise Services** at Sea World's Atlantis Theater (☎ 407/351–3600) and an **Easter Parade** down Main Street during mid-April at Walt Disney World (☎ 407/939–7814). From the end of April until early May, the **Orlando International Fringe Festival** brings 200 artists and theater troupes to perform in downtown Orlando. Cypress Gardens' Spring Flower Festival also wraps up in early May. Leading into June, the annual **Up, Up and Away" Airport Art Show** takes place at Orlando International Airport (☎ 407/826–2055).

JUNE➤ Late in the month and early in July is the **Silver Spurs Rodeo** (☎ 407/847–5000); there's another in early February.

JULY➤ The Fourth of July is a big day in and around Orlando. Walt Disney World's fireworks are legendary; recent years have brought record crowds (☎ 407/939–7814). In downtown Orlando, huge crowds gather around Lake Eola for the city's fireworks (☎ 407/363—5871). There are also fireworks in Kissimmee as part of its old-fashioned celebration in Lakefront Park, which also features games, rides, entertainment, and food (☎ 407/932–7223), and in Cypress Gardens, which mounts special ski shows as well (☎ 813/324–2111).

SEPTEMBER➤ **Oktoberfest at Church Street Station** (☎ 407/422–2434) means oompah bands and German folk dancers, food, and beer.

OCTOBER➤ Early in the month, the **Universal Art Show** is held on Orlando's Central Florida Fairgrounds (☎ 407/295–3247). Midmonth is the time for the **Walt Disney World Oldsmobile Golf Classic,** played on three of Walt Disney World's 18-hole golf courses (☎ 407/824–2250); for Cypress Gardens' **Annual Mustang**

Roundup (☎ 800/282–2123), which draws aficionados of that most famous Ford to exhibit and ogle models from 1965 to the present; and for the **Winter Park Autumn Art Festival** at Rollins College (☎ 407/644–8281). Later on is the **Pioneer Days Folk Festival,** with craftspeople and musicians on the grounds of the Folk Art Center on East Fairlane Avenue in suburban Pine Castle (☎ 407/855–7461). For Halloween, there are several October weekends of **Halloween Horror Nights** at Universal Studios, and a street party at Church Street Station (☎ 407/422–2434).

NOVEMBER➤ Early in the month, there's **Festival in the Park,** an arts and crafts show around the shores of downtown Orlando's Lake Eola; the **American Indian Powwow** (☎ 407/295–3247) takes place at the Central Florida Fairgrounds. Midmonth is the **Festival of the Masters,** with 230 top artists exhibiting their creations at Disney Village Marketplace (☎ 407/934–6743). **Light Up Orlando** (☎ 407/648–4010) is a street party downtown with live entertainment. Cypress Gardens hosts its month-long **Chrysanthemum Festival** (☎ 813/324–2111).

2 Exploring Walt Disney World®

By Catherine
Fredman

Updated by
Marianne
Camas

MILLIONS OF VISITORS, even those who place Pirates of the Caribbean and Space Mountain among the wonders of the world, are hard pressed to come up with an accurate definition for Walt Disney World. When you take a Walt Disney World exit off I–4 or U.S. 192 and begin traveling across empty land devoid of billboards or any other promotional materials, you're already on the grounds, even though there's no Cinderella Castle in sight. It's a very big place. And it's crammed with pleasures: from swooping above a starlit London in the Magic Kingdom's Peter Pan's Flight to simply sitting under the shade of a Callary pear tree frosted with blooms in Epcot Center.

The sheer enormity of the property—27,400 acres near Kissimmee, Florida—suggests that WDW is more than a single theme park with a fabulous castle in the center and the most dazzling rides on earth. The property's acreage translates to 43 square miles—twice the size of Manhattan or Bermuda, 60 times larger than Monaco, and just a shade smaller than Nantucket or Liechtenstein. If you were to drive at 60 miles per hour from one side of the property to the other, it would take close to 45 minutes. On a tract that size, 98 acres is a mere speck, yet that is the size of the Magic Kingdom. When most people imagine Walt Disney World, they think only of those 98 acres, but there is much, much more.

More than 2,500 acres of the property are occupied by hotels and villa complexes, each with its own theme and each equipped with recreational facilities, such as swimming pools and golf courses. Epcot Center, a little more than twice the size of the Magic Kingdom, is the second major theme park. A combination of a science exploratorium and a world's fair, Epcot offers visions of the future and celebrations of the world's cultural diversity. In 1989, the Disney-MGM Studios Theme Park, devoted to the machinations of the film business, opened nearby. In addition, there are thousands of acres of undeveloped land—grassy plains and pine forests patrolled by deer, and swamps patched by thickets of palmettos and fluttering with white ibis—even now, 25 years after opening day.

As Walt Disney himself decreed, WDW has never been completed; as one new confection welcomes its first guests, another begins construction, and still others are under study. Even as you read this, construction on WDW's fourth major theme park—Disney's Wild Animal Kingdom—is well underway. So do plenty of research before you go; call ahead to find out what's new, and make a plan. Then relax—and have a wonderful time.

MAGIC KINGDOM

For most people, the Magic Kingdom *is* Walt Disney World. Certainly it is both the heart and soul of the Disney empire. The Magic Kingdom is comparable to California's Disneyland; it was the first Disney outpost in Florida when it opened in 1971, and it is the park that traveled, with modifications, to France and Japan.

For a park that wields such worldwide influence, the Magic Kingdom is surprisingly small: At barely 98 acres, it is the tiniest of Walt Disney World's Big Three. However, the unofficial theme song—"It's a Small World After All"—doesn't hold true when it comes to the Magic Kingdom's attractions. Packed into six different "lands" are nearly 50 major crowd pleasers, and that's not counting all the ancillary attrac-

Walt Disney World

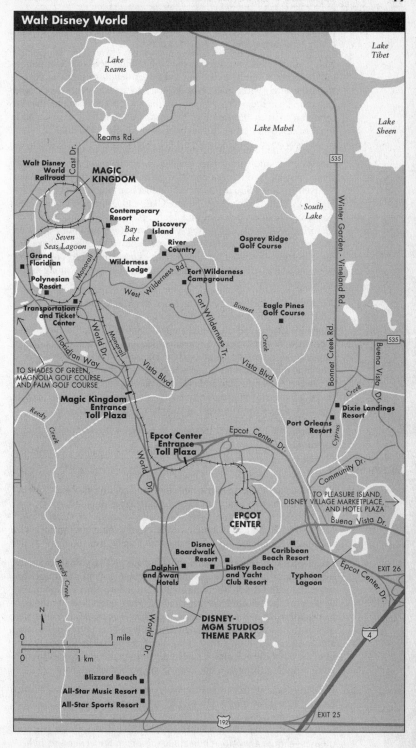

Lake Tibet

Lake Reams

Lake Mabel

Lake Sheen

Reams Rd.

535

Walt Disney World Railroad

MAGIC KINGDOM

Cast Dr.

South Lake

Contemporary Resort

Discovery Island

Bay Lake

Osprey Ridge Golf Course

Seven Seas Lagoon

River Country

Grand Floridian

Wilderness Lodge

Fort Wilderness Campground

Winter Garden - Vineland Rd.

Polynesian Resort

West Wilderness Rd.

Bonnet

Eagle Pines Golf Course

Monorail

Transportation and Ticket Center

Fort Wilderness Tr.

Creek

535

Floridian Way

World Dr.

Monorail

Vista Blvd.

Vista Blvd.

Bonnet Creek Rd.

Buena Vista Dr.

TO SHADES OF GREEN, MAGNOLIA GOLF COURSE, AND PALM GOLF COURSE

Magic Kingdom Entrance Toll Plaza

Creek

Cypress

Dixie Landings Resort

Reedy Creek

Port Orleans Resort

Epcot Center Dr.

Epcot Center Entrance Toll Plaza

Community Dr.

World Dr.

TO PLEASURE ISLAND, DISNEY VILLAGE MARKETPLACE, AND HOTEL PLAZA

EPCOT CENTER

Buena Vista Dr.

Reedy Creek

Disney Boardwalk Resort

Caribbean Beach Resort

Epcot Center Dr.

EXIT 26

Dolphin and Swan Hotels

Disney Beach and Yacht Club Resort

Typhoon Lagoon

N

World Dr.

DISNEY-MGM STUDIOS THEME PARK

0   1 mile

0   1 km

4

Blizzard Beach

All-Star Music Resort

All-Star Sports Resort

192

EXIT 25

tions: shops, eateries, live entertainment, cartoon characters, fireworks, parades, and, of course, the sheer pleasure of strolling through the beautifully landscaped and manicured grounds.

Many of the rides are geared to the young, but the Magic Kingdom is anything but a kiddie park. The degree of detail, the greater vision, the surprisingly witty spiel of the guides, and the tongue-in-cheek signs that crop up in the oddest places—for instance, in Fantasyland, the rest rooms are marked "Prince" and "Princess"—all contribute to a delightful sense of discovery that's far beyond the mere thrill of a ride.

The park is laid out on a north–south axis, with Cinderella Castle at the epicenter and the various lands surrounding it in a broad circle. Upon passing through the entrance gates, you immediately discover yourself in Town Square, a central connection point containing City Hall, Sun Bank, Tony's Town Square Café, and Disneyana Collectibles. Town Square directly segues into Main Street, a boulevard filled with Victorian-style stores and dining spots. Main Street runs due north and ends at the Hub, a large tree-lined circle, known as Central Plaza, located in front of Cinderella Castle. Rope Drop, the ceremonial stampede that kicks off each day, occurs at various points along Main Street and the Hub.

As you move clockwise from the Hub, the Magic Kingdom's various lands begin with Adventureland—home of Pirates of the Caribbean, the Jungle Cruise, and the Swiss Family Robinson Treehouse. Next come Frontierland and Liberty Square, containing Splash Mountain, Big Thunder Mountain Railroad, and the Haunted Mansion. Fantasyland is located directly behind Cinderella Castle—in the Castle's courtyard, as it were. Mickey's Starland is set off the upper right-hand corner—that's northeast, for geography buffs—of Fantasyland. And Tomorrowland, directly to the right of the Hub, rounds out the circle.

Numbers in the margin correspond to points of interest on the Magic Kingdom map.

Main Street

With its pastel Victorian-style buildings, antique automobiles "oohga-oohga"-ing as they stop to offer you a lift, sparkling sidewalks, and atmosphere of what one writer has called "almost hysterical joy," Main Street is more than a mere conduit to the other enchantments of the Magic Kingdom. It is where the spell is first cast.

Like Dorothy waking up in a technicolor Oz or Mary Poppins jumping through the pavement painting, you emerge from the tunnel beneath the Walt Disney World Railroad Station into a realization of one of the most tenacious American dreams. The perfect street in the perfect small town in a perfect moment of time is burnished to jewellike quality thanks to a ⅘-scale reduction, nightly cleanings with a fire hose, and constant repainting; neither life-size nor so small as to appear toylike, the carefully calculated size is meant to make you feel as though you're looking through a telescope into another world.

Everyone's always happy in this world, their spirits kept sunny thanks to outpourings of music: Dixieland jazz, barbershop quartets, brass-band parades, and scores of Disney films and American musicals played over loudspeakers. Old-fashioned horse-drawn trams and omnibuses—horns a-tootle—chug along the street. Street vendors in Victorian-era costumes sell balloons and popcorn. And to complete the illusion of the perfect dream, Cinderella Castle floats at the end of Main Street: the Holy Grail that is for once within reach.

❶ **City Hall.** This is information central, where you can pick up maps, guide-books, and inquire about all things Disney.

❷ **Disneyana Collectibles.** This bright yellow, Victorian-style gingerbread building is a trivia buff's delight with animation art and other memorabilia.

Although attractions with a capital "A" are minimal on Main Street, there are plenty of inducements to spend more than the 40 minutes most visitors usually take. The stores that most of the structures contain range from the **Main Street Athletic Shop,** which sells a variety of "Team Mickey" clothing; to the **Harmony Barber Shop,** where you can have yourself shorn; to a milliner's emporium stocking Cat-in-the-Hat fantasies; to all sorts of snacks and souvenirs. If the weather looks threatening, head for the **Emporium** to purchase those signature mouse-eared umbrellas and bright yellow ponchos with Mickey emblazoned on the back. The best time to shop is midafternoon, when the lines at the rides resemble a malevolent anaconda taking a nap. During the afternoon parade, store clerks have actually been seen twiddling their thumbs; if you're looking for a hard-to-find item, this is the time to ask for sales assistance. If you go at the end of the day, you'll be engulfed by the rush-hour crowds.

Main Street is also full of in-jokes for those in the know. For instance, check out the proprietors' names above the shops: Crystal Arts honors Roy Disney, Walt's brother; the Shadow Box—nod, nod, wink, wink—is the domain of Dick Nunis, chairman of Walt Disney Attractions; at the House of Magic, Card Walker—the "Practioner of Psychiatry and Justice of the Peace"—is the company's former chairman of the Executive Committee. At last glance, today's Head Mouseketeer, Michael Eisner, still doesn't have his own shop.

❸ **Walt Disney World Railroad.** Step right up to the elevated platform above the Magic Kingdom's entrance for a ride into living history. Walt Disney was a railroad buff of the highest order—he constructed a ⅛-scale train in his backyard and named it Lilly Belle, after his wife. Another Lilly Belle rides the rails here, as do Walter E. Disney; Roy O. Disney, named for Walt's brother; and Roger Broggie, named for a Disney Imagineer and fellow railroad aficionado. All the locomotives date from 1928, coincidentally the same year Mickey Mouse was created. Disney scouts tracked these vintage carriers down in Mexico, where they were used to haul sugarcane in the Yucatán, brought them back, and completely overhauled them to their present splendor. And splendid they are, with striped awnings, brightly painted benches, authoritative "choo-choo," and hissing plumes of steam. They are also quite useful. Their 1½-mile track runs along the perimeter of the Magic Kingdom, through the woods and past Tom Sawyer Island and other attractions; stops are in Frontierland and Mickey's Starland. It's a great introduction to the layout of the park and a much-welcome relief for tired feet and dragging legs. The four trains run at five- to seven-minute intervals. *Duration: 21 min. Crowds: Can be substantial beginning in late morning through late afternoon. Strategy: Go in midafternoon if you don't see a line; otherwise, skip on a first-time visit. Audience: All ages. Rating:* ★

❹ **Main Street Cinema.** Six screens run continuous vintage Disney cartoons in cool, air-conditioned quiet. It's a great opportunity to see the genius of Walt Disney and to meet the endearing little mouse that brought Disney so much fame. *Steamboat Willie,* the first sound cartoon, was also the first chance America had to meet Mickey Mouse, who, in his silver-screen debut, meets Minnie and is inspired to serenade her using a cow's udder. Disney said that he loved his creation more than any

22

The Magic Kingdom

Fort Sam Clemens

Rivers of America

WDW Railroad Frontierland Depot

Columbia Harbour House

Aunt Polly's Landing

FRONTIERLAND

LIBERTY SQUARE

Liberty Tree Tavern

Caribbean Plaza

Adventureland Bazaar

Crystal Palace

First Aid Station

ADVENTURELAND

Automatic Teller

Newsstand

KEY

🍴 Restaurants

🚻 Restrooms

—— Rail Line

•••• Skyride

═══ Monorail

Monorail

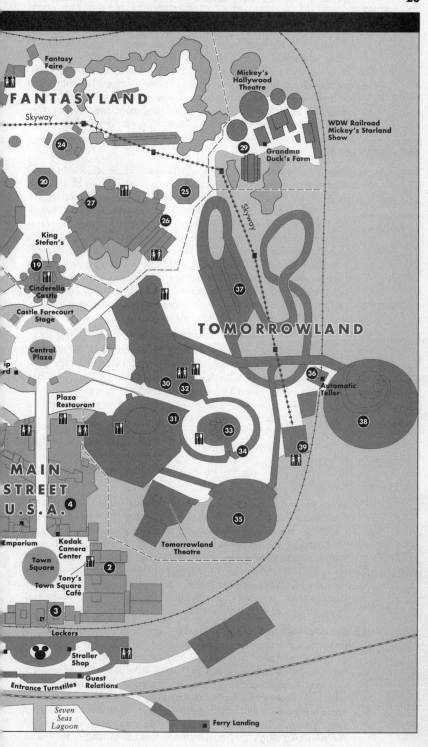

23

Fantasy
Faire

Mickey's
Hollywood
Theatre

FANTASYLAND

Skyway

WDW Railroad
Mickey's Starland
Show

24

29

Grandma
Duck's Farm

20

27

25

Skyway

26

King
Stefan's

37

19

Cinderella
Castle

Castle Forecourt
Stage

TOMORROWLAND

Central
Plaza

36

Automatic
Teller

ip
rd

Plaza
Restaurant

30

32

38

31

33

39

34

MAIN
STREET
U.S.A.

4

35

Emporium

Kodak
Camera
Center

Tomorrowland
Theatre

Town
Square

2

Tony's
Town Square
Café

3

Lockers

Stroller
Shop

Entrance Turnstiles

Guest
Relations

Seven
Seas
Lagoon

Ferry Landing

woman, which could make one wonder how Lilly Belle felt about this, especially since it was she who convinced her husband to change the character's name from Mortimer. Standing room only and the lure of other attractions farther inside the park keep Main Street Cinema from ever being too crowded, and in fact you can sit on the raised platform in the center of the screening room and still see all the films—all of them silents, without dialogue, screened with organ music. *Duration: Stay as long as you like. Crowds: Negligible. Strategy: A refuge on hot, crowded afternoons. Audience: All ages. Rating:* ★★

Adventureland

From the scrubbed brick, manicured lawns, and meticulously pruned trees of the Central Plaza, an artfully dilapidated wooden bridge leads to Adventureland, Disney's version of jungle fever. The landscape artists went wild here: South African Cape honeysuckle droops; Brazilian bougainvillea drapes; Mexican flame vines cling; spider plants clone; and three different varieties of palm trees sway, all creating a seemingly spontaneous mess. The bright, all-American, singalong tunes that fill the air along Main Street and Central Plaza are replaced by the recorded repetitions of trumpeting elephants, pounding drums, and squawking parrots. The architecture is an eclectic mishmash of the best of Thailand, the Caribbean, Africa, and Polynesia, arranged in an inspired disorder that recalls comic-book fantasies of far-off places. The message is that though the natives may be restless, the kids are all right.

Adventureland surrounds its own oblong central plaza. To the right as you cross the bridge is the **Adventureland Bazaar,** whose six shops have names like Bwana Bob's, Traders of Timbuktu, Zanzibar Shell Company, and Elephant Tales; they sell exotic—and generally quite affordable—safari-theme clothing, sharks'-teeth jewelry, elephant-hair bracelets, and other trinkets from the erstwhile Dark Continent as well as a menagerie's worth of life-size tropical critters. To the left are the spreading branches of the Swiss Family Robinson's banyan tree. Continuing around the plaza are the entrances to the Jungle Cruise, the Pirates of the Caribbean, and the Polynesian greathouse containing the Enchanted Tiki Birds.

In the far end of the plaza is another conglomeration of shops, the **Caribbean Plaza,** selling treasures inspired by the Pirates of the Caribbean: tropical clothing, costume jewelry (how about some pineapple earrings?), pirates' swords, hats embroidered with skull and crossbones, and, in a surprising lapse in kitsch, delicate crystal and blown glass. Be advised that many of these crystal items are also for sale in the King's Gallery inside the archway of Cinderella Castle. At **Lafitte's Portrait Deck,** you can stick your head through a pirate cutout and bring home a picture of yourself as the Scourge of the Spanish Main.

⑤ Swiss Family Robinson Treehouse. Few New York City apartments can boast the light, the airiness, the number of rooms, and all the services of this arboreal abode. In fact, the only thing lacking here is an elevator. Based on the classic novel by Johann Wyss about the adventures of a family shipwrecked on the way to America, the treehouse shows what you can do with a big banyan and a lot of imagination. The rooms are furnished with patchwork quilts and mahogany furniture. Disney detail abounds: The kitchen sink is made of a giant clamshell; the boys' room, strewn with clothing, has two hammocks instead of beds; and an ingenious system of rain barrels and bamboo pipes provides running water in every room. Small wonder that in the 1960 film, when offered the chance to leave their island, all but one Robinson decided to stay on. As you clamber around the narrow wooden steps and rope bridges that connect the rooms in this split-level dwelling, take a look at the Spanish moss. It is real, but the tree itself—some 90 feet in diameter, with more than 600 branches—was constructed by the props department. The 800,000 leaves are made of vinyl and cost $1 per leaf in the early 1970s. It all adds up to a species of tree unofficially called *Disneyodendron eximus,* or "out-of-the-ordinary Disney tree." *Duration: Up to you. Crowds: Artfully camouflaged so you may not see them—and the lines move slowly. Strategy: Go first thing in the morning or after dark. Audience: All ages; toddlers unsteady on their feet may have trouble with the stairs. Rating:* ★★

6 Jungle Cruise. During this ride, you cruise through three continents and along four rivers: the Congo, the Nile, the Mekong, and the Amazon. The canopied launches pack in visitors tighter than sardines, the safari-suited guides make a point of checking their pistols, and the *Irrawady Irma* or *Mongala Millie* is off for another "perilous" journey. The guide's spiel is surprisingly funny, with just the right blend of cornball humor and the gently snide; unfortunately, some guides' tendencies to imitate the unintelligible Chuck Yeager drawl patented by airline pilots is all too successful, and you can't understand half of what they're saying. Nitpicking aside, you'll encounter animals of the African veldt, elephants bathing, slinky pythons, an irritated rhinoceros, a bunch of hyperactive hippos (good thing the guide's got a pop pistol), and a tribe of hungry headhunters. Then there's Old Smily, the crocodile, who's always waiting for a handout—or, as the guide quips, "a foot out." Kids who might be terrified by the Pirates of the Caribbean will love this ride, and adults love the patter and all the detail—listen for what's playing on the radio of the overturned Jeep. *Duration: 10 min. Crowds: Huge, from late morning until supper time. Strategy: Go first thing in the morning or during the daily parade, but not after dark—you'll miss a lot. Audience: All ages. Rating:* ★★★

NEED A BREAK? Among the fast munchies here, some of the best are the fresh pineapple spears at Adventureland's **Aloha Isle.**

7 Pirates of the Caribbean. This boat ride is Disney at its best: memorable vignettes, incredible detail, a gripping story, and catchy music whose relentless "Yo-Ho!"-ing can only be eradicated by "It's a Small World." One of the pirate's "Avast, ye scurvy scum!" is the sort of greeting your kids will proclaim for the next week—which gives you an idea of the ride's impact.

The gracious arched entrance soon gives way to a dusty dungeon, redolent of damp and of a spooky, scary past. Lanterns flicker as you board the boats and a ghostly voice intones, "Dead men tell no tales." Usually, at this point, a much higher, younger voice quavers, "Mommy, can we get off?". A deserted beach, strewn with shovels, a skeleton, and a disintegrating map indicating buried treasure, is the preface to this story of greed, lust, and destruction.

Emerging from a pitch-black time tunnel, you're literally in the middle of a furious battle. A pirate ship, cannons blazing, is attacking a stone fortress. Cannonballs splash into the water just off your bows, and Audio-Animatronic pirates hoist the Jolly Roger while brave soldiers scurry to defend the fort—to no avail. Politically correct nerves may twinge as the women of the town are rounded up and auctioned. "Strike your colors, ye brazen wench, no need to expose your superstructure!" shouts one pirate, but the scene is terrific: pirates chasing chickens, ducking the town mayor in the well, and collapsing into a snoring stupor with a couple of pigs. Check out the hairy legs of the two carousers straddling the wall. The wild antics of the pirates result in a conflagration; the town goes up in flames, and all go to their just reward amid a chorus of "Yo-ho! Yo-ho! A pirate's life for me." There's a moral in there somewhere, if you want to look for one—or you can just enjoy the show. *Duration: 10 min. Crowds: Waits seldom exceed 30 min, despite the ride's popularity. Strategy: A good destination even during the busy afternoon hours. Audience: All ages. Rating:* ★★

8 **Enchanted Tiki Birds.** Don't expect much when your preshow host is a mechanical toucan called Claude Birdbrain. Inside the blessedly air-conditioned Polynesian longhouse that houses the birds, the avian intelligence quotient doesn't improve markedly, and ethnic stereotyping runs rampant. Four parrots run the joint—Pierre, José, Fritz, and Michael, the Irish one whose plumage is green—each of which has an appropriately ethnic accent. "Tropical Serenade" is sung and whistled by hundreds of Audio-Animatronic figures: exotic birds, swaying flowers, and Tiki god statues with blinking red eyes. Toddlers love the repetition of the song "In the Tiki, Tiki, Tiki, Tiki, Tiki Room." Older folks tend to roll their eyes along with the statues. This was Disney's first Audio-Animatronic attraction, and the animatronics still hold up fine, but the audio could use an update. *Duration: 17 min. Crowds: Waits seldom exceed 30 min. Strategy: Go when you need to sit in an air-conditioned room. Audience: All ages. Rating:* ★

Frontierland

Frontierland, in the northwest quadrant of the Magic Kingdom, invokes the American frontier. The period seems to be the latter half of the 19th century, and the West is being won by Disney staffers dressed in checked shirts, leather vests, cowboy hats, and brightly colored neckerchiefs. Banjo and fiddle music twang from tree to tree.

The screams that periodically drown out the string-sawing are not the result of a cowboy surprising an Indian. They come from one of the Magic Kingdom's big guns, **Splash Mountain,** an elaborate water flume. Opened in October 1992, it quickly eclipsed all the other attractions in popularity. **Big Thunder Mountain Railroad,** one of the park's two roller coasters, also gives vocal cords a workout. Other Frontierland attractions are somewhat tamer: **Tom Sawyer Island,** an enormous landscaped playground perfect for games of hide-and-go-seek; the **Frontierland Shooting Arcade,** an electronic shooting arcade that pleases even the sulkiest adolescent; and two musical revues—the *Country Bear Jamboree* and the *Diamond Horseshoe Jamboree.*

The rust-red rock spires of Thunder Mountain and Splash Mountain serve as local landmarks and set a landscaping tone best described as "Arid, Extra Dry." In contrast to the lush vegetation of Adventureland, Frontierland is planted with mesquite, twisted Peruvian pepper trees, slash pines, and many varieties of cactus. The unpainted buildings and wooden sidewalks have a ramshackle quality, and even though you know that no dust is allowed in Walt Disney World, the setting evokes dusty thoughts.

Shops and eateries are along the avenue bordering the southern curve of a lake that, because it variously represents the Mississippi and Missouri rivers and their tributaries, is called Rivers of America. It still looks like a lake. Emporia here are generally referred to as "posts," as in the Frontierland Trading Post and Prairie Outpost, which sell sheriff badges, leatherwork, cowboy hats, and southwestern, Indian, and Mexican crafts. Then there's Big Al's, for genuine Davy Crockett coonskin hats. Yee-haw!

The Walt Disney World Railroad makes a stop at Frontierland. It tunnels through Splash Mountain and drops you off between Splash Mountain and Thunder Mountain.

⑨ Splash Mountain. At Rope Drop, the hordes hoof it to this incredibly popular log-flume ride. Based on the animated sequences in Disney's 1946 film *Song of the South,* it features Audio-Animatronic creations of Brer Rabbit, Brer Bear, Brer Fox, and a menagerie of Brer beasts (including Brer Frog and a Heckle-and-Jeckle duo of Brer Crows). No matter what time you get there, you *will,* repeat, *will* wait in line. So the Disney folks have made the waiting area here as entertaining and comfortable as possible, with lots of large shade trees, little critters in tiny houses, and toe-tappin' country music wafting from speakers hidden in rocks. When you finally do settle into the eight-person hollowed-out logs, Uncle Remus's voice growls, "Mark mah words, Brer Rabbit gonna put his foot in Brer Fox's mouth one of these days." And this just might be the day.

As the boat carries you through a lily pond—just bopping with Brer Frogs merrily singing the ride's theme song, "Time to Be Moving Along"—past signs for Brer Fox's lair and Brer Bear's den, Brer Rabbit's silhouette hops along in front, always just ahead of you. Every time some critter makes a grab for the bunny, the log boats drop out of reach. But Brer Fox has been studying his book *How to Catch a Rabbit,* and our lop-eared friend looks as if he's destined for the pot. Things don't look so good for the flumers either, as the boats creak up and up the mountain, past a pair of pessimistic crows. You get one heart-stopping pause at the top—just long enough to grab the safety bar—and then the boat plummets down the world's longest and sharpest flume drop right into a gigantic briar patch. In case you want to know what you're getting into, the drop is 52½ feet—that's about five stories—at a 45-degree angle, enough to reach speeds of 40 miles per hour and make you feel weightless. From the boat—especially if you are in the front seat—it looks truly as if you are going to be impaled on those enormous spikes. Try to smile through your clenched teeth: As you begin to drop, a flashbulb pops, so you can purchase a photographic memento of the experience before exiting the ride. Brer Rabbit escapes—and so do you, wet and exhilarated—to the tune of "Zip-a-Dee-Doo-Dah," whose bouncy melody has become something of a Disney theme song. If you want to get really wet—and you will get splashed from almost every seat—ask the ride attendant to seat you in the front row.

Knowing how much we all like to watch people getting the pants scared off them, Disney constructed the flume so that spectators can see the plunge into the briar patch from the footbridge between Splash Mountain and Thunder Mountain. In an especially neat touch, it looks as if the log boats disappear into the pond below the briar patch with a giant splash—leaving only bubbles in their wake. *Duration: 11 min. Crowds: Yes! Strategy: If you're not in line by 9:45, your only hope is during meals or a parade. Audience: All except very young children. No pregnant women or guests wearing back, neck, or leg braces; minimum height 44". Rating:* ★★★

⑩ Big Thunder Mountain Railroad. As any true roller-coaster lover can tell you, this three-minute ride is a tame one; despite the posted warnings, you won't stagger off, you won't throw up, and you won't vow never to subject yourself to the experience again. The thrills are there, however, thanks to the intricate details and stunning scenery along every inch of the 2,780-foot-long wooden track.

Set in gold-rush days, the runaway train rushes and rattles past 20 Audio-Animatronic figures—including donkeys, chickens, a goat, and a grizzled old miner surprised in his bathtub—$300,000 of genuine antique mining equipment, tumbleweeds, a derelict mining town, hot springs, and a flash flood.

The ride was 15 years in the planning and took two years and close to $17 million to build. This price tag, give or take a few million, equaled the entire cost of erecting California's Disneyland in 1955. The 197-foot mountain is based on the monoliths of Utah's Monument Valley, and thanks to 650 tons of steel, 4,675 tons of cement, and 16,000 gallons of paint, it closely resembles the real thing. *Duration: 4 min. Crowds: Large. Strategy: Thunder Mountaineers swear that the ride is even better at night, when you can't anticipate the curves and the track's rattling sounds as if something's about to give. But then you'd miss the scenic details. The solution—go twice. Audience: All except young children. No pregnant women or guests wearing back, neck, or leg braces; minimum height 40″. Rating:* ★★★

⑪ **Tom Sawyer Island.** An artfully misspelled sign, signed by Tom Sawyer, conveys the island's attractions: "If'n you like dark caves, mystry mines, bottomless pits, shakey bridges 'n' big rocks, you have came to the best place I know." Aunt Polly would have walloped Tom for his orthography, but she couldn't have argued with the truth. The 6-mile-long island—actually two islands connected by an old-fashioned swing bridge—is a natural playground, all hills and trees and rocks and shrubs. Other guidebooks suggest that parents sit this one out on the porch of Aunt Polly's Landing, sipping lemonade; we say, why let the kids have all the fun?

Most of the attractions are on the main island, where the boats dock and where Aunt Polly's Landing and the rest rooms are. These include the mystery cave, an almost-pitch-black labyrinth where the wind wails in a truly spooky fashion; Injun Joe's cave, all pointy stalactites and stalagmites and endowed with lots of columns and crevices from which to jump out and startle younger sisters and brothers; Harper's Mill, an old-fashioned grist mill; and, in a clearing at the top of the hill, a rustic playground. As you explore the shoreline on the dirt paths, keep an eye out for the barrel bridge—every time someone takes a step, the whole contraption bounces.

On the other island is Fort Sam Clemens, a log fortress from which you can fire air guns with great booms and cracks at the soporific passengers on the Liberty Square Riverboat. It's guarded by an equally soporific Audio-Animatronic sentry, loudly snoring off his last bender. Both islands are sprinkled with lookouts for great views to Thunder Mountain and Frontierland, as well as nice natural niches—often furnished with benches and water fountains. *Duration: Up to you. Crowds: Seldom overwhelming, but it wouldn't matter—here, the more the merrier. Strategy: Try it as a refreshing afternoon getaway. Audience: All ages. Rating:* ★★

⑫ **Country Bear Jamboree.** In this stage show, wisecracking, cornpone Audio-Animatronic bears joke, sing, and play country music and 1950s rock and roll. The show stars Henry, the massive but debonair master of ceremonies; the robust Trixie, the Tampa Temptation, who laments a love lost while perched in a swing suspended from the ceiling; Bubbles, Bunny, and Beulah, harmonizing on "All the Guys That Turn Me On Turn Me Down"; and Big Al, a cult figure who has inspired postcards, stuffed animals, and his own shop next door. *Duration: 16 min. Crowds: Large, considering the relatively small theater.*

Strategy: Visit before 11 AM, during the daily parade, or after most small children have left for the day. Stand to the far left in the anteroom where you wait to end up in the front rows; to the far right if you want to sit in the last row, where small children can perch on top of the seats to see better. Audience: All ages. Rating: ★★★

⓭ Frontierland Shootin' Arcade. At this classic shooting arcade, laser beams sub for bullets, as genuine Hawkins 54-caliber buffalo rifles have been refitted to emit electronic beams. When they strike, tombstones spin and epitaphs change, ghost riders gallop out of clouds, and skulls pop out of graves, accompanied by the sounds of howling coyotes, creaking bridges, and the cracks of the rifles blasted over the digital audio system. *Cost: 25¢ per 5 shot. Strategy: Bring a pocketful of change. Audience: Older children and adults. Rating:* ★★

⓮ Diamond Horseshoe Jamboree. "Knock, knock." "Who's there?" "Ya." "Ya who?" "Yaaahooo!" And they're off, with another riproaring, raucous, corny, nonstop, high-kicking, elbow-jabbing, song-and-dance-and-fiddling show staged in a re-creation of an Old West saloon. The show features a sextet of dance-hall girls and high-spirited cowboys; Sam, the stagestruck and lovelorn saloon keeper; and Lily, a shimmying, feather-boa-toting reincarnation of Mae West, whose throaty version of "A Good Man Is Hard to Find" brings down the house. At other times, Lily swishes around the hall, tickling noses with her boa and uttering such lines as "Watch it, honey, this is Frontierland, not Fantasyland!" The cowboys leap from the balconies and swing around columns; Lily's Girls perform an exuberant cancan, and everyone has a hand-clapping good time. Seating begins half an hour before curtain time, and snacks and light refreshments may be purchased at your table. *Showtimes: 10:45, 12:15, 1:45, 3:30, and 4:45; reservations essential. Duration: 30 min. Crowds: Full house for most performances. Strategy: Book in early morning at Disneyana Collectibles (12:15 show fills up first) or show up 30 min before showtime to wait for cancellations. But give it a miss if you're on a tight schedule and have plans to see the Hoop-Dee-Doo Revue in Fort Wilderness. Audience: All except young children. Rating:* ★★

Liberty Square

The weathered siding gives way to neat clapboard and solid brick; the mesquite and cactus are replaced by stately oaks and masses of azalea, and the rough-and-tumble Western frontier gently slides into Colonial America. Liberty Square picks up where Frontierland leaves off, continuing around the western shore of Rivers of America and forming the eastern boundary of Fantasyland.

The theme is Colonial history, which northerners will be happy to learn is solid Yankee. The small buildings, topped with weather vanes and exuding comfortable prosperity from every rosy brick and every spiffy shutter, are pure New England. And in a delightful literary wink, the silversmith shop lists as its proprietor J. Tremaine, hero of the Esther Forbes novel about the Revolutionary War that's required reading in most junior high schools. There's even a **Liberty Tree**, a 130-year-old live oak actually found on Walt Disney World property and moved to the Magic Kingdom. Just as the Sons of Liberty hung lanterns on trees as a signal of solidarity after the Boston Tea Party, the Liberty Tree's branches are decorated with 13 lanterns representing the 13 original Colonies.

After the crowds in Frontierland, Liberty Square seems relaxed and peaceful—perhaps because its attractions tend to be sedentary. There's the **Hall of Presidents,** an Audio-Animatronic view of the history of the United States; **Keel Boats** and **Liberty Square Riverboat**—two ways to waste time on the Rivers of America; and the **Haunted Mansion,** Disney's ne plus ultra spook show. The shops in this area tend to sell more arts than kitsch; in addition to the silversmith shop, there's Olde World Antiques's one-of-a-kind objects and reproductions as well as custom-blended perfumes; the Yankee Trader's gourmet food and cooking items; the Silhouette Cart's profiles, hand-cut and framed while you wait; and the Umbrella Cart, with personalized products that are sure to come in handy during the daily summer afternoon thundershower. There are plenty of tree-shaded tables for picnicking and plenty of carts and fast-food eateries supplying the goods. **Liberty Tree Tavern,** a gracious, table-service restaurant that could have been airlifted from Colonial Williamsburg, is one of the best at the Magic Kingdom; reservations are essential.

⑮ The Hall of Presidents. This multimedia tribute to the Constitution, caused quite a sensation when it opened, because it was here that the first refinements of the Audio-Animatronic system of computerized robots could be seen. Now surpassed by Epcot Center's American Adventure, it's still well worth attending, as much for the two-part show as for the spacious, air-conditioned theater.

It starts with a film, narrated by writer Maya Angelou, that discusses the Constitution as the codification of the spirit that founded America. Visitors learn about threats to the document, ranging from the 18th-century Whiskey Rebellion to the Civil War, and hear such famous speeches as Benjamin Franklin's plea to the Continental Congress delegates for ratification and Abraham Lincoln's warning that "a house divided cannot stand." The shows conveying Disney's brand of patriotism may be ponderous, but they're always well researched and lovingly presented; this film, for instance, was revamped to replace a lingering subtext of Cold War paranoia with the more progressive assertion that our democracy is a work in progress, that liberty and justice still do not figure equally in the lives of all Americans.

The second half is a roll call of all 42 U.S. presidents. Each chief executive rises and responds with a nod—even those who blatantly attempted to subvert the Constitution. The detail is lifelike, right down to the brace on Franklin Delano Roosevelt's leg. The robots can't resist nodding, fidgeting, and even whispering to each other while waiting for their names to come up. The last to be called is Bill Clinton, who, unlike other contemporary presidential robots, has a speaking part. Audio-Animatronic Clinton's speech was written for Disney by *Lion King* lyricist Tim Rice, of *Jesus Christ Superstar* and *Evita,* in collaboration with the President's chief speechwriter; the audio was provided—in one take—by human Bill Clinton himself. *Duration: 30 min. Crowds: Usually moderate. Strategy: Go in the afternoon, when you'll appreciate the air-conditioning. Audience: Older children and adults. Rating:* ★★

NEED A   **Liberty Square Market** carts sell fresh fruit—a welcome change from the
BREAK?   Magic Kingdom's ubiquitous french fries and burgers.

⑯ Liberty Square Riverboat. A real old-fashioned steamboat, the **Richard F. Irvine**—named for a key Disney designer—is authentic, from its calliope whistle and the gingerbread trim on its three decks to the boilers that produce the steam that drives the big rear paddlewheel. In fact, the boat misses authenticity on only one count: There's no mustachioed captain to guide it during the ride around the Rivers of America. That task is performed by an underwater rail. The trip is slow and not exactly thrilling, except, perhaps, to the kids getting shot at by their counterparts at Fort Sam Clemens on Tom Sawyer Island. But it's a relaxing break for all concerned, and some lucky parents can take a load off on the few chairs scattered around the upper deck while their offspring explore the boat. *Duration: 15 min. Crowds: Moderate, but capacity is high so waits are seldom trying. Strategy: Go when you need a break from the crowds. Audience: All ages. Rating:* ★

17 **Keel Boats.** They're short and dumpy and you have to sit on a bench, wedged tightly between fellow visitors, and listen to a heavy-handed, noisy spiel about those roistering, roustabout days along the Missouri. And the Tom Sawyer Island crowd doesn't even bother to shoot you. Just for that we're going to tell you the answer to the guide's extraordinarily lackluster joke: "Firewood." So there—make our day. *Duration: 10–15 min. Crowds: Lines move slowly because of boats' low passenger capacity. Strategy: Skip this on your first visit. Audience: All ages. Rating:* ★

18 **Haunted Mansion.** The repository of special effects here is a howl. Or do we mean a scream? You are greeted at the creaking iron gates of this Hudson Gothic mansion by a lugubrious attendant, who has the only job at Walt Disney World for which smiling is frowned upon, and ushered into a spooky picture gallery. A disembodied voice echoes from the walls: "Welcome, foolish mortals, to the Haunted Mansion. I am your ghost host." A scream shivers down, and you're off on one of the best attractions at Walt Disney World.

Part walk-through, part ride on a "doom buggie," the Haunted Mansion is scary but not terrifying, and the special effects are phenomenal. Catch the glowing bats' eyes on the wallpaper—a riveting twist in interior decorating; the suit of armor that comes alive; the shifting walls in the portrait gallery that make you wonder if they are moving up or if you are moving down; the strategically placed gusts of damp, cold air; the marble busts of the world's greatest ghost writers in the library; the wacky inscriptions on the tombstones as you wait in line; the spectral xylophone player who enlivens the graveyard shift with bones instead of mallets; and, of course, the chattering head of the woman in the crystal ball. If you look at her hard enough, you'll see she's a hologram. Just when you think the Imagineers have exhausted their bag of ectoplasmic tricks, along comes another one. They've saved the best for last, as you suddenly discover that your doom buggie has gained an extra passenger. As you approach the exit, your ghoulish guide intones, "Now I will raise the safety bar and the ghost will follow you home." Thanks for the souvenir, pal.

An interesting piece of Disney trivia: One of the biggest jobs for the maintenance crew here is not cleaning up but keeping the 200-odd trunks, chairs, harps, dress forms, statues, rugs, and other knickknacks appropriately dusty. Disney buys its dust in 5-pound bags and scatters it throughout the mansion from a special gadget resembling a fertilizer spreader. According to local lore, enough dust has been dumped since the park's 1971 opening to completely bury the mansion. Where does it all go? Perhaps the voice is right in saying that something will follow you home. *Duration: 8 min. Crowds: Substantial, but high capacity and fast loading usually keep lines moving. Strategy: Go early, late, or during the nighttime parade; at any other time, check line and go back later if it's long. Audience: All except young children, who may be frightened. Rating:* ★★★

Fantasyland

Photographers will want to take advantage of one of the least-traveled byways in the Magic Kingdom. If you're coming to Fantasyland from Liberty Square, turn left at the Sleepy Hollow snack shop. Just past the outdoor tables you'll find a shortcut that provides about the best unobstructed ground-level view of Cinderella Castle. It's a great spot for a family photo.

Once you're here you'll know why Walt Disney called this "a timeless land of enchantment." Fantasyland's aura does conjure up the sprinkling of pixie dust. Perhaps that's because Fantasyland's fanciful gingerbread houses, gleaming gold turrets, and, of course, its rides based on Disney-animated movies are what the Magic Kingdom is all about.

With the exception of the slightly spooky **Snow White's Adventures** and **Mr. Toad's Wild Ride,** the attractions here are imaginative rather than heart-stopping. Like the animated classics on which they are based, rides that could ostensibly be classified as kiddie rides are, in fact, packed with enough delightful detail to engage adults. While the kids are awed by the bigger picture, their parents are amused by the road signs at Mr. Toad's Wild Ride or enchanted by the view of moonlit London in Peter Pan's Flight.

You can enter Fantasyland on foot from Frontierland or by skyway from Tomorrowland, but the classic introduction is through the **Cinderella Castle.** To get in an appropriately magical mood—and to provide yourself with a cooling break—turn left immediately after you exit the Castle's archway. Here you'll find one of the most charming and most overlooked touches in Fantasyland: **Cinderella Fountain,** a lovely brass casting of the Castle's namesake, who's dressed in her peasant togs and surrounded by her beloved mice and bird friends. Water splashing from the fountain provides a cooling sensation on a hot day—as do the very welcome brass drinking fountains at the statue's base. Don't forget to toss in a coin and make a wish; after all, you're in Fantasyland, where dreams do come true. Straight ahead from the Castle you'll find **Cinderella's Golden Carrousel.** The land's other attractions are arranged around it in a somewhat bulging circle.

Fantasyland is always the most heavily trafficked area in the park, and its rides are almost always crowded. Luckily, its rides sometimes open early for guests at WDW-owned resorts. Or you can take your chances during the afternoon parade. Visitors without children should save Fantasyland for evening, when a sizable number of the little ones will have departed for their own private dreamland.

⑲ Cinderella Castle. The royal blue turrets, gold spires, and glistening white towers are every child's fairy-tale castle come true. It was inspired by the castle built by the mad Bavarian king Ludwig at Neuschwanstein, as well as by drawings prepared for Disney's animated film of the classic French fairy tale. Although often confused with Disneyland's Sleeping Beauty Castle, at 180 feet this castle is more than 100 feet taller; and with its elongated towers and lacy fretwork, it is immeasurably more graceful. It's easy to bypass the elaborate murals on the walls of the archway as you rush toward Fantasyland, but they are worth a stop. The five panels, measuring some 15 feet high and 10 feet wide, were created by Disney artist Dorothea Redmond and realized in a million bits of multicolored Italian glass, real silver, and 14-karat gold by mosaicist Hanns-Joachim Scharff. Following the images drawn for the Disney film, the mosaics tell the story of the little cinder girl from pumpkin to prince and happily ever after.

The fantasy has feet, if not of clay, then of solid steel beams, fiberglass, and 500 gallons of paint. Instead of dungeons, there are service tunnels for the Magic Kingdom's less-than-magical quotidian operations. These are the same tunnels that honeycomb the ground under much of the park. And upstairs does not hold, as rumor has it, a casket containing the cryogenically preserved body of Walt Disney but instead mundane broadcast facilities, security rooms, and the like.

Within the Castle's archway, on the left as you face Fantasyland, is the **King's Gallery,** one of the Magic Kingdom's finest and priciest shops. Here you'll find exquisite hand-painted models of carousel horses, delicate crystal castles, and other symbols of fairy-tale magic, including Cinderella's glass slipper in a variety of colors and sizes.

㉒ Cinderella's Golden Carrousel. This is the whirling, musical heart of Fantasyland—and maybe even of the entire Magic Kingdom. This ride encapsulates the Disney experience in 90 prancing horses and then hands it to you on a 60-foot platter. Seventy-two of the dashing steeds date from the original carousel built in 1917 by the Philadelphia Toboggan Company; 12 additional mounts were made of fiberglass. All are meticulously painted—at a rate of about 48 hours per horse—and like real horses, each one is completely different. One steed sports a collar of bright yellow roses, another a quiver of Indian arrows, and yet another, for some completely mysterious reason, a portrait of Eric the Red. They gallop ceaselessly beneath a wooden canopy, gaily striped on the outside and muraled on the inside with 18 panels depicting scenes from Disney's 1950 film *Cinderella.* As the platter starts to spin, the mirrors sparkle, the fairy lights glitter, and the rich notes of the band organ— no calliope here—play favorite tunes from Disney movies. If you wished upon a star, it couldn't get more magical than this. *Duration: 2 min. Crowds: Lines during busy periods. Strategy: Go early, during the daily parade, or in the evening. Audience: All ages. Rating:* ★★

㉑ Legend of the Lion King. Featuring an advanced form of puppeteering, the elaborate stage show is further boosted by special effects and Elton John's lyrical music. It brings to vivid life Simba, Mufasa, Scar, and the rest of the characters from Disney's 32nd animated feature. Unlike many of the stage shows in the Magic Kingdom, this one showcases "humanimals," Disneyspeak for bigger-than-life-size figures that are manipulated by human "animateers" hidden from the audience's view. The adult Simba, for instance, is nearly eight feet tall! The preshow consists of the opening "Circle of Life" overture from the film. It's a perfect stage-setter for the fun and drama to come. *Duration: 15 min. Crowds: Rendered insignificant by large theater capacity. Strategy: Save this for mid- or late-afternoon, when you want to sit down and cool off. Audience: All ages. Note that last show is 30 minutes to one hour before park closing; check with show attendant. Rating:* ★★

㉒ Peter Pan's Flight. Kids of all ages love this truly fantastic indoor ride, inspired by Sir James M. Barrie's story about the boy who wouldn't grow up. Disney animated it in 1953. You board two-person magic sailing ships, with brightly striped sails that catch the wind and soar into the skies above London en route to Never-Never-Land. Along the way, you watch as Wendy, Michael, and John are sprinkled with pixie dust while Nana barks below, wave to Princess Tiger Lily, meet the evil Captain Hook, and cheer for the tick-tocking, clock-swallowing crocodile who's breakfasted on Hook's hand and is more than ready for lunch. Despite the lack of '90s high-tech special effects, kids love this ride. Adults will especially enjoy the dreamy views of London by moonlight, a galaxy of twinkling yellow lights punctuated by Big Ben, London Bridge, and a moonlit Thames River. There's so much to see that the ride seems much longer than it is. *Duration: 2½ min. Crowds: Always heavy, except in the evening and early morning. Strategy: Go early, during the daily parade, or in the evening. Audience: All ages. Rating:* ★★

㉓ It's a Small World. Visiting Walt Disney World and not stopping for this tribute to terminal cuteness—why, the idea is practically un-American. Disney raided the remains of the 1964–65 New York World's Fair for this exhibit, which was originally sponsored by Pepsi-Cola long before soft drinks were "It" or "The Right One, Baby, Uh-Huh." Disney then appropriated the theme song of international brotherhood and friendship for its own.

This ride strains the patience more than the adrenal glands. Moving somewhat slower than a snail, the barges inch through several barnlike rooms, each crammed with musical moppets, all madly singing the theme song, "It's a Small World After All." It's the revenge of the Audio-Animatrons, you think, as rather simplistic dolls differentiated only by their national costumes—Dutch babies in clogs, Spanish flamenco dancers, German oompah bands, Russian balalaikas, sari-wrapped Indians waving temple bells, Tower of London guards in scarlet Beefeater uniforms, yodelers and goatherds, Japanese kite fliers, and juvenile cancan dancers, to name just a few—parade past, smiling away and wagging their heads in time to The Song. But somehow by the time you reach the end of the ride, you're grinning and wagging too. You just can't help it—and small children can't wait to ride it again. By the way, there is only one verse to The Song and it repeats incessantly, tattooing itself indelibly into your brain. Now all together: "It's a world of laughter, a world of tears. It's a world of hope and a world of fears . . ." *Duration: 11 min. Crowds: Steady, but lines move fast. Strategy: Look for the line to the left—it's usually the shorter of the two. Go anytime but mid-afternoon. Audience: All ages. Rating:* ★★

㉔ Dumbo the Flying Elephant. Hands down, this is one of Fantasyland's most popular rides. While the story has one baby elephant with gigantic ears who accidentally downs a bucket of champagne and learns he can fly, the ride has 16 jolly Dumbos flying around a central column, each pachyderm packing a couple of kids and a parent. A joystick controls each of Dumbo's vertical motions, so you can make him ascend or descend at will. Alas, the ears do not flap. *Duration: 2 min. Crowds: Perpetual, except in early morning. Strategy: If accompanying small children, make a beeline here at Rope Drop; otherwise, skip it, especially on a first visit. Audience: Young children. Rating:* ★

㉕ Mad Tea Party. A staple in carnivals, where it's known as "Tubs o' Fun," this Fantasyland icon is for the vertigo addict looking for a fix. The Disney version is based on the 1951 film *Alice in Wonderland,* in which the Mad Hatter hosts a tea party for his un-birthday. You hop into oversize, pastel-colored teacups and whirl around a giant platter. Add your own spin to the teacup's orbit with the help of the steering wheel in the center. If the centrifugal force hasn't shaken you up too much, check out the soused mouse that pops out of the teapot centerpiece and compare his condition to your own. *Duration: 2 min. Crowds: Steady from late morning on, with slow-moving lines. Strategy: Skip this on your first Magic Kingdom visit. Rating:* ★

㉖ Mr. Toad's Wild Ride. Based on the 1949 Disney release *The Adventures of Ichabod and Mr. Toad*—itself derived from Kenneth Grahame's classic children's novel *The Wind in the Willows*—this ride puts you into the jump seat of the speed-loving amphibian's flivver as he floors the accelerator on a jolting, jarring jaunt through the English countryside. At the entrance, notice the ride's two lovingly adhered-to mottoes: *Toadí Acceleratio* and *Semper Absurda;* and inside keep an eye out for such whimsical touches as signposts indicating "Worcestershire" and "Notsoshire" as well as your own destination, "Nowhere in Particular." Along the way you'll crash through walls, scatter chickens, nearly get clobbered by a falling suit of armor, go hurtling through haystacks, and end up on a collision course with a freight train. *Duration: 3 min. Crowds: Steady from late morning until evening. Strategy: Go very early, during the daily parade, or after dark. Audience: All ages. Marginally less scary than Snow White's Adventures; may startle young children. Rating:* ★★

㉗ Snow White's Adventures. What was previously an unremittingly scary three-minute, indoor spook-house ride is now a kinder, gentler experience. Where once the dwarves might as well have been named Anxious and Fearful, the revamped ride—now with six-passenger cars and a mini-version of the movie—has been tempered. There's still the evil queen, her nose wart, and her cackle, but joining the cast at long last are the prince and Snow White herself. The trip is still packed with plenty of scary moments, but an honest-to-goodness kiss followed by a happily-ever-after ending might even get you "heigh-ho"-ing on your way. *Duration: 3 min. Crowds: Steady from late morning until evening. Strategy: Go very early, during the daily parade, or after dark. Audience: All ages; may frighten young children. Rating:* ★★

㉘ Skyway to Tomorrowland. Take a one-way aerial trip to Tomorrowland from an enchanted attic perched above the trees in the far left corner of Fantasyland. This is also the terminus for those taking the Skyway from Tomorrowland to Fantasyland. You soar above the turquoise lagoon dotted with Captain Nemo's weird boats, the striped canopy of Cinderella's Golden Carrousel, the crowds thronging around Fantasyland, the Grand Prix Raceway at the edge of Tomorrowland, and the extraordinarily mundane tar-paper rooftops of the buildings that house the magic. Although this is a quick shortcut to Tomorrowland, it's actually more fun to take it in the other direction. That way you'll preview the sights of Fantasyland, hear the happy music ascending, and then alight in the attic terminus, in the mood for magic. *Duration: 5 min. Crowds: Moderate from late morning until evening but usually not a problem. Strategy: Bypass this on a first visit until you've seen the major attractions. Audience: All ages. Rating:* ★

㉙ Mickey's Starland. For a company that owes its fame to a certain endearing, big-eared little fellow, Walt Disney World is astonishingly mouse-free. Until, that is, you arrive here, a concentrated dose of adulation built in 1988 to celebrate Mickey Mouse's 60th birthday. Rarely crowded, the 3-acre niche set off to the side of Fantasyland is like a scene from a cartoon, and everything is child size. The attractions are in the imaginary town of Duckburg, where you'll find Donald and Huey, Dewey, and Louie, along with a cast of other Disney characters. Its pastel houses are positively Lilliputian, with miniature driveways, toy-size picket fences, and signs scribbled with finger paint. The best way to arrive is on the Walt Disney World Railroad, the old-fashioned choo-choo that also stops at Main Street and Frontierland.

It looks as if the Mickster himself has just left mustard-colored clapboard **Mickey's House.** Sad to say, despite Minnie's ministrations, her mate is a slob—to say nothing of a pack rat. Mickey's red pants are carelessly tossed over a chair; his slippers and golf clubs lie nearby; he leaves the radio on when he's not here; and his diet, to judge from the shopping list tacked to the fridge, is decidedly one-dimensional. Check out the mouse-ear-shaped andirons in the fireplace.

You can visit with Minnie in the kitchen, then slip out the back to tour her own neat and separate dwelling, as well as Donald Duck's houseboat and Goofy's ramshackle abode. Though this is primarily a children's attraction, adults will get a kick out of the imaginative architecture and the Disney attention to detail.

Mickey's Starland Show and Hollywood Theater, held under a yellow-and-white-striped big top, presents the television stars of "The Disney Afternoon" in a cheerful sing-along musical comedy that kids adore. There are Chip and Dale, Scrooge McDuck, the ever-bumbling Launchpad McQuack, and Gadget of the "Rescue Rangers." A video cartoon of pop star Cyndi Lauper singing "Hey Mickey, You're So Fine" kicks off the performance in high gear. Afterward, all the kids dash around backstage to **Mickey's Dressing Room,** where the star graciously signs autographs and poses for pictures with his adoring public.

Diagonally across the street from Mickey's House you'll find a delightful play area. Here the kids can climb, jump, slide, explore, and have a plain old good time in **Mickey's Treehouse** and **Minnie's Doll House** while Mom and Dad take a rest on benches that have a clear view of the climbing areas. For toddlers and preschoolers, there's the **Mouse-Ka-Maze,** a scaled-down version of the maze from *Alice in Wonderland.*

Next to the play area at **Grandma Duck's Farm**—a petting zoo with real live animals—the star is Minnie Moo, a placid Holstein cow whose distinctive black splotches just naturally arranged themselves into Disney's mouse logo. Like the rest of Mickey's Starland, the animals are pint-size, too, and a more cuddly bunch of baby chicks, sheep, calves, rabbits, pigs, and goats couldn't be imagined. How Walt Disney World manages to keep this imaginative barnyard so spick-and-span is completely beyond us. *Duration: Up to you. Crowds: Moderate and seldom a problem. Strategy: Go anytime. Audience: Young children, mainly. Rating:* ★★

New Tomorrowland

As the "new" added to this land indicates, it's a redesigned Tomorrowland. The stark, antiseptic future forecasted by the original design had become embarrassingly passé: Bare concrete and plain white walls, plus such outdated rides as Star Jets and Mission to Mars, said more about Eisenhower-era aesthetics, or lack thereof, than third-millennium progress. To revitalize what had become the least appealing area of the Magic Kingdom, Disney artists and architects created new facades, restaurants, and shops for an energized Future City, which is more similar in mood to the themed villages of other lands. And this time around the creators showed that they had learned their lesson: Rather than predict a tomorrow destined for obsolescence, they focused on "the future that never was"—the future envisioned by sci-fi writers and moviemakers in the '20s and '30s, when space flight, laser beams, and home computers belonged in the world of fiction, not fact.

With two completely new attractions—**Alien Encounter** and **Timekeeper** in the **Metropolis Science Centre**—an overhauled version of the Star-Jets now reincarnated as **AstroOrbiter,** and an updated **Carousel of Progress,** Tomorrowland is certain to be high on the list of returning Disneyphiles as well as first-timers. Eateries here have also been revamped inside and out; however, while the menus and decor may have changed, they're still heavy on the fast-food side of things. In addition to all the new goodies, this land is home to one of the park's perennial favorites, the **Space Mountain** roller coaster, so count on lines at just about all hours of the day and night. Main Street's Penny Arcade, which was rechristened the **Tomorrowland Arcade,** has moved here, too, and it's been souped-up with the latest video games. There's even an ATM here for parents who need to replenish their supply of quarters.

30 **The Timekeeper.** Disney Imagineers have pulled out the stops on this tribute to time travel. Located in the Transportarium in the Metropolis Science Centre, it combines CircleVision 360 filmmaking with Audio-Animatronic figures and takes visitors on a time-traveling adventure to the past and on into the future. Don't plan on a relaxing voyage, however; there are no seats in the theater—only lean rails. Hosted by Time Keeper, a C-3PO clone whose frenetic personality is given voice by Robin Williams, and Nine-Eye, a slightly frazzled droid, time-travelers meet famous inventors and visionaries of the machine age. *Duration: 20 min. Crowds: Moderate; moves steadily since theater capacity is nearly 900. Strategy: Go when the lines at Alien Encounter are long. Audience: All ages. Rating:* ★★

31 **Delta Dreamflight.** There's almost never a wait here, which should put your suspicions on red alert. It's in the same building complex as Timekeeper and, in fact, the entrances can be easily confused—Dreamflight is farther along and to the right. Sponsored by Delta Airlines, this ride takes a look at the adventure of flying by showing a series of scenes of pop-up figures and photos of Delta's destinations. The idea is cute, but the execution—surprising given Disney's experience with special effects—falls far short of thrilling. At its best, the attraction screens special 70mm film segments showing barnstorming wing walkers performing such stunts as hanging off the wing and picking a ribbon off the ground and then sends you through a jet engine. You can ride past the rest of the plane's body at Disney-MGM's Backstage Studio Tour. At its worst, the photography looks as if it came from the local tourist information bureau. *Duration: 4½ min. Crowds: Light. Strategy: Go in the afternoon when everything else is crowded. Audience: All ages. Rating:* ★

32 **Alien Encounter.** Although Disney spent millions developing this attraction, it had difficulties getting off the ground. Rumor has it that when Michael Eisner first viewed it, he was not amused and decreed an overhaul. The revamped version contains more special effects and is scarier than the first go-around. The show provides a welcome change from its stodgy predecessor, Mission to Mars. Old-time Disneyphiles will note, though, that the room in which the "encounter" takes place is in exactly the same circular configuration as the Mars misadventure. Playing on Tomorrowland's new Future City theme, this attraction has guests enter what is ostensibly the city's convention center to watch a test of a new teleportation system. Representatives from the device's manufacturer, an alien corporation called XS-Tech— pronounced *excess,* their motto is "If something can't be done with XS, it can't be done at all"—try to transport the company's CEO from their planet to Earth to demonstrate the product. The attempt fails, however, and the resulting catastrophe consists of a very close encounter with an "extraTERRORrestrial" creature. *Duration: 20 min. Crowds: Expect lines. Strategy: Go first thing in the morning, during the afternoon parade, or during the evening fireworks. Audience: Definitely not suitable for small children or those afraid of the dark. Rating:* ★★

33 **AstroOrbiter.** This gleaming superstructure of revolving planets has come to symbolize the new Tomorrowland as much as Dumbo represents Fantasyland. The ride itself, however, hasn't changed much from its previous life as StarJets. Ride vehicles—now looking more like Buck

Rogers toys than space shuttles—sail past the whirling planets during a swing through space where you control the altitude if not the velocity. *Duration: 2 min. Crowds: Humongous, and line moves slowly. Strategy: Skip on your first visit if time is short, unless there's no line. Audience: All ages. Rating:* ★★

34 Tomorrowland Transit Authority—TTA. A reincarnation of the WEDway PeopleMover, the TTA takes a nice, leisurely ride around the perimeter of Tomorrowland, circling the AstroOrbiter and eventually gliding through the middle of Space Mountain. Some faint-hearted TTA passengers have no doubt chucked the notion of riding the roller coaster after being exposed first-hand to the screams emanating from the mountain—it sounds worse than it really is, though. Disney's version of future mass transit is smooth and noiseless, thanks to an electromagnetic linear induction motor that has no moving parts, uses little power, and emits no pollutants. *Duration: 6 min. Crowds: Not one of the park's popular attractions, so lines are seldom long. Strategy: Go to preview Space Mountain, but skip on a first-time visit until you've been through all the major attractions. Audience: All ages. Rating:* ★

35 Carousel of Progress. Originally seen at the 1964–65 World's Fair in New York, this revolving theater traces the impact of technological progress on the daily lives of Americans from the turn of this century into the near future. In each decade, there's an Audio-Animatronic family that sings the praises of the new gadgets that technology has wrought. Fans of the holiday film *A Christmas Story* will recognize the voice of its narrator, Jean Shepard, who injects his folksy, all-American humor as father figure through the decades. A pre-show, seen on overhead video monitors while you're waiting to enter the theater, details the design of the original carousel and features Walt himself singing the theme song. Speaking of which, gone is the irritating theme of years' past, "The Best Time of Your Life"; it's been replaced by the ride's original ditty, "There's a Great Big Beautiful Tomorrow"—very fitting for New Tomorrowland. *Duration: 20 min. Crowds: Moderate. Strategy: Skip on a first-time visit. Audience: All ages. Rating:* ★

36 Tomorrowland Arcade. Main Street's Penny Arcade has been moved to a new locale inside the Tomorrowland Light and Power Company and updated to reflect its new surroundings. With the move, however, much of the charm that was in the Main Street digs has been lost; gone are the antique Mute-o-scopes and Cail-o-scopes that cost a nickel. In their place are a bank of video games, with a heavy emphasis on Formula One racing. There is one tribute to the past left—an antique Candy Crane, where kids can fish for toys. Alas, it never has a line.

37 Grand Prix Raceway. This is one of those rides that incite instant addiction among kids and immediate antipathy among parents. The reasons for the former are easy to figure out: the brightly colored, Mark VII model, gasoline-powered cars that swerve around the four 2,260-foot tracks with much vroom-vroom-vrooming. Like real sports cars, the vehicles are equipped with rack-and-pinion steering and disc brakes; unlike the real thing, these run on a track. However, the track is so twisty that it's hard to keep the car on a straight course—something the race car fanatics warming the bleachers love to watch. If you're not a fanatic, the persistent noise and pervasive smell of high-test on a muggy central Florida afternoon can quickly rasp your nerves into the danger zone. Furthermore, there's a lot of waiting: You wait up to an hour to get on the track; you wait again for your turn to climb in a car; then you wait one more time to return your vehicle after your lap. All this for a ride in which the main thrill is achieving a top speed of 7 miles per hour. *Duration: 5 min. Crowds: Steady and heavy from* *late morning to evening. Strategy: Go in the evening or during a parade; skip on a first-time visit until you've been through all the major attractions. Audience: Older children. Minimum height for drivers 52". Rating:* ★

38 **Space Mountain.** The needlelike spires and gleaming white concrete cone of this attraction are almost as much of a Magic Kingdom landmark as Cinderella Castle. Towering 180 feet high, the structure has been called "Florida's third-highest mountain." Inside is arguably the world's most imaginative roller coaster. Although there are no loop-the-loops, gravitational whizbangs, or high-speed curves, the thrills are amply provided by Disney's masterful brainwashing as you take a trip into the depths of outer space—in the dark.

The mood for your space shot is set in the waiting area, as long lines are inevitable, so milk the mood for all it's worth. A dim blue light reflects off the mirror-and-chrome walls, while above planets and galaxies and meteors and comets whirl past; strobe lights flash, and the fluorescent panels on the six-passenger rockets streak by, leaving phosphorescent memories. Screams and shrieks echo in the chamber, piercing the rattling of the cars and the various otherworldly beeps and buzzes. Meanwhile, you can't help overhearing gossip about how earrings have been known to be ripped out of earlobes by the centrifugal force, pocketbooks shaken open and upended, and so on. Although it's a good idea to stow personal belongings securely, Disney staffers in a control booth constantly monitor the ride on a battery of closed-circuit televisions; at the first sign of any guest having trouble, the ride can be stopped.

That rarely happens. Instead, you wedge yourself into the seat. The blinking sign in front switches from "boarding" to "blast off," and you do. The ride lasts only 2 minutes and 38 seconds and attains a top speed of 28 miles per hour, but the devious twists and invisible drops, and the fact that you can't see where you're going, make it seem twice as long and many more times as thrilling. People of all ages adore this ride; there is, however, a bail-out area just before boarding in case you have second thoughts. *Duration: 3 min. Crowds: Large and steady, with long lines from morning to night despite high capacity. Strategy: Go either at the end of the day, during a parade, or at Rope Drop (in which case wait at the Plaza Restaurant rather than at the top of Main Street to get a 120-yd head start on the crowd). Audience: All except young children. No pregnant women or guests wearing back, neck, or leg braces; minimum height 44". Rating:* ★★★

39 **Skyway to Fantasyland.** The brightly colored cable cars of this one-way ride can be picked up at the station right outside Space Mountain for the commute to the far western end of Fantasyland. Not only a great shortcut, the open-air cars offer magnificent views of Cinderella Castle and many of the Fantasyland rides; that is, you can scope out the lines from above and plan your strategy accordingly. Last but not least, those aerial tramlets provide one of the few opportunities for a little peace and quiet among the madding crowd. If you can time things right, there's no better way to view the 10 PM fireworks. *Duration: 5 min. Crowds: 10- to 20-min wait, except in early morning and during parades. Strategy: Skip this on your first visit. Audience: All ages. Rating:* ★

Shopping

Everywhere you turn in the Magic Kingdom there are shops and stalls urging you to take home a little piece of the magic. The big daddy of all shops in the Magic Kingdom is the enormous **Emporium,** which stocks thousands upon thousands of Disney character products, from keychains to T-shirts to stuffed animals. Although perpetually crowded and absolutely mobbed at closing time, the Emporium is, hands down, one of the best places in which to find souvenirs, especially for hard-to-buy-for Aunt Tilly. Hang on to the kids in here; they're likely to wander away as they discover new delights.

Trinkets and treasures that are theme-related to their home base are also very popular in the Magic Kingdom. The **Main Street Athletic Club,** where the House of Magic used to be is a source for all things sports-related with character logos. The **Collector's Nook** sells autographed baseballs, footballs, magazine covers, and posters of famous athletes. Prices are not cheap, averaging about $200, and some items can be much higher. A visit here unearthed a Joe DiMaggio glove priced at $20,000. Serious collectors of Disney memorabilia will want to stop at **Disneyana,** across the square from City Hall. Limited-edition sculptures, dolls, posters, and sometimes even park signs are available for purchase.

Inside Cinderella Castle is the **King's Gallery,** where you can buy imported European clocks, chess sets, and tapestries while artisans perform intricate metalwork. Another nifty nook is **Harmony Barber Shop,** on the west side of Main Street, where old-time shaving items like mustache cups are sold. At **Olde World Antiques,** in Liberty Square, you can find expensive antique jewelry, hutches, pewter, and brass.

Here are some of the all-time best Magic Kingdom souvenirs: pirate hats, swords, and plastic hooks-for-hands sold at the **House of Treasure** just outside Pirates of the Caribbean in Adventureland. Creepy-crawly rubber snakes and lizards, just the sort of thing to spook a younger sibling, are available at **Bwana Bob's** kiosk next to the entrance to the Jungle Cruise in Adventureland. Davy Crockett coonskin hats, personalized sheriff badges, and Big Al memorabilia is sold at **Big Al's** across from the Country Bear Jamboree in Frontierland. To get monogrammed mouse ears, stop at the **Chapeau,** on the east side of Main Street, or at the **Mad Hatter,** in Fantasyland. Children's clothing with Disney characters is sold at **Tinkerbell's Treasures** in Fantasyland. The **Briar Patch,** next door to Splash Mountain, handles all things Winnie-the-Pooh, as well as those distinctive canary yellow umbrellas with black mouse ears on top and the signature yellow ponchos adorned with a smiling Mickey on the back—a bargain at $4.51.

Magic Kingdom A to Z

Baby Care
The Magic Kingdom's soothing, quiet **Baby Care Center** is next to the Crystal Palace at the end of Main Street. Furnished with **rocking chairs,** it has a low-lighting level that makes it comfortable for nursing. There are **toddler-size toilets,** and supplies such as **formula, baby food, pacifiers,** and **disposable diapers** for sale. You'll find changing tables here, as well as in all women's rooms and some men's rooms. You can also buy disposable diapers in the Emporium on Main Street. The **Stroller Shop** near the entrance to the Magic Kingdom, on the east side of Main Street, is the place for stroller rentals ($6 fee; $1 deposit required).

Barbershop
Tucked in a corner just off Main Street, where the Emporium ends, the **Harmony Barber Shop** isn't just for show—it's a for-real place to get a **haircut** from Disney cast members dressed in 19th-century costumes.

Cameras and Film
Kodak's disposable Fun Saver cameras are widely available in shops throughout the theme parks and hotels. Or, at the **Camera Center** on

Main Street, you can rent **35mm cameras** or **video camcorders** ($5 and $25, respectively; a $300 deposit is required for camcorders; deposit for 35mm cameras varies from $5–$30). Multiple-day rentals of camcorders are available. Be advised that camcorders are full-size models.

For minor **camera repairs,** the Camera Center on Main Street is the place.

For **two-hour film developing,** look for the Photo Express sign throughout the park; drop your film in the container, and you can pick up your pictures at the Camera Center as you leave the park. Instant gratification.

Dining

Alas, the gustatory offerings are mostly fast food—and mundane fast food at that. Every land has its share of restaurants serving burgers, hot dogs, and nachos, with chef's salad thrown in as the token "health food" for the on-the-go crowd. In addition, the walkways are peppered with carts dispensing popcorn, ice cream, lemonade, and soda.

FULL-SERVICE RESTAURANTS

There are three full-service restaurants in the Magic Kingdom; reservations are essential and can be made at all restaurants.

Liberty Square: Liberty Tree Tavern. Decorated in lovely Williamsburg colors, with Early American antiques and lots of brightly polished brass, it's a pleasant place even when jammed to the gills. The menu is all-American, with the oversize salads and assorted sandwiches a good bet at lunch, and fresh fish, prime rib, and chicken the best choices at dinner. You can also order a full Thanksgiving turkey feast with all the trimmings—even in July. But then you'd miss out on the idiosyncratic garnish that decorates the sandwiches: a slice of watermelon cut to resemble Mickey Mouse's profile, ears and all.

Fantasyland: King Stefan's Banquet Hall. No Magic Kingdom visitor can consider dining in the park without contemplating this venue. The food covers the basic choices of seafood salad or roast beef sandwiches at lunch, with chicken or seafood or prime rib at dinner. But the real attraction is that you get to eat inside Cinderella Castle in an old mead hall, where Cinderella herself is sometimes on hand, and serving wenches whisk around in long medieval gowns and 13th-century-style wimples. How they prevent their veils from dragging in the mayonnaise is one of those secrets revealed only to the adepts. A character breakfast here—complete with Mickey Mouse waffles—is a mighty special treat for the entire family.

Main Street: Tony's Town Square Café. It's named after the Italian restaurant in *Lady and the Tramp* where Disney's most famous canine couple share their first kiss over a plate of spaghetti. In fact, the video plays on a TV in the restaurant's waiting area. Lunch and "Da Dinner" menus offer pasta, of course, along with seafood, steak, and chicken.

CAFETERIA

Crystal Palace. This buffeteria makes for as pleasant a dining experience as the full-service places do. The offerings in this glass-roofed conservatory are varied, generous, and surprisingly good. The black bean soup is especially noteworthy, as are the burritos and the herb-roasted chicken, and there's a sizable choice of pasta dishes and hearty salads. The place is huge, but its barn-size dimensions are softened by numerous nooks and crannies, comfortable banquettes, cozy cast-iron tables, and lots of sunlight. It's also one of the few places in the Magic Kingdom that serve breakfast.

For Travelers with Disabilities
ATTRACTIONS

Main Street: To board the **Walt Disney World Railroad** at the Main Street Station, you must transfer from your wheelchair, which can be folded to ride with you or left in the station. Alternatively, board at Frontierland or Mickey's Starland. The **Main Street Cinema** is barrier free for guests using wheelchairs—a definite miss for visually impaired guests, since the cartoons are silents, played without dialogue, and set to theater organ music. The **Main Street Vehicles** can be boarded by guests with limited mobility who can fold their wheelchair and climb into a car. There are curb cuts or ramps on each corner.

Adventureland: The **Swiss Family Robinson Treehouse,** with its 100 steps and lack of narration, gets low ratings among those with mobility and visual impairments. At the **Jungle Cruise,** boarding requires that a guest step down into the boat; those who can lip-read will find the skippers' punny narration, delivered with a handheld mike, difficult to follow, though sitting up front may make it easier to see. Boarding **Pirates of the Caribbean** requires transferring from a nonfolding to a folding wheelchair, available at the entrance; the flume drop may make the attraction inappropriate for those with limited upper-body strength or who wear neck or back braces, and because of gunshot and fire effects, service animals should stay behind. The theater-style **Enchanted Tiki Birds** is barrier free for guests using wheelchairs.

Frontierland: To ride **Big Thunder Mountain Railroad** and **Splash Mountain,** you must be able to step into the ride vehicle and walk short distances, in case of an emergency evacuation; those with limited upper-body strength should assess the situation on site, and those wearing back, neck, or leg braces should not ride. Ditto for service animals. **Tom Sawyer Island,** with its stairs, bridges, inclines, and narrow caves, is not negotiable by those using a wheelchair. The **Diamond Horseshoe Jamboree** and the **Country Bear Jamboree** are completely wheelchair accessible; if you lip-read, ask to sit up front, especially at the Diamond Horseshoe, (its script is not in the guide for guests with hearing impairments). The **Frontierland Shootin' Gallery** has two guns at wheelchair level. Frontierland is the only area of the park, aside from Main Street, that has sidewalk curbs; there are ramps by the Mile Long Bar and east of Frontierland Trading Post.

Liberty Square: The **Hall of Presidents** is completely barrier free for guests using wheelchairs. The **Liberty Square Riverboat** is completely wheelchair accessible; to ride the **Mike Fink Keel Boats,** guests must negotiate two steep steps. At the **Haunted Mansion,** guests using wheelchairs must transfer to the "doom buggies" and take one step; however, if you can walk as much as 200 feet, you will enjoy the great preshow as well as the sensations and eerie sounds of the rest of the ride. **Mickey's Starland** is completely accessible.

Fantasyland: Boarding the **Skyway** is impossible for guests who use a wheelchair unless they can transfer to the ride cabins. Go for the round-trip, because stairs are a chief feature of the Tomorrowland Station. And if you're visually impaired, don't waste your time; there's no narration, and the panoramic view is the ride's chief raison d'être. The stage show **Legend of the Lion King** has wheelchair seating; for guests with visual impairments, the chief attraction is the music by Elton John. **It's a Small World** can be boarded without leaving your wheelchair, but only if it's a standard-size one; guests using a scooter or an oversize chair must transfer to one of the attraction's standard chairs, available at the ride entrance. To board **Peter Pan's Flight, Dumbo the Flying Elephant, Cinderella's Golden Carrousel, the Mad Tea Party, Mr.**

Toad's Wild Ride, and **Snow White's Adventures,** guests using wheelchairs must transfer to the ride vehicles. Mr. Toad's, Dumbo, and Peter Pan's are inappropriate for service animals.

Tomorrowland: Alien Encounter, The Timekeeper, and **Carousel of Progress** are barrier-free for those using wheelchairs. To board **Delta Dreamflight, AstroOrbiter,** and the **Tomorrowland Transit Authority,** you must be able to walk several steps and transfer to the ride vehicle. The TTA has more appeal to guests with visual impairments, Dreamflight greater charm for those with hearing impairments. To drive **Grand Prix Raceway** cars, you must have adequate vision and be able to steer, press the gas pedal, and transfer into the low car seat. The cautions for Big Thunder Mountain Railroad and Splash Mountain (☞ Frontierland, *above*) also apply to **Space Mountain.** In the **Tomorrowland Arcade,** the machines may be too high for guests using wheelchairs and not of much interest for some guests with visual impairments.

SHOPS AND RESTAURANTS

All restaurants and shops throughout the park have level entrances or are accessible by ramps.

Entertainment

DAYTIME

Particularly along Main Street, you'll come upon all sorts of shows and happenings: a **barbershop quartet, ragtime pianist, brass bands, banjo pickers.** Every day just after 5, homing pigeons wing their way to Cinderella Castle from Town Square as part of a **flag ceremony.** There are usually **song-and-dance revues** in the Cinderella Castle forecourt and in Fantasyland and Tomorrowland as well.

Still, **Disney characters** are the main event, especially if you're traveling with children, but even if you're not. They sign autographs and pose for snapshots throughout the park—line up at City Hall for your turn to pose for a picture, or snag Mickey's autograph in the star's own dressing room in the Hollywood Theater in Mickey's Starland. You can get another eyeful at the 30-minute-long **daily parade** that proceeds down Main Street through Frontierland beginning at 3; it shows off floats, balloons, cartoon characters, dancers, and singers who are usually lip-synching to music played over the public-address system. It's as good as the Macy's Thanksgiving Day Parade—and the streets are cleaner. There's usually some thematic rubric attached; recently, it's been billed as Mickey Mania, with oversize mouse-ear icons covering floats, costumes, toys, clocks, and balloons. Note that lines at popular attractions often disappear during the parade.

AFTER DARK

The former Main Street Electrical Parade was shipped overseas to France and replaced by **SpectroMagic,** a 30-minute extravaganza of battery-lighted floats, sequined costumes, sparkling decorations, and twinkling trees. This parade runs only during peak holiday periods and during the summer. There are staffers dressed as dragonflies, carrying battery packs that light up their emerald-and-sapphire wings. Shimmering, oversize Christmas-tree ornaments roll down the street. Mickey Mouse and Minnie—in silver sequins—ride an ornate peacock, and Cinderella s coach is outlined in hundreds of fairy lights.

For a blast, visit **Fantasy in the Sky,** the Magic Kingdom fireworks display. Heralded by a dimming of all the lights along Main Street, the camouflaged loudspeakers play "When You Wish upon a Star." A single spotlight illuminates the top turret of the Cinderella Castle and—poof!—Tinkerbell emerges in a shower of pixie dust. Thanks to an invisible guy wire, she appears to fly over the treetops and the crowds, on her way to a Never-Never-Land touchdown located, appropriately enough, in Tomorrowland. Her disappearance signals the start of the fireworks, which fill the sky with some pixie dust of their own. It's a magical way to end an enchanted idyll.

First Aid

The Magic Kingdom's **First Aid Center,** staffed by registered nurses, is alongside the Crystal Palace.

Getting Around

Once you're in the Magic Kingdom, distances are generally short, and the best way to get around is on foot. The Walt Disney World Railroad, the Main Street vehicles, the Skyway between Fantasyland and Tomorrowland, and the Tomorrowland Transit Authority do help you cover some territory and can give your feet a welcome rest, but they're primarily forms of entertainment, not transportation.

Take note of the following tips that might make your travels in Magic Kingdom a bit more orderly. From Adventureland, you can go on to Frontierland or to Liberty Square. For the latter, go to the left as you exit the Tiki House in Adventureland, into the passageway between the Sunshine Tree Terrace and the Tiki Tropic shop. For Frontierland—and a shortcut to Splash Mountain—look for the rest rooms in the Caribbean Plaza as you exit the Pirates of the Caribbean. They open onto a tiled arcade that divides the two lands. Note, however, that rest room patrons get easily confused upon exiting and end up in the wrong land. In other words, this is a prime place to misplace your children or your partner, so station someone right outside the rest rooms in the arcade to keep watch.

Guided Tours

A good way to get a feel for the layout of the Magic Kingdom and what goes on behind the scenes is to take the "Keys to the Kingdom" tour, a 3½- to 4-hour guided orientation tour ($25 adults and children 10 and up; no younger children allowed). Tours leave from City Hall daily between 9:15 and 9:30 AM and are on a first-come, first-served basis. Included are visits to some of the "backstage" zones: the parade staging area and parts of the underground "Tunnel," including the wardrobe area.

Lockers

You'll find them in an arcade underneath the Main Street Railroad Station (50¢). If what you need to store won't fit in the larger lockers, inquire at City Hall.

Lost and Found

City Hall is the place to report losses and finds (☎ 407/824–4521). If nobody claims what you turn in, you may get to keep it.

Lost Children and Adults

If you're worried about your children getting lost, you can get them **name tags** at the Magic Kingdom—at City Hall or at the Baby Center next to the Crystal Palace. If your fears are realized, immediately ask any cast member and try not to panic; obviously lost children are usually taken to City Hall or the Baby Care Center, where lost children's logbooks are kept, and everyone is well trained to effect speedy reunions.

City Hall also has a computerized **Message Center,** where you can leave notes for your traveling companions, both those in the Magic Kingdom and in other parks.

Money

For cash or currency exchange, go to the Guest Relations window in the turnstile area, to City Hall, or to the SunTrust branch in Town Square (open daily 9–4), with an ATM nearby.

Package Pickup

Ask the shop clerk to send any large purchase you make to Guest Relations in the Entrance Plaza so you won't have to carry it around all day. Allow three hours.

Reservations

One of the most frequently asked questions at City Hall is whether this is the place to make reservations for the Diamond Horseshoe Jamboree. The answer is no. That's done across Town Square at Disneyana Collectibles. In order to ensure reservations at the handful of other full-service restaurants, take advantage of the **Disney reservation hot line,** ☎ 407/WDW–DINE.

Visitor Information

City Hall (☎ 407/824–4521) is the principal information center. Here you can pick up the *Magic Kingdom Guide Book* and a schedule of daily events (if you haven't requested one by mail in advance), search for misplaced belongings or companions, and ask questions of the omniscient staffers.

At the end of Main Street, on the left as you face Cinderella Castle, just before the Hub, is the **Tip Board,** a large chalkboard with constantly updated information about attractions' wait times—fairly reliable except for those moments when everyone follows the "See It Now!" advice and the line immediately triples. A cast member is usually at hand.

Other cast members throughout the park can be helpful, too. In fact, providing information for visitors is part of the job description of the young men and women who sweep the pavement and faithfully keep litter in its place.

Wheelchair Rentals

Go to the gift shop to the left of the ticket booths at the Transportation and Ticket Center or the Stroller and Wheelchair shop inside the main entrance to your right ($6 plus $1 deposit); the latter also has motor-powered chairs ($30 plus $20 deposit). Electric scooters are available by reservation (☎ 407/824–4321) the cost is $30 plus a $20 deposit. If your rental needs replacing, ask a host or hostess.

EPCOT CENTER

Walt Disney World was created because of Walt Disney's dream of EPCOT, an "Experimental Prototype Community of Tomorrow." Disney envisioned a future in which nations coexisted in peace and harmony, reaping the miraculous harvest of technological achievement. He suggested the idea as early as October, 1966, saying, "EPCOT will be an experimental prototype community of tomorrow that will take its cue from the new ideas and new technologies that are now emerging from the creative centers of American industry." He wrote of the never completed, always improving Epcot, "Epcot . . . will never cease to be a living blueprint of the future . . . a showcase to the world for the ingenuity and imagination of American free enterprise."

But with Disneyland hemmed in by development, Disney had to search for new lands in which to found his new world. He found it in central Florida. Many of the technologies incorporated into the Walt Disney World infrastructure were cutting-edge at the time. But the permanent

Epcot Center

WORLD SHOWCASE

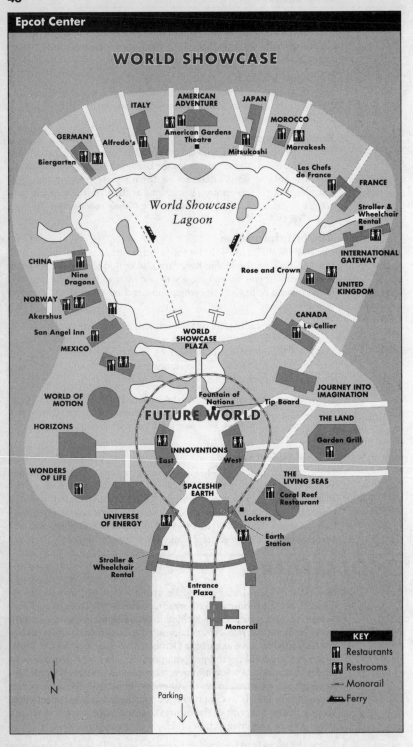

ITALY
AMERICAN ADVENTURE
JAPAN
MOROCCO
GERMANY
Alfredo's
American Gardens Theatre
Mitsukoshi
Marrakesh
Biergarten
Les Chefs de France
FRANCE

World Showcase Lagoon

Stroller & Wheelchair Rental

CHINA
Nine Dragons
Rose and Crown
INTERNATIONAL GATEWAY
NORWAY
UNITED KINGDOM
Akershus
San Angel Inn
CANADA
Le Cellier
MEXICO

WORLD SHOWCASE PLAZA

WORLD OF MOTION
Fountain of Nations
Tip Board
JOURNEY INTO IMAGINATION

FUTURE WORLD
THE LAND
Garden Grill

HORIZONS
INNOVENTIONS
East   West

WONDERS OF LIFE
THE LIVING SEAS

SPACESHIP EARTH
Coral Reef Restaurant

UNIVERSE OF ENERGY
Lockers

Earth Station

Stroller & Wheelchair Rental

Entrance Plaza

Monorail

N

Parking

| KEY |
| Restaurants |
| Restrooms |
| Monorail |
| Ferry |

community that he envisioned has not yet come to be. Instead, we have Epcot Center—which opened in 1982, 16 years after Disney's death— a showcase, ostensibly, for the concepts that would be incorporated into the EPCOTs of the future. Then, as now, it was composed of two parts: **Future World,** where the majority of its 10 pavilions are sponsored by major U.S. corporations and demonstrate their technological advances; and **World Showcase,** where 11 exhibition areas each represent a different country.

Epcot Center today is both more and less than Walt Disney's original dream. Less because some of the Future World pavilions are stuck in a 1965 World's Fair mentality, their driving vision, like the companies that sponsored them, eerily out of touch with today's values. Less because World Showcase presents idealized views of its countries, as an Epcot guide put it: "as Americans perceive them." Less because the missionary zeal that infuses the park backfires occasionally; young children get bored and adults start to wonder if they have to take a short test at the exit.

But these are minor quibbles in the face of the major achievement: Epcot is that rare paradox—an educational theme park—and a very successful one, too. The amount of imagination concentrated in its 230 acres is astounding and can't help rubbing off on the visitors. Through ingenious architecture, intriguing exhibits, amusing and awe-inspiring movies, and lively rides, Epcot Center inspires curiosity, rewards discovery, and encourages the creative spark in each of us.

Although rides have been added over the years to amuse young 'uns, the thrills are mostly in the mind. Consequently, because it helps to have a well-developed intelligence that one can exercise, Epcot is best for older children and adults.

The two parts of Epcot are separated by the 40-acre World Showcase Lagoon. The northern half, comprising Future World, is where the monorail drops you off and which is considered the official entrance. The southern half, at whose International Gateway the trams from the Dolphin and Swan hotels and Disney's Yacht Club Beach Club and Boardwalk resorts drop you off, comprises World Showcase.

Future World

Future World is made up of two concentric circles of pavilions. The inner core is composed of the **Spaceship Earth** geosphere and, just beyond it, the new **Innoventions** exhibit and Innoventions Plaza. The large Fountain of Nations serves as a dividing point between the inner core and the pavilions beyond.

Seven pavilions compose the outer ring of the circle. On the east side they are, in order, **Universe of Energy, Wonders of Life, Horizons,** and **World of Motion.** With the exception of the Wonders of Life, the pavilions present a single, self-contained ride and an occasional post-ride showcase; a visit rarely takes more than 30 minutes, but it depends on how long you spend in the post-ride area. On the west side there's the **Living Seas, The Land,** and **Journey into Imagination.** Like the Wonders of Life, these blockbuster exhibits contain both rides and interactive displays; count on spending at least 1½ hours per pavilion—and wanting to stay longer.

Horizons

This pavilion is a relentlessly optimistic look at the once and future future. After being enjoined to "live your dreams," you ride a tram past visions of the future, where former great minds imagine what the world might have been like in a hundred years or so. There's the 19th-century French artist Albert Robida's vision of Paris in the 1950s, with dirigible taxis, and Jules Verne's picture of spaceships as bullets with microscopic portholes. Visitors slathered with sunscreen will get a kick out of the 1930s view of the 1990s home, which includes personal tanning centers where you could choose between Hawaiian, Floridian, or Bahamian shades of brown. The tram then moves past a series of tableaux of life in a future space colony. This pavilion was built more than a decade ago, and the magnetic levitation trains it envisioned are now being tried out in Japan. Who knows whether the holographic telephones will soon be marketed? Visitors who have already gone through Living Seas and The Land will find Mesa Verde's future farming sequence and the Sea Castle section especially interesting; at Horizons you get the idea of what innovations are being imagined, and then you see them being tested in other pavilions. The Omega Centuri tableau, portraying a free-floating space colony, prefigures virtual reality, with its games of zero-gravity basketball and simulated outdoor sports. *Duration: 15 min. Crowds: Often large because of its location near Innoventions, but the only time the wait exceeds 15 min is when the megaride at the nearby Universe of Energy lets out, and usually swift-moving trams keep wait times down. Strategy: Keep an eye on the line, and if it's long, just go back later. Audience: All ages. Note that this pavilion may be closed for renovation during the time you visit. Rating:* ★★

Innoventions

Disney's latest addition to Future World is **Innoventions,** a two-building, 100,000-square-foot attraction situated at the center of the complex. Repeat visitors will remember this attraction as Communicore East and West. Live stage demonstrations, interactive hands-on displays, and exhibits highlight new technology that affects daily living. Each major exhibition area is presented by a leading manufacturer. **Innoventions East** will appeal more strongly to adults, with manufacturers such as General Electric, Hammacher Schlemmer, and Honeywell displaying products for the home of the not-too-distant future. There's also a hands-on display of Apple computer software that will keep your kids entertained—provided they can get to a PC. **Innoventions West** is hugely popular with pre-teens, and no wonder. It features an enormous display of Sega toys and games. One of the most popular is an eight-car Formula-One Grand Prix race in which you get to drive a full-size car through a turn-filled course that's projected onto a huge screen in front of each vehicle. You'll be hard-pressed to pull the kids out of here. *Duration: Up to you. Crowds: Largest around the popular computer displays. Strategy: Go first thing in the morning or during the evening IllumiNations laser show. Audience: All ages, although young children will tend to be bored. Rating:* ★★★

NEED A
BREAK?

Two large fast-food emporiums dominate the Innoventions Plaza area. In Innoventions East you'll find the **Electric Umbrella.** The fare here is chicken sandwiches, burgers, and salads. If you hit this side of Innoventions later in the day, you might want to check out the snacks offered at **Desserts & Things.** Those who are tempted by things high in calories will be happy to note that this treatery is open only during peak seasons. Innoventions West offers the **Pasta Piazza Ristorante.** As its name suggests, it's heavy on the Italian side, with pizza, pasta, and salads. It's also one of the few places in Epcot that serve breakfast. On certain days, breakfast with Disney characters is on the menu. Morning fare includes omelets and the Sunrise Scramble, a tasty Egg McMuffin clone. Adjacent to the Sunrise Terrace is **Fountainview Expresso,** a café with freshly ground coffees, scrumptious croissants, fruit tarts, crème brulée, and éclairs. You can eat at the circular counter or perch on a chair at one of the high tables. There's also a patio with tables and umbrellas that offers a fine view of the fountain. In the afternoon, this is a great place to sip wine and watch the Fountain of Nations Water Ballet Show without having to stand in the blazing sun and crane your neck.

Journey into Imagination

The big attraction here is the 3-D film *Honey, I Shrunk the Audience,* and the Image Works, a computer-enhanced creative playground. Don't miss the quirky fountains outside: the **Jellyfish Fountains,** which spurt streams of water that flatten at the top into their namesake shape, and the **Serpentine Fountains,** whose random squirts arc from one garden bed to another, over paths and—most of the time—over the people standing on them. Count on spending at least 1½ hours here, more if you become addicted to the Stepping Tones section of the Image Works.

The stars of the **Journey into Imagination** pavilion are a jolly, red-headed, full-bearded, top-hatted professorial type called Dreamfinder and his sidekick, the ever-inquisitive, pop-eyed purple dragon, Figment, who often show up outside the pavilions to welcome visitors. They guide you on the dreamy exploration of how creativity works. It begins with Dreamfinder's creating this Figment of his imagination, by combining a lizard's body, a crocodile's nose, a goat's horns, two big yellow eyes, two small wings, and an ineffable sense of wonder. Your most important stop is the **Dreamport,** which stores data collected by the senses for use by the imagination. Subsequent scenes show the data being spun into dreams that influence all areas of life, from science and technology to literature and the performing arts. Laser beams zing back and forth; lightning crackles; letters leap out of a giant typewriter, and an iridescent painting unfolds across a wall. Smile when you see flashing lights—about ¾ of the way through the ride—you're on candid camera. You'll see the results at the end of the ride. *Duration: 13 min. Crowds: Steady during crowded periods. Strategy: Go early or late. Audience: All ages. Rating:* ★★★

No other theme park has anything that compares with the **Image Works,** an electronic funhouse crammed with interactive games and wizardry that will give your imagination a real workout. There's the **Electronic Philharmonic,** best done with a partner, in which you can take turns conducting an orchestra by waving your hands over a console to increase or decrease the sound of an indicated batch of musical instruments. These, in turn, are spotlighted on a giant screen so that everyone can tune in. At the **Magic Palette,** you can use an electronic paintbrush to make video images and washes of color that resemble psychedelic northern lights. Jumping up and down on the magic carpet at the **Stepping Tones** produces lights and music; each hexagonal splotch of colored light corresponds to a sound—a drumroll, a harp throb, a choral blast—and with a little bit of fancy dancing, you can create an étude. Though it's lots of fun to try out all the activities, it's equally entertaining to watch other people. *Duration: Allow at least ½ hr. Crowds: Thick in late morning and afternoon, but there's plenty of room. Strategy: Go during busy periods; because there's a separate entrance; you don't have to enter through the Journey into Imagination ride. Audience: All ages. Rating:* ★★★

Honey, I Shrunk the Audience is one of the most popular attractions in Epcot, and it's not hard to understand why. This 3-D adventure utilizes the futuristic "shrinking" technologies demonstrated in two hit films that starred Rick Moranis. Moranis reprises his role as Dr. Wayne

Szalinski, who is about to receive the Inventor of the Year Award from the Imagination Institute. While Dr. Szalinski is demonstrating his latest shrinking machine, though, things go really, really wrong. It'll cut into your fun too much if we give anything else away. Just be prepared to laugh and scream your head off, courtesy of the special in-theater effects, moving seats, and 3-D film technology. Don't miss this one. *Duration: 14 min. Crowds: Large theater capacity should mean a relatively short wait, but the ride's popularity can make for big crowds. Strategy: Go first thing in the morning or just before closing. Audience: All but the youngest children. Rating:* ★★★

The Land
Shaped like an intergalactic greenhouse, the enormous skylighted The Land pavilion dedicates 6 acres and a host of different attractions to everyone's favorite topic: food. You can easily spend two hours exploring here. The main event is the **Listen to the Land** boat ride.

Piloted by an informative, overalls-clad guide, you cruise through three biomes in Listen to the Land—rain forest, desert, and prairie ecological communities—and into an experimental greenhouse that demonstrates how food sources may be grown in the future, not only on the planet but also in outer space. Sunshine bass, tilapia, pacu—the piranha's vegetarian cousin—and shrimp are raised in controlled aquacells; and tomatoes, peppers, and squash thrive in the Desert Farm area through a system of drip irrigation that delivers just the right amount of water and nutrients to their roots. Gardeners will be interested in the section on integrated pest management, which relies on "good" bugs like ladybugs to control insect predators. Many of the growing areas are actual experiments-in-progress, in which Disney and the U.S. Department of Agriculture have joined forces to produce, say, a sweeter pineapple or a faster-growing pepper. Interestingly, while the plants and fish in the greenhouse are all quite real—and are regularly harvested for use in The Land's restaurants—those in the biomes are artful fakes, manufactured by Disney elves out of flexible, lightweight plastic. The grass is made out of glass fibers and is implanted into rubber mats—a useful deterrent to barefooted trespassers, perhaps. *Duration: 14 min. Crowds: Large, all day. Strategy: Go during mealtimes. Audience: Teens and adults. Rating:* ★★★

Food Rocks is a rowdy concert where recognizable rock 'n' roll performers take the shape of favorite foods and sing about the joys of nutrition. There are performances by the Peach Boys, Chubby Cheddar, and Neil Moussaka, among others. *Duration: 20 min. Crowds: A large theater erases them. Strategy: Go when the line at Listen to the Land is too long. Audience: Children. Rating:* ★

Circle of Life is a film featuring three stars of *The Lion King*—Simba the lion, Timon the meerkat, and Pumbaa the waddling warthog—in a powerful message about protecting the world's environment for all living things. Part animation, part *National Geographic*–like film using spectacular 70mm live-action footage, *Circle of Life* tells a fable about a "Hakuna Matata Lakeside Village" that Timon and Pumbaa are developing by clearing the African savanna. Simba cautions about mistreating the land by telling a story of a creature who occasionally forgets that everything is connected in the great Circle of Life. "That creature," he says, "is man." The lilting accompaniment, of course, is Elton John's award-winning song. *Duration: 20 min. Crowds: Large, all day. Strategy: Hit this first at The Land. Audience: Enlightening for children and adults but a nap opportunity for some toddlers. Rating:* ★★

Guided **Greenhouse Tours** of the greenhouses and aquacell areas in The Land cover the same topics as the boat ride but in much more detail—and you have the chance to ask questions. Reservations are essential and can be made on the lower floor, in the corner opposite the boat ride entrance, behind **Broccoli and Co.,** a delightful shop stocking hydroponic plants, gardening books, vegetable refrigerator magnets, place mats, and cheerful aprons. *Duration: 45 min; available daily every ½ hr 9:30–4:30. Strategy: Reserve ahead. A good activity for busy times of day—late morning through afternoon. Audience: Adults and budding horticulturists. Rating:* ★★

NEED A
BREAK?

Talk about a self-contained ecosystem: The pavilion grows its own produce and houses the **Farmer's Market** food court, composed of a dozen or so stands—a soup-and-salad stand, bakery (with great jumbo-size cinnamon rolls and corn muffins before 11 AM and brownies and cheesecake afterward), barbecue store, sandwich stand, ice cream stand, potato store, and beverage house, which bolsters the usual soft drinks with milk shakes, buttermilk, vegetable juice, and exotic fruit nectars. The brownies are legendary, and Epcot staffers have been known to make a special trip to pick up some of the bakery's chocolate chip cookies. Just remember that at this pavilion, you must eat all your vegetables. Try to avoid this very popular eatery during the prime meal hours of noon–2; lines are huge and tables are hard to come by.

Living Seas

On Epcot Center's western outer ring is the first satellite pavilion, Living Seas, a favorite among children. Epcot Center is known for its imaginative fountains; the one at Living Seas flings surf in a never-ending wave against a rock garden beneath the stylized marquee. Time and technology have caught up with the 5.7-million-gallon aquarium at the pavilion's core—thrilling when it first opened—so that what was once revolutionary has now been equaled by top aquariums around the country and at Sea World. Still, the three-minute **Caribbean Coral Reef Ride** encircling the acrylic tank may be too short. Sometimes you'll catch sight of a diver, testing out the latest scuba equipment, surrounded by a cloud of parrot fish while scattering a mixture of dry dog food, chicken's laying pellets, amino-acid solution, and B-complex vitamins or carefully placing a head of lettuce within reach of a curious sea turtle.

If you really want to get into the swim—and you have a SCUBA open-water certificate—there's **Epcot Divequest,** a program that allows you to take a dive in the aquarium under the watchful supervision of one of the Living Seas' master divers. Cost is $120 plus tax for a 45-minute session. Call ☎ 407/WDW–TOUR for information and reservations.

After the reef ride, you may want to circumnavigate the tank at your own speed on an upper level, pointing out barracudas, stingrays, parrot fish, sea turtles, and even sharks, before exploring the two levels of **Sea Base Alpha,** a prototype undersea research facility that is a typical Epcot Center playground. Each of its six modules is dedicated to a specific subject: the history of robotics, ocean exploration, ocean ecosystems, dolphins, porpoises, and sea lions. Fully interactive, these contain films, touchy-feely sections, miniaquariums, and video quizzes; there's even a deep-sea diving suit that visitors can try on. *Duration: 45 min and up, including the 3-min ride, depending on how long you leer at angelfish and play Diver Dan at the modules. Crowds: Large, all day long. Strategy: Stop in first thing in the morning or after 5. Audience: All but young children. Rating:* ★★★

Spaceship Earth

Balanced like a giant golf ball waiting for some celestial being to tee off, the multifaceted silver geosphere of Spaceship Earth is to Epcot Center what the Cinderella Castle is to the Magic Kingdom. As much a landmark as an icon, it can be seen on a clear day from an airplane flying down either coast of Florida. Spaceship Earth contains both the **Spaceship Earth ride** and **Earth Station,** the principal source of Epcot Center information.

Everyone likes to gawk at the golf ball, but here are some truly jaw-dropping facts: It weighs 1 million pounds, measures 164 feet in diameter and 180 feet in height—aha! you say, it's not really a sphere! Altogether it encompasses more than 2 million cubic feet of space, and is balanced on six pylons sunk 100 feet into the ground. The anodized aluminum sheath is composed of 954 triangular panels, not all of equal size or shape. And, last, because it is not a geodesic dome, which is only a half sphere, the name "geosphere" had to be invented; no other like it existed when it was built.

Spaceship Earth explores human progress and the continuing search for better forms of communication. Scripted by science fiction writer Ray Bradbury and now narrated by Jeremy Irons (who replaced Walter Cronkite as the disembodied voice of the past, present, and future), the journey begins in the darkest tunnels of time. It then proceeds through history, and ends poised on the edge of the future, including a dramatic look at a "virtual reality" classroom.

Audio-Animatronic figures present in astonishing detail Cro-Magnon man daubing mystic paintings on cave walls, Egyptian scribes scratching genuine hieroglyphics on papyrus, Roman centurions building roads, Islamic scholars mapping the heavens, and 11th- and 12th-century Benedictine monks hand-copying ancient manuscripts in order to preserve the wisdom of the past. One monk, not as tireless as history would have us believe, is conked out at his carrel, his candle smoking in the gusts of his snores. As you move into the Renaissance, Michelangelo paints the Sistine Chapel, Gutenberg invents the printing press, and in rapid succession, the telegraph, radio, television, and computer come into being. The pace speeds up, you're bombarded with images from our communication age, and, just as you begin to think you can't absorb another photon, you're shot through a tunnel of swirling lights into serene space, its velvety darkness sparkling with thousands of stars. In one corner, hanging like the jeweled toy envisioned by Milton in *Paradise Lost,* is our own Earth as photographed by the astronauts on one of the *Apollo* moon shots. It's breathtaking. Toward the conclusion of the ride, visitors arrive in a "Global Neighborhood" that ties all of the peoples of the earth together through an interactive global network. Special effects, animated sets, and audience-enclosing laser beams are used to create the experience. *Duration: 15 min. Crowds: Longest during the morning and shortest just before park closing time. Strategy: Ride first thing in the morning or just before leaving. Audience: All ages. Since a portion of the ride is in total darkness, Disney recommends that persons who experience anxiety in dark, narrow, or enclosed spaces do not ride. Rating:* ★★★

Universe of Energy

Two large topiary dinosaurs stand guard over Universe of Energy. The first of the pavilions on the left, or east, side of Future World, it occupies a large, lopsided pyramid, sheathed in thousands of mirrors, which serve as solar collectors to power the ride and films within. One of the most technologically complex shows at Epcot Center, the exhibit combines one ride, two films, the largest Audio-Animatronic animals ever built, 250 prehistoric trees, and enough cold, damp fog to make you think you've been transported to the inside of a defrosting refrigerator. "We don't want to go through that fog again," one child announced after emerging from a particularly damp vision of the Mesozoic era. About the rest of the ride, however, he had few qualms.

The preshow film about the different forms of energy—nuclear, solar, electric, mechanical, and thermal—has been recently updated to reflect the changes that have taken place since Epcot's 1982 opening. The 14-by-90-foot projection surface is made up of 100 separate screens, which rotate according to complicated computerized directions to form what their creator, Czech filmmaker Emil Radok, described as a "kinetic mosaic."

Then there's a film depicting the eras in which today's fossil fuels originated. No cute Disneyesque dinosaurs populated this earth; these animals are hulking, shadowy figures, lumbering across a steamy landscape of volcanoes, lush plants, and eerie insects. Even more eerie is the moment at the conclusion of the movie when the blocks of seats shift and rotate, then break up, and move forward into the ride.

The ride lurches into the forest primeval—and do we ever mean primeval. Huge trees loom out of the mists of time; ominous blue moonbeams waver in the fog; sulfurous lava burbles up, and the air smells distinctly of Swamp Thing. Through this unfriendly landscape brontosauruses wander trailing mouthfuls of weeds; a tyrannosaurus fights it out with a triceratops; pterodactyls swoop through the air, and a truly nasty sea snake emerges from the swamp to attack the left side of the tram.

The ride concludes with another film about the search for alternative forms of energy. Dramatic shots of North Sea drilling platforms and a space-shuttle blastoff sequence so unusual that even NASA requested a copy that will serve to underline rather than mask the message. An interesting fact here: The 96-passenger, 30,000-pound "traveling theaters" are guided along the concrete floor by a wire only ⅛-inch thick and are powered by the 80,000 solar cells on the roof so that you have been, as they say, "riding on sunshine." *Duration: ½ hr. Crowd: Steady but never horrible; 600 people enter every 15 min. Strategy: To be at the front of the ride and have your experience of the primeval landscape unspoiled by rows of modern heads in front of you; sit in the seats to the far left and front of the theater. Audience: All ages. Rating:* ★★★

Wonders of Life

A towering statue of a DNA double helix outside the gold-crowned dome of the Wonders of Life welcomes you to one of Epcot Center's most popular attractions. Truly one of the wonders of Epcot Center, it takes an amusing but serious and educational look at health, fitness, and modern lifestyles. One improvisational theater revue, two films, and dozens of interactive gadgets that whiz, bleep, and blink make up the **Fitness Fairground.** Walt Disney World's first flight simulator—**Body Wars**—takes visitors on a bumpy platelet-to-platelet ride through the human circulatory system. And the entertaining multimedia presentation, **Cranium Command,** reveals the workings of the mind of a typical 12-year-old boy during the course of an ordinary day.

The flight-simulator technology that is used to train commercial and military pilots adapts perfectly to thrill rides. By synchronizing the action on a movie screen with the movement of the capsule, the simulator tricks your mind into thinking that you're experiencing a wild ride without your ever leaving your seat. Probably the mildest flight simulator in central Florida, Body Wars still offers a thrilling ride, thanks to the fascinating film and the ingenious idea. You and your fellow scientists enter a the simulator chamber that, like something out of *Honey, I Shrunk the Kids,* will be miniaturized and injected into the body's bloodstream. "How's the weather in there?" calls out one of the specialists on the screen. "Clear and warm, temperature about 98.6," comes the reply from within. And in a couple of seconds, you experience it yourself: shooting through the heart, wheezing through the lungs, and picking up a jolt of energy in the brain. *Duration: 5 min. Crowds: Sometimes discouraging, with occasional 45-min waits. Strategy: Go as soon as the park opens, during the hour before closing, or between 6 and 7 PM, the peak dinnertime in World Showcase. Audience: All but young children. Not recommended for pregnant women or guests who have neck or back injuries, heart problems, or motion sickness. Rating:* ★★★

Showtimes at Wonders of Life are staggered to pick up as soon as another lets out, so with a little luck you can segue right into **The Making of Me,** a valuable film on human conception and childbearing. Starring Martin Short as a man who, in search of his origins, journeys back in time to his parents' childhood, youth, marriage, and, eventually, their decision to have him, the film uses both animation and actual footage from a live birth to explain where babies come from. Some scenes are explicit, but all the topics are handled with gentle humor, as when the sperm race for the egg to the tune of "The Ride of the Valkyries" and with great delicacy. Children tend to be dumbstruck; many adults find the film affecting enough to get out the handkerchiefs for a quick swipe at overflowing eyes. *Duration: 14 min. Crowds: Long lines all day because the theater is so small. Strategy: Save this one for after 6 PM. Audience: All ages. Rating:* ★★★

The theater housing **Cranium Command** seats 200 at a shot. Combining a fast-paced movie with an elaborate set, this engaging show looks at how the cranium manages to make the heart, the uptight left brain, the laid-back right brain, the stomach, and an ever-alert adrenal gland all work together as their host, a 12-year-old boy, surmounts the slings and arrows of a typical day. The star is Buzzy, a bumbling Audio-Animatronic Cranium Commando for whom adolescent boys are the last chance before being consigned to run the brain of a chicken. Buzzy's is not an easy job; as the sign on the way to the theater warns, you are entering "The Home of the Flying Endorphins." In the flick, Buzzy's 12-year-old wakes up late, dashes off without breakfast, meets the new girl in school, fights for her honor, gets called up before the principal, and, finally, returns home and has a much-needed snack. Buzzy attempts to coordinate a heart, operated by "Saturday Night Live"'s muscle-team, Hans and Franz; a stomach, run by George Wendt, formerly of "Cheers," in a sewer worker's overalls and rubber boots; and all the other body parts. He succeeds—barely. *Duration: 20 min. Crowds: Long lines, but the big theater can quickly erase 'em. Strategy: Go when everyone else is at Body Wars. Audience: All ages. Rating:* ★★★

The **Fitness Fairground,** an educational playground that teaches both adults and children about good health, takes up much of Wonders of Life. There are games in which you can test your golf and tennis prowess, pedal around the world on a stationary bicycle while watching an ever-changing view on video, and guess your stress level at an interactive computer terminal. "Goofy about Health," an eight-minute multiscreen montage, follows Goofy's conversion from a foul-living dog to a fun-loving guy. **The Anacomical Players Theater,** seating 100 people, is a corny but funny improvisational show with lots of audience participation. **The Frontiers of Medicine,** the only completely serious section of the pavilion, demonstrates leading-edge developments in medicine. *Duration: Up to you. Crowds: Shifting, but they don't af-*

fect your visit. Strategy: Hang loose and take turns. Audience: All ages. Rating: ★★★

NEED A
BREAK?

Pure & Simple, a food stall offering healthful snacks and full meals, proves that nutritious can also be delicious. While cholesterol addicts pig out on basic burgers and fries, those who take the Wonders of Life message to heart can sample the venison chili spiked with fresh herbs, the salads with a choice of zippy dressings including the beta-carotene salad with tomato-basil vinaigrette, and sandwiches that for once are better than what you'd make at home. Follow lunch up with a slice of angel food cake or a fruit or yogurt smoothie. The wholewheat waffles with berry toppings are somewhat overrated but a nice touch. The prices won't give you indigestion either, although overhearing the Ana-comical Players ask—and answer—as you eat, "Why do some people pick their nose?" may give you pause.

World of Motion

This attraction is currently undergoing a major renovation and is not scheduled to be open until at least mid-1997. When it does reopen, expect long lines, mostly of teenagers, because the World of Motion will be a small-scale version of a General Motors test track, where riders will get to sample life in the fast lane, aboard race cars that will accelerate up to 60 mph. There also will be hot and cold chambers modeled on the ones used at GM to test their vehicles' durability under tightly controlled weather conditions. Be prepared to fasten your seat belt.

NEED A
BREAK?

Handsome, hexagon-shape **Odyssey** restaurant looks like a pleasant sit-down eatery, but the food comes a lot faster.

World Showcase

The 40-acre World Showcase Lagoon is 1⅓ miles around, but in that space, you circumnavigate the globe, or at least explore it, in pavilions representing 11 different countries in Europe, Asia, North Africa, and the Americas. In these, native food, entertainment, art and handicrafts, and usually a multimedia presentation showcase the culture and people; architecture and landscaping re-create well-known landmarks. France has a scaled-down model of the Eiffel Tower; America's display is housed in Liberty Hall; Japan glories in a pagoda; Italy has a reproduction of Venice's Piazza San Marco, and Morocco's minaret is practically a landmark of its own. Impressive as they are by day, the structures are truly fantastical at night, when they are outlined in literally miles of tiny lights. Instead of amusement park rides, you have breathtaking films at the Canadian, Chinese, French, and Norwegian pavilions; several art exhibitions; and the chance to chat in the native language of the friendly foreign staff, all of whom are part of a Disney exchange program. Live entertainment is an integral part of the pavilions' presentations.

The focal point of World Showcase is the American Adventure. The pavilions of other countries fan out from both sides, encircling the lagoon. Counterclockwise from World Showcase Plaza as you enter from Future World are **Canada,** the **United Kingdom, France, Morocco, Japan,** the **American Adventure, Italy, Germany, China, Norway,** and **Mexico.**

American Adventure

In a scrupulous reproduction of Philadelphia's Liberty Hall, Disney's Imagineers prove that their kind of fantasy can beat reality hands-down.

The 110,000 bricks, made by hand from soft pink Georgia clay, sheathe the familiar structure, which acts as a beacon for Epcot Center visitors across the lagoon. Talk about symbolism. And when those colored lights start flashing and the lasers zing from Spaceship Earth to Liberty Hall during the sound-and-light-and-fireworks IllumiNations show after dark, it's difficult not to feel patriotic.

The pavilion's superlative attraction is a 100-yard dash through history called the **American Adventure.** To the music of a piece called the "Golden Dream," performed by the Philadelphia Orchestra, it combines evocative sets, the world's largest rear-projection screen (72 feet wide), enormous movable stages, and 35 Audio-Animatronic players, which are some of the most lifelike ever created—Ben Franklin even climbs up stairs. Beginning with the arrival of the Pilgrims at Plymouth Rock and their grueling first winter, Ben Franklin and a wry, pipe-smoking Mark Twain narrate the episodes—both praiseworthy and shameful—that have shaped the American spirit. Disney detail is so painstaking that you never feel rushed, and, in fact, each speech and each scene seems polished like a little jewel. You feel the cold at Valley Forge and the triumph when Charles Lindbergh flies the Atlantic; are moved by Nez Perce Chief Joseph's forced abdication of Native American ancestral lands and by women's rights campaigner Susan B. Anthony's speech; laugh with Will Rogers's aphorisms and learn about the pain of the Depression through an affecting radio broadcast by Franklin Delano Roosevelt; and recognize such popular figures as John Wayne, Lucille Ball, Muhammed Ali, and, yes, Mickey Mouse, epitomizing the American spirit. *Duration: 30 min. Crowds: Large, but the theater is huge, so you can almost always get into the next show. Strategy: Go when everything else is busy and you want to sit down and cool off. Audience: All ages. Rating:* ★★★

While waiting for the American Adventure show to begin, be sure to read the quotes on the walls of the **Hall of Presidents.** They include thought-provoking comments from Wendell Wilkie, Jane Addams, Charles Lindbergh, Ayn Rand, Archibald MacLeish, and Thomas Wolfe, and they offer far from standard patriotic pablum. Directly opposite the pavilion, on the edge of the lagoon, is the **American Gardens Theatre,** the venue for concerts and shows of the Yankee Doodle Dandy variety.

NEED A
BREAK?   **Liberty Inn,** a counter-service restaurant, serves burgers, sandwiches, apple pie, and other all-American fare.

Canada

"Oh, it's just our Canadian outdoors," said a typically modest native guide upon being asked the model for the striking rocky chasm and tumbling waterfall that represent just one of the high points of Canada. The beautiful formal gardens do have an antecedent: Butchart Gardens, in Victoria, British Columbia. And so does the Hôtel du Canada, a French Gothic mansion with spires, turrets, and a mansard roof; anyone who's ever stayed at Quebec's Château Frontenac or Ottawa's Château Laurier will recognize the imposing style favored by architects of Canadian railroad hotels. Like the size of the Rocky Mountains and the Great Canadian North, the scale of the structures seems immense; unlike the real thing, it's managed with a trick called forced perspective, which exaggerates the smallness of the distant parts to make the entire thing look humongous. Another bit of design legerdemain: The World Showcase Rockies are made of chicken wire and painted concrete mounted on a movable platform similar to a parade float. Ah, wilderness!

The top attraction is the CircleVision film *O'Canada!* And that's just what you'll say after the stunning opening shot of the Royal Canadian Mounted Police literally surrounding you as they circle the screen. From there, you whoosh over waterfalls, saunter through Montreal and Toronto, sneak up to bears and bison, mush behind a husky-pulled dog sled, and land pluck—or, should we say, puck—in the middle of a hockey game. This is a standing-only theater, with lean rails. *Duration: 17 min. Crowds: Can be thick in late afternoon. Strategy: Go in the morning or evening. Audience: All ages, but no strollers permitted and toddlers have to be held aloft to see. Rating:* ★★★

Canada also contains shops selling maple syrup, lumberjack shirts, and other trapper paraphernalia to help you survive in the Far North or even the Deep South.

NEED A BREAK? **Le Cellier,** a buffeteria with some style—vaulted, stone ceilings and a cozy, subterranean air—serves such hearty fare as pork pie, poached fresh salmon, and bread custard with maple sauce.

China

A shimmering red-and-gold, three-tiered replica of Beijing's **Temple of Heaven** towers over a serene Chinese garden, an art gallery displaying treasures from the People's Republic, a spacious emporium devoted to Chinese goods, and two restaurants. The garden, planted with rosebushes native to China, a 100-year-old mulberry tree, and water oaks whose twisted branches look Asian but are actually Florida homegrown, is one of the most peaceful spots in the World Showcase, with its piped-in traditional Chinese music.

Think of the Temple of Heaven as an especially fitting movie theater for showings of the *Wonders of China*, a sensational panorama of the land and people dramatically portrayed on a 360° CircleVision screen. The only drawback is that the theater has no chairs; lean rails are provided. *Duration: 19 min. Crowds: Steady from late morning through late afternoon, but the theater's high capacity means you can usually get into the next show. Strategy: Go anytime. Audience: All ages, but no strollers permitted and small children have to be held aloft to see. Rating:* ★★★

NEED A BREAK? **Lotus Blossom Café** has egg rolls and stir-fries that you can wash down with cold TsingTao beer. The food is a nonthreatening introduction for Occidental tastes, but more sophisticated palates will find it bland—and overpriced at that.

France

You don't need the scaled-down model of the Eiffel Tower to tell you that you've arrived in France, specifically Paris. There's the poignant accordion music wafting out of concealed speakers, the trim sycamores pruned in the French style to develop signature knots at the end of each branch, and the delicious aromas surrounding the Boulangerie Pâtisserie bakeshop. This is the Paris of dreams, a Paris without the problems of parking, the numerous dogs, and all those irascible French people. We can understand how Disney remedied the parking situation but still can't figure out where they found such a collection of pleasant, helpful, English-speaking natives who retain their inherited pertness. It's a Paris of La Belle Epoque (the beautiful age) just before World War I, when solid mansard-roofed mansions were crowned with iron filigree, when the least brick was drenched in romanticism. Here's a replica of the conservatory-like Les Halles—the iron-and-glass-barrel-roofed market that no longer exists in the City of Light; there's an arching footbridge, and all around, of course, there are shops. You can inspect artwork, Limoges porcelain, and crystal sold in the exquisite Plume et Palette, buy decorated writing paper Proust would have envied and a pen to match at La Signature, pick up a baking pan to make those famous madeleine cookies at Tout pour le Gourmet, and acquire a bottle of Bouzy Rouge to wash it all down at La Maison du Vin, where wine tastings are frequently held for a small charge.

The intimate **Palais du Cinema,** inspired by the royal theater at Fontainebleau, screens the film *Impressions de France,* an homage to the glories of the country. Shown on five screens spanning 200° in an air-conditioned, sit-down theater, the film takes you to vineyards at harvesttime, Paris on Bastille Day, the Alps, Versailles, Normandy's Mont-St-Michel, and the stunning châteaus of the Loire Valley. The musical accompaniment also hits high notes, with familiar segments from Offenbach, Debussy, and Saint-Säens, all woven together by longtime Disney musician Buddy Baker. *Duration: 18 min. Crowds: Considerable from late morning through late afternoon. Strategy: Come before noon or after dinner. Audience: Adults. Rating:* ★★★

NEED A BREAK?	Stop in for a snack at Boulangerie Pâtisserie or **Au Petit Café,** a Parisian-style sidewalk café that serves sandwiches and omelets (☞ Chapter 7).

Germany

Germany, a make-believe village that distills the best folk architecture from all over that country, is so jovial that you practically expect the Seven Dwarfs to come "heigh-ho"-ing out to meet you. Instead, you'll hear the hourly chimes from the specially designed glockenspiel on the clock tower, musical toots and tweets from multitudinous cuckoo clocks, folk tunes from the spinning dolls and lambs sold at Der Teddybär, and the satisfied grunts of hungry visitors chowing down on hearty German cooking. Other than the four-times-a-day oompah band show in the Biergarten restaurant, Germany doesn't offer any specific entertainment, but it does boast the most shops of any pavilion. Our favorites: **Die Weinachts Ecke,** for nutcrackers and other Old World Christmas ornaments; **Süssigkeiten,** for cookies and not-to-be-believed animal crackers; and **Volkskunst,** with a folk crafts collection that includes cuckoo clocks ranging from hummingbird scale to the size of an eagle.

NEED A BREAK?	The **Sommerfest** pretzel-and-bratwurst cart is one of the rare snacking options in this part of the World.

Italy

In Italy, the star is the architecture: a reproduction of Venice's Piazza San Marco; a recreation of Venice's Doge's Palace that's accurate right down to the gold leaf on the ringlets of the angel perched 100 feet atop the Campanile; the seawall stained with age with barbershop-stripe poles to which two gondolas are tethered; and the Romanesque columns, Byzantine mosaics, Gothic arches, and stone walls that have all been carefully "antiqued" to look historical. Mediterranean plantings such as cypress, kumquat, and olive trees add to the verisimilitude. Inside, shops sell Venetian beads and glasswork, leather purses and belts, and Perugina cookies and chocolate "kisses."

Japan

A brilliant vermilion torii gate, derived from the design of Hiroshima Bay's much-photographed Itsukushima shrine, frames the **World Showcase Lagoon** and epitomizes the striking yet serene mood that pervades Japan. Disney horticulturists deserve a hand here for their achievement in constructing out of all-American plants and boulders a very Japanese landscape, complete with rocks, pebbled streams, pools, and hills. At sunset, or during a rainy dusk, the sharp edges of the evergreens and twisted branches of the corkscrew willows frame a perfect Japanese view of the five-story winged pagoda that is the heart of the pavilion. Based on the 8th-century Horyuji Temple in Nara, the brilliant blue pagoda has five levels, symbolizing the five elements of Buddhist belief—earth, water, fire, wind, sky. As you wander along the twisting paths, listen for the wind chimes and the soothing clack of the water mill, and watch a fiery sunset—Walt Disney World seems 5,000 miles away.

The peace is occasionally disturbed by performances on drums and gongs by the **Genroku Hanamai players.** Other entertainment is provided by demonstrations of traditional Japanese crafts, such as kite making or snipping brown rice toffee into intricate shapes; these take place outdoors on the pavilion's plaza or in the **Bijutsu-Kan Gallery,** where there are also changing art exhibitions. Mitsukoshi department store, an immense three-centuries-old retail firm known as "Japan's Sears," carries everything from T-shirts to kimonos and row upon row of Japanese dolls.

NEED A BREAK?	Westerners with a yen for Japanese tastes will be satisfied here at **Yaki-tori House,** which serves broiled chicken and beef on skewers and batter-fried seafood and vegetables, as well as such Japanese specialties as clear soup and pickled ginger. Despite the fact that this is basically a gussied-up fast-food place, the food tastes authentic and is reasonably priced (☞ Chapter 7).

Mexico

Housed in a spectacular Mayan pyramid surrounded by a tangle of tropical vegetation, Mexico contains the El Río del Tiempo boat ride, an exhibit of pre-Columbian art, a restaurant, and, of course, a shopping plaza, where you can unload many, many pesos.

True to its name, *El Río del Tiempo* takes you on a trip down the river of time. Your journey from the jungles of the Yucatán to modern-day Mexico City is enlivened by video images of feathered Toltec dancers, by Spanish-colonial, Audio-Animatronic, dancing puppets, and by film clips of the cliff divers in Acapulco, the speed boats in Manzanillo, and snorkeling around Isla Mujeres. The puppets are garish and reprise "It's a Small World," without the brain-numbing ditty. But this ride is still one of the major attractions in World Showcase. *Duration: 9 min. Crowds: Long, slow-moving lines from late morning through late afternoon. Strategy: Skip this one on a one-day first-time visit. Audience: All ages. Rating:* ★

Modeled on the mercado (market) in the town of Taxco, **Plaza de los Amigos** in the Mexico pavilion is well named: There are lots of friendly people—the women dressed in off-the-shoulder, ruffled, peasant blouses and bright skirts, the men in white shirts and dashing sashes—all eager to sell you trinkets from a cluster of canopied carts. The perimeter is rimmed with stores with tiled roofs, wrought-iron balconies, and window boxes drooling flowers. What to buy? Brightly colored paper blossoms, sombreros, baskets, pottery, leather goods, and colorful papier-mâché piñatas, which are so popular that Epcot Center imports them by the truckload.

NEED A BREAK?	For burritos and margaritas, go outside to the counter-service **Cantina de San Angel.**

Morocco

You don't need a magic carpet to be instantaneously transported into an exotic culture—just walk through the pointed arches of the Bab Boujouloud gate into Morocco. A gift from the kingdom of Morocco, they are ornamented with beautiful wood carvings and encrusted with intricate mosaics made of nine tons of handmade, hand-cut tiles; 19 native artisans were sent to Epcot Center to install them and to create the dusty, stucco walls that seem to have withstood centuries of sandstorms. Look closely and you'll see that every tile has a small crack or some other imperfection, and no tile depicts a living creature—in deference to the Muslim belief that only Allah creates perfection and life.

Koutoubia Minaret, a replica of the prayer tower in Marrakesh, acts as Morocco's landmark. Traditional, winding alleyways, each corner bursting with carpets, brasses, leatherwork, and other North African craftsmanship, lead to a beautifully tiled fountain and lush gardens. You can take a guided tour of the pavilion by inquiring of any cast member, check out the ever-changing exhibit in the **Gallery of Arts and History**, and entertain yourself examining the wares at such shops as Casablanca Carpets, Jewels of the Sahara, Brass Bazaar, and Berber Oasis.

Norway

Here there are rough-hewn timbers and sharply pitched roofs designed so the snow will slip right off, softened and brightened by bloom-stuffed window boxes, figured shutters, and lots of smiling, blond and blue-eyed young Norwegians, all eager to speak English and show off their country. The pavilion complex contains a 14th-century stone fortress that mimics Oslo's Akershus, cobbled streets, rocky waterfalls, and a wood stave church, modeled after one built in 1250, with wood dragons glaring from the eaves. The church houses an exhibit called "To the Ends of the Earth," which tells the story of two early 20th-century polar expeditions by using vintage artifacts. It all puts you in the mood to handle wood carvings, glass artworks, and beautifully embroidered woolen sweaters, which sell briskly despite Florida's heat, in the pavilion's shops.

Norway also has a dandy boat ride: **Maelstrom.** Visitors pile into 16-passenger, dragon-headed longboats for a voyage through time that, despite its scary name and encounters with evil trolls, is actually more fascinating than frightful. The journey begins in a 10th-century village where a boat, much like yours and the ones used by Eric the Red, is being readied for a Viking voyage. You glide steeply up through a mythical forest populated by trolls, who cause the boat to plunge backward down a mild waterfall, then cruise amid the grandeur of the Geiranger fjord, experience a storm in the North Sea, and, as the presence of oil rigs signals a return to the 20th century, end up in a peaceful coastal village. Disembarking, you proceed into a theater for a quick and delightful film about Norway's scenic wonders, culture, and people. *Duration: 10 min. Crowds: Steady, with slow-moving lines from late morning through early evening. Strategy: Go in the evening. Audience: All ages. Rating:* ★★

NEED A BREAK?	Open-face sandwiches can be washed down with Norwegian Ringnes beer at **Kringla Bakeri og Kafe.** Go early or late for speediest service (☞ Chapter 7).

United Kingdom

Never has it been so easy to cross the English Channel. A pastiche of "There-will-always-be-an-England" architecture, the United Kingdom rambles between the elegant mansions lining a London square to the bustling, half-timbered shops of a village High Street to the thatched-roof cottages from the countryside. Their thatch is made of plastic broom bristles in consideration of local fire regulations. And of course there's a pair of the scarlet phone booths that used to be found all over the United Kingdom, now on their way to being historic relics. The pavilion has no single major attraction. Instead, you can wander through shops selling tea and tea accessories, Welsh handicrafts, Royal Doulton figurines, and woolens and tartans from Pringle of Scotland; Lords and Ladies sells fragrances, bath accessories, and heraldic plaques—only the British would see a connection between these three. Outside, the strolling Old Globe Players coax audience members into participating in their definitely low-brow versions of Shakespeare. There's also a lovely garden and park with benches in the back that's missed by many visitors. It's a scene right out of the street on which Mary Poppins lived; in fact, Ms. Poppins often makes appearances there along with another lovely British lass, Alice from Wonderland.

NEED A BREAK? Revive yourself with a pint of the best—although you'll be hard put to decide among the offerings—at **Rose & Crown Pub,** which also offers traditional afternoon tea on the outside terrace. The adjacent dining room serves more substantial fare, but reservations are required.

Shopping

World Showcase is nothing if not crammed with souvenirs, because each pavilion shelters shops galore. Many of their wares are also sold in shop branches and department stores around the United States. But among the more exotic items are leather belts and purses from Morocco's **Tangier Traders,** beautiful writing paper from **Plume et Palette** in France, heraldic plaques at **Lords and Ladies** in the United Kingdom, Inuit and Native American crafts at **Northwest Mercantile** in Canada, nutcrackers at **Die Weinachts Ecke** in Germany, piñatas at **Plaza de los Amigos** in Mexico, and kimonoed and obi-sashed dolls at **Mitsukoshi** in Japan.

If your shopping time is limited, check out the two shops at the entrance to World Showcase: **Disney Traders,** as its name suggests, features Disney character dolls dressed in the national costumes of the World Showcase participants and the requisite T-shirts and sweatshirts. Kids love the flags from around the world. Also sold here—and only here—is a great keepsake for youngsters: a World Showcase Passport ($7.95). At each pavilion, kids can present their passports to be stamped—it's a great way to keep their interest up in this more adult area of Epcot. At **Port of Entry,** there are products from around the world; a recent shopping expedition there revealed a new theme, "Preserve and Protect," with ecologically sound products. In keeping with the green theme, our favorite item was the small topiary Mickey Mouse.

As for shopping at Future World, frankly, it's difficult to spend money a lot of money here, although there are all sorts of kitchen- and garden-related knickknacks at The Land's **Green Thumb Emporium** and marine merchandise at Living Seas, but after that the pickings are slim indeed. The standard range of Epcot Center logo souvenirs is available at the **Centorium,** and you can pick up an aid to healthy living, including sweats emblazoned with Disney characters working up a sweat, at **Well & Goods Limited** in the Wonders of Life. On the way out of Epcot stop at **Centorium** in Future World's Innoventions, which has the largest selection of goodies with Epcot Center logos. The **Epcot Discovery Center** features educational items for teachers and students alike. Young guests can bring back gifts to their teachers for allowing them to miss a few days of class.

Strategies for Your Visit

Epcot Center is now so vast and varied that a dedicated visitor really needs two days to explore it all. However, if you want to attempt the whole thing in a day, the first rule is: Don't sleep late. Not only are there so many attractions, but you'll want to arrive early to beat the lines and to make reservations at the restaurants. The second rule is: Don't spend time eating. Instead, have a big breakfast and tote a snack to tide you over so that you can have a late lunch. The third rule is: Walk fast, see the shows when the park is empty, and slow down and enjoy the shops and the live entertainment when the crowds thicken.

Blitz Tour

When you arrive at Epcot Center, your first task is to send the speediest member of your party ahead to the **WorldKey Information System** terminals at Guest Relations to make reservations for a 5:30 dinner, because after your marathon day, you'll be ready to sit down. Thus, dining early will give you time to zip through the attractions you've missed while everyone else is dawdling over dinner. Reservations made, you can smugly proceed to **Spaceship Earth** with nothing more on your mind than to have it expanded. Everyone else will also be lining up at Spaceship Earth, but the first-thing-in-the-morning lines move along snappily, and this attraction really is the best introduction to Future World.

Upon leaving Spaceship Earth, everyone else will head for the first pavilion they see: either Universe of Energy or the Living Seas. Skip 'em, we say, and go directly to the **Wonders of Life.** Once here, stay to your left; if the lines are minimal, you can segue from Body Wars to *The Making of Me* to Cranium Command with barely a pause.

Then head to Future World's western pavilions. Visit **Journey into Imagination** first; while most other visitors are breathing Mesozoic fog at Universe of Energy, you can meet Dreamfinder on the ride and then, with a little good luck and timing, walk right into *Honey, I Shrunk the Audience.* Don't linger in the Image Works—you can always come back.

Now enter **The Land**; take the boat ride and see Circle of Life and Food Rocks. By this time there may be a line at Living Seas, but if there isn't, go on in and stay as long as you like. Outside, things should be getting crowded. Head counterclockwise into World Showcase, toward **Canada,** while everyone else is hoofing it toward Mexico. Then see **France** and the **American Adventure.** If there are lines at **Norway** by the time you get there, head for **Innoventions** and the **Image Works.**

After dinner, see any World Showcase attractions you missed, plus the **Universe of Energy, Horizons,** and **World of Motion** (if the latter has reopened by the time you visit). Lines are practically nonexistent then, and, because rides are continuous at the last two pavilions, you can literally run from one to another, detouring at the **Wonders of Life** for a fruit-yogurt smoothie. World Showcase empties after 5, and there's a truly magical quality to the lush plantings at dusk.

If you have a day and a half or two days, plan to do just the opposite of what most visitors do: Explore World Showcase in the late morning, Future World in the early evening.

Epcot Center A to Z

Baby Care

Epcot Center has a **Baby Care Center** as peaceful as the one in the Magic Kingdom; it's near the Odyssey Restaurant in Future World. Also furnished with **rocking chairs,** it has a low lighting level that makes it comfortable for nursing, and cast members have supplies such as **formula, baby food, pacifiers,** and **disposable diapers** for sale. You'll find **changing tables** here, as well as in all women's rooms and some men's rooms. You can also buy disposable diapers near the park entrance at Baby Services. For **stroller rentals** ($6 a day; $1 deposit required), look for the special stands on the east side of the Entrance Plaza and at World Showcase's International Gateway.

Cameras and Film

Kodak's disposable Fun Saver cameras are widely available. Or you can borrow a Kodak **disk camera** or rent **35mm cameras** or **video camcorders** ($5 and $25 respectively; refundable $300 deposit required for video cameras.); sources include the Kodak Camera Center, in the Entrance Plaza; the lagoon's-edge World Traveler, at the end of the promenade between Future World and World Showcase; and Cameras and Film at Journey into Imagination.

For **two-hour film developing,** look for the Photo Express signs throughout the park: at the Kodak Camera Center and Cameras and Film at Journey into Imagination in Future World, and in World Showcase at Northwest Mercantile in Canada, World Traveler at International Gateway, Heritage Manor Gifts in the American Adventure, at the booth on the right as you enter Norway, and Artesanias Mexicanas in Mexico. Drop your film in the container, and you can pick up your pictures at the Kodak Camera Center as you leave.

Dining

In World Showcase every pavilion sponsors at least one and often two or even three eateries. Where there's a choice, it is between a full-service restaurant with commensurately higher prices, a more affordable ethnic fast-food spot, and carts and shops selling snacks ranging from French pastries to Japanese ices—whatever's appropriate to the pavilion. Reservations are essential at the formal restaurants (☞ Reservations, *below,* and Chapter 7).

Future World is not bursting with eateries. You won't starve here, but you do need to plan ahead. In addition to the counter-service spots, your options include **The Land Grille Room** in The Land pavilion, a revolving restaurant that serves solid, American food, and **Coral Reef,** a seafood restaurant in the Living Seas with a windowed wall onto the pavilion's enormous aquarium.

For Travelers with Disabilities

Accessibility standards in this park are high. Many attractions and most restaurants and shops are fully wheelchair accessible. Not only does the *Guidebook for Guests with Hearing Impairments* give scripts and story lines for all Epcot Center attractions with sound tracks, personal translator units can be rented ($4 plus $40 deposit) to amplify sound in some of the theater shows.

ATTRACTIONS

Future World: To ride the **Spaceship Earth ride,** you must be able to walk four steps and transfer to a ride vehicle; in the unusual case that emergency evacuation may be necessary, it is by way of stairs. Service animals are not appropriate. Although much of the enchantment is in the visual details, the narration is interesting as well. The Epcot Discovery Center here is wheelchair accessible. **Innoventions** is completely wheelchair accessible. **Universe of Energy** is accessible to guests using standard wheelchairs and those who can transfer to them; especially because this is one of the attractions which has sound tracks amplified by rental personal translator units, it is slightly more interesting to those with hearing impairments than to those with visual impairments. **Wonders of Life,** Cranium Command, *The Making of Me,* Goofy about Health, and the Anacomical Theater are all totally wheelchair accessible, with special seating sections for guests using wheelchairs. Guests with visual impairments may wish to skip Goofy about Health; Cranium Command and *The Making of Me* are both covered in the guidebook for guests with hearing impairments. To ride the turbulent Body Wars, you must transfer to a ride seat; those who lack upper-body strength should request extra shoulder restraints. It's inappropriate for service animals. **Horizons** is accessible to guests who can walk three paces and step up one step. Service animals should not ride. In **Living Seas,** guests using wheelchairs typically bypass the three-minute ride and move directly into the SeaBase Alpha and aquarium area—the best part of the pavilion. In **The Land,** the Harvest Theater, Food Rocks, and the Greenhouse Tour are completely wheelchair accessible. Rental personal translator units amplify sound in the Harvest Theater film *Symbiosis,* and those who can read lips will enjoy the Greenhouse Tour. As for the Listen to the Land boat ride, guests using an oversize wheelchair or a scooter must transfer to a Disney chair. At **Journey into Imagination,** the ride requires guests to take three steps and step up into a ride vehicle. The Magic Eye theater, home to *Honey, I Shrunk the Audience,* is completely accessible. The hands-on activities of Image Works are wheelchair accessible; there's something for everyone in here.

World Showcase: Most people stroll about Epcot Center, but there are two forms of transportation here: Friendship boats, which require guests using oversize wheelchairs or scooters to transfer to Disney chairs; and the omnibuses that chug along the promenade, which require guests to walk up four steps and have a folding wheelchair. The **American Adventure, France, China,** and **Canada** are all wheelchair accessible; personal translator units amplify the sound tracks here. **Germany, Italy, Japan, Morocco,** and the **United Kingdom** all have live entertainment, most with strong aural as well as visual elements; the plaza areas where the shows are presented are wheelchair accessible. In **Norway,** you must be able to step down into and up out of a boat to ride the Maelstrom, and an emergency evacuation would require the use of stairs; service animals should not ride. In **Mexico,** the El Río del Tiempo boat ride is accessible to guests using wheelchairs, but those using a scooter or oversize chair must transfer to a Disney model.

ENTERTAINMENT
Certain areas along the lagoon's edge at Showcase Plaza, the United Kingdom, and Italy are reserved for guests using wheelchairs during IllumiNations.

INFORMATION
(☞ Access for Travelers with Disabilities *in* Walt Disney World Essentials, *below.*)

SHOPS AND RESTAURANTS
With a few exceptions, all are wheelchair accessible. In both the Land Grille Room and Living Seas' Coral Reef Restaurant, only one level is accessible to guests using wheelchairs, and France's Bistro de Paris is accessible only via staircase.

Entertainment

ABOVE THE LAGOON
First there are the all-out spectaculars we've come to expect at the Disney parks. Figuring "Why waste a perfectly good lagoon?" Walt Disney World uses its watery stage for the spectacular **IllumiNations** show every night before closing. Be sure to stick around. Lasers, lights, fire-

works, fountains, and music from every host nation fill the air over the lagoon; the show is so over the top that it's got to be seen to be believed. Although there's generally good viewing from all around the lagoon, the best spots are on the bridge between France and the United Kingdom, the promenade in front of Canada and Norway, and the bridge between China and Germany, which will give you a clear shot, unobstructed by trees. A sweet touch after the show: Concealed loudspeakers play the theme from "It's a Small World" manipulated into salsa, polka, waltz, and even—believe it or not—Asian rhythms. Talk about a total experience.

AT THE PAVILIONS

Some of the most enjoyable entertainment takes place outside the national pavilions in their courtyards and along the promenade by the lagoon. Live shows with actors, dancers, singers, mime routines, and demonstrations of folk arts and crafts are presented at varying times of day; get times from the WorldKey terminals in Earth Station or look for signs posted outside the pavilions. Italy's farcical **Commedia di Bologna,** France's **Theatre du Fromage,** and the United Kingdom's **Old Globe Players** each enlists audience members as heroes and villains, princes and princesses, to the hilarity of all.

First Aid

The park's **First Aid Center,** staffed by registered nurses, is near the Odyssey Restaurant in Future World.

Getting Around

It's a big place; a local joke suggests that Epcot is an acronym for "Every Person Comes Out Tired." But still, the most efficient way to get around is to walk. Just to vary things, you can cruise across the lagoon in one of the air-conditioned, 65-foot water taxis that depart every 12 minutes from World Showcase Plaza at the border of Future World. There are two docks: Boats from the one on the left zip to the Germany pavilion, from the right to Morocco. In World Showcase, you can board the slow-moving, double-decker buses that depart every 5–8 minutes and stop in front of every other pavilion.

If you think the huge distances involved may be a problem, start out by renting a stroller or wheelchair.

Guided Tours

Reserve up to three weeks in advance for the two, four-hour, behind-the-scenes tours, led by knowledgeable Disney cast members and open to guests 16 and older (☎ 407/560–6150); the cost is $25 plus park admission. Both offer up-close views of the phenomenal detail involved in the planning and maintenance of Epcot Center. **Hidden Treasures of World Showcase,** featured Sunday, Wednesday, and Friday at varying times, tells you everything from the provenance of the boulders in Japan's garden to the number of bricks in the U.S. pavilion. **Gardens of the World,** run Monday, Tuesday, and Thursday at varying times, explains World Showcase's realistic replicas of exotic plantings.

Lockers

You'll find them to the west of Spaceship Earth; outside the Entrance Plaza; and in the Bus Information Center by the bus parking lot (50¢). If what you need to store won't fit into the larger lockers, go to Guest Relations in the Entrance Plaza or at Earth Station.

Lost and Found

Go to the west edge of the Entrance Plaza. If nobody claims what you turn in, you may get to keep it.

Lost Children and Adults

If you're worried about your children getting lost, get them name tags at either Earth Station or the Baby Care Center. If the worst happens, immediately report it to any cast member and try not to panic; the staff here is experienced at reuniting families, and there are lost-children logbooks at Earth Station and the Baby Care Center.

Earth Station also has a computerized Message Center, where you can leave notes for your traveling companions, both those in the Magic Kingdom and other parks.

Money

For cash and currency exchange, go to the Sun Bank branch at Epcot Center (open daily 9–4), the Guest Relations window, or Earth Station. There is an American Express ExpressCash machine on the left side of the Entrance Plaza.

Package Pickup

Ask the shop clerk to forward any large purchase you make to Guest Relations in the Entrance Plaza so that you won't have to carry it around all day. Allow three hours.

Reservations

Lunch or dinner reservations for Epcot Center full-service restaurants may be made in advance by calling 407/WDW–DINE or in person at the WorldKey terminals at the park—only on the day of the meal—or at the restaurants themselves when they open for lunch at 11. For complete information, *see* Reservations at Epcot Center *in* Chapter 7, or call Guest Relations (☎ 407/824–4321).

Visitor Information

Earth Station, underneath Spaceship Earth, is the principal information center, the place to pick up schedules of live entertainment, park brochures, and the like. The computerized WorldKey Information System kiosks, in Earth Station and in World Showcase near Germany, are another resource. Using the touch-sensitive screens, you can obtain detailed information about every pavilion, leave messages for companions, and get answers to almost all of your questions. If the computer can't give you the answer, you can request the assistance of a host or hostess.

Wheelchair Rentals

You'll find them inside the Entrance Plaza on the left, to the right of the ticket booths at the Gift Stop, and at World Showcase's International Gateway. Standard models are available ($6 plus $1 deposit); you can also reserve an electric scooter (☎ 407/824–4321; $30 plus $20 deposit).

DISNEY-MGM STUDIOS THEME PARK

When Walt Disney company chairman Michael Eisner opened Disney-MGM Studios in May 1989, he welcomed visitors to "the Hollywood that never was and always will be." Inspired by southern California's highly successful Universal Studios tour, an even more successful version of which is just down I–4, Disney-MGM combined Disney detail with MGM's motion-picture expertise. The result is an amalgamation that blends theme park with fully functioning movie and television production center, breathtaking rides with instructional tours, nostalgia with high-tech wonders.

The rosy-hued view of the moviemaking business takes place in a dreamy stage set from the 1930s and 1940s, amid sleek Art Moderne buildings in pastel colors, funky diners, kitschy decorations, and sculptured gardens populated by roving actors playing, well, roving actors. Thanks to a rich library of film scores, Disney-MGM is permeated with music, all familiar, all happy, all evoking the magic of the movies and all constantly burbling through the camouflaged loudspeakers at a volume just right for humming along. And watching over all, like the penthouse suite of a benevolent genie, is the Earfful Tower, a 13-story water tower adorned with giant mouse ears.

Although some of the attractions will interest young children, Disney-MGM is really best for teenagers old enough to watch old movies on television and catch the cinematic references. Not quite as fantasy oriented as the Magic Kingdom or as earnestly educational as Epcot Center, Disney-MGM could almost be said to have attitude. Not a lot, mind you, but enough to add a little sizzle to the steak.

Disney-MGM Studios is divided into sightseeing clusters. **Hollywood Boulevard** is the main artery to the heart of the park: the glistening red-and-gold, multiturreted replica of Grauman's Chinese Theater, home of the **Great Movie Ride.** Encircling it in a roughly counterclockwise fashion are **Sunset Boulevard,** which features the **Twilight Zone of Terror;** the **Animation Courtyard,** which houses the entrance to the **Backstage Studio Tour,** the **Inside the Magic** special effects and production tour, the **Magic of Disney Animation,** and **The Voyage of the Little Mermaid;** the **New York Street** area, with Henson's Muppet*Vision 3D, *Honey, I Shrunk the Kids* Movie Set Adventure playground, and the **Backlot Theater;** **Echo Lake,** containing the **Indiana Jones Epic Stunt Spectacular, Star Tours, SuperStar Television,** and the **Monster Sound Show.**

Surprisingly, the entire park is rather small—only 110 acres, ¼ the size of Universal Studios—with barely a dozen major attractions, as opposed to 45 in the Magic Kingdom and 23 in Epcot Center. When the lines are minimal, the park can be easily covered in a day with time for repeat rides. And even when the lines seem to stretch clear to Epcot Center, a little careful planning should allow you to see everything on one ticket.

Hollywood Boulevard

With its palm trees, pastel buildings, and flashy neon, Hollywood Boulevard paints a rosy picture of Tinseltown in the 1930s. The sense of having walked right onto a movie set is enhanced by the art-deco storefronts, strolling brass bands, and roving actors dressed in costume and playing everything from would-be starlets to nefarious agents. They are frequently joined by characters from Disney movies new and old, who pose for pictures and sign autographs. *Beauty and the Beast*'s Belle is a favorite, as are Jafar, Princess Jasmine, and the Genie from *Aladdin.*

Hollywood Boulevard, like Main Street, has souvenir shops and memorabilia collections galore. **Oscar's Classic Car Souvenirs & Super Service Station** is crammed with fuel pump bubble-gum machines, photos of antique cars, and other automotive knickknacks. At **Sid Cahuenga's One-of-a-Kind** antiques and curios, you might find and acquire Brenda Vaccaro's shawl, Liberace's table napkins, or autographed stars' photos. Down the street at **Cover Story,** don the appropriate costume and have your picture put on the cover of a major magazine. Next door, check out the movie memorabilia crammed into the **Celebrity 5 & 10.** At the end of the street, at the corner of Sunset Boulevard, you'll find loads of kid-size character clothing at **L.A. Cinema Storage.** The

40-something crowd will also appreciate this shop's collection of old Mickey Mouse Club black-and-white production stills.

NEED A
BREAK?
For a sweet burst of energy, snag a cinnamon swirl at **Starring Rolls Bakery,** near the Brown Derby. Or try the croissants, the turnovers, or the almost-authentic bagels.

Numbers in the margin correspond to points of interest on the Disney-MGM Studios Theme Park map.

① Great Movie Ride. At the head of Hollywood Boulevard is the fire-engine-red, pagodaed replica of Grauman's Chinese Theater, which houses this attraction. Disney-MGM pulls out all the stops on this tour of great moments in film.

The lobby, really an ingenious way to spend time standing in line, slots you past such icons as Dorothy's ruby slippers from *The Wizard of Oz*, a carousel horse from *Mary Poppins*, and the piano played by Sam in *Casablanca*. You then shuffle into the preshow area, an enormous screening room with continuously running clips from *Mary Poppins, Raiders of the Lost Ark, Singin' in the Rain, Fantasia, Footlight Parade,* and, of course, *Casablanca*. The line continues snaking through the preshow, which itself is so much fun that you almost resent that you'll miss favorite clips once the great red doors swing open and it's your turn to ride.

Disney cast members dressed in 1920s newsboy costumes usher you onto open trams and you're off on a tour—through Audio-Animatronics, scrim, smoke, and Disney magic—of cinematic climaxes. First comes the world of musical entertainment, with Gene Kelly clutching that immortal lamppost in one hand and a useless umbrella in the other as he sings the title song from *Singin' in the Rain* and Mary Poppins, with her umbrella, and her sooty admirers reprising "Chim-Chim-Cher-ee," among others. The lights dim, and you move into gangsterland, with James Cagney snarling in *Public Enemy*. Then it's on to a western shootout à la John Wayne as Calamity Jane tries to rob the Miners' and Cattlemen's Bank and hijack the tram—and succeeds.

Nothing like a little time warp to bring justice. With pipes streaming fog and alarm klaxons whooping, the tram meets some of the slimier characters in *Alien*—look up for truly scary stuff—and then eases into the cobwebby, snake-ridden and slithering set of the Temple of Doom, where Calamity Jane attempts to bluff an idol threat—and gets vaporized.

Each time you think you've seen the best scene, the tram moves into another set: Tarzan yodels and swings on a vine overhead; then Bogey toasts Bergman in front of the plane to Lisbon. The finale has hundreds of robotic Munchkins cheerily enjoining you to "Follow the Yellow Brick Road," despite the cackling imprecations by the Wicked Witch of the West. Remember to check out Dorothy's tornado-tossed house—those on the right side of the tram can just spot the ruby slippers. The tram follows the Yellow Brick Road, and there it is: Emerald City.

As icing on the cake, there's one more movie presentation with three screens all going at once to display yet more memorable moments, including great kisses ranging from Rhett Butler and Scarlett O'Hara embracing to Roger and Jessica Rabbit engaging in an animated smooch. Then the lights come up, and the announcer calls you for the final scene: The Exit. *Duration: 22 min. Crowds: Steady and large all day long; when the inside lines start spilling out the door, expect at least a 25-min wait. Strategy: Go first thing in the morning or at the end of the day. If the lines still look long, ask before you slink away discouraged—*

Disney-MGM Studios Theme Park

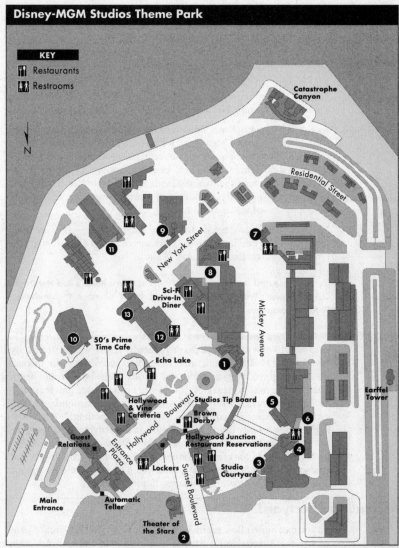

KEY

🍴 Restaurants

🚻 Restrooms

N

Catastrophe Canyon

Residential Street

New York Street

Sci-Fi Drive-In Diner

Mickey Avenue

Earffel Tower

50's Prime Time Cafe

Echo Lake

Hollywood & Vine Cafeteria

Studios Tip Board

Brown Derby

Hollywood Junction Restaurant Reservations

Guest Relations

Entrance Plaza

Hollywood Boulevard

Sunset Boulevard

Lockers

Studio Courtyard

Main Entrance

Automatic Teller

Theater of the Stars

Backstage
Studio Tour, **4**

Great Movie Ride, **1**

*Honey, I Shrunk the
Kids* Movie Set
Adventure, **8**

Indiana Jones Epic
Stunt Spectacular, **10**

Inside the Magic
Special Effects and
Production Tour, **7**

Jim Henson's
Muppet*Vision 3D, **9**

Magic of Disney
Animation, **3**

Monster Sound
Show, **13**

Star Tours, **11**

SuperStar
Television, **12**

Twilight Zone Tower
of Terror, **2**

Voyage of the Little
Mermaid, **5**

Walt Disney Theater, **6**

Disney staffers often "stack" people up outside to clear up the crowds inside and to prepare for closing. Audience: All but young children, for whom it may be too intense. Rating: ★★★

Sunset Boulevard

This newest of Disney-MGM's theme avenues pays tribute to famous Hollywood monuments with facades derived from the Cathay Circle, the Beverly Wilshire Theatre, and other City of Angels landmarks.

As guests turn onto Sunset Boulevard from Hollywood Boulevard, first stop for the hungry hordes is **Hollywood Junction Station,** where reservations can be made for restaurants throughout the park. Starstruck shoppers should find something to feed their fandom at **Legends of Hollywood,** which brims with books, videos, and posters of classic films, while the young at heart should stop by **Once upon a Time,** which showcases displays of vintage character toys.

The wildly popular stage show, *Beauty and the Beast—Live on Stage,* takes place in **The Theater of the Stars,** a re-creation of the famed Hollywood Bowl (☞ Entertainment, *below*).

NEED A BREAK?
Sunset Boulevard features three fast-food eateries: **Rosie's Red Hot Dogs, Catalina Eddie's Frozen Yogurt,** and, for a healthful snack, the **Anaheim Produce Company.**

❷ **Twilight Zone Tower of Terror.** Ominously overlooking Sunset Boulevard is a 13-story structure that's reputedly the now-deserted Hollywood Tower Hotel. You take an eerie stroll, especially at night, through the dimly lighted lobby and decaying library to the boiler room before boarding the hotel's giant elevator. As you head upward past seemingly deserted hallways, ghostly former residents appear around you, until suddenly—faster than you can say "Where's Rod Serling?"—the creaking vehicle abruptly plunges downward in a terrifying, 130-foot free-fall drop! *Duration: 10 min. Crowds: Yes! Strategy: Go early or, even better, wait until the evening dinner hours when the crowds thin out. Audience: Older children and adults. No pregnant women or guests with back, neck, or heart problems. Rating: ★★★*

Animation Courtyard

As you exit Sunset Boulevard, veer right through the high-arched gateway to the Animation Courtyard. You're now at one end of Mickey Avenue, and straight ahead are the Magic of Disney Animation, the Backstage Studio Tour, and the Voyage of the Little Mermaid, often combined with Inside the Magic at the other end of Mickey Avenue for a two-hour, whiz-bang revelation of cinematic secrets.

NEED A BREAK?
The Animation Courtyard also houses **Catwalk Bar** and **Soundstage Restaurant,** a food court in an aptly named barn of a building with an attic's worth of furniture dangling from the ceiling. This stuff would be a great source of conversation—if you could hear anything. Burgers, fajitas, chef's salads, and the like are on the menu.

❸ **The Magic of Disney Animation.** This self-guided tour through the Disney animation process is one of the funniest and most engaging attractions at the park. More than any backstage tour, more than any revelation of stunt secrets, this tour truly takes you inside the magic as you follow the many steps of animation from concept to charisma.

Although you can move at your own pace, the staff tries to keep crowds to a minimum, so groups assemble in a lobby. Take the opportunity to check out the collection of drawings and original cels, the clear celluloid sheets on which the characters were drawn for *Snow White, Fantasia,* and other Disney classics. Here, too, are the Academy Awards that Disney has won for its animated films.

From a designated lobby in the Animation Courtyard, you segue into the **Disney Animation Theater** for a hilarious eight-minute film in which Walter Cronkite and Robin Williams explain animation basics. A Peter Pan sequel called *Back to Neverland,* with Walter Cronkite as Walter Cronkite and Robin Williams as a Little Lost Boy. The irrepressible Robin really wants it to be called *Peter Pan: First Blood,* but the title was voted down. The film was almost impossible to complete because the steadfast, avuncular Cronkite kept cracking up. You might, too, if you suddenly discovered Tinkerbell in your jacket pocket. Robin Williams discovers the potential range of animation: "Hey," he proclaims as he's redrawn into a familiar rodent, "I can be a corporate symbol!", while we learn about cel- making, layout artists, background artists, cleanup artists, sound effects, and more.

From the theater, you follow walkways with windows overlooking the **working animation studios,** where you see salaried Disney artists at their drafting tables doing everything you just learned about. Their desks are strewn with finished drawings of Simba, Scar, Aladdin, Genie, and other famous characters, and you can peer over their shoulders at soon-to-be-famous characters. This is better than magic—this is real.

Meanwhile, Robin and Walter continue their banter on overhead monitors, explaining the processes as you saunter from story room, where animators develop story lines; to the drawing boards, where ideas metamorphose from sketch to colorful characters; to the cleanup room, the special effects area, and the special camera that transfers drawings to cels. To produce one 24-minute film, the 70-plus members of the animation team must create 34,650 drawings and add scenes from at least 300 background paintings. No wonder everyone wears headphones, although one doubts they're listening to "Whistle While You Work."

The penultimate attraction on the tour is a continuously running video, *Animators on Animation.* "You believe the character *is* alive," confesses one of the geeky-looking animators who so identify with their characters that they can take on their personalities. Watching a low-key, pleasant Asian man become the blowsy, evil Ursula from *The Little Mermaid* right before your eyes makes you wonder if pixie dust is in the air.

Upon completion of the tour there's a valedictory quip from Robin Williams, and you head into the **Disney Classics Theater** for a presentation of the best moments from animated films. It's fascinating to see the evolution of the art from the bright colors and straightforward drawings in *Snow White* and *Pinocchio* to the rainbow hues and complex panoramas of *Beauty and the Beast, Aladdin, The Lion King,* and *Pocahontas.* Best of all, you know that here the characters always will live happily ever after. *Duration: Usually around 30 min. Crowds: Steady all day. Strategy: Go in the morning or late afternoon, when you can get in with less waiting and still see the animators at work (they leave by 6 and are not always around on weekends). Audience: All but toddlers. Rating:* ★★★

➍ The Backstage Studio Tour. A combination tram ride and walking tour, it takes you on a tour of the back-lot building blocks of movies: set design, costumes, props, lighting, and the de rigueur Catastrophe

Canyon. Disney-MGM outdoes Universal Studios on this ride because it's got an ace in the hole: a real moviemaking environment. You literally ride through working offices, peering through windows as Foley artists mix sound, lighting crews sort cables, costumers stitch seams, and so on. The motor pool boasts the usual bunch of beat-up automobiles, including a series of old blue Plymouths from *Who Framed Roger Rabbit?* The greens department is a gardener's delight, with its elephant topiaries, trellised roses, and the faux tree trunk used in *Honey, I Shrunk the Kids*; most of the greens are used to camouflage unsightly parts of movie sets, so the next time you see a particularly verdant tree on film, think about what's behind it.

The residential street gives new meaning to the term "open house," as the tram winds past false fronts in styles ranging from Frank Lloyd Wright to generic suburban. New Yorkers will get the usual kick out of seeing the litter-free, graffiti-free depiction of their fair city on New York Street. The tram rumbles past the boneyard, where the helicopter from *Blue Thunder* and the orange-and-red Pacific Electric trolley car used in *Who Framed Roger Rabbit?* are permanently parked; a live egret now uses the trolley car as its perch.

Then it's on to Catastrophe Canyon. The tram's announcer swears that the film that's supposedly shooting in there is taking a break. Not! The next thing you know, the tram is bouncing up and down in a simulated earthquake, an oil tanker explodes in gobs of smoke and flame, and a water tower crashes to the ground, touching off a flash flood, which douses the oil tanker but threatens to drown the tram. Although the earthquake is more like a shimmy, the water and fire provoke genuine screams. As the tram pulls out, you see the backstage workings of the catastrophe: The canyon is actually a mammoth steel slide wrapped in copper-colored cement, and the 70,000 gallons of flood water—enough to fill 10 Olympic-size swimming pools—is recycled 100 times a day, or every 3½ minutes.

Let your heartbeat slow down as the tram takes another pass through the Big Apple. This time you're close enough to see that brownstones, marble, brick, and stained glass are actually expertly painted two-dimensional facades of fiberglass and Styrofoam. Grips can slide the Empire State and Chrysler buildings out of the way anytime. Note the storefronts carefully; you'll encounter them again in a Bette Midler film on the Inside the Magic tour.

Hop off the tram and walk through the **Studio Showcase,** a continually updated exhibit of film and television memorabilia, including models from such Disney TV programs and films as *The Nightmare Before Christmas* and *The Santa Clause.* Then follow Roger Rabbit's pink footsteps to the **Loony Bin,** where kids can have their pictures taken in front of directional signs indicating "Thisaway" and "Thataway," or open Pandora's boxes containing such sound effects as boinks, toots, squeaks, chugs, clunks, and speeding trains. Roger Rabbit souvenirs are sold here, as are palm buzzers and other magic tricks. *Duration: 25 min. Crowds: Steady through the afternoon, but lines seem to move quickly. Strategy: As you enter the tram, remember that people sitting on the left get seared and wet; people on the right get crushed as the people on the left leap into their laps. Go early. Closes at dusk. Audience: All but young children. Rating: ★★★*

❺ Voyage of the Little Mermaid. A boxy building on Mickey Avenue invites you to join Ariel, Sebastian, and the underwater gang in this stage show, which condenses the movie into a marathon presentation of the greatest hits. In an admirable effort at verisimilitude, a fine mist sprays the stage; visitors sitting in the front rows will get refreshed. *Duration: 15 min. Crowds: Perpetual. Strategy: Go first thing in the morning or wait until the stroller brigade's exodus after 5. Audience: All ages. Rating:* ★★★

6 **Walt Disney Theater.** Tucked behind the Voyage of the Little Mermaid, is this movie theater, which usually runs *The Making of . . .* a behind-the-scenes look at Disney's latest smash hit. The films are shows that have been produced for The Disney Channel, so if you're a subscriber, you may have already seen it. Programs have included *The Lion King, Pocahontas,* and, most recently, *Toy Story. Duration: 30 min. Crowds: Rendered insignificant due to theater size and relatively remote location. Strategy: Go in the afternoon when other lines are too long. Audience: All ages. Rating:* ★★★

NEED A
BREAK?

The **Studio Catering Company Commissary** here will provide you with sustenance for the next tour: hot dogs, burgers, pizza, and fries.

---

7 **Inside the Magic Special Effects and Production Tour.** This walking tour explains how clever cameramen make illusion seem like reality through camera angles, miniaturization, matte backgrounds, and a host of other magic tricks. While you're waiting in line, Goldie Hawn and Martin Short appear on overhead video screens, hosting a humorous overview of the processes you're about to see. Then you're off to the first stop, an outdoor special-effects water tank. Here two willing, if unwary, members of the audience don bright yellow slickers. One gets to play the skipper of the ill-fated SS *Miss Fortune,* while the other unsuspecting soul assumes the role of submarine commander, "Captain Duck," about to pilot his craft into battle. As the audience watches, the skipper nearly gets drowned in a thunderstorm, and the doughty Duck gets strafed, torpedoed, and doused with 400 gallons of water from a depth charge while a video records the scenario and plays it back with music and background.

To show how miniature props are filmed to look life-size, two children from the audience climb up on a hairy bumblebee to shoot a scene from *Honey, I Shrunk the Kids.* A matte, blue screen background is used to combine their scene with realistic shots of the bee's flight, and the audience sees the end result on overhead monitors.

Three soundstages are used for filming the *Mickey Mouse Club, Ed McMahon's Star Search,* and assorted movies. Specially soundproofed catwalks let visitors eavesdrop as overhead video monitors explain what goes on. It takes five hours to shoot a 30-minute episode of the *Mickey Mouse Club*; most of the taping takes place in the afternoon and evening. *Star Search,* on the other hand, tapes two or three shows a day from summer through Thanksgiving.

Then it's on to the sets of a complicated and hilarious sequence from *The Lottery,* a short film in which Bette Midler chases a pigeon that has stolen her winning $1-million lottery ticket. Now New Yorkers can feel aggrieved at the graffiti-covered subway car, since no one else around the country realizes that the subways are now mostly graffiti-free. The actual sequence is subsequently shown on overhead video screens. The 2½-minute scene took five days and 100 people to create; the work was done exclusively at Disney-MGM Studios, and you may recognize many of the scenes from the Backstage Studio Tour.

In the Post-Production area, George Lucas, aided by R2D2 and C-3PO, explains how computers are used for editing, and Mel Gibson and Pee-Wee Herman switch voices in a lecture on sound tracks. *Duration: 1 hr. Crowds: Large but constantly moving. Strategy: Don't assume that crawling into the tour guide's back pocket will give you the best view: Stay in the middle to remain in the center of the action, and aim for the right if you want a front-row view and the left if you want to stay dry. Audience: Older children and adults. Rating:* ★★★

New York Street

In addition to New York Street sets that can be toured on foot as long as crews aren't filming—and are worth it, for the wealth of detail to be seen in the store windows—this area also comprises a live show, either *Ace Ventura, Pet Detective—Live in Action* or *Jim Henson's Muppet*Vision 3D*; the *Honey, I Shrunk the Kids* Movie Set Adventure, a playground; and the Backlot Theater, currently home to the *Spirit of Pocahontas* stage show.

⑧ **Honey, I Shrunk the Kids Movie Set Adventure.** Let the kids run free in this state-of-the-art playground based on the movie about Lilliputian kids in a larger-than-life world. They can slide down a gigantic blade of grass, crawl through caves, climb a mushroom mountain, inhale the scent of a humongous plant and have it spit water back in their faces, and dodge sprinklers set in the resilient flooring, which is made of ground-up tires. All the requisite playground equipment is present: net climbs, ball crawls, ingenious caves, and slides. Because this is an enclosed area, there's often a line to get in, which seems rather restrictive for a playground. *Duration: Up to you. Crowds: Steady. Strategy: Come early or come back when there's no line. Audience: Children and those who love them. Rating:* ★★★

⑨ **Jim Henson's Muppet*Vision 3D.** You don't have to be a Miss Piggyphile to get a kick out of this combination of 3-D movie and musical revue. In the waiting area, Muppet movie posters advertise Miss Piggy in *Star Chores* and *To Have and Have More,* and Kermit the Frog in an Arnold Schwarzenegger parody, *Kürmit the Amphibian,* who's "so mean, he's green." The theater was constructed especially for this show, with special effects built into the walls. All the Muppet characters make appearances, with Miss Piggy in the role of the Statue of Liberty. Guided by a new character, Waldo, the spirit of 3-D, the technology is at its best here. In fact, the 3-D effects are coordinated with other sensory stimulation so you're never sure what's coming off the screen and what's being shot out of vents in the ceiling and walls. An equal-effect theater, the house has no bad seats. *Duration: 10-min preshow, 20-min show. Crowds: Steady from morning through late afternoon, and because the waiting area is carefully hidden, you don't know how long the line is until you've waited for too long. Strategy: Go early or late. Audience: All ages. Rating:* ★★★

Echo Lake

Segue from New York Street into Echo Lake, an idealized California. In the center is cool, blue Echo Lake, an oasis fringed with trees and benches and ringed with landmarks: pink-and-aqua restaurants trimmed in chrome, presenting sassy waitresses and television sets at the tables; Min and Bill's Dockside Diner, which offers fast food in a shipshape atmosphere; and Gertie, a Sinclair gas station dinosaur that dispenses ice cream, Disney souvenirs, and the occasional puff of smoke in true magic-dragon fashion. Look for Gertie's giant footprints in the sidewalk. Here, too, you'll find two of the Studios' biggest attractions, the **Indiana Jones Epic Stunt Spectacular** and **Star Tours.** On the north side of the pond are two more of Echo Lake's attractions: **SuperStar Television** and the **Monster Sound Show.**

⑩ **Indiana Jones Epic Stunt Spectacular.** The rousing theme music from the Indiana Jones movies blares out like a clarion call, summoning visitors to see this show that features the stunt choreography of veteran coordinator Glenn Randall, boasting *Raiders of the Lost Ark, Indiana Jones and the Temple of Doom, E.T.,* and *Jewel of the Nile* among his credits. Presented in a 2,200-seat amphitheater, the show starts with a series of near-death encounters in an ancient Mayan temple. Clad in his signature fedora and looking cute enough for front-row viewers to consider painting "Love You" on their eyelids, just like Professor Jones's adoring student did in *Raiders of the Lost Ark,* Indiana slides down a rope from the ceiling, dodges spears that shoot up from the floor, avoids getting chopped by booby-trapped idols, and snags a forbidden gemstone, setting off a gigantic boulder that threatens to render him two-dimensional.

It's hard to top that opener, but Randall and his pals do just that with the help of 10 audience participants. "Okay, I need some rowdy people," the casting director calls. While the lucky few demonstrate their rowdiness, behind them the set crew casually wheels off the entire temple: two people roll the boulder like a giant beach ball and replace it with a Cairo street, circa 1940. Nasty Ninja-Nazi stuntmen roll out a mat and bounce around performing flips and throws in the background. This is one of those times when it's better to be in the audience.

The scene they're working up to takes place on a busy Cairo street, down which saunter Indy and his redoubtable girlfriend, Marian Ravenwood, portrayed by a Karen Allen look-alike. She is to be kidnapped and tossed in a truck while Indy fights his way free with bullwhip and gun, and bad guys tumble from every corner and cornice. Motorcycles buzz around; the street becomes a shambles; and as a stunning climax, the truck carrying Marian flips and bursts into flame. Viewers sitting up front can feel the heat.

Randall and his gang do a great job at explaining the stunts. The audience sees how they are set up, watches the stars practice them in slow motion, and learns how cameras are camouflaged behind imitation rocks for trick shots. Only one stunt remains a secret: How do Indy and Marian escape the explosion? That's what keeps 'em coming back. *Duration: 30 min. Crowds: Large, but the theater's high capacity means that everyone who wants to get in usually does. Strategy: Go at night, when the idols' eyes glow red. Audience: All but young children. Rating:* ★★★

NEED A
BREAK?

At the **Backlot Express,** you don't need a reservation to chow down on the burgers, fajitas, and chef's salads.

---

⑪ **Star Tours.** Although the flight-simulator technology used for this ride was long-ago surpassed by other thrill rides, most notably Universal Studios' Back to the Future, the Ride, Star Tours is still a pretty good trip. Guarded by an otherworldly metallic monster, Star Tours is inspired by the *Star Wars* films. "May the force be with you," says the attendant on duty, "'cause I won't be!" Piloted by *Star Wars* characters R2D2 and C-3PO, the 40-passenger StarSpeeder that you board is supposed to take off on a routine flight to the moon of Endor. But with R2D2 at the helm, things quickly go awry: You shoot into deep space, dodge giant ice crystals and comet debris, innocently bumble into an intergalactic battle, and attempt to avoid laser-blasting fighters as you whiz through the canyons of some planetary city before coming to a heart-stopping halt. *Duration: 7 min. Crowds: Legendary, with*

near-perpetual 40- to 60-min waits. Strategy: Try shortly before clos-
ing time. Although you can always get in first thing in the morning,
it'll spoil you for the rest of the park. When you line up to enter the
simulation chamber, keep to the right to sit in the back rows, where
you'll get a rougher ride, to the far left to sit up front and closer to the
screen for more realistic sensations. Audience: Older children and
adults. No pregnant women, children under 3, or guests with motion
sickness or neck, back, or heart problems; children under 7 must be
accompanied by an adult. Rating: ★★★

⑫ **SuperStar Television.** "I need a woman over 21 who can tell a guy off,"
the casting director proclaims, and at least 25 candidates scream for
attention. Twenty-eight are chosen and through judicious dubbing appear to play the starring roles on shows from "I Love Lucy" to "Gilli-
gan's Island."

While the volunteers are led off to makeup and costume, the audience
files into a 1,000-seat theater reminiscent of the days of live television
broadcasting. Most important, eight, six-foot-wide monitors hang in
front of a stage that has three movable sets. Through blue-screen electronic techniques, the onstage action appears on the screen to have
merged with clips from classic shows.

The pace is fast and furious, and a good director can make all the difference, coaching the volunteer actors with words and body language,
then running on to the next skit. Soap opera fans get a special kick
from a love-triangle scene in "General Hospital." Then a woman volunteer, outfitted in white apron and tall, white chef's hat, desperately
tries to wrap chocolates on an ever-speedier assembly line in one of
the best-known episodes from "I Love Lucy." Other scenes include the
"Vonzells" singing "Da Doo Run Run" on "The Ed Sullivan Show,"
Neil Armstrong landing on the moon and reading his famous "One
step for a man, one giant step for mankind" line from a placard held
by yet another volunteer, and an extremely young New York Yankee
getting interviewed by Howard Cosell after hitting a grand slam homer.
The latter role almost always goes to cute little kids, especially girls
with pigtails.

Each show is flavored differently by the volunteer cast. It's not easy to
get chosen—only about 12 out of 1,000 make it. To even the odds, arrive 15–30 minutes before starting time, go to the front of the waiting
area, and let a staffer know that you would love to be in the show. Dressing outrageously and having a loud cheering section helps. By the way,
unlike Indiana Jones volunteers, SuperStar actors can watch the action
on monitors. *Duration: 30 min. Crowds: Large, but the large theater*
keeps waiting minimal. Audience: All but young children. Rating: ★★

NEED A   **Min & Bill's Dockside Diner** is the spot for sandwiches—step right up
BREAK?   to the counter. Be sure to save room for "Ice Cream of Extinction" at
              Gertie's.

⑬ **Monster Sound Show.** Despite its name, this show is anything but
scary. Rather, it's a delightful, multifaceted demonstration of the use
of movie sound effects. The show features many of the gadgets created by soundmaster Jimmy Macdonald, who became the voice of
Mickey Mouse during the 1940s and invented some 20,000 sound effects during his 45 years at Walt Disney Studios. Most qualify as giz-
mos—a metal sheet that, when rattled, sounds like thunder; a box of
sand for footsteps on gravel; and other noises made from nails, straw,
mud, leather, and other ordinary components.

The 270-seat theater is small enough for volunteer Foley artists to be seen as they dash around trying to coordinate their sound effects with the short movie being shown simultaneously. "Foley artist," the movie name for sound effects specialists, was named for Jack Foley, the man who created the system. The audience sees the scene—a hilariously klutzy Chevy Chase playing an insurance man on a visit to a haunted house— three times: once with the original sounds, once without any sound as the Foleys-for-a-day try to fill in, and then once more with the volunteer product. Somehow the boinks and bangs never seem to come in on time. Gonnng!

The postshow is a treat consisting of hands-on exhibits called **Sound-Works.** There are buttons that go "boing" and knobs you push to alter your voice. Earie Encounters lets you imitate flying-saucer sounds from the 1956 film *Forbidden Planet.* At Movie Mimics, you can try your chords at dubbing Mickey Mouse, Roger Rabbit, and other Disney heroes.

Soundsations is a "3-D audio" experience in which you enter a sound-proofed room, don a pair of earphones, and . . . you're a movie executive on the first day of work at Walt Disney Studios. A face-to-face chat with Mickey Mouse is just one thrill; wait until you meet the studio barber. It's literally hair-raising. *Duration: as long as you're interested. Crowds: Steady. Audience: All ages. Rating:* ★★★

Just past the Miss Piggy Statue of Liberty in Jim Henson's Muppet*Vision 3-D, you'll find the **Studio Arcade,** Disney-MGM's collection of video games, which replaced the collection of movie and TV props now in the Studio Showcase. Older kids will enjoy a stop here, perhaps while adults browse in nearby shops.

Shopping

Budding animators can hone their talents with Paint-a-Cel, a kit with two picture cels ready to be illustrated. It's sold at the **Animation Gallery** in the Animation Building. For movie memorabilia, there's the cleverly named **Movieland Memorabilia,** located to the left of the park entrance. Check out Sid Cahuenga's **One-of-a-Kind** shop, to the left as you enter the park. Alongside old movie posters, autographed pictures, and assorted, one-of-a-kind knickknacks are original costumes once worn by stars in feature movies. Strategically positioned shops and push-carts adjacent to Voyage of the Little Mermaid, the Beauty and the Beast stage show at the Theater of the Stars, and the *Making of . . .* will satisfy the kids' lustings for character merchandise from these wildly popular films. Genuine Indiana Jones bullwhips and fedoras are sold at the **Indiana Jones Adventure Outpost** next to the stunt amphitheater. All sorts of Roger Rabbit magic tricks are just waiting to buzz, explode, squish, and trick you at the **Loony Bin.** At the conclusion of Star Tours, **Endor Vendors** stocks Darth Vader and Wookie masks as well as other out-of-this-world paraphernalia. For Disney-themed Christmas ornaments, try **It's a Wonderful Shop,** which is tucked in a corner near the Muppets on Location. The **Costume Shop,** near one of the entrances to the New York Street, features getups of Disney villains and villainesses, including favorite outfits of *Sleeping Beauty*'s wicked Maleficent and *101 Dalmatians*' Cruella De Vil Who could resist a pair of Mickey Mitts, an easy-to-pick-up last-minute gift sold at **Legends of Hollywood** on Hollywood Boulevard. Use them to wave at the Earful Tower on your way out.

Strategies for Your Visit

Blitz Tour

Pick up an entertainment schedule on your way into the park. Then run, do not walk, right up Hollywood Boulevard, hang a right at Sunset Boulevard, and dash to the 13-story **Twilight Zone Tower of Terror.** You won't be the only one with this plan, so if the lines look too awful, consider swinging back during the quieter evening hours. Next, head back to the Chinese Theater for the **Great Movie Ride.** It'll put you in the mood for a day at the Disney-MGM Studios like nothing else— and help you brush up on the songs pouring out of the hidden speakers. So suitably armed, head to the **Backstage Studio Tour** and spend the rest of the morning backstage and **Inside the Magic.**

Beat the crowds to an early lunch at one of the lakeside beaneries. Keep your eyes tuned to the Indiana Jones Epic Stunt Spectacular and SuperStar Television schedules. As soon as they have magnetized enough people, take your cue and zip over to the **Monster Sound Show.** Nothing like some simple arithmetic to realize that 2,000 seats in the Indiana Jones amphitheater and 1,000 seats at SuperStar Television won't fit into the 270 seats at the Monster Sound Show without one humongous line, right? This way, you avoid it. Then you can go to **SuperStar Television.** However, save Indiana for later—it's especially dramatic at night.

Instead, amble over to **Jim Henson's Muppet*Vision 3D,** checking the lines at **Star Tours** on the way. If you can't see a line, nip in now. If the line looks appalling, the Muppets are a great consolation prize. Especially because Muppet*Vision lets out in a back corner and while everyone is milling around and thinking of wandering up New York Street, you can whip right back to Star Tours for a second try. You could also try to catch a performance of the **Spirit of Pocahontas** stage show at the Backlot Theater.

You'll need a little downtime after Star Tours. Take the opportunity to explore **Sunset Boulevard,** where the shops sell much of the same merchandise as those on Hollywood Boulevard, but they are less crowded here. Grab a healthful snack at the Anaheim Produce Company, and try to catch a late-afternoon performance of **Beauty and the Beast** at the **Theater of the Stars.** That will put you in the right mood for the **Magic of Disney Animation,** and the time will be right, too— the crowds here will have begun to thin, but the animators won't have gone home yet. Spend all the time you want, but make sure that you catch the last show at the **Indiana Jones Epic Stunt Spectacular.** We love the way the idol's eyes glow in the dusk, and the gobs of flame from the exploding truck make you understand just why this attraction is called "spectacular." Then there's the music, which will carry you all the way back to the parking lots. Remember to turn at the gate for one last look at the Earful Tower, whose perky appendages are outlined in gold lights.

Disney-MGM Essentials

Baby Care

At the small **Baby Care Center,** you'll find facilities for nursing as well as **formula, baby food, pacifiers,** and **disposable diapers** for sale. There are **changing tables** here and in all women's rooms and some men's rooms. You can also buy disposable diapers in the Guest Services building. Oscar's, just inside the entrance turnstiles and to the right, is the place for **stroller rentals** ($1 rental fee; $6 deposit required).

Cameras and Film

If you want something more than a disposable Kodak Fun Saver camera, walk through the aperture-shaped door of the Darkroom on Hollywood Boulevard, and rent a **35mm camera** or **video camcorder** ($5 and $25 respectively; refundable $300 deposit required on camcorders). Be advised that camcorders are full-size models only.

For **minor camera repairs,** the Darkroom on Hollywood Boulevard is the place.

Drop off your film at the Darkroom for **one-hour film developing** or at any Photo Express container for **two-hour film developing**; you can pick up your pictures at the Darkroom or have them delivered to your hotel if you're staying on-site.

Dining

CAFETERIA

Hollywood & Vine Cafeteria of the Stars. The usual menu of upscale fast foods—baby back ribs, roasted chicken, and tortellini at lunch, prime rib, veal chops, and mesquite-grilled pork chops at dinner—constitutes this fare. The usual complement of downscale fast-food spots is also available.

FULL-SERVICE RESTAURANTS

Although the glow often gets tarnished at mealtime, Disney-MGM's full-service restaurants are so much fun that the magic continues. Once you're inside, that is. Unfortunately, visitors never seem to want to leave their tables—after all, would you if you could watch television monitors airing '50s sitcoms while chowing down on veal-and-shiitake-mushroom meatloaf? Consequently, the lines can be enormous and reservations are routinely late.

Brown Derby. With its staff in black tie and its airy, palm-fronded room positively exuding suave, the 235-seat restaurant is one of the nicest—and most expensive—places to eat in the park. The cobb salad, a conglomeration of salad greens, tomato, bacon, turkey, egg, blue cheese, and avocado—invented at the restaurant's Hollywood namesake—is alive and well here, as you can see from the numerous orders getting tossed tableside. The all-California wine list is wide-ranging enough to keep an oenophile happy. The butter comes in molds shaped like miniature derby hats, and patrons seated in booths can even have a '40s-style dial telephone brought to their tables.

'50s Prime Time Café. You'll certainly want to spend a leisurely lunch at this eatery, where video screens constantly show sitcoms, where place mats pose television trivia quizzes, and where waitresses play "Mom" with convincing enthusiasm. The menu is what your own mom might have made were she a character on one of those video screens—meatloaf, broiled chicken, pot roast, hot roast beef sandwich—all to be washed down with root beer floats and ice cream sodas. Don't go to Star Tours immediately afterward—the time warp might be too much to endure.

Sci-Fi Dine-In Theater. If you don't mind zombies leering at you while you slurp up sloppy joes, more meatloaf, chef's salad, and the like, then head here for a re-creation of an actual drive-in. All the tables, which are contained within candy-colored '50s vintage convertibles, face a large screen, where a 45-minute reel of the best and worst of science fiction trailers plays in a continuous loop. Only here would popcorn be considered an appropriate appetizer.

Mama Melrose's Ristorante Italiano. To replace the energy you've no doubt depleted by miles of theme park walking, you'll want to load up on carbs here. The menu features pasta, chicken, steak, and seafood dishes, as well as pizza baked in a gourmet brick oven.

Reservations are required at all the full-service restaurants and, for popular seating times, must be made in person at the restaurant or first thing in the morning at Hollywood Junction Restaurant Reservations, just to the right of the Studios Tip Board, at the intersection of Hollywood and Sunset boulevards.

For Travelers with Disabilities
Almost everything in this park is wheelchair accessible.

Disney-MGM attractions are wheelchair accessible, with certain restrictions on the Star Tours thrill ride and Twilight Zone Tower of Terror.

Sunset Boulevard: To board the **Twilight Zone Tower of Terror** you must be able to walk unassisted to a seat on the ride and have full upper-body strength. The ride's free-falls make it inappropriate for service animals. The **Theater of the Stars** is completely accessible to guests using wheelchairs.

Hollywood Boulevard: To board the **Great Movie Ride,** you must transfer to a Disney wheelchair if you use an oversize model or a scooter; the gunshot, explosion, and fire effects make the attraction inappropriate for service animals.

Animation Courtyard: The **Voyage of the Little Mermaid** show, the **Magic of Disney Animation,** and the **Walt Disney Theater** are all wheelchair accessible, with terrific entertainment value for all guests with disabilities. The **Backstage Studio Tour** is also wheelchair accessible. Guests with hearing impairments who lip-read should request a seat near the tour guide. The earthquake, fire, and water effects of the Catastrophe Canyon scene make the attraction inappropriate for some service animals. The **Inside the Magic Special Effects and Production Tour** are similarly accessible by those in wheelchairs.

New York Street: The *Honey, I Shrunk the Kids* **Movie Set Adventure** is barrier free for most guests using wheelchairs, although the uneven surface may make maneuvering difficult. **Jim Henson's Muppet*Vision 3D** is also completely wheelchair accessible. Guests with hearing impairments may request a personal audio link that will amplify the sound here.

Echo Lake: The **Indiana Jones Epic Stunt Spectacular** is completely wheelchair accessible. Explosions and gunfire may make it inappropriate for service animals. **Star Tours,** a turbulent ride, is accessible by guests who can transfer to a ride seat; those lacking upper-body strength should request an extra shoulder restraint. Service animals should not ride. **SuperStar Television** is completely wheelchair accessible, as is the **Monster Sound Show.** However, the entertainment value there is derived from the timing of different sound effects, so guests with hearing impairments may decide to skip this one.

Most live entertainment locations, including those used at the **Ace Ventura, Pet Dectective** show and **Beauty and the Beast—Live on Stage,** are completely wheelchair accessible. Certain sections of parade routes are always reserved for guests with disabilities. **Tapings** of television shows are wheelchair accessible, but none of the sound stages currently have sign-language interpreters.

INFORMATION
(☞ Access for Travelers with Disabilities *in* Essential Information, *below.*)

RESTAURANTS AND SHOPS
All are fully wheelchair accessible, but there are no braille menus or sign-language interpreters.

Entertainment

The Theater of the Stars on Sunset Boulevard is modeled after the famed Hollywood Bowl. Among the popular presentations is the long-running **Beauty and the Beast—Live on Stage,** a skillful condensation of the animated film. The show is almost always crowded; queue up at least 30 minutes prior to show time for good seats, especially if you're with children.

The Backlot Theater in the New York Street area is now home to the **Spirit of Pocahontas** stage show. The outdoor theater has been decorated to recapture the setting of the popular animated film. To recreate the enchanted willow glade from the film, trees adorn the stage. Instead of a condensed retelling of the film, this show presents the story of Pocahontas through dance, song, giant puppets, and other props. The film's songs are featured, most notably "Colors of the Wind." A particularly uplifting finale shows the audience what is possible if humans live in peace with one another.

The daily parade that wends its way up Hollywood Boulevard is usually tied to the latest Disney hit film. The long-running Aladdin parade was replaced by an all-new **Toy Story Parade.** Originally conceived as a Christmas holiday parade to tie in with the film's holiday season opening, it proved so popular that it's still going strong. All the characters from the film, including Woody and Buzz Lightyear, appear in larger-than-life incarnations.

The **fireworks** in Disney-MGM may be the best. Revisiting Mickey as he appeared in the "Sorcerer's Apprentice" in *Fantasia,* a giant balloon of the great star floats amid the starbursts and chrysanthemums raining down on Grauman's Chinese Theater. Traditionally these are presented on Friday and Saturday nights and nightly in summer and during year-end holidays.

First Aid

It's in the Entrance Plaza adjoining Guest Services.

Getting Around

Inside Disney-MGM Studios Theme Park, distances are small and walking is the optimal way to get around.

Lockers

You'll find them alongside Oscar's Classic Car Souvenirs, to the right of the Entrance Plaza after you pass through the turnstiles.

Lost and Found

Report your loss or find at Guest Services in the Entrance Plaza. If nobody claims what you turn in, you may get to keep it.

Lost Children and Adults

If you're worried about your children getting lost, get them name tags at Guest Services. If you do get separated, ask any cast member before you panic; lost children's logbooks are kept at Guest Services.

Guest Services also has a computerized Message Center, where notes can be left for traveling companions not only at Disney-MGM but also at other parks.

Money

There is an ATM near the Production Information Window, outside Disney-MGM's Entrance Plaza. Currency exchange is available at the Guest Relations window.

Package Pickup

Ask the shop clerk to forward any large purchase you make to Guest Services in the Entrance Plaza so you won't have to carry it around all day. Allow three hours.

Reservations

Make dining reservations at the Hollywood Junction kiosk, located just to the right of the Studio Tip Board at the intersection of Hollywood and Sunset boulevards. If you're staying at one of the Disney hotels, you can make reservations from one to three days in advance (☎ 407/824–4321). Reservations are also required for the popular Aladdin's Breakfast Adventure, held each morning from 8:30 to 10:30 at Aladdin's Soundstage Restaurant (☎ 407/824–4321). Disney resort guests can reserve seats through their hotel's guest services desk.

Visitor Information

The **Crossroads of the World** kiosk in the Entrance Plaza dispenses maps, entertainment schedules, brochures, and the like. Take specific questions to **Guest Relations,** inside the turnstiles on the left side of the Entrance Plaza.

The **Production Information Window** (☎ 407/560–4651), also in the Entrance Plaza, is the place to find out what's being taped when and how to get into the audience.

At the corner where Hollywood Boulevard intersects with Sunset Boulevard is the **Studios Tip Board,** a large chalkboard with constantly updated information about attractions' wait times—reliable except for those moments when everyone follows the "See It Now!" advice and the line immediately triples. Studio staffers are on hand.

Wheelchair Rentals

Go to Oscar's, to your right in the Entrance Plaza ($6 plus $1 deposit); Oscar's also has motor-powered chairs ($25 plus $20 deposit). No electric scooters are available in this park. If your rental needs replacing, ask a host or hostess.

DISCOVERY ISLAND

Originally conceived as a re-creation of the setting of Robert Louis Stevenson's *Treasure Island,* complete with wrecked ship and Jolly Roger, Discovery Island evolved gradually into its contemporary status. It began as an animal preserve and member of the American Association of Zoological Parks and Aquariums, where visitors could see and learn about some 100 different species of exotic birds and animals amid 11½ lushly landscaped acres. Its long, white-sand beaches, its hills, and its hidden groves were sculpted and planned by Disney Imagineers, who brought in 15,000 cubic yards of sandy soil, added 1,000 tons of boulders and trees, and planted 20 types of palm trees, 10 species of bamboo, and dozens of other plants whose original habitats ranged from Argentina, Trinidad, and Costa Rica to the Himalayas and South Africa. Despite all that work, Discovery Island remains the least artificial attraction in Walt Disney World. Although it is barely a 15-minute boat ride from the dock at the Magic Kingdom, surprisingly few visitors take the time to explore it.

One of the special features of Discovery Island is the large and airy enclosures holding birds and animals along the boardwalk throughout the island. More animals are allowed to roam free, so you're likely to surprise a male peacock spreading his iridescent fan in an attempt to woo an unimpressed female, or you can watch 500-pound Galápagos tortoises inch along the beach. Informative signs explain the animal's characteristics and point out particularly interesting plants.

Although it's possible to "do" Discovery Island in less than an hour, anything more than a stop-and-start saunter would do it injustice. You can wander along the shady boardwalks at your own pace, stopping to inspect the bougainvillea or visit with a rhinoceros hornbill. You can picnic on the beach or on one of the benches in the shade and watch trumpeter swans glide by. You can simply sit and read without being disturbed by the ecstatic screams of thrill riders. The only thing you may not do is go swimming—the Water Sprites and motor launches on Bay Lake come just too close for safety.

Pick up a map and a schedule of bird shows at the entrance kiosk and then start exploring. It's truly impossible to get lost, because the boardwalks, however twisty and no matter how many detours, essentially trace a circle around the island. It may take a while, but you'll always get back to your starting place.

Sights to See

The **Discovery Island** menagerie contains areas dedicated to specific species. **Monkey Point** is home to a family of golden-lion tamarins from South America. **Avian Way,** one of the largest walk-through aviaries in the world, houses both a colony of scarlet ibis, whose brilliant color is enhanced by a special carotene-rich diet, and a bunch of blush-colored roseate spoonbills. It's especially amusing to watch the spoonbills scoop up fish in their lagoon—as well as to eavesdrop on the peanut gallery. More carotene helps the Caribbean flamingos in **Flamingo Lagoon** keep their characteristic tropical coral color. Dainty demoiselle and gold-crested African crowned cranes delicately pick their way around **Crane's Roost,** while alligators loll about in slothful splendor in the **Alligator Pool.** The pool also hosts another Animal Encounter: "Reptile Relations" looks at the habits of snakes and alligators. And what would Florida be without pelicans? You don't have to imagine, thanks to a protected flock in **Pelican Bay.**

Discovery Island Bird Show. Aviary "Animal Encounters" shows are presented in an open amphitheater equipped with benches and numerous perches. "Feathered Friends" features macaws and cockatoos, including the tricky green trio of Larry, Curly, and Moe. **"Birds of Prey"** demonstrates the behaviors of such predatory birds as owls, hawks, and king vultures. There's usually a show every hour from 11 to 4; most last about 15 minutes.

NEED A
BREAK?

Sandwiches, hot dogs and burgers, ice cream sandwiches and bars, frozen juice bars, and both beer and soft drinks are sold at the **Thirsty Perch,** at the entrance dock.

Discovery Island A to Z

For Travelers with Disabilities

All paths and boardwalks are accessible by wheelchair. No signage is in braille, and no signing is available.

Getting Around

Boardwalks and well-beaten paths wind through the island's lush vegetation.

Guided Tours

Reserve ahead for **Discovery Island Kidventures** (☎ 407/824–3784), four-hour guided tours for children aged 8–14, offered Wednesday and Sunday in summer, but Wednesday only the rest of the year. The $32 cost includes lunch, transportation, craft materials, and a souvenir photo.

Visitor Information

Disney hosts and hostesses at the entrance kiosk can answer most questions you may have and can give you maps and show schedules.

Wheelchairs

Available for rent throughout Walt Disney World; wheelchairs are available here on loan—with no charge.

TYPHOON LAGOON

According to Disney legend, Typhoon Lagoon was created when the quaint, thatched-roof, lushly landscaped Placid Palms Resort was struck by a cataclysmic storm. It left a different world in its wake: Surfboards sundered trees; once-upright palms imitated the Leaning Tower of Pisa; a great buoy crashed through the roof of one building; a small boat was blown through the roof of another; and part of the original lagoon was cut off, trapping thousands of tropical fish—and a few sharks. Nothing, however, topped the fate of *Miss Tilly,* a shrimp boat from "Safen Sound, Florida," which was hurled high in the air and became impaled on Mount Mayday, a magical volcano that periodically tries to dislodge *Miss Tilly* with huge geysers of water.

Ordinary folks, the legend continues, would have been crushed by such devastation. But the resourceful residents of 56-acre Placid Palms were made of hardier stuff—and from the wreckage they created Typhoon Lagoon, the self-proclaimed "world's ultimate water park."

Four times the size of River Country, Typhoon Lagoon offers a full-day's worth of activities: bobbing in four-foot waves in a surf lagoon the size of two football fields, speeding down arrow-straight water slides and around twisty storm slides, bumping through rapids, and snorkeling. More mellow folks can float in inner tubes along the 2,100-foot Castaway Creek, rubberneck from specially constructed grandstands as human cannonballs are ejected from the storm slides, or merely hunker down in one of the many hammocks or lounge chairs and read a book. A children's area replicates adult rides on a smaller scale. It's Disney's version of a day at the beach—complete with lifeguards in spiffy red-and-white-striped T-shirts.

The layout is so simple that it is truly impossible to get lost—trust us. The eponymous wave and swimming lagoon is at the center of the park; the waves break on the beaches closest to the entrance and are born in Mount Mayday at the other end of the park. Castaway Creek encircles the lagoon. Anything requiring a gravitational plunge—storm slides, speed slides, and raft trips down rapids—starts around the summit of Mount Mayday. Shark Reef and Ketchakiddie Creek flank the head of the lagoon, to Mount Mayday's right and left, respectively.

Sights to See

Numbers in the margin correspond to points of interest on the Typhoon Lagoon map.

❶ **Typhoon Lagoon.** This is the heart of the park, a swimming area that spreads out over 2½ acres and contains almost 3 million gallons of clear, chlorinated water. It's scalloped by lots of little coves, bays, and inlets, all edged with white-sand beaches—spread over a base of white concrete, as body surfers will soon discover when they try to slide into shore. Ouch! The main attraction is the waves. Twelve, huge water-collection chambers hidden in Mount Mayday dump their load with a resounding "whoosh" into trap doors to create waves large enough for Typhoon Lagoon to host amateur and professional surfing championships. A piercing hoot from *Miss Tilly* signals the start and finish of wave action: Every even hour, for 10 minutes on and 10 minutes off, 4-foot-plus waves issue forth every 90 seconds; every odd hour is devoted to moderate bobbing waves. Even during the big-wave periods, however, the waters in Blustery Bay and Whitecap Cove are protected enough for timid swimmers.

❷ **Castaway Creek.** This circular, 15-foot-wide, 3-foot-deep waterway is everyone's water fantasy come true. Snag an inner tube and float along the creek that winds around the entire park, a wet version of the Magic Kingdom's Walt Disney World Railroad. You pass through a rain forest that showers you with mist and spray, you slide through caves and grottos, you burble by overhanging trees and flowering bushes, and you get dumped on at the Water Works whose "broken" pipes the Typhoon Lagooners never got around to fixing. The current ambles at 2½ feet per second; it takes about 30 minutes to make a full circuit. There are exits along the way, where you can hop out and dry off or do something else—and then pick up another inner tube and jump right back in.

❸ **Shark Reef.** Anyone who wanted to leap onto the stage at Disney-MGM's Voyage of the Little Mermaid or jump into the tank at Epcot Center's Living Seas will make tracks for this 360,000-gallon snorkeling tank. The coral reef is artificial, but the 4,000 tropical fish—including black-and-white striped sergeant majors, sargassum trigger fish, yellowtail damselfish, and amiable nurse and bonnet-head sharks—are quite real. So are the southern stingrays that congregate in the warmer, shallower water by the entrance. To prevent algae growth, Shark Reef is kept at a brisk 72°, which is 18° colder than the rest of Typhoon Lagoon. A sunken tanker divides the reef; its portholes give landlubbers access to the underwater scene and let them go nose to nose with snorkelers. Unless the reef is practically deserted—almost never—you are supposed to swim in a counterclockwise circle around the tanker; one circuit takes about 15 minutes. Go first thing in the morning or at the end of the day if you want to spend more time. Chilly air and water temperatures close the reef from November through April.

❹ **Humunga Kowabunga.** There's no time to scream, but you'll hear just such vociferous reactions as the survivors emerge from the catch pool opposite Shark Reef. The basic question is: Want to get scared out of your wits in three seconds flat—and like it enough to go back for more? "Do that?" asked one observer. "I'm not crazy!" The two side-by-side Humunga Kowabunga speed slides rightly deserve their four-pennant designation, as they drop more than 50 feet in a distance barely four times that amount. For nonmathematicians, that's very steep. Oh yes, and then you go through a cave. In the dark. Awesome, indeed. The average speed is 30 miles per hour; however, you can really fly if you lie flat on your back, cross your ankles, wrap your arms around your chest, and arch your back. Just remember to smile for the rubberneckers on the grandstand at the bottom—and to readjust your bathing suit

Typhoon Lagoon

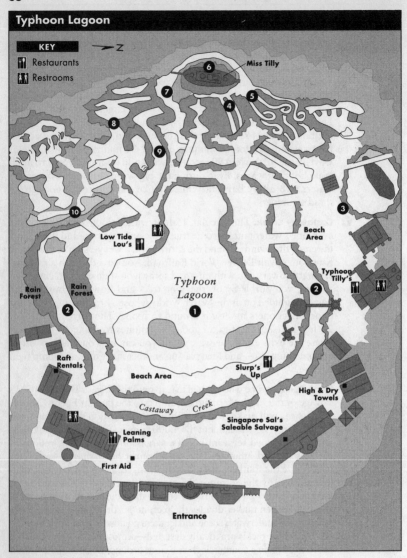

KEY

🚹 Restaurants
🚻 Restrooms

N

6 Miss Tilly

7

5

4

8

9

3

Beach Area

Low Tide Lou's 🚻🍴

Typhoon Tilly's 🚻

10

2

Typhoon Lagoon

1

Rain Forest

Rain Forest

2

Raft Rentals

Beach Area

Slurp's Up

High & Dry Towels

Castaway Creek

Singapore Sal's Saleable Salvage

🚻 Leaning Palms

First Aid

Entrance

before leaving the water. *No pregnant women or guests with back or heart problems or other physical limitations.*

5 **Jib Jammer, Rudder Buster, and Stern Burner.** Each of these three body slides is about 300 feet long and snakes in and out of rock formations, through caves and tunnels, and under waterfalls, but each has a slightly different view and offers an idiosyncratic twist. We'll only say that the one in the middle has the longest tunnel; the others' secrets you'll have to discover for yourself. Maximum speed is about 20 miles per hour, and the trip takes about 30 seconds.

6 **Mount Mayday.** What goes down can also go up—and up and up and up and up. "It's like climbing Mount Everest," wailed one teenager about a climb that seems a lot steeper than this 85-foot peak would warrant. However, it's Mount Everest with hibiscus flowers, a shivering rope bridge, stepping-stones set in plunging waters, and—remember that seminal typhoon?—a broken canoe scattered over the rocks near the top. The view encompasses the entire park.

Mayday Falls, Keelhaul Falls, Gangplank Falls—white-water raft rides that you experience in oversize inner tubes—plunge down the left side of Mount Mayday. Like the storm slides, they feature caves and waterfalls and intricate rock work but add some extra elements.

7 **Mayday Falls.** The 460-foot slide over Mayday Falls in blue inner tubes is the longest and generally acclaimed the bumpiest; it's a straight slide over the falls into a catchment area, which gives you just enough time to catch your breath before the next plunge.

8 **Keelhaul Falls.** This spiraling, 400-foot ride in yellow inner tubes seems faster than the purported 10 miles per hour.

9 **Gangplank Falls.** Designed for groups and families, this ride features four-person, 6½-foot inner tubes that travel down 300 feet of rapids.

10 **Ketchakiddie Creek.** Typhoon Lagoon's children's area has scaled-down versions of the big people's rides. There are slides, minirapids, squirting whales and seals, bouncing barrels, waterfalls, sprinklers, and all the other ingredients of splash heaven. The bubbling sand ponds, in which kids can sit in what seems like an enormous Jacuzzi, are special favorites. *All adults must be accompanied by a child under 4' and vice versa.*

NEED A BREAK? Standard fast-food beach fare—burgers, dogs, chef's salads, and, of course, ice cream and frozen yogurt—is what's cooking at **Leaning Palms,** to the left of the entrance, and **Typhoon Tilly's Galley & Grog Shop,** on the right just south of Shark Reef. Tilly's grog is mostly carbonated, but she also sells Davy Jones lager. **Let's Go Slurpin',** a beach shack on the edge of Typhoon Lagoon, dispenses frozen margaritas as well as wine and beer. Food carts purveying lemonade, soda, ices, and snow cones are scattered around the park.

Strategies for Your Visit

There's really only one problem with Typhoon Lagoon—it's popular. In the summer and on weekends, the park often reaches its capacity of 7,200 people by midmorning. By this time Castaway Creek is a bank-to-bank carpet of tangled arms and legs; Typhoon Lagoon resembles the Times Square subway station at rush hour, and the lines for Humunga Kowabunga, the storm slides, and Shark Reef can top an hour. In that time, you could have driven to the Atlantic Ocean. Now that

Blizzard Beach has opened, however, crowds will be able to breathe more freely here.

If you must go during the summer, go for a few hours during the dreamy late afternoons or when the weather clears up after a thundershower. Typically, rainstorms drive away the crowds, and lots of people simply don't come back. If you plan to make a whole day of it, avoid weekends—Typhoon Lagoon is big among locals as well as tourists. Instead, visit on a Monday, or on Sunday morning, when the locals are in church. Arrive 30 minutes before opening time so you can park, buy tickets, rent towels, and snag inner tubes before the hordes descend. Set up camp and hit the slides, white-water rides, and Shark Reef first. Then bobble along Castaway Creek and save the lagoon itself for later.

If you're visiting at a relatively unpopulated time of year, go in the afternoon, when the day will have warmed up a bit. Do Castaway Creek first to get a sense of the park.

There are plenty of lounge chairs, a number of hammocks, and definitely not enough beach umbrellas. If you crave shade, commandeer a spot in the grassy area around Getaway Glen on the left side of the park just past the raft-rental concession. If you like lots of action, people-watching, and sand in your face, go front and center at the surf pool. For sand and relative quiet, head for the coves and inlets on the left side of the lagoon.

Typhoon Lagoon A to Z

For Travelers with Disabilities

Wheelchair rentals are available in the entrance turnstile area and are free with ID. All of the paths that connect the different areas of Typhoon Lagoon are wheelchair accessible. Guests who use a wheelchair can also float in Typhoon Lagoon and on Castaway Creek, provided it's possible to transfer to a raft or inner tube. The park is head and shoulders above River Country in the accessibility department.

Facilities

Men's and women's thatch-roofed **dressing rooms** and two sizes of full-day **lockers** ($5 and $7) are in two areas—to the right of the entrance and near Typhoon Tilly's Galley & Grog Shop. The latter area is usually less crowded. You can also rent **towels** (50¢ at the stand to the right of the main entrance), but they're a little skimpy; bring your own beach towel or buy one at Singapore Sal's. The Typhoon Lagoon Imagineers thoughtfully placed **rest rooms** in every available nook and cranny. Most are equipped with showers, and they are much less crowded for clothes-changing than the main dressing rooms are.

First Aid

The small first-aid stand is left of the entrance, not far from the Leaning Palms food stand.

Lost Things or People

Ask after your misplaced people or things at the Guest Relations window just outside the entrance turnstiles, to your left.

Picnicking

Picnicking is permitted. Tables are set up at Getaway Glen and Castaway Cove, near Shark Reef. Bring a box lunch from your hotel—and you'll eat well without having to line up with the masses.

Supplies

The rental **rafts** concession, the building with the boat sticking through the roof to the left of the entrance, past the Leaning Palms food concession, also rents **inner tubes.** You need to rent tubes only for the lagoon; they are provided for Castaway Creek and all the white-water rides. You can borrow **snorkels and masks** at Shark Reef, and **life vests** are available at High and Dry Towels (25¢ deposit). You may not bring your own equipment into Typhoon Lagoon.

Singapore Sal's, to the right of the main entrance, is the place to acquire sunscreen, hats, sunglasses, and other beach paraphernalia.

Visitor Information

The **Guest Relations** window just outside the entrance turnstiles, to your left, can answer many questions. Inside, a chalkboard gives water temperature and surfing information, and all rides and attractions are marked with red nautical pennants indicating the thrill level: One pennant equals "laid back," two means "radical," three means "hot stuff," and four equals "awesome." Because the semantical differences between "radical" and "awesome" are minimal, assume that one and two pennants means you can keep your sunglasses on, and three or four pennants suggests that you should hand them to someone for safekeeping and then secure the knot on your swimsuit.

BLIZZARD BEACH

The newest entry in the Disney water park universe is a real chiller—literally and figuratively. With its oxymoronic name, Blizzard Beach promises the seemingly impossible—a seaside playground with an Alpine theme. As with its older cousin, Typhoon Lagoon, the Disney Imagineers have created an entire legend around the park's origin. In the case of Blizzard Beach, the story goes like this: After a freak winter storm dropped snow over the western side of Walt Disney World property, entrepreneurs decided to create Florida's first downhill ski resort. The plan, alas, was short-lived: The snow melted as Central Florida's weather returned to its usual sauna-like temperatures. Just as the resort's operators were ready to close up shop, however, they spotted a playful alligator sliding down the "liquid ice" slopes. The realization that the melting snow had created the tallest, fastest, and most exhilarating water-filled ski and toboggan runs in the world gave birth to the ski-resort/water-adventure park.

With that premise in mind, the Disney Imagineers have gone all-out to create the paradox of a ski resort in the midst of a tropical lagoon. Playing with the snow-in-Florida water motif, there are lots of verbal puns and sight gags. Most of the park's attractions have names that playfully follow through on the beach-ski theme. The park's centerpiece is Mt. Gushmore, which features the 120-foot-high Summit Plummet, as well as other toboggan and water sled runs with names such as Teamboat Springs, a white-water raft ride; Toboggan Racer; Slush Gusher; and Runoff Rapids. Swim-skiers can also ride an actual chairlift converted from ski-resort to beach-resort use—with umbrellas and snow skis on their undersides—over the face of Mt. Gushmore, from its seaside base to its summit.

Sights to See

Blizzard Beach Ski Patrol Training Camp. The pre-teens in your crowd will probably want to spend most of their time at this venue, where they can use bungee-cord slides, a T-bar drop, and culvert slides. In addition, there's a chance to challenge **Mogul Mania,** a wide-open slide area filled with wet and slippery moguls.

Chair Lift. If you're waterlogged, take a ride on this conveyor, which transports visitors from the beachfront base of Mt. Gushmore up over its face and on to the summit. While most riders will probably want to body-"ski" down via one of the water slides, you can opt to take the lift back to the beach. Few do, however.

Cross-Country Creek. Circling the entire park is this creek down which guests float on inner tubes. Along the way, there is a bone-chilling ice cave, where trespassers are splashed with "melting ice" from overhead—pure heaven on a steamy Florida day!

Melt-Away Bay. The park's main pool is a one-acre oasis that's constantly fed by "melting snow" waterfalls. The waves in the pool are man-made, of course, and create the desired ocean-like effect. If you're not a strong swimmer, though, stay away from the far end of the pool, where the waves emanate. You can get temporarily "stuck" in a pocket—a feeling not unlike getting caught in an ocean's undertow—even if your head is still above water.

Mt. Gushmore. The park centers on this 90-foot "snow-capped" mountain. Here, "skiers" slide down the face of the mountain, tackling moguls, slalom courses, and toboggan and water-sled runs. At the base of the mountain, there's a sandy beach featuring the de rigueur wave pool, a lazy river, and play areas for both young children and pre-teens.

Runoff Rapids. For the slightly less adventurous, guests can slide down three different twisting, turning flumes.

Slush Gusher. A speed slide that drops through a snow-banked mountain gully is a real thriller. It's shorter and less severe than Summit Plummet but gives quite a rush nonetheless. *Must be 48″ to ride.*

Snow Stormers. No water park would be complete without a flume ride, and Blizzard Beach has one: it's actually three flumes that descend from the top of Mt. Gushmore. Riders follow a switchback course through ski-type slalom gates.

Summit Plummet. This is Mt. Gushmore's big gun, which Disney bills as "the world's tallest, fastest, free-fall speed slide." From Summit Plummet's "ski jump" tower, it's a wild 55-mph plunge straight down to a splash landing at the base of the mountain. From far, far below, park visitors can see the first part of this "run." It looks almost like a straight vertical drop. If you're watching from the beach below, you can't hear the yells of the participants, but rest assured, they're screaming their heads off.

Teamboat Springs. Six-passenger rafts zip along in this "white-water raft ride" that follows a a twisting, 1,200-foot series of rushing waterfalls.

Tike's Peak. Disney is never one to leave the little kids out of the fun, and this junior-size version of Blizzard Beach features scaled-down elements of Mt. Gushmore. A snow-castle fountain play area is here as well. Kids can also swing across a pool via an overhead rope while stepping across floating icebergs.

Toboggan Racer. On this ride, guests slither down an eight-lane water slide over Mt. Gushmore's "snowy" slopes.

Lottawatta Lodge—a North American ski lodge with a Caribbean accent—is the park's main food emporium, offerings an array of the fast-food variety. Lines are long at peak feeding times.

You can also satisfy your food cravings at **Avalunch,** where hot dogs, snow cones, and ice cream are offered. The **Warming Hut** has Italian sausage heroes, popcorn, and ice cream. In addition, stands around the park sell ice cream, soft drinks, bottled water, and beer.

Strategies for Your Visit

Blizzard Beach is just as popular as Typhoon Lagoon—and even more crowded, since it's the new kid on the block. As with every other mecca, your best bet is to get there early, before the gates fling open. Expect long lines at the major attractions, such as the **Summit Plummet.** If you go during the summer, try to arrive in the late afternoon, just after the daily thunderstorm. The air will be hot and humid, but you'll be cool as a cucumber because the hordes will have already departed for indoor pursuits. If thrill rides aren't your top priority, though, there's plenty of room in **Melt-Away Bay**'s wave pool. A relaxing inner tube ride on **Cross-Country Creek** is a cool alternative as well.

Blizzard Beach A to Z

For Travelers with Disabilities

A limited number of wheelchairs are available for rent near the park entrance. Most of the paths in the park are wheelchair accessible. Guests who use a wheelchair can also float in Cross-Country Creek, provided they can transfer to a large inner tube. Some guests with limited mobility might also be able to use the inner tubes at some of the park's tamer slides.

Facilities

Dressing rooms—for "Sleigh Belles" and "Snowmen"—are located in the Village area, just past the main entrance. Here you'll find showers and rest rooms as well. **Lockers** can be found in two strategic locations: near the entrance—next to Snowless Joe's Rentals—and near Tike's Peak, the children's area, which could prove to be more convenient for adults with little swimmers in tow. Get locker keys at Snowless Joe's. Rentals for lockers are $5 for small and $7 for large, but you'll receive $2 back at the end of the day when you turn in your key; small lockers only are available at Tike's Peak. **Rest rooms** are conveniently located throughout the park; there are facilities in the Village area near the entrance, in Lottawatta Lodge, at the Ski Patrol Training Camp, and just past the Melt Away Bay Beach Area. **Towels** are also available for rent at Snowless Joe's ($1) but they aren't beach towel size. Bring your own if you can.

First Aid

The first aid stand is in the Village, between Lottawatta Lodge and the Beach Haus.

Lost Things or People

Get reunited with lost children at Snowless Joe's.

Picnicking

Picnicking is allowed, but don't bring in any alcoholic drinks or glass containers in your cooler. There are several areas that lend themselves to picknicking, most notably the terrace outside Lottawatta Lodge and its surrounding environs.

Supplies

Personal flotation devices, or life jackets, for both children and adults are available free of charge at Snowless Joe's. A refundable deposit is required—either $25 or the photo ID of a Disney multiday passport; credit card imprints are also taken. No inner tubes are available for rent; you'll find tubes provided at the various rides in the park.

Sundries, including sunglasses, sunscreen, bathing suits—even waterproof disposable cameras—are available at the Beach Haus, located within the Village. Check out the ski equipment hanging from the ceiling. Not surprisingly, a large variety of Blizzard Beach logo merchandise is available here as well.

Visitor Information

Disney staffers at the **Guest Relations** window, located to the left of the ticket booth, can answer most of your questions. Unlike Typhoon Lagoon, there's no rating system for the slides; however, the two speediest slides, Summit Plummet and Slush Gusher, have a minimum height requirement of 48″.

RIVER COUNTRY

Imagine a mountain in Utah's red-rock country. Put a lake at the bottom, and add a verdant fuzz of maples and pines here and there on the sides. Then plant some water slides among the greenery, and call it a "good ole fashion' swimmin' hole." That's River Country.

It was the first of Walt Disney World's water parks. Whereas larger, glitzier Typhoon Lagoon is balmy and tropical, this one is rustic and rugged. Some of the activities are the same, but the mood is different. River Country is smaller and in many ways has more charm. Appropriately enough, it's the only one that gives visitors an unobstructed view of Cinderella Castle. It's quite lovely to lie on a chaise longue and gaze at this icon glinting in the sunlight.

When you're ready to get out of the water, follow one of the nature trails that begin at the edge of the property and skirt the shore of Bay Lake.

Sights to See

Bay Cove. Encompassing the roped-off corner of Bay Lake, this cove is the main section of River Country. Rope swings hang from a rustic boom, and there are various other woody contraptions from which kids dive and cannonball.

Bay Lake. This massive pool is bright blue and concrete paved, like something out of a more modern Midwest. There are a couple of short, steep water slides here.

White Water Rapids. For a leisurely trip down, follow the series of short chutes and swirling pools in a jumbo inner tube. Laughs, not thrills, are what this one is all about, as your tube gets caught in the pool's eddies and you spin around, stuck, until someone slides down and bumps you out.

Whoop 'n' Holler Hollow. Consisting of the two big water slides—100 and 260 feet long—and descending from down the side of the mountain, this is truly the main event.

NEED A BREAK?   You can pick up burgers, hot dogs, and fries at **Pop's Place** or, in summer and over Easter break, buy nachos, ice cream, soda, and beer at the **Watering Hole.** Picnicking is permitted.

Strategies for Your Visit

Go early in the morning to avoid the crowds that sometimes close River Country altogether on busy days. Alternatively, in summer, wait until 4 and take advantage of the reduced-price admission ticket.

River Country A to Z

For Travelers with Disabilities

Wheelchairs are available at Guest Services at no charge (with ID as deposit), but very little of the park is wheelchair accessible; you're better off at Typhoon Lagoon.

Facilities

There are **dressing rooms** for men and women near the entrance, with coin-op **lockers** (50¢) and **towel rentals** ($1). Bring quarters to avoid having to wait in line for change, and bring your own towel since the ones here are skimpy. You'll also need your own beach towel.

First Aid

It's in the white building next to the guest pay phone, but it's open only during Easter break and in summer. At any other time, go to Guest Services.

Lost Children

Lost youngsters are usually taken to the towel window and then walked around until they spot their folks. River Country is small enough for that system to work fine.

Visitor Information

The **Guest Services** window, at the entrance turnstiles, can answer most of your questions. It's also the spot to take finds and report losses.

STRATEGIES FOR YOUR VISIT TO WALT DISNEY WORLD

Arriving at least 30 minutes before Rope Drop is essential to get your bearings and explore the shops on Main Street. If you are staying at a Disney resort, check your passport to see whether you are entitled to early admission; this is vital, especially for parents with small children, who will be able to visit most of the Fantasyland rides before the park officially opens, thereby offering the option of an afternoon trip to Discovery Island.

Blitz Tours

WITH SMALL CHILDREN

Go directly to Fantasyland and start with a ride on **Dumbo, the Flying Elephant.** Then ride **Cinderella's Golden Carrousel** and, moving clockwise, the other attractions. Check the line at **Legend of the Lion King**; if it's moving briskly, join the crowd. You'll get into the next show. Leave **It's a Small World** until last; its continuously moving lines keep crowds shuffling along and it's a nice end to a Fantasyland visit.

Proceed to Liberty Square and have an early lunch at Liberty Tree Tavern. Take an after-meal tour of **Tom Sawyer Island** and follow it up with the next show at Frontierland's **Country Bear Jamboree.** By now it should be about time to find a place on the pavement to watch the three o'clock parade—Frontierland is one of the best places in the park in which to do it.

Upon exiting the Country Bear Jamboree, turn right, as the crowds tend to go left, to Splash Mountain and Big Thunder Mountain Railroad.

Then make another right at Frontier Woodcarving at the end of the row of false-fronted shops and take the shortcut to Adventureland.

Proceed directly across the Adventureland plaza to the **Jungle Cruise.** If your arms and legs are up to it, scramble around the **Swiss Family Robinson Treehouse.** We don't really recommend the **Enchanted Tiki Birds** unless you're in need of an air-conditioned place to sit down or want to inoculate your children against terminal kitsch.

Now stroll through the rest-room arch next to Plaza del Sol Caribe by the **Pirates of the Caribbean** back to Frontierland, round the corner of Splash Mountain to the **Walt Disney Railroad** station. Take the train to **Mickey's Starland.** From here, depending on your stamina, either proceed to Tomorrowland for **Carousel of Progress** or hop back on board the train to Main Street.

If you're really determined to eke out every penny, leave the park for Discovery Island, perhaps, or your hotel. Come back for dinner at the **Crystal Palace.** Many kids want to repeat the rides in Fantasyland, so now is a good time to do that. At about eight o'clock, claim a piece of pavement to watch the nine o'clock **SpectroMagic** parade.

FOR EVERYONE ELSE

Upon entering the gates of the Magic Kingdom, go right over to **Disneyana Collectibles** on the right side of Town Square and make reservations for a late-morning show of the **Diamond Horseshoe Jamboree.** Position yourself for the Rope Drop at the southwestern spur off the Hub that leads to Adventureland. Then sprint right over to **Splash Mountain** via the Adventureland plaza. This route is marginally shorter than going through Frontierland, which is what everyone else is doing. From Splash Mountain, everyone naturally goes to **Big Thunder Mountain Railroad**; buck the trend and go instead to Adventureland. Here you can visit **Pirates of the Caribbean, Jungle Cruise,** and the **Swiss Family Robinson Treehouse** before the crowds, as well as knock off this relatively remotely located land.

Proceed to Frontierland through the exit near the **Enchanted Tiki Birds.** You should have just enough time to get oriented before going to the **Diamond Horseshoe Jamboree,** located to your left as you enter Frontierland. Have a snack here—you'll be having a late lunch. At this point, everyone else is beginning to think about lunch—so it's a good time to visit the **Haunted Mansion.** If the lines look too daunting, backtrack to the **Hall of Presidents** and try again later.

From the Haunted Mansion or Hall of Presidents it's a quick slide over to Fantasyland. Hit one or two of the more accessible attractions while those with younger kids are at the feeding trough—you'll be back. When it looks as though the postlunch crowd is swelling, head out through **Cinderella Castle** and take a right to the Crystal Palace for your own relaxed, late lunch. You'll also be perfectly positioned to grab a piece of pavement for viewing the three o'clock parade.

Head straight across the Hub to Tomorrowland. Again, count on the fact that everyone else had an early lunch and therefore will need an early dinner—which is when you can ride **Space Mountain** and take in **Alien Encounter.** Whet your appetite in the meantime, and take a little break on the **Tomorrowland Transit Authority, AstroOrbiter,** or **Carousel of Progress,** and the **Timekeeper.**

Hop on the **Skyway** right outside of Space Mountain for a journey back to Fantasyland. By now, it should be getting on in the day—a good time to visit some more attractions, now that tired children are being taken home. Wander back to Liberty Square for dinner at the Liberty

Tree Tavern, give yourself time to digest—the **Country Bears Jamboree** is a good spot for this—and then head over to **Big Thunder Mountain Railroad** for a nighttime ride. After that, it's time to find a place to watch the **SpectroMagic** parade, which wends its way up Main Street, around the Hub and—how fortuitous!—into Frontierland.

You've still got about an hour or so before the fireworks. This is a good time to visit attractions that were just too mobbed earlier, such as Alien Encounter or Space Mountain, if you missed one during your first pass; or attractions that are easy on the adrenaline and light on the mood, like **Cinderella's Golden Carrousel** or **It's a Small World.** Again, you'll want to stake out a place to view the fireworks about 30 minutes before ignition—the southwest corner of the Hub is good because you can see over the trees and get a great view of Tinkerbell as she wafts along her wire to tomorrow and tomorrow and Tomorrowland. Or try the central court of Fantasyland, where you can watch sitting down, nursing a soft-ice-cream sundae from one of the stands.

Rainy Days

If you visit during a busy time of year, pray for rain. Rainy days dissolve the crowds here. Unlike those at Disney-MGM and Epcot Center, however, many of the Magic Kingdom's attractions are outdoors. If you don't mind getting damp, pick up a bright yellow poncho on Main Street ($4.25 adults, $3.75 children) and soldier on.

WALT DISNEY WORLD ESSENTIALS

Access for Travelers with Disabilities

Attractions in all the Disney parks typically have both a visual element that makes them appealing without sound and an audio element whose charm remains even without the visuals; many are accessible by guests using wheelchairs, and most are accessible by guests with some mobility. Guide dogs and service animals are permitted, unless a ride or special effect could cause the animal to be spooked or traumatized.

At many rides and attractions, guests with mobility, hearing, and visual impairments do not use the main entrance and sometimes even bypass lines; to find out where to enter or if you have specific questions, ask any host or hostess.

WDW's *Guidebook for Guests with Disabilities* details many specific challenges and identifies the special entrances. In addition, story notes, scripts, or song lyrics are covered in the *Guidebook for Guests with Hearing Impairments*. Both publications are available at the main visitor information locations in every park, along with **cassette tapes** and **portable players** that provide audio narration for most attractions (no charge, but refundable deposit required). There are also **wheelchair rentals** in every park.

Admission

Visiting Walt Disney World is not cheap, especially if you have a child or two along. Everyone 10 and older pays adult price; reductions are available for children 3–9. No discounted family tickets are available.

Passports and Tickets

In Disneyspeak, "ticket" refers to a single day's admission to the Magic Kingdom, Epcot Center, or the Disney-MGM Studios. If you want to spend two or three days visiting the attractions, you have to buy a separate ticket each day. A ticket is good in the park for which you buy it only on the day you buy it; with single-day admission tickets, you can't park-hop. If you buy a one-day ticket and later decide to extend your visit, you can apply the cost of it toward the purchase of any passport. Exchanges can be made at City Hall in the Magic Kingdom, at Guest Relations in Epcot Center, or at Guest Relations at Disney-MGM.

If you want to spend more than three days, you have several options, called passports. The **Four-Day Value Pass** allows admission to each of the three parks on any three days. You can then visit one of the parks again on one more day. You cannot visit more than one park on one day. There is a way to avoid this restriction: the **Four-Day Park Hopper,** a personalized photo ID pass that allows unlimited visits to the three parks on any four days. The **Five-Day World Hopper** is also a photo ID; it includes unlimited visits to the three theme parks over five days, plus seven consecutive days' admission—dated from first entry to WDW—to WDW's minor parks, including Blizzard Beach, Discovery Island, Pleasure Island, River Country, and Typhoon Lagoon. Disney says it introduced the photo IDs as a way to prevent counterfeiting; however, these park-hopping passes were introduced after Disney weathered a storm of controversy over its decision to allow park-hopping only to guests registered at hotels on Disney property.

These three passports can save you money. In fact, if you plan to visit the minor parks or go to Typhoon Lagoon or Blizzard Beach more than once, it may pay to buy a Five-Day World Hopper Pass even if you're staying only four days. Each time you use a passport, the entry date is stamped on it; remaining days may be used even years in the future. A variety of annual passes are also available, at a cost only slightly more than a World Hopper Pass; if you plan to visit twice in a year, these are a good deal. Guests at Disney resorts can also purchase Length of Stay Passes, which are good from the time of arrival until midnight of the departure day. Length of Stay Passes may be purchased at the front desks of all resorts as well as in Guest Services at the three theme parks. Prices, not including tax, are based upon the number of room nights and range from $87.98 for a 1-night/2-day adult pass to $288.32 for 9-nights/10 days. The pass is good for all three theme parks, as well as the three water parks, Pleasure Island, and Discovery Island.

Prices

Disney changes its prices at least once a year and without much notice. At press time, WDW admission prices, including 6% tax, were as follows, but call as close as possible to the time of your trip for the most current information. Note that admission prices to Blizzard Beach and Typhoon Lagoon have now been combined into one **Water Park Hopper,** which entitles you to use both water parks in one day; separate admission is needed to River Country.

	ADULTS	CHILDREN
One-day ticket	$39.22	$31.80
Four-Day Value Pass	$131.44	$102.82
Four-Day Park Hopper	$145.22	$115.54
Five-Day World Hopper	$197.16	$156.88
River Country	$15.64	$12.19
Discovery Island	$10.60	$5.83
Combined River Country/ Discovery Island	$19.61	$14.05
Combined Blizzard Beach/ Typhoon Lagoon	$23.85	$18.02
Pleasure Island	$16.91	$16.91

Purchasing Tickets and Passports

Tickets and passports to Walt Disney World, Epcot Center, and Disney-MGM Studios Theme Park can be purchased at admission booths at the TTC, in all on-site resorts if you're a registered guest, and at the Walt Disney World kiosk on the second floor of the main terminal at Orlando International Airport. American Express, Visa, and Master-Card are accepted, as are cash, personal checks with ID, and traveler's checks. Discounted tickets are also sold at many offices of the American Automobile Association, but check with your local office before you leave home. Four- and five-day passports are also available in many Disney Stores located in malls throughout the country. By purchasing tickets before you leave for Orlando, you can also obtain current park entertainment schedules.

You can also buy your Passports by mail, which will allow you to be waiting at the turnstiles, ready to get a jump on the day, while everyone else is lining up at Guest Services in the Disney hotels or at the theme park ticket booths. Send a check or money order to Ticket Mail Order Dept., Walt Disney World, Box 10000, Lake Buena Vista, FL 32830. Note that this is only for multiday admissions. Allow four–six weeks for processing.

HAND STAMPS

If you want to leave the Magic Kingdom, Epcot Center, and Disney-MGM and return on the same day, be sure to have your hand stamped on the way out. You'll need your ticket and the hand stamp to be readmitted.

Arriving and Departing by Car

Walt Disney World has three exits off I–4. For the Magic Kingdom, Disney-MGM Studios, Fort Wilderness, and the rest of the Magic Kingdom resort area, take the one marked **Magic Kingdom–U.S. 192.** From here, it's a 4-mile drive along Disney's main entrance road to the toll gate, and another mile to the parking area; during peak vacation periods, be prepared for serious bumper-to-bumper traffic both on I–4 nearing the U.S. 192 exit and on 192 itself.

For access to Disney Village Marketplace, Pleasure Island, Typhoon Lagoon, the Crossroads Shopping Center, and the establishments on Hotel Plaza Boulevard, use the **Route 535–Lake Buena Vista** exit.

The **Epcot Center–Disney Village** exit is the one to use if you're bound for those destinations or for hotels in the Epcot Center and Disney Village resort areas; you can also get to Disney Village Marketplace and Disney-MGM from here.

Auto Needs

The gas islands at the **Disney Car Care Center** near the Magic Kingdom are open daily until 90 minutes after the Magic Kingdom closes.

Parking

Every theme park has a parking lot—and all are huge. In fact, Disney prides itself on noting that the Magic Kingdom's parking lot, with its 12,000 parking spaces, is the second-largest lot in the universe, next to Houston's Astrodome. Always write down exactly where you park and take the number with you. Although in theory Goofy 45 is unforgettable (sections of the Magic Kingdom lot are named for Disney characters; Epcot's are named after environments, such as Space and Energy; Disney-MGM Studios' are film genres), a day full of unforgettable experiences in the Disney parks may prove otherwise. Trams make frequent trips between the parking area and the parks' turnstile areas.

For each lot, admission is $5 for cars, $6 for RVs and campers, and free for Walt Disney World resort guests with ID. Save your receipt; if you want to visit another park the same day, you won't have to pay to park twice. Parking is always free at Typhoon Lagoon, River Country, and Blizzard Beach.

Dining

Walt Disney World is full of places to snack and eat. The theme parks are chockablock with fast-food spots; all have full-service, sit-down restaurants, and in Epcot Center's World Showcase, these eating-and-drinking spots are part of the show. On-site hotels offer still other options, including buffeterias as well as full-service restaurants.

This book does not describe and rate every eating spot. Best bets for quick meals are described as "Need a Break?" in the theme park sections of this chapter, and top options for meals in full-service restaurants are in the theme parks' Dining sections. For reviews of restaurants in Disney hotels and at Epcot Center, *see* Chapter 7.

Fresh fruits, salads, steamed vegetables, and low-fat foods are more widely available than you might expect. In full-service restaurants, for instance, you can usually get skim milk, and many fast-food operations have low-fat milk.

Beer, Wine, and Spirits

The Magic Kingdom's no-liquor policy does not extend to the rest of Walt Disney World, and in fact, most restaurants and watering holes, particularly those in the on-site hotels, mix elaborate fantasy drinks based on fruit juices or flavored with liqueurs.

Entertainment

Live entertainment adds texture to visits to the Disney theme parks. Although the jokes may be silly, the humor broad, and the themes sometimes excessively wholesome, the level of professionalism is high and the energy of the performers unquestionable. Be sure to pick up a performance schedule on your way into the theme parks.

Getting Around

Walt Disney World has its own transportation system that can get you wherever you want to go. It's fairly simple once you get the hang of it. All charges for transportation are included in the price of your multiday passport.

By Boat

Motor launches connect WDW destinations located on waterways. Specifically, they operate between the Epcot Center resorts—except the Caribbean Beach—and Disney-MGM Studios and between Discovery Island in Bay Lake and the Magic Kingdom, Fort Wilderness, the Wilderness Lodge, and the Polynesian, Contemporary, and Grand Floridian resorts.

By Bus

Buses provide direct service from every on-site resort to both major and minor theme parks, and express buses go directly between the major theme parks. To Typhoon Lagoon, you can go directly from or make connections at the Transportation and Ticket Center—called TTC—Disney Village Marketplace, Epcot Center, and the Epcot Center resorts including the Beach Club and Yacht Club, the Caribbean Beach Resort, the Swan, and the Dolphin.

By Monorail

The elevated monorail serves many important destinations. It has two loops: one linking the Magic Kingdom, TTC, and a handful of resorts, including the Contemporary, the Grand Floridian, and the Polynesian Village, and the other looping from the TTC directly to Epcot Center. Before this monorail line pulls into the station, the elevated track circles through Future World—Epcot Center's northern half—and circles the giant silver geosphere housing the Spaceship Earth ride to give you a preview of what you'll see.

By Tram

From the Epcot Center resort area, trams operate to the International Gateway of the park's World Showcase.

Hours

Monorail, launches, buses, and trams all operate from early in the morning until at least midnight, although hours are shorter during early closing periods. Check on the operating hours of the service you need if you plan to be out later than that.

Important Contacts

Financial Services

Fulfill your banking needs at either the SunTrust branch in the Magic Kingdom (☎ 407/299–4786) or the one in Lake Buena Vista, across the street from the Disney Village Marketplace (☎ 407/299–4786). There are **automatic teller machines** located at the entrances to the Magic Kingdom, Epcot Center, Disney-MGM Studios, and in Pleasure Island.

Information

For **general information,** contact Guest Relations or Guest Services in any Disney theme park or hotel (☎ 407/824–4321) or the central WDW switchboard (☎ 407/824–2222). For **accommodations and shows,** call WDW Central Reservations (☎ 407/W–DISNEY). To inquire about **resort facilities,** call the individual property.

To get very specific information, call the attraction or department directly: **Blizzard Beach** (☎ 407/560–3400), **Discovery Island** (☎ 407/824–3784), **Disney Village Marketplace** (☎ 407/828–3058), **Fort Wilderness** (☎ 407/824–2900), **KinderCare** child care (in-room, ☎ 407/827–5444; drop-off, ☎ 407/827–5437), **learning programs** (☎ 407/354–1855), **Pleasure Island** (☎ 407/934–7781), **River Country** (☎ 407/824–2760), **Disney-MGM Studios TV-show tapings** (☎ 407/560–4651), **Typhoon Lagoon** (☎ 407/560–4141).

Lost and Found

There are same-day lost-and-found offices at **Epcot Center** (☎ 407/560–6166 or 407/560–6236), in the **Magic Kingdom** at City Hall (☎ 407/824–4521), and in **Disney-MGM Studios** (☎ 407/560–4668). After one day, all items are sent to the **Main Lost & Found** office at the Magic Kingdom's Ticket and Transportation Center (☎ 407/824–4245).

Reservations

To make reservations at restaurants in Walt Disney World, including the heavily booked **Epcot Center restaurants,** call 407/WDW–DINE; to reserve **golf tee times and lessons** call 407/824–2270.

Tips for Your Visit

The order in which you tour each of the Disney parks has everything to do with your priorities, the time of year you visit, (which is in turn related to the opening and closing hours and the size of the crowds), how long you're staying in Walt Disney World, and whether you're staying on or off WDW property. The "Strategies for Your Visit" section included for each of the various Disney theme parks assumes that you want to see that park in a single day and that you're traveling during a period of good-size crowds and long hours. The italicized "Crowds" and "Strategy" information that follows each attraction's review should help you draw up alternative plans. No matter where you go, you will have a smoother time of it if you follow certain basic rules.

- Arrive in the theme parks early—well ahead of the published opening times—so that you can check belongings into lockers, rent strollers, and otherwise take care of business before everyone else.

- See the three-star attractions either first thing in the morning, during a parade, or at the very end of the day.

- Whenever possible when you're visiting the theme parks, eat in a restaurant that takes reservations, or have meals before or after meal-time rush hours (from 11 AM to 2 PM and again from 6 to 8 PM). Or leave the theme parks altogether for a meal in one of the hotels. Early meals are particularly advantageous; you'll be resting up and cooling off while the rest of the world is waiting in line; while they're all waiting to order, you'll be walking right into many attractions.

- Spend afternoons in high-capacity sit-down shows or catching live entertainment—or leave the park entirely for a swim in your hotel pool.

- If you plan to take in Blizzard Beach or Typhoon Lagoon, go early in your visit (but not on a weekend). You may like it so much that you'll want to go again.

- If a meal with the characters is in your plans, save it for the end of your trip, when your youngsters will have become accustomed to these large, looming figures.

- If you're planning a meal at an Epcot Center World Showcase restaurant, reserve in advance by calling 407/WDW–DINE. If you can only make reservations in person, try to get to Epcot Center's World Key Information booths located inside Spaceship Earth as early in the day as possible (☞ Chapter 7).

- Familiarize yourself with all age and height restrictions—and don't let your younger children get excited about rides they're too short or too young to experience.

Opening and Closing Hours

Major Theme Parks

Operating hours for the **Magic Kingdom, Epcot Center,** and **Disney-MGM Studios** theme parks vary widely throughout the year and change for school and legal holidays. In general, the longest days are during the prime summer months and over the year-end holidays, when the Magic Kingdom is open until midnight, later on New Year's Eve; Epcot Center is open until 11; and Disney-MGM is open until 9.

At other times, Epcot Center and Disney-MGM are open until 8 and the Magic Kingdom until 7—but there are variations, so call ahead.

Note that though the Magic Kingdom, Epcot Center's Future World (Epcot's World Showcase opens at 11), and Disney-MGM officially open at 9, visitors may enter at 8:30, and sometimes at 8. The parking lots open at least an hour before the parks do. Arriving at the Magic Kingdom turnstiles before the official opening time, you can breakfast in a restaurant on Main Street, which opens before the rest of the park, and be ready to dash to one of the popular attractions in other lands at

Rope Drop, the Magic Kingdom's official opening time. Arriving in Epcot Center or Disney-MGM Studios, you can make dinner reservations before the crowds arrive and take in some of the attractions and pavilions well before the major crowds descend, which is usually at about 10.

Guests who stay at an on-site Disney-owned hotel can enter one of the three parks on alternating days a full hour and a half before the official opening time of 9. They can get a jump on some of the main attractions, which open for them at 8.

Minor Parks

Hours at **Discovery Island, River Country, Typhoon Lagoon,** and **Blizzard Beach** are 10–5 daily (until 7—occasionally 10—in summer).

Ratings

Every visitor leaves the Magic Kingdom, Epcot Center, and Disney-MGM Studios with a different opinion about what was "the best." Some attractions get raves from all visitors, whereas others are enjoyed most by young children or older travelers. To take this into account, our descriptions rate each attraction with ★, ★★, or ★★★, depending on the strength of its appeal to the visitor group noted by the italics preceding the stars. A three-star attraction, standing out for its imaginative qualities or technical wizardry, elicits the most enthusiastic responses in that group; see it even if your time is limited.

At Epcot Center's World Showcase, the national pavilions are enjoyed by audiences of all ages; however, young children may consider such cultural fare less exciting than the fantasy-oriented attractions in the Magic Kingdom or Disney-MGM, and they may be exhausted by all the walking required.

3 Universal Studios, Sea World, and Beyond

THEME PARKS GROW SO WELL in the sandy central Florida soil that one might almost imagine a handful of seeds, scattered across the fertile I–4 belt, waiting for the right combination of money and vision to nurture them into the next . . . Walt Disney World. WDW is, in fact, something of an upstart latecomer. Long before the strains of "It's a Small World" echoed through the palmetto scrub, other theme parks tempted visitors away from the beaches into the scruffy interior of central Florida.

By Catherine
Fredman

Updated by
Mary Meehan

None was anywhere near the scale of today's megaparks. I–4 hadn't even been built when Dick and Julie Pope created Cypress Gardens, which now holds the record as central Florida's oldest continuously running attraction, having just celebrated its 60th anniversary. Busch Gardens was founded a quarter-century later, in 1959, as an exotic-animal sideshow attached to a brewery and beer garden.

But when the Magic Kingdom opened on October 1, 1971, and was immediately successful, the central Florida theme park scene went from mom-and-pop operations to big business. Sea World filled its tanks two years later. Epcot Center debuted in 1982. Disney-MGM Studios Theme Park threw down the movie gauntlet in 1989; Universal Studios answered the challenge one year later. Splendid China joined the fray in 1993. And meanwhile, Busch Gardens has steadily expanded, spawning the Busch Entertainment Corporation (BEC), which, with the 1989 acquisition of Cypress Gardens and Sea World, became the second-largest theme park owner and operator in the world. Its neighbor down the interstate remains number one. And slated for the near future is a major expansion at Universal Studios, including the addition of a nighttime entertainment complex.

Growth engendered more growth. Whereas it used to be that you could do a whole park—any park—in about six hours, a thorough visit now can barely be contained in a day—and a full day, too. As competition sharpened and tastes grew more sophisticated, a sort of "me-too" mentality became prevalent. If one park has a flight simulator, then all parks must have one—but for now the best are Disney-MGM's Star Tours and Universal Studios' Back to the Future . . . The Ride. Ditto Broadway-style music-and-dance shows, distinguished for their professional presentation, snazzy costumes, high-kicking dancers, and completely forgettable plots. A blessing for parents, every park now has a sophisticated children's play area; ball crawls, four-story net climbs, bouncing rooms, water tricks, and twisty slides—all designed to match a preconceived theme—are de rigueur. So, too, thankfully, are lighter gustatory offerings that, though not exactly heart-healthy, are a welcome alternative to the usual greasy burnt offerings.

Prices have risen accordingly. Busch Gardens, Cypress Gardens, and Sea World match Walt Disney World's pass system with discounts on tickets to BEC parks purchased at other BEC parks, and Sea World has also teamed with Universal and Wet 'n Wild to offer an $89.95 unlimited-admission five-day Value Pass.

The problem for visitors with a tight schedule or a slim wallet is that each of the parks is worth a visit. But if you're staying in the Orlando area, a decision can be made on the basis of distance. Busch Gardens is 75 miles away, a good 90-minute commute each way; Cypress Gardens is a little closer, but the 60-minute drive through the dusty citrus groves seems to take forever. Coincidentally, these two parks offer few high-tech, gasp-producing spectacles. If you want to take in a park that has more cultural substance than blockbuster style, try Splendid China; this new attraction is only a few miles from WDW, but the emphasis here is on expert craftsmanship, not astounding effects. In any case, Sea World and Universal Studios are not to be missed. Universal Studios is best seen after visiting Disney-MGM; it definitely gilds Mickey's lily.

UNIVERSAL STUDIOS FLORIDA

Film fans know that Disney has no copyright on movie magic. Universal Studios has worked celluloid wizardry since 1915, and it wasn't long afterward that it offered visitors behind-the-scenes tours of what was to become the world's biggest and busiest motion picture and television production studio—that of Universal Studios Hollywood. So it wasn't surprising that Orlando's entertainment park expansion should pique the interest of that other candidate from California. Universal Studios Florida opened in June 1990.

Far from being a Disney-MGM Studios–wannabe, Universal Studios Florida is a theme park with plenty of personality of its own. And its personality can be summed up in one word: attitude. It's saucy, sassy, and hip—and doesn't hesitate to invite comparisons with the competition. Where Disney-MGM has the Muppets trilling "Great Balls of Fire," Universal's Beetlejuice Graveyard Revue, a new take on the Grateful Dead, sports a transfunkified Dracula belting "I'm Gonna Wait 'til the Midnight Hour" and a miniskirted Frankenstein's Bride getting down to "You Make Me Feel Like a Natural Woman." Disney-MGM's strolling actors are pabulum compared to the Blues Brothers peeling rubber in the Bluesmobile. And let's face it, even the Muppets are matched by E.T., Tickli Moot Moot, and other inventions of Steven Spielberg, Universal's genius-on-call. Universal's even figured out a way to keep people entertained while they wait in line: From arcade games at Nickelodeon to news shows on overhead screens in the *Jaws* line, Universal makes the most of its video connection.

In short, Universal Studios is the bad boy of central Florida entertainment parks. It's come a long way from the public relations nightmare of its opening days, when almost none of the highly touted rides functioned. Now they do, and so-called blockbuster rides such as Kongfrontation, Back to the Future . . . The Ride, E.T. Adventure, Earthquake—The Big One, and even the much-maligned Jaws—so glitch-haunted in its early days that it had to be closed for two years for repairs—are running. And judging from the delighted shrieks and groans issuing forth, they're running just fine. Universal Studios Florida is now the third most popular entertainment park in the United States, after Walt Disney World with its three theme parks and Disneyland; Universal Studios Hollywood, by the way, is a close fourth. Look forward to further expansion as Universal takes advantage of its Hollywood connections and opens rides and exhibits that tie in with hit movies. In 1994, a *Jurassic Park* exhibit opened. Could a ride be far behind?

The lofty adult ticket prices raise expectations very high indeed. They are met most of the time, but resentment can set in if you're confronted by too many long lines and the movie theater–like price gouging at ubiquitous concession stands and snackeries. We know, we know, it's a free country.

With Disney-MGM just down the road, is Universal worth the visit? Absolutely—they're not the same thing: If Disney-MGM is the introductory course, Universal Studios is graduate school. As such, the attractions are geared more to older kids than the stroller set. If your party is prepared for some loud and scary entertainment, then you should have a wonderful time.

The 444 acres of Universal Studios are a bewildering conglomeration of stage sets, shops, reproductions of New York and San Francisco, and anonymous soundstages housing theme attractions, as well as genuine moviemaking paraphernalia. On the map, these sets are neatly divided into six neighborhoods: Expo Center, taking up the southeastern section of the park; the Front Lot; Hollywood, situated just inside the Universal entrance; New York, with its excellent street performances at 70 Delancy; Production Central, marked in green on the park map and spreading over the entire left side of the Plaza of the Stars—practically encircling Hollywood; and San Francisco/Amity, which lazily wend their way around a huge blue lagoon, the setting for the Dynamite Nights Stunt Spectacular. On foot, it's a different story. There is no prominent central edifice by which to orient yourself, and the street names change depending on which "neighborhood" you're in. In other words, expect to get lost early and often. Rather than trying to figure out whether you're on Sunset Boulevard, Hollywood Boulevard, or Rodeo Drive, look for official staffers; their snappy, surprisingly classy pink-and-white-striped oxford-cloth shirts and white walking shorts stand out.

Expo Center

Numbers in the margin correspond to points of interest on the Universal Studios map.

❶ Back to the Future . . . The Ride. If there's one ride that's on top of everyone's list it's this one—a flight simulator to beat all others, probably even those yet to be built. Michael J. Fox, star of the 1985 movie, said that the ride actually delivered what the script imagined. When popstar Michael Jackson was visiting Walt Disney World, he made a special detour specifically to experience this ride—and rode it three times in a row. Even Disney-MGM's Star Tours, which easily outranks most other flight simulators, can't compare with this one. The cause of all the unbridled enthusiasm is a seven-story, one-of-a-kind Omnimax screen, which surrounds your De Lorean-shaped simulator vehicle so that you lose all sense of perspective as you rush backward and forward in the space-time continuum. It also helps that this simulator's motion is the most aggressive of all flight simulators—and there are no seat belts. Having your wallet slide out of your pocket is the least of your worries and a stiff neck is a distinct possibility. *Duration: 5 min. Crowds: Up to 2 hrs in busy seasons at peak times (between 11 and 3). Strategy: Arrive in the park at opening and dash on over—or be prepared to wait (and wait . . . and wait); lines drop off a hair about ½ hour after the mad mass rope-drop rush. Or go late. For view and motion, sit smack-dab in the middle of the car. Audience: Older children and adults. No pregnant women, guests under 40" tall, or guests with motion sickness or heart, back, or neck problems. Rating:* ★★★

NEED A BREAK? The **International Food Bazaar** is an efficient, multi-ethnic cafeteria serving Italian, American, German, Greek, and Chinese dishes at affordable prices (most of the entrées cost either $5.95 or $6.75). The Italian Caesar salad and Greek salads are especially welcome on a muggy day.

❷ A Day in the Park with Barney. "I love you, you love me . . ." If you can't get enough of the big, purple dinosaur at home, here he is at Universal, in a setting filled with brilliantly colored trees and indoor clouds and stars. The big guy sings and does his TV schtick, and, although

106

Universal Studios

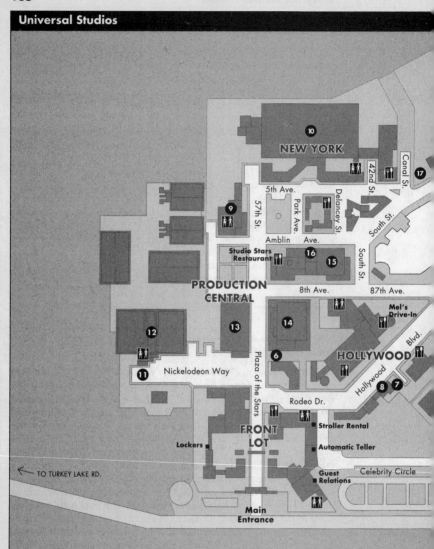

A Day in the Park
with Barney, **2**

AT&T at the
Movies, **5**

"The Adventures of
Rocky &
Bullwinkle", **16**

Alfred Hitchcock's
3-D Theatre, **14**

Back to the
Future...The Ride, **1**

Beetlejuice's
Graveyard Revue, **17**

Dynamite Nights
Stunt Spectacular, **21**

E.T. Adventure, **4**

Earthquake—The
Big One, **18**

Fievel's Playland, **3**

Funtastic World of
Hanna-Barbera, **13**

Ghostbusters, **9**

Gory, Gruesome &
Grotesque Horror
Make-Up Show, **7**

Jaws, **19**

Jurassic Park: Behind
the Scenes, **8**

Kongfrontation, **10**

Lucy: A Tribute, **6**

"Murder, She Wrote"
Mystery Theatre, **15**

Nickelodeon
Studios, **12**

Production Tram
Tour, **11**

Wild, Wild, Wild
West Stunt Show, **20**

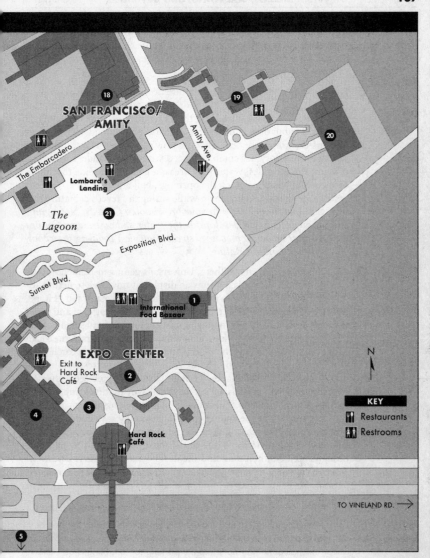

SAN FRANCISCO/
AMITY

The Embarcadero

Lombard's
Landing

*The
Lagoon*

Amity Ave.

18

19

20

21

Exposition Blvd.

Sunset Blvd.

International
Food Bazaar

1

EXPO CENTER

Exit to
Hard Rock
Café

2

3

4

Hard Rock
Café

N

KEY

🍴 Restaurants

🚻 Restrooms

TO VINELAND RD. →

5

his star has dimmed a bit with the popularity of the Power Rangers, little kids still go crazy. There are plenty of nifty things to play with once the show is over, too. *Crowds: Room for all. Strategy: Arrive 10–15 min early on crowded days for a good seat. Audience: Families with children. Rating:* ★★

❸ Fievel's Playland. For parents who are doing the baby swap on Back to the Future, or for younger children who need some time out, this play area is a true gift. Based on the adventures of Steven Spielberg's mighty, if miniature, mouse, this gigantic playground incorporates state-of-the-art amusements that are now de rigueur in entertainment parks: a four-story net climb equipped with tubes, ladders, and rope bridges; tunnel slides; water play areas; a harmonica slide that plays music when you slide along the openings; ball crawls; and a 200-foot water slide that you whiz down while sitting in Fievel's signature sardine can. *Duration: It's up to your preschooler. Crowds: Not significant, though waits do develop for the water slide. Strategy: On hot days, go after supper, or prepare to sweat. Audience: Toddlers, preschoolers, and their parents. Rating:* ★★

❹ E.T. Adventure. Steven Speilberg, Universal's genius-in-residence, puts one of his most-beloved creations on display at this large structure adjoining Fievel's Playland. To the hoarsely murmured mantra of "Home, home," you board bicycles mounted on a movable platform and pedal through fantastic forests floating in mists of dry-ice fumes, magic gardens populated by such whimsical new Spielberg characters as the Tickli Moot Moot, and across the moon—remember to turn to catch your shadow—in an attempt to help the endearing extraterrestrial find his way back to his home planet. Though part of the ride seems like an outer-space version of Disney's It's a Small World, it picks up enough to have a thrill-ride bite. The music is as tear-jerking as ever, and so is the little surprise at the end when E.T. personally says good-bye. Another surprise, the waiting area—a pine-scented forest complete with E.T. beckoning you on—is one of the most pleasant at this park, although small children may find the darkness a little scary. *Duration: 5 min. Crowds: Sometimes not bad, but up to 2-hr wait during crowded periods. Strategy: Go early. Audience: All ages. No one suffering from motion sickness or heart, back, or neck problems. Rating:* ★★★

NEED A BREAK?

For all-American burgers and shakes in a full-service restaurant, one of the best choices is the guitar-shaped **Hard Rock Café.** The neck of the guitar extends out of the park into the parking lot, enabling area visitors to take their teenagers without buying an admission ticket. The rock music is classic but earsplitting, which makes conversation next to impossible—not always a bad thing when dining with teenagers. The walls are crammed with rock-and-roll memorabilia, a treat for hard-core fans who can recognize many of the items' obscure provenance. Allow some time for picking up that Hard Rock tee. So popular is the restaurant's store, you may well find yourself standing in line to get in a line inside the store. The music, however, is cool.

❺ AT&T at the Movies. Though this attraction doesn't seem to actually have much connection to the movies, it is a nifty collection of interactive computer games. What's interactive mean, anyway? In this case, it means you can hear your words spoken by television characters. For example, check out Grandpa Munster running through Shakespeare. It also means putting computer disguises on your face or hearing your voice as it would have sounded on a Victrola. Sneak into one of the sound booths for a vintage radio thriller and probably one of the few, quiet, private moments you will have all day. *Strategy: Go near the end of the* *day while others are hustling to make the big rides. Crowds: It can be busy, but usually not a problem. Audience: All ages. Rating:* ★★

The Front Lot

Like Disney-MGM's Hollywood Boulevard, Universal Studios' Front Lot is essentially a scene-setter, a mood manipulator, the first of many opportunities to squander the contents of your savings account on merchandise or snacks, and the place to find many services. Its main drag, the Plaza of the Stars, stretches from the marble-arched entrance gateway straight down to the other end of the lot, affording a great trompe-l'oeil view of New York City's public library painted on a wall in the New York neighborhood. One thousand miles in as many yards—how's that for magic?

Hollywood

❻ **Lucy: A Tribute.** As the first attraction you meet after promenading through the grandiose gateway, this one occupies a prime corner at Rodeo Drive and Plaza of the Stars. A walk-through collection of Lucy's costumes, accessories, and other memorabilia; trivia quizzes; and 20-second spots from the series shown on overhead video screens, the exhibition doesn't quite match the value of the real estate. Fans of the ditzy redhead may want to reminisce over every item, however. *Duration: About 15 min. Crowds: Seldom a problem. Strategy: Save this for a peek on your way out or for a hot afternoon. Audience: Adults. Rating:* ★

❼ **Gory, Gruesome & Grotesque Horror Make-Up Show.** Just past the bend where Rodeo Drive turns into Hollywood Boulevard is this scary attraction that's especially appreciated by young children and teens, showing as it does what goes into and oozes out of the most mangled monsters in movie history. There's a delicious irony in the fact that you settle into comfortable seats in an air-conditioned theater to find out how an actor's mouth turned into a roach motel in the movie *Creep Show,* how man-to-wolf transmogrification is effected in *American Werewolf in London,* and, of course, the secret of the famous spinning-head scene in *The Exorcist.* The Horror Make-Up Show demystifies without disillusioning—although you never do learn the exact proportions of shrimp sauce, oatmeal, and red dye that go into making a gallon of blood and guts. *Duration: 25 min. Crowds: Not daunting. Strategy: Go in the afternoon or evening. Audience: All but young children, who may be frightened; older children eat up the blood-and-guts stories. Rating:* ★★

❽ *Jurassic Park:* **Behind the Scenes.** This collection of memorabilia from the largest-grossing movie ever is surprisingly small given the film's blockbuster status. Nonetheless, it's worth dropping by if only to see the triceratops lying in the entryway. The rest of the exhibit includes some Jurassic Jeeps, costumes, and stills from the production process. Although park officials aren't promising anything, look for an accompanying dinosaur-themed thrill ride sometime in the near future. *Duration: 10–15 min. Crowds: Not a problem. Strategy: Go anytime. Audience: All ages. Rating:* ★★

NEED A BREAK?

At the corner of Hollywood Boulevard and 8th Avenue—which turns into Sunset Boulevard along the bottom shore of the lagoon—is **Mel's Drive-In,** a flashy '50s eatery with a menu and decorative muscle cars straight out of *American Graffiti.* For burgers and fries, this is one of the best choices in the park. It's complete with a roving doo-wop group, and—unlike at the Hard Rock Café, which serves a similar menu—the decibel level allows normal conversation. You're on vacation—go ahead and have that extra-thick shake.

New York

⑨ Ghostbusters. New York is home to those paranormal problem-solvers first introduced in the 1984 movie. The pre-show, which takes place in a stand-up theater designed as a cluttered store, is a sales pitch for a Ghostbusters franchise, with some hands-on lessons in slime control from volunteers from the audience. Don't worry, the stuff slides right off your clothes without leaving any stains. Then everyone files into the ectoplasmic containment chamber—that is, a large sit-down theater—for an equipment demonstration that's suitably mismanaged to send spooks slithering through the auditorium. All the movie favorites—even the Stay Puft Marshmallow Man—are here amid ghostly explosions and arcing lasers, and the climax is breathtaking. We're not giving anything away when we say it involves the sprinkler system. *Duration: 15 min. Crowds: Steady, but the auditorium can hold almost everyone. Strategy: A good bet for crowded periods; check show times at Guest Relations before you enter the park. Audience: Older children and adults. Rating:* ★★★

⑩ Kongfrontation. The thrill quotient peaks at this Universal power-punch, just down 5th Avenue from Ghostbusters. The waiting area reproduces a New York subway station, complete with graffiti. In fact, one former New York mayor objected to the set on the grounds that it painted a picture of a much-bruised Big Apple. As you board the trams for the escape from the ape-threatened city to Roosevelt Island, police radios crackle with news of Kong-sightings. Then you round a corner and . . . you're in the middle of mayhem. King Kong grabs the tram, helicopter gunships swoop in for a shot, everyone's screaming joyously, and the distinctive odor of banana-breath fills the air. Somehow you escape, but the quavering voice of the tram operator implies that the beast still lurks, waiting for a second chance. *Duration: 5 min. Crowds: Lines ebb and flow throughout the day and move slowly because of the ride's small capacity. Strategy: Go early or late; if your time is limited, opt for Jaws and Earthquake, because they provide more thrill for the time spent in line. Audience: Older children and adults; Kong is too realistic for youngsters. No pregnant women or guests with motion sickness or heart, back, or neck problems; must be 40″ tall to ride alone. Rating:* ★★

Production Central

⑪ Production Tram Tour. To the left of the Plaza of the Stars opposite Lucy: A Tribute is Nickelodeon Way. Take it past the Green Slime Geyser, which welcomes you to Nickelodeon Studios and is the embarkation point for the tour. It's actually an updated version of the old Hollywood Glamortram that takes you on a nonstop ride around the park on which you can gloat at folks wearing out the soles on their Reeboks. The guide is full of nifty trivia about movies filmed on the giant soundstages: for instance, check out the continuity glitch in *Parenthood,* when Steve Martin extols the joys of living in St. Louis while driving past a sign that reads "Florida's Turnpike, 6 miles." You'll also see props now slowly rusting in the boneyard—yes, this is where *Jaws*'s dorsal fin washed up—but the ride neither orients you nor takes you inside any of the soundstages. *Duration: 20 min. Crowds: Ebb and flow. Strategy: Go in the morning to get a feel for the place and mentally mark* *must-visit shops and photo-ops. Try to nab a seat in the front; exhaust fumes perfume the rear cars. Audience: All ages. Rating:* ★

⑫ **Nickelodeon Studios.** If you take the Production Tram Tour, it lets you off where the Green Slime Geyser is going strong, enticing visitors into these studios. This tour, showing how a television show is produced, is akin to Disney-MGM's Inside the Magic. About 90% of Nickelodeon's original programming is produced on the soundstages you'll walk through. The banks of lights, concrete floors, and general-warehouse feel go a long way toward demystifying movie magic, but it's exactly that behind-the-scenes perspective that makes the tour interesting. You may even end up in the taping of a pilot. You'll get a peek at wardrobe and make-up studios, as well as a tour of the kitchen where Slime is made. The tour winds up in the **Game Lab**, an even wackier version of the interactive wonders in the Image Works at Epcot Center's Journey into Imagination. Kids of all ages who watch Nick will love it. *Duration: 30 min. Crowds: Steady, long lines. Strategy: Skip it on a first-time visit or if no shows are taping. Audience: All ages but especially grade-schoolers. Rating:* ★★

⑬ **Funtastic World of Hanna-Barbera.** This combination ride-video-interactive display at the corner of Nickelodeon Way and Plaza of the Stars is Universal's answer to Disney-MGM's Animation Building and one of the most popular attractions at Universal Studios. Before the show, Yogi Bear appears on overhead video monitors to explain how cartoons are constructed. The "dynamically aggressive ride," as the park puts it, puts you inside a *Jetsons* cartoon in a hint of what you might expect at the Back to the Future . . . The Ride flight simulator. But the best part is the interactive electronic magic booths at the end of the attraction, in which you provide the studio voice for a *Flintstone* cartoon, paint Pebbles's hair green with a computerized brush, and twirl dials and push buttons to mix up a sound-salad of boinks, splats, and plops. *Duration: 8 min. Crowds: Usually stunning, despite high capacity. Strategy: Go as soon as the gates open or at night. Audience: All ages; frightening for some toddlers. Young children can opt for stationary seats in the front of the theater. No pregnant women or guests with motion sickness or heart, neck, or back problems; must be 40″ tall to ride. Rating:* ★★★

⑭ **Alfred Hitchcock's 3-D Theatre.** "Have you ever had a premonition?" asks the superbly cultured and ever-so-slightly spooky voice of Alfred Hitchcock, the star of the high-capacity theater, located across the Plaza of the Stars from Hanna-Barbera. It starts off a dandy multimedia tribute to the master of suspense, who made 53 films for Universal Studios. Thanks to 3-D glasses, you learn what it's like to be a citizen of Bodega Bay on a day of abnormal avian activity. Audience participation reveals the secret of *Psycho*'s famous shower scene as well as some previously unseen 3-D footage from *Dial M for Murder*. As in any good Hitchcock film, this attraction engages your mind as well as your adrenaline—and has a characteristic twist of an ending. *Duration: 40 min. Crowds: Sizable but fairly fast moving because of the theater size. Strategy: Try to negotiate seats in the middle of the theater for best 3-D viewing. Audience: All but young children, who may be frightened. Rating:* ★★★

⑮ **"Murder, She Wrote" Mystery Theatre.** A harried TV producer gives you the rundown during one of Universal's patented pre-shows. The crew is running out of time and, well, you know Hollywood—there have been some artistic differences on the set. So now, you're in charge. Armed with any manager's key phrase—NO, ABSOLUTELY NOT—you try to beat the clock. Using footage of senior super-sleuth

Jessica Fletcher, it's no mystery why this is one of the best shows in the place. The rows of screaming, laughing tourists make this big fun. When they ask for volunteers, raise your hand and help them make some joyful noise. *Duration: 40 min. Crowds: Substantial, but waits are seldom discouraging. Strategy: Go in the afternoon, when you feel like sitting down and cooling off. Audience: Older children and adults. Rating:* ★★★

⑯ **"The Adventures of Rocky & Bullwinkle."** Friends of Frostbite Falls follow the call of the moose around the back of the "Murder, She Wrote" soundstage to a musical revue starring Bullwinkle the Moose, his faithful friend Rocky Squirrel, the dashing and ineffably dense Canadian Mountie Dudley Doright, and those two Russian no-goodniks, Boris Badenov and his slinky sidekick, Natasha. The action takes place on an animated set at the edge of Universal's New York backlot and involves lots of songs, corny jokes, and trademark explosions when Boris and Natasha's nefarious plot backfires. Kaboomski. *Duration: 15–20 min. Crowds: Never a problem. Strategy: Shows every hr, usually beginning around 11; go anytime. Audience: All ages. Rating:* ★★

San Francisco/Amity

⑰ **Beetlejuice's Graveyard Revue.** Ease your transcontinental switch at this live sound-and-light spectacle in an open-air amphitheater in which the ghoul with groove transfunkifies a group of scary monsters into a rhythm-and-blues band. Based on the 1991 movie starring Michael Keaton, it has a graveyard rock-and-roll call that includes a hot, earring-wearing Dracula, Frankenstein playing bass guitar, and his miniskirted bride street-dancing. The amplification is enormous, and what with the noise, the smoke, and the monsters, kids often seem confused, if not downright scared. But adults will enjoy the music and the high-energy performances. *Duration: 25 min. Crowds: Steady, but high capacity of amphitheater means no waiting. Strategy: Go when rides' lines are at capacity or after dark on hot days. Audience: Older children and adults. Rating:* ★★★

⑱ **Earthquake—The Big One.** Along with Kongfrontation and Jaws in Universal's Adrenaline Alley is another headliner. The pre-show is almost as good as the main attraction; using audience volunteers, matte paintings, and video cameras, it reproduces choice scenes from the movie *Earthquake.* "This is not a happy disaster, so no smiling," cautions the staffer running the show, as tourists shake and tremble in a mock tremor. Raise your hand to volunteer; it is part of the fun. Suitably glum, everyone troops onto Bay Area Rapid Transit subway cars to ride out an 8.3 Richter scale tremor and its consequences: fire, flood, blackouts. Unlike in Disney-MGM's Disaster Canyon, there are no "safe" seats on this ride; catastrophe strikes from every angle—including above and below—so everyone gets a few months shaved off his or her life. This ride is a technological marvel that resets itself in a matter of minutes. *Duration: 20 min. Crowds: Heavy. Strategy: As with most blockbuster rides, if you want to ride it you will have to wait. The pre-show helps ease the tedium. Audience: All but young children. No pregnant women or guests with motion sickness or heart, neck, or back conditions; those under 40″ must ride with an adult. Rating:* ★★★

⑲ **Jaws.** This is Universal's second attempt at the terror-filled boat-ride, since the first incarnation had an embarrassing tendency to get stuck midattack. Bide your time watching Amity TV on WJWS, a station piped into the waiting line, complete with commercials for used recreational vehicles and candied blowfish. Just when you think it's safe to go back into the water, along comes the finny fiend attempting to turn you into saltwater taffy. This time your boat is under attack, with concomitant explosions, noise, and shaking, in addition to the gnashing of sharp shark teeth. Don't think you're safe when the boat escapes into the boathouse, either. The special effects on this ride really shine, especially the fire and electrical explosions that allow you to feel the heat. Try it after dark for an extra thrill. *Duration: 7 min. Crowds: Lines are long most of the day, but nothing like those at Back to the Future. Strategy: Go early or after dark for an even more terrifying experience— you can't see the attack but can certainly hear and feel it. For the shortest lines, cast off for Jaws during the stunt show. Audience: All but young children, who will be frightened. No pregnant women or guests with motion sickness or heart, neck, or back conditions. Rating:* ★★★

⑳ Wild, Wild, Wild West Stunt Show. The sign "Square Dance and Hanging, Saturday Night," lets you know what kind of town you've moseyed into, and the repeated playing of the theme from *Bonanza* confirms your hunch. The show involves trapdoors, fistfights, bullwhips, water gags, explosions, shoot-outs, horseback riding, and one tough mama who proclaims, "Listen, poptart, I've been falling off barns since I was three." She then demonstrates her inimitable style by hurling herself off the ridgepole. By the end of the show, the set is in shambles and every other theme park in central Florida has been skewered in jokes and snide remarks: "Look, Ma, I'm Shamu," yells one sopping stuntman as he emerges, spitting water, from a well. The panting stuntpeople take time out from rebuilding the set for photographs, autographs, and questions. They will not, however, explain how you can replicate the stunt at home. *Duration: 16 min. Crowds: Large, but its 2,000-seat amphitheater means no waiting. Strategy: On hot days go after dark, when it will be cooler in the amphitheater. Note the splash zone near the well, if you want to stay dry. Audience: All ages. Rating:* ★★★

㉑ Dynamite Nights Stunt Spectacular. The lagoon at the heart of Universal's layout is the setting for the show presented nightly at 7. This is a shoot-'em-up stunt show with a difference: It's performed on water skis and in motorboats and at night. As far as theme park finales go, this one pales in comparison with Disney's fireworks or Sea World's watery, holographic Neptune. There are a few noisy boats, some loud explosions, and much ado about nothing. If you're worried about getting stuck in parking-lot gridlock, skip it. Children may enjoy seeing the kind of chase scenes live they've seen on television. If you do decide to stay, amble back along the lagoon and pick your spot for the evening show. There are definitely bad and good views: The best are from the footbridge, at the opposite end of the lagoon on New York's South Street, as well as along Exposition Boulevard, the avenue along the lagoon adjoining Expo Center. Prime locations fill up at least 30 minutes before show time, so be warned. *Duration: 20 min. Crowds: Large, but there's plenty of room for all. Strategy: Bring a snack and claim your spot 30 min before show time. Audience: All ages. Rating:* ★

Strategies for Your Visit

When to Go

As in the Disney parks, Mondays through Wednesdays are the busiest days of the week at Universal Studios. The pace slows down on Thursdays and Fridays and builds again over the weekend. Saturdays and Sundays are usually busy, but especially during holiday weeks.

Blitz Tour

Universal estimates that 14 hours are needed to experience the entire park. So if you want to attempt to see everything in one day, arrive early so that you can take care of business and see the fabled attractions before the park gets very crowded.

Don't be distracted by the faux Hollywood streets, don't be lured into those shops calling to you as you go through the gate. Walk past all those inviting doorways straight back to **E.T. Adventure.** After flying to alien worlds, zip over to **Back to the Future . . . The Ride,** and streak through Hill Valley, the town where the movie was set. Catch the animal show, then traipse over to Amityville, where the terrifying star of **Jaws** will try to catch you. Mosey over to the **Wild, Wild, Wild West Stunt Show.** Next, get a healthy dose of disaster with **Earthquake—The Big One** and **Kongfrontation;** see if the Blues Brothers are performing, and then have a little lunch. The Turkey Leg is the best bargain you will find. Skitter over to **Ghostbusters** in New York; then take the short walk to **Production Central,** tour **Nickelodeon,** catch "**Murder, She Wrote" Mystery Theater,** dodge the birds in **Hitchcock's 3-D Theatre,** and zoom through a cartoon world at the **Funtastic World of Hanna-Barbera.**

You will have made a circle around the park. Now, with all those people who didn't read this guide still standing in line to hit the big rides, you can enjoy **Lucy: A Tribute,** *Jurassic Park*: **Behind the Scenes,** the **Gory, Gruesome & Grotesque Horror Make-Up Show,** and **AT&T at the Movies.** With the day waning, you'll have some time to shop. If Hard Rock souvenirs beckon, let the kids play at **Fievel's Playland** or **A Day in the Park with Barney** while you stand in line to get into the store. This will put you in a good position to find a prime spot for the **Dynamite Stuntacular,** which allows you to end your day with a bang.

On Rainy Days
Except during Christmas week, rainy days at Universal are less crowded—even though the park is in full operation. Only a couple of street shows get canceled at Universal Studios because of bad weather.

Other Tips
- Call the day before your visit to get official park hours.

- Arrive in the parking lot 30–45 minutes early and see the biggest attractions first.

- Lunch before 11 and dine at 5. Or have a filling snack at 10:30, lunch after 2, and dinner at 8 or later. Or lunch on the early side at a place that takes reservations: Lombard's Landing and Studio Stars are good bets. Be sure to make your reservations ahead of time or, at the very least, when you enter the park.

- If you're traveling with small children, avoid backtracking. Universal is just too big.

- Set up a rendezvous point at the start of the day, just in case you and your companions get separated.

- Be sure to mark your parking location by some permanent landmark. Universal Studios' parking lots do not have overhead signs designating parking areas.

- When entering the park, everyone naturally walks to the right. Go to the left and avoid the crowds. This strategy is especially effective early in the day

Shopping

Every ride and every attraction has its affiliated theme shop; in addition, Rodeo Drive and Hollywood Boulevard are pockmarked with money pits. Choice souvenirs include the Universal Studios' trademark movie clipboard; sepia prints of Richard Gere, Mel Gibson, and Marilyn Monroe; supercool sunglasses à la Blues Brothers; and, of course, all the gak you want to eat. The little plush King Konglets at **Kongfrontation** and a variety of stuffed animals from the **Hanna-Barbera** folks are among the unique gifts available. Stop by Hollywood's **Brown Derby** for the perfect topper, from fedoras à la Indiana Jones to bush hats from *Jurassic Park*. Be advised that few of the attraction-specific souvenirs are sold outside of their own shop, so if you're struck by Fred Flintstone "yabba dabba doo" boxer shorts at the Hanna-Barbera Shop, seize the moment—and the shorts.

Universal Studios A to Z

Admission

Tickets for Universal Studios, excluding tax, cost $37 for one day, $55 for two days; $30 and $44, respectively, for children 3–9. They're available in advance by mail through TicketMaster (☎ 800/745–5000).

DISCOUNTS

Making your Universal purchase at the Orlando/Orange County Convention and Visitors Bureau ticket office at the Mercado International Market (✉ 8445 International Dr.) will save you about $4 per adult ticket ($3 on children's prices). When you buy your ticket at the gate, you can save $2.50 by using the Orlando Magicard, available free on request (☎ 800/551–0181) or in person at the Mercado. AAA members get 10% off (sometimes more at AAA offices). If you're also visiting Sea World and Wet 'n Wild, buy the multi-day, multi-park Value Pass ($89.95 plus tax; $72.95 plus tax for kids 3–9).

HAND STAMPS

If you want to leave the park and come back the same day, have your hand stamped when you leave, and show your hand and your Studio Pass when you return.

TICKET UPGRADES

If you decide that one day is not enough, buy your next day's ticket at Guest Relations, just inside the Main Entrance before you leave the park, and you'll pay only the two-day ticket price.

Baby Care

There are **diaper-changing tables** in both men's and women's rest rooms; there are **nursing facilities** at Guest Relations just inside Universal Studios Main Entrance and to the right, as well as at First Aid, adjoining Louie's Italian restaurant between San Francisco and New York. No **diapers** are sold on the premises; instead, they're complimentary—to guests in need—at Animal House, Dock's Candy Store, the Universal Studios Store, and other locations. You will find **strollers**—which look like Jurassic Park Jeeps—for rent in Amity and just inside the Main Entrance to the right, next to the First Union National Bank (singles $6, doubles $12; no deposit required). No formula or baby food is sold on the premises; the nearest sources are K-mart on Sand Lake Road, Walgreen's on Kirkman Road, and Publics supermarkets on Sand Lake and Kirkman roads.

Baby Exchange

All rides have Baby Exchange areas, so that one parent or adult party member can watch a baby or toddler while the other enjoys the ride or show. The adults then change roles, and the former caretaker rides without having to wait in line all over again.

Cameras and Film

At the Lights, Camera, Action shop in the Front Lot, just inside the Universal Studios Main Entrance, you'll find **rental video cameras** ($29.95 per day; deposit or credit-card imprint required) and **loaner cameras.** You must show a valid driver's license and a major credit card.

For **minor camera repairs,** go to the Dark Room on Hollywood Boulevard.

For **one-hour film developing,** the Dark Room is the spot.

Car Care

You can fill 'er up at the '40s-vintage Texaco station at the Turkey Lake Road entrance. If you need a battery jump, raise your hood and speak to the nearest employee.

Dining

Most eateries are on Plaza of the Stars and Hollywood Boulevard. And their stellar locations are often matched by astronomical prices. Several restaurants accept reservations: Production Central's **Studio Stars** (☎ 407/363–8769), which has an all-you-can-eat buffet; San Francisco/Amity's **Lombard's Landing** (☎ 407/362–9955), designed to resemble a warehouse from 19th-century San Francisco; and the **Hard Rock Café** (☎ 407/351–7625).

For Travelers with Disabilities

As in Walt Disney World's major parks, each attraction has an audio portion that will appeal to those with visual impairments and a visual portion to interest those with hearing impairments. But Universal Studios has also made an all-out effort not only to make the premises physically accessible for those with disabilities but also to lift attitudinal barriers. Power-assist buttons were added to heavy, hard-to-open doors, lap tables were provided for guests in shops, and already-accessible bathroom facilities were modified with niceties such as insulating under-sink pipes and companion rest rooms. In addition, all the employees now attend disability awareness workshops to remind them that people with disabilities are people first. And you can occasionally spot staffers using wheelchairs. Parts of the park with cobblestone streets now have paved paths, and photo spots have been modified for wheelchair accessibility. Various attractions have been retrofitted, so that most attractions can be boarded directly in a standard wheelchair; those using oversize vehicles or scooters must transfer to a standard model—these are available at the ride's entrance—or into the ride vehicle.

ATTRACTIONS

Alfred Hitchcock's 3-D Theatre, "Murder, She Wrote" Mystery Theater, Ghostbusters, Animal Actors Stage Show, the **Gory, Gruesome & Grotesque Horror Make-Up Show, Beetlejuice's Graveyard Revue,** and the **Wild, Wild, Wild West Stunt Show** are all completely wheelchair-accessible, theater-style attractions. Guests with visual impairments will enjoy all of these shows, but sound and special effects make all but Alfred Hitchcock's 3-D Theater and "Murder, She Wrote" inappropriate for service animals.

Expo Center: To ride **E.T. Adventure,** you must transfer to the ride vehicle or to a standard-size wheelchair if you're not already using one. Service animals are not permitted. There is some sudden tilting and accelerating, but anyone with back, neck, or heart conditions can ride in E.T.'s orbs (the spaceships) instead of the flying bicycles.

Hollywood: Lucy: A Tribute is wheelchair accessible, but the TV show excerpts shown on overhead screens are not close-captioned.

New York and San Francisco/Amity: If you use a standard-size wheelchair or can transfer to one or to the ride vehicle directly, you can board **Kongfrontation, Earthquake—The Big One,** and **Jaws** directly. If their turbulence will be a problem for you, you shouldn't ride. Service animals should not ride. Note that guests with visual impairments as well as those using wheelchairs should cross San Francisco with care.

Production Central: Guests using an oversize wheelchair or scooter must transfer to a standard wheelchair to board the **Production Tram Tour.** The information in the narrative—interesting to those with visual impairments—is written down in the guidebook for the hearing-impaired. The **Nickelodeon Studios** tour is also completely accessible by guests using wheelchairs and enjoyable for guests with other disabilities. If you lip-read, ask to stay up front. The **Funtastic World of Hanna-Barbera** is completely accessible by guests using wheelchairs. However, your experience will be more intense if you can transfer to a ride seat and tolerate your vehicle's sudden sharp accelerations, climbs, stops, dives, and banked turns. If you can't, you can still experience the attraction, albeit from a stationary seat. Guests with other disabilities who enjoy other thrill rides will enjoy this one as well.

RESTAURANTS

All restaurants are wheelchair accessible. However, you can't take into the Hard Rock Café wheelchairs or scooters rented in the park.

ENTERTAINMENT

There are special viewing areas at all of the outdoor shows, including **Dynamite Nights Stunt Spectacular.**

SERVICES

Many Universal Studios employees have had basic sign-language training; even some of the animated characters speak sign, albeit—because many have only four fingers—an adapted version. Like Walt Disney World, Universal Studios Florida supplements the visuals with a special **guidebook** containing story lines and scripts in all of the attractions described below, unless otherwise noted. There is an **outgoing TTY** on the counter in Guest Relations, just inside the Main Entrance and to the right.

Universal Studios also publishes the **"Studio Guide for Guests with Disabilities,"** which pinpoints the special entrances available for those with disabilities; these routes often bypass the attraction's line. In addition, cassettes with narrative descriptions of the various attractions can be borrowed, along with portable tape players. You can get these and the various booklets at Guest Relations.

WHEELCHAIR RENTALS

Wheelchairs ($5 a day) and electric wheelchairs ($25 a day) can be rented in Amity and just inside the Main Entrance, to the right, next to the First Union National Bank. You must leave a valid driver's license or $25 as a deposit. If the wheelchair breaks down, disappears, or otherwise needs replacing, speak to any shop attendant.

First Aid

Universal Studios' First Aid Center is between New York and San Francisco, next to Louie's Italian Restaurant.

Getting There

Universal Studios is about ½ mile north of I–4 Exit 30B (Kirkman Rd. or Rte. 435), near the intersection of I–4 and the Florida Turnpike. Be warned, however, that getting from the 30B/Kirkman exit to the park is confusing—you have to drive past the entrance gates and then loop back. It's much easier to reach Universal Studios if you get off I–4 at

Exit 29, which is slightly south of the park. From Exit 29, directions are as follows: If traveling westbound on I–4, make a right onto Sand Lake Road and another right onto Turkey Lake Road; if traveling eastbound, make a left onto Sand Lake Road and then a right onto Turkey Lake Road. Numerous billboards and signposts mark the way.

Guided Tours

Universal has two VIP tours, which offer what's called "back-door admission" or, in plain English, the right to jump the line. No other theme park has anything like this, which we suppose is the ultimate capitalist fantasy. In any case, they're definitely worthwhile if you're in a hurry, if the day is crowded, and if you have the money to burn—from $90 for an individual four-hour VIP tour, including park admission, to $900 for an eight-hour tour for up to 15 people, again including park admission.

Hours

Universal Studios is open 365 days a year, from 9 to 7, with hours extended as late as 10 during summer and holiday periods.

Lockers

Lockers are across from Guest Relations (50¢).

Lost and Found

Misplaced possessions go to Guest Relations near the Main Entrance.

Lost Children and Adults

If you lose your children or traveling companions, speak up immediately at Guest Relations or at Security—behind Louie's, between New York and San Francisco.

Money

The First Union National Bank, just inside the Main Entrance, cashes traveler's checks, makes cash advances on credit cards, and exchanges foreign currency. There's one ATM at the bank and another outside the Main Entrance, to the right of the Guest Relations window; they're linked to Plus, Honor, Cirrus, Visa, and MasterCard.

Parking

The cost for parking at Universal Studios is $5 for cars, $7 for campers. Valet parking is also available for $11.

Reservations

Reservations at the Universal Studios restaurants that accept them can be made as far in advance as you want to make them; just call the restaurant or go there in person first thing in the morning.

Visitor Information

Contact Universal Studios (✉ 1000 Universal Studios Plaza, Orlando 32819-7610, ☎ 407/363–8000, TTY 407/363–8265).

Stop by **Guest Relations,** in the Front Lot to the right after you pass through the turnstiles, for brochures, maps, and a schedule of the day's entertainment, tapings, and filmings.

Studio Information Boards in front of Studio Stars Restaurant and Mel's Drive-In provide up-to-the-minute ride and show operating information—including the length of lines in minutes at the Studios' major attractions.

If you want to watch a production filming or taping, consult the Production Schedule at the entrance turnstiles or stop in at Guest Relations. Attendants at the Nickelodeon studio can tell you how to get studio audience tickets.

SEA WORLD

Many visitors are surprised to discover that there's a lot more to Sea World than Shamu, its mammoth killer-whale mascot. Aptly named, 135-acre Sea World is the world's largest zoological park and is devoted entirely to the mammals, birds, fish, and reptiles that live in the ocean and its tributaries. Sure, you can be splashed by Shamu and his other orca buddies, but you can also be spat at by a walrus, stroke a stingray, experience life as a manatee, and learn to love an eel.

What's even more astonishing is that the fun factor is closely tied to educational elements. Every attraction is designed to teach visitors about the beauty of the marine world and how that world is being threatened by human thoughtlessness. It's all very politically and environmentally correct. Yet the presentations are rarely dogmatic, never pedantic, and almost always memorable as well as enjoyable.

After a rough adolescence under previous owner Harcourt Brace Jovanovich, which included a threat of bankruptcy amid rumors that stressed-out killer whales had turned on their trainers, Sea World was purchased by Anheuser-Busch in 1989 and added to that company's stable of entertainment theme parks, whose Florida representatives now are Busch Gardens, Adventure Island, and Cypress Gardens. Sea World turns 24 in 1997 and, thanks to Anheuser-Busch's new management, is bigger and better than ever. Recent years have seen annual additions from polar bears to sea lions. Sea World seems to have at last found an identity that makes it shine.

The park rivals Disney properties for sparkling cleanliness, smiley staff, and attention to detail—the nautical flags flying over the entrance spell out "Sea World" in semaphore, and the strollers are shaped like upended dolphins with tails as handles.

It used to be you could whip through Sea World and still have time to play a few rounds of golf. No more. Count on spending an entire day—and wanting to return. It's organized around the nucleus of a 17-acre central lake. Rather than being divided into sections or "lands," as is the case at other Florida entertainment parks, Sea World's attractions flow into each other. As you enter, the lake is to your right. The right side of the park contains Shamu Stadium, Shamu Breeding Pool and Nursery, Shamu's Happy Harbor play area, Wild Arctic, Atlantis Water Ski Stadium, and Anheuser-Busch Hospitality Center, home of the hulking Clydesdale horses. The left side of the park is considerably denser, with all the other attractions stacked one on top of another. You can orient yourself by the Sky Tower ($3), whose revolving viewing platform is generally visible even above the trees; it's directly opposite Shamu Stadium.

The computerized, color-coordinated map handed out at the entrance makes the park look much larger than it is. It's actually quite compact, but artful landscaping, curving paths, and concealing greenery make it very easy to get disoriented. When that happens, don't try to figure out the sometimes confusing signs; just find an aqua-shirted staff member and ask for directions. If you're panicked about missing a Shamu performance, just remember that the key is finding the lake; Shamu Stadium is no more than a 10-minute walk away.

Numbers in the margin correspond to points of interest on the Sea World map.

❶ Tropical Reef. Sea World goes head to head here with Walt Disney World's Epcot Center and the older Living Seas pavilion . . . and scores lots of points. The centerpiece of this indoor, air-conditioned attraction is a cylindrical 160,000-gallon mega-aquarium where more than 1,000 tropical fish swim around a man-made coral reef. Identification photos of Tinker's butterfly fish, black-and-white Moorish idols, bright blue-striped yellow sergeant majors, and their piscine pals are displayed just above eye level, but because the pesky things don't stay put under their portraits, matching fish to picture is like playing connect-the-dots with moving dots. Kids especially like to run circles around the tank in search of one particular species. There are also 17 miniaquariums set in pillars and around the perimeter, displaying king crabs, moray eels, and other single species as well as vignettes of undersea life. *Crowds: Not usually a problem. Strategy: Go the end of the day (because it's near the entrance, most people stop here on their way in). Audience: All ages. Rating:* ★★★

② **Caribbean Tide Pool.** This is the touchy-feely version of the Tropical Reef. Under the watchful eye of a Sea World guide, you can reach into the lukewarm water, pick up a starfish or a sea anemone, and ask such basic questions as "What do they do?" Answer: "Not much." *Crowds: Make it hard to get to the animals. Strategy: Go early or late. Audience: All ages. Rating:* ★★

NEED A
BREAK?

The full-service **Bimini Bay Café** dishes up light and tasty tropical cuisine in a pale pastel setting that would be refreshing even without the air-conditioning. The veranda tables have a great view of the action "backstage" at the water-ski show, the floats where the water-ski tow boats pick up their next load of daredevil stuntmen and stuntwomen.

---

③ **Whale & Dolphin Stadium.** One of two gleaming white-and-navy-blue structures, this one is located just beyond Stringray Lagoon. The dolphin show spotlights one lucky child from the audience—to get yours picked, come early and ask one of the stadium attendants—six Atlantic bottlenose dolphins, and two false killer whales. The dolphins wave, leap, and do backflips; in one sequence, the trainer rides on their backs and then gets torpedoed into the air. The child from the audience stands on the side of the tank, commands the dolphins with hand gestures, and gets splashed. *Duration: 20 min. Crowds: You'll always get in. Strategy: Sit in the first four rows if you want to get splashed. Audience: All ages. Rating:* ★★★

④ **Sea Lion & Otter Stadium.** Inside the "sister" stadium to the Whale & Dolphin are wildly inventive, multilevel balconies—used as diving boards—and staircases—used as water slides. The "Hotel Clyde and Seamore" is the current setting, located on the left side of the park, just to the left of the spot where the central lake begins to curve. The comedy features break-dancing sea lions, an environmentally sensitive otter, and a heroic walrus that lumbers in and saves the day from blundering, littering humans. Show times are staggered so that there's time to explore the attractions between the two stadiums between shows. *Duration: 40 min, including the 15-min pre-show. Crowds: No problem. Strategy: Sit toward the center for the best view, and don't miss the show's opening minutes. Audience: All ages. Rating:* ★★★

⑤ **Manatees: The Last Generation?** Sea World's commitment to the conservation of Florida's manatees, a gentle cross between a walrus and an oil barrel, is especially striking. Visitors tramp down a Plexiglas tunnel beneath the naturalistic, 3½-acre lagoon to **Manatee Theater,** where a film examines manatees' lifestyle and describes how human encroachment is threatening the species' survival. You can snoop at the lettuce-chomping giants and native fish, including tarpon, gar, and snook,

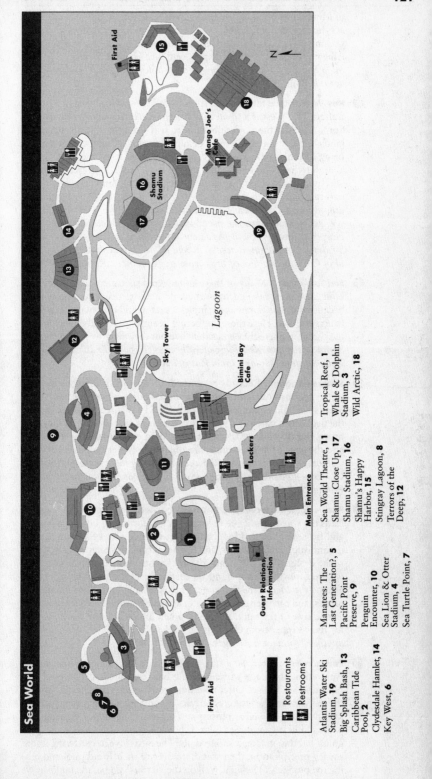

Sea World

First Aid

N

First Aid

Shamu
Stadium

Mango Joe's
Cafe

Lagoon

Sky Tower

Bimini Bay
Cafe

Lockers

Main Entrance

Guest Relations/
Information

First Aid

■ Restaurants

♦♦ Restrooms

Atlantis Water Ski
Stadium, **19**
Big Splash Bash, **13**
Caribbean Tide
Pool, **2**
Clydesdale Hamlet, **14**
Key West, **6**

Manatees: The
Last Generation?, **5**
Pacific Point
Preserve, **9**
Penguin
Encounter, **10**
Sea Lion & Otter
Stadium, **4**
Sea Turtle Point, **7**

Sea World Theatre, **11**
Shamu: Close Up, **17**
Shamu Stadium, **16**
Shamu's Happy
Harbor, **15**
Stingray Lagoon, **8**
Terrors of the
Deep, **12**

Tropical Reef, **1**
Whale & Dolphin
Stadium, **3**
Wild Arctic, **18**

in **Manatee Habitat,** a 300,000-gallon tank with a 126-foot seamless acrylic viewing panel; keep an eye out for mama manatees and their nursing calves. Other animals that share the manatee's world live in **Alligator Habitat,** a marsh display, and **Bird Habitat.** *Strategy: Go during a Shamu show, and not right after a dolphin show. Audience: All ages. Rating:* ★★★

❻ Key West. Made famous by artists from Ernest Hemingway to Jimmy Buffett, Key West is a town that's been re-created here for those who don't have the time or inclination to traverse that long stretch of islands to the home of the most beautiful sunset in America. Of course, being a family park, Sea World doesn't attempt to mimic the drunken abandon that is stereotypically the heart of the Keys' allure. The park, wisely, sticks to what it does best—nature. **Dolphin Cove,** a 2.5-acre naturalist habitat is home to nearly two dozen Atlantic bottlenose dolphins. As a new Sea World feature, special school and tour groups will get to wade into the pseudosurf for an up-close encounter with Flipper's friends. *Crowds: As a new attraction, the crowds can get thick. Strategy: For premium access, attend a late Shamu show and hit Dolphin Cove during one of the earlier performances. Rating:* ★★★★

❼ Sea Turtle Point. Many of these endangered specimens at this new exhibit have been rescued from the wild and are residents at this park because they have permanent injuries that would otherwise keep them from surviving. Here these lumbering beauties peacefully dwell in natural habitat where they can safely live out their lengthy lives. *Crowds: Sporadically crowded, but generally enough space for all to get a good view. Strategy: Go any time. Rating:* ★★★

❽ Stingray Lagoon. Recently revamped, this pool is now twice the size of the previous one and features a special nursery pool for baby rays. Smelts are sold at concession stands for $1 for three, so you can feed the fish. Buy a batch and stroke the stingrays' velvety skin as they flap up to you. It's one of the most rewarding experiences for everyone, and the snack-happy animals are obligingly hungry all day. *Crowds: Can make it hard to get to the animals during busy seasons. Strategy: Go early—the smelt concession stand closes at dark. Audience: All ages. Rating:* ★★★

❾ Pacific Point Preserve. The nonstop chorus of "aarrrps" and "yawps" leads the way to the 2½-acre home for California sea lions and harbor and fur seals. Located just behind Sea Lion & Otter Stadium are the naturalistic beaches, waves, and huge outcroppings of upturned coastal rock, designed to duplicate the rocky northern Pacific coast. The weather, on the other hand, is distinctly Floridian. Viewers stroll around the edge of the surf zone, a favorite hangout for fun-loving pinnipeds, and can peep at underwater activities through the Plexiglas wall at one side of the tank. Buy some smelt and watch the sea lions sing for their supper from close up. *Crowds: Not a problem. Strategy: Go anytime. Audience: All ages. Rating:* ★★★

❿ Penguin Encounter. Scooting around a refrigerated re-creation of Antarctica, at a large white building between Whale & Dolphin Stadium and Sea Lion & Otter Stadium, are 17 species of penguin. Among the residents are the little crested fairy penguin to the large orange-striped king penguin, as well as puffins and murries. The indoor viewing area is the chilliest spot in Sea World, but it's even colder inside the penguins' habitat; in fact, it snows daily. The birds love it, clustering under the icy precipitation, then waddling over to their frigid pool and taking the plunge. A Plexiglas wall on the viewers' side of the tank shows that the penguins are as graceful in the water as they are awkward on land. Sea World's penguin-breeding program has been so successful that it routinely supplies birds to other zoos. *Crowds: Frequently grid-locked, despite a moving walkway tactfully nudging visitors past the glassed-in habitat. Strategy: Go while the dolphin and sea lion shows are on. Audience: All ages. Rating:* ★★

⓫ **Sea World Theatre.** Between Penguin Encounter and the central lagoon, is the screening of *Window to the Sea,* a brief overview of the park's re-search, conservation, and breeding efforts. It highlights the efforts of Sea World's emergency teams that routinely save beached whales, injured manatees, and other water animals. The film starts out like a dreary PBS special but picks up enough to keep even children entertained. Footage of a killer-whale attack increases the gore factor that's so appreciated by some adolescents. If a behind-the-scenes tour seems more interesting now that you've had a look at the park's scientific side, skitter right back to the entrance—groups leave every half hour until 3.

Later in the afternoon, usually starting at 5, the film presentation in Sea World Theatre is replaced with *Water Fantasy,* a delightfully kitschy demonstration of what you can do with a really state-of-the-art sprin-kler system and some colored lights. The stage floor, a sort of giant wading pool, contains 36 revolving nozzles that spray water into foun-tains, waving plumes, and helices, all in time to a sound track of pop tunes. Still, this undemanding show and air-conditioned theater are a pleasant relief after all the intense animal interaction, and the young-sters will love it. *Windows to the Sea duration: 20 min. Crowds: No problem. Audience: All but young children. Rating:* ★★ *Water Fan-tasy duration: 20 min. Crowds: Not a problem. Strategy: Go when you want to sit down and cool off. Audience: All ages. Rating:* ★

⓬ **Terrors of the Deep.** Within this large, innocuous white structure are some thoroughly nasty critters that Sea World attempts to make you love—or at least no longer be repulsed by. Included are dangerous sea creatures such as eels, barracuda, venomous and poisonous fish, and sharks. Each animal is profiled via a video screen and educational posters—"There is little to love about the eel," one says, backing up its point by explaining how a slimy coat of mucus makes so-called blue eels appear green. Then you walk through a series of four Plexiglas tubes—surrounded by tanks—containing the world's largest collection of such animals. Sharks slide just feet overhead and eels slither out from their hiding places. Stop to absorb this neatly contained underwater nightmare in a large viewing theater with benches. Even at its most crowded—and this is another one of Sea World's most popular at-tractions—the walk-through tubes and overhead videos mean that even small children can get an eyeful. *Duration: Plan to spend 40 min. Crowds: Most significant when adjacent sea lion show gets out. Strat-egy: Go during the sea lion shows. Audience: All ages. Rating:* ★★★

⓭ **Big Splash Bash.** Featuring 14 dancers, 2,400 seats, 45 set pieces, an 80-foot curtain of water, a school of ultraviolet fishes, and three 10-foot puppet-worms singing "Hey, Big Spender," this presentation touts big numbers and delivers an earnest but ordinary show. *Duration: Kids get restless during the 30-min performance. Crowds: Not a problem. Strategy: Good when you need a rest. Rating:* ★★

⓮ **Clydesdale Hamlet.** A feature of all Anheuser-Busch parks, the walk-through hamlet houses hulking Clydesdale horses and provides a bu-colic corral for their ponderous romping. A statue of a heroically endowed stallion, which youngsters are encouraged to scramble up on, makes a perfect generic theme-park photo opportunity. The Clydes-dales are so incongruous in this marine-oriented setting that you have to agree with one teenager, who wisecracked, "Look, Dad, surf 'n' turf." *Crowds: Never significant. Strategy: Go anytime. Audience: All ages. Rating:* ★

The **Anheuser-Busch Hospitality Center,** far from espousing the Teutonic overtones of its Busch Gardens cousin, is light and airy, combining cafeteria-style service with a bar serving Anheuser-Busch beverages.

⑮ **Shamu's Happy Harbor.** Little ones love to scramble around this 3-acre outdoor play area with crawlable, climbable, explorable, bounceable, and get-wetable activities, including a four-story net climb. Youngsters go wild for the "ball rooms," which are two tents—one for toddlers and one for grade schoolers—filled with thousands of Styrofoam balls that children can wade through. There's also a tent with an air-mattress floor, which is like a giant trampoline, and pipes to crawl through, and much more. With big sailing ships to explore and water to play in and around, it's different but just as dramatic as Disney-MGM's *Honey, I Blew Up the Kids* Movie Set Adventure Playground. Plus, Shamu's Happy Harbor is much more spacious and airy. Tip: Bring a bathing suit or change of clothes. *Crowds: Often a challenge. Strategy: Don't go first thing in the morning or you'll never drag your child away (but if you go in midafternoon, expect plenty of hubbub). Audience: Toddlers through grade schoolers. No height or age restrictions. Rating:* ★★

⑯ **Shamu Stadium.** Home to Sea World's orca mascot, the stadium is hands-down the most popular feature in the park. Several shows daily showcase the whales' acrobatic, spectator-drenching antics. Fantastic flips and jumps are combined with video footage of orcas in the wild and gently educational factoids about the care and training of the giant mammals. After an unprecedented two births in late 1993—a baby boom by orca standards—Sea World revamped the show to focus on "Baby Shamu." Because killer whales do not reach their full size for four years, the kids are likely to be part of the show for a while. For a funkier version catch **Shamu's Night Magic.** Watching an orca bop to Madonna is not to be missed. Come early to get a seat. Sitting in the first tier will help you become part of the pre-show via a closed-circuit screen. Your head will be roughly the size of a Volkswagen. Snap a picture for a unique souvenir. *Duration: 25 min. Crowds: Sometimes a problem. Strategy: Go 45 min early for the early afternoon show. Close-up encounters through the Plexiglas walls are not to be missed, so trot on down. Audience: All ages. Rating:* ★★★

⑰ **Shamu: Close Up.** For unprecedented up-close-and-personal underwater viewing of the breeding and nursery area, this is the place to be. Follow the signs around to the underground viewing stations for a unique glimpse of favorite whale pastimes, tummy-rubbing and back-scratching. The 1.7-million-gallon outdoor tanks are on the same level as the main pool in Shamu Stadium and have similar Plexiglas walls and viewing setups. Sea World can never predict when its whales will get pregnant, but its breeding program has been astonishingly successful. There's a good chance that you'll see a miniature Shamu cavorting after its mother. *Crowds: Sometimes so large you'll have to edge your way to viewing areas. Strategy: Ideal time is during a Shamu show; otherwise, go early or late, or be patient. Audience: All ages. Rating:* ★★★

⑱ **Wild Arctic.** Walruses hoist themselves onto half-inch-thick ice with a groan as sea lions lazily lounge nearby, blinking their round, long-lashed eyes. A polar bear roars in the distance as a blast of cold air hits your face and you spy salmon skim through clear, frigid water. A wide array of live animals, a simulated trek through the frozen Arctic, a chance to help with a little sub-zero research, Wild Arctic—Sea World's most ambitious project to date—is part ride, part educational adventure, with 28 viewing stations and exhibits. Since opening in the spring of 1995, it's become a Sea World must-see. The atmosphere created in this pseudo-ice station and the interactive, educational elements are the among the best in the park. Watching the hulking polar bears up close is a treat. *Crowds: Expect a wait during peak season. Strategy: Go early, late, or during a Shamu show. Audience: All ages. Rating:* ★★★

NEED A BREAK?

Mango Joe's Café, a speedy, tropical-colored cafeteria between Shamu Stadium and Atlantis Water Ski Stadium, serves fresh fajitas, hefty salads, and delicious key lime pie, and the place has plenty of umbrella-shaded tables, many right on the lake. Some tables have a great view of the show.

⑲ Atlantis Water Ski Stadium. The last attraction on the lagoon circuit presents "Baywatch at Sea World," a themed water-skiing show on Sea World's central lagoon. With the voice of David Hasselhoff in the background, Sea World tries to recreate some of the magic that made the beauties and the beach key elements to the world's most popular television show. This extravaganza is to Cypress Gardens' performance what the Ice Capades is to Olympic figure-skating competitions. The Baywatch connection and the speeding boats are new, but the basic water ski stunts are the same. *Duration: 35 min. Crowds: Not a problem. Strategy: Be warned—the splash factor is significant in the first 10 rows; the terrace at neighboring Mango Joe's Café and the deck at the Bimini Bay Café are alternative viewing spots. Audience: All ages. Rating:* ★★★

Mermaids, Myths & Monsters. Sea World has wisely decided not to compete directly with the can't-be-beat bang of Disney's legendary closing fireworks. Instead, this new show caps off a nautically themed day using lasers, fountains, and a few well-timed pyrotechnics. More a montage than a miniseries, the show has a loose theme allowing you to witness huge, seemingly 3-D versions of King Neptune, and a host of other characters walk, dance, and leap across the water. *Duration: 20 min. Crowds: Room for all. Strategy: Follow the crowd after the last Shamu show, sitting on the second tier to avoid getting wet from wind-borne spray. Audience: All ages, although young children may be a little frightened by the sheer size of the holograph-like images. Rating:* ★★★

Strategies for Your Visit

When to Go

Friday, Saturday, and Sunday are usually busier than the rest of the week, except during weeks that include Easter, July 4, and Dec. 25, when every day is equally busy.

Blitz Tour

The recommended itinerary and show schedule printed on the park map make a lot of sense. There's only one problem: Everyone else will be following them, too. Although there's room for all at the stadiums, the other attractions—especially Penguin Encounter and the Dolphin Community Pool—can get unpleasantly crowded, and there will be lines at Wild Arctic.

Instead, walk straight through the park to the **Sea World Theatre** to see *Windows to the Sea,* both to orient yourself and to get a sense of the larger vision of the park. Then whip into **Penguin Encounter** early, to visit one of the most spectacular attractions at its least crowded. While you are in the area, catch "Big Splash Bash," the park's revamped, Broadway-style song-and-dance show. Stop by Key West; then proceed to **Terrors of the Deep** to spend some quality time with a moray eel. Follow the crowds across the bridge to **Shamu Stadium**; while they're watching the first Shamu show, glimpse Orlando's only polar bears in a chilly tour of the park's newest and most elaborate attraction, **Wild Arctic.** Pick up a cuddly likeness of the northern version of a teddy bear from a nearby concession; then beat the crowds to lunch at Mango Joe's Café. Get a lakeside table and catch the early "Baywatch at Sea World."

While on this side of the lagoon, visit the sea lions at **Pacific Point Preserve,** plus **Manatees: The Last Generation?** and the **Shamu Breeding Pool and Nursery.** That should put you right in place for the afternoon Shamu show.

Wander back across the bridge and treat yourself to some interactive exhibits: There's the **Caribbean Tide Pool,** where fondling the starfish is not to be missed; visit these exhibits during the day because the herring and smelt concessions close at dusk. Keep an eye on the time: You'll want to intersperse these with the shows at the **Whale & Dolphin Stadium** and the **Sea Lion & Otter Stadium.**

By now, you'll be feeling a little frayed. The soothing New Age music at the **Tropical Reef** strikes just the right note, especially once cranky children and their families have left for the day. The "Water Fantasy" is another good option. During high season, stick around for the closing laser and fireworks show, entitled "Mermaids, Myths & Monsters," and watch King Neptune walk on water and dance across the central Florida sky.

On Rainy Days

Although Sea World gives the impression of open-air roominess, almost a third of the attractions are actually indoors, and all the others are shielded from the elements by canopies, cantilevered roofs, or tautly stretched tarpaulins. Pick up a signature poncho—it's clear, with a black-and-white orca on the back—at one of the ubiquitous concession stands, and dive right in.

Other Tips

- Try to arrive early for Shamu shows, which generally fill to capacity on even the slowest days. They're not kidding about that splash zone, either. If you simply must experience an orcan belly flop, pack a set of dry clothes, especially in chilly weather.

- When the park hours are extended, wait until midafternoon to arrive. Then you can do most of your touring during the less steamy parts of the day and have dinner in the park.

- You may want to budget ahead for food for the animals—a major part of the close-up Sea World charm. A small carton of fish is usually $2.

- Set up a specific rendezvous time and location at the start of your visit in case you and your companions get separated.

Shopping

There are some hard-hearted souls who can pass up a plush Shamu, but they are few and far between. These are available all over the park. Also extremely cuddly are the stuffed manatees sold at **Manatee Cove,** near the manatee exhibit; proceeds from the toys go to benefit a manatee preservation organization. The **Friends of the Wild** shop near Penguin Encounter carries various items, including tropical fish earrings and hair ornaments. If you've left the park before realizing that your Aunt Betsy simply must have a Shamu slicker, visit the shop just outside the entrance, where you can also pick up a variey of knick-knacks featuring the Budweiser label.

Sea World A to Z

Admission

Regular one-day tickets cost $37.95 for adults, $31.80 for children 3–9, including tax. Two-day tickets, which must be used within one week, are available. Discounted and multi-park single-day tickets to Cypress Gardens and Busch Gardens may be purchased at the ticket booth at the exit. AAA members who present their membership card receive a 10% discount. And if you're also visiting Universal Studios and Wet 'n Wild, buy the multi-day, multi-park Value Pass ($89.95 plus tax; $72.95 plus tax for kids 3–9).

Baby Care

There are **diaper-changing tables** in or near most women's rest rooms, and in the men's rest room at the front entrance, near Shamu's Emporium. You can buy **diapers** at machines located in all changing areas and at Shamu's Emporium. A special area for **nursing** is alongside the women's rest room at Friends of the Wild gift shop, equidistant from Sea World Theater, Penguin Encounter, and Sea Lion and Otter Stadium. You will find **stroller rentals** at the Information Center ($5 for single, $10 for double; no deposit). However, no formula or baby food is sold on the premises; the nearest sources are a five-minute drive away at Gooding's Supermarket on International Drive, Publix supermarket and Eckerd's drugs on Central Florida Parkway, and Kmart on Turkey Lake Road.

Cameras and Film

Disposable Kodak Funsaver cameras are for sale on the premises, as are film and blank videotapes. There were neither camera nor camcorder rentals nor camera repairs on the premises at press time.

Dining

In addition to burgers, barbecue, and the usual burnt offerings sold at restaurants and concessions throughout the park, Sea World has two dandy places for lunch: **Mango Joe's Café** and **Bimini Bay Café,** from which you have a close-up view of the frenetic activity on the floats where the water-ski show stunts are set up.

Pickings are slim for dinner. Mango Joe's closes down, alas, leaving a meager choice of barbecued chicken and ribs at **Buccaneer Smokehouse** and sandwiches and salads at **Anheuser-Busch Hospitality Center.**

LUAU

Alternatively, you can opt for entertainment in the form of the **"Aloha!" Polynesian Luau Dinner and Show** at Bimini Bay Café. In an Anheuser-Busch family version of *Blue Hawaii,* scantily clad dancers undulate across the floor, bearing lei-draped platters of roast pig, mahimahi, piña coladas, and hula pie. Reservations are required for this two-hour, culinary island voyage and may be made the same day either at the luau reservations counter in the information center at the entrance or by telephone (☎ 407/363–2195 or 800/227–8048). The cost is $27.95 adults, $18.95 children 8–12, $9.95 children 3–7, including one cocktail and all nonalcoholic drinks. Although the restaurant is inside the park, you do not have to pay park admission to attend only the feast.

For Travelers with Disabilities

ATTRACTIONS

Because many of the shows are in theaters and stadiums, guests using wheelchairs will have an easy day at Sea World. With reserved seating areas, the **Nautilus Showplace, Sea Lion & Otter Stadium, Sea World Theatre, Shamu Stadium,** and **Whale & Dolphin Stadium** are completely accessible, though entry usually requires an uphill climb along sloping ramps. The stadium shows usually fill to capacity, so plan to arrive 30–45 minutes before each show, or 45–60 minutes in peak seasons. At Shamu Stadium, the reserved seating area is inside the splash zone, so if you don't want to get soaking wet, get a host or hostess to recommend another place to sit. There is entertainment value in all of the theater and stadium shows for both hearing-impaired and visually impaired guests with a single exception: Performances in the Nautilus Showplace may be unrewarding for guests with visual impairments.

Penguin Encounter, Terrors of the Deep, and **Tropical Reef** are all wheelchair accessible. To ride the moving-sidewalk viewing areas in Penguin Encounter and Terrors of the Deep, guests must transfer to a standard wheelchair, available in the boarding area, if they do not already use one. Tropical Reef and Penguin Encounter have minimal entertainment value for guests with visual impairments. All will be enjoyable for guests with hearing impairments.

The **Anheuser-Busch Hospitality Center** is completely accessible. **Shamu's Happy Harbor** has some activities that are accessible to children using wheelchairs and anyone else who wants to climb, crawl, or slide.

The **"Aloha!" luau** is completely accessible.

SERVICES
There are **TTYs for outgoing calls** at Bimini Bay Café, across from Whale & Dolphin Stadium.

SHOPS AND RESTAURANTS
Restaurants are accessible, but drinking straws are not provided here; this is out of concern for the safety of the animals. Bring your own. Shops are level, but many are so packed with merchandise that maneuvering in a wheelchair can be a challenge.

WHEELCHAIR RENTALS
Both standard and electric wheelchairs are available at Sea World ($5 and $25 daily with driver's license).

First Aid
First Aid Centers are behind Stingray Lagoon and near Shamu's Happy Harbor. Registered nurses are on duty.

Getting There
Sea World is just off the intersection of I–4 and the Bee Line Expressway, 10 minutes south of downtown Orlando and 15 minutes from Orlando International Airport. Of all the central Florida theme parks, it's the easiest to find. Signs direct you to Exit 28 off I–4 and guide you the short distance to the parking lot.

Guided Tours
Even if you already know the answer to the frequently asked question, "Do you paint Shamu?," it's worth spending the nominal extra fee to sign up for the 90-minute behind-the-scenes guided tours—**"Backstage Explorations"** or **"Animal Lover's Adventure"**—or the 45-minute **"Animal Training Discoveries,"** in which Sea World trainers discuss animal behavior and training techniques ($5.95 adults, $4.95 children 3–9). Tours leave every 30 minutes until 3. Register at the guided tour center to the left of the Guest Relations/Information Center at the park entrance. Sign-language interpreters can be provided with advance notice.

Hours

Sea World is open daily 9–7; during the summer and on holidays, the park may stay open as late as 10.

Lockers

They're inside the park entrance and to the right, next to Shamu's Emporium. The cost is $1.

Lost and Found

Go to the Information Center to reclaim your misplaced items or to drop off somebody else's.

Lost Children and Adults

Lost parents and lost children should rendezvous at the Information Center just inside the park entrance. All employees who see lost-looking children have been trained to take them to the Information Center. A park-wide paging system helps reunite guests.

Money

Foreign currency can be exchanged at the Special Services Window at the Main Gate (daily 10–3). An ATM linked to various bank and credit-card networks is at the exit gate.

Package Pickup

When you make purchases anywhere in the park, your clerk can send them to Package Pickup, in Shamu's Emporium, on request. Allow an hour between making your purchase and your departure.

Parking

Parking costs $5 per car, $7 per RV or camper.

Visitor Information

Contact Sea World (✉ 7007 Sea World Dr., Orlando 32821, ☎ 407/351–3600).

You're given a computer-generated map at the park entrance. An especially neat and considerate touch is the recommended show schedule, personalized according to your arrival time, which is printed out on it. In the park, a large board at the entrance lists all show times.

Inside the park, the main information center is **Guest Relations,** near the park entrance.

BUSCH GARDENS

When Anheuser-Busch opened a small hospitality center adjacent to its Tampa brewery in 1959, the company couldn't foresee the day that a couple of somnolent koalas and a ride called Kumba would be more of a draw than a draught would be. Busch Gardens, as the tropical biergarten was called, was seen as a useful place to stash the Busch family's collection of exotic animals and birds while tending to the real business: making and selling beer.

But 12 years later, the call of the wild proved so strong that Anheuser-Busch began to develop Busch Gardens into a multifaceted, Africa-themed park and zoo, with the brewery increasingly relegated to a sideshow. Rising profits demanded the creation of a separate corporate umbrella, and as a profit center spun off from the parent company, Busch Entertainment Corporation (BEC) was endowed with the mandate to expand and multiply in the field of leisure-time entertainment. Now owners of Busch Gardens; The Old Country in Williamsburg, Virginia; Adventure Island in Tampa; Sesame Place in Langhorne, Pennsylvania; the Sea World parks in Orlando, San Antonio, Aurora (Ohio) and San Diego; and Cypress Gardens in Winter Haven, BEC has become the second-largest theme park owner-operator in the world, right behind the Walt Disney Company.

There is little of the crowd and bustle of the Disney parks here. The animal displays and lush landscaping help to create a softer mood. The personnel are equally casual; they seem less stiff and programmed than some of the clean-shaven assembly-line workers at the home of the Mouse. Their relaxed attitude can seem disrespectful or charming, depending on your point of view. Another odd note is that some of the attractions, such as the Show Jumping Hall of Fame and the Questor flight simulator, have nothing to do with the African theme that led Busch Gardens to be dubbed "The Dark Continent"—a name later dropped in the interest of political correctness; in fact, they seem like a theme park version of monkey-see, monkey-do.

But that's merely a case of smudged icing on what's still a very satis-fying cake. A member of the American Association of Zoological Parks and Aquariums, Busch Gardens ranks among the top four zoos in the United States. More than 3,400 birds, mammals, and reptiles are spread out on its 335 acres; the aviary houses some 600 rare and ex-otic birds, and about 500 African big-game animals roam uncaged on the 60-acre Serengeti Plain. Busch Gardens participates in the Species Survival Program, lending animals to other zoos for breeding as well as recording tremendous success with breeding endangered animals on the premises. Top of the program's wish list is to host a pair of rare Chinese pandas.

The park itself is divided into nine areas linked to the common theme of turn-of-the-century Africa, plus the brewery. Animals are exhibited wherever possible—on islands, near concession stands, in spacious cages in the middle of a maze of lines, and in displays and shows in which they are the stars. But there's more than enough for the non–an-imal lover to do, what with numerous roller coasters and other gut-wrenching rides—namely the Kumba, water attractions, a Skyride, and shops galore. And there's always the brewery, whose self-guided tour is rarely crowded—a nice, if ironic, touch, considering it is the park's raison d'être.

Busch Gardens' 10 different areas plus brewery are laid out in two con-centric circles with an occasional appendage. The center is Timbuktu, an open-air carnival and bazaar. The main entrance is through Mo-rocco; going counterclockwise along the winding paths, you'll en-counter **Egypt, Myombe Reserve, Nairobi, the Serengeti Plain, the Congo, Stanleyville, Bird Gardens,** and the **Brewery,** which abuts Mo-rocco. A sharp elbow to the right from Myombe Reserve and Nairobi is the **Crown Colony.** Each of the areas is distinguished by its own dis-tinctive architectural styles as well as regional music pumped through carefully camouflaged loudspeakers.

Egypt

The most notable attraction in this section of the park is the awesome **Montu.** Since its opening in 1996, the ride that snakes like an asp over 4,000 feet of track dominates everything else. This is not to say, how-ever, that the shops and the tour through a replica of the tomb of King Tutankhamen (Tut to his friends) aren't interesting—they are. But the real reason visitors cross the border from Busch Garden's version of Morroco is the ride.

A three-minute trip, a G-force of 3.85, and speeds in excess of 60 miles per hour add up to a gut-wrenching, adrenaline-pumping thrill ride that is not for the faint hearted. Like its cousin **Kumba,** the mere sound and the sheer size of **Montu** is intimidating. But take the chance. *Crowds: Lines can get long on busy days. Strategy: Go early in the morning or late in the day. Most of the time, settle in for a wait that will be worth it. Rating:* ★★★★

Morocco

The park's Main Entrance leads you through the gates of the tiled and turreted Moroccan fort, which houses the park administrative offices, and into a land of swirling colors and skirling music. Morocco itself contains two eateries—the Zagora Café and the Boujad Bakery—a resident snake charmer, the **Moroccan Palace Theater,** and numerous souvenir stands, arranged in a replica of an Arabic souk (open-air marketplace). A recent addition in **Tangiers Theatre** is "Harris & Co.," the filming of a local television talk-variety show that invites park patrons to be audience members.

It's hard not to fall into the shekel-flinging mode; Middle Eastern music wails through the speakers, brightly colored wool tassels droop overhead, brass urns glimmer, bangles shimmer, veils waft in the wind, and mouthwatering smells issue from the Boujad Bakery. Follow the main drag past the **Sultan's Tent,** a raised platform hung with multicolored striped curtains, where a snake charmer snuggles up to a python and wraps it around her arms, waist, and neck. Show schedules are posted next to the Sultan's Tent. The snake charmer's main audience is a group of indifferent alligators, who loll about in a pond to the right of the Sultan's Tent. No hungry audience this: The alligators are so well fed and lazy that they ignore the plump koi fish that share their pond.

Numbers in the margin correspond to points of interest on the Busch Gardens map.

❶ Moroccan Palace Theater. When you step into the blue-tiled, iron-fretted theater, situated catercorner to the alligators, you enter the cool comfort of an ice rink. An African-inspired park featuring an ice show? Go figure. It sounds really weird but works really well. Ten skaters and two singers join together to create these frigid follies in a chorus line production backed by clips from Hollywood's golden age. You have to see it to understand the presence of the 17-foot inflatable dinosaur. This is one of the most unique shows in the whole theme-park realm and it offers a rare chance to see close up some Olympic-quality spins and jumps. *Duration: 30–40 min. Crowd: Sizable, but there's always enough room. Strategy: Shows four times daily; check schedules posted outside. Go when you want to sit down and cool off. Audience: All ages. Rating:* ★★★★

NEED A BREAK? | Morocco's **Zagora Café** dishes out basic burgers, fajitas, and turkey sandwiches in an enormous open-air cafeteria. **Boujad Bakery** is the place for a cup of cappuccino and a *churro* (Mexican deep-fried sweet dough liberally dusted with confectioner's sugar). Breakfast is also available.

Crown Colony

The Crown Colony is a transportation and hospitality center with two distinctly non-African attractions that couldn't be accommodated elsewhere: the home of BEC's signature Clydesdale horses—a staple at every BEC park—and the requisite flight simulator. The **Monorail** has only one station, and this is it. The lines snake past airy cages containing

132

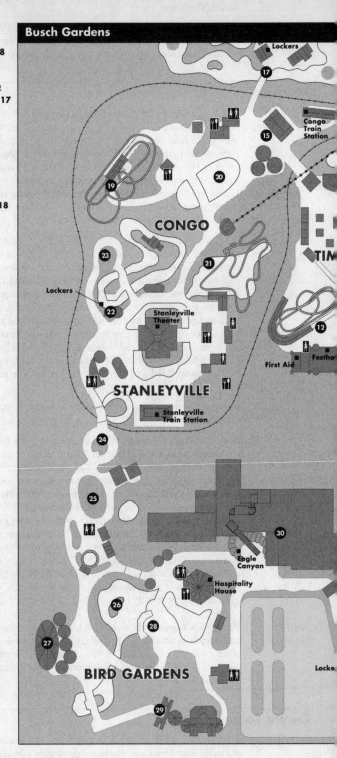

Busch Gardens

SERENGETI
PLAIN

16

14

13

11

BUKTU

10

Kenya
Kanteen

9

7
8

Elephant
Wash

NAIROBI

Nairobi
Train
Station

6

CROWN
COLONY

Colony
Club

MYOMBE
RESERVE

5

The Great Ape
Domain

Skyride
and Monorail
Station

Sultan's
Tent

EGYPT

Montu

2

3

Stroller/
Wheelchair Rental

Automatic
Teller

1

MOROCCO

Guest
Relations

Main
Entrance

Marrakesh
Theater

KEY

Restaurants

Restrooms

Rail Line

Skyride

Monorail

Roller Coaster

N

curious lemurs, which set the mood for the ride itself: a journey around the adjacent Serengeti Plain. The station is the Crown Colony terminus for a seven-minute **Skyride** above the Serengeti and through Timbuktu; except in bad weather, when it sometimes closes, it's a useful shortcut to the Congo, its other terminus.

② **Clydesdale Hamlet.** This attraction presents the usual batch of oversize beasts galumphing around a corral and stables; a particularly patient one is periodically led out for photographs.

③ **Questor.** Keeping pace with the other theme parks, this is Busch Gardens' flight simulator, whose gimmick theme is that you are helping a mad scientist search for a magic crystal, a search that takes you to the center of the earth. As flight simulators go, the shake-up is pretty good but no competition for Disney-MGM's Star Tours or Universal's Back to the Future and certainly not worth what can be a long wait. But if the line is manageable, then give it a whirl. *Duration: 5 min. Crowds: Up to 1½ hr on crowded days. Strategy: In summer and holiday periods, go early or late. Audience: Older children and adults. Must be 42" to ride. Rating:* ★★

| NEED A BREAK? | The **Colony Club,** done up to resemble a veddy British eatery from the good old *Out of Africa* days with portraits of top-hatted sahibs, used polo mallets, and nicely faded Oriental carpets, serves sandwiches, salad platters, and pizza in a downstairs, counter-service restaurant. There's full service upstairs. |

Serengeti Plain ④

The 80-acre, open-air zoo features about 500 animals running free in a re-creation of their natural habitats—all of which look remarkably similar to Florida pastureland. You'll see zebras, camels, impalas, giraffes, lions, gazelles, Cape buffalo, and kudus (a heftier impala), among other species. Don't be dismayed if it's raining; in fact, hasten right over to the Monorail to catch sight of all the animals instinctively turning their heads up into the rain. Though the Trans-Veldt Railroad skirts the eastern edge of the Serengeti, there are basically two ways to explore it: the **Skyride** and the **Monorail.** The Skyride takes you 49 feet above the Serengeti on a 1.1-mile one-way ride to the Congo; it gives you a great overview but not much detail. The Monorail is a classic Busch Gardens' experience; unlike Disney's monorail, it's suspended from an overhead rail and trundles around the veldt at eye level to a zebra. A guide tells you a little about the animals as you edge along the track. If you believe the hype about seeing the animals in their natural environments, the omnipresent fence lines will be a shock. Busch Gardens could take some tips from sister-park Sea World about displaying animals. *Duration: Monorail 20 min, Skyride 7 min. Monorails leave every 5 min; Skyrides operate continuously. Crowds: You can always walk right on. Strategy: Go anytime. Audience: All ages. Rating:* ★★★

Myombe Reserve: The Great Ape Domain ⑤

Easily overlooked is this reserve, thanks to superbly luxuriant rainforest landscaping and a modest entrance opposite the Moroccan Palace Theater. Completed in 1992, it's one of the park's newer and much-heralded animal attractions. Some 3 acres have been lovingly landscaped into a home for an extended family of chimpanzees—formerly of Chimp Island in the Serengeti—and another family of Western lowland gorillas whose scientific name is, according to an educational plaque, Gorilla gorilla gorilla. There's always a well-informed guide on hand to explain that gorillas rest 40 percent of the day and feed another 30 percent, or to point out the almost infinitesimal differences and complicated relationships between Sally, Smokey, and Samantha. Check out the Aldabra tortoises, which can weigh more than 500 pounds and live to be 100. *Crowds: Not significant. Strategy: Visit either first thing in the morning or late in the afternoon; both are close to feeding time, when both apes and chimps are more active. Audience: All ages. Rating:* ★★★

Nairobi

Myombe's rain-forested path leads you to Nairobi, a collection of buildings containing the animal nursery, the petting zoo, the Show Jumping Hall of Fame, the elephant display, and the Nairobi train station—a gingerbread clapboard structure straight out of *Out of Africa*.

❻ Animal Nursery. Within this long, low building are glass cages holding convalescing animals wrapped in nests of blankets; through the glass on the other side of the cages, you can see the laboratories and food preparation. Animals are fed at various times, so there's usually something going on.

❼ Petting Zoo. Nubian and African pygmy goats, Barbados black-bellied sheep, ducks, rabbits, turtles, roosters, and hens are all gathered in this zoo. Visitors are allowed to feed only the goats and sheep, both of which are rotated throughout the day to keep them from being overfed; for the others, food is brought out on a tray for the twice-daily handout. *Crowds: Never significant. Strategy: Go anytime. Audience: All ages. Rating:* ★

❽ Show Jumping Hall of Fame. Although it has nothing to do with Africa, this attraction has everything to do with colonialism and family ties. Elizabeth Busch, a family member and a horse jumping fanatic, needed a place to house her collection of antique riding saddles, horseshoes, ribbons, and portraits of famous horses, and this minuscule corner was found, right next to the reptiles. *Crowds: Not a problem. Strategy: Go anytime. Audience: Adults. Rating:* ★

❾ Elephant Display. The big attraction in Nairobi is the building housing 22 Asian elephants; the most attractive part of the display is their swimming pool, in which elephant parents and children snort, swim, and clean off before getting dusty again. Every couple of hours, some of the elephants troop out to the Elephant Wash area next to the Kenya Kanteen, where a schedule is posted and where they take a garden hose and give each other showers while a keeper explains elephant habits. *Crowds: Can be significant for the Elephant Wash, but you can usually see. Strategy: Go anytime. Audience: All ages. Rating:* ★★★

The Kenya Kanteen is a good place to watch out for the **Trans-Veldt Railroad,** an authentic reproduction of an East African steam locomotive with, as the tour guide points out, an American cowcatcher for those pesky impala—none of which actually can come near the tracks. The train chugs around the Serengeti and then circumnavigates the park in a 2½-mile journey, making stops near the Congo River Rapids and Stanleyville—about 10 minutes to the Congo Train Station and another 10 minutes to Stanleyville. It's a dandy way to see the Serengeti. *Duration: 30 min. Crowds: Steady, but you almost always find a seat. Strategy: It comes only every 30 min, so watch the mother elephants dunking the little ones in the elephant pool until you hear the whistle, then dash for the station. Audience: All ages. Rating:* ★★

Timbuktu

The entrance to Timbuktu is a blindingly white mud fort, inside which is a claustrophobic walled area housing at least three rides that are guaranteed to make you lose your lunch; a video arcade; the Festhaus, an incongruous little piece of Germany, with dirndled maidens and lederhosen-clad youth dancing around a beer-swilling, sausage-chomping crowd; numerous games of chance; the Crazy Camel carousel; kiddie rides; and the Dolphin Theater.

⑩ Sandstorm. "The number-one ride for making guests throw up," is how a Busch Gardens staffer eloquently describes this attraction. It doesn't look all that menacing, but the constant rotation of both your seat and the arm to which it's attached should prove the point. *Duration: 2½ min. Crowds: Not a problem. Strategy: Go anytime. Audience: Older children, teens, adults. Rating:* ★★

⑪ ⑫ Phoenix and **Scorpion.** Not for the faint of heart is the **Phoenix,** whose crescent swings back and forth, higher and higher until it swoops sickeningly over the top. The **Scorpion,** 1,805 feet of steel roller coaster twisted into a gigantic hoop with a 65-foot drop, reaches a maximum speed of 50 mph. *Duration: Phoenix 2 min, Scorpion 2 min. Crowds: Lines can build at midday in busy periods. Strategy: Go early or late. Audience: Older children, teens, adults. No riders under 48" on Scorpion. Rating:* ★★

⑬ Crazy Camel. Among the tamer diversions in Timbuktu is this delightful carousel with brightly painted camels dancing alongside the traditional horses. Although not for thrill-seekers, other very enjoyable attractions here include carnival-type games of chance from basketball to fishing with a magnet and children's rides, as well as a pint-size version of the Phoenix. For similar rides for little ones, check out **Dwarf Village,** outside Stanleyville.

⑭ Dolphin Theater. Although it's modeled after Sea World's theater, this dolphin tank is smaller and lacks the Plexiglas sides that let you peer at the underwater activities during the show. But the two-dolphin show here is similarly delightful, and, in fact, the dolphins and trainers are borrowed from Busch Gardens' fishy cousin. Mick and Bud more than earn their 35 pounds of raw fish, jumping and waving their flippers and thoroughly enchanting everyone, including the one lucky child chosen to come up and play with them. If your child is between 5 and 8, outgoing, and not scared by dolphins, arrive 15 minutes early and ask an usher if your child can be picked for the show. He or she will, however, be backstage learning the proper hand signals during a dandy section of the show when the trainer plays in the water with the dolphins. *Duration: 20 min. Crowds: Never a problem. Strategy: Go in the middle of the day, when the other animals in the park are snoozing. Audience: All ages. Rating:* ★★★

Congo and Stanleyville

The entrance to the Congo and adjacent Stanleyville is practically indistinguishable from the Congo. Unlike the open, dusty plains of the Serengeti and Nairobi, the section is delightfully shaded by lush plantings and lofty, leafy trees, under whose branches nestle African fetish statues and piles of expedition-supply boxes for that "Dr. Livingstone, I presume" touch. Hysterical shrieks from the area's several thrill rides remind you that the visitors, if not the natives, are perpetually restless.

⑮ Ubanga-Banga Bumper Cars. Aptly named, this popular attraction has a carnival allure, and young kids, along with big kids who have never grown up, love them. *Duration: About 4 min. Crowds: Never signif-icant enough to cause a wait except in midafternoons during busy pe-riods. Strategy: Go anytime—and if there's a line, don't bother to wait. Audience: Older children, teens, adults. Rating:* ★★

16 **Kumba.** The nearly 4,000 feet of twisting turquoise steel supports cars going up to 60 mph through three, first-of-a-kind coaster maneuvers: a "diving loop" that plunges you from 110 feet into a loop; a camel-back, with a 360° spiral and three seconds of weightlessness; and the world's largest loop, with a height of 108 feet. That's in addition to spirals, cobra rolls, and a corkscrew ride in the dark. Kumba offers a surprisingly smooth ride without the neck-wrenching of most similar efforts. Catch a replay of your screaming face on three TV monitors near the exit. *Duration: 3 min. Crowds: Can mean long lines. Strat-egy: Go as soon as the park opens. Audience: Older children, teens, adults. No riders under 52". Rating:* ★★★

17 **Congo River Rapids.** Visitors who love water rides consider this one of the all-time best. The watery version of bumpers cars, this ride takes 12 people in each inner tube-like raft. As you go bumping and bucketing through nearly ¼ mile of rapids and waterfalls and through a dark cave, be sure your camera is wrapped in a waterproof bag—and remember to smile for the spectators taking pictures from the bridge. *Duration: 5 min. Crowds: There's usually a line. Strategy: Go early to avoid waits and have the best time. Audience: Older children, teens, adults. Rating:* ★★★

18 **19** **Monstrous Mamba** and **Python.** This octopus ride and steel roller coaster are among the big hits, the latter of which has 1,250 feet of track and hurls passengers through two hoops at 50 mph. *Duration: Monstrous Mamba, 70 sec, Python, 70 sec. Crowds: Significant only in busy seasons. Strategy: Go early or late in holiday periods. Audi-ence: Older children, teens, adults. No riders under 47" on Mamba, must be 39" and accompanied by adult on the Python. Rating:* ★★

20 **Claw Island.** Somehow all the hoopla at the park doesn't seem to bother the somnolent Bengal tigers. If you want to see them when they're most active, come in the early morning or the late afternoon. Some par-ticularly pleasant shady benches overlook the island and are a nice place to recuperate before hitting the next rides.

21 **22** **Stanley Falls Log Flume Ride** and **Tanganyika Tidal Wave.** The 40-foot and 55-foot drops, respectively, into splash pools, are among the park's most popular rides, due as much to the certainty of getting wet as to their gut-turning falls. In fact, the tidal wave offers two possibilities for dunking: the ride itself and, for those who are chicken, the view-ing bridge at the bottom of the drop, where a recording of Tchaikovsky's *1812 Overture* heralds the next wave. A sign posted nearby politely reads, "This bridge is part of a water attraction. You will get soaked. Thank you." Either huddle behind the Plexiglas shelter on the bridge or skitter off—fast. *Duration: Stanley Falls, 3½ min, Tanganyika Tidal Wave, 6 min. Crowds: Significant, with lines even on average days. Strat-egy: Ride early in the morning or in the evening. Audience: Older chil-dren, teens, adults. Rating:* ★★★

23 **Orchid Canyon.** This lovely, 100-yard walk winds through 200-odd, cascading orchids and bromeliads native to South Africa, the Philip-pines, and South America—it's a welcome respite from the sensory over-load you'll get in the rest of the park. Meanwhile, placidly ignoring riders' screeches and distant pleas of "Aw, c'mon, Melissa, you need to go on this ride," lemurs, rhinoceroses, eland, and orangutans peace-fully snooze away in spacious enclosures naturalized with rocks, trees, and, in the case of the orangutans, gymnastic equipment. A couple of thatched huts scattered throughout the Congo and Stanleyville contain snakes in wire boxes and inquisitive parrots perched in cages. Keepers are on hand to explain their behavior and hold them for you to stroke.

Stanleyville is also home to the **Stanleyville Theater,** where youngsters are exposed the Big Band era, music that will sound familiar to the young at heart. **Stanleyville Bazaar** and **Air Africa,** something like a Moroccan souk, presents craftspeople fashioning their wares outside. Some interesting handcrafted wares are available for sale.

NEED A
BREAK?

The **Stanleyville Smokehouse** cafeteria serves slow-cooked chicken, beef, and ribs with corn on the cob and all the trimmings; the **Bazaar** Café offers hearty barbecued beef sandwiches. Between the two, the Stanleyville air is redolent of barbecue.

When in Stanleyville you can move on by catching the train at the **Stanleyville Train Station**—a twin of Nairobi's station—located behind the **Stanleyville Theater** and near the orangutans' island. Or follow the path past the orangutans, onto the bridge over the train tracks, and down to Bird Gardens.

Bird Gardens

Bird Gardens is home to Land of Dragons, the koala habitat, and 1,883 exotic birds representing 218 species, including one of the largest managed flocks of Caribbean flamingos—fed beta-carotene supplements to maintain their bright coral color.

㉔ Parrots of the Pacific. Situated just over the ramp from Stanleyville is where multicolored parrots, macaws, and cockatoos are arranged in a circle, in cages, beneath two sprawling, live oaks. A staffer is usually on hand to answer questions.

㉕ Land of the Dragons. Busch Gardens replaced the old Dwarf Village with this colorful, elaborate attraction. In the center is a three-story treehouse filled with rope climbs and bouncing walkways. Adults tromp along with the kids in one of the best children's areas of any theme park. Loudspeakers merrily belt out happy kiddie songs, lending a cheerful air to the zone. Several times daily, conservation specialists tell animal stories, sometimes with live animals as props. The youngsters' seats: fake toadstools. *Crowds: Seldom a problem. Strategy: Wait until later in the day, or you may never get your youngsters away; or go at midday for a respite from the heat. Audience: Young children. Rating:* ★★★★

㉖ Flamingo Island. The dollar value on the flock of Caribbean flamingos nesting here is worth well over $1 million. The flamingos are part of a national breeding program, so the number of birds in the flock is constantly changing. *Crowds: Not a problem. Strategy: Go early or late to see birds at their most active. Audience: All ages. Rating:* ★★

㉗ Aviary. Situated to the right of Flamingo Island, is a lushly landscaped walk-through cage in which 194 species flutter freely among the trees and stalk along the ground. *Crowds: Not a problem. Strategy: Go early or late to see birds at their most active. Audience: All ages. Rating:* ★★

㉘ Bird Show Theater. An open amphitheater just behind Flamingo Island displays macaws, condors, and eagles performing natural behaviors; bird enthusiasts rate it one of the best shows anywhere. You can have your photo taken with one of the squawking stars at the adjacent pos-ing area just after each show. *Duration: 30 min. Crowds: Sometimes significant during holiday periods. Strategy: Arrive 15 min before show time in busy seasons. Audience: All ages. Rating:* ★★

㉙ Koala House. A very elaborate display with Chinese motifs down the boardwalk past the aviary once housed a pair of pandas; now it's home to a breeding group of four—one male and three females. You can usually spot some joeys (baby koalas), although a look at the impassive parents makes it hard to imagine that any two of them ever get worked up enough to procreate. For close-up viewing by visitors, the exhibit offers a people-mover and an elevated observation gallery. Also, pay a few quarters for pellets to feed the huge, decorative fish in the adjoining pool. They beg. Really. *Crowds: Not a problem. Strategy: Go in late afternoon to see the animals at their most active. Audience: All ages. Rating:* ★

Brewery ㉚

Take the self-guided walk through a working brewery that produces 2.7 million barrels of Budweiser annually. You'll occasionally spot the big tanker cars on the freight trains that rumble out of the park bearing beer for a thirsty nation. Using automatic video and audio displays, educational placards, and labels, the tour covers every step of the process, from choosing the hops to canning the product. You don't have to be a beer fanatic to enjoy yourself, but people with a special interest in the inception of Bud Light do tend to linger. Some people gallop along, peering from the glassed-in walkways at the aging vats and bottling lines. But the printed and audio displays provide abundant beer trivia, from George Washington's favorite recipe to the secret behind how the aluminum tabs get put on top of flip-top cans. *Duration: Allot around 20 min. Crowds: Never a problem. Audience: Older children and adults. Rating:* ★★

NEED A BREAK?
You won't be able to snap a cold one at the Brewery, but the **Hospitality House** right outside provides whistle-wetting wuffo on tap. After a full day at Busch Gardens, you'll need it. You can also order a delicious hero sandwich, called a Tampa Sandwich Platter. Even the outdoor setting is pleasant, with Dr. Dave's Trio and their ragtime renditions.

Strategies for Your Visit

When to Go

Mondays are least crowded in summer, and other times when local schools are out; weekdays are the most tranquil the rest of the year.

Blitz Tour

Figuring out the most efficient way of visiting Busch Gardens is only lightly less complicated than planning a safari. Pick up a list of shows at the entrance gate and loosely schedule your day around them; they are welcome sit-down breaks in a full day on your feet and some are even air-conditioned. Must-sees are the **dolphin show,** the **bird show,** the **elephant wash,** and the **Hollywood Live on Ice** in the Moroccan Palace Theater. Roller coaster enthusiasts should also be sure to ride the **Kumba,** one of the best roller coasters around; and the **Montu,** the largest, inverted steel roller coaster in the world.

Make **Myombe Reserve** your first stop. Then hop on the **Trans-Veldt Railroad** at Nairobi Station and take it all around the park to Stanleyville. People on foot get to Stanleyville and the Congo in the afternoon; by visiting in the morning, you'll beat the lines on the rides—including the

Stanley Falls Log Flume, the **Kumba,** and the **Tanganyika Tidal Wave**—and the animals will be more lively. Work your way north through the Congo to the **Congo River Rapids**—a refreshing splash at midday—and then catch the show at **Dolphin Theater.**

Busch Gardens is laid out so that the crowds tend to shuffle counterclockwise. Now go against the flow—through Timbuktu and back to Nairobi—to visit the **Elephant Wash,** et al. You're close enough to the **Moroccan Palace Theater** to make an afternoon show of **Hollywood Live on Ice** or to wile away the time before the next one with a **Monorail** ride. If the line's not too long, try **Questor;** otherwise, save it until the end of the day.

Wander back through Morocco, past the brewery, and to the **Bird Gardens.** Time your visit for the last bird show; remember that the brewery tour is self-guided, so you can do that anytime.

Walk back up to Stanleyville and consider your late-afternoon options: You can go on the tidal wave again, see the rare white Bengal tigers get frisky at Congo's **Claw Island,** roar with Kumba; then ride the **Skyride** back to Nairobi. You'll be dropped off right opposite Questor. Now is the time to tour Egypt, and zoom on the roller coaster to end all roller coasters, **Montu.** Take a well-deserved rest with a ride on the train, or take the train for a late-afternoon tour of the **Serengeti.** This is a worthwhile trip, although this often seems to be the time of day when the kudus get randy and ardently embrace other kudus. If you end up at Nairobi, have a restorative drink on the balcony of the **Colony Club,** where Budweiser, Bud Light, and O'Doul's are on tap; red and white wine and soft drinks are also available. Then hit the Moroccan souk on your way out.

On Rainy Days
The Skyride may close temporarily because of lightning or high winds, but otherwise it's business-as-usual in the park.

Other Tips
- Keep in mind that the animals nap through most of the day, and you'll see the most action first thing in the morning and in the late afternoon.

- Unlike most central Florida parks, Busch offers national fast-food restaurants literally across the street. Readmission is allowed, so you can easily duck out for a burger.

- The water rides are designed to get you wet, very wet. There is no seat on the ride that will allow you to escape. If it's a cold or overcast day and you don't want to freeze, purchase a thin plastic poncho for about $3.50 or bring your own.

- If you want to snap loved ones in mid-ride, look for photo staging spots at Congo River Rapids, Kumba, and the Tanganyika Tidal Wave.

- As soon as you arrive in the park, set up a specific rendezvous location and time in case you and your companions get separated.

Shopping

There are three, must-have stuffed animals on the central Florida theme-park circuit, and two of them are here: white tiger puppets sold at the **Stanleyville Bazaar,** and cuddly gorillas sold at **J.R.'s Gorilla Hut,** just outside Myombe Reserve. The latter also stocks a delightfully long-limbed chimpanzee, whose Velcroed palms attach in an everlasting hug. In Stanleyville, the aforementioned **Stanleyville Bazaar** and **Air Africa** are chockful of pseudo-African schlock—along with some authentic, imported treasures—but you can find the perfect birthday trinket or Yuletide stocking-stuffer in the form of a set of carved wooden zoo animals, perhaps, or brilliantly colored, elephant-shaped napkin rings. The **Souk** is the stop for inexpensive bangles, moderately priced brass, and exorbitantly pricey Moroccan leather, not to mention a rainbow of gauze veils to swathe your own little Salome. If all you want to do is shop, 30-minute shopping passes are available for a deposit equaling the price of admission.

Busch Gardens A to Z

Admission
Adults pay $34.60, children 3–9, $28.20. Senior citizens receive a 15% discount, and AAA members get 10% off. Tickets are also available for sister parks, Sea World and Cypress Gardens.

Baby Care
Facilities for **nursing** and **diaper-changing tables** are in Dwarf Village; only women's rest rooms have changing tables. You'll find **stroller rentals** at Stroller and Wheelchair Rental in Morocco ($4 for singles, $8 for doubles, including $1 deposit; doubles are safari trucks!). No **formula, baby food,** or **disposable diapers** are sold on the premises, but there are shopping centers all around the park, as well as a K-mart and Kash 'N' Karry about 1 mile east of the Main Entrance on Busch Boulevard.

Cameras and Film
Disposable **Kodak Funsaver cameras** are for sale at Safari Foto, near the Main Entrance, as well as at other stores throughout the park. You can rent **35mm cameras** ($6.95 per day with $50 deposit) at the One-Hour Photo Shop, also near the Main Entrance.

Car Service
If you have car trouble, raise your hood and the parking patrol will assist you.

Dining
The majority of the gustatory offerings are of the red-meat variety, smoked, wursted, or burgered. They are routinely washed down with Anheuser-Busch products, which are sold parkwide: Budweiser, Bud Light, Michelob, and nonalcoholic O'Doul's. Ice cream and popcorn stands are ubiquitous.

Steak, chicken, and pasta dishes are on the menu upstairs in the Crown Colony's **Colony Club,** a white-tableclothed, full-service dining area whose huge windows give a great view of the Serengeti. The change in altitude affects the price only minimally, and the setting is one of the most relaxing in the park. It's also the fanciest place in the park. Unfortunately, the number of window tables is limited, so you have to eat very early or late to get one. When the park closes early, seating may end around 4, though this varies.

For Travelers with Disabilities
To many wheelchair users, the Busch Gardens experience will be represented less by the wild rides than by the animals, which are on display at almost every turn. Of the rides that make up a significant part of the experience for many other visitors, almost all are accessible by guests who can transfer from their own wheelchair into the ride vehicles.

ATTRACTIONS
All attractions are wheelchair accessible in **Morocco, Myombe Reserve,** and **Nairobi.**

Bird Gardens: To play in **Land of the Dragon,** children must be able to leave their wheelchairs. The **Brewery** is not wheelchair accessible; the tour involves walking limited distances and several flights of stairs.

Congo, Stanleyville: Guests using wheelchairs must transfer to ride vehicles at **Congo River Rapids, Ubanga Banga Bumper Cars, Monstrous Mamba,** and **Python** in Congo and at **Stanley Falls** and **Tanganyika Tidal Wave** in Stanleyville; you must also be able to hold lap bars or railings for these, as well as sit upright and absorb sudden and dramatic movements. Transferring out of a wheelchair is also required for **Congo kiddie rides.**

Crown Colony, Timbuktu: For **Questor** in the Crown Colony and for **Crazy Camel, Phoenix, Sandstorm,** and **Scorpion** in Timbuktu, you must be able to transfer from your wheelchair into the ride vehicle, and you must also be able to continuously hold on to lap bars or railings, hold yourself upright, and absorb sudden and dramatic movements. Timbuktu's other rides also cannot be boarded in a wheelchair.

SERVICES

The park publishes a leaflet describing each attraction's accessibility. It's available at Guest Relations.

SHOPS AND RESTAURANTS

All shops and restaurants in Busch Gardens are wheelchair accessible.

WHEELCHAIR RENTALS

At **Stroller and Wheelchair Rental** in Morocco, you can rent standard chairs ($4, with $1 deposit) and motorized wheelchairs ($20, with $5 deposit). If yours disappears and needs replacing, ask in any gift shop.

First Aid

The infirmary is alongside the Festhaus in Timbuktu.

Getting There

Busch Gardens is at the corner of Busch Boulevard and 40th Street, 8 miles northeast of downtown Tampa, 2 miles east of I–275, and 2 miles west of I–75. It will take you an hour and 15 minutes to drive the 81 miles from Orlando on I–4. Contrary to declarations in the brochures, Busch Gardens is not easy to find. The printed directions are fine until you get to Fowler Avenue, and then the signs indicating your route disappear and you are guaranteed to miss 40th Street, where you are supposed to turn. A better route is to follow the brochure directions to Fowler Avenue (Exit 54 off I–75 from Orlando; Exit 33 off I–275 from Tampa), then turn left onto 30th Street—a well-marked intersection with a bank of traffic lights. Then make another left onto Busch Avenue—another well-marked intersection with traffic lights. You will finally see Busch Gardens signs telling you to make another left onto 40th Street for the entrance to the parking lot.

Guided Tours

Numerous tours and programs here are designed to fan the animal conservation spark. One of the most popular is the three-hour **Behind-the-Scenes Tour,** daily at 8:30 AM, in which you ride the feeding truck and see just how many carrots those gorillas go through in one day. You can also reserve ahead to join periodic four-hour **Senior Safaris** as well as wonderful, age-specific half-day, full-day, and multiday programs for children (☎ 813/987–5555); the cost is $18–$100.

Hours

The park is open daily from 9:30 to 6, except during summer and selected holidays when hours are extended.

Lockers

You'll find them in the Moroccan Village, near the Congo River Rapids; in Stanleyville, near the Tanganyika Tidal Wave; and in the Congo, at the Kumba and Congo River Rapids rides. The cost is 50¢. There are change machines near the lockers.

Lost and Found

Report losses and finds of material goods at the Main Entrance's Security office.

Lost Children and Adults

Go to Security at the Main Entrance or speak to any security officer. Security personnel wear white shirts, badges, and hats and look vaguely like sheriffs.

Money

For currency exchange, go to the Guest Relations window near the Main Entrance in Morocco. There is an ATM just inside the Main Entrance, in Morocco; it's linked to the Plus, Honor, and Cirrus networks.

Package Pickup

If you'd rather not lug around your purchases all day, have them sent from any store in the park to **Sahara Traders,** in the Moroccan village area near the entrance. You can pick them up on your way out. The service is free, but do allow an hour for delivery.

Parking

The cost for parking is $3 for cars, $4 for trucks or campers and $2 for motorcycles.

Visitor Information

Contact Busch Gardens (✉ Box 9158, Tampa 33674, ☎ 813/987–5283).

On-site park information is available at **Guest Relations,** near the Main Entrance in Morocco.

A large signpost at the entrance lists performances scheduled for that day; show times for each performance are also posted in front of the individual stages and theaters.

CYPRESS GARDENS

A botanical garden, amusement park, and waterskiing circus rolled into one, Cypress Gardens is a uniquely Floridian combination of natural beauty and utter kitsch. It was founded during the Depression by Dick and Julie Pope; she was a southern belle from Alabama with a green thumb, and he was a short, fast-talking real estate promoter and public relations whiz addicted to flashy jackets: "If I didn't wear the jackets," he once confided to *Life* magazine, "people would think I was a tall fire hydrant." They created their dream in a snake- and alligator-infested cypress swamp on the shores of Lake Eloise in what are euphemistically referred to as the central Florida "highlands," and they opened for business on January 1, 1936. Ticket receipts that day totaled $38, less than the price of a day's admission for two adults today. Cypress Gardens has been open ever since and is central Florida's oldest, continuously running attraction.

Despite Dick's self-designated status as "Swami of the Swamps" and "The Man Who Invented Florida," Cypress Gardens owes its two best-known traditions to Julie. In charge of the park during World War II while Dick was in the Armed Forces, Julie promised free water-ski shows for the soldiers at a nearby military base. What started with some stunts by Dick, Jr. and his friends quickly expanded into a fully chore-ographed program with a bevy of "aquamaids" and stunt skiers, who originated the flips, barefoot skiing, and pyramids now a part of all waterskiing shows—both at Cypress Gardens and at other entertain-ment parks. When a winter storm devastated the plantings at the en-trance to the park, Julie dressed the women on the staff in antebellum-style hoopskirts and had them stand in strategic locations, waving and smiling to draw visitors' attention away from the blighted blooms. These "Flowers of the South" provide photo-ops to this day.

The park now encompasses more than 200 acres and contains more than 8,000 varieties of plants gathered from 75 countries. More than half of the grounds are devoted to flora, ranging from natural land-scaping to cutesy-poo topiary to chrysanthemum cascades. A staff of more than 50 horticulturalists manages a 7-acre nursery complex, which turns out some 10,000 plants a week, and they produce annual chrysanthemum shows, poinsettia pageants, and a three-month spring flower extravaganza.

The souvenir-shop-ridden main entrance funnels visitors straight to the water-ski stadiums. To the right are the Botanical Gardens; to the left are the Exhibition Gardens and the amusement area.

Numbers in the margin correspond to points of interest on the Cypress Gardens map.

❶ Botanical Gardens Cruise. One of the first things to do at Cypress Gar-dens is to get on the boat and float through the cypress-hung canals of the Botanical Gardens, passing waving belles, flowering shrubs, 27 different species of palm, and the occasional baby alligator. Doing this first gives you a sense of Cypress Gardens' slightly schizoid history.

❷ Water Ski Stadium. Don't miss one of Cypress Gardens' true special-ties, the stunt-filled waterski revue. Unlike the splashy song-and-dance extravaganzas at other parks, the show at Cypress Gardens is purely athletic—and those sitting in the front rows don't get wet here! The Mardi Gras theme can be counted on year after year to provide great enjoyment. Smiling aquamaids whiz along on one leg; the Rampmas-ters pivot, flip, and jump over each other at 35 mph; Corky the Clown skis backward; and the grand finale involves a four-tier pyramid. The show can get a little corny, but it's lively enough to keep everyone en-tertained. *Duration: 30 min (presented every 2 hrs). Crowds: Not usu-ally a problem. Strategy: Arrive 5–10 min before show time and sit in either stadium; the view is equally good from both. Audience: All ages. Rating:★★★*

❸ Exhibition Gardens. For a great photo-op catch one of the famous belles sashaying through here to freshen up at the Southern Mansion, a.k.a. Tara South. The landscaping philosophy is heroic in intent and hilar-iously vulgar in execution, especially for the special flower festivals: During the annual November Mum Festival, 2 million multicolored chrysanthemums cascade over the ledges of the 40-foot-high Mediter-ranean waterfall, decorate the walls of an Italian-style fountain, color four gargantuan floral hearts, and drape two topiary swans in an eye-spinning display of pink, purple, yellow, orange, and red. The yearly Poinsettia Festival runs from December through early January and fea-tures flying-reindeer topiaries and Christmas trees made of more than 40,000 red, pink, and white blooms. A new addition is the Garden of Lights, which gilds the park's natural beauty with thousands of twin-kling strands.

Cypress Gardens

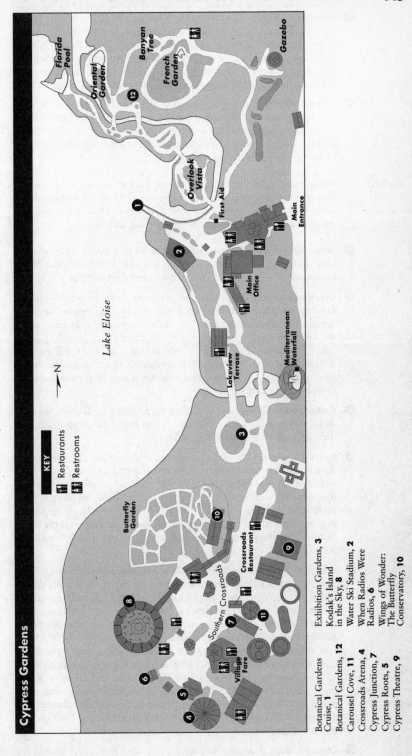

KEY
🍴 Restaurants
🚻 Restrooms

Lake Eloise

N

Florida Pool

Oriental Garden

Banyan Tree

French Garden

Gazebo

12

Overlook Vista

First Aid

1

2

Main Office

Mediterranean Waterfall

Main Entrance

Lakeview Terrace

3

Butterfly Garden

10

9

Crossroads Restaurant

Southern Crossroads

8

7

11

Village Fare

6

5

4

Botanical Gardens
Cruise, **1**

Botanical Gardens, **12**

Carousel Cove, **11**

Crossroads Arena, **4**

Cypress Junction, **7**

Cypress Roots, **5**

Cypress Theatre, **9**

Exhibition Gardens, **3**

Kodak's Island
in the Sky, **8**

Water Ski Stadium, **2**

When Radios Were
Radios, **6**

Wings of Wonder:
The Butterfly
Conservatory, **10**

❹ **Crossroads Arena.** The far southern end of the park is home to a rotating collection of circus-themed acts from acrobats to trained birds. If you get there before the show, you can often watch the performers rehearse. *Duration: 25 min, plus 15-min pre-show. Crowds: Not significant. Strategy: Try for the first or last show of the day, because the tent gets wickedly hot at midday. Audience: All ages. Rating:* ★★★

❺ **Cypress Roots.** This unprepossessing clapboard shack is chockful of fascinating memorabilia about the "Maharaja of the Marshes" and his fair bride. Save a good 20 minutes for the video interview of the Popes and the same amount of time to read all the *Life* magazine clippings of Dick, Sr.'s promotional exploits.

....

NEED A
BREAK?

Village Fare, a conglomeration of fast-food outlets, serves pizza, salads, burgers, and roast beef on picnic tables covered with green-trellised tablecloths in an air-conditioned arena. The **Cypress Deli,** a hop and skip away, features submarine sandwiches and big salads.

....

❻ **When Radios Were Radios.** Nostalgia gets a firm nudge at this antique radio museum, with its collection of hundreds of 1920s Philcos, Westinghouses, and their successors dating through the 1950s.

❼ **Cypress Junction.** One of the nation's most elaborate model railroad exhibits bridges the generation gap with its whistling freights, sleek expresses, tunnels, weather hazards, and all sorts of other knick-knacks. At any given time, you'll see nearly two dozen trains operating on its 1,100 feet of track; nearly 5,000 miniature figures of people and animals add that extra bit of detail. Oddly enough, this menagerie of miniatures was originally created as a Christmas exhibit for the *National Enquirer* in Lantana, Florida.

❽ **Kodak's Island in the Sky.** A 153-foot-high revolving platform provides aerial views of the park's seasonal flower spectaculars and lush gardens, as well as of nearby Winter Haven.

❾ **Cypress Theatre.** One of the most popular attractions at Cypress Gardens is the bird show. Not only is it colorful and amusing, but it's air-conditioned! Bird tricks are now referred to as "behaviors," although the behaviors exhibited by the parrots and macaws lean more toward such tricks as riding a bicycle or singing "Oh, What a Beautiful Morning" than the natural responses demonstrated by the raptors at the Busch Gardens bird show. Still, there's rousing audience response to "sing along with Grackles."

❿ **Wings of Wonder: The Butterfly Conservatory.** Anheuser-Busch Corporation's purchase of Cypress Gardens has resulted in both the installation of its signature statue of a hulking Clydesdale and a significant investment of money. The latter has been put to good use in this newest exhibit. More than 1,000 butterflies representing more than 50 species flit about an enclosed Victorian-style greenhouse, whose 5,500 square feet contain three waterfalls, educational displays, and a couple of chrysalis chambers where you can watch new butterflies struggling out of their cocoons. Four new gardens surround the conservatory: a butterfly garden constructed in the shape of a butterfly wing, with great aerial shots from Kodak's Island in the Sky; an herb and scent garden, complete with cooking demonstrations; a vegetable and fruit garden; and a rose garden.

⓫ **Carousel Cove.** Catering to fidgety kids who demand a reward for traipsing past antique radios and inanimate shrubbery, this attraction is perfectly geared to grandparents and grandchildren, with none of Sea World's athletic net climbs. Most of the rides are closer to the old-fashioned, county-fair variety than to the high-tech wonders at most theme parks. There are the ball crawls and bouncing pads, where kids can work off excess energy while their weary relatives watch, as well as skee ball, ball tosses, swings, and classic kiddie rides such as the Red Baron (airplanes). Some carnival games ($1 a chance) are also available.

⑫ **Botanical Gardens.** If you can, make this the last stop on your tour—for the same reason that you save room for dessert. Most of the plants are labeled, as part of the park's education program; the plantings are naturalized; and a saunter on winding paths beneath shady, live oaks or the quiet chamber created by a giant banyan's hanging roots provides a respite from the usual entertainment park rush. Photo-ops abound.

Strategies for Your Visit

There's no sense of amusement-park anxiety at Cypress Gardens. The slow pace is partly because few people dash to gape at a banyan tree and partly due to the clientele, most of whom are older. In any case, there's no need to rush; even at a sedate pace, you can see just about everything in six hours. In summer, when the park stays open past the usual 5:30 closing time, you can arrive at noon and not miss anything. Lines are seldom a consideration. However, lines do build up at the Electric Boat Rides in fine weather on weekends and during winter, a favorite traveling time of the older visitors that Cypress Gardens tends to attract. Therefore, start with the boat-rides and save a pedestrian perambulation of the gardens for later in the day.

Other Tips

- There are mailboxes near all exhibits, saying "Please Take One." Please do. The fliers inside contain interesting background on the attractions.

- If you have allergies, come prepared with antihistamines. The beautiful floral arrangements wreak havoc on susceptible sinuses.

Shopping

Before entering the park, buy a straw fan at the **Bazaar Gift Shop** at the entrance—it's invaluable for hot afternoon performances at the Crossroads Arena and on steamy days. Once inside, pick up minitopiaries and tastefully flowered T-shirts and sweatshirts at **Gardening, Etc.,** in Southern Crossroads. On your way out, stop in the gift shop again for pastel parasols for the baby-belle in your life, a pair of flowered gardening gloves, or an all-too-apt copy of *Allergy Plants* to find out what just ambushed your sinuses. The **Butterfly Shop,** near Wings of Wonder, has a unique collection of fluttery fancies for collectors and some nifty things for bug-loving children.

Cypress Gardens A to Z

Admission

Daily rates of $26.95 for adults, $16.45 for children 6–12, and a senior rate of $22.95 all exclude tax. AAA members get 10% off. Discounted tickets for Sea World and Busch Gardens can also be purchased here.

Baby Care

You'll find **stroller rentals** at the Bazaar Gift Shop ($4 per day, with no deposit). Baby needs such as **baby food, formula, diapers,** and **wipes** can be purchased at the Winn-Dixie supermarket, across the street from the park. There are no designated facilities for nursing.

Dining

The food is fast and the service friendly, but don't expect much more than basic refueling choices on the menu. At the Southern Crossroads hub, **Crossroads Restaurant** is fairly upscale, with a sit-down restaurant and a similar salad-quiche-sandwich menu with touches of southern cooking. **Lakeview Terrace,** on the upper level of the more southerly of the pair of water-ski stadiums, has a terrific view of the waterskiing show, as well as food that won't diminish your attention. Cypress Gardens is located plunk in the middle of central Florida's citrus plantations, so you can always pick up some freshly squeezed orange juice at **Baker's Dozen, Village Fare,** and most other food locations in the park.

For Travelers with Disabilities

All of the garden attractions at Cypress Gardens are wheelchair accessible, as are all restaurants and shops. Children with disabilities may not be able to negotiate some of the rides in Carousel Cove without assistance.

WHEELCHAIR RENTALS
You can rent **standard wheelchairs** ($4 a day, with no deposit) and **motorized wheelchairs** ($5 per hour, with a $10 minimum and a $25 maximum, plus a $25 deposit).

First Aid

First aid is near the entrance to the Botanical Gardens.

Getting There

To get here, take I–4 west to the U.S. 27S exit. From there, the route is well signed: Follow signs to Winter Haven; at Waverly, turn right (west) on Route 540, and go 5 miles. It's a 45-minute drive from Walt Disney World.

Guided Tours

Behind-the-scenes tours of the nursery, as well as botanical tours of the gardens, are available by special request. Call the main park information number (☎ 813/324–2111) to arrange such tours.

Hours

The park is open daily 9:30–5:30; extended during peak seasons.

Lockers

They're near the main office, just inside the park entrance (50¢).

Lost Things or People

Report **lost children and adults** as well as **lost possessions** at the main park office.

Money

There are no ATMs or currency exchange facilities.

Parking

The grassy parking area is divided into the North Lot and the South Lot; within these, rows are marked numerically. Parking is free.

Visitor Information

Contact Cypress Gardens (✉ Box 1, Cypress Gardens 33884, ☎ 813/324–2111 or 800/237–4826; in FL, 800/282–2123).

Within the park, the principal **information booth** is just inside the main gate.

SPLENDID CHINA

The Orlando area's newest attraction is more a superlative open-air museum than a theme park in the Mickey Mouse tradition. Instead of standing in long lines at thrill rides and glitzy shows, visitors here stroll among painstakingly re-created versions of China's greatest landmarks. Tinkling, meditative music plays in the background, and Chinese artisans demonstrate traditional woodworking, weaving, and other crafts. Think of a park featuring scaled-down versions of the Grand Canyon, the Alamo, and the White House, plus roping shows and high school marching bands, and you'll get an idea of what a "Splendid America" might be like.

It took $100 million and 120 Chinese craftspeople working for two years to craft the 60-plus replicas, which include both man-made structures, such as the Imperial Palace, and natural phenomena, such as the rock formations of the Stone Forest. Some of the monuments are lifesize, while others have been greatly reduced in scale—each brick in the Great Wall, for example, is only 2 inches long. These detailed reproductions are even more impressive when you consider that the artisans used historically accurate building materials and techniques whenever possible. Whereas Universal Studios and WDW are working to out-automate each other, Splendid China is content to stress tradition over technology; the most advanced electronics you'll see here are the tiny lights that glow inside the buildings after dark.

Park developers had planned to let the park consist solely of the miniature monuments, thereby re-creating the successful formula that has brought millions of visitors to the prototype park, Shenzhen Splendid China, which opened near Hong Kong in 1989. U.S. advisers convinced them, however, that theme park-savvy Western visitors expected more bang for their buck, so a playground area for children and live entertainment were added. Despite the awareness that Florida's Splendid China needed to be tailored for different demographics, problems still arose that neither the Chinese creators nor their U.S. friends had foreseen.

Park officials certainly didn't figure on demonstrators, who showed up on opening day to protest China's occupation of Tibet. The park includes a representation of Potala Palace, the official seat of the Dalai Lama, Tibet's exiled spiritual and secular leader. And they never dreamed that early guests would trample through the displays, kick over hundreds of handmade clay figurines, or try to take home the delicately painted decorations that are cemented onto many structures. The park suffered more damage in its first few days than its cousin in Shenzhen did in six years of operation. The first stage shows were an equally uncomfortable meeting of Asian and Western sensibilities: Chinese announcers read from stilted text that seemed to describe every other performer as "breathtaking and elegant." Some park-goers simply walked out.

Things have evened out considerably since opening day, but the difficulties are a reminder that cultural differences can be extremely powerful. Maybe it is the unrelenting Florida rain and sunshine, but after only a year in operation, the park was looking a bit worn. Officials continue to try and find a way to make the root differences a foundation for Splendid China's appeal. They also claim that many of the customers are repeat visitors. It may be true. Many guests come to the park out of curiosity and find themselves fascinated by the delicate craftsmanship that went into creating the displays, the thousands of years of history that the structures represent, and the religious mythology attached to many of the re-created shrines. Splendid China turns out to be just their cup of tea. Others are still just trying to figure it out.

Besides the star attractions like the Great Wall and the Summer Palace, Splendid China also has reproductions of Chinese temples, pagodas, typical Chinese homes, and grottoes filled with religious statuary. Each display is accompanied by a short, written explanation or a recorded message or both, explaining its significance and history.

As you come through the turnstile, you enter Splendid China's version of Main Street: **Suzhou Gardens** is a re-creation of a 14th-century Chinese village. Inside the tile-roofed structures, you'll find most of the park's shops, several restaurants, and **Guest Services.**

Acrobatic Show. In the **Golden Peacock Theater** are some cheesy magic tricks followed by truly incredible feats of balance and flexibility. One woman stands on a bench about six feet off the ground and bends backward to pick up a coin with her mouth. That is just the beginning of these amazing, Asian acrobatics. This is easily the most entertaining show in the park. Don't miss it. *Duration: 20 min. Crowds: Not significant. Audience: All ages. Rating:*★★★

The Great Wall. Take a walk along the wall and keep in mind that the 6.5 million tiny bricks used to make the wall were mortared into place by hand. This ½-mile-long expanse cannot begin to replicate the size of the original—the 1,500-mile-long behemoth that is the only man-made structure visible from space. As in China itself, Mongolia lies on the other side of this wall. While over here, check to see if a wrestling demonstration is scheduled near the **Mongolian Yurt.** Mongolia's capital city, Ulan Bator, has a population of 500,000, more than half of whom live in yurts like these.

Grotto 257. This cave shrine features a dark interior with rich colors. It's authentic down to the smudges in the artwork and the missing digits on some of the statues. A number of the exhibits appear worse for wear because their prototypes were damaged during the Cultural Revolution or simply by the passage of time; the craftspeople chose to replicate these originals as authentically as possible, warts and all.

Harmony Hall. Best visited as your first stop, this is where the *This Is Splendid China* film is screened every 20 minutes. Although it contains some lovely footage of China and useful background information on the buildings and statues on whic the exhibits here are based, the film does not explore the meticulous construction that went into building the park. The **closing parade,** which kicks off each night at about 6:30, starts near the main entrance and then winds through Suzhou Gardens. Featuring colorfully painted wooden floats, flotillas of traditional sedan chairs, and a slew of ornately adorned ladies, it's worth a watch. *Duration: 15 min. Crowds: Not a problem. Strategy: See it first so you'll better understand the exhibits. Audience: All ages. Rating:*★★ *Parade duration: 25 min. Crowds: Nothing significant. Audience: All ages. Rating:*★★

Imperial Palace. The centerpiece of Beijing's famed **Forbidden City,** this is one of the most impressive sights at Splendid China. The compound in Beijing, built in the early 1400s as the home of the royal family, was constructed of materials brought from all over China and decorated with centuries' worth of loot; it housed so many people that as many as 6,000 cooks were needed to feed them. No commoner stepped inside the walls of its inner sanctum until the mid-20th century; some of China's emperors never stepped outside. Even the scale model here gives a sense of the immense size and the artistry that made such a lifestyle possible.

Leshan Buddha. A re-creation of the largest man-made statue in the world, this version stands 35 feet compared to the original, which took 90 years to build, and stands 24 stories high.

Panda Playground. Here is Splendid China's attempt to compete with all other elaborate children's playgrounds, with its ball crawls, slides, and a maze. The amusements are likely to entertain smaller children who are less than captivated by exhibits that don't move, make noise, or light up. Compared with other central Florida theme park playgrounds, however, this one is nothing to write home about. *Crowds: Not significant. Audience: Young children. Rating:* ★

Potala Palace. The Water Village—China's version of Venice—and the Lijiang River Scenery area are the backdrops for the controversial reproduction of the palace, a dusty-rose-and-white structure situated far in the back of the park. The original in Lhasa, Tibet's capital, is an amalgam of two palaces—the Red and the White—both commissioned by the fifth Dalai Lama (1617–82); it stands 13 stories high but seems even taller because the walls were constructed to lean inward, creating a false perspective.

Stone Forest. With its maze of odd obelisks, this unusual formation replicates a 200-acre park in southern Yunan Province, where pillars have been whittled out of the limestone by eons of erosion.

Summer Palace. One of Splendid China's most impressive exhibits represents the traditional home of China's dowager empress. Aristocrats and other members of the court would come to stay during the summer to escape the heat in Beijing. As at the original, the many palace structures are reflected in a smooth pool. After the complex fell into ruins during the 19th century, the Empress Dowager Ci Xi had it rebuilt with money that was supposed to be used to expand the navy. The stone boat that you see moored at the water's edge—the prototype is made from marble—therefore takes on a certain ironic meaning.

Temple of Heaven. Past Dr. Sun Yat-sen's Mausoleum is a striking, blue-tiled structure. It was at this site in Beijing that the emperor, as high priest of his people, would spend time in fasting and prayer.

Temple of Light Amphitheater. A costume show and a demonstration of music, folk dances, and martial arts are each presented on alternating hours. Both are slow-moving affairs compared to other, flashy theme park fare. The **Costume Show** amounts to a bunch of attractive young Asian women in high heels and silk who parade back and forth in time to music. The **National Art Ensemble Show** is a performance of traditional folk dances and music from across China and is considerably more interesting than the costume show. The dancers are skilled, and the music intriguing. *Duration of each: 40 min. Crowds: Not significant. Audience: All ages. Costume show rating:* ★*; Art Ensemble show rating:* ★★

Terra Cotta Warriors. Modeled on 7,000 life-size clay figurines unearthed by archaeologists in 1974, this exhibit is quite impressive. The original figures were realistic portraits of servants, soldiers, and cavalry in the employ of Emperor Ch'in Shih Huang Ti. When the emperor died, almost 2,000 years ago, the figures were buried with him as an honor guard. Splendid China's warriors—replicas of replicas, as it were—are housed in a cool cave.

1,000 Eyes and 1,000 Hands Guanyin Buddha Statue. The many hands of the original are said to ease the troubles of the world. At the very least, it promises to provide you with a great photo opportunity.

Wind and Rain Court. When you're ready to take a break from the miniatures, head past Jingzhen Octagonal Pavilion, Dai Village, and Manfeilong Pagoda to the the place for Cantonese and Shanghai cuisine, along with a limited Western selection, served in this ersatz pagoda.

One park staffer said this is the place to get good hamburgers if your taste buds aren't in the mood to mu shu.

Strategies for Your Visit

You can probably tour every exhibit in under four hours, but once you add some time for shopping, eating, and taking in a few shows, Splendid China makes for a good, one-day trip. Park officials say it should take 4–6 hours to complete a leisurely stroll. The park is really at its most magical at night. Try not to arrive until after noon; that way you'll be in plenty of time to catch the shows, eat some dinner, watch the final parade, and then wander the exhibits until closing time.

When you get to the park, go to Harmony Hall and watch the 15-minute film *This Is Splendid China,* which explains the history behind the park. Also check with Guest Services for show times and any special events. Since lines are not an issue here, there's no pressing strategy needed for touring the attractions. One thing to note: The park map numbers the exhibits counterclockwise; if you tour in that direction, you'll end up at the underwhelming mausoleum of Dr. Sun Yat-sen in the middle of the park. If you head clockwise, you'll finish up your day with the most impressive sites—the Imperial Palace and the Great Wall.

One final caveat: The passive nature of the park makes it suitable mostly for older children and adults. Young kids and even restless teens may get bored because there's plenty to see but not much to do.

Rainy Days
Splendid China is very much an outdoor exhibit; once you're out among the displays there is little shelter from the elements. If rain is forecast, stay home or bring a poncho.

Shopping

As with the food, the merchandise available at Splendid China is a cut above typical theme-park tourist souvenirs. Of Suzhou Gardens' 11 shops, only **Nine Dragon Gifts** offers pedestrian goodies like T-shirts and key chains. For more exotic offerings, check out **Ancestral Artifacts'** handcrafted Chinese furniture, the nursery at **Pen Jing Gardens,** which sells bonsai trees, and **Loomed Creations'** lovely linens. Other unusual treasures such as teas, works of calligraphy, silk embroidery, hand-painted porcelain, and jade may make you wish you had more time and money to spend.

Splendid China A to Z

Admission
Regular admission is $23.55 for adults, $13.90 for children 5–12, $21.50 for AARP members and senior citizens. AAA members receive a 10% discount, as do senior citizens over 55.

Auto Needs
Should you experience car trouble, head for **Central Reception,** just outside the gate, and an attendant will call an auto service for you.

Baby Care
There are **diaper-changing tables** available in women's rest rooms. No **diapers** are sold on the property, but they can be purchased at Eckerd's, just off U.S. 192 near the park's entrance. **Strollers** are for rent at Guest Services (single $4, double $7, no deposit).

It helps to be pushy in airports.

Introducing the revolutionary new TransPorter™ from American Tourister® It's the first suitcase you can push around without a fight. TransPorter's™ exclusive four-wheel design lets you push it in front of you with almost no effort–the wheels take the weight. Or pull it on two wheels if you choose. You can even stack on other bags and use it like a luggage cart.

Stable 4-wheel design.

TransPorter™ is designed like a dresser, with built-in shelves to organize your belongings. Or collapse the shelves and pack it like a traditional suitcase. Inside, there's a suiter feature to help keep suits and dresses from wrinkling. When push comes to shove, you can't beat a TransPorter™. For more information on how you can be this pushy, call 1-800-542-1300.

Shelves collapse on command.

American Tourister®

Making travel less primitive®

Use your MCI Card® for the easy way to call when traveling.

MCI ‖ Calling Card

415 555 1234 2244
J.D. SMITH

Convenience on the road

- Your MCI Card® number is your home number, guaranteed.
- Pre-programmed to speed dial to your home.
- Call from any phone in the U.S.

MCI

1 - 8 0 0 - 7 5 4 - 8 9 4 1

http://www.mci.com

Cameras

Film for most cameras is sold at Guest Services, as are **disposable 35mm cameras.** Guest Services also rents **video cameras** ($25 per day, $150 deposit).

Dining

Splendid China has some splendid food. Even the cafeteria-style offerings at Suzhou Gardens' **Seven Flavors Court** are far better than normal park fare, and probably at least as good as your neighborhood take-out place. Try the nearby **Suzhou Pearl** if you're more in the mood for attentive service, elegant atmosphere, and gourmet versions of traditional Chinese dishes. If you're out among the exhibits proper, try **Great Wall Terrace,** near the 1,000 Hands Guanyin Buddha statue; it serves Mandarin and northern Chinese cuisine and has table service. Reservations are recommended at all the sit-down restaurants and can be made at Guest Services when you first arrive. If you want just a hot dog and a soda, carts are scattered throughout the park.

For Travelers with Disabilities

There are no special programs or guides available for guests with disabilities. Most of Splendid China's attractions are wheelchair accessible, but Sun Yat-sen's Mausoleum and the Guanyin Buddha Statue have stairs. Visitors must be able to transfer to a golf-cart-like tram for the VIP guided tour. Recorded messages in both English and Spanish discuss the various exhibits but probably do not provide enough information for visually impaired guests to have a full experience. All of the shops and dining areas are wheelchair accessible, although the stone streets in Suzhou Gardens may make for some rough riding.

WHEELCHAIR RENTAL

You can rent **standard wheelchairs** ($5) and **electric scooters** ($25, with $50 deposit) from Guest Services.

First Aid

First-aid services are immediately inside the main entrance.

Getting There

Splendid China is about 12 miles from Orlando, or 2½ miles west of the I–4/U.S. 192 junction. From Orlando, take I–4 west toward WDW, and get off at Exit 25B—the signs will say "Disney," "Fort Wilderness," and so on. You are now on U.S. 192; continue west past all of the exits leading to Disney. Stay in the far-left lane and look for the dragon.

Guided Tours

A four-hour walking tour of the park is $5 per person. Or, a VIP golf-cart tour will whip you, a guide, and up to four friends around the park in about 90 minutes; the tour is $45, regardless of the number of people.

Hours

The park is open daily 9:30–7; shops and restaurants in the Suzhou Gardens area stay open until 9. Hours may be extended in peak seasons.

Lockers

Lockers are located near Guest Services ($1).

Lost Things and People

If you lose someone or something go to Guest Services. There is a park-wide public-address system that can be used for contact in an emergency.

Money

You'll find an ATM at Guest Services, but no currency exchange facilities.

Package Pickup

If you do your shopping before checking out the exhibits, ask the merchant about holding the item or having it sent to Guest Services; there's no official package pickup, but most vendors will be happy to oblige.

Parking

There's no charge for parking at Splendid China.

Travel Agency

One thing Splendid China offers that's not found at any other park is a full-service travel agency. **China Travel Services** (☎ 407/397–8868), one of the largest travel agencies in China and a major investor in the park, has an office on-site. If the re-creations make you want to see the real thing, make reservations before you go home.

Visitor Information

Contact Splendid China (✉ 3000 Splendid China Blvd., Kissimmee 34747, ☎ 407/397–8800). Once you're at the park, **Guest Services** is located inside the main entrance to the right.

4 Away from the Theme Parks

WHEN YOU'RE READY TO PUT SOME DISTANCE between you and Mickey, you'll find that Orlando and the surrounding Central Florida

Updated by
Val Meyer

area offer much more than theme parks. Nature buffs like to escape to the Ocala National Forest or the Florida Audubon Society Madlyn Baldwin Center for Birds of Prey. Art devotees head for Rollins College's Cornell Fine Art Museum or the Charles Hosmer Morse Museum of American Art. New-Agers check out Cassadaga—more than half the residents of this town are psychics, mediums, and healers. And since this is Central Florida, you'll also find such attractions as Wet 'n Wild and Terror on Church Street. Indeed, you'll discover an abundance of sights—natural, unnatural, and supernatural—that are equally enjoyable and often less crowded and less expensive than those at the theme parks.

Take this opportunity to explore one or more of the many neighborhoods throughout Central Florida. But don't make the mistake of darting into a museum in one neighborhood and bee-lining it to a great restaurant in another. Enjoy each town's unique personality and linger for a while. This is your day off!

GREATER ORLANDO

Downtown and Vicinity

Downtown is a dynamic community that's constantly growing and changing, but still has lovely, loyal locals who live here year-round and are more than happy to share with visitors some of their favorite spots—new and old.

Numbers in the margin correspond to point of interest on the Away from the Theme Parks map.

Sights to See

⑩ Harry P. Leu Gardens. A popular spot for local weddings, this former estate of citrus entrepeneur Harry P. Leu provides a quiet respite from the artificial world of the theme parks. On the grounds' 50 acres are a collection of historical blooms, many varieties of which were established before 1900. You'll see ancient oaks, a 50-foot floral clock, an orchid conservatory, and one of the largest camellia collections in eastern North America (in bloom October–March). Mary Jane's Rose Garden, named after Leu's wife, is filled with more than 1,000 bushes; it is the largest formal rose garden south of Atlanta. The simple 19th-century **Leu House Museum,** once the Leu family home, preserves the furnishings and appointments of a well-to-do, turn-of-the-century Florida family. ⊠ *1920 N. Forest Ave.,* ☎ *407/246–2620,* 𝔽𝔸𝕏 *407/246–2849.* ☞ *$3 adults, $1 children 6–16.* ☉ *Garden daily 9–5; museum Tues.–Sat. 10–3, Sun. and Mon. 1–3.*

⑬ Lake Eola Park. In the heart of downtown Orlando, you'll find this picturesque lake with its signature fountain in the center. The park represents an inner-city victory over decay. Established in 1892, the family park experienced a series of ups and downs that left it very run-down by the late '70s. With the support of determined citizens, the park gradually underwent a renovation, which restored the fountain and added a wide brick walkway around the lake. The security there is now such that families with young children use the well-lighted playground in the evening and downtown residents walk their dogs late at night in safety. The **Walt Disney Amphitheater,** perched on the lake, is a dramatic site

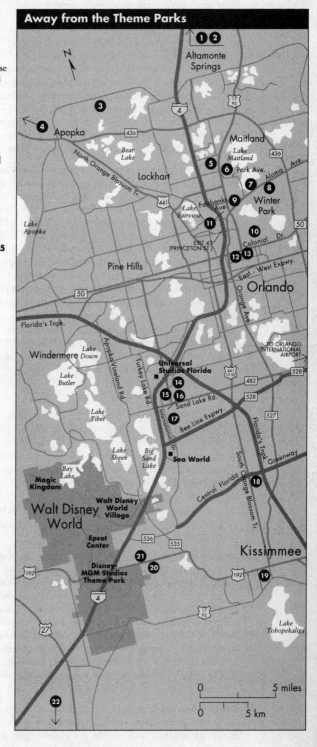

Away from the Theme Parks

for the annual Shakespeare Festival (April and May) as well as for weekend concerts and *FunnyEola*, a free, family comedy show performed the second Tuesday of every month. However, the most fun to be had in the park is a ride in a swan-shaped pedal boat, one of which frequent Disney World visitor Michael Jackson is reputed to have ordered for his personal use at his ranch. The view at dusk, as the fountain lights up and the sun sets behind Orlando's ever-growing skyline, is spectacular. ⊠ *Robinson St. and Rosalind Ave.,* ☎ *Park, 407/246–2827; swan boats, 407/841–9856.* ☉ *Park, daily 7–midnight; swan boats, winter daily 11–6, summer daily 11–9; café, weekdays 10–8, weekends 10–9.* ⛵ *Boat rental $5.30 per ½ hr, maximum 3 people per boat.*

⑭ Mystery Fun House. There are a variety of ways to attack this place. You might just want to bring your quarters and visit the video arcade, for which there's no admission charge. Paying admission to the actual **Fun House** entitles you to a walk through the 18-chamber Mystery Maze, which comes with the warning that it is "90% dark" and full of gory and distorted images. Outside, there's the 18-hole **Jurassic Golf,** a basic putt-putt course, laid out flat and simple, with, as you might expect, a dinosaur motif. The real highlight is the **Starbase Omega** laser-tag game. Equipped with laser guns and wearing reflector belts, players are transported on a simulated spaceship ride to the arena, where they score points by zapping each other and try to avoid being zapped by the UFO spaceship hovering overhead. Underfoot, the playing surface feels like an air mattress, adding a simulated low-gravity element to the game. Take I–4 to Exit 34B (Universal Studios). Turn right on Kirkman Road and right again on Major Boulevard. ⊠ *5767 Major Blvd.,* ☎ *407/351–3355.* ⛵ *Maze $7.95, miniature golf $4.95, laser game $6.95, all 3 for $13.85.* ☉ *Sun.–Thurs. 10–9, Fri. and Sat. 10–10, until midnight in peak seasons.*

Orange County Historical Museum. This is a storehouse of Orlando memorabilia, photographs, and antiques. Exhibits explore Native American and native Floridian culture, and they show off a country store, Victorian parlor, and print shop; call for an update on the always-changing traveling exhibits. **Fire Station No. 3,** an actual 1926 brick firehouse behind the museum, houses antique fire trucks, firefighting memorabilia, and collectibles. Though most items are for looking only, there are some firefighters' bunks, hats, and jackets for youngsters to investigate. ⊠ *812 E. Rollins St.,* ☎ *407/897–6350.* ⛵ *$2 adults, $1 children 6–11.* ☉ *Mon.–Sat. 9–5, Sun. noon–5.*

Orlando Museum of Art. The museum's rather limited collection includes 19th- and 20th-century American art, displayed on a rotating basis year-round. There's also a permanent exhibit of pre-Columbian artifacts from a Mayan excavation. Young children will enjoy the first-class **Art Encounter,** created with the help of Walt Disney World. Hands-on activities, such as dressing up in colorful handwoven clothing from South America, stimulate imaginations and enhance children's understanding of the works in the galleries. Call for information on special exhibits. ⊠ *2416 Mills Ave.,* ☎ *407/896-4231.* ⛵ *$4 adults, $2 children 4–11.* ☉ *Tues.–Sat. 9–5, Sun. noon–5; tours Sept.–May, Wed. and Sun. 2; Art Encounter Tues.–Fri. and Sun. noon–5, Sat. 10–5.*

Orlando Science Center. This is a place for action; best of all, touching is encouraged here. The **Tunnel of Discovery** has a variety of clever hands-on activities to teach the principles of physical science. Special traveling exhibits with themes ranging from dinosaurs to space travel all have interactive components. For preschoolers there's **WaterWorks,** where children, secured in plastic smocks, are turned loose to explore the properties of water. **NatureWorks** features an extensive collection of rocks and insects, as well as live demonstrations with resident snakes, other reptiles, and amphibians. Films in the dome-shaped planetarium take viewers on a journey through the stars, and on weekend evenings Cosmic Concerts, a local favorite, combine lasers and rock music in a psychedelic light show. There's a snack bar, too. ⊠ *810 E. Rollins St.,* ☎ *407/896–7151.* ⊡ *Science center $6.50 adults, $5.50 children 3–11, children under 2 free; Cosmic Concerts $6.50.* ☉ *Science Center Mon.–Thurs. and Sat. 9–5, Fri. 9–9, Sun. noon–5; Cosmic Concerts Fri. and Sat. 9, 10, 11, and midnight.*

⑰ Pirate's Cove Adventure Golf. You can play the crème de la crème of miniature golf at the two locations of this shrine to putt-putt golf. Each site offers two 18-hole courses that wind around artificial mountains, through caves, over waterfalls, and into lush foliage. The beginner's course is called Captain Kidd's Adventure; a more difficult game can be played on Blackbeard's Challenge. The courses are opposite Mercado Mediterranean Village and in the Crossroads of Lake Buena Vista shopping plaza. ⊠ *8501 International Dr.,* ☎ *407/352–7378; Crossroads Center, I–4 Exit 27,* ☎ *407/827–1242.* ⊡ *Captain Kidd's Adventure, $6.50 adults, $5.50 children 4–12; Blackbeard's Challenge, $7 adults, $6 children 4–12; both courses $11 adults, $10 children 4–12; all-day (9–5) admission to either course $12 adults, $9 children; Group discounts available.* ☉ *Daily 9–11:30.*

⑯ Ripley's Believe It or Not! Museum. A 10-foot-square section of the Berlin Wall. A pain and torture chamber. A Rolls-Royce constructed entirely of matchsticks. A 26-foot-by-20-foot portrait of Van Gogh made from 3,000 postcards. These and almost 200 other oddities speak for themselves in this museum-cum attraction in the heart of tourist territory on International Drive. It is said that the fruits of Robert Ripley's explorations are to reality what Walt Disney World is to fantasy. The building itself is designed to appear as if it's sliding into one of Florida's notorious sinkholes. Give yourself an hour or two to soak up the weirdness here, but remember this is a looking, not touching, experience, which may drive antsy youngsters—and their parents—crazy. Take I–4 to Exit 29 (Sand Lake Rd.); turn left. Turn right on International Drive (second traffic light); museum is ¼ mile on left. ⊠ *8201 International Dr.,* ☎ *407/363–4418 or 800/998–4418.* ⊡ *$9.95 adults, $6.95 children 4–11.* ☉ *Daily 9–11, extended for tour groups.*

⑫ Terror on Church Street. This showcase of horror in the heart of downtown, a few blocks east of Church Street Station, is a 25-minute walking tour through a high-tech labyrinth featuring 23 scenes from horror films with live actors and state-of-the-art sound effects. Lines are long on weekends, but they move along quickly because groups of eight leave every five minutes. The gift shop is stocked with gargoyles, eyeballs, and blood, as well as masks and makeup for re-creating your favorite slasher scenes. Terror targets the 12–22 age group but won't disappoint horror-film fans of any age. Follow signs off I–4 to the Church Street Historic District. ⊠ *Church St. and Orange Ave.,* ☎ *407/649–3327.* ⊡ *$12 adults, $10 students 17 and under; Florida residents $10 adults, $8 students 17 and under.* ☉ *Sun.–Thurs. 7 PM–midnight, Fri. and Sat. 7 PM–1 AM.*

⑮ Wet 'n Wild. This watering hole is probably best known for its outrageous water slides, especially the Black Hole—a 30-second, 500-foot, twisting, turning ride on a two-person raft through total darkness propelled by a 1,000-gallon-a-minute blast of water. There's also an elaborate **Kid's Park**—for those 4′ and under—full of miniature versions of the bigger rides. The latest addition is the **Bubba Tub,** a six-story, triple-dip slide with a tube big enough for the entire family. Teens like the **Top-40 concerts** that take place frequently in summer. The park has snack stands, but visitors are allowed to bring their own food and picnic around the pool or on the lakeside beach. Take I–4 Exit 30A and make a left. ⊠ *6200 International Dr.,* ☎ *407/351–3200.* ⊒ *$24.33 adults, $19.03 children 3–9 (half-price after 3; after 5 in peak season); joint 5-day pass available with Sea World and Universal Studios.* ☉ *Daily 10–5, until 9 in summer.*

Maitland

Maitland is a suburb north of Orlando with an interesting mix: It's home to both the Florida Save the Manatee Society and one of Central Florida's larger office parks. A number of spectacular homes grace the shores of this town's various lakes.

Sights to See

❻ **Florida Audubon Society Madlyn Baldwin Center for Birds of Prey.** More than 20 different species of hawks, eagles, owls, falcons, and vultures make their homes here. There is an earnestness to this humble, working facility on Lake Sybelia in Maitland, which takes in 500–600 injured wild birds of prey each year. About 43% are able to return to the wild; permanently injured birds continue to live at the center and can be seen in the aviaries along the pathways and sitting on outdoor perches. The center also tracks eagles and occasionally sets up a closed-circuit monitor to observe a nest, so visitors can watch a genuine nature show. Take I–4 Exit 47A, then Maitland Boulevard East; turn right on Maitland Avenue, right on U.S. 17–92, right on Kennedy Boulevard, and right on Audubon Way. ⊠ *921 S. Lake Sybelia Dr.,* ☎ *407/645–3826.* ⊒ *$2 adults, $1 children 6–12.* ☉ *Tues.–Sat. 10–4.*

❺ **Maitland Art Center.** It's local lore that this historic art museum near Lake Sybelia, is inhabited by the spirit of its artist-architect founder, André Smith. He began constructing his studio retreat in 1937, and the grounds and buildings themselves are works of art. The seemingly infinite reliefs and other details reflect Smith's fascination with Mayan and Aztec influences and further account for the mystical aura. An outdoor chapel is a favorite spot for weddings, and romantic gardens blend harmoniously with the natural surroundings. Inside, the galleries display an extensive collection of Smith's work as well as changing exhibits by local and national artists. From Orlando, take I–4 east to Exit 47A—Maitland Boulevard East; turn right on Maitland Avenue and after ¾ mile, right again on Packwood Avenue. ⊠ *231 W. Packwood Ave.,* ☎ *407/539–2181.* ⊒ *Donations accepted.* ☉ *Weekdays 10–4:30, weekends noon–4:30.*

Winter Park

Winter Park has a somewhat more upscale, independent identity. A pleasant day can be spent here shopping, eating, or taking in the scenery along Park Avenue. Away from the Avenue, the moss-covered trees form a canopy over brick streets, and old estates surround canal-linked lakes.

A Good Walk

Numbers in the text below correspond to numbers in the margin and on the Away from the Theme Parks map.

This stroll takes you through the heart of Winter Park's downtown. To get there, exit I–4 at the Fairbanks Avenue exit. Head east 3 miles on Fairbanks. Turn right at Park Avenue. Go one block to Holt, and turn left. You're now on the campus of **Rollins College**; park in a nearby lot. Begin your walk on the campus, a private liberal arts school. Among the school's alumns are Mister (Fred) Rogers—yes, this was once his neighborhood. You'll see the **Knowles Memorial Chapel,** built in 1932, and the **Annie Russell Theatre,** a 1931 building that's often the venue for local theatrical productions. Head east on Holt to the **Cornell Fine Arts Museum** ⑧, which houses a small but interesting collection that features 19th- and 20th-century American and European paintings and sculpture. Outside the musuem, there's a small but charming garden that overlooks Lake Virginia. Retrace your steps to **Park Avenue,** with its collection of chic boutiques, cozy cafés, and delightful nooks and crannies. Turn right (north) on Park; on your left, at the intersection of Park and Fairbanks, you'll see a 7-11. Construction of this store raised the hackles of Winter Park's image-conscious city fathers, who feared an invasion of the fast-food joints. Their fears were groundless, however. The Avenue is still very tony. Among the shops you'll see are Orvis (of duck fame) at number 528. You'll also see the Colony, a former movie palace that's now a jewelry store. Continuing north, you'll pass Park Plaza Gardens, a chic restaurant that's part of the Park Plaza Hotel. Just past Lyman Avenue, you'll find the Village Bistro, one of a number of cafés that line the street. When the weather's warm—and it almost always is—there are several streetside tables that are great for people-watching while you enjoy a drink, sandwich, or salad.

Heading north, you'll see a pretty park on the left side of the street. It's **Central Park,** Winter Park's gathering place. This lovely green space with a stage and gazebo is often the scene of concerts. If you don't want to browse in the shops across the street, a stroll through the park is a delightful alternative.

For shoppers and nonshoppers alike, the real fun of Park Avenue, is exploring the little nooks and crannies that divert you from the main drag. Between Wellborne and Morse avenues, around the corner from Barnie's Coffee, you'll find **Grenada Court.** A walk to the back reveals a delightful fountain and wrought iron tables and chairs where you can sit and relax with a cappucino from Barnie's. Of course, the antique store hidden there could keep you on your feet. In the middle of the next block, wedged in between Victorian Joy (Number 316) and The Rune Stone, a European toy store that adults enjoy as much as the kids, you'll find **The Garden Shops,** which houses Pooh's Corner, a delightful children's bookstore that prides itself on being "the best little bookstore in the world." The friendly and knowledgable staff here will help you locate hard-to-find children's titles. Here, too is Maison des Crêpes, where you can enjoy a light repast in a garden setting. But there's still more to discover in the Hidden Garden Shops. Wood, Stone and Steel specializes in culinary tools and tabletop items. Scott Laurent Gallery showcases the works of more than 150 Central Florida artists and artisans, including paintings, original jewelry, original and limited edition framed art, sculpture, art glass, fountains, and decorative gifts. Just before exiting the Hidden Gardens, check out Valerie's Tiny Gift Shop, which lives up to its name. This Lilliputian shop specializes in tiny treasures, especially in pewter.

Make a right, rounding the corner from the alcove back onto Park. Cross Canton Avenue, then cross Park to the **Charles Hosmer Morse Museum of American Art** ⑨. Here you'll see many of the works of Louis Comfort Tiffany, including stained glass windows, lamps, watercolors, and desk sets. From the museum, make a right and explore the shops of Brandywine Square. Madelaine's Antiques offers a wide variety of furniture as well as bric-a-brac.

From Brandywine Square, make a right and cross Park Avenue at Swoope. Walk one block on Swoope to Knowles Avenue, and make a right. Continue down Knowles, passing some of Winter Park's most unique residences. A look at number 340 reveals an old church; across the street is a private home that was once the rectory. As you walk, look up, too; you'll see leafy live oak trees draped with Spanish moss. Continue to Morse Avenue, and make a right. At the end of Morse you'll find the dock for the **Scenic Boat Tour** ⑦, a Winter Park tradition that's been in continuous operation for nearly 60 years. If time permits, the tour (every hour on the hour) is a delightful way to see the lakefront mansions of Winter Park. Retrace your steps on Morse and make a left onto Interlachen Avenue. At the corner of New England Avenue you'll pass the Langford Hotel, a Winter Park mainstay for generations of snowbirds. Continue on Interlachen to Fairbanks and make right. Make a left at Park Avenue and head back to your car in the Rollins lot.

WHEN TO TOUR

To browse the shops, allow 1½ hours minimum; if you plan to eat and/or visit the museums, you'll need at least three hours.

Sights to See

Numbers in the margin correspond to points of interest on the Away from the theme Parks map.

⑧ **Cornell Fine Arts Museum.** Located on the Rollins College Campus, this high-quality small museum houses permanent and changing exhibits of American and European paintings, decorative arts, and sculpture. Artists represented include William Merritt Chase, Childe Hassam and Louis Comfort Tiffany. ⊠ *Rollins College Campus, end of Holt Ave.,* ☎ *407/646–2526.* ☞ *Free.* ☉ *Tues.–Fri. 10–5, weekends 1–5; closed holidays.*

⑨ **Charles Hosmer Morse Museum of American Art.** This Winter Park favorite is home to an outstanding collection of stained-glass windows, blown glass, and lamps made by Louis Comfort Tiffany for his Long Island, N.Y., mansion. There's also a collection of paintings by 19th- and 20th-century American artists, as well as jewelry and pottery. ⊠ *445 Park Ave. N,* ☎ *407/644–3686.* ☞ *$2.50 adults, $1 students with ID.* ☉ *Tues.–Sat. 9:30–4, Sun. 1–4; closed holidays.*

⑦ **Scenic Boat Tour.** Narrated, relaxing one-hour tours cruise by 12 miles of Winter Park's opulent lakeside estates. One of Central Florida's oldest attractions, tours have been given for almost 60 years. ⊠ *312 E. Morse Blvd.,* ☎ *407/644–4056.* ☞ *$6 adults, $3 children 2–11.* ☉ *Tours leave daily hourly 10–4; closed Dec. 25.*

⑪ **Mead Gardens.** The 55 acres in this unusual park have been intentionally left to grow as a natural preserve. Walkers and runners are attracted to the trails that wind around the creek, and a boardwalk provides a better view of the delicate wetlands. ⊠ *S. Denning Ave., Winter Park,* ☎ *407/623–3334* ☞ *Free.* ☉ *Daily 8–sundown.*

OFF THE BEATEN PATH — **Winter Park Farmer's Market.** A longstanding tradition, this market shows the real community that exists behind the upper-crust facade. Friends and neighbors gather to shop for fresh fruits and vegetables, breads and pastries, herbs, coffees, and plants. ⊠ *W. Lyman and New York Aves.,* ☎ *407/623-3275.* ☉ *Sat. 7–noon.*

KISSIMMEE

Although Kissimmee is primarily known as being the gateway to Walt Disney World, its non-WDW attractions just might tickle your fancy.

Sights to See

⑲ Flying Tigers Warbird Air Museum. Old warbirds never die—they just become attractions at this Kissimmee museum. The working aircraft restoration facility is nicknamed "Bombertown USA" because most of the planes here are bombers. Once they are operational, they are usually flown away by private collectors, but the museum also houses a permanent collection of about 30 vintage planes in its hangar, with a few big ones out on the tarmac. Tour guides are full of facts and personality and have an infectious passion for the planes. Go south on U.S. 441 to U.S. 192; turn right. After the Kissimmee Airport entrance, turn left on Hoagland Boulevard, a.k.a. Airport Road. *231 Hoagland Blvd.,* ☎ *407/933–1942.* ✉ *$6 adults, $5 children 5–12.* ☉ *Mon.–Sat. 9–5:30, Sun. 9–5, extended hours for tour groups.*

⑱ Gatorland. Long before Walt Disney World, there was Gatorland. This campy attraction south of Orlando on U.S. 441 has endured since 1949 without much change, despite competition from major attractions. Through the monstrous aqua, gator-jaw doorway—a definite photo op—lie thrills and chills in the form of thousands of alligators and crocodiles, swimming and basking in the Florida sun. In addition to the gators and crocs, there is a zoo that houses many other reptiles, mammals, and birds. A free train ride provides an overview of the park, and a three-story observation tower overlooks the breeding marsh, which is swamped with gator grunts, especially come sundown during mating season.

Don't miss the Gator Jumparoo show, in which gators leap out of the water for their food. The best Jumparoo is the first one in the morning, when the gators are hungriest. There's also a Gator Wrestling show, and though there's no doubt who's going to win the match, it's still fun to see the handlers take on those tough guys with the beady eyes. In the educational Snakes Alive show, high drama is provided by the 30–40 rattlesnakes that fill the pit around the speaker. Don't look for scrupulous Disney-style cleanliness here, and the personnel aren't polished with pixie dust either. This is a real Florida experience, and you'll walk out those aqua gator jaws knowing the difference between a gator and a croc. ✉ *14501 S. Orange Blossom Trail between Orlando and Kissimmee,* ☎ *407/855–5496 or 800/393–5297.* ✉ *$10.95 adults, $7.95 children 3–11.* ☉ *Daily 8–dusk.*

⑳ Green Meadows Farm. Friendly farmhands keep things moving on the two-hour, guided tour of this Kissimmee attraction. There's little chance to get bored and no waiting in line because tours are always starting. Everyone who wants to gets to milk the fat mama cow, and chickens and geese are turned loose in their yard to run and squawk while city slickers try to catch them. Kids take a quick pony ride, and everyone gets jostled about on the old-fashioned hayride. Kids come away saying: "I milked a cow, caught a chicken, pet a pig, and fed a goat." Take I–4 Exit 25A, Kissimmee; go east on U.S. 192 for 3 miles to Poinciana Boulevard; turn right and drive 5 miles. ✉ *1368 Poinciana Blvd.,* ☎ *407/846–0770.* ✉ *$12 age 2 and over.* ☉ *Daily 9:30–5; last tour at 4.*

㉑ WaterMania. This park has all the requisite rides and slides without Walt Disney World aesthetics. However, it's the only water park around to have **Wipe Out,** a surfing simulator, where you grab a body board and ride a continuous wave form. The giant Pirate Ship in the **Rain Forest,** one of two children's play areas, is equipped with water slides and water cannons. The **Abyss,** similar to Wet 'n' Wild's Black Hole, is an enclosed tube slide through which you twist and turn on a one- or two-person raft for 300 feet of deep-blue darkness. The park also offers a sandy beach, a picnic area, snack bars, gift shops, and periodic concerts, which can be enjoyed while floating in an inner tube. Its 18-hole miniature golf course won't win any local prizes, considering the competition, but does give you another way to pass the time while you're out of the water. It's in Kissimmee (½ mile east of I–4 and 1½ miles from Walt Disney World). ✉ 6073 W. *Irlo Bronson Memorial Hwy.*, ☎ 407/239–8448, 407/396–2626, or 800/527–3092. ✆ *$23.95 adults, $17.95 children 3–12, children under 2 free.* ☯ *Feb. 14–29, daily 11–5; Mar. 1–29, daily 10–5; Mar. 30–Apr. 14, daily 10–7; Apr. 15–May, daily 10–5; Memorial Day weekend, 10–7; June–Aug. 18, weekdays 9:30–7, weekends 9:30–8; Aug. 19–Sept. 9, daily 9:30–6; Sept. 10–Oct., daily 10–5; Nov. daily 11–5.*

LAKE COUNTY

As you drive northwest out of Orlando on U.S. 441, you head into aptly named Lake County, an area renowned for its pristine water and excellent fishing. Watch the flat countryside, thick with scrub pines, take on a gentle roll through citrus goves and pastures with live oaks. The lean orchards still show signs of the devastation caused by the freeze of 1989. Unusually cold weather in 1996 hasn't helped their regeneration.

Mount Dora

About 45 minutes northwest of Orlando is the quaint valley community of Mount Dora. There are two ways to get there: take U.S. 441—Orange Blossom Trail in Orlando—north or take I-4 to exit 51—Sanford/Mt. Dora—and take Hwy. 46 west and follow the signs.

Built around the unspoiled Lake Harris chain of lakes, the town has a slow and easy pace, a rich history, New England-style charm and excellent antiquing. Although the population of Mount Dora is less than 8,000, there is plenty of excitement here, especially in fall and winter. The first weekend in February is the annual **Mount Dora Art Festival,** which opens Central Florida's spring art fair season. Attracting more than 50,000 visitors over a 3-day period, it is one of Central Florida's major outdoor events. During the year, there's a sailing regatta, a bicycle festival, a crafts fair, and many other events. **Palm Island Park** offers nature trails and fishing, and **Gilbert Park** has a public dock and boat-launching ramp, picnicking facilities, and a playground. The Mount Dora Chamber of Commerce provides a self-guilded tour map that tells you everything you need to know—from historic landmarks to restaurants—just in case you forget to bring this book along. ✉ *341 Alexander St.,* ☎ *352/383–2165,* ₣ₐₓ *352/383–1668.* ☯ *Welcome Center weekdays 9–5, Sat. 10–4, Sun. noon–4; after hrs, maps on display at kiosk.*

A Good Walk

Begin your tour in the heart of Mount Dora, in Donnelley Park, between 5th and 6th avenues and Donnelley and Baker streets. During the holidays, this is the site of Mount Dora's annual lighting ceremony in which 80,000 twinkles illuminate the night. Head towards Donnelly Street, where you'll see a Queen Anne–style mansion. This is **Donnelley House,** an 1893 architectural gem that now serves as the local Masonic Temple Lodge. Notice the details on the leaded glass windows. At 413 Donnelly Street, you'll see the **Dora Hotel,** built in the 1920s and now used as restaurant and office space. Continue down Donnelley to Third Street and make a right. At the intersection of Third and Alexander you'll see Mount Dora's **historic train depot,** which now serves as the offices of the Chamber of Commerce. Stop in to pick up a guided tour map and to get the latest information on shops and restaurants.

From the train depot, make a right, continuing on Alexander to the **Lakeside Inn,** an historic country inn built in 1883 that's been restored to its original grandeur. Stop in for tea or something stronger here. A stroll around the grounds will make you feel like you've stepped out of the pages of *The Great Gatsby*; there's even a croquet court. From the Lakeside Inn, head out towards Lake Dora along Third Avenue. Make a right on McDonald Street and stroll around the **Mt. Dora Yacht Club,** the oldest inland yacht club in Florida. On a misty day here, the lakes seem to go on forever.

From the Yacht Club, head back to 5th Avenue and make a right. Along the way, you'll pass several of the town's historic buildings: the **Princess Gallery Theatre** at number 130 is a 1920s movie palace that's now home to several small boutiques; number 115, the **Simpson Hotel,** was built in 1925 by descendants of the Simpson family, Mount Dora's first home-steaders. Continue on 5th, and you'll pass a number of charming an-tiques and gift shops. Along the way, you'll pass the **Park Bench Restaurant,** the perfect spot for a late lunch or early dinner.

WHEN TO TOUR
To fully enjoy the town and its rich architectural details, allow two hours minimum, longer if you plan to shop and take a meal break.

Sights to See

Alexander Springs. Located about 30 minutes north of Mount Dora, this park is favored by the locals in the summer for its cold, fresh water. After hiking down to its small beach, swim out, preferably with a snorkel and fins, to the steep drop-off at the head of the spring, where the water rushes out from rock formations below. Although it's not unusual to see friendly alligators sitting on the bank opposite the sandy beach, re-member that they are still wild and should not be provoked. You'll no-tice that the natives leave the water before sundown–feeding time. From Ocala National Forest Visitor Center, 45621 Rte. 19, Altoona, go north on Rte. 19 and turn right on Rte. 445. Entrance is on the left. ☎ 352/669–7495. ☐ $2. ☉ *Springs daily 8–8, center daily 9–5.*

Lakeside Inn. On the shores of Lake Dora, this elegant, 1883 hostelry provides the charm and hospitality of a bygone era. The Inn has an award-winning restaurant that's open for lunch and dinner. ✉ *100 N. Alexander St., Mount Dora, 32757,* ☎ *352/383–4104 or 800/556–5016,* FAX *352/735–2642. AE, D, MC, V.*

❹ **Ocala National Forest.** This 366,000 acre area between the Oklawaha and the St. Johns rivers is known for its canoeing, hiking, swimming, camping, and invigorating springs. ✉ *Ocala National Forest Visitor Center, 45621 Rte. 19, Altoona,* ☎ *352/669–7495.* ☉ *Center daily 9–5.*

EAST OF ORLANDO

Christmas

There really is a Santa Claus in this tiny hamlet about 18 miles east of Orlando on Highway 50, Colonial Drive. Locals zipping to the beach can miss this town if they blink their eyes; even so it's hard not to re-sist a look at the permanent Christmas tree. Area residents also flock here during December to have their holiday missives postmarked at the local post office.

Sight to See

Fort Christmas Museum. If the kids have been cooped up in the car for a while, this is a great place for them to let off steam. There's a large play area and picnic area, plus a restored 1837 fort, built during the Second Seminole War as part of preparations to take the fighting to South Florida. Inside the fort is a museum that details Florida pioneer life in the mid-19th century. During the week the fort is often brimming with local school children who visit on Florida history field trips. ⊠ *2 mi. north of S.R. 50 on C.R. 420 (Ft. Christmas Rd.)* ☎ *407/568–4149* ☒ *Free* ⊙ *Tues.–Sat. 10–5, Sun. 1–5; closed Orange County holidays.*

NORTH OF ORLANDO

Apopka

Sight to See

❸ Wekiva Springs State Park. Where the tannin-stained Wekiva River meets the crystal-clear Wekiva headspring, there is a curious and visible exchange—like strong tea infusing in water. Wekiva is a Creek Indian word meaning "flowing water," and the park sprawls around this area on 6,400 acres. The parkland is well-suited for camping, hiking, and picnicking; the spring for swimming, and the river for canoeing and fishing. Canoe trips can range from a simple hour-long paddle around the lagoon to observe a colony of water turtles to a full-day excursion through the less-congested parts of the river that haven't changed much since the area was inhabited by the Timacuan Indians. Take I–4 Exit 49 (Longwood) and turn left on S.R. 434. Go 1¼ miles to Wekiva Springs Road; turn right and go 4½ miles to the entrance, on the right. ⊠ *1800 Wekiva Circle,* ☎ *407/884–2009.* ☒ *$3.25 per vehicle.* ⊙ *Daily 8–sundown.*

Cassadaga ❶

This tiny town of Cassadaga, about 35 miles northeast of Orlando, is headquarters of the Southern Cassadaga Spiritualist Camp Meeting Association. More than half of the 300 residents are psychics, mediums, and healers, which makes it the nation's largest such community. To get here, take I–4 to Exit 54 (Cassadaga and Lake Helen). Turn right on Route 472 and right again at the first traffic light marked Route 4139; continue 2 miles. ⊠ *Cassadaga Spiritualist Camp, Box 319, Cassadaga,* ☎ *904/228–2880.*

Sight to See

Colby Memorial Temple. Church services are held 10:30–11:45 AM Sunday and 7:30–8:15 PM Wednesday, and visitors are very welcome. Spiritualist services are nonsensational, meditative gatherings, with the most unconventional aspect being the "message" portion, during which certified mediums deliver specific messages to attendees from spirits in the beyond. Visitors are also encouraged to get a reading from a camp member; it is suggested that the best way to find a medium who is right for you is by walking or driving through this rustic, 5-block-by-5-block neighborhood and stopping at a house that is giving off the right energy. ⊠ *Stevens St.,* ☎ *904/228–3171.*

Southern Cassadaga Bookstore. This community rich in spirit doesn't offer much to the material world, except this modest bookstore. People here and in the community are friendly and wholesome and accustomed to curiosity seekers, but they do request respect for their community. ⊠ *1112 Stevens St.,* ☎ *904/228–2880.* ⊙ *Mon.–Fri. 9:30–5, Sat. 9:30–6, Sun. noon–6.*

Sanford

This growing community on the shores of Lake Monroe has attracted a number of Orlandoans seeking a respite from Orlando's burgeoning urban sprawl. First Street, with buildings that date from the 1880s to the 1920s, offers antiques and second-hand shops, and a few galleries.

Sight to See

❷ Central Florida Zoological Park. A visit here will disappoint if you're expecting a grand metro zoo. However, this is a respectable display of about 230 animals tucked under pine trees, and, like the city of Orlando, it continues to grow. The elephant exhibit is popular, as are the tortoises and the exotic and native snakes housed in the herpetarium. The zoo is becoming specialized in small and medium-size exotic cats, including servals, caracals, and jaguarundis, and there is an aviary that houses American bald eagles that have been grounded due to injury. Children love the Animal Adventure, which has domestic and farm animals to pet and feed; pony rides are offered from 10 to 4. Take I–4 Exit 52, and drive 1 mile east on U.S. 17–92 to the entrance, on the right. ⊠ *3755 N. U.S. 17–92, Sanford,* ☎ *407/323–4450.* ⊑ *$5 adults, $2 children 3–12.* ☉ *Daily 9–5.*

SOUTH OF ORLANDO

Lake Wales

If, after several days at the theme parks, you find that you're in need of a back-to-nature fix, head south of Orlando, along U.S. 27 south. Along the way, you'll see what's left of Central Florida's citrus groves (there's still quite a lot of them); plus you'll get away from the congestion of the city.

Sight to See

㉒ Bok Tower Gardens. This quirky, yet appealing sanctuary of plants, flowers, trees, and wildlife is overlooked by most visitors, but it's worth a look. Shady paths meander through pine forests in this peaceful world of silvery moats, mockingbirds and swans, blooming thickets, and hidden sundials. You'll be able to boast that you stood on the highest measured point in the state, a colossal 324 feet above sea level. The majestic, 200-foot Bok Tower is constructed of conquina—from seashells—and pink, white, and gray marble. The tower houses a carillon with 57 bronze bells that ring every half hour after 10 AM. Each day at 3 there is a 45-minute recital, which may include Early American folk songs, Appalachian tunes, Irish ballads, or Latin hymns. There are also moonlight recitals.

The landscape was designed in 1928 by Frederick Law Olmsted, Jr., son of the planner of New York's Central Park. On the grounds you'll find the 20-room, Mediterranean Revival-style Pinewood House, built in 1930. Take I–4 west to U.S. 27 south. About 5 miles past the Cypress Gardens turnoff, turn right on Route 17A to Alternate U.S. 27. Past the orange groves, turn left on Burns Avenue and follow it about 1½ miles to the gardens. ⊠ *Burns Ave. and Tower Blvd.,* ☎ *941/676– 1408.* ⊑ *$4 adults, $1 children 5–12, free Sat. 8 AM–9 AM.* ☉ *Pinewood House tours Sept. 15–May 15, Tues. and Thurs. 12:30 and 2, Sun. 2.* ⊑ *Suggested donation for Pinewood House: $5.*

5 Shopping

SHOPPING IS PART OF THE ENTERTAINMENT at Walt Disney World and throughout the Greater Orlando area. There's something in every price range in virtually every store, so even kids on allowances can get in on the act. You'll find everything from specialty stores, gift shops, and flea markets to factory outlets, department stores, and, of course, malls. Shop-till-you-droppers will be delighted to know that Orlando is packed with malls—and every year there are more and more. It is virtually impossible to step outside your hotel room without seeing a mall or a sign advertising one. Whatever your shopping interests—Pongo and Perdita stuffed toys, Ralph Lauren blue jeans, flea-marketesque finds—the area provides a great opportunity to do a lifetime of shopping in a few days. Most stores accept traveler's checks and major credit cards.

Updated by
Marianne
Camas and
Val Meyer

WALT DISNEY WORLD

You'll be able to find Disney trinkets in every park, but there are a few shops throughout the property that carry unique items, like Magic Kingdom's Frontier Trading Post, where you can find western-style gifts. For top suggestions—such as the Emporium, the Magic Kingdom's largest gift shop—*see* the Shopping sections *in* Chapter 2. In addition, keep your eye out for wonderful finds tailored to special interests—tennis balls with Mickey Mouse logos, for instance, are available in the pro shops at the Contemporary and other hotels.

GREATER ORLANDO AREA
AND KISSIMMEE

Antiques

Although not known as a mecca for antiques hunters, Orlando has a small but thriving antiques row just north of downtown on North Orange Avenue. The charming town of Mount Dora, about a 45-minute drive north, has a thriving antiques trade, with dozens of shops within a few square blocks.

A&T Antiques. Located in the middle of Orlando's "Antique Row" on North Orange Avenue, A&T prides itself on having the area's largest selection of antiques. Items for sale include European and country pine furniture and decorative pieces. ⊠ *1620 N. Orange Ave. (I–4 Exit 43 to Princeton Ave. east to N. Orange Ave. and turn right), Orlando,* ☎ *407/896–9831.* ⊙ *Weekdays 9–6, Sat. 10–5.*

Flo's Attic. A wonderful neighborhood store, Flo's sells furniture, pottery, china, jewelry, and other treasures. There's lots of stuff to sort through. ⊠ *1800 N. Orange Ave. (I–4 Exit 43 to Princeton Ave. east to N. Orange Ave. and turn right),* ☎ *407/895–1800.* ⊙ *Mon.–Sat. 9–6.*

Ivanhoe Row. This group of shops near downtown Orlando sells mostly delightful but pricey antiques. The Fly Fisherman specializes in accoutrements for the angler; you can often spot salesperson and customer testing out a rod and reel in Lake Ivanhoe, across the street. Swanson's Antiques carries a fine selection of 19th- and 20th-century furniture and bric-a-brac. Wildlife Gallery offers paintings and sculptures of various members of the animal kingdom. After antiquing, cross the street and take a stroll in the beautiful park surrounding Lake Ivanhoe. ⊠ *1213–1303 N. Orange Ave. (I–4 Exit 43 to Princeton Ave.*

170

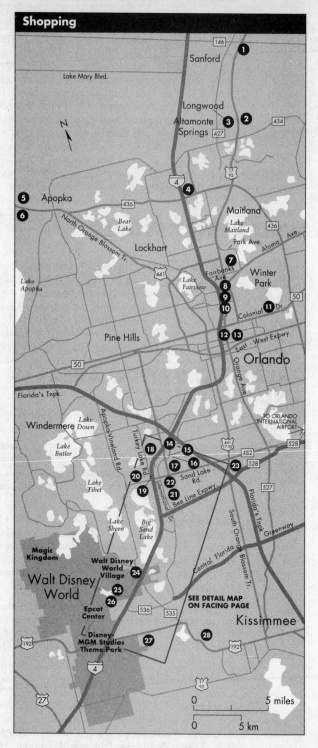

Shopping

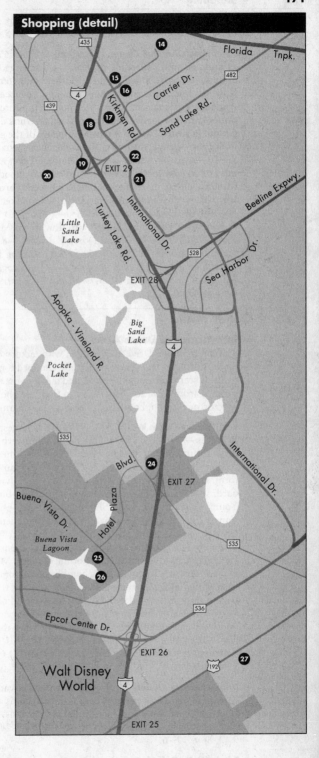

Shopping (detail)

435

14

Florida Tnpk.

15

16

Carrier Dr.

482

4

439

Kirkman Rd.

Sand Lake Rd.

18

17

22

19

EXIT 29

21

Beeline Expwy.

20

International Dr.

Little
Sand
Lake

Turkey Lake Rd.

528

Sea Harbor Dr.

EXIT 28

Big
Sand
Lake

Apopka - Vineland R.

4

Pocket
Lake

International Dr.

535

Blvd.

24

EXIT 27

Buena Vista Dr.

Hotel Plaza

535

Buena Vista
Lagoon

25

26

536

Epcot Center Dr.

EXIT 26

27

Walt Disney
World

4

192

EXIT 25

east to N. Orange Ave. and turn right), Orlando, ☎ *407/896–9230 or 407/898–6050.* ☉ *Weekdays 10–6, Sat. 10–5.*

Renninger's Antique Center. Advertised as Florida's biggest gathering of antiques and collectible dealers, it's one large building with 150 booths, similar to a flea market. **Mother Daughter** and the **Victorian Rose** sell fine 19th-century American and European furniture, **Lyons Antiques** specializes in American country furniture, and **Lismore Antiques** carries a large selection of steamer trunks. The aptly named **Grandma's Attic,** which is typical of many of the shops, offers china, quilts, toys, lamps, furniture, and collectibles from the 1890s through the 1950s. At bimonthly weekend **Antique Fairs,** as many as 500 antiques and collectibles dealers set up outdoor booths on the adjacent wooded, hilly acres. At the adjacent **Renninger's Farmers' and Flea Market,** 500 merchants sell fresh produce, meats, baked goods, crafts, and new and used household items. The best plan is to spend the morning at Renninger's and then move on to downtown Mount Dora in time for lunch. ⊠ *U.S. 441, Mount Dora,* ☎ *352/383–8393 (Thurs.–Sun.).* ▣ *Extravaganzas only, $10 Fri., $5 Sat., $2 Sun.* ☉ *Weekends 9–5; Antiques Fairs 7 weekends per year 8–5; Extravaganzas once each in Nov., Jan., and Feb., Fri. 10–5, weekends 7–5; Farmers' and Flea Market weekends 8–5.*

Factory Outlet Malls

International Drive Area

The International Drive area is filled with factory outlet stores, most on the northeast end. These outlets are clumped together in expansive malls or scattered along the drive, and much of the merchandise is discounted from 20% to 75%. You can find just about anything, some of it top quality, but be advised: These are not charming places to shop.

Belz Factory Outlet World. This is the area's largest collection of outlet stores—nearly 170, in two malls and four nearby annexes. A good place to find discount name-brand clothes for the whole family, the complex includes such stores as Carole Hockman Lingerie, Maidenform, Danskin, Anne Klein, Jonathan Logan, Calvin Klein, Harvé Benard, Van Heusen, Burlington Brands, Just Kids, Bugle Boy, Oshkosh, Young Generations, Bally Shoes, Bass Shoes, Etienne Aigner, and Capezio. Especially popular are the outlets for athletic shoes: Converse, Reebok, and Sneakee Feet, which sells Reebok, Nike, and Adidas. There are also good buys in housewares and linens in such outlets as Fieldcrest/Cannon, Pfaltzgraff, Corning/Revere, Mikasa, and Fitz & Floyd. Don't worry about carting home breakable or cumbersome items; these stores will ship your purchases anywhere in the United States by UPS. Although the mall isn't fancy, it is clean and pleasant. Mall 2 offers a carousel for children and an adequate food court. The information booth sells discount tickets to all the non-Disney theme parks and offers a foreign currency exchange service. ⊠ *5401 W. Oakridge Rd., northern tip of International Dr.,* ☎ *407/352–9600.* ☉ *Mon.–Sat. 9:30–9:30, Sun. 10–6.*

Dansk Factory Outlet. All the dinnerware, flatware, glassware, and cookware you can imagine is here—and all of it is at discount prices. Many of these items are seconds, limited editions, and discontinued styles. ⊠ *7024 International Dr.,* ☎ *407/351–2425.* ☉ *Mon.–Sat. 9–7, Sun. 11–6.*

Edwin Watts Golf Shop. Local duffers love all the locations of this no-handicap shop for golfing equipment. ⊠ *Shop, 7501 Turkey Lake Rd.; clearance center, 7048 International Dr.,* ☎ *Shop, 407/345–8451;*

clearance center, 407/352–2535. ☼ *Shop weekdays 9:30–8, Sat. 9:30–6, Sun. noon–5; clearance center weekdays 9:30–7, Sat. 9:30–6, Sun. noon–5.*

Quality Outlet Center and **Quality Center East.** These two interconnected strip shopping centers contain more than 20 brand-name, factory-outlet stores, including American Tourister, Great Western Boots, Corning/Revere, Royal Doulton, Villeroy & Boch, Florsheim Shoes, Laura Ashley, Magnavox, and Mikasa. ⊠ *5409 and 5529 International Dr., 1 block north of Kirkman Rd.,* ☎ *407/423–5885.* ☼ *Mon.–Sat. 9:30–9, Sun. 11–6.*

Special Tee Golf. Discounted golf and tennis equipment and sportswear will be found in this store's several locations. Two are located along the International Drive tourist corridor. ⊠ *5400 International Dr.,* ☎ *407/352–3673.* ☼ *Mon.–Sat. 10–9, Sun. 11–5:30.* ⊠ *8747 International Dr.,* ☎ *407/363–1281.* ☼ *Mon.–Sat. 10–9, Sun. 11–5:30.*

World of Denim. A great place for jeans, this shop carries Levi's, Lee, Bugle Boy, Jordache, and Wrangler and often offers two-for-one deals on shirts. Although the selection in children's sizes is limited, most women's and men's sizes can be found. There are plenty of salesclerks to help you dig through the stacks of jeans, and a seamstress will make alterations while you wait. It only takes 10 minutes if you're first, but much longer if there's a line. Parking is limited. ⊠ *7623 International Dr.,* ☎ *407/351–5704.* ☼ *Daily 9–midnight.*

U.S. 192 Area

Kissimmee Manufacturers' Outlet Mall. It doesn't look too appealing from the road, but this strip shopping center contains a nice selection of shops. The approximately 20 stores include Bass Shoes, American Tourister, Van Heusen, Bon Worth, London Fog, Levi's, Fieldcrest/Cannon, Manhattan, Totes, Acme Boots, and Brandname Shoes, carriers of Reebok and L.A. Gear. ⊠ *2511–2557 Old Vineland Rd. off U.S. 192 (Irlo Bronson Memorial Hwy., 1 mi east of Rte. 535),* ☎ *407/396–8900.* ☼ *Mon.–Sat. 10–9, Sun. 11–5.*

Flea Markets

Flea World. This Sanford fixture claims to be America's largest flea market under one roof. More than 1,600 booths lend credence to the claim, but so much abundance sometimes means only that good bargains are hiding under unusually large piles of junk. Unlike flea markets in some areas, this one sells only new merchandise—everything from car tires, Ginsu knives, and pet tarantulas to gourmet coffee, leather lingerie, and beaded evening gowns. It's also a great place to buy cheap Florida and Mickey Mouse T-shirts. A free newspaper, distributed at the parking lot entrance, contains a map and directory. Kids love **Fun World** next door, which offers two unusual miniature golf courses, arcade games, go-carts, bumper cars, bumper boats, kiddie rides, and batting cages. Located 3 mi east of I–4 Exit 50 on Lake Mary Blvd., then 1 mi south on U.S. 17–92, *Sanford,* ☎ *407/321–1792.* ☼ *Fri.–Sun. 8–5.*

192 Flea Market Outlet. With 400 booths, this shopping stop is about one-quarter the size of Sanford's Flea World, but it's much more convenient to the major Orlando attractions and is open daily. The all-new merchandise includes toys, luggage, sunglasses, jewelry, clothes, beach towels, sneakers, and the obligatory T-shirts. ⊠ *4301 W. Vine St. (also known as Irlo Bronson Memorial Hwy.), Kissimmee,* ☎ *407/396–4555.* ☼ *Daily 9–6.*

Historic Shopping Towns

Longwood. History buffs will especially enjoy shopping in the quaint little shops in this typical late-19th-century Florida town of towering, live oak trees and brick-paved streets. At its heart is the 1886 **Longwood Hotel,** now an office building, but originally a winter resort for sun-seeking northerners. The turreted **Bradley-McIntyre House** (1885), open for tours on the second and fourth Wednesdays of each month from 11 to 4, was a winter "cottage" in Victorian days. The shops, many of which are housed in historic homes, are scattered throughout this quiet neighborhood. The **Apple Basket** specializes in folk art, hand-thrown pottery, braided rugs, country furnishings, and hand-blown glass ornaments at holiday time. The **Enchanted Cottage** stocks country and Victorian furniture. The **Culinary Cottage** sells wonderful gourmet foods, decorative accessories, and rubber stamps. In the **Browser's Barn** you can find antiques and collectibles. **Transformations** sells one-of-a-kind jewelry, as well as gifts and decorative items. Have lunch or afternoon tea in The **Magnolia Tea Room & Gift Boutique,** a charming, old-fashioned tearoom where you can quite literally buy the teapot that's on your table. 2½ mi east of I–4 Exit 49 on Rte. 434, then north on Rte. 427 to first traffic light (Church Ave.), then left. Most shops are open Monday–Saturday 10–5.

Mount Dora. If you love antiques or if you're just tired of amusement parks, treat yourself to a day here. Founded by homesteaders in 1874, this charming little town has 19th-century stores and houses tucked into rolling hills that overlook Lake Dora. There are dozens of crafts shops, boutiques, galleries, and antiques shops here. **Schwab Antiques** offers furniture, glass, china, silver, and clocks. **Country Pine Newtiques** has an extensive selection of Tom Clark gnomes, David Winter cottages, and other collectibles. The **Art and Antique Union** is a 16-dealer minimall. Arrive in time for lunch at **Eduardo's Mexican & American Cantina** or **Windsor Rose Tea Room**; stay for dinner at the **Park Bench Restaurant,** the **Gables,** or the **Beauclaire Dining Room** in historic **Lakeside Inn,** a famous turn-of-the-century resort that was later a favorite vacation spot of President and Mrs. Calvin Coolidge. ⊠ *West off U.S. 441 on Old U.S. 441 or Rte. 44B,* ☎ *Chamber of Commerce, 352/383–2165.*

Malls and Department Stores

Central Orlando

Orlando Fashion Square. Gayfers, JC Penney, Burdines, and Sears are the anchors for the 165 specialty shops, including such chain stores as Camelot Music, the Gap, Lerner, and Lechters. Bebe's has special children's wear, including mother-daughter outfits, christening gowns, and dresses for big occasions. The White House sells women's lingerie, sportswear, and formal dresses, but only in shades of white and ivory. And, just in case you missed something at the home of the Mouse, there's a large Disney store. Souvenir prices are the same as in the park; however, the store stocks some clothing items and memorabilia not found anywhere else. There's a large and popular food court. ⊠ *3201 E. Colonial Dr., 3 mi east of I–4 Exit 41, Orlando,* ☎ *407/896–1131.* ☼ *Mon.–Sat. 10–9, Sun. noon–5:30.*

International Drive Area

Florida Mall. The largest in central Florida, it includes Sears, JC Penney, Gayfers, Dillard's, a new Saks due to open by winter 1997, 200 specialty shops, seven theaters, and one of the better food courts around. The specialty stores are mostly those you've seen before:

County Seat, the Limited, Radio Shack, Waldenbooks, Athlete's Foot, and Gordon's Jewelers. One recent addition is yet another Warner Brothers Store. At the Barefoot Mailman, however, you can purchase something special—authentic autographed pictures of Madonna, John Wayne, Michael Jackson, Elvis, and many others. Although the mall is supposedly divided into three distinct architectural areas—Victorian, Mediterranean, and Art Deco—you will probably not be aware of any striking differences. Because the mall attracts crowds of tourists, it offers many services, including car rental, airline reservations, check cashing, and currency exchange. Discount tickets to Universal Studios and other area attractions are also available here, as are brochures—many containing money-off coupons—describing local spots of interest. ✉ *8001 S. Orange Blossom Trail, 4½ mi east of I-4 and International Dr., Orlando,* ☎ *407/851-6255.* ⊗ *Mon.–Sat. 10–9:30, Sun. 11–6.*

Northern Suburbs

Altamonte Mall. With its renovation in 1989 and the addition of a food court in 1990, this mall has kept pace with the others in the area. Sears, Gayfers, Burdines, and JC Penney department stores anchor the two-level property; its 175 specialty shops include branches of such chain stores as J. Riggings, Victoria's Secret, Foot Locker, Kay Bee Toys, B. Dalton, and Limited Express. To buy something unusual, try the San Francisco Music Box Company or, if you're really ready to splurge, the Wentworth Gallery, which has a fine selection of original art from around the world. Unlike the one-level malls in the area, this one has a light, airy, and spacious feeling. The many benches, central fountain, and towering palm trees invite you to relax. The neighboring **Renaissance Center** includes eight theaters, Byrons, Linens & Things, and Bookstop. ✉ *451 Altamonte Ave., ½ mi east of I-4, Exit 48 off Rte. 436, Altamonte Springs,* ☎ *407/830-4400.* ⊗ *Mon.–Sat. 10–9, Sun. noon–5:30.*

Seminole Towne Center. Opened in September 1995, this mall answers the shopping needs of Orlando's burgeoning northern suburbs. Anchored by Dillard's, Sears, JC Penney, Burdines, and the area's first Parisian, the mall contains more than 100 retailers, including branches of major chain stores including Ann Taylor, County Seat, the Gap, Foot Locker, and Victoria's Secret. For something tropical, try A Shop Called Mango, owned by singer Jimmy Buffet. And just in case you missed something in the theme parks, there's a branch of the Disney Store here. For information on mall specials, pick up a copy of *The Saving Times,* available throughout the mall. Strollers and wheelchairs are available for rent. There's a pretty good food court, too. ✉ *200 Towne Center Circle, ¼ mi east of I-4 Exit 51, south of Rte. 46, Sanford,* ☎ *407/323-2262.* ⊗ *Mon.–Sat. 10–9, Sun. noon–6.*

Shopping Centers and Villages

Central Orlando and Winter Park

Church Street Exchange. This decorative, brassy, Victorian-theme "festival marketplace" is filled with more than 40 specialty shops; still others are across the street and in the nearby Church Street Marketplace. Among the standouts are The Ark, which specializes in collectibles with an antedeluvian theme; Historic Families, featuring mugs with thousands of surnames; the Old Town Magic Shop, with its collection of gags and pranks; and Destination Orlando, which offers an eclectic selection of Orlando Ts and sweats without the ubiquitous Mouse. You can also find many of the requisite upscale shops, such as Victoria's Secret. Across the street from the complex is Bumby Emporium, a Church Street souvenir shop, and Buffalo Trading Company, where you can buy string ties, cowboy hats, and snakeskin boots; and across the railroad tracks is yet another collection of unusual shops and pushcarts, known as the Historic Railroad Depot. The Exchange has a small food court on the second floor, but remember there are some great restaurants in Church Street Marketplace; children can spend some money on arcade and video games on the top floor at **Commander Ragtime's Midway of Fun, Food and Games.** ⊠ *Church St. Station, 124 W. Church St., Orlando,* ☎ *407/422–2434.* ⊙ *Daily 11–11.*

Church Street Marketplace. It's lots of tourists, lots of locals, and lots of fun. This shopping and dining complex is almost single-handedly responsible for revitalizing downtown Orlando's nightlife. Many staples of the festival marketplace-genre, such as Brookstone and The Sharper Image are here, along with a smattering of other retailers, such as B. Dalton, Express, and Hit or Miss. Dining and drinking options include Pizzeria Uno, Olive Garden, Hooter's, and Jungle Jim's. For entertainment, there's Howl at the Moon, a sing-along nightclub. But the real show is the people-watching. ⊠ *55 W. Church St., Orlando,* ☎ *407/872–3500.* ⊙ *Mon.–Sat. 10–10, Sun. noon–6, restaurant and bar hours vary.*

Park Avenue. Longtime residents complain that Winter Park's tony shopping street is beginning to resemble a mall, as local one-of-a-kind stores are replaced by chains such as Banana Republic, B. Dalton, the Gap, Orvis, Laura Ashley, and Ann Taylor. Visitors, however, are usually charmed by this posh shopping district, with its tiny courtyards ringed by restaurants, galleries, bookstores, and other little shops. Perfumery on Park specializes in hard-to-find fragrances. Country Life and Park Avenue Gallery feature gift items and collectibles, Victorian Joy is a children's boutique with designer clothing, and Madelaine's Antiques offers furniture and collectibles. *Pooh's Corner* is a delightful children's bookstore specializing in hard-to-find titles. ⊠ *Park Ave. between Fairbanks Ave. and Canton, 3 mi east of I–4 Exit 45, Winter Park,* ☎ *407/644–8281.* ⊙ *Most shops Mon.–Sat. 10–5:30, some also Sun. noon–5.*

International Drive and WDW Area

The Crossroads of Lake Buena Vista. This conveniently located shopping center near Disney World contains restaurants and more than 25 shops that are convenient for tourists. Upscale and casual shops are geared toward sun and surf, electronics, and children, but the necessities, such as a 24-hour grocery and pharmacy, post office, bank, and cleaners, are also there. Though you'll find the usual franchised restaurants, there are also some local spots like the casual Pebbles. While you shop, your offspring can entertain themselves at **Pirate's Cove Adventure Golf.** ⊠ *12545–12551 Rte. 535, I–4 Exit 27, Orlando,* ☎ *407/ 827–7300.* ⊙ *Stores daily 10–10, restaurant hours vary.*

Gooding's Plaza International. In a shopping plaza that caters to tourists, there's a 24-hour Gooding's Supermarket with a food court, one-hour photo developing, and an aisle devoted to Disney merchandise. Also here are several restaurants, including a branch of the popular Jungle **Jim's.** ⊠ *8255 International Dr., Orlando,* ☎ *407/352–4215.* ⊙ *Hours vary.*

The Marketplace. This neighborhood shopping center provides all the basic necessities in one spot near International Drive. Stores include a pharmacy, post office, one-hour film processor, stationery and card store, bakery, dry cleaner, hair salon, optical shop, natural-food grocery, and 24-hour supermarket. Also in the Marketplace are three popular restaurants: Christini's, Enzo's, and the Phoenician. ⊠ *7600 Dr. Phillips Blvd., west of I–4 Sand Lake exit, Orlando,* ☎ *407/345–8668.* ⊙ *Hours vary.*

Mercado Mediterranean Village. This Spanish-style shopping center, a relaxation stop for many bus tours, houses more than 60 specialty shops, such as Beach Club Orlando, which sells swimsuits and beach accessories; American Cola Company, which offers Coca-Cola and An-heuser-Busch memorabilia; and Earth Matters, a shop for environmentalists that sells items with a wildlife theme. A dinner theater and five restaurants are found along the walkway that circles the festival courtyard, where live entertainment can be enjoyed at various times throughout the day. Near Mercado's front entrance is an office of the **Orlando/Orange County Convention and Visitors Bureau.** Here you'll find racks and racks of brochures on just about every conceivable area attraction. Discounted tickets to Universal Studios, dinner shows, and the water parks are sold here. The clean, quick, and large food court offers a selection of food from around the world. Although there is a variety show with animated birds for children every 20 minutes, this isn't a place you'll want to linger with your offspring. ⊠ *8445 International Dr., Orlando,* ☎ *407/345–9337.* ⊙ *Visitors bureau daily 8– 8, stores daily 10–10.*

U.S. 192

Old Town. This shopping-entertainment complex features a 1928 Ferris wheel, a 1909 carousel, and more than 70 specialty shops re-creating a turn-of-the-century Florida village. You can buy a 25¢ Pepsi at the General Store or gourmet popcorn at the Kissimmee Popcorn Company, watch the taffy maker at Coffelt's Taffy & Chocolates or the candlemaker at Kandlestix, and, at Black Market Minerals, pan for gemstones and sharks' teeth or buy agate, onyx, quartz, or even dinosaur fossils. Every Saturday night there is a parade of classic automobiles. ⊠ *5770 Irlo Bronson Memorial Hwy., east of I–4, Kissimmee,* ☎ *407/396–4888 or 800/843–4202.* ⊙ *Daily 10–11.*

6 Sports and the Outdoors

ACTION!

ORLANDO IS THE PLACE TO VISIT if you want to be outside, whether you canoe, hike, fish, or beachcomb. You'll find just about every outdoor sports opportunity here—unless it involves a ski lift—that you'll find anywhere else in the country. There are plenty of tennis courts and more than 60 golf courses in a 30-mile radius, staffed by nearly three dozen PGA pros. Anglers have their own place in the Orlando sun, as well, on the dozens of small lakes. Predictably, boating is big, both on these lakes and on backcountry rivers fed by clear, sweet springs.

Another aspect to the Orlando area sports scene is its good fortune of being a solid professional sports town. The Orlando Magic are big-time, and true baseball fans love the minor-league action. And recently, Disney upped the ante, adding the 51,000-seat Walt Disney World Speedway, home of the annual Indy 200 and other big races on the professional circuit.

Bicycling

At WDW

The most scenic bike riding in Orlando is on Walt Disney World property, along roads that take you past forests, lakes, golf courses, and Disney's wooded resort villas and campgrounds. Bikes are available for rent at: **Caribbean Beach Resort Marina** (☎ 407/934–2850) for $3.50 an hour or $8 a day; at **Fort Wilderness Bike Barn** (☎ 407/824–2742) for $3 per hour, $10 a day, or $15 for 24 hours; and at **Walt Disney World Village Resort** (☎ 407/827–6905) for $3 an hour, $7 a day, or $15 for 24 hours. Theoretically, bike rentals are only for those lodging on WDW property; in practice, rental outfits usually check IDs only in busy seasons. However, bikes must be used only in the area in which you rent them.

Elsewhere

Despite the presence of two large schools—the University of Central Florida and Rollins College—where you would expect to find large numbers of enthusiastic bicyclists, the Orlando area doesn't offer a lot in the way of biking opportunities. It's illegal to ride bikes on Orlando sidewalks—the police will issue tickets, and bike trails are few and far between. Moreover, local motorists are often not particularly accommodating when it comes to sharing the road with two-wheeled traffic. There are some scenic routes, however.

The area near **Rollins College,** in Winter Park, offers views of lakes, tree-lined streets, and the homes of much of the area's old money. Most riders prefer to go west of town to the **Clermont–Lake County** area. Since it's out in the boonies, there isn't much traffic to worry about. There are lots of orange groves and some hills.

Florida Backroad by Robert Howard ($14.95 in bookstores), contains detailed descriptions of biking areas, plus maps with mileage markers and routes for 40 excursions.

Fishing

Central Florida is covered with freshwater lakes and rivers teeming with all kinds of fish, especially largemouth black bass, but also perch, catfish, sunfish, and pike.

Licenses

To fish in most Florida waters—but not at Walt Disney World—anglers over 16 need a fishing license, available at bait-and-tackle shops, fishing camps, most sporting-goods stores, and Walmarts and K-marts. Some of these locations may not sell saltwater licenses, or they may serve non-Florida residents only; call ahead to be on the safe side. The cost is $16.50 for seven days and $31.50 for one year (freshwater); $7 for three days, $17 for seven days, and $32.50 for one year (saltwater).

At WDW

Two-hour fishing trips on regularly stocked **Bay Lake** departing from Fort Wilderness, Contemporary, Polynesian, and Grand Floridian Resort marinas include boat, equipment, coffee and pastries, and guide for up to five anglers. These organized trips are the only way you're allowed to fish on the lake. Reservations are required. ⊠ *Bay Lake Fishing Trips,* ☎ *407/824–2621.* ☎ *$137.* ☉ *Trips daily 8, 11:30, and 3.*

Bass specialists will head for the two-hour fishing expeditions for up to five anglers that depart from the Disney Village Marketplace marina. ⊠ *Captain Jack's Guided Bass Tours,* ☎ *407/828–2461.* ☎ *$120–$175.* ☉ *Trips daily 6:30, 9:00, and 11:30.*

There's fishing off the dock at the **Ol' Man Island Fishing Hole.** Catch and release is encouraged, but you can have your fish packed in ice to take home. You'll have to clean them yourself, though. ⊠ *Dixie Landings,* ☎ *407/934–5409.* ☎ *Cane poles and bait $3.50 per hour per person, $12.50 per hour for family of up to 6; no fee to use dock with pole rental.* ☉ *Daily 9–3.*

A two-hour fishing trip down the **Sasagoula River** at Dixie Landings includes guide, rod, bait, and soft drinks. Reservations must be made in advance. ⊠ *Dixie Landings,* ☎ *407/934–5409.* ☎ *$4 per person.* ☉ *Daily 6:30 AM.*

Fishing without a guide is permitted in the **canals** in Disney Village (Dixie Landings, Port Orleans resorts) and at **Fort Wilderness resort and campground.** Poles and tackle can be rented from one of the "trading post" grocery stores located on the Fort Wilderness campground.

Elsewhere

Top central Florida fishing waters include **Lake Kissimmee,** the **Butler** and **Conway** chains of lakes, and **Lake Tohopekaliga**—don't bother to pronounce it, instead call it "Lake Toho," like the locals do. Your best chance for trophy fish is between November and April on Toho or Kissimmee; for good creels, the best producer is usually the Butler area, which has the additional advantage of its scenery—lots of live oaks and cypresses, plus the occasional osprey or bald eagle. Toho and Kissimmee are also good for largemouth bass and crappie. The Butler chain yields largemouth, some pickerel, and the occasional huge catfish. A variety of services are available, from equipment and boat rental to full-day trips with guides and guarantees.

FISHING CAMPS

There are a number of excellent fishing camps in the area in the form of lakeside campgrounds that draw a more outdoorsy crowd than you find elsewhere in the area.

East Lake Fish Camp on East Lake Tohopekaliga has a restaurant and country store, sells live bait and propane, and rents boats. You can also take a ride on an airboat. It has 243 RV sites, 40 tent sites, and 24 cabins. Try to make reservations for the cabins at least two weeks in advance during the winter and spring. ⊠ *3705 Big Bass Rd., Kissimmee,*

☎ *407/348–2040.* ⌧ *RV sites $16 (2 people), tent sites $12, cabins $45 (2 people, $5 each additional).*

Red's Fish Camp, on West Lake Tohopekaliga, has 100 RV sites. Most of the full hookups are booked year-round, but electrical and water hookups are usually available, as are live bait, food, and drinks. ⌧ *4715 Kissimmee Park Rd., St. Cloud,* ☎ *407/892–8795.* ⌧ *RV sites $12 per night or $195 per month plus electricity.*

Richardson's Fish Camp, on West Lake Tohopekaliga, has 9 cabins with kitchenettes, 16 RV sites, 12 tent sites, boat slips, and a bait shop. ⌧ *1550 Scotty's Rd., Kissimmee,* ☎ *407/846–6540.* ⌧ *RV sites $19.50; tent sites $15; cabins $36 for 1 bedroom, $55 for 2 bedrooms, $65 for 3 bedrooms.*

GUIDES

Guides fish out of the area's fishing camps, and you can usually make arrangements to hire them through the camp office. Rates vary, but for two people $125 for a half day and $175 for a full day are good rules of thumb. Many area guides are part-timers who fish on weekends or take a day off from their full-time job to guide, hitting a variety of local state and private lakes.

Bass Bustin' Guide (BBG), in business 15 years, provides boat, tackle, transportation, and ice and soft drinks for bass fishing on local lakes. Live bait is included in the price—and BBG guarantees fish! ⌧ *5935 Swoffield Dr., Orlando,* ☎ *407/281–0845.* ⌧ *½ day from $150, full day from $200, extra adult $25.*

Bass Challenger Guide (BCG) takes you out in boats equipped with tackle and drinks. Transportation can be arranged between fishing spots and local hotels. Bass is the only quarry, and they guarantee "No bass, no pay!" ⌧ *Box 679155, Orlando,* ☎ *407/273–8045 or 800/241–5314.* ⌧ *½ day from $150, full day from $200.*

Cutting Loose Expeditions goes after bass, but also arranges saltwater expeditions to the Indian River flats to light-tackle-cast for redfish, sea trout, tarpon, and snook. They'll arrange deep-sea charters out of Port Canaveral, too. All trips can include everything but food. They'll even pick you up at the hotel and take you to the fishing hole. ⌧ *Box 447, Winter Park,* ☎ *407/629–4700 or 800/533–4746.* ⌧ *½ day from $175, full day $200–$300, offshore $500–$600.*

Golf

With sunny weather practically year-round, Florida is a golfer's haven, offering more golf courses than any other state. Most of Florida is extremely flat, but many of the courses listed here have been sculpted by their designers to create rolling hills that make them more challenging. Many resort hotels let nonguests use their golf facilities. Some country clubs are affiliated with particular hotels, and their guests can play at preferred rates. If you're staying near a course you'd like to use, call and inquire.

In general, even public courses have dress codes, so call to find out the specifics at each, and be sure to reserve tee times in advance. The yardages quoted are those from the blue tees. Greens fees usually vary by season, but the highest and lowest figures are provided, and all include mandatory cart rental.

Golfpac (⌧ Box 162366, Altamonte Springs 32716–2366, ☎ 407/260–2288 or 800/327–0878) packages golf vacations and prearranges tee times at more than 40 courses around Orlando. Rates vary based on hotel and course, and at least 60–90 days' advance notice is recommended to set up a vacation.

At WDW

Where else would you find a sand trap shaped like the head of a well-known mouse? Walt Disney World has five championship courses—all on the PGA Tour route. Eagle Pines and Osprey Ridge are the newcomers, flanking the Bonnet Creek Golf Club just north of Fort Wilderness. They join WDW's original courses, the Palm and the Magnolia, which flank the Shades of Green Resort, to the west, and the Lake Buena Vista course, near Disney Village Marketplace.

GREENS FEES

The three original Disney courses have the same fees and discount policies: Guests at WDW resorts pay $85; all others pay $95 regardless of season. Prices at Eagle Pines and Osprey Ridge go up to $105 and $120 from January through April. The twilight discount rate is $50 for everyone; this rate goes into effect at 2PM during the winter and peak seasons, at 3 from March through May, and during the summer months after 4, the rate is $40.

TEE TIMES AND RESERVATIONS

Tee times are available from 7:3AM until dark on weekdays and from 7 until dark on weekends. You can book them up to 30 days in advance if you're staying at a WDW-owned hotel, 7 days ahead if you're staying elsewhere from May through December, and 4 days in advance from January through April. For tee times and private lessons at any course, call 407/824–2270.

Eagle Pines, one of two new courses, was designed by golf-course architect Pete Dye. Greens are small and undulating, and fairways are lined with pines and punctuated by bunkers that broaden the challenge. ⊠ *Golf View Dr., Bonnet View Golf Club, north of Fort Wilderness. 6,722 yds. Par: 72. USGA: 72.3. 18 holes. Restaurant, private lessons, club and shoe rental, lockers, driving range, putting green.*

The **Lake Buena Vista** course winds among Disney Village Resort town houses and villas; greens are narrow—and hitting straight is important, since errant balls risk ending up in someone's bedroom. ⊠ *Lake Buena Vista. 6,829 yds. Par: 72. USGA: 72.7. 18 holes. Restaurant, private lessons, club and shoe rental, lockers, driving range, putting green.*

The Magnolia, played by the pros in the Walt Disney World Golf Classic, is long but forgiving, with extra-wide fairways. ⊠ *Shades of Green. 7,190 yds. Par: 72. USGA: 73.9. 18 holes. Restaurant, private and small-group lessons, club and shoe rental, lockers, driving range, putting green.*

In designing **Osprey Ridge,** Tom Fazio leavened the challenge of the course with a relaxing tour into some of the still-forested, as yet undeveloped portions of the huge WDW acreage. Tees and greens as much as 20 feet above the fairways keep competitive players from getting too comfortable, however. Osprey Ridge opened in 1992 along with Eagle Pines. ⊠ *Golf View Dr., Bonnet Creek Golf Club. 7,101 yds. Par: 72. USGA: 73.9. 18 holes. Restaurant, private lessons, club and shoe rental, lockers, driving range, putting green.*

The Palm, one of WDW's original courses, has been confounding the pros as part of the annual Walt Disney World Golf Classic for years. It's not as long as the Magnolia, or as wide, and there are more trees. And don't go near the water! ⊠ *Shades of Green Resort. 6,957 yds.*

Par: 72. USGA: 73. 18 holes. Restaurant, private and small-group lessons, club and shoe rental, lockers, driving range, putting green.

Elsewhere

Greens fees at most non-Disney courses fluctuate with the season. A twilight discount applies after 2 in busy seasons and after 3 during the rest of the year; the discount is usually half off the normal rate.

Cypress Creek Country Club is a demanding course with 16 water holes and lots of trees. ⊠ *5353 Vineland Rd., Orlando,* ☎ *407/351–2187. 6,955 yds. Par: 72. USGA: 70.9. 18 holes.* ✑ *Greens fees $34–$39. Special policies: tee times 7 days in advance. Restaurant, private lessons, club rental.*

Falcon's Fire Golf Club, designed by golf-architect Rees Jones, has one of Orlando's newest courses. Its strategically placed fairway bunkers demand accuracy off the tee. ⊠ *3200 Seralago Blvd., Kissimmee,* ☎ *407/397–2777. 6,473 yds. Par: 72. USGA: 72.5. 18 holes.* ✑ *Greens fees $52–$78. Special policies: tee times 7 days in advance. Restaurant, lounge, private and group lessons, club rental, lockers, driving range, putting green.*

Located about 45 minutes from Orlando, **Grenelefe Golf and Tennis Resort** has three 18-hole courses amid gentle hills. Length is the key here. The West Course, designed by Robert Trent Jones, Sr., plays to 7,325 yards from the championship tees. An absence of water hazards—there are just two ponds—softens the course somewhat. The East Course is very tight, with small greens and lots of changes in elevation. Designed by Ed Seay, it requires accuracy. The South, designed by Ron Garl and Andy Beane, has plenty of sand and water but wider fairways and larger greens. ⊠ *3200 Rte. 546, Haines City,* ☎ *813/422–7511 or 800/237–9549. West Course 7,325 yds, par 72, USGA 75; East Course 6,802 yds, par 72, USGA 72.5; South Course 6,869 yds, par 71, USGA 72.6. 54 holes.* ✑ *Greens fees $39–$110. Special policies: tee times 3 days in advance, but courses often closed to public at busiest time of year (Jan.–Apr.). 3 restaurants, 2 lounges, snack bar, fitness club, sports lounge, spa, marina, private lessons, club and shoe rental.*

The Lloyd Clifton–designed **Hunter's Creek Golf Course** has large greens and 14 water holes. ⊠ *14401 Sports Club Way, Orlando,* ☎ *407/240–4653. 7,432 yds. Par: 72. USGA: 75.2. 18 holes.* ✑ *Greens fees $35–$60. Special policies: tee times 3 days in advance. Snack bar, private lessons, club rental.*

Marriott's Orlando World Center has a Joe Lee–designed course with 14 water holes and lots of sand. ⊠ *1 World Center Dr., Orlando,* ☎ *407/238–8660. 6,307 yds. Par: 71. USGA: 69.8. 18 holes.* ✑ *Greens fees $60–$110. Special policies: tee times 7 days in advance for public, 90 days in advance for World Center guests. 4 restaurants, sports bar, private and group lessons, club and shoe rental.*

MetroWest Country Club has a rolling Robert Trent Jones, Sr. course, with few trees but lots of sand. ⊠ *2100 S. Hiawassee Rd., Orlando,* ☎ *407/299–1099. 6,500 yds. Par: 72. USGA: 70.3. 18 holes.* ✑ *Greens fees $55 for residents, $70 for non-residents. Special policies: tee times 7 days in advance. Restaurant, private and group lessons, club rental.*

About five minutes from Walt Disney World's main entrance is **Orange Lake Country Club.** It has three 9-hole courses, all very similar. Distances aren't long, but fairways are very narrow, and there's a great deal of water, making the course very difficult. ⊠ *8505 W. Irlo Bronson Memorial Hwy., Kissimmee,* ☎ *407/239–0000 or 800/877–6522.*

Lake/Orange: 6,551 yds, par 72, USGA 72.2. Orange/Cypress: 6,680 yds, par 72, USGA 72.6. Cypress/Lake: 6,535 yds, par 72, USGA 72.3. ⊠ *Greens fees $42–$75. Special policies: tee times 2 days in advance. Restaurant, cafeteria, pizzeria, driving range, putting green, private and group lessons, club rental.*

About 18 miles southeast of Disney World is the **Poinciana Golf & Racquet Resort**—69 bunkers and water on 12 holes nestled in a cypress forest. ⊠ *500 E. Cypress Pkwy., Poinciana (near Kissimmee),* ☎ *407/933–5300 or 800/331–7743. 6,700 yds. Par: 72. USGA: 72.2 18 holes.* ⊠ *Greens fees $40–$50. Special policies: tee times 7 days in advance, discount coupons accepted off season. Restaurant, lounge, driving range, putting green, private and group lessons, club rental.*

Timacuan Golf and Country Club has a two-part course designed by Ron Garl. Part I, the front nine, is open, with lots of sand; part II, the back nine, is heavily wooded. ⊠ *550 Timacuan Blvd., Lake Mary,* ☎ *407/321–0010. 6,582 yds. Par: 72. USGA: 71.5. 18 holes.* ⊠ *Greens fees $40–$85. Special policies: tee times 3 days in advance. Restaurant, snack bar, club rental, driving range, putting green.*

Health Clubs

At WDW

Although most of the Walt Disney World health clubs accept only guests at Walt Disney World hotels—and some accept only guests of that particular hotel—some clubs have been known to stretch the rules. This is a fact worth noting if you're desperate for your workout.

Body by Jake, at the Dolphin, has step and regular aerobics classes, weights, personal trainers, treadmills, and stationary bikes. ⊠ *The Dolphin,* ☎ *407/934–4264.* ⊠ *$10 per individual.* ☉ *Daily 6 AM–9 PM. Guests at other hotels admitted only by the day; must pay cash. Dry Sauna, coed Jacuzzi.*

The Olympiad Health Club has Nautilus and hand weights, stairclimbers, cross-country ski machines, and treadmills, plus a tanning bed and booth. Massages are offered at the club or in your room. ⊠ *Contemporary Resort,* ☎ *407/824–3410.* ⊠ *$8.48 per day; massage $37 per ½ hr, $55 per hr, $70–$95 per hour in room.* ☉ *Daily 6:30 AM–8 PM. Open to all Disney guests. Sauna.*

The glittering **St. John's Health Spa** has Nautilus, cardiovascular equipment, treadmills, stairclimbers, rowing machines, and a sauna. ⊠ *Grand Floridian,* ☎ *407/824–3000, Ext. 2433.* ⊠ *$6 per day; $12 per individual or $18 per family for length of stay; massage $37 per ½ hour, $55 per hour.* ☉ *Daily 5:30 AM–9 PM. Sauna.*

Exercise machines, a sauna, spa, and steam room are available at the **Ship Shape Health Club.** ⊠ *Yacht and Beach Club,* ☎ *407/934–3256.* ⊠ *$7 per day, $10 per individual or $20 per family for length of stay; massage $37 per ½ hour, $55 per hour, $70 per hour in room.* ☉ *Daily 6:30 AM–10 PM. Disney guests only.*

Elsewhere

To find out what's hot in exercise facilities when you visit, the best bet is to ask at your hotel, because clubs outside WDW come and go. And don't forget about the local YMCAs, longtime local favorites. To find the one nearest where you're staying, phone the Metropolitan YMCA office (☎ 407/896–9220). Most accept guests on a single-visit basis, for $5–$10, and you don't have to be a Y member.

The **Downtown YMCA** has Nautilus, Cybex machines, free weights, racquetball, an Olympic-size pool, two gyms, and aerobics classes. It's an older property, but the weight room facilities were just revamped. ⊠ *433 N. Mills Ave., Orlando,* ☎ *407/896–6901.* ⊞ *$7 per day, $3.50 to YMCA members from outside Orlando.* ☉ *Weekdays 5 AM–9:30 PM, Sat. 8–6:30, Sun. 1–5.*

The **International Drive YMCA** is definitely more posh than the Downtown Y. It has Nautilus, free weights, racquetball, two swimming pools (one Olympic-size), and a diving well. Members can call ahead to reserve racquetball courts. ⊠ *8422 International Dr., Orlando,* ☎ *407/363–1911.* ⊞ *$10 per day, $4 to YMCA members from outside Orlando, $20 per week.* ☉ *Weekdays 6 AM–9 PM, Sat. 8–5 , Sun. noon–4.*

Horseback Riding

At WDW

Fort Wilderness Campground offers tame trail rides through backwoods. Children must be at least nine, and adults must be under 250 pounds. The campground is open to the public. ⊠ *Fort Wilderness Campground Resort,* ☎ *407/824–2832.* ⊞ *Trail rides $17 for 45 min.* ☉ *Rides daily 9, 10:30, noon, and 2.*

Elsewhere

Private lessons in hunter, jumper, and dressage are given at **Grand Cypress Equestrian Center.** Supervised novice and advanced group trail rides are also available. Call at least a week ahead for reservations in winter and spring. ⊠ *Grand Cypress Resort, 1 Equestrian Dr., Orlando,* ☎ *407/239–4608.* ⊞ *Trail rides $30 per hour for novice, $45 per hour for advanced; private lessons $45 per ½ hour, $75 per hour.* ☉ *Daily 8–5.*

Poinciana Riding Stables offers basic and longer, more advanced nature trail tours along old logging trails near Kissimmee. Pony rides are also available, and the stable area has picnic tables, farm animals you can pet, and a pond to fish in. Reservations a day in advance are recommended for the popular advanced trails. ⊠ *3705 Poinciana Blvd., Kissimmee,* ☎ *407/847–4343.* ⊞ *Trail rides $29.95 for basic, $39.95 for advanced; pony rides $4 for 10 min.* ☉ *Daily 9–5.*

Ice Skating

Orlando sees frost only about once every other year, so ice-skating fever is not taking the city by storm. There are a couple of options, however, if you feel the urge to chill out.

Orlando Ice Skating Palace is either grungy or a look into pre-Disney Orlando, depending on your point of view. But if you are homesick for a winter chill, this should do the trick. ⊠ *3123 W. Colonial Dr., Parkwood Shopping Plaza, Orlando,* ☎ *407/299–5440.* ⊞ *Weekdays and Sun. $5.95 adults, $4.95 children under 12; skate rental $1.50.* ☉ *Summer, Mon.–Sat. 12:30–3:30, 4–7, 7:30–10:30, Sat. also 11 PM–1 AM, Sun. 2–5, 7:30–10:30; winter, closed Mon. and Tues., reduced hours Wed.–Sun.*

Rock on Ice is definitely spiffier but seems touristy. ⊠ *Dowdy Pavilion, 7500 Canada Ave., Orlando,* ☎ *407/363–7465.* ⊞ *Skate rental $2; admission prices and open-skating times vary; call for information.*

Jogging

At WDW

Walt Disney World has several scenic jogging trails. Pick up jogging maps at any Disney resort. **Fort Wilderness Campground** (☎ 407/824–2900) has a 2.3-mile jogging course with plenty of fresh air and woods, as well as numerous exercise stations along the way. Early in the morning all the roads are fairly uncrowded, however, and make for good running. The roads that wiggle through Disney's Village Resorts are pleasant, as are the cart paths on the golf courses.

Elsewhere

Turkey Lake Park (✉ 3401 S. Hiawassee Rd., Orlando, ☎ 407/299–5581), not far from Disney, has a 3-mile biking trail that's also popular with joggers. Several wooded hiking trails also make for a good run. The park closes at 5, and fees are $2 adults, $1 children under 12.

In Winter Park, around **Rollins College,** you can jog along the shady streets and around the lakes, inhaling the aroma of old money. The Orlando Runners Club meets in the area every Sunday morning at 7AM for 3-, 6-, and 12-mile jaunts; for details, call the **Track Shack** (✉ 1322 N. Mills Ave., Orlando, ☎ 407/898–1313). The Track Shack is open weekdays 10–7, Saturday 10–5.

Tennis

At WDW

You can play tennis at any number of Disney hotels, and you'll find the courts a pleasant respite from the milling throngs in the parks. All have lights and are open from 7AM to 10PM, and most have lockers and rental racquets ($4–$5 an hour). There seems to be a long-term plan to move from hard courts to clay, and the Contemporary has already converted. All courts are open to all players, but court staff can opt to turn away nonguests when things get busy. However, that doesn't often happen.

The **Contemporary Resort** is the center of Disney's tennis program, with its sprawl of six clay courts. It has three backboards and an automatic ball machine. Reservations are available up to 24 hours in advance, and there is an arrange-a-game service. ☎ 407/824–3578. 🎾 *Courts $12 per hour, $40 for length of stay; clinics with video replay ($35); private lessons $40 per hour, $25 per ½ hour; ball machines $20 per hour, $10 per ½ hour; racquet rental $4.*

The **Dolphin and Swan** share eight asphalt courts. Call for private lessons with a pro. ☎ 407/934–4396. 🎾 *Courts free; private lessons $45 per hour; racquet rental $10.*

Fort Wilderness Campground has two courts out in the middle of a field; they're popular with youngsters. If you hate players who are too free about letting their balls stray across their neighbors' court, this is not the place for you. There are no court reservations and no instruction. ☎ 407/824–2900. 🎾 *Free.*

At the **Grand Floridian,** the two clay courts attract a somewhat serious tennis-minded crowd. Court reservations are available up to 24 hours in advance. ☎ 407/824–2438. 🎾 *$12 per hour, private lessons $35 per hour.*

The **Yacht and Beach Club** has two blacktop courts. Court reservations are available up to 24 hours in advance. Three is no instruction available. ☎ 407/934–3256. 🎾 *Free.*

Elsewhere

Lake Cane Tennis Center has 13 lighted hard courts. Four pros provide private and group lessons. ⊠ *5108 Turkey Lake Rd., Orlando,* ☎ *407/352–4913.* 🖾 *Courts $3 per hour weekdays, $5 per hour weekends and evenings; lessons $35 per hour, $18 per ½ hour.* ☉ *Daily 8 AM–10 PM.*

In addition to its golf courses, **Orange Lake Country Club** has 15 all-weather hard tennis courts, 9 of them lighted. It is five minutes from Walt Disney World's main entrance. Court reservations are unnecessary. ⊠ *8505 W. Irlo Bronson Memorial Hwy., Kissimmee,* ☎ *407/239–0000.* 🖾 *Courts free for guests, $4 per hour for nonguests; private lessons $30 per hour; clinics $10 per ½ hour; racquet rental $2.* ☉ *Daily dawn–11 PM for guests, 8–5 for nonguests.*

Orlando Tennis Center offers 16 lighted tennis courts (9 HarTru and 7 asphalt), 2 racquetball courts, and three tennis pros. Court reservations are unnecessary. ⊠ *649 W. Livingston St., Orlando,* ☎ *407/246–2162.* 🖾 *Courts $5.80 for 1½ hour on HarTru, $3.68 for 1½ hour on asphalt; racquetball $2.12 per hour; private lessons $30 per hour, group lessons $5.* ☉ *Weekdays 8 AM–10 PM, weekends and holidays 8–3.*

Red Bug Park has 16 lighted Plexipave courts and 8 outdoor covered four-wall racquetball courts. Court reservations are available up to 24 hours in advance. ⊠ *3600 Red Bug Lake Rd., Casselberry,* ☎ *407/695–7113.* 🖾 *Tennis courts $2 per hour before 5, $4 per hour after; racquetball $4 per hour; private lessons $34 per hour.* ☉ *Daily 8 AM–10 PM.*

Sanlando Park has 25 lighted Plexipave courts and 8 covered, fan-cooled racquetball courts. Court reservations are available up to 24 hours in advance. ⊠ *401 W. Highland St., Altamonte Springs,* ☎ *407/869–5966.* 🖾 *Tennis courts $2 per hour before 5, $4 per hour after on weekdays; racquetball $4 per hour; private lessons $32 per hour, $16 per ½ hour.* ☉ *Daily 8 AM–10 PM.*

Water Sports

At WDW

Boating is big at Disney, with the largest fleet of for-rent pleasure craft in the nation. There are marinas at the Caribbean Beach Resort, Contemporary Resort, Disney Village Marketplace, Fort Wilderness Campground, Grand Floridian, Polynesian Village, and Yacht and Beach Club, where you can rent Sunfish, toobies, catamarans, motor-powered pontoon boats, pedal boats, and tiny two-passenger Water Sprites—a hit with kids—for use on **Bay Lake** and the adjoining **Seven Seas Lagoon, Club Lake, Lake Buena Vista,** or **Buena Vista Lagoon.** Most rent Water Sprites; otherwise, each hotel has its own rental roster, and you're sure to find something of interest. The Polynesian Village marina rents outrigger canoes. Fort Wilderness rents canoes for paddling along the placid canals in the area. And you can sail and water-ski on Bay Lake and the Seven Seas Lagoon; stop at the Fort Wilderness, Contemporary, Polynesian, or Grand Floridian Resort marinas.

Elsewhere

Orange Lake, a private lake at the Orange Lake Country Club next to Walt Disney World, has all types of boating—in rowboats, paddleboats, canoes, wave runners, water skiing, and jet boats. You can even sign up for waterskiing school. Rentals at Orange Lake Water Sports. ⊠ *8505 W. Irlo Bronson Memorial Hwy., Kissimmee,* ☎ *407/239–4444.* 🖾 *$5 per ½ hour for canoes, $35 per ½ hour for Waverunners, $60* *per ½ hour for powerboats; $45 per hour, including instruction; waterskiing $35 per ½ hour, $60 per hour.* ☉ *Daily 10–6.*

There's a ski ramp and slalom course on 140-acre **Sand Lake,** a fairly quiet scenic expanse of water rimmed mainly by villas. Jet Skis keep swimmers firmly in the restricted swimming area. Rentals available at Splash 'n' Ski. ⊠ *10000 Turkey Lake Rd., west off I–4 Exit 29 on Sand Lake Rd., Orlando,* ☎ *407/352–1494.* ⊞ *Jet Skis $35 per ½ hour, sailboards $25 per ½ day, waterskiing $45 per ½ hour.* ☉ *Mon.–Sat. 10–5:30.*

A boat ride on **Shingle Creek** provides views of giant cypress trees dripping with Spanish moss. You can get around by airboat or rent a quiet electric swampboat or a canoe. ⊠ *Airboat Rentals, 4266 Irlo Bronson Memorial Hwy., Kissimmee,* ☎ *407/847–3672.* ⊞ *Airboats $25 per hour, swamp boats and electric boats $16 per hour, canoes $5 per hour.* ☉ *Daily 9:30–5.*

The **St. Johns River** winds through pine and cypress woods and past pastures where cows graze placidly, skirting the occasional housing development. There's good bird- and wildlife-watching; herons, ibis, storks, and sometimes bald eagles can be spotted, along with alligators and manatees. It's a favored local boating spot, for everything from a day of waterskiing to a weeklong trip in a houseboat. Rentals are available in DeLand (west of I–4 Exit 56 via U.S. 44). ⊠ *Holly Bluff, 2280 Hontoon Rd., DeLand,* ☎ *904/822–9992 or 800/237–5105.* ⊞ *Pontoon boats $75 for 4 hours, $125 per day; 44-foot houseboats $400 per day, $750 per 2 days (weekend), $1,150 per week; rates lower Dec.–Feb.* ⊠ *Hontoon Landing Resort and Marina, 2317 River Ridge Rd., DeLand,* ☎ *904/734–2474; in FL, 800/248–2474.* ⊞ *Luxury houseboats $400–$1,395 per day, $1,095–$2,195 per week (Oct.–Mar.), $1,495–$2,595 per week (Apr.–Sept.); ski boats $150 per day or $30/hour not including gas and oil; pontoons $30 per hour, $100 per day (weekdays), $125 (weekends) including gas and oil; deckboat $175 per day or $50 per hour.*

Another great waterway for nature lovers is the **Wekiva River,** which runs through 6,397-acre Wekiva State Park into the St. Johns River. Bordered by cypress marshlands, its clear, spring-fed waters showcase a rich array of Florida wildlife, including otters, raccoons, alligators, bobcats, deer, turtles, and numerous birds. Canoes and battery-powered motorboats, whose quiet engines don't disturb the wildlife, are the best way to get around; they're available for rent. ⊠ *Katie's Wekiva River Landing and Campground, 190 Katie's Cove, Sanford,* ☎ *407/628–1482.* ⊞ *Canoes $12 per hour (2-hour minimum), $2 each additional hour, $20 per day. Group trips, campsites, 4 cabins, picnic tables.*

Alexander Creek and Juniper Creek, in Ocala National Forest just north of the greater Orlando area, also offer wonderful wilderness canoeing, with abundant wildlife and moss-draped oaks and bald cypresses canopying the clean, clear waters. Some of these runs are quite rough— lots of ducking under brush and maneuvering around trees. Do not bring any disposables. ⊠ *Alexander Springs Canoe Rental, County Rd. 445,* ☎ *904/669–3522.* ⊞ *Canoes $10–$22 with $20 deposit and ID.* ☉ *Daily 8–dark.* ⊠ *Juniper Springs Canoe Rental, State Rd. 40,* ☎ *904/625–2808.* ⊞ *Canoes $20–$25 with $20 deposit and ID.*

FROM THE SIDELINES

Not everything in Orlando is wholesome, Disney-style family fun. Wagering a wad of cash at the fronton or the dog track is guaranteed to wipe the refrain from "It's a Small World" right out of your head. And even if you bet and lose steadily, you won't necessarily spend more than you would at most of the attractions. In addition, there are teams in various sports and leagues that play their regular seasons in and around Orlando, as well as major-league baseball clubs that make their spring-training homes in the area.

Baseball

Watching a minor-league or spring-training game in a small ballpark can take you back to a time when going to a game didn't mean bringing binoculars or watching the big screen to see what was happening. Minor-league teams play from April to September, and spring training lasts only a few weeks in March and early April, but it can be a thrill to watch stars up close while you, and they, enjoy a spring break before getting back to work. Tickets to the minors usually run $3–$6; spring training seats cost $8–$10.

Minor Leagues
The **Orlando Cubs** are Chicago's Class AA Southern League affiliate. They play 69 home games at Tinker Field. ⊠ *287 S. Tampa Ave., west off I–4 Colonial Ave. exit, Orlando,* ☎ *407/872–7593.*

The **Kissimmee Cobras** are Houston's Class A team in the Florida State League and play at Osceola County Stadium. Arrive early because tickets are sold only at the stadium on a same-day, first-come basis. ⊠ *1000 Bill Beck Blvd., west of I–4 Exit 65, Kissimmee,* ☎ *407/933–5500; spring-training tickets, 407/933–2520.*

Spring Training
Major-league baseball teams hold spring training all over Florida: in **Baseball City** (Kansas City Royals), **Bradenton** (Pittsburgh Pirates), **Clearwater** (Philadelphia Phillies), **Dunedin** (Toronto Blue Jays), **Fort Lauderdale** (New York Yankees), **Fort Myers** (Boston Red Sox and Minnesota Twins), **Kissimmee** (Houston Astros), **Lakeland** (Detroit Tigers), **Melbourne** (Florida Marlins), **Plant City** (Cincinnati Reds), **Port Charlotte** (Texas Rangers), **Port St. Lucie** (New York Mets), **St. Petersburg** (Baltimore Orioles and St. Louis Cardinals), **Sarasota** (Chicago White Sox), **Vero Beach** (Los Angeles Dodgers), **West Palm Beach** (Atlanta Braves and Montréal Expos), and **Winter Haven** (Cleveland Indians). For dates and more information, get a copy of the free *Florida Spring Training Guide,* published each year in early February by the Florida Sports Foundation (⊠ 107 W. Gaines St., Tallahassee 32399, ☎ 904/488–8347).

Basketball

The **Orlando Magic** joined the National Basketball Association in the 1989–90 season and play in the 15,077-seat Orlando Arena. Seven-foot-one center Shaquille O'Neal and teammates have since driven the city to new heights of hoop fanaticism. Tickets to the '94 season sold out in one day, and the current waiting period for season tickets is 10 years. Your best bet for seeing a game is probably a sports bar. ⊠ *Box 76, 600 W. Amelia St., 2 blocks west of I–4 at Amelia St. exit, Orlando,* ☎ *TicketMaster, 407/839–3900; box office, 407/649–2255; season tickets, 407/896–2442.* 🎟 *$19–$35.*

Dog Racing

Sanford Orlando Kennel Club has dog-racing and betting, as well as South Florida horse-racing simulcasts and betting. ⊠ *301 Dog Track*

Rd., Longwood, ☎ 407/831–1600. ☒ $1. ⊘ Nov.–May, Mon.–Sat. 7:30 PM; matinees Mon., Wed., and Sat. 12:30.

Seminole Greyhound Park, a newer, larger, and prettier track, is your other option for wagering on greyhounds and simulcast horse-racing. ☒ *2000 Seminola Blvd., Casselberry, ☎ 407/699–4510. ☒ $1 general, $2 clubhouse, children half price. ⊘ May–Oct., Mon.–Sat. 7:30 PM; matinees most recently Mon., Wed., and Sat. 12:30.*

Football

The **Orlando Predators** play in the indoor Arena Football League, which differs from the National Football League in that teams have only eight players, each of whom holds both offensive and defensive positions. Games are held May to August at the Orlando Arena. ☒ *600 W. Amelia St., Orlando, ☎ 407/648–4444 or 407/872–7362. ☒ $10–$33.*

Jai Alai

Orlando-Seminole Jai-Alai, about 20 minutes north of Orlando off I–4, offers south Florida horse-racing simulcasts and betting in addition to jai alai at the fronton. ☒ *6405 S. U.S. 17–92, Fern Park, ☎ 407/331–9191. ☒ $1 general, $2 reserved seating. ⊘ Wed.–Sat. 7:30 PM; matinees Thurs. and Sat. noon, Sun. 1.*

7 Dining

Updated by
Rowland
Stiteler

TOURIST STRIPS SUCH AS IRLO BRONSON HIGHWAY in Kissimmee and International Drive in Orlando are fast-food heaven: it seems that every chain in the United States has at least one location near Disney. Since Orlando is America's number-one tourist destination, it makes sense that corporate America test drives its new Burger Barns and Lasagna-on-a-Bun outlets here to see if they'll make it. If they can batter it, fry it, microwave it, torture it, and serve it with a side of fries, you'll find it in central Florida.

The same concept is applied to more upscale eateries in the midprice range, as well. Fabulous cuisine—from designer pizzas to newer-than-now *nouvelle classique*—is available throughout Walt Disney World and the surrounding area; it just takes a little pleasant homework to find it. As for fancier establishments, outlooks for the future are exciting, as Orlando looks forward to such famous restaurants as Wolfgang Puck's Café, settling into the neighborhood.

Restaurateurs build monuments here, and most of them try to offer good food. The result is a fiercely competitive dining market, which also brings out the best from the hometown eateries that predate Disney. Keep in mind that the dining choices here, like the entertainment choices, are far more than you can sample on any one trip.

Local Specialties

Grouper—fried, blackened, or broiled—is the closest thing central Florida has to a local dish. Most natives don't eat much alligator tail, but almost every fish restaurant offers it for the tourists—and it's fun to give it a try. Also worthy are some of the treats imported from the Florida Keys and billed as local fare. Try the stone crabs in season October through March, the small, tasty Keys lobsters, and conch chowder. Fresh hearts of palm, served in the more upscale restaurants, are also a treat. One tip on key lime pie: If it's green, especially fluorescent green, you've been had. Authentic key lime pie is yellow, even if the fruit isn't.

Dinner Shows

Dinner shows are popular and quite numerous in Orlando, although as a rule the meal won't be as memorable as the entertainment. Walt Disney World has several tableside extravaganzas, like the extremely popular Hoop-Dee-Doo Musical Revue at the Fort Wilderness Campground area. If you can't score a reservation for the Disney hoop-along, there are Arabian nights–, Wild West–, king-and-queen-, and medieval-theme shows, to name just a few. For our assessment and all the details, *see* After Dark *in* Chapter 9.

Dress

Because tourism is king here, casual dress is the rule, and very few restaurants require jackets or other dress-up attire for men. Unless an eating establishment is in the higher end of the price range, you'll be safe wearing anything that wouldn't get you thrown out of a Burger King. And if your child is the only one wearing a hat with Goofy ears, you probably made a wrong turn and ended up in Georgia.

Reservations

Reservations are always a good idea in a market where the phrase "Bus drivers eat free" is emblazoned on the city's coat of arms. Without reservations, the entire Ecuadorian soccer team or the senior class from Platt City High School may arrive moments before you and keep you waiting a long, long time. Save that experience for your visit to the attractions.

For restaurants within Walt Disney World, reservations are especially easy to make, thanks to its central reservations lines, ☎ 407/WDW–DINE and 407/560–7277. In addition, the WorldKey Information Center can be used for the very popular restaurants of Epcot Center (☞ Epcot Center, *below*). Remember that while Orlando is not a big town, getting to places is frequently complicated, so always call for directions.

Price

CATEGORY	COST*
$$$$	over $40
$$$	$30–$40
$$	$20–$30
$	under $20

per person, excluding drinks, service, and 6% sales tax

IN AND AROUND WALT DISNEY WORLD

Eateries abound in and near Walt Disney World. On the tourism warp drive called U.S. 192, between Walt Disney World and Kissimmee, most of the restaurants are either chains or large, overrated, and overpriced, with a few worthwhile exceptions. On the other hand, Lake Buena Vista—around Exit 27 on I–4—is full of good eating opportunities. International Drive is internationally known for its tackiness, but in recent years some good restaurants have popped up on the southern end of the boulevard, around the cavernous Orange County Convention Center.

American

$$$$ ✕ **Victoria and Albert's.** All the servers work in man-woman pairs, call-
★ ing themselves "Victoria" and "Albert," and they recite the day's specials in tandem, like some surrealistic recitation out of a Lewis Carroll fantasy—you almost expect them to start smashing pocket watches on the table. But don't let the strange theatrics scare you away. You are in for a real experience at this lavish, romantic dining room that many Disney executives consider to be the top restaurant they have to offer. The intimate room seats about 60 and fits the Victorian theme, with a domed ceiling, fabric-covered walls, marbleized columns, and lots of fresh-cut flowers. A harpist adds an ethereal touch. The seven-course, prix fixe menu for $65 changes substantially day to day. Chef Scott Hunnel loves creating exotic dishes but always offers something for more proletarian palates. Appetizers might include velvety veal sweetbreads and rare New Zealand venison, artichokes in a lusty *duxelles* (mushroom-based) sauce, or jumbo sea scallops served over seaweed salad with warm beet vinaigrette. Entrées range from sautéed breast of duck or tournedos of veal on braised onions to well-prepared sirloin or broiled Maine lobster. A deluxe version of the meal comes with four glasses of wine, each selected by the sommelier to complement a particular course. Two seatings—6 and 9—are offered nightly. Expect to spend about $100 a person with drinks. Prix fixe for children 2–11 is $45. You leave with a menu with your name printed on it. ✉ *Grand Floridian Beach Resort, Walt Disney World Magic Kingdom Resort Area,* ☎ *407/WDW–DINE. Reservations essentials. Jackets required. AE, MC, V. Kosher and vegetarian meals by advance order.*

$$$ ✕ **Artist Point.** The Wilderness Lodge—a huge, jauntily brawny, hunt-
★ ing-lodge-style hotel—is definitely worth a look, and this excellent restaurant offers those not booked at the Wilderness a good excuse to see the place. The northwestern salmon sampler is a good start, but you

194

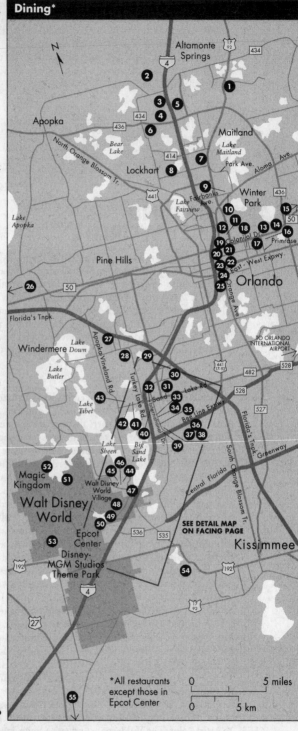

Dining*

*All restaurants except those in Epcot Center

0   5 miles

0   5 km

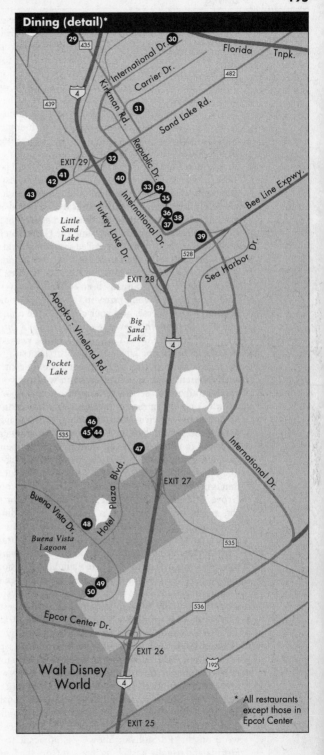

Dining (detail)*

29 435
30
International Dr.
Carrier Dr.
Florida Tnpk.
482
4
439
Kirkman Rd.
31
Sand Lake Rd.
Republic Dr.
EXIT 29
32
41
42
40
33 34
43
35
Bee Line Expwy.
Turkey Lake Dr.
International Dr.
36 38
37
Little
Sand
Lake
39
528
Sea Harbor Dr.
Apopka - Vineland Rd.
EXIT 28
Big
Sand
Lake
4
Pocket
Lake
46
535
45 44
47
International Dr.
EXIT 27
Buena Vista Dr.
Hotel Plaza Blvd.
48
535
Buena Vista
Lagoon
536
50 49
Epcot Center Dr.
Walt Disney
World
EXIT 26
192
4
* All restaurants
except those in
Epcot Center
EXIT 25

might also try the smoked duck breast, the maple-glazed steak, or the sautéed elk sausage. Most meats are hardwood grilled. The house specialty is the "trail dust shortcake," a buttermilk biscuit with strawberries, vanilla-bean ice cream, and whipped cream. Just to make sure you get that *North by Northwest* feeling, the sommelier can offer a suggestion from the selection of Washington state and Oregon vintage wines. Breakfast is an experience at the other restaurant in the hotel, **Whispering Canyon Cafe,** which features all-you-can-eat family meals with selections like smoked buffalo sausage and warm apple cakes. ⊠ *Wilderness Lodge Resort, Walt Disney World Magic Kingdom Resort Area,* ☎ *407/WDW–DINE. AE, MC, V.*

$$ ✕ **Austin's.** That cameo on the front of the menu is Stephen F. Austin, kids, founder of the Republic of Texas and the inspiration for this ersatz Southwest eatery. Like many things in Orlando, Austin's is a fantasy, a Florida restaurant chain dedicated to Floridians' visions of what a Texas beef palace should be. But it's a good fantasy. The barbecued ribs and chicken are quite tasty, and the Galveston Bay—half a pound of ribs and a skewer of hickory-grilled shrimp—should satisfy those buckaroos who can't settle the age-old surf vs. turf quandary for themselves. The hickory-grilled fish is also good, especially when Norwegian salmon is available. If you've already been to Walt Disney World, the $6 price tag for the burgers won't faze you. This version comes with cheddar or Monterey Jack cheese, and your choice of the ubiquitous sesame seed bun or a healthy, whole-wheat edition. ⊠ *8633 International Dr., Orlando,* ☎ *407/363–9575. AE, D, DC, MC, V.*

$$ ✕ **Cafe Tu Tu Tango.** This très-chic bistro doesn't have a dance floor, ★ but there's plenty of choreography here. Multiple kitchens bombard you with different courses, which arrive in waves if you follow the house custom and order a series of appetizers. Actually, you end up doing this anyway, since the entrées are appetizer-size. The menu gives the address—on International Drive—a new meaning. Try the Cajun chicken egg rolls, for instance, with blackened chicken, Greek goat cheese, Creole mustard, and tomato salsa, if you want to get a compendium of the major cuisines of the world at one go. Trendy dishes like sun-dried tomato pizza and smoked chicken quesadillas give this place a certain hip spin that is in keeping with its origins in Miami's ultra-cool quarter, Coconut Grove. For added atmosphere, or perhaps just for the surrealism factor, artists work on paintings on easels while diners watch and sip drinks like the Matisse margarita and the Renoir rum runner. This place is part of the empire of Orlando-based restaurant magnate Robert Earl, who created Planet Hollywood and always wants to entertain customers as well as feed them. There's a limited selection of nonfancy food like burgers and pizza on the children's menu. Even though nothing on the entire menu is more than $8, it's not hard to spend $50 for lunch for two, especially if you follow your server's suggestion and order sangria early and often. ⊠ *8625 International Dr., Orlando,* ☎ *407/248–2222. Reservations not accepted. AE, D, MC, V.*

$$ ✕ **Hard Rock Café Orlando.** The motto at this place is "Save the Planet," but that was before Hard Rock Orlando founder Robert Earl jumped ship and moved on to found Planet Hollywood with a galaxy of star partners. Both chains purvey a similar fantasy: a few hours of being cool just for standing in line and getting inside the restaurant. The Hard Rock Orlando, a huge, guitar-shaped building that is loaded down with memorabilia—including the collarless suits the Beatles wore on the"Ed Sullivan Show"—is adjacent to Universal Studios Florida and usually has a long line just from the Universal visitors. It's also a popular hangout for members of the Orlando Magic NBA basketball team, and, yes, food is even served here. Best bets are the pig sandwich, made of pork shoulder hickory-smoked for 14 hours, and

the reliable ⅓-pound charbroiled cheeseburger with all the trimmings. There is an extensive selection of beers. This place is a rock club and proud of it, so don't go if you can't tolerate the noise, which approaches the level of a 747 take-off. ⊠ *Universal Studios Florida, 5800 Kirkman Rd., Orlando,* ☎ *407/351–7625. Reservations not accepted. AE, MC, V.*

$$ ✕ **Pebbles.** In the past few years this restaurant has become one of the most popular dining spots among Orlandoans—so popular that there are now four locations. They offer just the right blend of elegance and informality. Management says it targets the "casual gourmet" as its customer base. This is California cuisine, dude, with a Florida touch that brings grouper and other regional favorites into the picture. The Lake Buena Vista location will give you a chance to see how the locals live. Good entrée choices include angel-hair pasta smothered with smoked duck, scallops, and Asian spices, and the Mediterranean salad, in which sun-dried tomatoes put in their obligatory appearance. The Caesar salad, tossed at tableside, is memorable. Good burgers, with your choice of several excellent cheeses, are also served here. This place is perennially voted best restaurant in the city by the readers of the daily *Orlando Sentinel* newspaper. Desserts here are worth the calories, and the wine list is intelligent without being a wallet-breaker. ⊠ *Crossroads Shopping Center near Lake Buena Vista entrance to Walt Disney World, Orlando,* ☎ *407/827–1111;* ⊠ *17 W. Church St., Orlando,* ☎ *407/839–0892;* ⊠ *2516 Aloma Ave., Winter Park,* ☎ *407/678– 7001;* ⊠ *2100 Rte. 434, Longwood,* ☎ *407/774–7111. Reservations not accepted. AE, D, DC, MC, V.*

$$ ✕ **Planet Hollywood.** On weekend nights, when the nearby Pleasure Island clubs are jumping, the line is extremely long because patrons come here to see a piece of history. In this case, it's movie history, as assembled by club owners Demi Moore, Arnold Schwarzenegger, Sylvester Stallone, and Bruce Willis, and the biggest showman among the partners, restaurateur Robert Earl. It was Earl who brought Hard Rock Café to Orlando, and it's easy to see a lot of Hard Rock at the Planet. Memorabilia, like the bus that was used in the movie *Speed* and the leather jacket worn by Schwarzenegger in *The Terminator,* rotate between the Orlando Planet Hollywood and its 17 sister restaurants around the country. There's also a souvenir shop just outside, where you can buy a few T-shirts while you wonder when you will actually get inside the restaurant. The wait is typically about two hours on most evenings. If you want to minimize your wait, go in midafternoon: The menu doesn't change. Food is secondary to the 20,000-square-foot building, complete with an indoor waterfall. The 110-foot-tall "planet" cost $15 million, as much as Disney or Universal Studios Florida might spend to add a new attraction. The menu is built around fresh, healthful dishes like turkey burgers, smoked and grilled meats, unusual pastas and salads, and a wide range of desserts. Among the better offerings are a Creole pizza with shrimp, chicken, and Cajun sausage, and a tasty $7.50 burger, a bargain in these parts. If someone else is driving, you should try a "Comet," the gargantuan souvenir-glass drink with vodka, rum, tequila, orange juice, and pineapple juice, for $13. ⊠ *Pleasure Island, Walt Disney World Village,* ☎ *407/363– 7827. Reservations not accepted. AE, DC, MC, V.*

$$ ✕ **White Horse Saloon.** Cattle ranchers would love this, the only hoedown kind of place we know of in a four-star hotel. They would be mighty pleased at the way this western-theme saloon in the Hyatt Regency Grand Cypress sells their products: You can get a barbecued half-chicken for 20 bucks or pay a dollar more for prime rib. If you want to go for the 28-ounce beef-worshiper's cut—that's 1½ pounds of corn-fed beef—it's $46. All entrées come with sourdough bread, baked

or mashed potatoes, and your choice of creamed spinach or corn on the cob. A hearty, hot apple pie with cinnamon-raisin sauce awaits those desperadoes who can still handle dessert. You also get music with your vittles. The Hand-Picked Trio, which has been here for years, plays in the evenings. ⊠ *Hyatt Regency Grand Cypress, 1 Grand Cypress Blvd., Orlando,* ☎ *407/239–1234. AE, DC, MC, V.*

Chinese

$$ ✕ **Ming Court.** In Orlando, restaurateurs know that if the chef doesn't get high marks, be sure the architect and interior designer do. Here, all parties concerned have done a fine job. Even though this place is on International Drive, a wall designed to look like a dragon's back gives an enclosed courtyard-like serenity to this Chinese palace of a restaurant. Diners look out through glass walls over a beautifully arranged series of floating gardens. Inside, little touches like rosewood chopsticks and linen tablecloths add to the classy feeling of the place. If you eat Chinese food often, the menu probably doesn't have any dishes you haven't heard of, but the versions here are expertly prepared. The jumbo shrimp in lobster sauce, flavored with crushed black beans, costs more than you may be used to paying ($15), but it's very worthwhile. Another popular dish is the Hunan *kung pao* chicken, sautéed with red and green peppers and served with cashews and walnuts. Ming Court is within walking distance of the Orange County Convention Center and, incidentally, just across the street from several other good restaurants. ⊠ *9188 International Dr., Orlando,* ☎ *407/351–9988. AE, DC, MC, V.*

Continental

$$$$ ✕ **Arthur's 27.** The view from the 27th floor of the Buena Vista Palace Hotel, overlooking all of Walt Disney World and its environs, is breathtaking, but you may be even more lightheaded when you get a look at your check if you are not prepared to pay top dollar for a top-notch Continental meal. Handle the fiscal traumas up front with one of two prix-fixe dinner options: $60 (not including drinks and gratuities) for a six-course meal or $45 for a four-course special. Order à la carte and you will probably leave behind a couple of bills with Ben Franklin's picture on them. What you get for your money, however, is a well-prepared meal and a formal dining experience that will last two to three hours. But if you love haute cuisine, and enjoy watching the sun go down behind the Epcot dome, you'll want to savor every minute at this place. All entrées come with some kind of heavenly sauce, like the rich, creamy cognac-based mixture that is spooned over the tenderloin of beef or the herb-rich garlic sauce that accompanies the roast loin of lamb. Desserts include a credible crème brûlée with raspberries and a chocolate cake to die for. Service can be pretentious, with waiters uttering clichés like "Excellent choice, sir" and making the changing of the plates seem like a Tomb of the Unknown Soldier ritual. Because there's only one seating a night, reservations as early as a month in advance are recommended. ⊠ *Buena Vista Palace Hotel, Walt Disney World Village, Lake Buena Vista,* ☎ *407/827–3450. Reservations essential. Jacket required. AE, D, DC, MC, V.*

Fast Food

$ ✕ **McDonald's.** The nation's largest McDonald's is no plain-Jane burger joint. Although the menu is standard, the frills are pure Orlando: a 7,500-square-foot playground full of slides, tunnels, and seesaws; a theater where musicians and magicians perform; even a gift shop, called Mickey D's, full of T-shirts. You can chow down in the tiki-bar-style Sunset Terrace area; the Maui Room, with a 600-gallon saltwater aquarium; or the Rock and Roll Room, featuring '50s memorabilia and a jukebox. ✉ *6875 Sand Lake Rd. and International Dr., Orlando,* ☎ *407/351–2185. Reservations not accepted. AE, MC, V.*

French

$$$ ✕ **La Coquina.** This gourmet restaurant bills itself as French with an Asian influence, and if you sample the pheasant and truffle wonton with foie gras and chives, you'll think this culture combo is quite worthwhile. The Hyatt Regency Grand Cypress culinary staff uses this restaurant as a showcase for its skills, and if you want a closer look, there's a special chef's table dining experience that can be arranged through the restaurant manager, in which your party eats in the kitchen. If your children can't quite scarf down all their wasabi-seared tuna with soy or their glazed roast squab and foie gras, smaller portions at half the price are available for diners 12 and under. The high-point meal here is Sunday brunch, with a generous selection of goodies like waffles, omelets, tropical fruits, smoked fish, poached salmon, quartered duck, and pastries that make the $38 per person price seem like a real bargain. Brunch is truly a pleasant experience here, with nice touches like black swans swimming on the lake outside the window and a harpist calmly thrumming—excellent preparation for an assault on Space Mountain a little later in the morning. Lose the tank tops; men must wear shirts with collars and women must dress "appropriately," according to the printed dress code. ✕ *Hyatt Regency Grand Cypress, 1 Grand Cypress Blvd., Orlando,* ☎ *407/239–1234. Jacket required. AE, DC, MC, V.*

Italian

$$–$$$ ✕ **Capriccio's.** Corporate executives and conventioneers, who make up a good part of the Peabody Hotel's clientele, like the relaxed atmosphere of this place as a nice departure from the rubber-chicken circuit. The marble-topped tables are arranged on the tile floors so that everyone can view the open kitchen and wood-burning pizza ovens, which turn out whole-wheat-flour pies ranging from *pizza margherita* (made with sun-dried tomatoes and smoked mozzarella, fontina, provolone, and Parmesan cheeses) to healthy *pizza bianca* (with mozzarella, goat cheese, and fresh thyme). If you're not in the mood for pizza, try one of the mesquite-grilled fish, beef, or chicken entrées, like the *pollo gonzo* (chicken in a lemon sage sauce). There's also a popular brunch offered on weekends. ✉ *Peabody Orlando Hotel, 9801 International Dr., Orlando,* ☎ *407/352–4000. AE, DC, MC, V. Closed Mon.*

$$ ✕ **Ciao Italia.** This is an odd place for a quiet, charming little Italian eatery, almost in the shadow of Sea World. But even though this quaint restaurant is in the middle of tourism's fast lane, nothing is hurried here. Every item on the menu is made to order, so you might want to bring along that dog-eared copy of *War and Peace* you never finished. Your patience will be rewarded, however: The Italian-speaking proprietors have managed to re-create a piece of Italy in central Florida. The proof is in the sweet New Zealand mussels, served with either white garlic or marinara sauce, and the light, colorful *pollo alla Tonino* (chicken breast with red and yellow peppers). For dessert, try the *tartufo* (chocolate-coated ice cream). ✉ *Across from Sheraton World Resort, 6149 Westwood Blvd., Orlando,* ☎ *407/354–0770. AE, D, DC, MC, V. Beer and wine only. No lunch.*

$$ ✕ **Portobello Yacht Club.** Operated by Chicago's venerable restaurateurs, the Levy brothers, this eatery has a much better lineage than the one the Disney brain trust made up. According to Disney Imagineers, the building was the home of Merriweather Adam Pleasure, the man for whom Pleasure Island was named. Of course, the man never existed, but that doesn't mean you won't find great pleasure dining here. Start with something simple—the chewy, tasty sourdough bread, served

with roast garlic. Then move on to bigger and better things like the spaghettini *alla portobello* (a stick-to-your-ribs pasta dish with scallops, clams, shrimp, mussels, tomatoes, garlic, portobello mushrooms, and herbs). There's always a fresh-catch special of the day. Since Pleasure Island is in Disney's own nightclub district, where party animals are a protected species, the people-watching can be quite interesting here, especially after a little sangria. This is a good spot for a late meal; it's open until midnight. ⊠ *Pleasure Island, Walt Disney World,* ☎ *407/934–8888. AE, DC, MC, V.*

$–$$ ✕ **Rosario's.** This little place, in a New England–style clapboard house that looks refreshingly out of place in the unsightly jumble of motels known as Kissimmee, is understated and cheerful and serves Italian food that's above average, such as the spaghetti *aglio olio* (with fresh garlic, basil, and diced tomatoes sautéed in olive oil) and the hearty pasta *e fagioli* soup (filled with Italian white beans, prosciutto, escarole, and pasta and flavored with both brandy and a touch of marinara sauce). ⊠ *4838 W. Irlo Bronson Hwy., Kissimmee,* ☎ *407/239–0118. AE, D, DC, MC, V. Beer and wine only. No lunch.*

Japanese

$$ ✕ **Ran-Getsu.** The surroundings are definitely a Disney version of the Orient—but the food is fresh and carefully prepared. Sit at the curved, dragon-tail-shaped sushi bar and order the *matsu* platter (an assortment of *nigiri-* and *maki*-style sushi). Or, unless you're alone, you can have your meal Japanese-style at the low tables overlooking a carp-filled pond and decorative gardens. Specialties include sukiyaki and *shabu-shabu* (thinly sliced beef prepared tableside in a simmering seasoned broth and served with vegetables). If you feel more adventurous, try the deep-fried alligator tail. ⊠ *8400 International Dr., Orlando,* ☎ *407/345–0044. AE, DC, MC, V. No lunch.*

Seafood

$$$ ✕ **Ariel's.** The centerpiece of this favorite of Disney executives, named for the Little Mermaid, is a 2,500-gallon saltwater tank. The finny fare comes from Florida, the Northeast, and the Northwest, and it's most often simply grilled over a hardwood fire. Want something more exotic? Start with the Tuckernut shellfish gumbo with andouille sausage and then have Ariel's strudel (chicken and ricotta wrapped in a flaky basil-perfumed pastry). ⊠ *Disney's Beach Club Resort, Lake Buena Vista,* ☎ *407/WDW–DINE. AE, MC, V. No smoking.*

$$–$$$ ✕ **Hemingway's.** There's usually a wait at this popular, elegant eatery
★ that overlooks the huge Hyatt Regency Grand Cypress pool, but when you begin to sample the wide variety of seafood specialties, you'll forget about the wait. Try the Old Man and the Sea special, which offers you a choice of grouper, swordfish, tuna, mahimahi, red snapper, pompano, or salmon, charbroiled or blackened, with Cajun, tartar, or béarnaise sauce. You can sample dishes that were inspired by all the phases of Hemingway's life, like the Spanish paella he might have eaten in Madrid before he wrote *For Whom the Bell Tolls*. The kitchen assumes you have a Papa-style appetite and includes mussels, clams, scallops, lobster, chicken, and sausage in this version. Beer-batter coconut shrimp with orange marmalade horseradish sauce is a house specialty. ⊠ *Hyatt Regency Grand Cypress Resort, 1 Grand Cypress Blvd., Orlando,* ☎ *407/239–1234. Reservations essential. AE, DC, MC, V.*

$$ ✕ **Nick's on the Water.** One of Orlando's great mysteries is why the
★ city, which seems to have more lakes than Minnesota, has such a dearth of waterfront restaurants. In the case of Nick's, the waterfront location is almost a technicality, as the lake is actually across the street from the restaurant, and Crane's Roost Lake is merely postage-stamp size by Central Florida standards. But guests don't come to Nick's for

its proximity to the water: It's one of the best way-too-small restaurants. This Italian seafood restaurant, with a central grill, serves all sorts of tasty tuna, grouper, snapper, and salmon entrées, as well as some decent landlubber options. Veal dishes are a house specialty, as are steaks cooked over wood on the open grill. Don't leave the property without trying the tasty vodka sauce, made with cream, herbs, and marinara. It's available on a tasty rigatoni a la vodka, and also on a gourmet pizza topped with scallops and fresh basil. Save room for another house specialty, the sweet and creamy cannoli, which, like all of Nick's desserts, are made at the restaurant. The upstairs patio overlooks the water, and is a wonderful place to wile away an afternoon. ⊠ *309 N. Lake Blvd., Altamonte Springs,* ☎ *407/834–5880. AE, D, MC, V.*

$–$$ ✕ **Atlantis.** It would be surprising if someone didn't choose this name for a seafood restaurant in a major hotel near Sea World of Florida, but rest assured, the food is more original than the moniker. The restaurant is elegant and moderately formal—men don't need a jacket—and offers good fish selections, like various lobster dishes and grilled yellowfin tuna. ⊠ *Stouffer Orlando Resort, 667 Sea Harbor Dr., Orlando,* ☎ *407/351–5555. AE, D, DC, MC, V. No lunch.*

Epcot Center

Epcot's World Showcase offers some of the finest dining to be found not only in Walt Disney World but in the entire Orlando area. The problems are that you have to pay Epcot admission to eat in these establishments; the top-of-the-line places, such as those in the French, Italian, and Japanese pavilions, can be expensive, and reservations hard to come by. On the other hand, most of them have a limited-selection children's menu with dramatically lower prices. Dress is informal—no one expects you to go all the way back to your hotel to tidy up. And if you have unruly youngsters in tow, you probably won't be alone. Kosher and vegetarian meals are available on request.

Reservations

All restaurants, unless otherwise noted, are open for both lunch and dinner daily. For both meals, reservations are a must. At Epcot, there are two ways of making reservations: either by calling the central reservations lines (☎ 407/WDW–DINE or 407/560–7277) or, when actually on site at Epcot, by going to the WorldKey Information Centers—a system of interactive computer screens. To use the WorldKey system, here's the drill: As soon as you get to Epcot, head for Guest Services, at the base of Spaceship Earth, and line up in front of the WorldKey Information Center. Or better still, go to the WorldKey kiosks located throughout the park, and avoid the logjam at the main location. Just ask any cast member, as all Disney employees are called, where to find the nearest kiosk. There's one near the Port of Entry shop, near the dock for the water taxi to Morocco, and another just before the bridge to World Showcase.

To make reservations using WorldKey, you should arrive early, because the most popular seating times in the busier restaurants are filled up within an hour of Epcot Center's official opening time, which may be as much as 30 minutes ahead of the published opening time. To avoid the battle of WorldKey, remember you can always book by phone using numbers listed above. You can also opt to eschew the computer reservation bit and walk straight to the restaurant of your choice, where someone will be on hand to take reservations at 11 when they open for the day.

Alternatively, be flexible about your mealtimes. For the more popular establishments, it is much easier to get a reservation for lunch than for dinner, to get lunch reservations before noon, and to get dinner reservations for seatings before 6 and after 8. And it's always worth stopping by the restaurant of your choice during the day in hopes of a cancellation.

No matter how you book, try to show up a bit early to be sure of getting your table. You can pay with cash; charge with American Express, MasterCard, or Visa; or, if you're a guest at an on-site hotel on Disney property, charge the tab to your room.

British

$$ ✕ **Rose and Crown.** If you are an Anglophile and you love nothing more than a good, thick beer, this friendly pub is the place to soak up both the suds and the British street culture. As with all World Showcase restaurants, the staff has been brought in from the appropriate country, so you can get a great foreign affairs lesson for the price of a meal. At day's end, visitors mingle with Disney employees while knocking down pints of Bass Ale and Guinness Stout with Stilton cheese. "Wenches" serve up simple pub fare, such as steak-and-kidney pie and fish-and-chips. Dark wood floors, sturdy pub chairs, and brass lamps create a warm, homey atmosphere. At 4, a traditional tea is served. The food is relatively inexpensive, especially at lunch, and the terrace has a splendid view of IllumiNations. All things considered, it's one of the best bets in Epcot.

French

$$$ ✕ **Les Chefs de France.** To create this sparkling French café-restaurant, three of France's most famous culinary artists came together: Paul Bocuse, who operates one restaurant north of Lyon and two in Tokyo; Gaston Lenôtre, noted for his pastries and ice creams; and Roger Vergé, proprietor of France's celebrated Mougins, near Cannes. The three developed the menu, trained the chefs, and look in—apparently not as frequently as they should, according to some reviewers—to make sure the food and service stay up to snuff. Start with a chicken-and-duck pâté in a pastry crust, follow up with a classic coq au vin or broiled salmon with sorrel sauce, and end up with chocolate-doused, ice-cream-filled pastry shells. Some people feel transported back to fin-de-siècle France, if only for an hour or two.

$$–$$$ ✕ **Bistro de Paris.** The great secret at the France pavilion—and, indeed, ★ in all of Epcot—is the Bistro de Paris, located around the back of the Chefs de Paris and upstairs. The sophisticated menu changes regularly and contains exciting offerings that reflect the cutting edge of French cooking. The dining salon is serene—and often filled with well-dressed French people, the mark of a successful transplant. Come late, ask for a window seat, and plan to linger to watch IllumiNations. The French wines are moderately priced and available by the glass.

German

$$ ✕ **Biergarten.** In this popular spot, Oktoberfest runs 365 days a year. The cheerful—some would say raucous—atmosphere is what you would expect in a place with an oompah band. Waitresses in typical Bavarian garb serve hot pretzels, hearty German fare such as sauerbraten and bratwurst, and stout pitchers of beer and wine, which patrons pound on their long communal tables—even when the yodelers, singers, and dancers aren't egging them on.

Italian

$$$ ✕ **L'Originale Alfredo di Roma Ristorante.** This is the most popular restaurant at Epcot, and its namesake dish, made with mountains of butter flown in from Italy, is one of the principal reasons. This restaurant was created, with the help of Disney, by the descendants of Al-

fredo de Lelio, who in 1914 founded Rome's Alfredo all'Augusteo restaurant and invented the now-classic dish—fettuccine sauced with cream, butter, and loads of freshly grated Parmesan cheese. But the true secret to the dish here is the butter. Insiders say the only Parmesan that goes into the mixture is what your waiter sprinkles on at the table. A very good variation of the trademark dish is the fettuccine *alla carbonara* (with lots of rich, crushed bacon that might make your cardiologist scream, but it's oh, so tasty). Stick with pasta, for the other menu items are undistinguished. Or try *lo chef consiglia* (the chef's selection—a spaghetti or fettuccine appetizer, a mixed green salad, and a chicken or veal entrée). In addition, during dinner the Italian waiters skip around singing Italian songs and bellowing arias, a show in itself.

Japanese

$$–$$$ ✕ **Mitsukoshi.** This complex of dining areas overlooking tranquil gar-
★ dens is actually three restaurants. The **Yakitori**, a fast-food stand in a small pavilion modeled on a teahouse in Kyoto's Katsura Summer Palace, offers broiled skewers of chicken basted with teriyaki sauce, and *gyudon* (paper-thin beef simmered in a spicy sauce and served with noodles). At the Tempura Kiku, two dozen diners sit around a central counter and watch the chefs prepare sushi, sashimi, tempura, batter-dipped deep-fried shrimp, scallops, and vegetables. In the Mitsukoshi's third area—a series of five **Teppanyaki Rooms**—chefs skillfully chop vegetables, meat, and fish at lightning speed and then stir-fry them at grills set into communal dining tables. The Matsunoma Lounge to the right of this area pours Japanese sake, plum wine, and *saketinis* (martinis made with sake rather than vermouth). If you just want sushi, go to the lounge and you can usually avoid a wait.

Mexican

$$ ✕ **San Angel Inn.** The lush, tropical surroundings—cool, dark, and almost surreal—make this restaurant in the courtyard inside the Mexican pavilion perhaps the most exotic in Walt Disney World. It's popular among Disney execs as well as tourists, who treasure this place because it offers a great respite, especially when the humid weather outside makes central Florida feel like equatorial Africa. Don't expect to see a Disney employee, even off duty, ordering one of the margaritas: They are so bad as to be legendary. Candlelit tables are companionably close together, and the restaurant is open to a midnight-blue "sky" in the inside of the pavilion and filled with the music of folk singers, guitars, and marimbas. The best seats are along the restaurant's outer edge, away from the entrance and directly alongside the pavilion's "river," where boatloads of sightseers stream by; above looms an Aztec pyramid and volcano, whose soft, fiery light evokes a sense of the distant past. On the roster of authentic dishes, one specialty is mole *poblano* (chicken simmered until tender in a rich sauce of different kinds of chilies, green tomatoes, ground tortillas, cumin, and 11 other spices mixed with cocoa). Fresh tortillas are made every day and served with beef, chicken, and cheese fillings, as well as with fresh salsa *verde* (spicy green sauce).

Moroccan

$$–$$$ ✕ **Marrakesh.** This is the least popular of any of the World Showcase restaurants, possibly because the average American hasn't heard much about Moroccan food. Consequently, it's relatively easy to get seated, and once inside, you'll find belly dancers and a three-piece Moroccan band set a North African mood that feels almost like a set for a Disney Casablanca. The building itself, painstakingly constructed by artisans brought in from Morocco to handcraft the extensive carving, is impressive. The food is mildly spicy and relatively inexpensive. Try the couscous, the national dish of Morocco, served with vegetables; or *bastila* (an appetizer made of alternating layers of sweet-and-spicy pork and a thin pastry, redolent of almonds, saffron, and cinnamon).

Norwegian

$ ✕ **Restaurant Akershus.** Norway's tradition of seafood and cold-meat dishes is highlighted at the *koldtboard* (Norwegian buffet) in this restaurant, comprising four dining rooms that occupy a copy of Oslo's Akershus Castle. Hosts and hostesses explain the dishes and suggest which ones go together, then send you off to the buffet table. There is no need to shovel everything you see onto your plate at one time—it is traditional to make several trips. First, take your appetizers—usually herring, which comes several ways here; then go for cold seafood such as gravlax. Pick up cold salads and meats on your next trip; and then, on your last foray, fill up on hot lamb, veal, or venison. The selection of desserts, offered à la carte, includes cloudberries (delicate fruits that grow on the tundra in season).

Other Options

Future World's two full-service restaurants are Living Seas' tiered **Coral Reef Room,** which serves a finny menu and has a view of the pavilion's jumbo aquarium through 8-foot-high windows, and the **Garden Grill,** where you can eat American fare with a twist as the restaurant revolves, giving you an ever-changing view of each of the biomes of the Living with the Land boat ride. In World Showcase, there's also China's **Nine Dragons,** which offers Chinese fare representing several regions—modified for American tastes—in a large, comfortable room decorated with Oriental motifs. If your hometown has a thriving Chinese community, you'll find the fare here uninspired, though the restaurant does seem to attract a large Asian following.

Meals with Disney Characters

At these breakfasts, brunches, and dinners staged in hotel and theme park restaurants all over Walt Disney World, kids can snuggle up to all the best-loved Disney characters. Sometimes the food is served buffet style, sometimes it's sit-down. Prices and times vary, so call ahead. Reservations are often required; places where they are not are crowded, so show up on the early side if you hate to wait. Smoking is not permitted at any of these.

Breakfast

No reservations are required for many of these events. You can drop in from 8 to 10:30 on Sundays at the **Buena Vista Palace** (☎ 407/827–2727, $10.95 adults, $5.95 children under 11); from 8 to 11 for a no-holds-barred buffet at the Contemporary Café in the **Contemporary Resort** (☎ 407/WDW–DINE, $12.95 adults, $7.95 children 3–11); from 7:30 to 11 in the Cape May Café at **Disney's Beach Club** ($12.95 adults, $7.95 children under 12); from 7:30 to 10:15 daily at the **Polynesian Resort**'s Papeete Bay Verandah (☎ 407/WDW–DINE, $12.95 adults, $7.95 children 3–11); Saturdays from 8 to 11 in the Garden Grove at the **Walt Disney World Swan** (☎ 407/934–1281, about $11 for adults, $7 for children, depending on whether you choose buffet or order from menu); and at the counter-service Stargate Restaurant in Future World's Innoventions East in **Epcot Center.** There, the characters are on hand from park opening until 10, with breakfast served for another hour; you don't have to buy food to enjoy the goings-on. Reservations are required for other breakfasts, including the one hosted by Mary Poppins, from 7:30 to noon in the 1900 Park Fare Restaurant in the **Grand Floridian** (☎ 407/824–2383, $14.95 adults, $9.75 children 3–11).

Sunday Brunch

The Disney characters show up for the lavish Sunday brunch from 8:30 to 12:30 at the Ristorante Carnivale at the **Walt Disney World Dolphin** (☎ 407/934–4025, $12.95 adults, $7.95 children 4–12). You can help yourself to everything from bacon and eggs and seafood crepes to pancakes and chocolate chip waffles in the distinctive circle-with-ears shape. Reservations are a good idea.

Dinner

Mickey's Tropical Revue, a luau character show, is presented daily at 4:30 at the **Polynesian Resort** (☎ 407/WDW–DINE, $29 adults, $22 young adults 12–20, $13 children 3–11). Mickey and Minnie are at the buffet served from 5 to 9 daily at the 1900 Park Fare Restaurant in the **Grand Floridian** (☎ 407/WDW–DINE, $18.50 adults, $9.95 children 3–11). Mickey also appears during dinner, served 5–10 daily, at **Chef Mickey's Village Restaurant** (☎ 407/WDW–DINE, entrées $9.75–$18.25, children's menu entrées from $8.75). You will need reservations for all of these. Every night at 8 (7 in winter months), near Fort Wilderness's Meadow Trading Post, there's also a **Character Campfire** and free sing-along.

THE ORLANDO AREA

American

$$ ✗ **Sam Snead's Tavern.** The prototype for a golf-theme grill, this lively restaurant is a tribute to the venerable pro champion Sam Snead. The wood-paneled walls are chockablock with pictures and memorabilia of his illustrious career. The kitchen does well with an eclectic variety of foods ranging from hamburgers and grilled chicken to veal chops and fish. The Caesar salad is excellent, as are the barbecued spareribs. The chocolate sack sounds weird but isn't: It's pound cake, ice cream, strawberries, and whipped cream packed into what looks like a paper bag made of chocolate, and it's much too much for one person. This is one of the few restaurants in town open as late as 1 AM. ☒ *2461 S. Hiawassee Rd., Orlando,* ☎ *407/295–9999. AE, DC, MC, V.*

$ ✗ **Dexter's.** This hip college bar is so nondescript from the outside that the facade almost blends into the coin laundry next door. But inside you'll find a popular, trendy eatery and winery sophisticated enough to offer its own wine label and publish a monthly newsletter for those who appreciate a good vintage. Much of the clientele comes from Rollins College, a liberal arts school a block away, and the SoHo-like menu reflects that. If you are over 40, however, you won't feel out of place. One of the best entrées is chicken tortilla pie (a stack of cheese-laden tortillas that looks more like a spaceship than a pie); equally popular is the ratt pie (like the tortilla pie but filled with provolone and ratatouille). Jazz is featured frequently at night. ☒ *200 W. Fairbanks Ave., Winter Park,* ☎ *407/629–1150. AE, MC, V.*

$ ✗ **White Wolf Café.** Located in Orlando's small but vibrant antique-and art-gallery district, this warm, informal place reflects the eclectic character of the neighborhood around it. Light fare includes about a dozen salads: the Caribbean chicken salad (with spicy chicken breast, apricot vinaigrette and fresh coconut) is a solid choice. Menu mainstays include an array of sandwiches, including standards such as turkey clubs and B.L.Ts., as well as a strange-but-worthy pita sandwich called the Mighty Joe Mango (with fresh fruits, vegetables, and mango salsa). Entrées change often, but usually include some well-prepared pasta dishes and a deep-dish lasagna. White Wolf, which is named for Casper, the now-deceased German Shepherd that belonged to the owner, serves a good variety of drinks ranging from gourmet coffees to wines available by the glass. Tuesday through Saturday evenings there's live music. For outdoor dining, there's a small sidewalk seating section, or the staff will happily prepare a picnic basket for you to take to the lakeside park a block down the street. ⊠ *1829 N. Orange Ave., Orlando,* ☎ *407/895-9911. AE, MC, V.*

American-International

$$$$ ✕ **Manuel's on the 28th.** How's this for one-upmanship? For a decade, ★ Arthur's 27 was Orlando's loftiest restaurant in terms of altitude, with a spot on the 27th floor of the Buena Vista Palace Hotel. In 1994, Manuel's on the 28th—as in 28th floor of the downtown Barnett Bank building—opened its doors and was almost immediately hailed by local dining critics as a culinary landmark. In many cases, restaurants with a view offer only that, but the cuisine here is excellent, with stellar offerings like seared loin of lamb in a cayenne-Scotch-whiskey sauce, wood-roasted chicken and lobster in a coconut-lime sauce, and hickory-grilled muscovy duck breast with plum-ginger sauce. There is an extensive wine list and, an unusual offer, wines by the half glass. The restaurant offers several tasting packages. Though it's open only at dinner, you may be allowed to come in during the day and just gawk ・ at the view across the flat, green central Florida landscape. ⊠ *390 N. Orange Ave., Orlando,* ☎ *407/246–6580. Jacket required. AE, D, DC, MC, V. Closed Sun. and Mon. No lunch.*

$$–$$$ ✕ **Chatham's Place.** This is one of Orlando's best. The Chatham ★ brothers, Culinary Institute of America graduates, prepare everything to order here, and the staff is genuinely concerned that every patron has a perfect experience. The professional office building that the restaurant calls home, across the street from the Marketplace shopping mall, lends nothing in the way of atmosphere; nor is the decor anything to get excited about—hanging plants, glass-topped, paisley tablecloths, and a view of the kitchen. But the meticulously prepared food rises above the setting. Try the black grouper with pecan butter, the rosemary-infused rack of lamb, or the duck breast, grilled to crispy perfection. ⊠ *7575 Dr. Phillips Blvd., Orlando,* ☎ *407/345– 2992. MC, V. No lunch.*

$$ ✕ **Harvey's Bistro.** In the Barnett Bank building downtown, within walking distance of the arena and the Centroplex, this clubby newcomer, with paneled walls and white tablecloths, has quickly collected an enthusiastic business crowd at lunch and concert-, theater-, and arenagoers after dark. The menu offers a good selection of bistro and comfort foods. Soups are good, as are the oven-roasted saffron scallops, the duck cassoulet with white and black beans, and the thin-crusted pizza with caramelized onions, fresh spinach, and goat cheese. Late hours are a plus. ⊠ *390 N. Orlando Ave., Orlando,* ☎ *407/246–6560. AE, D, DC, MC, V. Closed Sun. No lunch Sat.*

$$ ✕ **Moorefield's.** The trendy menu and fresh, sophisticated but home- ★ made dishes make you think Martha Stewart might be in the kitchen somewhere, but in this case it's owner-chef Elizabeth Moorefield. The menu changes constantly, but you can always find some variation of grilled salmon; roast pork; and perhaps the most popular dish on the menu, angel-hair pasta with artichoke hearts, hearts of palm, chevre, sun-dried tomatoes, and Parmesan. Vegetarians are always satisfied with the selection offered. A popular appetizer is a minipizza topped with mushrooms and roasted garlic. About 20 carefully selected wines are offered by the glass. This place attracts a highly urbane clientele, and is usually crowded before and after live theater events and concerts. ⊠ *123 S. Orange Ave., Orlando,* ☎ *407/872–6960. AE, MC, V.*

Chinese

$–$$ ✕ **Forbidden City.** The Hunan-style food at this restaurant in a recon-structed gas station is terrific. Start with the diced chicken with pine seeds in a package—icy lettuce cups wrapped around spicy chicken, which offer a delightful mix of cold and hot sensations. The sesame chicken—large chunks of sesame-coated poultry sautéed in a sweet sauce—goes perfectly with bright-green broccoli in a subtle garlic sauce. The traditional 10-ingredient lo mein is full of fresh shrimp, chicken, beef, and pork. You're in for a treat if you can get past the decor, or lack thereof; the former gas station's marquee is still there, and inside there are utilitarian tables and booths, with a few plastic plants to add that fresh, natural note. ⊠ *948 N. Mills Ave., Orlando,* ☎ *407/894–5005. MC, V. Closed Sun. No lunch Sat.*

$–$$ ✕ **4-5-6.** With its mirrored walls and emerald green carpet, this restau-rant is sleek and clean-looking, setting the stage for the food, which is made without MSG or preservatives. Dumplings sautéed in hot peanut butter sauce is a must for peanut butter fans. Specialties include chicken-three-ways (one platter that includes portions of General Tso's chicken, lemon chicken, and sliced chicken breast with snow peas), as well as Five Fresh Herbs Steamed Fresh Fish, made with sea bass. The friendly staff tries hard to accommodate, so be sure to speak up if you want your food spicy or served in a special casserole to keep it warm. ⊠ *657 N. Primrose Dr., Orlando,* ☎ *407/898–1899. AE, MC, V. Beer and wine only.*

Continental

$$$$ ✕ **Chalet Suzanne.** If you like to drive or are returning from a day at
★ Cypress Gardens, consider making a dinner reservation at this family-owned country inn and restaurant. Because of its charm and original-ity, Chalet Suzanne has earned praise from restaurant critics. It might provide one of the most memorable dining experiences of your Orlando stay. Expanded bit by quirky bit since it opened in the 1930s, this un-likely country inn looks like a small Swiss village—right in the middle of the orange groves. As an appetizer, try the broiled grapefruit, basted with a butter, cinnamon, and sugar mixture and served with a grilled chicken liver; then move on to shrimp curry, lobster Newburg, or filet mignon. Crepes Suzanne are a good bet for dessert. All meals are prix fixe, with seven courses; prices begin at $40 and are determined by the cost of your entrée. There's also an excellent Sunday brunch, with stel-lar eggs benedict. ⊠ *3800 Chalet Suzanne Dr., U.S. 27 north of Lake Wales, about 10 mi past Cypress Gardens turnoff,* ☎ *813/676–6011. Jacket required. AE, DC, MC, V. Closed Mon. in summer.*

$$ ✕ **Dixie Crossroads.** When you first pull into the parking lot, you may
★ think this a newly-opened gambling operation, like one of Florida's highly popular and ubiquitous bingo halls. The outside is always over-flowing with crowds waiting to be seated. But quick money doesn't draw the throngs, its the basic but uniformly excellent seafood feast. The specialty here is the difficult-to-cook rock shrimp, which the Crossroads crew shells and fries or broils to perfection. Other stand-outs on the menu include the clam strips, and the all-you-can-eat cat-fish. The Indian River combo includes rock shrimp, cod or other saltwater fish, scallops, and crab. Not a fancy place, but well worth a stop, especially if you are taking a side trip to the Kennedy Space Cen-ter, which is about 20 minutes away. If you don't want to wait for lit-erally hours to get a table here, you can order take-out. ⊠ *1475 Garden St., Titusville, 2 mi east of Interstate 95 Exit 80,* ☎ *407/268-5000. Reservations not accepted. AE, DC, MC, V.*

Cuban

$ ★ **✕ Numero Uno.** To the followers of this long-popular Latin restaurant, the name is quite appropriate. Downtowners have been filling the place up at lunch for years. It bills itself as "the home of paella," and that's probably the best dish. If you have time and a good appetite, try the paella Valenciana, which takes an hour and 15 minutes on special order, with yellow rice, sausage, chicken, fish, Spanish spices, and a side order of plantains. If you don't have that long, go for traditional Cuban fare like shredded flank steak or the dish that half of Latin America eats daily, arroz con pollo (chicken and rice). ⊠ *2499 S. Orange Ave., Orlando,* ☎ *407/84–3840. Reservations essential for 4 or more. AE, D, MC, V.*

French

$$$ **✕ Le Cordon Bleu.** Over the past two decades, Georges and Monique Vogelbacher have assembled a loyal clientele, who come back night after night for French cuisine with a Swiss touch. With its print wallpaper, lace curtains, and white tablecloths, the room is comfortable, and so is the menu, which offers the kitchen's well-prepared version of Caesar salad, superb roast rack of lamb (for two) with an array of seasonal vegetables, and poached Norwegian salmon. In keeping with the trend toward lighter cuisine, Le Cordon Bleu has placed a number of low-fat dishes and fresh fish specials on the menu as well. The bread is really good. ⊠ *537 W. Fairbanks Ave., Winter Park,* ☎ *407/647– 7575. AE, D, DC, MC, V. Closed Sun. No lunch Sat.*

$$ ★ **✕ Le Coq au Vin.** Louis Perrotte deserves a medal, not just for his culinary achievements in serving excellent French cuisine in Orlando for more than 15 years but for remaining modest. This French chef could run a stuffed-shirt kind of place with the best of 'em because his food is as expertly prepared as any haute cuisine you'll find in the Orlando area. Instead, he chooses the self-effacing route, running a modest little kitchen in a small but charming house in south Orlando. Perrotte and his wife, Magdalena, who acts as hostess, make the place feel warm and homey, and it is usually filled with friendly Orlando residents. The traditional French fare is first-class and roused *Vogue*'s restaurant critic to raves: homemade chicken liver pâté, fresh rainbow trout with champagne sauce, and Long Island duck with green peppercorns. For dessert, try the crème brûlée, and pat yourself on the back for discovering a place that few tourists know about. The menu changes quarterly, as Perrotte celebrates the regional cuisines of his native France. Ask to be seated in the main dining room—it's the center of the action. ⊠ *4800 S. Orange Ave., Orlando,* ☎ *407/851–6980. AE, DC, MC, V.*

$$ **✕ Le Provence Bistro Français.** This charming, two-story restaurant in the heart of downtown Orlando does a fine imitation of an out-of-the-way bistro on the Left Bank in Paris. Reasonable prices and first-rate service add to the delightful surroundings and excellent food. For lunch try the *salade Niçoise* (made with fresh grilled tuna, French string beans, and hard-boiled eggs), or the cassoulet *toulousain* (a hearty mixture of white beans, lamb, pork, and sausage). At dinner you can choose between a six-course prix fixe menu, a less pricey four-course version, or à la carte options. ⊠ *50 East Pine St., Orlando,* ☎ *407/843–1320. Reservations advised. AE, DC, MC, V. Closed Sun. No lunch Sat.*

Italian

$$$ **✕ Christini's.** Orlando is short on the kind of upscale Italian restaurant you find so often in New York, so locals, tourists, and Disney execs gladly pay the price at Christini's, one of Orlando's best for northern Italian cuisine. As a result, the place always feels as if there's a party going on, particularly in the center of the room. Owner Chris Christini is on hand

nightly to make sure that everything is perfect. Try the pasta with lobster, shrimp, and clams or the huge veal chops, perfumed with fresh sage. Note: This is no place to be in a hurry; dinner, with its various courses, will often take a couple of hours or more. But Christini assumes you are there for more than a meal, so he makes it an event. Frequently, live music is offered by a strolling violinist. ⊠ *7600 Dr. Phillips Blvd., in Marketplace, Orlando,* ☎ *407/345–8770. AE, DC, MC, V.*

$$$
★ ✕ **Enzo's on the Lake.** Enzo's is one of Orlando's most popular restaurants, even though it's located on a tacky stretch of highway filled with used car lots. The Roman charmer who owns the place, Enzo Perlini, has turned a rather ordinary lakefront house in suburban Longwood, about 30 minutes' drive from I-Drive, into an Italian villa. It's worth the trip to sample the antipasto. The mussels, cooked in a heady broth of white wine and garlic, and the mild *bufalo* mozzarella cheese, flown in from Italy, make equally good starters. The *bucatini à la Enzo* (a combination of sautéed bacon, mushrooms, and peas served over long hollow noodles) is a very popular house specialty. The electricity in the air is such that even people with reservations don't mind waiting at the bar; they simply get into the party mood. ⊠ *1130 S. U.S. 17–92, Longwood,* ☎ *407/834–9872. Reservations essential. AE, DC, MC, V. Closed Sun.*

$$–$$$ ✕ **Antonio's La Fiamma.** The wood-burning grill and oven give the place a charming smell that greets you when you walk in the door. But they aren't just for ambience, as the chef uses them to turn out great grilled fish dishes, gourmet pizzas, and homemade bread. The main section of the restaurant is upstairs, where diners can watch the cooks at the back of the building working their magic. Try the fennel and radicchio salad topped with orange zest, cracked pepper, shavings of Gruyère, and extra-virgin olive oil. The linguine *alla cine di rapa* (linguine served with sautéed bitter greens, sausage, and slivered garlic) is a tantalizing marriage of tastes and textures. The *anitra con rosmarino all'agrodolce* (fully deboned and roasted duck with a sweet-sour sauce made of balsamic vinegar, rosemary, and honey) is heavenly. ⊠ *611 S. Orlando Ave., Maitland,* ☎ *407/645–1035. AE, MC, V. Closed Sun.*

$$–$$$ ✕ **La Scala.** Mirrored walls and gracious, sophisticated decor make this one of Orlando's most romantic restaurants. The fact that owner Joseph del Vento, a former opera singer, who once worked in New York's Tre Scalini, breaks into song every so often only adds to the charm. For pasta, order the dish called Chop, Chop, Chop (fresh seafood sautéed tableside, doused in marinara sauce, and served over fettuccine). ⊠ *205 Loraine Dr., Altamonte Springs,* ☎ *407/862–3257. AE, DC, MC, V. Closed Sun. No lunch Sat.*

$$–$$$ ✕ **La Sila.** Although located in one of Orlando's ubiquitous strip shopping centers, La Sila offers consistently fresh, northern Italian cuisine in a gracious, sophisticated setting. Pasta lovers will appreciate the large and original selection of dishes, including a penne with arugula and fresh tomato sauce that's an ideal mixture of bitter and sweet. Because the restaurant's popularity continues to grow and because it's so convenient to WDW and Universal Studios, reservations are a must. ⊠ *4898 Kirkman Rd., Orlando,* ☎ *407/295–8333. AE, DC, MC, V.*

$–$$ ✕ **Gargi's Italian Restaurant.** You can feel the building vibrate when Amtrak rolls by a few feet away, but that just adds charm to this delightful, downhome ma-and-pa pasta place. If you crave old-fashioned spaghetti and meatballs, lasagna, or manicotti made with sauces that you know have been simmering all day, this storefront hole-in-the-wall in Orlando's antiques district just a little north of downtown is the place. If you want more than basic pasta, try some of the specialties like the veal marsala or the tasty shrimp with marinara sauce and peppers, served over linguini. Well-heeled Orlandoans eat here before Orlando Magic games; it's also a favorite of waterskiers from Lake Ivanhoe across the street. Located off the beaten tourist track, but only a couple of hundred yards from I-4, it's a welcome change from I-Drive. Get off I-4 at Ivanhoe (Exit 42); it's three minutes away. You should know, however, that this place is notorious for slow service—but worth it!. ⊠ *1421 N. Orange Ave., Orlando,* ☎ *407/894–7907. MC, V. Beer and wine only. Closed Sun.*

$–$$ ✕ **Romano's Macaroni Grill.** This Texas-based chain of Italian restaurants has thrived in Orlando, and now there are three locations in the metro area. So much is right about Romano's, beginning with the friendly family-run service. It's also a casual, comfortable setting, which is immediately obvious when the waitress brings over a pile of crayons for you to scribble on the giant sheets of white wrapping paper serving as table cloths. Let your creative juices flow, no matter what your age. They sure let theirs go in the kichen, spinning out a whole spectrum of popular pastas, complete with toppings and sauces made with everything from sausage to eggplant, and topped with freshly grated parmesan cheese. Excellent home-made breads are cooked in a wood-burning oven on premises. House wines, selected from a decent list, are brought to the table in gallon bottles. You serve yourself and then tell the waiter how many glasses you had. Good desserts, too. ⊠ *884 W. State Road 436, Altamonte Springs,* ☎ *407/682–2577;* ⊠ *5320 W. Irlo Bronson Hwy., Kissimmee,* ☎ *407/396-6155;* ⊠ *12148 S. Apopka-Vineland Rd., Orlando,* ☎ *407/239-6676. AE, DC, D, MC, V.*

Mexican

$ ✕ **Amigo's.** There are those who say the best Mexican food in central Florida is at Amigo's, two restaurants run by a family of transplanted Texans. Their strategy consists of building on good basics, like refried beans that would play well in San Antonio. Go for the Santa Fe dinner, so big it almost takes a burro to bring it to your table; you'll be able to sample tamales, enchiladas, chiles rellenos, and those heavenly frijoles and wash it down with a Mexican beer. ⊠ *120 Westmoreland, Altamonte Springs,* ☎ *407/774–4334;* ⊠ *494 N. Semoran, Winter Park,* ☎ *407/657–8111. AE, MC, V.*

$ ✕ **L.A. Tacos.** The name seems to imply that this is a fast food place with a limited menu, but it's neither. Although you order at the register and your meal is brought to you on a plastic tray, the sitdown meals are satisfying and well prepared. The menu offers some excellent Mexican staple items like good homemade tamales; numerous variations of soft tacos, with pork, chicken, beef and other ingredients of your choice; chiles rellanos; enchiladas; and a tasty, freshly made guacamole. House specialties are sometimes creative, like fish tacos, and the more mainstream but delicious mole *poblano* (Mexican chicken topped with a chocolate sauce). Regardless of what you order, be sure to pop a quarter in the plastic piggy bank at the register and then dish yourself up some of the tasty *pico de gallo.* Desserts include a flan with fresh coconut, which, like everything else served here, is made on premises. ⊠ *2117 E. Colonial Dr.,* ☎ *407/894-5590; take-out orders* ℻ *407/894-1581. No credit cards. Beer and wine only.*

Pizza

$–$$ ✕ **Donato's.** This family-owned restaurant, the only one on the north end of International Drive, is just steps away from the Belz Factory Outlet Mall. There's a takeout deli and grocery store as you walk in. But taking the time to eat in one of the two large dining rooms is worthwhile. Although the decor is delicatessen, the food is abundant and well prepared. ⊠ *5159 International Dr., Orlando,* ☎ *407/363–5959. AE, DC, MC, V.*

$–$$ ✕ **Enzo's at the Marketplace.** This pizzeria and deli combines the real Italian flavor of its Longwood sister with an atmosphere that's casual and a location that's more convenient for tourists. Owner Enzo Perlini, a food purist, imported the pizza ovens from Italy to ensure that his pizza Napoli would have the proper thin, crispy crust. It does. The toppings are Italian style—fresh tomatoes and mozzarella, seafood, or grilled vegetables. ⊠ *7600 Dr. Phillips Blvd., in the Marketplace, Orlando,* ☎ *407/351–1187. AE, D, DC, MC, V.*

$–$$ ✕ **Positano.** One side of this cheerful restaurant is a bustling family-
★ style pizza parlor; the other is a more formal dining room. Although you can't order pizza in the dining room, you can get anything on the entire menu in the pizzeria, which serves some of the best New York–style pies in central Florida. Try the unusual and piquant ziti *aum* (mozzarella, Parmesan, eggplant, and basil in a tomato sauce). ⊠ *8995 W. Colonial Dr., in Good Homes Plaza, Orlando,* ☎ *407/291–0602. AE, D, DC, MC, V.*

Seafood

$$ ✕ **Straub's Fine Seafood.** One school of economic thought in Orlando is that the farther you drive from Disney, the less you pay for everything. Straub's holds up the culinary part of the equation with items like escargot to go (or to stay) for $6—less than you'd pay for a burger 30 miles away on U.S. 192 in Kissimmee. Straub's is one of those minimalist restaurants that put their emphasis on food, not atmosphere. Tablecloths are covered with Plexiglas, and when you walk into the place, you know there won't be a string quartet playing in the background. But owner Robert Straub, a fishmonger of many years, knows how to prepare a mean mesquite-grilled Atlantic salmon with a little béarnaise on the side. Straub fillets all his own fish and won't serve anything he can't get fresh. Blackened dolphin Cajun–style is quite good here, as is the angel-hair pasta with sautéed shrimp, pine nuts, capers, artichoke hearts, and fresh spinach. The menu states the calorie count and fat content of every fish item, but for the coconut-banana cream pie, made on premises, you just don't want to know. ⊠ *5101 E. Colonial Dr., Orlando,* ☎ *407/273–9330;* ⊠ *512 E. Altamonte Dr., Altamonte Springs,* ☎ *407/831–2250. AE, D, DC, MC, V.*

Steak

$$$ ✕ **Del Frisco's Prime Steak House.** Orlando finally has a genuine New York–style steak house to call its own. The sound of Ol' Blue Eyes belting the standards swirls about a clubby dining room, where big, juicy sirloins and porterhouses are the entrées of choice. Scalloped potatoes and chopped spinach mixed with melted cheddar cheese and bacon bits come with the steaks and are sure to blow your low-fat diet. ⊠ *729 Lee Rd., Orlando,* ☎ *407/645–4443. AE, DC, MC, V. Closed Sun.*

$$$ ✕ **Ruth's Chris Steak House.** If you've never eaten in a country club but always wanted to, this sublime restaurant, with dark wood paneling, starched white tablecloths, and little lamps at each table, will give you the same feeling. Although it's part of a chain, this is a place for beef purists. The sirloins are panfried in butter and served à la carte only. Baked potatoes, spinach au gratin, and other accompaniments are all $3 to $5 extra. Even though the atmosphere makes you feel as if you should be wearing a blazer with a crest on it, jackets aren't required for men. ⊠ *999 Douglas Ave., Altamonte Springs,* ☎ *407/682–6444. AE, DC, MC, V.*

$$ ✕ **Lindas La Cantina.** They take their beef very seriously at this place, as you can tell by the disclaimer at the top of the menu's entrée list: "We cannot be responsible for steaks cooked medium-well and well done." Despite that stuffed-shirt sounding caveat, this place is really a down-home eatery, a favorite among locals for 40 years. The menu is short and to the point, including about a dozen steak dishes and just enough ancillary items to fill up a single page. What has packed in the locals since the Eisenhower administration is the straight-forward approach to well-prepared, tender beef. Among the best is the La Cantina large t-bone—more beef than most can handle, for $22. With every entrée you get a heaping order of spaghetti or baked potato. Being the friendly, Southern kinda of restaurant that it is, La Cantina will bake your birthday cake for $5. ⊠ *4721 E. Colonial Dr., Orlando*, ☎ *407/ 894–4491. AE, D, MC, V.*

Thai

$$ ✕ **Siam Orchid.** One of Orlando's several elegant Asian restaurants, Siam Orchid occupies a gorgeous structure a bit off I-Drive. Waitresses, who wear costumes from their homeland, serve authentic fare such as Siam wings (a chicken wing stuffed to look like a drumstick) and *plalad prig* (a whole, deep-fried fish covered with a sauce flavored with red chili, bell peppers, and garlic). If you like your food spicy, say "Thai hot" and grab a fire extinguisher. ⊠ *7575 Republic Dr., Orlando*, ☎ *407/ 351–0821. AE, DC, MC, V.*

24-Hour

$$ ✕ **Beeline Diner.** This slick, 1950s–style diner in the Peabody Hotel is not exactly cheap, but the salads, sandwiches, and griddle foods are tops. Though very busy at times, it can be fun for breakfast or a late-night snack. And for just a little silver, you get to play a lot of old tunes on the jukebox. ⊠ *9801 International Dr., Orlando*, ☎ *407/352–4000. AE, DC, MC, V.*

Vietnamese

$ ✕ **Little Saigon.** As Orlando flourishes, so grow the ethnic restaurants,
★ including a variety of Vietnamese eateries and shops, about 1½ miles east of I–4's U.S. 50 exit. The folks at Little Saigon are friendly and love to introduce novices to their healthy and delicious national cuisine. Sample the spring rolls or the summer rolls (spring roll filling in a soft wrapper); then move on to the grilled pork and egg, served atop rice and noodles, or the traditional soup, filled with noodles, rice, vegetables, and your choice of either chicken or seafood; ask to have extra meat in the soup if you're hungry, and be sure they bring you the mint and bean sprouts to sprinkle in. Ask for an English-speaking waiter if you're unfamiliar with the cuisine. ⊠ *1106 E. Colonial Dr., Orlando*, ☎ *407/423–8539. MC, V. Beer and wine only.*

8 Lodging

ORLANDO IS YOUR BRIGHTEST FANTASY, an escape to the sun and the still waters of a lake-size swimming pool, a week of sipping fruity drinks topped with whipped cream and served by fit waiters at some of America's largest and most imaginative hotels. To hotel owners, however, the vision is more complex. Business is good here, as 13 million-plus visitors a year create a market that can finance some outrageous projects. But the competition is fierce for hoteliers, since nearly every investor in America wants to build here. The number of rooms has raced past 85,000, and will reach more than 110,000 by the end of this decade. Too much supply for builders, but great news for travelers who are looking for low rates.

Adding to the sprawl are two big new hotels that recently opened, the Omni Rosen Hotel and Disney World's BoardWalk Inn and BoardWalk Villas. From a tourism and marketing perspective, that's put a couple of thousand more rooms in the hotel inventory; for the tourist, it means that poolside mai-tai just got that much more affordable. Cheers.

The first big decision: to stay at a hostelry within WDW or one outside the property. There are advantages to each option. To help in finding your perfect room, we've reviewed hundreds of offerings throughout the main hotel hubs both in and surrounding WDW.

How to Choose

When examining your options, give careful thought to the kind of vacation you want. Consider what you want to see during your Orlando visit and how long you want to stay. Within a given price category, compare the facilities of the available establishments to make sure that you get exactly what you want; our charts (☞ *below*) will help you do this. Don't overlook the savings to be gained from cooking your own breakfast and maybe a few other meals as well, which you can do if you choose an establishment with cooking facilities. If you're traveling with children, remember to ask about the cut-off age, the age at which the management considers your offspring to be adults—and makes you pay accordingly, even when they share your room. Finally, don't overlook time spent in transit; if you're not staying at a property in or near WDW, you can waste a few hours a day sitting in traffic.

Staying in WDW

If you are coming to Orlando for only a few days and are interested solely in the Magic Kingdom, Epcot Center, and the other Disney attractions, the resorts on Disney property—whether or not they're owned by Disney—are the most convenient. Put aside your car keys, because Walt Disney World buses and monorails—free to guests at on-site resorts—are efficient enough to make it possible to visit one park in the morning and another after lunch, with a Park- or World-Hopper admission ticket. You have the freedom to return to your hotel for R&R when the crowds are thickest, and if it turns out that half the family wants to spend the afternoon in one of the parks and the other half wants to float around Typhoon Lagoon, it's not a problem.

On-site hotels were built with families in mind. Older children can travel on their own on the transportation system without inviting trouble. Younger children get a thrill from knowing that they're actually living in Walt Disney World. Rooms are usually large enough to accommodate up to five; villas sleep six or seven. All accommodations offer cable TV with the Disney Channel and a daily events channel.

If you're an on-site guest at a Disney hotel, a major perk is free transportation to the various Disney parks, either by monorail—which services three of the leading hostelries—or by motor launch, bus, or tram; the most frequent mode of transportation is buses, which depart every 15 minutes. Disney hotels offer other benefits to their guests. Each day on-site guests can get in to one of the three parks one hour before regular park opening—and even when the theme parks or water parks have reached capacity, as Blizzard Beach, Typhoon Lagoon, and Disney-MGM Studios sometimes do, on-site guests are guaranteed entry. Then there are the small conveniences: Guests at Disney-owned properties are able to charge to their room most meals and purchases throughout WDW. To golfers, it's important to know that Disney guests get first choice of tee times at the golf courses and can also reserve them up to 30 days in advance.

Staying Around Orlando

If you're planning to visit attractions other than WDW or if the Disney resorts seem too rich for your blood, then staying off-site holds a number of advantages. You'll enjoy more peace and quiet and may have easier access to Sea World and Universal Studios—as well as to Orlando's shopping, dining, and entertainment facilities. You're almost certain to save money.

The hotels closest to Walt Disney World are clustered in several principal areas: along International Drive within Orlando city limits; within the boundaries of Kissimmee, the town that is actually closest to Walt Disney World and with hotels that tend to be small and cheap; and in the Disney Maingate area around WDW's northernmost entrance, just off I–4. Nearly every hotel in these areas provides frequent transportation to and from Walt Disney World. In addition, there are some noteworthy—if far-flung—options in the suburbs, the U.S. 192 area, and the Greater Orlando area. Since the city isn't so big, even apparently distant properties are seldom much more than a half hour's drive from Disney toll plazas, when traffic is running smoothly. If you're willing to make the commute, you're likely to save a bundle: Whereas accommodations at the Embassy Suites near Lake Buena Vista will cost you upwards of $120 a night, the sister property about 35 minutes away in Altamonte Springs charges around $80 for equally luxurious quarters. Some of the simpler motels with Kissimmee addresses will put you up for $40 a night or even less.

Reservations

All on-site Disney accommodations may be booked through the Walt Disney World Central Reservations Office (✉ Box 10100, Suite 300, Lake Buena Vista 32830, ☎ 407/W–DISNEY); persons with disabilities can call WDW Special Request Reservations (☎ 407/354–1853, TTY 407/939–7670) to get information or book rooms. Rooms at most non-Disney, chain hotels can be reserved by calling either the hotel itself or the toll-free number for the entire chain. Be sure to tell the reservationist exactly what you are looking for—Disney-owned property or not, price range, the number of people in your party, and the dates of your visit. If possible, stay flexible about dates; many hotels and attractions offer seasonal discounts of up to 40%.

Deposits

You must give a deposit for your first night's stay within three weeks of making your reservation. At many hotels you can get a refund if you cancel at least five days before your scheduled arrival. However, individual hotel policies vary, and some properties may require up to 15 days' notice for a full refund. Check before booking.

When to Book

Reserve your WDW or non-Disney hotel several months in advance—as much as a year ahead if you want to snag the best rooms during high season.

Other Options

If neither the WDW Central Reservations Office nor the off-site hotels have space on your preferred dates, look into packages from American Express, Delta, or other operators, who have been allotted whole blocks of rooms. In addition, because there are always cancellations, it's worth trying even at the last minute; for same-day bookings, call the property directly.

Packages, including cruises, car rentals, and hotels both on and off Disney property, can be arranged through your travel agent or Walt Disney Travel Co. (✉ 1675 Buena Vista Dr., Lake Buena Vista 32830, ☎ 800/828−0228).

Ratings and Rates

Rates are lowest from early January to mid-February, from mid-April to mid-June, and from mid-August to the third week in December; low rates often remain in place longer at non-Disney properties. Always call several places—availability and special deals can often drive room rates at a $$$$ hotel down into the $$ range—and don't forget to ask if you're eligible for a discount. Many hotels offer special rates for members of, for example, the American Automobile Association (AAA) or the American Association of Retired Persons (AARP).

CATEGORY	COST*
$$$$	over $180
$$$	$120–$180
$$	$65–$120
$	under $65

All rates are for two adults traveling with up to two children during high season, plus 10% tax.

IN WDW: DISNEY HOTELS

Traditionally, guests have had to take a heavy hit in the wallet to stay in Disney-owned hotels. During the past several years, however, the number of moderately priced properties has boomed. With a wide selection of price ranges available, most lodging decisions come down to what area of WDW or what style of hotel strikes your fancy. Resort hotels predominate, but there are also campsites, trailers, and kitchen-equipped suites and villas. These accommodations are clustered together in four sections of Walt Disney World.

The Magic Kingdom resort area has ritzy hotels, all of which lie on the Magic Kingdom monorail route and are only minutes away from the park. Fort Wilderness Campground Resort, with trailers and RV and tent sites, is just southeast of this area. The Epcot Center resort area, south of the park, includes the luxurious Beach and Yacht Club Resorts as well as the popular Caribbean Beach Resort. Disney's newest high-end property, the Boardwalk Resort—which has a turn-of-the-century Atlantic City atmosphere—is opening near Epcot Center by summer '96. The Disney Village resort area, east of Epcot Center, is near Pleasure Island and the Disney Village Marketplace. Accommodations include two midprice resorts with an Old South theme as well as the Disney Village Resort, made up of town houses and villas equipped with kitchens. The newest complex, All-Star Village, lies near the intersec-

In case you want to see the world.

At American Express, we're here to make your journey a smooth one. So we have over 1,700 travel service locations in over 120 countries ready to help. What else would you expect from the world's largest travel agency?

do more

Travel

http://www.americanexpress.com/travel

In case you want to be welcomed there.

We're here to see that you're always welcomed at establishments everywhere. That's why millions of people carry the American Express® Card – for peace of mind, confidence, and security, around the world or just around the corner.

do more ®

Cards

In case you're running low.

We're here to help with more than 118,000 Express Cash locations around the world. In order to enroll, just call American Express before you start your vacation.

do more ®

Express Cash

And just in case.

We're here with American Express® Travelers Cheques and Cheques *for Two.*® They're the safest way to carry money on your vacation and the surest way to get a refund, practically anywhere, anytime.

Another way we help you...

do more

Travelers Cheques

tion of World Drive and U.S. 192, south of Epcot Center and the Magic Kingdom.

Magic Kingdom Resort Area

Resort Hotels

$$$$ ⊞ **Contemporary Resort.** If the Jetsons ever came to WDW, this 15-
★ story, flat-topped pyramid is where they'd stay. Since the monorail runs right through the heart of this awkwardly modern A-frame, it looks like some intergalactic docking bay lifted straight out of a futuristic space age. The Contemporary is a high-class, ideally situated resort complex that seems to be bustling, in traditional Disney fashion, from the crack of dawn until after midnight. Half the rooms are in the Tower, the main building, and you'll have to pay extra for their spectacular views. Those in the front look out toward the Magic Kingdom's Cinderella Castle and Space Mountain, a great backdrop for the flaming Florida sunsets and the regular nighttime fireworks show; those on the back side have ringside views of the Electrical Water Pageant and the sun rising through the mists of Bay Lake. Some guests report that Tower rooms can be somewhat noisy at night—sounds rise through the busy atrium—so if you're a light sleeper, you may prefer a room in the hotel's North and South Gardens, where the other half of the rooms are located; the best are on the shore of Bay Lake, but all cost less than Tower rooms. Try to avoid units described as having a view of the Magic Kingdom—they have an even better view of the parking lot. Regardless of location, all rooms have a small terrace and most have two queen-size beds plus a small day bed. Main recreational facilities are right on the property; one of the swimming pools, WDW's largest at 20 by 25 meters, has been renovated and is now three, large, connected circles with a 10-foot slide. Kids happily disappear into the Fiesta Fun Center, one of the biggest game rooms known to childkind. A short hop on the monorail—which breezes right into the hotel every 10 to 15 minutes from 7 AM until two hours after park closing—takes you to the Polynesian and Grand Floridian hotels as well as to the Magic Kingdom and Epcot Center; other destinations can be reached by motor launch and bus. ⊠ *WDW Central Reservations, Box 10100, Lake Buena Vista 32830,* ☎ *407/934–7639; same-day reservations, 407/824–1000;* FAX *407/824–3539. 1,041 rooms, 80 suites. 3 restaurants, 1 snack bar, 3 lounges, room service, 3 heated outdoor pools, beauty salon, 6 lighted tennis courts, health club, game room, shuffleboard, volleyball, lakeside beach, marina, boat rentals, waterskiing, laundry, concierge services. AE, MC, V.*

$$$$ ⊞ **Grand Floridian.** At first you might think that a magical Disney time
★ machine transported this gilded-age masterpiece brick by brick from some turn-of-the-century coastal hot spot to the shores of the Seven Seas Lagoon. Actually, the gabled red roof, brick chimneys, rambling verandas, and delicate gingerbread are grand-old yet brand-new, all built from scratch on the site. Loving attention was paid to each detail, from the crystal chandeliers and stained-glass domes to the ornate balconies and aviary. Although equipped with every modern convenience, the moss-green and salmon-pink rooms, with Victorian wallpaper, deep carpets, and wall hangings, have real vintage charm, especially the attic nooks up under the eaves. Deluxe suites are available in the smaller building known as the Lodge. The Victorian theme extends to the resort's charming monorail station as well. The monorail itself makes it easy for guests to zip to the Magic Kingdom and Epcot Center from here; bus and motor launch lines also connect to the parks. ⊠ *WDW Central Reservations, Box 10100, Lake Buena Vista 32830,* ☎ *407/934–7639 or 407/824–3000,* FAX *407/824–3186. 900 rooms, 61 concierge*

Walt Disney World Lodging

Name of Property	Number of Rooms/Suites	Number of Restaurants	Number of Lounges	Room Service	Complimentary Breakfast	
$$$$						
Buena Vista Palace and Palace Suite Resort	1,028	5	4	✓		
Disney's Village Resort	592	4	4	✓		
Grand Cypress Resort	676	5	4	✓		
Hilton at WDW Village	814	7	2	✓		
Marriott's Orlando World Center	1,504	7	2	✓		
Peabody Orlando	891	3	2	✓		
Renaissance Orlando Resort	780	5	2	✓		
Vistana Resort	722	2	1			
WDW Beach and Yacht Club Resorts	1,158	4	3	✓		
WDW Boardwalk Resort	392	4	4	✓		
WDW Contemporary Resort	1,041	3	3	✓		
WDW Dolphin	1,510	8	3	✓		
WDW Fort Wilderness Resort Homes	408	2	1			
WDW Grand Floridian	905	6	3	✓		
WDW Polynesian Resort	865	3	1	✓		
WDW Swan	758	4	3	✓		
$$$						
Courtyard by Marriott	323	1	1			
Embassy Suites Hotel at Plaza International	246		1		✓	
Embassy Suites International Drive South	244	1	1		✓	
Embassy Suites Orlando—North	210	1	1	✓	✓	
Embassy Suites Resort Lake Buena Vista	280	1	1		✓	
Grosvenor Resort	633	2	1	✓		

In-Room Kitchenettes	In-Room Microwaves	In-Room Coffeemaker	In-Room VCR	No. Swimming Pools	No. Tennis Courts (Lighted)	On-Site Golf	Arcade Game Room	Health Club	Boating	Supervised Children's Program	Baby-Sitting	Guest Laundry
✓	✓	✓	✓	3	3(L)		✓	✓		✓	✓	✓
✓	✓	✓		5			✓	✓	✓		✓	✓
✓	✓	✓		2	12(L)	✓	✓	✓	✓	✓	✓	✓
				2	2(L)		✓	✓		✓	✓	✓
				4	8(L)	✓	✓	✓		✓	✓	✓
				1	4(L)		✓	✓		✓	✓	✓
				1	5(L)		✓	✓		✓	✓	✓
✓	✓	✓		5	13(L)		✓	✓		✓	✓	✓
				3	2(L)		✓	✓	✓	✓	✓	✓
✓				1	2		✓	✓	✓	✓	✓	✓
				3	6(L)		✓	✓	✓	✓	✓	✓
				4	8(L)		✓	✓		✓	✓	✓
✓	✓	✓		3	1(L)		✓		✓	✓	✓	✓
				1	2(L)		✓	✓	✓	✓	✓	✓
				2			✓		✓	✓	✓	✓
				2	4(L)		✓	✓		✓	✓	✓
		✓		2			✓	✓			✓	✓
✓	✓	✓		1			✓	✓			✓	✓
				1							✓	✓
✓	✓	✓		1				✓			✓	✓
				1	1(L)		✓	✓		✓	✓	
		✓	✓	2	2(L)		✓	✓			✓	✓

Walt Disney World Lodging

Name of Property	Number of Rooms/Suites	Number of Restaurants	Number of Lounges	Room Service	Complimentary Breakfast	
Guest Quarters Suite Resort	229	1	1		✓	
Parc Corniche Resort	210	1	1			
Sol Orlando Resort	150	1	1		✓	
Summerfield Suites Hotel	146		1		✓	
WDW Wilderness Lodge	697	3	1	✓		
Westgate Lakes	369	2	1			
$$						
All-Star Sports and All-Star Music Resorts	3,840	2*	2			
Best Western Kissimmee	282	1	1			
Caribbean Beach Resort	2,106	1*	1			
Clarion Plaza Hotel	810	2	1	✓		
Dixie Landings Resort	2,048	1/1*	1			
Enclave Suites at Orlando	321	1	1			
Holiday Inn Maingate East	614	6	2	✓		
Holiday Inn Sunspree Resort	507	1	1	✓		
Hyatt Orlando Hotel	922	4	1			
Orlando North Hilton	323	1	1	✓		
Park Plaza Hotel	27	1	1	✓	✓	
Perri House	6				✓	
Port Orleans Resort	1,008	1/1*				
Quality Suites Maingate East	225	1	1		✓	
Radisson Inn Maingate	583	1	1	✓		
Ramada Plaza Resort Maingate at the Parkway	583	1	2			
Residence Inn by Marriott on Lake Cecile	159				✓	

In-Room Kitchenettes	In-Room Microwaves	In-Room Coffeemaker	In-Room VCR	No. Swimming Pools	No. Tennis Courts (Lighted)	On-Site Golf	Arcade Game Room	Health Club	Boating	Supervised Children's Program	Baby-Sitting	Guest Laundry
		✓		2	2(L)		✓	✓			✓	✓
✓	✓	✓	✓	1		✓	✓				✓	✓
✓	✓	✓		1	1(L)		✓	✓			✓	✓
✓	✓	✓	✓	1			✓	✓				✓
				1			✓		✓	✓	✓	✓
✓	✓	✓		1	2(L)		✓	✓	✓	✓	✓	✓
				4			✓				✓	✓
✓				2		✓						
		✓		7			✓		✓		✓	✓
			✓	1							✓	✓
				6			✓		✓			✓
✓	✓	✓		3	1(L)			✓			✓	✓
✓	✓	✓	✓	2	2(L)		✓			✓		✓
✓	✓	✓	✓	1				✓		✓		
				4	3(L)		✓	✓			✓	✓
				1				✓			✓	✓
											✓	✓
				1								
				1			✓				✓	✓
✓	✓	✓		2			✓					✓
				1	2(L)			✓			✓	✓
				2	2(L)		✓	✓			✓	✓
✓	✓	✓	✓	1						✓		✓

Walt Disney World Lodging

Name of Property	Number of Rooms/Suites	Number of Restaurants	Number of Lounges	Room Service	Complimentary Breakfast	
Royal Plaza	418	2	2			
Sheraton Lakeside Inn	651	2	1	✓		
Travelodge Hotel	325	1	1			
Twin Towers Hotel and Convention Center	790	1	3	✓		
Wyndham Garden Hotel	167	1	1	✓		
$						
Comfort Inn Maingate	281	1	1			
Fairfield Inn by Marriott	135					
Fort Wilderness Resort Campsites	1,185	2	1			
Knights Inn—Maingate	120					
Park Inn International	197	1				
Quality Inn Lake Cecile	222					
Record Motel	57					
Red Roof Inn	102					
Sevilla Inn	46					
Shades of Green on WDW Resort	288	2	1	✓		
Wynfield Inn—Westwood	300					

In-Room Kitchenettes	In-Room Microwaves	In-Room Coffeemaker	In-Room VCR	No. Swimming Pools	No. Tennis Courts (Lighted)	On-Site Golf	Arcade Game Room	Health Club	Boating	Supervised Children's Program	Baby-Sitting	Guest Laundry
				1	4(L)		✓				✓	✓
				3	4(L)		✓		✓	✓	✓	✓
				1			✓				✓	✓
				1			✓	✓		✓	✓	✓
				1			✓	✓				
				1			✓					✓
				1			✓					
				3	2(L)		✓		✓			✓
✓				1			✓					✓
	✓			1			✓					✓
				1								✓
				1							✓	✓
				1								✓
				1								✓
				2	2(L)	✓	✓	✓				✓
				2			✓					✓

224

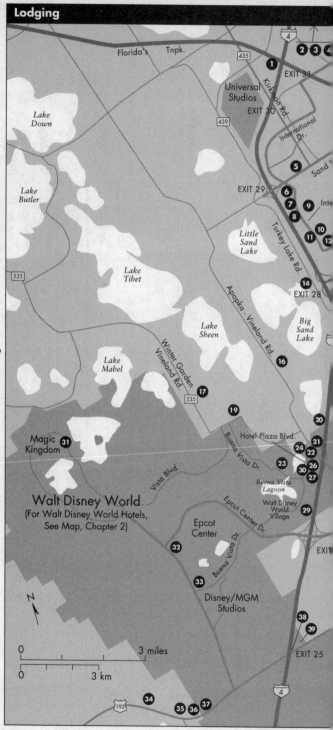

Lodging

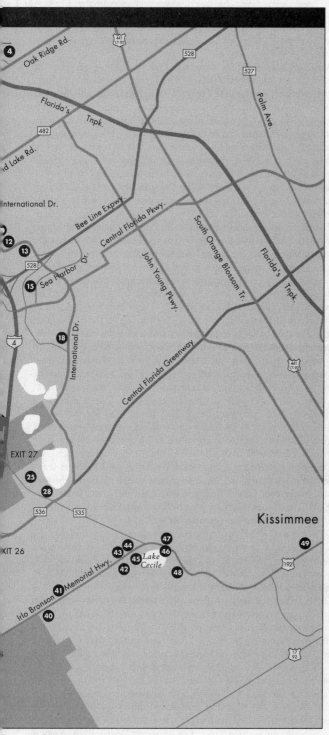

rooms, 71 suites. 6 restaurants, 3 lounges, room service, 2 lighted tennis courts, large outdoor heated pool, whirlpool, health club, beach, marina, boat rentals, baby-sitting, children's program, playground, laundry, concierge services. AE, MC, V.

$$$$ ▦ **Polynesian Resort.** When you arrive here you almost expect to be greeted with a conch-shell fanfare. The Great Ceremonial House, where visitors check in, sets the exotic mood at this resort, still the most popular of all owned by Disney. A three-story tropical garden, with more than 70 species of tropical plants, fills the lobby; orchids bloom alongside coconut palms and banana trees in the middle of the atrium, and volcanic rock fountains fill the arrival area with the harmonies of cascading water. If it weren't for the kids darting about in Mickey Mouse caps, you might think your travel agent sent you to Fiji by mistake. Rooms are in 11 two- and three-story "longhouses" arranged around this main building. All offer two queen-size beds and a twin bed in the living room to accommodate up to five, and except for some second-floor rooms, all have a balcony or patio. For the best view of the Magic Kingdom and the sandy, palm-trimmed Seven Seas Lagoon, stay in the Samoa and Maori sections, or the King Kamehameha rooms of Tonga, where guests enjoy special check-in and check-out service, valet parking, complimentary Continental breakfast, afternoon snacks, and wine and cheese in the evening. Lagoon-view rooms are the most peaceful and the priciest. They also have a perfect view of the sparkling, once-nightly Electrical Water Pageant. If you're staying in Tonga, you can sit in the three-story, glass conservatory and watch the nightly Magic Kingdom fireworks light the sky overhead. Rooms with garden and pool views are slightly less quiet and slightly less expensive; the least expensive rooms overlook the other buildings, the monorail, and the parking lot. One of the two pools is an extravagantly landscaped, free-form affair with rocks and caverns; both are great for—and beloved by—children, so if you want peace and quiet, head for the beach. Other recreational activities center on the hotel's marina, which rents boats. Exhausted parents never complain about the strict children-only policy at the Neverland Club, the hotel's child-care center, which even offers its young patrons their very own dinner show, Las Vegas style. No wonder more than half of the guests have been here before. Monorail, bus, and motor launch lines network the three parks from here. ⊠ *WDW Central Reservations, Box 10100, Lake Buena Vista 32830,* ☎ *407/934–7639; same-day reservations, 407/824–2000;* FAX *407/824–3174. 751 rooms, 102 concierge-served rooms in private building, 12 suites. 3 restaurants, snack bar, lounge, room service, 2 outdoor heated pools, game room, volleyball, lakeside beach, boating, baby-sitting, children's program, playground, laundry, concierge services. AE, MC, V.*

$$$ ▦ **Walt Disney World Wilderness Lodge.** You'll almost feel like Lewis ★ and Clark as you follow a long, pine-sheltered, out-of-the-way road to get to this pricey, seven-story Disney hostelry modeled after the turn-of-the-century structures in national parks of the West. Of course, Disney does everything bigger and grander than history ever could, and the sheer size of this lodge—which sits on the southwest shore of Bay Lake—tells you this is no ordinary backwoods cabin. It's really an homage to the Great Indoors and recalls the days when tycoons with names like Vanderbilt were "roughing it" in rustic palaces in the great American woods. The towering, five-story lobby is supported by pillars and beams that were once great tree trunks; the lobby's center-piece is a huge, three-sided, stone fireplace that Disney likes to say is 2 billion years old because it's constructed of rocks plucked from various strata of the Grand Canyon; and illumination is provided by enormous chandeliers shaped like tepees. A couple of authentic, 50-foot northwestern totem poles, real Indian headdresses, and other

craft items add to the splendor. The rooms are all decorated in western motifs, with hard-back leather chairs, patchwork quilts, and cowboy art on the walls. Each has either a balcony or a patio, and comes with two queen-size beds, or one queen and two bunk beds if requested. The hotel's showstopper is its Fire Rock Geyser, a sort of faux Old Faithful, near the large swimming pool area, which itself begins as a hot spring in the main lobby, flows under a window wall to become "Silver Creek," and then widens into a rushing waterfall. You can satisfy a hankerin' for buffalo, elk, or other unusual western-style dishes, as well as some fine wines from the great Northwest, at Artist Point, a dining room inspired by the Craftsman era. Motor launches and buses connect you to all three parks. ⊠ *WDW Central Reservations, Box 10100, Lake Buena Vista 32830,* ☎ *407/934–7639,* ℻ *407/824–3232. 697 rooms, 29 suites. 3 restaurants, lounge, room service, heated swimming pool, children's pool, golf, game room, baby-sitting, children's programs, laundry. AE, MC, V.*

Camp and Trailer Sites

$$$$ △ **Wilderness Homes.** In the old days people usually stayed in one of these when the rest of moderately priced Orlando was booked up. Then the word got out: cheap family accommodations available in a beautifully forested area. Now people are calling months in advance and requesting the same Wilderness Home they had last year. You won't find *House Beautiful* decor, but these perfectly comfortable accommodations put the relaxed friendliness of Fort Wilderness within reach of families who haven't brought their own RV and don't want to camp out. The larger trailers can accommodate four grown-ups and two youngsters; the bedroom has a double bed and a bunk bed, and the living room has a double sleeper sofa or Murphy bed. The smaller trailers, without the bunk beds, sleep four. Both types come with full kitchen, dishes, linens, a comfortable bathroom, air-conditioning, heat, daily housekeeping services, outdoor grill and picnic table, and even a color TV set with cable. *408 60- and 80-foot trailers.*

$–$$ △ **Fort Wilderness Resort and Campground.** If you're seeking a calm spot amid the theme-park storm, you need go no farther than the 700 acres of scrubby pine, tiny streams, and peaceful canals known as Fort Wilderness Resort and Campground on the shore of subtropical Bay Lake about a mile from the Wilderness Lodge Resort. This is about as relaxed as it gets in Walt Disney World. Sports facilities abound; bike trails are popular, and there's a marina where you can rent a sailboat to go out on Bay Lake. Nearby are WDW's River Country water playground and the Meadow Recreation Complex, which has lighted tennis courts and a fast-food snack bar. To experience this property, you can either bring your own tent or RV, or rent one of the fully equipped, air-conditioned Disney trailers, known as Wilderness Homes, that are parked on the property (☞ *below*). ⊠ *WDW Central Reservations, Box 10100, Lake Buena Vista 32830,* ☎ *407/W–DISNEY or 407/824–2900 for same-day reservations. Cafeteria, snack bar, grocery, 3 outdoor heated pools, game room, riding stable, volleyball, lakeside beach, canoe rentals, bike rental, bike paths, laundry, petting farm. AE, MC, V.*

$ △ **RV and Tent Sites.** Bringing a tent or RV to Walt Disney World is
★ one of the cheapest ways to actually stay on WDW property, especially considering that sites accommodate up to 10. Tent sites with water and electricity are real bargains. RV sites cost more but come equipped with electric, water, and sewage hookups as well as outdoor charcoal grills and picnic tables; you can even get maid service for your trailer. Three hundred "preferred sites," those closest to the lake—numbering from 100 to 500, in the 700s, and in the 1400s—have higher prices but also have cable-TV hookups. Each group of sites has restrooms, showers,

telephones, an ice machine, and a laundry room. *777 sites, including 300 preferred tent sites, 90 tent sites with water and electric hookups, and 387 trailer sites with water, electric, and sewage hookups.*

Epcot Center Resort Area

Resort Hotels

$$$$ 🏨 **Boardwalk Resort.** Disney's newest hotel brings back to life all the
★ candy-floss enchantment of America's great amusement piers. In the beginning, long before Disneyland ever existed, American holidaymakers unloosened their starched collars at amusement piers that dazzled with elaborately gingerbreaded structures, cotton-candy colors, and pavilions of extravagant design. The most famous was at Atlantic City, and now WDW's noted architectural master, Robert A. M. Stern, pays homage to Disney's amusement park roots while celebrating vintage Americana at its most madcap. Complete with New England–style verandas, painted marquee signs, and saltwater-taffy touts, it comprises several buildings—ranging from Victorian to Deco in style—all side-by-side on a lakeside boardwalk. An inn-side view, however, reveals the Inn at the Boardwalk: WDW's smallest and most intimate deluxe hotel, it's accented with courtyards and family-size garden cottages. Thanks to the Muscles and Bustles health club, 10-piece bands, the dueling pianos of the Crazy Fingers Piano Bar, and Luna Park—a pool with a 200-foot water slide in the form of a classic wooden roller coaster—one will never be bored on this boardwalk. Bus, tram, and motor launch lines access the parks. ⊠ *WDW Central Reservations, Box 10100, Lake Buena Vista 32830,* ☎ *407/W–DISNEY. 378 rooms, 14 cottages. 4 restaurants, room service, pool, tennis court, ESPN Sports Club, croquet court, 15 shops, nightclub, convention center. AE, MC, V.*

$$$$ 🏨 **Walt Disney World Beach and Yacht Club Resorts.** Straight out of a
★ Cape Cod summer, these two properties—sited on a 25-acre lake—are coastal inns on a grand Disney scale. The five-story Yacht Club recalls turn-of-the-century New England seacoast resorts, with its hardwood floors, lobby full of gleaming brass and polished leather, oyster-gray clapboard facade, and evergreen landscaping; there's even a lighthouse on its pier. Rooms are similarly nautical, with white and blue naval flags on the bedspreads and a small ship's wheel on the headboard. Drawing on similar inspirations is the blue-and-white, three- to five-story Beach Club, where a croquet lawn, cabana-dotted, white-sand beach, and staffers' 19th-century Jams and T-shirts set the scene. Guest rooms are summery, with wicker and pastel furnishings. Both establishments are refreshingly unstuffy, just right for families. Though each has its own restaurants and shops, the pair share certain facilities—including the Sand Castle Club for children and Stormalong Bay, a 3-acre water-recreation area, complete with a shipwreck to clamber over and a mast that is an exciting water slide. The hotels are both accessible from Epcot Center via motor launch, and tram and bus lines also travel to the parks. ⊠ *WDW Central Reservations, Box 10100, Lake Buena Vista 32830; Beach,* ☎ *407/934–7639 or 407/934–8000,* FAX *407/934–3850; Yacht* ☎ *407/934–7000,* FAX *407/934–3450. 1,098 rooms, 30 concierge-served rooms, 30 suites. 4 restaurants, snack bar, 3 lounges, room service, 2 pools, beauty salon, golf, 2 lighted tennis courts, croquet court, game room, health club, volleyball court, heated water recreation area, marina with boat rentals, baby-sitting, concierge services. AE, MC, V.*

$$ 🏨 **Caribbean Beach Resort.** Talk about tropical punch! Awash with
★ the bright, dizzying colors of the Caribbean, this hotel—the first of Disney's moderately priced accommodations—was a smash the moment it opened. Just east of Epcot Center and Disney-MGM Studios, and

surrounding 42-acre Barefoot Bay, this property is composed of five palm-studded island "villages." Each village is named for a different Caribbean island—Aruba, Barbados, Jamaica, Martinique, and Trinidad—and each has its own pool and guest laundry; all share a white-sand beach. Bridges over the lake connect the mainland with the 1-acre, path-crossed Parrot Cay, where there's a play area for children. A mile-long promenade circles the lake and is favored by bikers, joggers, and old-fashioned romantic strollers. The hub of the resort is a complex called Old Port Royale, which is decorated with pirates' cannons and tropical birds and has stores, a food court, and a tropical lounge. Each village has a different style of decor, but in general the rooms are pastel-hued and attractive and come equipped with mini-bars and coffee-makers. They are smaller than rooms in more expensive Disney resorts, but roomy enough for smaller families. You don't have the dining options that you do at other hotels in the same price range. Otherwise, the only thing missing is a supervised children's program. Bus lines network to all parks. ⊠ *WDW Central Reservations, Box 10100, Lake Buena Vista 32830,* ☎ *407/W–DISNEY,* FAX *407/934–3288. 2,106 rooms. Food court, lounge, large, heated outdoor pool with pirate fort, 6 smaller pools, wading pool, whirlpool, game room, jogging track, beach, marina with boat rentals, bike rentals, baby-sitting, playground, laundry. AE, MC, V.*

Disney Village Resort Area

Resort Hotels

$$ 🏨 **Dixie Landings Resort.** Disney's Imagineers drew inspiration from the antebellum splendor of the Old South's architecture for this sprawling, moderately priced resort northwest of Disney Village Marketplace and Lake Buena Vista, not far from Fort Wilderness. Rooms are in three-story plantation-style mansions and two-story, rustic, bayou dwellings. All rooms are the same size and accommodate up to four in two double beds; they are elegantly decorated with wooden armoires, and the faucets on the sinks are of gleaming brass. The guest registration area looks like the interior of an old steamboat. The quaintly designed food court offers burgers, sandwiches, breakfast items, and pizza. The pool, a 3½-acre, old-fashioned, swimming-hole complex called "Ol' Man Island," looks like an oversize version of something out of a Mark Twain novel; it has slides, rope swings, and an adjacent play area. A marina rents out Water Sprites and other craft. Alas, there's no children's program. Transportation is provided by bus and motor launch lines. ⊠ *WDW Central Reservations, Box 10100, Lake Buena Vista 32830,* ☎ *407/W–DISNEY,* FAX *407/934–5777. 2,048 rooms. Food court, restaurant, pizza delivery, 6 heated outdoor pools, wading pools, whirlpool, game room, boating, playground, laundry. AE, MC, V.*

$$ 🏨 **Port Orleans Resort.** Disney's version of New Orleans's French Quarter deftly emulates the charm and romance of the original. Ornate, row-house buildings with wrought-iron balconies overgrown with climbing vines are clustered around squares lushly planted with magnolia trees. If you choose to go for an evening walk on the lamp-lit sidewalks that edge the complex's alleyways, don't be surprised to find yourself on Bourbon Street, for all the routes are named after French Quarter thoroughfares. Crescent City specialties such as red beans and rice, jambalaya, Cajun chicken, *beignets* (fritters), and croissants are on the menu, as well as the usual burgers, deli sandwiches, and pizza, at the Sassagoula Floatworks Factory, the hotel's food court. Bonfamille's Café, the hotel's full-service dining room, offers Creole and other Louisiana-style fare. Kids love the large, free-form Doubloon Lagoon, which is one of the most exotic of all Disney hotel pools: The serpentine body of Neptune twists through the water and becomes a water slide; you zoom out through his mouth. The marina rents the usual assortment of boats. Note that most rooms here have two double beds to accommodate four; for quarters with one king-size bed, book early. Try to get one with a view over the garden, though these are a little more costly. The hotel does not have a child-care program. Bus and motor launch lines access all parks. ⊠ *WDW Central Reservations, Box 10100, Lake Buena Vista 32830,* ☎ *407/W–DISNEY or 407/934– 5502,* FAX *407/934–5777. 1,008 rooms. Food court, restaurant, pizza delivery, pool, children's pool, whirlpool, game room, bike rental, baby-sitting, laundry, concierge. AE, MC, V.*

Villas with Kitchens

$$$$ 🏨 **Disney's Village Resort.** The secret's out: You don't have to stay at a hotel if you come to WDW. If you're holidaying with your family or a group of friends you might favor the good-value, self-catering option presented by the five clusters of villas at Disney's Village Resort. These share a single check-in point, the Village Resort Reception Center. To get around within the village, a car or rented bike or golf cart is necessary, while buses offer transport to the parks. The accommodations are not quite as plush as those in the resort hotels, but they are more personal and homey. You certainly get more space than in a hotel room, not to mention proximity to great golf, WDW's most extensive shopping, and the lively after-dark action of Pleasure Island. ⊠ *WDW Central Reservations, Box 10100, Lake Buena Vista 32830,* ☎ *407/934–7639 or 407/827–1100,* FAX *407/934–2741. 4 restaurants, 4 lounges, full kitchens, room service, 5 outdoor pools (3 heated), whirlpools, game room, health club, boat rentals, baby-sitting, playground, laundry. AE, MC, V.*

$$$$ 🏨 **Fairways Villas.** The name hints at this complex's proximity to the links: These officially titled "Two-Bedroom Deluxe Villas" sit beside the Lake Buena Vista Golf Course, one of WDW's best. Built of cedar like the One-Bedroom Suites (☞ *below*), these guest quarters are more tastefully decorated than those of some of the other villas and are very spacious. Done in muted mauves and blues, each sleeps eight in two bedrooms with two double beds each, a loft with a queen-size bed, and a living room with a Murphy bed. *64 units.*

$$$$ 🏨 **Grand Vista Suites.** These attractively furnished accommodations, originally designed as two-story, 2,000-square-foot condominiums for a housing development, are now available to rent through WDW. All the comforts of a luxury hotel are offered, including nightly turndown service and stocked refrigerators. *4 units.*

$$$$ 🏨 **One- and Two-Bedroom Villas.** These facilities have fully equipped kitchens and either one or two bedrooms. The one-bedroom units have a king-size bed in one room and a double Murphy bed in the living room and sleep up to four. The two-bedroom units, which sleep six, have a sofa bed in the living room, a king-size bed in one bedroom, and a queen-size or two doubles in the other. *39 1-bedroom units, 89 2-bedroom units.*

$$$$ 🏨 **One-Bedroom Suites.** The smallest and least expensive of the villas, these were designed to meet the needs of business people attending meetings at the nearby WDW Conference Center. The accommodations are built of cedar and have one bedroom with two queen-size beds, a day bed in an adjacent parlor, microwave, coffee/tea maker, and a wet bar but no kitchen—they're the only villas without one. A few deluxe units with whirlpools sleep six, but most of the suites accommodate five. *316 units.*

$$$$ 🏨 **Treehouse Villas.** Take your vacation experience to a whole new level ★ with these out-of-the-way forest retreats on stilts, officially known as the "Two-Bedroom Resort Villas with Study." Isolated within a serene, heavily wooded area ribboned with canals, these won't exactly make you feel like Tarzan or Jane, but the woods do occasionally reverberate with a howl or two late at night. Each villa accommodates six and has a kitchen and breakfast bar, two bathrooms, and two bedrooms with queen-size beds on the main level, plus a double-bedded study. There is a utility room with washer and dryer on a lower level. *60 units.*

All-Star Village

Resort Hotels

$$ 🏨 **All-Star Sports and All-Star Music Resorts.** What could America possibly love more than Mickey Mouse? Sports and music, perhaps. The buildings at each resort carry out one of five sports themes, including baseball, football, tennis, surfing, and basketball; or five music themes such as Broadway, country, jazz, rock, and calypso. Don't worry about being able to tell one from the other; gargantuan exterior ornamentations define each themed area. Stairwells in the shape of giant bongos stand on each side of Calypso, a three-story silhouette of a sax player adorns Jazz, and so it continues in Sports with 30-foot tennis rackets striking balls the size of small cars, baseball bats as big as oak trees, and football helmets you could climb into. Each resort has two pools: In Sports, the Grand Slam pool is shaped like a baseball diamond, while Music's Calypso pool is in the form of a giant guitar. The Sports and Music resorts mark Disney's entry into the economy-priced hotel market, and so, under the elaborate packaging, the buildings are basically well-maintained motels. Each room has two double beds, a closet rod, an armoire, and a desk. The End Zone and Intermission food courts offer a predictable selection of fast foods, from pizza to barbecue. The complex is in the northwest quadrant of the World Drive/U.S. 192 interchange, southwest of Disney-MGM Studios and Epcot Center; transportation to other WDW sites is by bus. ✉ *WDW Central Reservations, Box 10100, Lake Buena Vista 32830; Sports, ☎ 407/W–DISNEY; Music, 407/939–7222; ℻ 407/939–7333. 1,920 rooms at each resort. 2 food courts, 2 bars, 4 pools, game room, 2 merchandise centers, baby-sitting, laundry. AE, MC, V.*

OTHER HOTELS IN WDW

Though not operated by the Disney organization, the Swan and the Dolphin just outside Epcot Center, the military's Shades of Green Resort near the Magic Kingdom, and the seven hotels along Hotel Plaza Boulevard near the Disney Village resort area call themselves "official" Walt Disney World hotels. While the Swan, Dolphin, and Shades of Green hostelries offer the special privileges of on-site Disney hotels, such as free transportation to and from the parks, the Hotel Plaza resorts do not; these hotels do offer their own transport systems, however.

Hotel Plaza

$$$$ 🏨 **Buena Vista Palace and Palace Suite Resort at Walt Disney World**
★ **Village.** This bold, sand-colored tower, the largest hotel at Lake Buena Vista, seems small and quiet when you enter its lobby. Don't be fooled. Better indications of its enormity are its sprawl of parking lots, the height of its taller tower, and its huge roster of facilities, right down to a business center with translation and secretarial service. Restaurants and lounges include the Australian-themed Outback and the Laughing Kookaburra Good Time Bar next door, the Top of the Palace Lounge, and the formal Arthur's 27 (☞ Chapter 7), which offer a ringside seat for the local sunsets and Epcot Center's nightly laser-and-fireworks show.

Upper-floor rooms in the main hotel are more expensive; the best ones look out toward Epcot Center's Spaceship Earth. Ask for a room in the main tower, where the original rooms are, to avoid the late-night noise that reverberates through the atrium from the Kookaburra. All bedrooms come with one king- or two queen-size beds. Suites in the adjacent Island Resort accommodate up to eight people—a nice alternative for larger families or people who just want extra space. All rooms have private balconies or patios; in the Island Resort section, rooms come with queen-size sleeper sofas and dining areas with coffee-maker and microwave. The hotel sits right on Lake Buena Vista, where a private marina provides Water Sprites, jet boats, sea cycles, and other craft. ⊠ *1900 Lake Buena Vista Dr., Lake Buena Vista 32830,* ☎ *407/827–2727 or 800/327–2990,* FAX *407/827–6034. 1,028 rooms. 5 restaurants, 4 lounges, snack bar, room service, indoor-outdoor heated pool, lap pool, wading pool, whirlpool, beauty salon, sauna, 3 lighted tennis courts, game room, health club, sand volleyball court, baby-sitting, children's program in summer, playground, laundry, business services. AE, DC, MC, V.*

$$$$ 🏨 **Hilton at Walt Disney World Village.** One of the leading establish-
★   ments along Hotel Plaza Boulevard, the Hilton is also among the most expensive. An ingeniously designed waterfall tumbles down off the covered entrance to the hotel and into a stone fountain surrounded by palm trees so hefty you'd think they were on steroids. Another fountain adorns the lobby, which is enlivened by floral carpeting, shell-shaped cornices, and two large tanks of tropical fish. Guest rooms positively sparkle in bright yellow and mauve and, although not huge, are cozy and contemporary. Each has a king-size bed or two double beds, and amenities include a minibar, cable TV, and in-room movies. Prices vary dramatically from one location, floor, and season to another. Keep in mind that if you must book a room at the lowest rate—on a lower floor with a mediocre view—the check-in clerk can assign you to a better room if one is available, at an extra charge of $30 to $40. The Vacation Station, a hotel-within-a-hotel, is aimed at the kids, with a video arcade, Sunday morning breakfast with Mickey and Minnie, and a supervised playroom with large-screen television and six-bed dormitory that operates every evening; meals are served on schedule, and the cost is $4 an hour. ⊠ *1751 Hotel Plaza Blvd., Lake Buena Vista 32830,* ☎ *407/827–4000; reservations, 800/782–4414,* FAX *407/827–3890. 787 rooms, 27 suites. 7 restaurants, 2 lounges, room service, 2 outdoor heated pools, outdoor whirlpool, 2 lighted tennis courts, health club, lobby shops, baby-sitting, children's program, laundry, business center, parking (fee). AE, DC, MC, V.*

$$$ 🏨 **Courtyard by Marriott.** Once under the Howard Johnson name, this hotel has undergone a recent multimillion-dollar renovation by the Courtyard arm of Marriott, which offers the chain's more moderately priced accommodations. The 14-story atrium is now accented with gazebos, white-tile trim, and tropical gardens, all creating a tranquilizing place where guests can enjoy a gourmet breakfast under white umbrellas. By evening, you'll find the energy center has shifted to the Tipsy Parrot, the hotel's welcoming bar. Guest rooms are Marriott-modern and feature handy coffee-makers. ⊠ *1805 Hotel Plaza Blvd., Lake Buena Vista 32830,* ☎ *407/828–8888 or 800/223–9930,* FAX *407/827–4623. 323 rooms. Restaurant, lounge, 2 heated pools, children's pool, whirlpool, exercise room, game room, baby-sitting, playground, laundry. AE, DC, MC, V.*

$$$ 🏨 **Grosvenor Resort.** Offering a wealth of facilities and comfortable rooms for a fair price, this attractive member of the Best Western chain is the best deal in the neighborhood. Rooms are average in size but colorfully decorated and have many amenities, including mini-refrigerator, coffee-maker, and VCR; rental movies are available in the lobby. Public areas are spacious, with a Colonial-Caribbean decor. Baskerville's, decorated with Sherlock Holmes memorabilia, serves traditional fare and hosts a weekly Saturday night murder mystery dinner show, with the Baker Street sleuth himself turning up to grill the witnesses and audience and sort out the clues. ⊠ *1850 Hotel Plaza Blvd., Lake Buena Vista 32830,* ☎ *407/828–4444 or 800/624–4109,* FAX *407/828–8192. 633 rooms, 6 suites. 2 restaurants, lounge, room service, 2 heated outdoor pools, children's pool, whirlpool, 2 lighted tennis courts, basketball court, game room, shuffleboard, volleyball court, baby-sitting, playground, laundry. AE, DC, MC, V.*

$$$ ★ 🏨 **Guest Quarters Suite Resort.** Lodgings in this modern, L-shaped, concrete-and-tinted-glass structure are all in one- or two-bedroom suites. That extra room can make all the difference when the kids—or the alleged grownups—decide they want to spend all night retelling and embellishing the adventures of the day gone by. Convenient for small families or groups who want to avoid the hassle of cots and the expense of two separate hotel rooms, each bedroom has a king-size or two double beds, and the separate living area is equipped with a sofa bed, so the suites can sleep up to 6 or 10 respectively, if not particularly comfortably. There's a television in each room plus another in the bathroom, as well as a refrigerator, wet bar, and coffee-maker; microwave ovens are available on request. ⊠ *2305 Hotel Plaza Blvd., Lake Buena Vista 32830,* ☎ *407/934–1000 or 800/222–8733,* FAX *407/934–1011. 229 units. Restaurant, ice cream parlor, lounge, pool bar, heated pool, children's pool, whirlpool, 2 lighted tennis courts, exercise room, baby-sitting, laundry. AE, DC, MC, V.*

$$–$$$ 🏨 **Royal Plaza.** Would you like to sleep in the same place Burt Reynolds and Barbara Mandrell do? When in Orlando, the two celebrities stay here, in suites named after them. The rest of the time you can book these rooms—complete with photos, gold records, and other memorabilia donated by the stars themselves. For the most part, this casual, lively establishment is popular among families. Each of the generously proportioned rooms has a terrace or balcony, and the best ones overlook the pool. Be sure your quarters aren't too close to the ground floor if you have any interest in sleeping late or napping in the afternoon. The Giraffe, the hotel's Top-40 nightclub, hops until the wee, wee hours. ⊠ *1905 Hotel Plaza Blvd., Lake Buena Vista 32830,* ☎ *407/828–2828 or 800/248–7890,* FAX *407/827–3977. 395 rooms, 23 suites. 2 restaurants, 2 lounges, heated outdoor pool, whirlpool, sauna, 4 lighted tennis courts, baby-sitting, laundry. AE, DC, MC, V.*

$$–$$$ 🏨 **Travelodge Hotel.** An old, black London taxi is parked outside the front entrance and the lobby is very British, with polished chandeliers, deep green carpet, a two-story winding staircase, and big, broad wicker chairs. Though otherwise unexceptional, this is a quality property and a good choice for families, especially now that its guest rooms have been refurbished with attractive furniture, touches of brass, and hues of baby blue, peach, and soft green. Each room comes with one king-size or two double beds and private balcony. For nightly entertainment—and great vistas of Epcot Center—head for Topper's, on the 18th floor. ⊠ *2000 Hotel Plaza Blvd., Lake Buena Vista 32830,* ☎ *407/828–2424 or 800/348–3765; in FL, 800/423–1022;* FAX *407/828–8933. 325 rooms. Restaurant, lounge, 2 snack bars, heated pool, game room, baby-sitting, playground, laundry. AE, DC, MC, V.*

Epcot Center Resort Area

$$$$ ★ 🏨 **Walt Disney World Dolphin.** Not everyone takes to this Sheraton-operated bit of whimsy, but no one denies that its wild, imaginative

ambience has made it a leading Disney landmark. Two mythical, 56-foot sea creatures—labeled dolphins by the hotel's noted architect, Michael Graves—perch atop each end of the building; between them soars a 27-story pyramid, one of the highest structures in Walt Disney World. A waterfall cascades down the facade from seashell to seashell and then into a 54-foot-wide clamshell supported by other giant dolphin sculptures; in true Florida spirit, the building's coral-and-turquoise facade displays a mural of giant banana leaves. Inside, chandeliers are shaped like monkeys, and room decor is equally jocular with palm tree-shaped lamps and wildly colorful bedspreads. The best rooms overlook Epcot Center and have a stunning view of its nightly fireworks show. Special registration and concierge services are available to those staying in the Tower—12th through 20th floors. The Grotto Pool features a high-speed water slide. With its emphasis on the convention trade, this hotel, despite its zany decor, is more urban and adult than many other on-site properties. Kids, however, will feel right at home at Camp Dolphin, the hotel's supervised program for children. Bus, tram, and motor launch lines access the parks. ⊠ *1500 Epcot Resorts Blvd., Lake Buena Vista 32830,* ☎ *407/934–4000 or 800/227–1500,* FAX *407/934–4884. 1,185 rooms, 140 suites, 185 Tower rooms. 8 restaurants, 3 lounges, room service, in-room safes, minibars, 4 outdoor heated pools, beauty salon, 8 lighted tennis courts, exercise room, game room, lakeside beach, boat rentals, baby-sitting, children's program, multilingual concierge services. AE, DC, MC, V.*

$$$$ ▣ **Walt Disney World Swan.** Facing its twin property, the Dolphin, across Crescent Lake, the Swan is another example of the postmodern "Learning from Las Vegas" school of entertainment architecture characteristic of design genius Michael Graves, the hotel's architect. Two 45-foot swans grace the rooftop of this coral-and-aquamarine hotel, which is connected to the Dolphin by a covered causeway. Inside, Graves canopied the ceiling with tall, gathered papyrus reeds and lined up a regiment of columns with palm-frond capitals. Guest rooms, located in the 12-story main building and in two seven-story wings, are decorated in floral and geometric patterns; the quirky theme continues with pineapples painted on the furniture and exotic bird-shaped lamps. As at the Dolphin, the atmosphere is more grown-up and less family oriented than that at many other on-site properties, though there are certainly plenty of facilities that families will appreciate, including Camp Swan, a supervised children's program. Bus, tram, and motor launch lines connect this Westin-managed hotel with the parks. ⊠ *1200 Epcot Resorts Blvd., Lake Buena Vista 32830,* ☎ *407/934–3000, 800/248–7926, or 800/228–3000,* FAX *407/934–4499. 717 rooms, 45 concierge rooms. 4 restaurants, 3 lounges, room service, in-room safes, refrigerators, 2 heated outdoor pools, 4 lighted tennis courts, game room, health club, beach, boat rentals, baby-sitting. AE, DC, MC, V.*

Magic Kingdom Resort Area

$–$$ ▣ **Shades of Green on Walt Disney World Resort.** Formerly the Disney Inn, this quiet resort, only two minutes by car from the Magic Kingdom, is now operated by the U.S. Armed Forces Recreation Center. Vacationing active-duty and retired personnel from all branches of the armed forces, as well as those in the reserves, National Guard, and Department of Defense, are eligible to stay here, and rates vary with your rank. Flanked by three, world-class golf courses, the hotel offers spacious, country-style rooms that accommodate up to five in two queen-size beds and a comfortable sleeper sofa. Choose among views of the fairways, lush gardens, or pools. ⊠ *WDW Central Reservations, Box 10100, Lake Buena Vista 32830,* ☎ *407/824–3600. 288 rooms. 2 restaurants, 2* *lounges, room service, 2 heated pools, children's pool, golf, 2 lighted tennis courts, game room, health club, laundry. AE, MC, V.*

INTERNATIONAL DRIVE

If you plan to visit other attractions besides Walt Disney World, the sprawl of newish hotels, restaurants, and shopping malls known as International Drive—"I-Drive" to locals and "Florida Center" in formal parlance—makes a convenient base. Parallel to I-4 and accessible from Exits 28, 29, and 30, it's just a few minutes south of downtown Orlando. It's also near Sea World, Universal Studios, Wet 'n Wild, and several popular dinner theaters.

Each part of the Drive has its own personality. The southern end is classier; the concentration of cheaper restaurants, fast-food joints, and inexpensive malls increases as you go north.

$$$$ 🏨 **Peabody Orlando.** At 11 every morning, the celebrated Peabody
★ Ducks exit a private elevator into the enormous marble-floored lobby and waddle their way across a special red carpet to the little marble fountain in which they pass the day, basking in the glory of high-class fame: Eat your heart out, Donald. At 5 PM, to the delight of gathered crowds, the royal marching mallards repeat the ritual in reverse. Built by the owners of the landmark Memphis, Tennessee, Peabody Hotel, this 27-story structure looks like three, high-rise, office blocks from afar. But don't be put off by its austere exterior. Inside, the place is very impressive and handsomely designed. The most panoramic of the oversize beige-and-cream rooms have views of Walt Disney World, and every one comes with minibar and hair dryer; those in the Peabody Club on the top three floors enjoy special concierge service. There are three noteworthy restaurants: Capriccio's, serving Italian fare; Dux, with new American cuisine ranked by some gourmands among the best in Orlando; and the Beeline, a 24-hour, 1950s–style diner (☞ Chapter 7). Located across the street from the Orange County Convention Center, the hotel attracts rock stars and other performers, as well as conventioneers and duck lovers. ⊠ *9801 International Dr., Orlando 32819,* ☎ *407/352–4000 or 800/732–2639,* 📠 *407/351–9177. 891 rooms. 3 restaurants, 2 lounges, room service, pool, children's pool, whirlpool, spa, golf privileges, 4 lighted tennis courts, health club, babysitting, children's program, concierge services. AE, D, DC, MC, V.*

$$$$ 🏨 **Stouffer Orlando Resort.** This bulky building directly across the street from Sea World looks more like a Federal Reserve Bank than a comfortable hotel. Longer than a football field—at 65,000 square feet, its atrium lobby is billed as the world's largest. Occupying the entire core of the building, it is full of waterfalls, goldfish ponds, and palm trees; as guests shoot skyward in sleek, glass elevators, exotic birds twitter in a large, hand-carved, gilded Victorian aviary. It's nice to be greeted with a glass of champagne when you register, but the spaciousness of the guest rooms, which are central Florida's largest, and the luxury of their marble bathrooms are even more pleasant. The most expensive rooms face the atrium, but if you're a light sleeper, ask for an outside room to avoid the music and party sounds that come from gatherings there. ⊠ *6677 Sea Harbor Dr., Orlando 32821,* ☎ *407/351–5555 or 800/327–6677,* 📠 *407/351–9991. 780 rooms. 5 restaurants, 2 lounges, room service, heated pool, children's pool, whirlpool, beauty salon, sauna, golf privileges, 4 lighted tennis courts, game room, volleyball, health club, baby-sitting, children's program, laundry, concierge services. AE, D, DC, MC, V.*

$$$–$$$$ 🖭 **Westgate Lakes.** Formerly the Sonesta Villa Resort, this complex
★ of multi-unit town houses not far from International Drive is like a huge luxury apartment complex on a lake. Each unit is small but homey and comfortable, with a kitchenette, dining area, living room, small patio, bedroom, one or two bathrooms, and private ground-floor entrance; some units are bilevel. Guests can sail and waterski on the lake, sun themselves on the sandy beach, or golf at nearby clubs. If you want to cook at "home" but are too busy to shop, the hotel will pick up groceries for you and deliver them while you're out. ✉ *10000 Turkey Lake Rd., Orlando 32819,* ☎ *407/352–8051 or 800/424–0708,* 𝔽𝔸𝕏 *407/345–5384. 369 units. 2 restaurants, lounge, pool bar and grill, ice cream parlor, grocery, heated outdoor pool, children's pool, 11 whirlpools, 2 lighted tennis courts, game room, health club, jogging, shuffleboard, vollyball, water sports (water-ski, Jet Ski, and paddleboat rental), baby-sitting, children's program, laundry. AE, D, DC, MC, V.*

$$$ 🖭 **Embassy Suites Hotel at Plaza International.** The concept of an all-suites hotel that serves a free buffet breakfast and complimentary cocktails, pioneered by the Embassy Suites chain, has proved very popular in Orlando. There are several reasons for this: The arrangement is comfortable—each unit has both a bedroom and a full living room equipped with wet bar, refrigerator, pull-out sofa and two TVs—and, more to the point, the cost is less than that of a single room in the top hotels. This member of the chain has a central atrium that contains a lounge where a player piano sets the mood. The two-room suites can sleep up to six, and their kitchenettes, equipped with microwave, refrigerator, and coffee-maker, make it possible to eat in. ✉ *8250 Jamaican Ct., Orlando 32819,* ☎ *407/345–8250 or 800/327–9797,* 𝔽𝔸𝕏 *407/352–1463. 246 rooms. Lounge, indoor-outdoor pool, whirlpool, sauna, steam room, exercise room, game room, baby-sitting. AE, D, DC, MC, V.*

$$$ 🖭 **Embassy Suites International Drive South.** Another of the all-suite chain of hotels, this member has an expansive lobby with marble floors, pillars, hanging lamps, and old-fashioned ceiling fans. Tropical gardens with mossy rock fountains and palm trees add to the atrium's distinctive southern ambience. Elsewhere, ceramic tile walkways and brick arches complement the tropical mood. ✉ *8978 International Dr., Orlando 32819,* ☎ *407/352–1400 or 800/433–7275,* 𝔽𝔸𝕏 *407/363–1120. 244 suites. Restaurant, lounge, indoor pool, whirlpool, sauna, steam room, baby-sitting. AE, D, DC, MC, V.*

$$$ 🖭 **Parc Corniche Resort.** This resort is a good bet for golf enthusiasts: It's framed by an 18-hole, Joe Lee–designed golf course. Each of the one- and two-bedroom suites is decked out in pastels and tropical patterns and has a patio or balcony with a golf course view, as well as a kitchen. The largest accommodations, with two bedrooms and two baths, can sleep up to six. The resort serves a complimentary Continental breakfast daily, and Sea World is only a few blocks away. ✉ *6300 Parc Corniche Dr., Orlando 32821,* ☎ *407/239–7100 or 800/446–2721,* 𝔽𝔸𝕏 *407/239–8501. 210 suites. Restaurant, lounge, heated pool, wading pool, whirlpool, golf, game room, baby-sitting, playground, laundry. AE, D, MC, V.*

$$$ 🖭 **Summerfield Suites Hotel.** "Time to go to bed, kids—yes!—in your own room." How many times have you wanted to say that on your vacation? Sleeping from four to eight people, the one- and two-bedroom units at the all-suites Summerfield are a great option for big families. Parents relish the chance for a little peace, and the youngsters enjoy the feeling of grown-up privacy and, more importantly, the chance to control their own TV fate—there's a box in each room. Two-bedroom units, the most popular, have fully equipped kitchens, plus a

living room with TV and VCR. Plush landscaping manages to give the place a secluded feel even though it's on International Drive. The courtyard shelters a small but pretty pool, with a poolside bar where you can get hot dogs and burgers. If you don't want the hassle of whipping up eggs in the morning, you can sample the hotel's free Continental buffet—or stop in at one of the restaurants in the Mercado Mediterranean Village across the street. ⊠ *8480 International Dr., Orlando 32819,* ☎ *407/352–2400 or 800/833–4353,* 𝔽𝔸𝕏 *407/352–4631. 146 suites (42 1-bedroom, 104 2-bedroom). Lounge, grocery, in-suite kitchen, heated outdoor pool, children's pool, whirlpool, exercise room, game room, laundry. AE, D, DC, MC, V.*

$$–$$$ ☷ **Enclave Suites at Orlando.** With three, 10-story buildings surrounding an office, restaurant, and recreation area, this all-suite lodging is less a hotel than a condominium complex. Here, what you would spend for a room in a fancy hotel gets you a complete apartment, with significantly more space than you'll find in other all-suite hotels. Accommodating up to six, the units have full kitchens, living rooms, two bedrooms, and small terraces. This is a great deal for families or small groups of good friends who don't mind skipping the hotel hustle, and the studio suites are wonderful for couples. The Enclave Beach Cafe is popular with local yuppies. ⊠ *6165 Carrier Dr., Orlando 32819,* ☎ *407/351–1155 or 800/457–0077,* 𝔽𝔸𝕏 *407/351–2001. 321 suites. Restaurant, lounge, in-suite kitchens, 2 heated outdoor pools, indoor pool, whirlpool, sauna, lighted tennis court, exercise room, babysitting, playground, laundry. AE, D, DC, MC, V.*

$$–$$$ ☷ **Twin Towers Hotel and Convention Center.** When it opened in the mid-1970s, this was the largest convention hotel between Miami and Atlanta. It's still a hotbed of business-trippers, but a $30 million renovation has targeted the huge theme-park tourist market. The we-try-harder attitude and the great location right at the entrance to Universal Studios Florida give it a head start. And don't worry about noisy conventioneers—the meeting and convention facilities are completely isolated from the guest towers. The comfortable, if nondescript, rooms are oversize and have wicker furnishings, one king- or two queen-size beds, cable TV, and in-room movies. Among the dining-and-drinking options are a deli open around the clock; the Palm Court Restaurant, which serves three meals daily; and the Everglades Lounge, with live entertainment and a large-screen TV. ⊠ *5780 Major Blvd., Orlando 32819,* ☎ *407/351–1000 or 800/327–2110,* 𝔽𝔸𝕏 *407/363–0106. 742 rooms, 6 executive suites (1- or 2-bedroom), 9 parlor suites (1-bedroom) 4 2-bedroom suites. Restaurant, 2 lounges, deli, room service, pool, children's pool, whirlpool, sauna, exercise room, game room, babysitting, children's program, playground, laundry. AE, D, DC, MC, V.*

$$ ☷ **Clarion Plaza Hotel.** You'll see no shortage of wide-eyed conventioneers sporting name tags at this 12-story hotel alongside the Orange County Convention Center. Yet leisure travelers are gradually discovering both the hotel's prime location, minutes from attractions, and its long list of amenities generally found only at more expensive properties. The guest rooms are simple but large and elegant, with two queen-size beds and a nice little extra: a video-game unit hooked up to the TV. The dining line-up is exceptional for a hotel in this price range: There's the 24-hour Lite Bite; the upbeat Café Matisse, a coffee shop that serves elaborate buffets; and the richly paneled Jack's Place, which serves steaks, seafood, and huge desserts on tables dressed in crisp white linens amid autographed caricatures of famous movie stars. ⊠ *9700 International Dr., Orlando 32819,* ☎ *407/352–9700 or 800/627–8258,* 𝔽𝔸𝕏 *407/352–9710. 810 rooms. 2 restaurants, lounge, coffee shop, lobby bar, room service, in-room safes, heated outdoor pool, whirlpool, game room, baby-sitting, laundry. AE, D, DC, MC, V.*

$$ **⊡ Country Hearth Inn.** Standing out like a curiosity among the very
★ modern car parks, gas stations, and high-rises of International Drive,
the exterior of this two-story, pale-pink structure was inspired by the
owner's love for *Gone with the Wind*. It has white railings on all bal-
conies, a first-floor veranda with big, wooden rocking chairs and four
brass ceiling fans, and, on top, a polished weather vane. Inside the lobby
atrium, the decor moves to imitate a later, Victorian-era Florida. In the
guest rooms, folk art hangs on walls, lace curtains adorn the double
French doors, and quilted spreads cover the beds. ⊠ *9861 International
Dr., Orlando 32819,* ☎ *407/352–0008 or 800/447–1890,* ℻ *407/352–
5449. 150 rooms. Restaurant, lounge, room service, in-room safes,
heated outdoor pool, laundry. AE, D, DC, MC, V.*

$–$$ **⊡ Wynfield Inn–Westwood.** If you don't want a room with just the
bare essentials yet don't have the budget for luxury, this two-story motel
is a find. Its cheerful, contemporary rooms are smartly appointed with
colorful, floral-print bedspreads, peach walls, and understated wall hangings. Complimentary coffee and tea are served in the lobby every day.
The staff is friendly and helpful and acts more like the staff of a "do-
anything-to-please" independent motel. Children 17 and under stay
free in their parents' room (with a maximum of four guests per room).
⊠ *6263 Westwood Blvd., Orlando 32821,* ☎ *407/345–8000 or
800/346–1551,* ℻ *407/345–1508. 300 rooms. Pool bar, 2 outdoor
pools (1 heated), game room, laundry. AE, D, DC, MC, V.*

$ **⊡ Fairfield Inn by Marriott.** This understated, few-frills, three-story
hotel—the Marriott Corporation's answer to the Motel 6 and
Econolodge chains—is a natural for single travelers or small families
on a tight budget. It's squeezed between International Drive and the
highway and doesn't have the amenities of top-of-the-line Marriott properties, but nice perks such as complimentary coffee and tea, free local
phone calls, and cable TV give a sense of being at a much fancier property. ⊠ *8342 Jamaican Ct., Orlando 32819,* ☎ *407/363–1944 or
800/228–2800,* ℻ *407/363–1944. 135 rooms. Heated outdoor pool.
AE, D, DC, MC, V.*

MAINGATE

Outside the northernmost entrance to WDW, just off I–4, the Maingate area is full of large hotels unaffiliated with Walt Disney World,
mostly sprawling, high-quality resorts catering to Walt Disney World
vacationers. Although they share a certain sameness with resorts the
world over, they vary in size and price. As a rule, the bigger the resort
and the more extensive the facilities, the more you can expect to pay.
If you're looking for a clean, modern room, you cannot go wrong with
any of them. All are equally convenient to Walt Disney World. One
may emphasize one recreational activity more than another, so your
ultimate decision may depend on how much time you plan to spend
at your hotel and which of your strokes—your drive or your backhand—
requires the most attention.

$$$$ **⊡ Hyatt Regency Grand Cypress Resort.** If you polled those familiar
★ with Orlando to name its most spectacular resort, few would hesitate
to name the Grand Cypress. With more than 1,500 acres, it is huge and
offers virtually every resort facility, and then some—even a 45-acre nature preserve. Golf facilities are first-class, with 45 Jack Nicklaus–
designed holes, with four courses and a high-tech golf school. The
huge, 800,000-gallon swimming pool resembles an enormous grotto,
has a 45-foot water slide, and is fed by 12 cascading waterfalls. And as
you'd expect of a first-class Hyatt resort, the hotel has a striking
18-story atrium filled with tropical plants. Accommodations are divided

between the 750-room Hyatt Regency Grand Cypress and the 146-unit Villas of Grand Cypress. The one-, two-, three-, and four-bedroom villas, near the fairways, are luxuriously furnished and include cathedral ceilings and tile floors; the larger ones have a full kitchen. The restaurants are excellent (☞ Chapter 7). There's just one drawback: the king-size conventions that the Grand Cypress commonly attracts. ⊠ *Hyatt Regency Grand Cypress, 1 Grand Cypress Blvd., Orlando 32836, ☎ 407/239–1234 or 800/233–1234, FAX 407/239–3800. 750 rooms. Villas of Grand Cypress, 1 N. Jacaranda, Orlando 32836, ☎ 407/239– 4700 or 800/835–7377. 146 villas. 5 restaurants, 4 lounges, room service, 2 outdoor pools (1 heated), 4 whirlpools, 45-hole golf complex with clubhouse and golf school, 12 tennis courts (6 lighted), croquet, game room, health club, horseback riding, jogging, water sports on lake (paddleboat, sailboat, and canoe rentals),bicycle rental, baby-sitting, children's program, laundry. AE, D, DC, MC, V.*

$$$$ ▥ **Marriott's Orlando World Center.** To call this Marriott massive would be an understatement. The lineup of amenities seems endless. One of the four swimming pools is the largest in Florida, and every other amenity you could imagine seems to be on-site, including a golf course. The lobby is a huge, opulent atrium, adorned with 16th-century Asian artifacts. Luxurious villas—the Royal Palms and Sabal Palms—are available for daily and weekly rentals. If you like your hostelries cozy, you'll consider the size of this place a definite negative; otherwise, its single unappealing aspect is the hordes of conventioneers it attracts. ⊠ *8701 World Center Dr., Orlando 32821, ☎ 407/239–4200 or 800/228– 9290, FAX 407/238–8777. 1419 rooms, 85 suites. 7 restaurants, 2 lounges, room service, 3 heated outdoor pools, heated indoor pool, children's pool, 4 whirlpools, beauty salon, 18-hole golf course, miniature golf course, 8 lighted tennis courts, game room, health club, volleyball, baby-sitting, children's program, laundry. AE, D, DC, MC, V.*

$$$$ ▥ **Vistana Resort.** Consider this peaceful resort if you're interested in tennis: Its clay and all-weather tennis courts can be used without charge; private or semiprivate lessons are available for a fee. It's also a good bet if your family is large or you're traveling with a group of friends. The spacious, tastefully decorated villas and town houses spread over 95 landscaped acres and have two bedrooms each plus a living room and all the comforts of home, including a full kitchen and a washer and dryer. The price may seem high, but considering that each unit can sleep six or eight, the place is a positive bargain. ⊠ *13500 State Rd. 535, Orlando 32821, ☎ 407/239–3100 or 800/877–8787, FAX 407/239–3111. 722 units. 2 restaurants, lounge, grocery, 5 heated outdoor pools, 5 children's pools, 6 whirlpools, minature golf, basketball, game room, health club, shuffleboard, baby-sitting, children's program, laundry. AE, D, DC, MC, V.*

$$$–$$$$ ▥ **Embassy Suites Resort Lake Buena Vista.** This is a typical example of the popular all-suite chain, although some local folks have been shocked by this hotel's wild turquoise, pink, and yellow facade. Clearly visible from I–4, it has become something of a local landmark. But it's an attractive option for other reasons. It's just 1 mile from Walt Disney World, 3 miles from Sea World, and 7 miles from Universal Studios Florida. The central atrium lobby, loaded with tropical vegetation and soothed by the sounds of a rushing fountain, is a great place to enjoy the complimentary breakfast and complimentary evening cocktails. ⊠ *8100 Lake Ave., Lake Buena Vista 32830, ☎ 407/239–1144, 800/257–8483, or 800/362–2779, FAX 407/238–0230. 280 suites. Restaurant, lounge, deli, indoor-outdoor heated pool, children's pool, whirlpool, lighted tennis court, basketball, exercise room, game room, shuffleboard, volleyball, baby-sitting, children's program, playground. AE, D, DC, MC, V.*

$$–$$$ ▦ **Holiday Inn Sunspree Resort Lake Buena Vista.** You might be impressed by the sweeping, covered entrance to its striking, terra-cotta-colored facade, but what really earns the kudos at this place is the way it seems to be built around the idea of family fun. All employees, including managers, have to graduate from Clown College—an eight-week intensive course in balloonology, magic tricks, costume design, clown ethics, and the seven clown commandments. This ensures that Camp Holiday—a free children's program of magic shows, arts and crafts, movies, cartoons, and other supervised activities day and night—is the finest program around. Children even have their own restaurant, the Kid's Kottage, where they eat for free if a parent is dining in the main restaurant, and the hotel rents beepers so that parents can have some time to themselves without worrying about the kids. It's also an excellent value. Furnished with two queen-size beds or one king-size bed and a sleeper sofa, all rooms have a TV and VCR plus a kitchenette. The showpiece of the hotel courtyard is a wonderfully huge pool. ⊠ *13351 State Rd. 535, Lake Buena Vista 32830,* ☎ *407/239–4500, 800/366–6299, or 800/465–4329;* ℻ *407/239–8463. 507 rooms. Restaurant, lounge, deli, snack bar, kitchenettes, room service, heated outdoor pool, wading pool, 2 whirlpools, billiards, health club, children's program, playground. AE, D, DC, MC, V.*

$$–$$$ ▦ **Ramada Plaza Resort Maingate at the Parkway.** The only Ramada
★ Resort to earn the title "Plaza," this bright, spacious Ramada may offer the best deal in the neighborhood: attractive setting, good facilities, and competitive prices. Its delicatessen comes in handy when you want to assemble a picnic. Generously proportioned rooms are decked out in tropical patterns, with pastel colors and pineapple shapes carved in white, wooden furniture; rooms with the best view and light face the pool. ⊠ *2900 Parkway Blvd., Kissimmee 34746,* ☎ *407/396–7000 or 800/634–4774; in FL, 800/225–3939;* ℻ *407/396–6792. 712 rooms, 6 suites. Restaurant, 2 lounges, deli, snack bar, 2 outdoor pools (one heated), children's pool, 2 whirlpools, sauna, 2 lighted tennis courts, exercise room, game room, volleyball, baby-sitting, laundry. AE, D, DC, MC, V.*

$$ ▦ **Hyatt Orlando Hotel.** Instead of a single tower, this very large hotel consists of 10, two-story buildings in four clusters. Each cluster is a community with its own heated pool, whirlpool, park, and playground at its center. The rooms are spacious but otherwise not memorable. The lobby is vast and mall-like, with numerous shops and restaurants; the Foi-Foi is upscale Italian, and there is also a very good deli. If you'll be spending most of your time attacking Orlando attractions, the reasonable rates and convenience—it's the closest independent property to WDW—will more than make up for the unremarkable nature of the place. ⊠ *6375 W. Irlo Bronson Memorial Hwy., Kissimmee 34746,* ☎ *407/396–1234 or 800/233–1234,* ℻ *407/396–5090. 888 rooms, 34 suites. 4 restaurants, deli, lounge, sports bar, 4 heated outdoor pools, 4 whirlpools, 3 lighted tennis courts, exercise room, game room, jogging, baby-sitting, 4 playgrounds, laundry. AE, D, DC, MC, V.*

$$ ▦ **Perri House.** Exactly 1 mile from the Magic Kingdom as the crow
★ flies, this six-room bed-and-breakfast on a serene side road is a unique lodging in build-it-bigger-and-they-will-come Orlando: Part-hostelry, part-bird preserve, Perri House will be, by 1996, an Audubon Society–recognized Bird Sanctuary, complete with observation paths, a pond, feeding station, and a small birdhouse museum. About 200 trees and more than 1,500 bushes have been planted—many awaiting the addition of birdhouses. Already you can awaken to the cries of bobwhites, downy woodpeckers, red-tail hawks, and an occasional bald eagle. Nick and Angi Perretti planned and built the circular house so that each room has an outside entrance. Guests dally

at will in the "swan-and-roses" living-room area and have free run of the kitchen, where a Continental breakfast buffet is served gratis. The bird- and blossom-themed bedrooms come with either two queen- or one king-size four-poster bed, private bathroom, and TV. The furnishings are childproof, and kids are welcome. ⊠ *10417 State Rd. 535, Lake Buena Vista 32830,* ☎ *407/876–4830 or 800/780–4830,* ℻ *407/876–0241. 6 rooms. Outdoor pool, spa. AE, D, MC, V.*

$$ 🏨 **Wyndham Garden Hotel.** After traipsing through Orlando's theme
★ parks and malls, what many visitors want most is to lounge around their living room just the way they do at home. Formerly the Doubletree Club Hotel, this six-story complex lets you do just that: It provides a 5,000-square-foot living room full of big couches, with a better-than-at-home, big-screen TV fitted with a Nintendo unit. Homey touches abound, and the in-room services and amenities, including hairdryers and coffee-makers, more than make up for the less-than-inspiring facade. ⊠ *8688 Palm Pkwy., Lake Buena Vista 32830,* ☎ *407/239–8500 or 800/996–3426,* ℻ *407/239–8591. 167 rooms. Restaurant, lounge, room service, heated outdoor pool, whirlpool, game room, health club, shuttle to WDW. AE, D, DC, MC, V.*

U.S. 192 AREA

If you're looking for anything remotely quaint, charming, or sophisticated, move on. The U.S. 192 strip—a.k.a. the Irlo Bronson Memorial Highway, the Spacecoast Parkway, and Kissimmee—is a neon-and-plastic theme park crammed with mom-and-pop motels, bargain-basement hotels, cheap restaurants, fast-food spots, nickel-and-dime attractions, gas stations, and minimarts in mind-numbing profusion. But if all you want is a decent room with perhaps a few extras for a manageable price, this is Wonderland. Room rates start at $20 a night—lower at the right time of year, if you can cut the right deal—with most costing $30 to $70 a night, depending on facilities and proximity to Walt Disney World. Among the chain hotels—Best Western, Comfort Inn, Econolodge, Holiday Inn, Radisson, Sheraton, Travelodge, and so on—are a pride of family-owned properties, many of which are run by recent immigrants.

Whatever your choice, you will find basic rooms, grounds, and public spaces that vary little from one establishment to the next. Keep in mind that the newer the property, the more comfortable your surroundings. Of course, the greater the distance from Walt Disney World, the lower the room rates. A few additional minutes' drive may save you a significant amount of money, so shop around. And if you wait until arrival to find a place, don't be bashful about asking to see the rooms. It's a buyer's market.

$$$ 🏨 **Sol Orlando Resort.** The brochure on this resort-hotel complex stretches a point when it says it has the charm of a small village in the Spanish region of Andalusia. The red-tile-and-stucco villas and palm-studded grounds are indeed attractive, but it's the spacious accommodations that are truly noteworthy. Each of the one-, two-, and three-bedroom units has a living and dining area, a kitchen, and two TVs; the three-bedroom villa has 1,200 square feet of living space and sleeps up to eight comfortably. Complimentary breakfast is also included. ⊠ *4787 W. Irlo Bronson Memorial Hwy., Kissimmee 34746,* ☎ *407/397–0555,* ℻ *407/397–0553. 150 villas. Restaurant, lounge, grocery, heated outdoor pool, wading pool, whirlpool, access to*

minigolf, lighted tennis court, game room, health club, racquetball, squash, laundry. AE, D, DC, MC, V.

$$–$$$ ⌂ **Quality Suites Maingate East.** This hotel, built in 1989, is an excellent option for a large family or group of friends. The spacious, green-and-mauve rooms, designed to sleep six or ten, come equipped with a microwave, refrigerator, and dishwasher. Suites have two bedrooms with two double beds each and a living room with a double pull-out couch. A complimentary Continental breakfast is offered, and free beer and wine are served afternoons at the pool-side bar. As an added bonus, guests get one free admission per suite to Cypress Gardens, Water Mania, or Splendid China. Kids will enjoy the motel's restaurant: A toy train chugs along overhead. No-smoking suites are available. ⊠ *5876 W. Irlo Bronson Memorial Hwy., Kissimmee 34746,* ☎ *407/396–8040 or 800/848–4148,* 𝖥𝖠𝖷 *407/396–6766. 225 units (113 one-bedroom, 112 two-bedroom). Restaurant, grocery, lounge, poolside bar, kitchenette, heated outdoor pool, children's pool, whirlpool, game room, playground, laundry. AE, D, DC, MC, V.*

$$–$$$ ⌂ **Residence Inn by Marriott on Lake Cecile.** Of the all-suite hotels on U.S. 192, this complex of four-unit town houses is probably the best. One side of the complex faces the highway; the other overlooks an attractive lake, where you can sail, waterski, Jet Ski, and fish. Forty units are penthouses accommodating four, with complete kitchens, small living rooms, loft bedrooms, and fireplaces. All others accommodate two and are laid out like studio apartments but still have full kitchens and fireplaces. Each suite has a private entrance. While the price may seem high considering the location, there is no charge for additional guests, so you can squeeze in the whole family at no extra charge, and both the Continental breakfast and a grocery shopping service are complimentary. ⊠ *4786 W. Irlo Bronson Memorial Hwy., Kissimmee 34746,* ☎ *407/396–2056 or 800/468–3027,* 𝖥𝖠𝖷 *407/396–2296. 159 units. Heated outdoor pool, whirlpool, basketball, playground, laundry. AE, D, DC, MC, V.*

$$ ⌂ **Best Western Kissimmee.** Overlooking a nine-hole, par-three, executive golf course, this independently owned and operated three-story hotel is a hit with golf-loving senior citizens as well as families. The two swimming pools in the garden courtyard are amply shaded to protect tender skin from the sizzling sun. The spacious rooms are done in soft pastels, with light wood furniture and attractive wall hangings. Units with king-size beds and kitchenettes are available. The hotel's restaurant, Casual Cuisine, serves breakfast and dinner buffet-style, as well as from a varied, full-service menu. ⊠ *2261 E. Irlo Bronson Memorial Hwy., Kissimmee 34744,* ☎ *407/846–2221 or 800/944–0662,* 𝖥𝖠𝖷 *407/846–1095. 282 rooms. Restaurant, lounge, picnic area, pool bar, 2 outdoor pools (1 heated), adjacent 9-hole golf course, playground. AE, D, DC, MC, V.*

$$ ⌂ **Holiday Inn Maingate East.** Everything seems to be the biggest something in Orlando, and Maingate East is the world's largest two-story Holiday Inn. The service is good, despite the size, but that's not the only reason to stay here. The whole interior recently got a multi-million-dollar makeover; all rooms now have a TV and VCR, and kitchenettes are fully equipped. You can rent videotapes and buy snacks and groceries in the lobby, and some of the restaurants serve buffet-style—an added convenience. For kids there's Camp Holiday's kids' program. ⌂ *5678 W. Irlo Bronson Memorial Hwy., Kissimmee 34746,* ☎ *407/ 396–4488, 800/366–5437, or 800/465–4329,* 𝖥𝖠𝖷 *407/396–1296. 584 rooms, 30 suites. 6 restaurants, café, 2 lounges, grocery, kitchenette, room service, 2 pools (1 heated), wading pool, 2 whirlpools, 2 lighted* *tennis courts, 2 game rooms, children's program, 2 playgrounds, laundry. AE, D, DC, MC, V.*

$$ 🏨 **Radisson Inn Maingate.** This sleek, twin-towered, seven-story mod-
★ ern hotel, just a few minutes from WDW's front door, has cheerful guest
rooms, large bathrooms, and plenty of extras for the price. It's not fancy,
but it is perfectly adequate. The best rooms are those with a view of
the pool. Two floors in each tower are reserved for nonsmokers. ✉
*7501 W. Irlo Bronson Memorial Hwy., Kissimmee 34746, ☎ 407/396–
1400 or 800/333–3333, ℻ 407/396–0660. 578 rooms, 5 suites.
Restaurant, lounge, deli, poolside bar, room service, heated outdoor
pool, whirlpool, 2 lighted tennis courts, basketball, exercise room, jog-
ging, baby-sitting, laundry. AE, D, DC, MC, V.*

$$ 🏨 **Sheraton Lakeside Inn.** This comfortable, if undistinguished, resort,
a complex of 15 two-story balconied buildings spread over 27 acres
by a small man-made lake, offers quite a few recreational facilities for
the money. The nondescript beige rooms are available in the standard
two double or one king-size bed configurations, and each has a refrigerator and safe. The children's program has arts and crafts, movies,
and miniature golf in a comfortable play area. ✉ *7769 W. Irlo Bronson Memorial Hwy., Kissimmee 34746, ☎ 407/239–2650 or 800/848–
0801, ℻ 407/396–2222. 651 rooms. 2 restaurants, lounge, deli, room
service, 3 outdoor pools (2 heated), wading pool, 4 lighted tennis
courts, miniature golf, 2 game rooms, paddleboat, fishing, baby-
sitting, children's program, laundry. AE, D, DC, MC, V.*

$ 🏨 **Comfort Inn Maingate.** This hotel is close to Walt Disney World—
just a mile away—so you can save a bundle without unduly inconve-
niencing yourself. Standard rooms are light and airy with a
mauve-and-soft-blue color scheme; deluxe rooms, overlooking a landscaped garden, have refrigerators, coffee-makers, and hair dryers. Children 18 and under stay free, and those 10 and under eat free. ✉ *7571
W. Irlo Bronson Memorial Hwy., Kissimmee 34746, ☎ 407/396–
7500 or 800/228–5150, ℻ 407/396–7497. 281 rooms. Restaurant,
lounge, outdoor pool, game room, laundry. AE, D, DC, MC, V.*

$ 🏨 **Knights Inn–Maingate.** Part of a national chain, this one-story motel,
with a prefab, Old-World facade, is not exactly an English charmer,
but it does offer spacious, clean rooms at budget prices; some have kitchenettes and sofas. ✉ *7475 W. Irlo Bronson Memorial Hwy., Kissimmee 34746, ☎ 407/396–4200 or 800/843–5644, ℻ 407/396–8838.
120 rooms. Heated outdoor pool, kitchenettes in some rooms, game
room, laundry. AE, D, MC, V.*

$ 🏨 **Park Inn International.** The Mediterranean–style architecture of
this property on Cedar Lake is not likely to charm you off your feet,
but the friendly staff might. Ask for a room as close to the water as
possible. There is a restaurant, but for an extra $10 you can get a room
with a kitchenette. ✉ *4960 W. Irlo Bronson Memorial Hwy., Kissimmee 34741, ☎ 407/396–1376 or 800/327–0072, ℻ 407/396–0716.
197 rooms. Restaurant, grocery, outdoor pool, whirlpool, game room,
beach, laundry.*

$ 🏨 **Quality Inn Lake Cecile.** Rooms at this plain-Jane inn are adequate,
not fancy—but those close to the lake are prettier as well as quieter.
✉ *4944 W. Irlo Bronson Memorial Hwy., Kissimmee 34746, ☎ 407/
396–4455 or 800/846–4855, ℻ 407/396–4182. 222 rooms. Outdoor
pool, lake, beach, laundry. AE, D, DC, MC, V.*

$ 🏨 **Record Motel.** This simple property is the kind of mom-and-pop op-
eration with few frills and rock-bottom rates that made U.S. 192 famous. Clean rooms with free HBO, continental breakfast, and a
solar-heated pool are the basic attractions here. What the place lacks
in luxuries and ambience, it more than makes up for with the friend-

liness of its staff, who'll gladly direct you to equally inexpensive restaurants. ✉ *4651 W. Irlo Bronson Memorial Hwy., Kissimmee 34746,* ☎ *407/396–8400 or 800/874–4555,* 𝔽𝔸𝕏 *407/396–8415. 57 rooms. Heated outdoor pool, baby-sitting. AE, D, MC, V.*

$ 🏨 **Red Roof Inn.** If you want a clean, quiet room but don't want to gamble on an independent, this three-story, chain motel delivers consistently. The small, comfortable rooms are decorated in blues and grays. A big plus are the many fast-food and budget-priced eateries within walking distance. The complimentary daily newspaper and coffee each morning are pleasant surprises. ✉ *4970 Kyng's Heath Rd., Kissimmee 34746,* ☎ *407/396–0065 or 800/843–7663,* 𝔽𝔸𝕏 *407/396–0245. 102 rooms. Outdoor pool, whirlpool, laundry. AE, D, DC, MC, V.*

$ 🏨 **Sevilla Inn.** This classy, family-operated motel built in 1985 and ex-
★ panded in 1990 is one of the best buys in the Orlando area. Stucco and wood on the outside, the three-story building has up-to-date rooms with colorful bedspreads, tasteful wall hangings, a fresh paint job, and cable TV. If you need a place to just drop your bags and get some rest between theme parks, this is a good bet. The pool area, encircled by palm trees and tropical shrubs, looks like something you'd find in a much fancier resort. Free coffee is available every morning. ✉ *4640 W. Irlo Bronson Memorial Hwy., Kissimmee 34746,* ☎ *407/396–4135 or 800/367–1363,* 𝔽𝔸𝕏 *407/396–4942. 46 rooms. Heated outdoor pool, laundry. AE, D, MC, V.*

ORLANDO SUBURBS

Travel farther afield and you can get more comforts and facilities for the money, and maybe even some genuine Orlando charm—of the warm, cozy, one-of-a-kind country inn variety.

Altamonte Springs

Staying among the suburban developments, office parks, and shopping malls of Altamonte Springs may not be as glamorous as dwelling with the Disney characters, but accommodations in this suburb, 30 to 40 minutes' drive from the theme parks, cost on average one-third less than comparable lodgings elsewhere in the Orlando area. The suburban atmosphere offers relief from the frantic tourist scene farther south. In addition, the area is convenient to Enzo's on the Lake, one of Orlando's best restaurants, as well as to the jumbo Altamonte Mall.

$$$ 🏨 **Embassy Suites Orlando—North.** What makes this member of the all-suite chain different from the others is its location right on the edge of Crane's Rost Lake. Otherwise, all the suites are up to the high Embassy Suites' standard and look out onto a lush, tropical atrium. Although the sound of the waterfalls can be soothing, the same can't be said for that of the conventioneers at the tables around them. So for guaranteed peace and quiet, choose a suite on one of the upper floors. The accommodations are spacious and flawlessly kept, the staff friendly and helpful, and the complimentary cooked-to-order breakfast makes a great send-off for your day in the theme parks. There's fishing on the lake, and a scenic 1-mile jogging trail surrounds it. ✉ *225 E. Altamonte Dr., Altamonte Springs 32701,* ☎ *407/834–2400 or 800/362–2779,* 𝔽𝔸𝕏 *407/834–2117. 210 suites. Restaurant, lounge, room service, kitchenettes, indoor heated pool, exercise room, fishing, baby-sitting, laundry. AE, D, DC, MC, V.*

$$ 🏨 **Orlando North Hilton.** Though the emphasis at this eight-story, concrete-and-glass tower is on the business traveler, tourists will also appreciate the hotel's quiet elegance. The comfortable rooms are decorated with peach and dark-green florals and brass accents. This hotel also has two floors of more pricey one- and two-bedroom Executive Suites and individual rooms with concierge service; most rooms have ironing boards and hairdryers. The pool is sunny and surrounded by palm trees, and the bar beckons at cocktail time. ✉ *350 S. Lake Blvd., Altamonte Springs 32715,* ☎ *407/830–1985,* FAX *407/331–2911. 318 rooms, 5 suites. Restaurant, lounge, room service, heated outdoor pool, whirlpool, health club, laundry. AE, D, DC, MC, V.*

Winter Park

Winter Park, a small college town and Orlando's most posh and best-established neighborhood, is full of chichi shops and restaurants. If its heart is the main thoroughfare of Park Avenue, then its soul must be Central Park, an inviting greensward dotted with huge trees hung with Spanish moss. It feels a million miles away from Orlando's tourist track, but it's just a short drive from the major attractions.

$$–$$$ 🏨 **Park Plaza Hotel.** Small and intimate, this 1922-vintage establishment—complete with wrought-iron balcony—feels almost like a private home, with nice touches including a newspaper slid under your door each morning and complimentary breakfast brought to your room. The key to a special stay here is a front garden suite, with a living room. These open onto a long balcony usually abloom with impatiens and bougainvillea and punctuated by wicker tables and chairs to enhance people-watching on chic Park Avenue or Central Park. All rooms have either a double, queen-, or king-size bed, but those in the back can be small and cramped. There's complimentary continental breakfast served in your room, and complimentary valet parking available. On the first floor is one of Orlando's most popular restaurants, the Park Plaza Gardens. This old-fashioned spot is definitely not for people who want recreational facilities or other amenities—nor is it suitable for young children. ✉ *307 Park Ave. S, Winter Park 32789,* ☎ *407/647–1072 or 800/228–7220,* FAX *407/647–4081. 27 rooms. Restaurant, lounge, room service, jogging, laundry. AE, DC, MC, V.*

9 After Dark

THE POWERS THAT BE HAVE FINALLY EMBRACED the fact that about half of Disney's 13 million travelers per year are adults without children. So Disney's nightlife has begun to take on a new identity, beginning with the Pleasure Island entertainment complex, including Planet Hollywood, which pulses with a Disney-controlled abandon. Meanwhile, Orlando is keeping up with the quickened pace on Church Street and Orange Avenue, among the main haunts of young, buff locals and tourists, alike. Outside of Disney, the onetime sleepy town of Orlando has awakened with its own Hard Rock Cafe and—scheduled to open by 1998—Universal Studios entertainment complex, featuring "Big Man" Shaquille O'Neal of the NBA's Orlando Magic fame.

Updated by
Mary Meehan

Although there are a few clubs that cater to the all-night, raving, bring-your-own-drugs crowd, for very-late-night action, head for Walt Disney World—believe it or not! By virtue of Disney's status as essentially a separate governmental entity, clubs on Disney property are allowed to stay open later than bars elsewhere; you can get served there until 2:45 AM.

WALT DISNEY WORLD

Inside Walt Disney World, every hotel has its quota of bars and lounges pushing specialty drinks in all colors of the rainbow. At the hotels and at Pleasure Island—Disney's dedicated after-dark destination—jazz trios and bluegrass bands, DJs and rockers tune up and turn on their amps after dinner's done. Plus, there are two long-run dinner shows that give you and your family an evening of song, dance, and dining, all for a single price.

Dinner Shows

The **Hoop-Dee-Doo Revue,** staged at Fort Wilderness's rustic Pioneer Hall, may be corny, but it is also the liveliest show in Walt Disney World. A troupe of jokers called the Pioneer Hall Players stomp their feet, wisecrack, and otherwise make merry while the audience chows down on barbecued ribs, fried chicken, corn on the cob, strawberry shortcake, and all the fixin's. There are three shows nightly, and the prime times sell out months in advance in busy seasons. But you're better off eating dinner too early or too late rather than missing the fun altogether—so take what you can get. And if you arrive in Orlando with no reservations, try for a cancellation. ⊠ *Fort Wilderness Resort; in advance,* ☎ *407/934–7639; day of show, 407/824–2748.* ⊡ *$36 adults, $18 children 3–11. Reservations essential. Seatings 5, 7:15, and 9:30. No smoking.*

The **Polynesian Luau** is an outdoor barbecue with entertainment appropriate to its colorful South Pacific setting at the Polynesian Resort. Its fire jugglers and hula-drum dancers are entertaining for the whole family, if never quite as endearing as the napkin-twirlers at the Hoop-Dee-Doo Revue. There are two shows nightly, plus an earlier wingding for children, called Mickey's Tropical Luau, wherein Disney characters do a few numbers, decked out in South Seas garb. Mickey's is also a little lighter on the Polynesian entertainement. ⊠ *Polynesian Village Resort,* ☎ *407/934–7639.* ⊡ *Polynesian Luau $34 adults, $17 children 3–11; Mickey's Tropical Luau $30 adults, $14 children 3–11. Reservations essential at least 1 month in advance. Polynesian Luau seatings 6:45 and 9:30. Mickey's Tropical Luau seating 4:30. AE, MC, V. No smoking.*

IllumiNations

You won't want to miss Epcot Center's grand finale, a laser show that takes place every night, just before the park closes, along the shores of the World Showcase lagoon. Orchestral music, including Tchaikovsky's 1812 Overture, fills the air. The show starts with laser images moving on screens mounted on barges in the middle of the lagoon. Later, multicolored, neon lasers streak across the sky in time to the music while fireworks explode high overhead and low to the water. More laser designs flicker on the clouds of smoke left behind. At the end, lasers trace the outline of the continents on Spaceship Earth, so that it looks like a slowly turning globe. It's a stellar performance.

Some places around the lagoon offer much better vantage points than others. The best locations are the Matsu No Ma Lounge in the Japan pavilion, the patios of the Rose and Crown in the United Kingdom pavilion, and Cantina de San Angel in Mexico. Another good spot is the World Showcase Plaza between the boat docks at the Showcase entrance, but this is often crowded with visitors who want to make a quick exit after the show. If you want to join them here, claim your seat at least an hour in advance. Because the fireworks create a good deal of smoke, use the old lick-the-finger test to see which way the wind is blowing, and position yourself accordingly.

Pleasure Island

Locals as well as tourists patronize this 6-acre after-dark entertainment complex, which, like many other Disney creations, has a fictitious history to go along with its craftily constructed facades. Ostensibly, the island's derelict factories and warehouses are left over from the sail-making business of 19th-century entrepreneur Merriweather Adam Pleasure. The complex is connected to Disney Village Marketplace and the mainland by three footbridges. In addition to seven clubs, including Planet Hollywood, the island has a few restaurants, shops, and a 10-screen AMC cinema that starts showing movies at 1:30 PM.

Things are always changing on Pleasure Island. New attractions include a '70s dance haven, a jazz club, and, adjoining the Pleasure Island complex, one of the glitziest of all Planet Hollywood restaurants; the nightly New Year's Eve party—complete with fireworks—that started a couple of years ago is still going strong. One thing hasn't changed, and that's the pay-one-price admission that gets you into all the clubs and shows except the movie house. There may be an opportunity to glimpse some stars or stars of the future. Star Search, based at Disney-MGM, films its band competitions at Pleasure Island. National acts also occasionally perform and film videos at the park. ⊠ *Pleasure Island, off Buena Vista Dr.,* ☎ *407/934–7781.* ▨ *$19.61 includes admission to all clubs, no charge for shops and restaurants.* ☉ *Clubs daily 7 PM–2 AM, shops daily 10 AM–1 AM, restaurants usually daily 11:30 AM–midnight. Children accompanied by parent or adult admitted to all clubs except Mannequins (same cover as adults).*

The **Adventurers Club** features the Audio-Animatronics showcased in many Disney rides and is supposed to re-create a private club of the 1930s. Apparently quiescent mounted trophies may start talking; your bar stool may begin sinking, and it's sometimes questionable if the person at the next table is a guest or part of the live entertainment. Guests under 18 must be accompanied by a parent or adult.

The **Comedy Warehouse** has evolved from a predictable troupe of comedians to an improvisational setup in which even Mickey and Walt are fair game. Nationally known acts perform in the club's Comics of the Month series, and Entertainment Television tapes its "Stand-Up/ Sit-Down Comedy Show" here. There are five shows nightly. Guests under 18 must be accompanied by an adult.

In case the lava lamps and disco balls don't tip you off, the '70s are back at **8trax,** one of Pleasure Island's newest clubs. Slip on your love beads, strap on your platform shoes, and groove to the recorded tunes of Iron Butterfly, the Village People, or Donna Summer. Guests under 18 must be accompanied by an adult.

Most of the locals who come to Pleasure Island can be found dancing to Top-40 hits at **Mannequins Dance Palace,** a high-tech nightclub with a revolving dance floor, elaborate lighting, and such special effects as bubbles and snow. Guests must be 21 or older.

Live country-and-western music is the focus of the southwestern-style **Neon Armadillo Music Saloon,** where you can also crack unshelled peanuts, drink a cold beer, or find a partner for the Texas two-step. Guests under 18 must be accompanied by an adult.

One of the better places for jazz in central Florida, the **Pleasure Island Jazz Company** presents nightly performances by accomplished soloists or six- or seven-piece bands. The decor recalls a '30s speakeasy, and the well-stocked tapas bar and assorted wines-by-the-glass add a smooth '90s touch. Guests under 18 must be accompanied by an adult.

The three-tier **Rock & Roll Beach Club** is always crowded and throbbing with the rock music of the 1950s and 1960s. The live band and disc jockeys never let the action die down. Guests under 18 must be accompanied by an adult.

They'll be back—that's what the stars promised as they left the December, 1994 opening of **Planet Hollywood.** Although we'd like to believe it, this latest satellite in the Stallone-Schwarzenegger-Willis universe doesn't seem to be a star magnet. Athough bad-boy actor Charlie Sheen of the Heidi Fleiss/Cheerleading fame did attend the premiere and came back later to marry a local girl-turned supermodel. There will, however, be an array of movie memorabilia, much of it with a central Florida connection: the motorcycle from Wesley Snipes's *Passenger 57,* which was filmed north of Orlando in Sanford, for example. Try a slab of Ebony and Ivory Brownie or some Cap'N Crunch Chicken. ⊠ *1506 E. Buena Vista Dr., next to Pleasure Island, Walt Disney World Resort,* ☎ *407/827–7828.* ☜ *No cover.* ⊙ *Restaurant daily 11 AM–1 AM, bar daily 11 AM–2 AM. AE, MC, V.*

Other After-Dark Doings

Clubs and Bars

The **Giraffe Lounge,** a flashy disco in the Hotel Royal Plaza at Lake Buena Vista, is full of spinning, colored lights. It's small, and classy it ain't, but there's a lot going on, including live bands five nights a week, happy hour daily, and themed buffets such as Mexican and Cajun; the place is usually packed on weekends. ⊠ *Hotel Royal Plaza, Lake Buena Vista,* ☎ *407/828–2828.* ☜ *No cover.* ⊙ *Daily 4 PM–2 AM, happy hour daily 4–9:30, buffet daily 4–8:30. AE, MC, V.*

Baja Beach Club is the two-story, inland answer to a beach party. Hits from the '60s to the '90s ring from the restaurant to the open deck where sandwiches and just-grilled burgers are served; a sand volleyball court is out back. Every 15 minutes a spunky, spandexed dance troupe performs. If it is any indication of the bar's allure, lots of locals tread into tourist territory to hit this beach. ⊠ *8510 Palm Pkwy., Lake Buena*

Vista, ☎ *407/239–9629.* ✉ *No cover.* ☺ *Tues.–Sat. 8* PM*–3* AM. *AE, DC, MC, V.*

Electrical Water Pageant

This is one of Disney's small wonders, a 10-minute floating parade of sea creatures outlined in tiny lights, with a terrific blipping, bleeping, toe-tapping electronic score. You can see it from key beaches on Bay Lake and the Seven Seas Lagoon beaches at the Polynesian (at 9), the Grand Floridian (9:15), Fort Wilderness (9:45), the Contemporary (10:05), and, in busy seasons, the Magic Kingdom (10:20). Times occasionally vary so check with Guest Services.

Fireworks

WDW is one of the earth's largest single consumers of fireworks. Traditionally, there have been spectacular short shows at the Magic Kingdom and Disney-MGM Studios at 10. Times vary during the year, so check with Guest Services just to be certain. You can also find them at Pleasure Island as part of the every-night-is-New-Year's-Eve celebrations—an event that's worth the wait into the wee hours.

Movies

With all the only-in-WDW activities, it seems a shame to do what you can always do at home. But there are nights when your feet won't walk even one more step. Try the tenplex theater at Pleasure Island (☎ 407/827–1309). It's state-of-the-art and plays all the latest.

Nightcaps

Even the busiest hotels have quiet corners. At the Contemporary Resort, try the **Top of the World Lounge,** with its view of the Magic Kingdom, the tiny white lights lining the Main Street roof lines, and, in busy seasons, nightly fireworks. This is one of the few Disney locales that require a jacket. At the Polynesian, Disney bartenders ring all the variations on rum punch and piña coladas at the **Tambu Lounge**[/r]. At the Grand Floridian, **Narcoossee's** serves jumbo beers. At the Caribbean Beach, **Captain's Hideaway** is the spot, with its tropical potables. At the Dolphin, try the **Copa Banana,** where the tabletops look like pieces of fruit. At the Beach Club, **Martha's Vineyard Lounge** pours a good selection of wines. At Disney Village Marketplace, drop in at **Cap'n Jack's** for huge, beautiful strawberry margaritas, which incorporate not only strawberries but also special strawberry tequila. The **Village Lounge,** at the Village Marketplace, is another friendly corner; here you can party till the wee hours.[/r]

SpectroMagic

The Disney Imagineers have outdone themselves once again with this Magic Kingdom parade incorporating the latest gee-whiz technology in sound and lighting. If you thought the Main Street Electrical Parade couldn't be topped, you just have to see this one: It proceeds down Main Street and through the park nightly at 9—and again at 11 during peak seasons, when the park stays open until midnight. Don't miss the blinking butterflies. Check with Guest Services. The early showing is for parents with children, while the later running ones get night owls and others with the stamina and the know-how to hang around in order to enjoy the Magic Kingdom's most pleasant, least crowded time of day. Stake out a spot about 30 minutes before the scheduled start of the parade.

THE ORLANDO AREA

Disneyesque street signs with bright colors and engaging graphics are not the only new things in downtown Orlando. Nightspots have sprung up and are thriving in areas that used to be deserted after the office workers went home. Orlando's club owners figured out that there's big money to be made by luring tourists into the city center. The result is a diverse collection of clubs and nighttime activities offering everything from cutting-edge dance palaces and quiet coffeehouses to jousting tournaments and murder-mystery buffets. Even locals who haven't ventured out in a few years are surprised when they brave a night out downtown. The streets are extra crowded when the Orlando Magic is playing at the O-rena—the locals' nickname for the Orlando Arena— or a college team is playing at the Citrus Bowl.

The Arts

If the fantasy wears thin, check out the Orlando fine arts scene in *The Weekly,* a local entertainment magazine, or the "Calendar" in Friday's *Orlando Sentinel,* both available at newsstands. The average ticket price for locally produced shows rarely exceeds $12 and is often half that. Shows at the Carr Performing Arts Centre, however, run more to the traveling-Broadway variety and ticket prices are much steeper.

Orlando has an active agenda of dance, classical music, opera, and theater, much of which takes place at the **Carr Performing Arts Centre** (⊠ 401 W. Livingston St., Orlando, ☎ 407/849–2020). With a stage that has been expanded to accommodate the 24-trailer production of *Phantom,* the Carr has opened up possibilities for other big Broadway extravaganzas. The Broadway Series, featuring top-notch touring shows is scheduled a year in advance. The **Civic Theater of Central Florida** (⊠ 1001 E. Princeton St., ☎ 407/896–7365) presents a variety of shows, with evening performances Wednesday through Saturday, and Sunday matinees.

During the school year, Winter Park's **Rollins College** (☎ 407/646– 2233) has a choral concert series that is open to the public and is usually free. During the last week in February there is a **Bach Music Festival** (☎ 407/646–2182), which has been a Winter Park tradition for nearly 60 years. Also at the college is the **Annie Russell Theater** (☎ 407/646–2145).

The **Orange County Convention and Civic Center** (☎ 407/345–9800), at the south end of International Drive, and the **Orlando Arena** (☎ 407/ 849–2020), downtown on West Amelia Street, play host to many big-name performing artists.

Church Street Station

Church Street Station is a complete entertainment complex, made up of old-fashioned saloons, dance halls, dining rooms, and shopping arcades that nearly match Disney in their attention to detail. It all started in the 1970s, when Church Street was distinguished by nothing more than a dilapidated hotel, a few run-down buildings, and a tired old train station. Developer Bob Snow started with just one bar, Rosie O'Grady's, then acquired neighboring properties as his business grew and boomed. Now both sides of the block are restored. The newest addition to the complex is the **Church Street Exchange,** a razzle-dazzle marketplace with more than 50 specialty shops and restaurants on the first two floors and a jumbo games parlor on another.

Unlike much of what you see in Walt Disney World, this place doesn't just look authentic—it actually is. The train on the tracks is an actual 19th-century steam engine; the calliope was especially rebuilt to whistle its original tunes. Just about everything down to the cobblestones that clatter under the horse-drawn carriages is the real McCoy.

You can either spend an entire evening in one part of the complex or wander from area to area, soaking up the particular atmosphere of each. Either way, you pay a single admission price. Food and drink cost extra and are not cheap. Parts of the complex are open during the day, but the area is usually quiet then; the pace picks up at night, especially on weekends, with crowds thickest from 10 to 11, when the streets can get insanely busy. Be forewarned that fall weekends, when a big football game is at the Citrus Bowl, will be very crowded. Also, there are special themed parties—crowded, alcohol-drenched, frat-type festivals—throughout the year on holidays such as St. Patrick's Day. Call ahead around holidays to check, especially if you're thinking of taking the children. The street scene alone is entertaining—saxophone players, singers, and balloon-bending clowns are among the street performers you're likely to spot. ⊠ *129 W. Church St., Orlando,* ☎ *407/422–2434.* ☞ *$15.95 adults, $9.95 children 4–12 (includes admission to all clubs; no cover for Church Street Exchange, Church Street Station, or Lili Marlene's). AE, MC, V.*

Rosie O'Grady's Good Time Emporium, the original bar on Church Street, is a turn-of-the-century saloon with dark wood, brass trim, a full Dixieland band blaring out from a gazebo stage, banjo shows, tap dancers, and vaudeville singers. Is this a set for *The Music Man* or an evening at the Moulin Rouge? It's difficult to say. Multi-decker sandwiches and hot dogs are available from 11 AM to 2 AM, along with sodas and such drinks as Flaming Hurricane Punch served in a souvenir glass. ☉ *Daily 11 AM–2 AM, shows 7:30, 9, 10:30, and midnight.*

Quiet **Apple Annie's Courtyard** offers recorded, easy-listening music from Jimmy Buffett to James Taylor for your enjoyment either before or after dinner. It's also a good place to rest your feet after you've finished walking through the Church Street Exchange, to have a drink, and to do some people-watching. ☉ *11 AM–2 AM.*

Lili Marlene's Aviator's Pub and Restaurant has the relaxed atmosphere of an English pub and the finest dining on Church Street. Food is hearty, upscale, and very American—mostly steaks, ribs, and seafood. Walls are wood-paneled and decked with biplane–era memorabilia; from the ceiling hangs a large-scale model aircraft. There's no music. ☉ *Lunch daily 11–4, dinner daily 5:30–midnight.*

Phineas Phogg's Balloon Works, a Top-40 dance club, plays tunes on a sound system that will blow your argyle socks off. It draws a good-looking yuppie tourist crowd and a few locals, mostly young singles over 21 but with a sprinkling of old-timers showing off their moves on the dance floor. Much of the young crowd feels it is worth the price of admission into the Station just to come here. The place is jammed by midnight. ☉ *Daily 7 PM–2 AM. Must be at least 21 to enter.*

In the **Orchid Garden Ballroom,** decorative lamps, iron latticework, arched ceilings, and stained-glass windows create a striking Victorian setting rather like an arcade where visitors sit, drink, and listen to a first-rate band pounding out popular tunes from the 1950s to the present. ☉ *Daily 7:30 PM–2 AM, shows daily 8:30, 9:30, 10:45, midnight; Fri. and Sat. also 1 AM.*

Cracker's Oyster Bar, behind the Orchid Garden, is a good place to get a meal of fresh Florida seafood and pasta or slam down a few oysters with a beer chaser. ☉ *Daily 11 AM–midnight, lunch daily 11–4, dinner daily 4–midnight.*

The **Cheyenne Saloon and Opera House** is the biggest, fanciest, rootin'-tootin' saloon you may ever see. Occupying a tri-level former opera house, the place is full of moose racks, steer horns, buffalo heads, and Remington rifles; the seven-piece country-and-western band that plays there darn near brings the house down. With all the pickin', strummin', fiddlin', hollerin', and do-si-do-in', it's a fun place to people-watch. It's also one of the few places at Church Street to draw a big crowd every night. Make sure you wear your best stompin' shoes and cowboy hat, and practice up on your catcalls. The upstairs restaurant serves chicken-and-ribs fare. ☉ *Daily 8:30 PM–2 AM; lunch daily 11–4; dinner daily 5–midnight; shows daily 8:30, 10, 11:30, Fri. and Sat. also 1 AM.*

Clubs and Bars

If you were to judge only by the bars and nightclubs around Kissimmee, Lake Buena Vista, and International Drive, you would think that no one from Orlando ever went out. Not so. It's just that locals go elsewhere—and they have no shortage of options. Early in the week, many of the clubs are mostly deserted much of the night. Depending on your tastes, the absence of wall-to-wall crowds might make a visit worth the trip.

Downtown Orlando

Zuma Beach, a sun-and-surf-themed dance club (formerly Dekko's) where it's not unusual to see a guy in a flatteringly snug wetsuit checking your ID, has a massive light show and an ear-splitting sound system. Check out the Lifeguard Station, the upstairs bar, for drink specials and games. A new look hasn't changed this dress-to-impress crowd—lots of minidresses and too-hip-to-touch ties. There are occasional progressive nights for the 20ish. ⊠ *46 N. Orange Ave.,* ☎ *407/648–8727.* ⊡ *$6.* ☉ *Mon. 8 PM–2 AM, Tues. and Wed. 9 PM–2 AM, Thurs. 9 PM–4 AM, Fri. and Sat. 5 PM–4 AM. AE, MC, V.*

The Edge, the current hot dance spot and concert venue in downtown Orlando, is a multilevel converted warehouse with light shows and smoke; the pounding dance music is played just below the pain threshold. The musical offerings are schizophrenic: They vary from night to night and will probably change by the time you get here. Big-name alternative and rock acts also perform frequently in an adjoining concert field. ⊠ *100 W. Livingston,* ☎ *407/426–9166.* ⊡ *$4–$5.* ☉ *Wed.–Sat. 9 PM–wee hours. AE, MC, V.*

Howl at the Moon has found the perfect solution to the rowdy bar patron who insists on crooning loudly with the band. Orlando's first sing-along bar encourages its patrons to warble the pop classics of yesteryear or favorites like the "Time Warp" and "Hokey Pokey." This isn't karaoke: Everybody sings at once, so the noise level is just below a sonic boom, but toss back a couple of long-neck beers or one of the house specialty drinks—served in souvenir glasses—and you won't care any more. Piano players keep the music rolling in the evening, and the World's Most Dangerous Wait Staff adds to the entertainment. No food is served, but the management encourages you to bring your own or order out; several nearby restaurants deliver. ⊠ *55 W. Church St., Church St. Marketplace, 2nd floor,* ☎ *407/841–4695.* ⊡ *$2–$4 Wed.–Sat., free Sun.–Tues.* ☉ *Daily noon–2 AM; piano players, Sun.–Thurs. 8 PM–2 AM, Fri. and Sat. 6 PM–2 AM. AE, D, MC, V.*

Pinkie Lee's, a jazz club with leather booths, a gourmet menu, and brass accents, is among the most grown-up of Orlando's downtown nightspots. The entertainment is usually top-notch, and the weekend cover charge reflects that. Quiet and not as crowded as some of the clubs catering to a younger crowd, it's a good place to get away alone, together. See if your hotel has a baby-sitting service. ⊠ *380 W. Amelia St.,* ☎ *407/ 872–7393.* ⊡ *$7.50 Tues.–Thurs., $10–$18 Fri. and Sat.* ☉ *Tues.– Thurs. 11 AM–midnight, Fri. 11 AM–2 AM, Sat. 6 PM–2 AM. AE, DC, MC, V.*

Elsewhere

Bennigan's, another young-singles spot, is a favorite of people who work in the area. Orlando Magic basketball star–rapper and national television persona extraordinaire Shaquille O'Neal supposedly eats here often. It draws crowds in the early evening and during happy hours from 2 to 7 PM and from 11 PM to midnight, with food served almost until closing. ⊠ *6324 International Dr., Orlando,* ☎ *407/351–4436.* ☉ *Daily 11 AM–2 AM, food served until 1:30. AE, D, MC, V.*

As you can tell from the name of this tiny bar-and-restaurant, **Dad's Road Kill Café** strives to be different. The bar area is littered with things to keep you busy as you drink your beer and wine: games, puzzles, a computer, plus the obligatory pool table and dart boards. On Friday and Saturday nights, there's low-key, live entertainment. The menu is eclectic, a little pricey, and better than most. To get there from I–4 take the Lee Road exit, head east to Orlando Avenue, turn left and go almost 1 mile, and look for the strip mall on the corner of Lake and Orlando. ⊠ *106 Lake Ave., Maitland,* ☎ *407/647–5288.* ⊡ *No cover.* ☉ *Tues.–Sat. 11 AM–2 AM, food served until 1. AE, MC, V.*

The Mill is a microbrewery and home to some of the best just-baked muffins you'll find in Orlando. Plus, it is a good venue to view some local rock bands in a casual, not horribly crowded atmosphere. The food is good, too. After the supper crowd, this place picks up some of the more laid-back students from Rollins College, which is just down the street. The bands usually start about 9:30 PM. ⊠ *330 W. Fairbanks Ave., Winter Park,* ☎ *407/644–1544;* ⊠ *5601 S. Kirkman Dr., Winter Park,* ☎ *407/345–4833.* ⊡ *$4–$5.* ☉ *Tues.–Sat. until 2 AM, Sun. until midnight; kitchen closes Tues.–Thurs. at 10, weekends at 11. Entertainment about 4 nights per week, never on Mon.; call for information. AE, MC, V.*

Sullivan's Entertainment Complex is a long-time Orlando hangout that a few years ago updated its image. It still is a country-and-western dance hall with much right-friendly charm, where people of all ages and many families come to strut their stuff. Even Yankees are welcome. Big-name performers entertain on occasion; a house band plays from Tuesday through Saturday. Free country-dance lessons are offered on Sunday, Monday, Tuesday, and Thursday. ⊠ *1108 S. Orange Blossom Trail (U.S. 441),* ☎ *407/843–2934.* ⊡ *$2 and up, depending on show.* ☉ *Mon.–Sat. 2 PM–2 AM, Sun. 6 PM–2 AM, with bands 8–2. AE, MC, V.*

Yab Yum is a bohemian refuge from the hustle and bustle of downtown Orlando. Local bands with names like Angel of the Odd or Gunga Din play on most Fridays and Saturdays. The crowd is heavy on aspiring-poet types, who hunch over espressos while giving form to their latest angst; luckily, you don't have to be tormented to enjoy a sandwich, the specialty coffees, or a tasty slab of fresh carrot cake or espresso flan. Beer, wine, and other drinks are also served. ⊠ *25 Wall St. Plaza, Orlando,* ☎ *407/422–3322.* ⊡ *Band nights $4.* ☉ *Mon.–Thurs. 8:30 AM–1 AM, Fri. 8:30 AM–2:30 AM, Sat. 11:30 AM–2:30 AM. No credit cards.*

Dinner Shows

Dinner shows are an immensely popular form of nighttime entertainment around Orlando. For a single price, these hybrid eatery-entertainment complexes deliver a theatrical production and a multiple-course dinner. Performances run the gamut from jousting to jamboree tunes and tend to be better than the usually forgettable meal; unlimited beer, wine, and soda are usually included, but mixed drinks will cost you extra. What the shows lack in substance and depth they make up for in color and the enthusiasm of the performers. The result is an evening of light entertainment, which youngsters in particular will enjoy. Shows have seatings between 7 and 9:30—usually one performance a night, but an extra show can be added during peak tourist periods—and at all but Mark Two, you sit with strangers at tables for 10 or more; that's part of the fun. Always call to make reservations in advance, especially for weekends. If you're in Orlando in an off-season, try to take in these dinner shows on a busy night—a show playing to a small audience can be pathetic and embarrassing. Also be on the lookout for discount coupons: You'll find them in brochure racks in malls, in hotels, and at the Orange County Convention and Visitor's Bureau in the Mercado Shopping Village on International Drive.

International Drive Area

King Henry's Feast. In a faux castle near the Orange County Convention Center, Orlando's own King Henry VIII holds court as a group of jesters, jugglers, dancers, magicians, and singers entertain; ostensibly, he is celebrating his birthday and commencing his quest for a seventh bride. Meanwhile, saucy wenches serve forth potato-leek soup, salad, chicken, and ribs. Reservations are advised. ⊠ *8984 International Dr., Orlando,* ☎ *407/351–5151 or 800/883–8181.* ☜ *$35.99 adults, $21.35 children 3–11.* ☉ *Performances daily 7 and 9:30, additional show occasionally added in high season. AE, D, DC, MC, V.*

Mark Two, Orlando's first true dinner theater, stages complete Broadway shows such as *Whose Life Is It, Anyway?*, *West Side Story*, and *George M.* throughout the year and musical revues chockablock with Broadway tunes during the Christmas holidays. For about two hours before curtain, you can order from the bar and help yourself at buffet tables laden with institutional-grade food; dessert arrives during intermission. Sets, costumes, music, and choreography are all done in-house; direction is by the theater's owner, and actors are mostly local. Under the circumstances, you wouldn't expect the world's best *Oklahoma!*, and you don't get it. But it can be a pleasure to revisit these old favorites while sitting comfortably with a drink in hand. Each show runs for six to eight weeks, with eight shows a week, including matinees. Note that unlike other dinner theaters, the Mark Two offers only tables for two and four. Young children usually find it impossible to sit through the shows, and the steep charge provides ample reason to leave them with a babysitter. Reservations are advised. ⊠ *Edgewater Center, 3376 Edgewater Dr., Orlando (west from I-4 Exit 44),* ☎ *407/843–6275 or 800/726–6275.* ☜ *$29–$33 adults, $24–$28 children under 12.* ☉ *Performances Wed.–Sat. 8; Wed., Thurs., and Sat. 1:15; Sun. 6:30. AE, D, MC, V.*

If Sherlock Holmes has always intrigued you, head for **Sleuths Mystery Dinner Show,** where your four-course meal and unlimited beer, wine, and soft drinks are served up with a healthy dose of conspiracy. The whodunit performance stops short of revealing the perpetrator; you get to question the characters and attempt to solve the mystery. Maybe it was the butler? Seven mysteries/comedies are rotated throughout the year. Reservations are essential. ⊠ *7508 Republic Dr., Orlando,* ☎ *407/363–1985 or 800/393–1985.* ☜ *$33.95 adults, $22.95 children.* ☉ *Performances Mon.–Sat. 6 and 9, Sun. 7:30. AE, D, MC, V.*

U.S. 192 Area

The **Arabian Nights** looks like an elaborate palace outside; inside it's more like an arena, with seating for more than 1,200 at long tables and a glass-enclosed skybox for private functions. The show features some 25 acts with more than 80 performing horses, music, special effects, and a chariot race; keep your eyes open for a unicorn. The three-course dinners offer entrees of prime rib or vegetarian lasagna. Reservations are advised. ⊠ *6225 W. Irlo Bronson Memorial Hwy., Kissimmee,* ☎ *407/396–7400 or 407/239–9223; in Orlando, 800/553–6116; in Canada, 800/533–3615.* ☎ *$36.95 adults, $23.95 children 3–11. AE, D, DC, MC, V.*

Capone's Dinner and Show returns to the gangland Chicago of 1931, when mobsters and their dames represented the height of underworld society. The evening begins in an old-fashioned ice cream parlor, but say the secret password and you'll be ushered inside Al Capone's private Underworld Cabaret and Speakeasy. Dinner is an unlimited Italian buffet that's heavy on pasta. Beer and sangria are included. Reservations are advised. ⊠ *4740 W. Irlo Bronson Memorial Hwy., Kissimmee,* ☎ *407/397–2378.* ☎ *$29.50 adults, $14.95 children under 12. AE, D, MC, V.*

Medieval Times, in a huge, ersatz-medieval manor house, portrays a tournament of sword fights, jousting matches, and other games on a good-versus-evil theme, featuring no fewer than 30 charging horses and a cast of 75 knights, nobles, and maidens. Sound silly? It is. Yet if you view it through the eyes of your children, this two-hour extravaganza is fabulous. That the show takes precedence over the hearty meat-and-potatoes fare is obvious from the dining setup: Everyone sits facing forward at long, narrow banquet tables stepped auditorium-style above the tournament area. Additional diversions, in the $2 million Medieval Life area, include a dungeon and torture chamber to tour, and demonstrations of antique blacksmithery, woodworking, and pottery-making. Reservations are essential. ⊠ *4510 W. Irlo Bronson Memorial Hwy., Kissimmee,* ☎ *407/239–0214 or 800/229–8300.* ☎ *Medieval Times $33.95 adults, $22.95 children 3–12.* ☉ *Castle daily 9* AM–*10* PM; *village daily 6:30–10; performances generally run each evening at 8* PM, *but call ahead to check. AE, D, MC, V.*

Wild Bill's Wild West Dinner Show, in the 22-acre Fort Liberty complex, has the kind of slapstick theatrics and country-western shindigging that children really enjoy, including can can girls, an authentic Texas lariat master, and Native American dancers. The chow, served by a rowdy chorus of cavalry recruits, is beef soup, fried chicken, corn on the cob, pork and beans, and pie and ice cream. Also part of the complex is an 1870s Main Street with shops, a stockade filled with western gifts and souvenirs. Between 11 AM and 2 PM, many of the acts in the dinner show perform in impromptu fashion in the courtyard. Reservations are advised. ⊠ *5260 W. Irlo Bronson Memorial Hwy., Kissimmee,* ☎ *407/351–5151 or 800/883–8181.* ☎ *$35.96 adults, $31.15 children 3–11.* ☉ *Performances daily 7. AE, DC, MC, V. No smoking in showroom.*

Sports Bars

So you're stuck in Orlando and the hotel bar isn't showing State U's biggest game of the year? No problem. Among about a dozen sports bars around town, the following pair offer dozens of games every week and are usually willing to tune their satellites in to pick up your requests.

With two big-screen televisions and a couple of satellite dishes, **Bloopers** is your regular high-testosterone sporting establishment. There is cold beer on tap and grunting, sweating men battling it out in vivid color. If it's not too crowded they sometimes oblige to flip through to find your favorite team. Don't ask, however, when Florida State or the University of Florida are playing. ⊠ *Delta Orlando Resort, 5715 Major Blvd.,* ☎ *407/351–3340.* ⊙ *Mon.–Thurs. 4–1, Fri. and Sat. noon–1 AM. AE, MC, V.*

Coaches Locker Room, a two-level sports palace, boasts 7 satellite dishes, 20 satellite receivers, 6 big-screen TVs, and 12 smaller monitors. Coaches shows every pro-football contest, plus every other kind of sport imaginable. The buffalo wings are worth trying. It's in the strip mall behind T.G.I. Friday's at the intersection of I–4 and Route 436. ⊠ *249 W. Rte. 436, Altamonte Springs,* ☎ *407/869–4446.* ⊙ *Daily 11 AM–2 AM. AE, D, DC, MC, V.*

10 The Cocoa Beach Area

Including the Space Coast

THE MOST DIRECT ROUTE from Greater Orlando to the coast, the Beeline Expressway (S.R. 528), is arrow straight, cut through forests of long-needle pine and laid across the yawning savannas of the south-to-north St. Johns River, which begins life as a tiny stream in a place called Hell and Blazes, Florida. In this countryside of cedars, red maples, and palmettos, American egrets, blue herons, and shy limpkin wade and fish for dinner; ibis tend their chicks; and anhinga perch where they can, spreading their wings to dry. High above watery prairies yellow with wild mustard and butterflies, hawks hunt and osprey soar over their nests that crown stately sabal palms, Florida's official tree. It feels a million miles from the artificial worlds of the theme parks, and it's one good reason to make the trip from Orlando to Brevard County, on the east coast, only an hour away.

Updated by
Val Meyer

The laid-back beach communities are another. Moreover, the area is home to Kennedy Space Center and Spaceport USA and offers water sports, fishing, golf, nature, nightlife, and some distinctive shopping.

Accommodations, restaurants, and shopping are relatively close to each other and to all of the region's points of interest. And if you're lucky enough to be in town during a space shot, you'll be treated to a spectacular sight.

Pleasures and Pastimes

Beaches
On Florida's mid-Atlantic coast from Ormond Beach south to Sebastian Inlet, there are about 100 miles of wide, sandy beaches. Although the winter season alone counts about 460,000 vacationers, the area's sands are much less densely developed than Daytona area beaches. Sun worshipers don't have to worry about being run over as they frolic or stroll—no cars are allowed on the sands. Although Central Florida's Atlantic beaches have some wave action, those looking for big surf will be much happier on the west coast—of the United States, not in Florida. Generally, beaches below Satellite Beach—south of Cocoa Beach—tend to be rocky, with an uneven bottom.

Dining
If you like fresh seafood, the Space Coast is your kind of place. The area is dotted with casual eateries with a heavy emphasis on the fruits of the sea. There are a few upscale dining establishments in Cocoa and Cocoa Beach, but for the most part the eatin' is easy. At some places, you can just walk up to a beachside window and order a burger and brew. For approximate costs, *see* the dining price chart *in* On the Road with Fodor's.

Lodging
Most lodging in Cocoa Beach is on U.S. A1A around its intersection with Route 520. Small motels abound; the few larger hotels are part of popular chains. There are also a few bed and breakfasts. For approximate costs *see* the dining price chart *in* On the Road with Fodor's.

Surfing
Cocoa Beach is the self-proclaimed East Coast Surfing Capital. Those who like to hang ten in the Pacific, however, will find the waves here quite tame. But, when there's a storm brewing and surf's up, you can get quite a ride. Cocoa Beach's main tourist attraction, Ron Jon's Surf Shop (*see below*) is a tribute to the town's principal claim to fame.

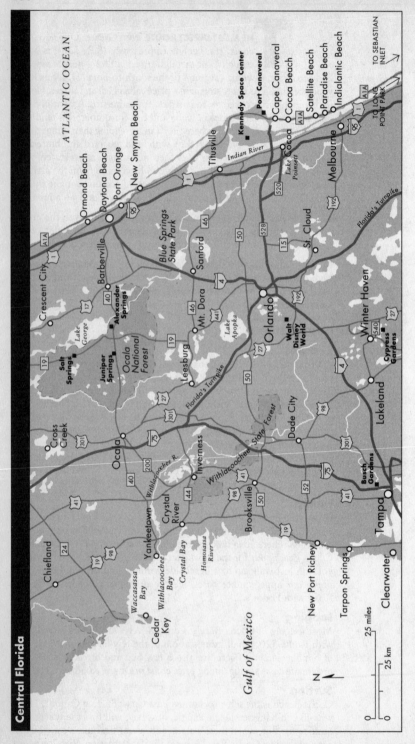

Central Florida

ATLANTIC OCEAN

Ormond Beach
Daytona Beach
Port Orange
New Smyrna Beach

Kennedy Space Center
Port Canaveral
Cape Canaveral
Cocoa Beach
Satellite Beach
Paradise Beach
Indialantic Beach

TO SEBASTIAN INLET

A1A
TO LONG POINT PARK

Titusville
Indian River

Cocoa
Melbourne

Lake Poinsett

95

Crescent City
A1A

11

Barberville

Blue Springs State Park
Sanford

46

St. Cloud

528

15

Florida's Turnpike

Winter Haven

27

Alexander Springs

40

Mt. Dora

Lake Apopka

Orlando

4

192

540

Cypress Gardens

Salt Springs

Juniper Springs

Ocala National Forest

19

Leesburg

46

441

Walt Disney World

27

Lakeland

4

Lake George

17

Cross Creek

301

Ocala

75

Inverness

Withlacoochee R.

Withlacoochee State Forest

Dade City

98

301

Busch Gardens

75

Chiefland

24

41

98

Yankeetown

Crystal River

44

Brooksville

98

50

52

41

Tampa

Waccasassa Bay

Cedar Key

Withlacoochee Bay

Crystal Bay

Homosassa River

New Port Richey

19

Tarpon Springs

Clearwater

Gulf of Mexico

N

25 miles

25 km

0

EXPLORING THE COCOA BEACH AREA

Although just 50 miles separate the Space Coast and Orlando, they're a world apart. In the small beachfront towns of Cocoa Beach, Titusville, and Cape Canaveral, you won't find a lot of glitz, glamour, or giddy attractions. Mainly, it's sun, sand, and surf. If you're looking to get away from it all, this could be the place.

Great Itineraries

Besides the beach, there is one major attraction in the area: Spaceport USA on the grounds of Kennedy Space Center. The other sites tend to be rather low-key, funky, and offbeat. Still, there's plenty to see and do—or not do. Probably the nicest thing about Cocoa Beach and its neighbors is their laid-back style, which is very easy to get used to.

If you have the time, the best plan is to set aside two or three days to enjoy the area. But the Space Coast can also be enjoyed as one or two day trips from Orlando.

IF YOU HAVE 2 DAYS

For a reprieve from Disney take this surf-and-turf tour of the Space Coast. From Orlando, drive the Beeline Expressway (S.R. 528) east. You'll pay a $1 toll, then just past mile marker 30, take the exit for S.R. 520. Watch carefully for the exit; during the summer, when the trees aren't pruned, the directional sign is often obscured. Take 520 east about 9½ miles to the **Lone Cabbage Fish Camp** for a touch of real down home Florida. Here you can fish from their dock, get some gator tail for lunch, and take an airboat ride—a genuine Florida experience. Continue east on 520 to **Cocoa Village,** a quaint restored neighborhood of shops and restaurants. Proceed farther east on 520 to **Cocoa Beach.** At the intersection of 520 and A1A, known as Atlantic Avenue in Cocoa Beach, make a right (south) and make an almost immediate left turn into **Ron Jon's Surf Shop,** a tribute to marketing genius and tourists' insatiable need for T-shirts and beach toys. Check into your hotel and spend the rest of the day soaking up the sun.

On day two, head north on A1A to Kennedy Space Center and **Spaceport USA.** Follow the signs to 528 (Orlando) and take the exit for the Spaceport, which is Route 3. From there, it's about a 20-minute drive. Spend the day learning the story of America's exploration of space. On your way back, retrace your route; at the end of S.R. 528, follow the signs for **Port Canaveral** and **Jetty Park.** Take a walk along the fishing pier and the beach here; it's a local hangout, and one of the least-discovered areas of the Space Coast. You'll get a good view of Cape Canaveral's launch pads, too.

IF YOU HAVE 3 DAYS

Allowing yourself that extra or two day will give you an opportunity to leisurely explore this lovely piece of Florida. This itinerary picks up on Day Three—your day to get back to nature. Follow the above itinerary to **Cocoa Beach.** From the beach head north on A1A and look for signs to **Merritt Island Wildlife Refuge.** Take a drive through before heading to one of the beaches at the **Canaveral National Seashore,** where you should spend the day. Be sure to look down the beach; you'll get some great views of the launch pads. Return to Cocoa Beach for day four. Jump-start the day with a brisk walk or jog along the beach to witness a spectacular sunrise. When you've had enough sun and sand, head for the shops and restaurants of Cocoa Beach Pier.

Cocoa

A Good Walk

Folks in a rush to get to the beach tend to overlook **Cocoa Village,** a charmingly restored 3-square-block area of brick sidewalks in the town of Cocoa. It's worth a stop. Head east on 520—named King Street in Cocoa—and make a right onto Brevard Avenue and follow the signs for the free municipal parking lot.

Walk east on Oleander Street, and your kids will surely come to a screaching halt at **We & De Farm Toys,** at 14 Oleander, which specializes in miniatures and antique farm toys. At the corner of Brevard Avenue and Oleander, look straight ahead and you'll see the **Cocoa Village Playhouse,** a restored 1924 brick building that's a registered national landmark. The Playhouse was originally The Aladdin Theater, a vaudeville house. It then did a turn as a movie theater before being purchased by Brevard Community College. Today it offers productions of Broadway plays and musicals. If you want to cheat on your walk, in front of the theater is the place to catch the **Cocoa Village Carriage,** a horse-drawn carriage that will take you on a 20-minute tour of the area.

If you are going to continue your walk, make a left on Brevard Avenue and wander in and out of the many boutiques and shops. Try the cappuccino and pastries at **Village Cappucino,** at 407 Brevard Avenue. Next door **The Piano Man** sells wonderful miniature musical instruments, as well as sheet music. Continue ½ block to Church Street, and make a left to Delannoy Avenue. At number 434 you'll find the **Porcher House,** the home of E.P. Porcher, one of Cocoa's original pioneers and the founder of the Deerfield Citrus groves. The Porcher Home, now a national historic landmark, is open for tours. Continue north on Delannoy Avenue to **S.F. Travis Hardware,** a genuine, old-fashioned hardware store with high tin ceilings and more nails than you've ever seen in your life.

Walk south on Delannoy to Harrison Street, where you'll find Cocoa Village's densest concentration of shops. Be sure to check out the **Monster Hole Surf Shop** in a narrow space at number 107. The shop prides itself on being the world's tiniest surf shop, with such items as the world's tiniest beach and bathing suit—a thong on a Barbie doll—that's displayed in the window. Monster Hole also boasts the world's smallest hours—noon to 5 on Saturdays only. Cool off with an ice cream at **Village Ice Cream** at 120-B Harrison Street. When you've checked out the shops on Harrison Street, make a left onto Brevard Avenue and walk through **Myrtle Tharpe Square** with its charming gazebo. Cut back to the parking lot, but before getting back into the car, walk to the left to Stone Street and check out **Martha's Gifts** at number 19. Here you'll find every kind of gift imaginable if you just happen to have a wedding coming up; there are lots of wonderful things to buy for yourself as well.

When to Tour

To walk the entire Cocoa Village area, allow at least 45 minutes; if you plan to do some serious browing in the shops or stop for a bite to eat, allow about two hours.

Sights to See

Astronaut Memorial Planetarium and Observatory. One of the largest public-access observatories in Florida, it features a 24-inch telescope through which visitors can view objects in the solar system and deep space. The planetarium has two theaters that offer a choice of films. The Science Quest Hall features an exhibit of scales that are calibrated to other planets. Weight watchers will be thrilled when they step on these. ⊠ *2½ mi east of Exit 75 off I–95 to S.R. 520, then 1¾ mi north on S.R. 501,* ☎ *407/634–3732.* ⬚ *Rooftop observatory and exhibit hall free; admission to 1 show $4, 2 shows $7.* ⊙ *Tues., Thurs., and Fri. 6:30 PM–9:30 PM; Sat. 1:30–4 and 6:30–9:30; Sun. 2–4:30.*

Brevard Museum of History and Natural Science. To see what the land was like in other eras, check out this museum. Not to be missed is the **Windover Archeological Exhibit** of 7,000-year-old artifacts indigenous to the region. Don't overlook the hands-on discovery rooms and the **Collection of Victoriana.** The museum's **nature center** has 22 acres of trails encompassing three distinct ecosystems—sand pine hills, lakelands, and marshlands. ⊠ *2201 Michigan Ave.,* ☎ *407/632–1830.* ⬚ *$3.* ⊙ *Tues.–Sat. 10–4, Sun. 1–4.*

Cocoa Village. A welcome respite from plastic and neon, Victorian-style Cocoa Village is a cluster of restored turn-of-the-century buildings and cobblestone walkways, where visitors can enjoy some 50 restaurants and specialty stores. ⊠ *South of Rte. 520 at Brevard Ave., Cocoa,* ☎ *407/631–9075.*

Lone Cabbage Fish Camp. It's a funky hole-in-the-wall that's the natural habitat of wildlife and local characters—Arnold Palmer loves the place, as the photos of him on the wall attest. There's a restaurant that serves no-nonsense catfish, gator, frog legs, and burgers and hot dogs. Even if you don't eat here, check out the gator souvenirs behind the bar. Our favorite was a gator-head backscratcher. Check out the Swamp Monster that's stuffed and mounted on the wall; it was "caught" by one of the owners, Charlie Jones. This one-of-a-kind spot also has a dock where you can buy your bait and fish. Airboat rides are also available. Reservations are essential. ⊠ *8199 Rte. 520,* ☎ *407/632–4199.* ⬚ *Airboat ride $10.10, nighttime ride. No credit cards.*

Porcher House. Here's a chance to see a real Florida "Cracker" house, built to keep the heat out and the cool inside. E.P. Porcher was one of Cocoa's original pioneers and the founder of the Deerfield Citrus groves. The Porcher Home, now a national historic landmark, is open for guided tours. ⊠ *434 Dellanoy Ave., Cocoa Village,* ☎ *407/639–3500.* ⬚ *Donations accepted.* ⊙ *Weekdays 9–5.*

S.F Travis Hardware. A hardware store, you say? Yes! This is the genuine article, complete with a high tin roof. This is no place for Tim the Toolman Taylor: there's not a power tool in sight. This is a good old-fashioned hardware store from your grandparents' era. Kids used to superstores will find Travis's a real throwback; Mom and Dad will think it's pretty cool, too. If you go there for thumbtacks or tape, you may not come out for four hours. ⊠ *300 Delannoy Ave.,* ☎ *407/636–1441.* ⊙ *Weekdays 7–5:30, Sat. 7–4.*

Dining

$$ ✕ **Black Tulip Restaurant.** At this romantic bistro, a tree provides the dining room's centerpiece; fresh flowers and candlelight reflected in mirrored walls enhance the Floridian cuisine, including mahimahi with scallops and herbs, as well as such Continental dishes as roast duckling with apples and cashews. The restaurant is in restored Cocoa Village. ⊠ *207 Brevard Ave.,* ☎ *407/631–1133. AE, DC, MC, V.*

$ ✕ **Lone Cabbage Fish Camp.** The catfish, frogs' legs, turtle, country ham, and alligator on the menu make the drive from either the beach or Orlando well worthwhile. On Friday nights, there's all-you-can-eat-catfish for $6.50. On the first and third Sunday of every month, there's a fish fry and spirited country-and-western hoedown—definitely not for the shy. ⊠ *8199 Rte. 520, 9 mi north of Cocoa city limits, 4 mi west of I–95.* ☎ *407/632–4199. No credit cards.*

Nightlife

Cocoa Village Playhouse. The area's community theater, located in Old Cocoa Village, mounts plays and musicals featuring local talent from September through March. The rest of the year the stage hosts touring professional productions, concerts, and, in summer, shows aimed at children on vacation. ✉ *300 Brevard Ave.,* ☎ *407/636–5050.*

Cocoa Beach

A Good Walk

The best place for walking here is the beach itself—a wide, sandy stretch that's great for jogging, power walking, or a leisurely stroll. Begin your walk north of the 520 extension. Head for the **Cocoa Beach Pier,** where you can take a break at one of several watering holes.

DISTANCE

It's over a mile from 520 to the Pier; count on the same distance to return to your car.

TIMING

Depending upon your gait, allow 45 minutes to get to the Pier; give yourself at least ½ hour to explore the pier; then take another 45 minutes to return to your starting point, for a total of two hours.

Sights to See

Cocoa Beach Pier. Stretching 840 feet into the Atlantic, the Pier is a local gathering spot as well as a beachside grandstand for space shuttle launches. There are several souvenir shops and watering holes here, among them **Marlin's,** a bar with a sports theme; **The Boardwalk,** an outdoor bar with live music; and **The Pier Restaurant,** a more upscale restaurant with great waterfront views. For the oyster lover, there's **Oh Shucks!** where you can slide down raw ones. And if you want to catch your own, there's a bait-and-tackle shop at the end of the pier. ✉ *401 Meade Ave.,* ☎ *407/783–7549.* 🍴 *Pier free, observers at fishing area 50¢.*

Jungle Village Family Fun Center. When the kids have had enough of the beach, take them here to tire them out. There are mazes for them to climb around and get lost in; go-cars for kids and adults; a "soft play" playground; and 36 holes of miniature golf with a jungle theme featuring Pinky, a lifesize elephant who sports pachyderm-size sunglasses. Hey, it's Florida. Don't go in the middle of the day; you will drop dead from the heat. ✉ *2½ mi north of S.R. 520 on A1A,* ☎ *407/783–0595.* ⊙ *Daily 10 AM–midnight.*

Ron Jon's Surf Shop. It's impossible to miss this emporium, probably the world's wildest tribute to surfer dudes anywhere. With an aqua, teal, and pink art-deco facade that looks like Cinderella Castle on acid, and a giant surfboard, Ron Jon's takes up nearly 2 blocks along A1A. What started in 1963 as a small T-shirt and bathing suit shop has evolved into a 52,000-square-foot superstore. Inside you'll find every kind of beachwear, plus the requisite T-shirts and flip-flops. There's also a wide variety of merchandise from Australia available, including boomerangs. In the center of the store there's even a waterfall and pond that can be viewed from within a glass elevator. There's also a **Ron Jon's Beach Outpost** that's even closer to the sand and surf. It features beach rentals: Surfboards, bodyboards, and beach bikes. For the truly adventurous, in-line skates can also be rented. ✉ *4151 N. Atlantic Ave. (S.R. A1A),* ☎ *407/799–8888;* ✉ *Beach Outpost, 199 E. Cocoa Beach Causeway, 407/868–7588.* ⊙ *Daily 9 AM–11 PM.*

Beaches

Cocoa Beach. This is one of the Space Coast's nicest beaches, with many wide stretches that are excellent for walking, jogging, and biking. In several places there are dressing rooms, showers, playgrounds, picnic areas with grills, snack shops, and surfside parking lots. Beach vendors offer necessities, and guards are on duty in summer. Cocoa Beach is considered the capital of Florida's surfing community.

Paradise Beach. Small and scenic, this 1,600-foot stretch of sand is part of a 10-acre park north of Indianlantic, about 20 miles south of Cocoa Beach on U.S. A1A. It has showers, rest rooms, a refreshment stand, and lifeguards in summer. Picnic tables must be reserved. ☎ 407/779–4008.

Satellite Beach. This is a sleepy little community just south of Patrick Air Force Base, about 15 miles south of Cocoa Beach. The only amenities are several picnic areas. Beaches are almost always uncrowded.

Dining and Lodging

$$$ ✕ **Bernard's Surf.** A nearly 50-year Cocoa Beach tradition, Bernard's is a family operation that has a faithful following of locals and seasonal visitors. The menu features a variety of seafood and mainland entrees, including fresh grouper, lobster, and snapper à la surf, which is topped with a creamy seafood sauce of crab, shrimp, and scallops. Be sure to try the Caesar salad, which is prepared right at your table. Try to save room for dessert—the cheesecake, topped with raspberries and chocolate is homemade by one of the restaurant's bartenders after she gets home from work. ⊠ 2 S. Atlantic Ave., ☎ 407/783–2401. AE, D, DC, MC, V. No lunch.

$$$ ✕ **Mango Tree Restaurant.** Candles, fresh flowers, white linen tablecloths, rattan basket chairs with fluffy cushions, and eggshell-color walls hung with tropical watercolors by local artists set a romantic mood here. The intimate dining room overlooks a garden aviary that is home to doves and pheasants. Try the broiled grouper topped with scallops, shrimp, and hollandaise sauce. ⊠ 118 N. Atlantic Ave., ☎ 407/799–0513. AE, MC, V. Closed Mon.

$$ ✕ **Ashley's.** The friendly servers in this snug wood-and-stucco restaurant will loan you the "U.S. Ghost Register" to read about the history of the place while you decide whether you want steak, seafood, or any of a wide range of other American favorites. Ladies may sense a presence in the powder room, purportedly the restless ghost of an ill-fated town girl; another spirit haunts the staircase, occasionally rudely pushing guests. Although Ashley's has a Rockledge address, it's only about 20 minutes from Cocoa Beach. ⊠ 1609 S. U.S. 1, Rockledge, ☎ 407/636–6430. MC, V.

$$ ✕ **Heidelberg.** Roast duck and fillet Madagascar are the specialties at this elegant establishment, with its crisp linens, fresh flowers, and dark-red color scheme. All the soups and desserts are homemade; try the apple strudel and the rum-zapped almond-cream tortes. ⊠ 7 N. Orlando Ave. opposite City Hall, ☎ 407/783–6806. AE, MC, V.

$$ ✕ **Pier House Restaurant.** In this elegant restaurant in the shopping, dining, and entertainment complex on Cocoa Beach Pier, you can enjoy fresh fish in a room with floor-to-ceiling windows that overlook the ocean. Try the mahimahi, or the grouper, which you can order broiled, blackened, grilled, or fried. ⊠ 401 Meade Ave., ☎ 407/783–7549. AE, D, DC, MC, V.

$ ✕ **Alma's Italian Restaurant.** Five crowded, noisy dining rooms keep the waitresses here busy. The specialties of the house are fresh-caught grouper Italian style and veal Parmesan. The cellar stocks more than 200 imported and domestic wines. The restaurant has a warm, casual atmosphere with red-checked tablecloths, stone floors, and a large stained-glass window. ✉ *306 N. Orlando Ave.,* ☎ *407/783–1981. AE, DC, MC, V.*

$ ✗ **The Boardwalk.** This open-air bar on Cocoa Beach Pier where finger food reigns and live music livens up weekend, is popular with locals and visitors alike. ✉ *Cocoa Beach Pier, 401 Meade Ave.,* ☎ *407/868–0420. AE, D, DC, MC, V.*

$ ✗ **Fischer's Seafood Bar and Grill.** This casual eatery, owned by the same family that runs the more upscale Bernard's Surf, features fresh catches as well as salads, pasta, and burgers. There's a happy hour from 4–7. It's a perfect spot for winding down after a tough day at the beach. ✉ *2 S. Atlantic Ave.,* ☎ *407/783–2401. AE, DC, MC, V.*

$ ✗ **Herbie K's.** This 1950s rock-and-roll diner has become a landmark since its 1987 opening. Servers dress, walk, and talk the '50s—you'll see saddle shoes and revisit such expressions as "Daddy-o" and "dollface." Famous for its burgers, Herbie K's also serves home-style blue plate specials and old-fashioned ice-cream desserts. It's great for families. ✉ *2080 N. Atlantic Ave.,* ☎ *407/783–6740. AE, D, DC, MC, V.*

$ ✗ **Marlin's.** This bar and grill on Cocoa Beach Pier serves burgers, sandwiches, and other pub fare. A band plays on weekends. ✉ *Cocoa Beach Pier, 401 Meade Ave.,* ☎ *407/783–7549. AE, D, DC, MC, V.*

$ ✗ **Oh, Shucks!** The main item here is—you guessed it—oysters, served on the half shell. Landlubbers can have burgers. ✉ *Cocoa Beach Pier, 401 Meade Ave.,* ☎ *407/783–7549. AE, D, DC, MC, V.*

$ ✗ **Rusty's Raw Bar.** This casual eatery with a Hooter's motif—waitresses are dressed in very short shorts—offers 20 different seafood dishes as well as burgers and fries. It's a popular watering hole for the locals. There are two locations: the first is in the same building as Bernard's Surf; the other is at Port Canaveral. ✉ *2 S. Atlantic Ave.,* ☎ *407/783–2401;* ✉ *628 Glen Cheek Dr., Port Canaveral,* ☎ *407/783–2033.*

$$–$$$ 🏨 **Cocoa Beach Hilton.** It's easy to pass by the Cocoa Beach Hilton, as the sign is sometimes hidden by the dense natural foliage that grows right out to the edge of A1A. But once you turn into the parking lot, it's impossible to miss. At seven stories, it's one of the tallest buildings in Cocoa Beach. The hotel provides more amenities than most properties in the area, with a lobby gift shop, waterfront dining and guest rooms, and concierge floors. Rooms are comfortably, but not lavishly, furnished. The hotel's best feature is its location, right on the beach. There's also a pool, where a band plays reggae on weekends. ✉ *1550 N. Atlantic Ave., 32931,* ☎ *407/799–0003 or 800/526–2609,* 🖷 *407/799–0344. 297 rooms. Dining room, pool, baby-sitting, concierge floor. AE, D, DC, MC, V.*

$$–$$$ 🏨 **Inn at Cocoa Beach.** The owners of this casually chic beachfront bed-and-breakfast make guests feel right at home. Rooms are delightfully furnished with antique reproductions and pastels. Green wicker furniture in the lobby invites you to sit and enjoy the nightly wine-and-cheese hour. Breakfast is served overlooking the ocean in a sunny dining room with French Country furniture and Oriental rugs. Couples can enjoy several honeymoon suites that feature jacuzzis and oceanfront balconies. Guests are invited to stay after they check out to use the pool and beach; a changing room with shower is provided. ✉ *4300 Ocean Beach Blvd., 32931,* ☎ *407/799–3460,* 🖷 *407/784–8632. 50 rooms. Pool. AE, D, MC, V.*

$$ 🏨 **Holiday Inn Cocoa Beach Resort.** When two adjacent beach hotels were redesigned and a promenade park landscaped between them, the Holiday Inn Cocoa Beach Resort was born. Public rooms are plush and modern, and there are many facilities. Options include standard, king, or oceanfront suites, which include a living room with sleeper sofa, or you can opt for a villa or bilevel loft. ✉ *1300 N. Atlantic Ave., 32931,*

☎ 407/783–2271, ⨐ 407/784–8878. *500 rooms. Pool, 2 tennis courts, baby-sitting, children's programs. AE, DC, MC, V.*

$$ ⌸ **Howard Johnson Plaza Hotel.** This oceanfront hotel, popular with families, is also a favorite of Orlandoans as a weekend getaway place. Rooms are comfortably furnished; many are oceanfront with private balconies. ⊠ *2080 N. Atlantic Ave., 32931,* ☎ *407/783–9222,* ⨐ *407/783–6514. 210 rooms. Restaurant, lounge, 2 pools, wading pool, exercise room. AE, D, DC, MC, V.*

$$ ⌸ **Ocean Suite Hotel.** A five-story building with a great location, this property is just ½ block south of Cocoa Beach Pier. Ideal for families, each room has a refrigerator and microwave. ⊠ *5500 Ocean Beach Blvd., 32931,* ☎ *407/784–4343,* ⨐ *407/783–6514. 50 rooms. Restaurant, lounge, pool. AE, D, DC, MC, V.*

$$ ⌸ **Wakulla Motel.** This motel has the best occupancy rate on the beach. Its completely furnished five-room suites, designed to sleep six, are ideal for families; they include two bedrooms, a living room, dining room, and fully equipped kitchen and have cable TV with HBO. The grounds are landscaped with tropical vegetation. ⊠ *3550 N. Atlantic Ave., 32931,* ☎ *407/783–2230,* ⨐ *407/783–0980. 116 suites. 2 pools, shuffleboard, laundry.*

$–$$ ⌸ **Cocoa Beach Oceanside Inn.** The name says it all: this property is right on the beach. Rooms are decorated in tropical pastels and many feature private balconies. You can swim in the heated pool and still have a view of the ocean without getting salt in your eyes. ⊠ *1 Hendry Ave., 32931,* ☎ *407/784–3126 or 800/874–7958,* ⨐ *407/799–0883. 76 rooms. Restaurant, refrigerators, lounge, pool, laundry service, parking (fee). AE, D, DC, MC, V.*

$ ⌸ **Best Western Ocean Inn.** This is a popular spot for families; it's a no-nonsense motel without a lot of frills. You'll have to walk ½ block to get to the beach, but the trek can be worth it to save your vacation dollars for other things besides an oceanfront room. ⊠ *5500 N. Atlantic Ave., 32931,* ☎ *407/784–2550 or 800/245–5225,* ⨐ *407/868–7124. 102 rooms, 14 efficiencies. Pool, in-room safe, coin laundry. AE, D, DC, MC, V.*

$ ⌸ **Comfort Inn and Suite Resort.** This hostelry is across the street from the ocean and within walking distance of more than a dozen restaurants. You can choose from standard double rooms, minisuites, one-bedroom ocean-view suites, and fully equipped efficiencies. All are clean, comfortable, and decorated in light, tropical colors. The poolside bar has a waterfall, and there's a pond full of tropical fish, in addition to the many facilities. ⊠ *3901 N. Atlantic Ave., 32931,* ☎ *407/783–2221,* ⨐ *407/783–0461. 40 rooms, 80 suites, 40 efficiencies. Lounge, pool, whirlpool, Ping-Pong, shuffleboard, volleyball court, playground. AE, D, DC, MC, V.*

$ ⌸ **Pelican Landing Resort on the Ocean.** This two-story beachfront motel is friendly and warm, so many guests call it a home away from home. Rooms have ocean views, microwaves, and TVs with cable and HBO; one even has a screened porch. Boardwalks to the beach, picnic tables, and a grill round out the amenities. ⊠ *1201 S. Atlantic Ave., 32931,* ☎ *407/783–7197. 11 units. Kitchenette, beach. D, MC, V.*

Nightlife

Bumpers. In this cozy '50s-style lounge, DJs spin oldies from a 1957 Chevy for happy dancers amid memorabilia of the Eisenhower era. Food is available from **Herbie K's,** the diner that shares the premises. ⊠ *2080 N. Atlantic Ave.,* ☎ *407/783–9222.* ⊘ *Mon.–Thurs. 4–midnight, Fri. and Sat. 4–2. AE, D, DC, MC, V.*

China Beach Lounge. A popular spot with locals, this bar features tropical citrus drinks that can be sipped poolside. Darts, big screen TV, and a pool table are available. There's a daily happy hour, too. ⊠ *1275 N. Atlantic Ave.*, ☎ *407/784–8008.*

Cocoa Beach Pier. This is one of the happening spots in the area. Several al fresco watering holes feature live music on weekends. Friday nights feature a "Boardwalk Bash," with live acoustic and rock and roll. There are also several casual eateries and The Pier, an upscale waterfront restaurant. ⊠ *401 Mead Ave.*, ☎ *407/783–7549.*

Coconuts on the Beach. This beachfront hangout, long a staple with locals, is popular with the younger crowd. It's the local party place: there are karaoke nights, ladies' nights, quarter beer nights, and live music on Thursday and Saturday nights. Burgers, salads, and sandwiches are on the menu. ⊠ *2 Minuteman Causeway*, ☎ *407/784–1422.*

Outdoor Activities and Sports

BIKING

Although there are no bike trails as such in the area, cycling is allowed on the beaches and the Cocoa Beach Causeway. Bikes can be rented hourly, daily, or weekly at Ron Jon Surf Shop in Cocoa Beach. ⊠ *4151 N. Atlantic Ave. (S.R. A1A)*, ☎ *407/799–8888;* ⊠ *annex, 199 E. Cocoa Beach Causeway, Cocoa Beach.*

FISHING

Check *Florida Today,* the local newspaper, or bait-and-tackle shops to find out what's biting where. There's surf casting for bluefish, pompano, sea bass, and flounder; success is mixed and depends on the season. Anglers fishing from piers sometimes pull in mackerel, trout, sheepshead, and tarpon; the Titusville pier has good shrimping. All major beach towns have lighted piers; admission is usually $1–$4. You can also fish from some bridges.

GOLF

Cocoa Beach Country Club. This extensive public sports complex along the banks of the Banana River offers a variety of sports facilities including a 27-hole championship golf course. Touching the shores of 17 lakes, the course is also home to much wildlife. The extensive complex offers an Olympic-size swimming pool, gymnasium, 10 lighted tennis courts, a restaurant, and a riverside pavilion with picnic tables. The clubhouse's restaurant has the best Sunday brunch in town. ⊠ *5000 Tom Warriner Blvd.*, ☎ *407/868–3361.*

WATER SPORTS

Boat America. The outfitter offers a variety of boat rentals and enough nautical knowledge to help you set your own course. Pack a lunch and explore Banana River's lovely unspoiled islands, seek out wildlife in Intercoastal Waterway canals, or fish the deep waters off Port Canaveral's harbor. Pontoons, runabouts, Jet Skis, and wave runners are available for half- or full-day rental. ⊠ *1891 E. Merritt Island Causeway, Cocoa Beach*, ☎ *407/678–2860.*

Shopping

Mai Tiki Gallery. Cocoa Beach may seem an unlikely place for a shop with a South Pacific theme, but, hey, why not? High-quality Tiki carvings, masks, and sculptures are offered; there's also a selection of souvenirs the kids will love. ⊠ *1 N. Atlantic Ave. (S.R. A1A)*, ☎ *407/783–6890.* ☉ *Mon.–Sat. 10–6.*

Merritt Square Mall. The Cocoa Beach area's only major shopping mall, on Merritt Island, is about a 20 minute ride from the beach. Anchors include Burdines, Dillard's, JC Penney, and Sears. There are more than 100 specialty shops; many are the usual suspects you'll find in any mall around the country, such as Casual Corner, Foot Locker, Lane Bryant, and Waldenbooks. There are two six-screen multiplexes, along with a food court and several popular restaurant chains—Jungle Jim's and the Outback Steak House. ✉ *777 E. Merritt Island Causeway (S.R. 520) Merritt Island*, ☎ *407/452–3272*. ⊙ *Mon.–Sat 10–9, Sun. noon–5:30.*

Ron Jon's Surf Shop. If you need anything for the beach, this is the place to go. There's also a nice selection of ladies' and men's sportswear, in addition to the T-shirts the kids will want to bring home as souvenirs. ✉ *4151 N. Atlantic Ave. (S.R. A1A)*, ☎ *407/799–8888.*

Melbourne

A decidedly laid-back atmosphere is the feeling in Melbourne, despite its dependence on the high-tech space industry. Recent cutbacks have led to closings of some popular eateries and nightspots, but Melbourne is adapting to the economic changes. Even though baseball's Marlins call South Florida's Joe Robbie Stadium home during the season, the team uses Melbourne's Space Coast Stadium for its spring training site.

Beaches

Sebastian Inlet State Recreation Area. This 576-acre park offers 3 miles of interesting beach good for swimming, surfing, and snorkeling. The beach is rocky and the sand coarser than elsewhere along the coast, and the underwater drop-off is often sharp. It's fun for treasure hunters, because storms occasionally wash up pieces of eight from the area's ancient Spanish shipwrecks. Sebastian is also a favorite destination for Florida anglers. Warning: Come seriously prepared for what Floridians call their state bird—the ubiquitous mosquito! The park has a bathhouse, a concession, a fishing jetty, a boat ramp, campsites (☎ 407/589–9659), and the **McLarty Treasure Museum** (☎ 407/589–2147), built to commemorate the loss of the Spanish Treasure Fleet of 1715. ✉ *12 mi south of Melbourne on U.S. A1A*, ☎ *407/984–4852.*

Port Canaveral

This once-bustling commercial fishing area is still home to a small shrimping fleet, charter, and party fishing boats. In recent years, a small but growing number of cruise ships have called Port Canaveral home. The port is currently expanding to make way for the two megaships that the Walt Disney Co. will be launching in the late '90s. Quaint in its own way, the port offers a glimpse into the Florida off the tourist path. Several restaurants wih great waterway views specialize in fresh-catch family fare.

Sight to See

Jetty Park. A place where friendly conversations are unavoidable, Jetty Park offers a wonderful experience in the real Florida. A long fishing pier jets out into the ocean. If you look north, you'll see the Vehicle Assembly Building and the launch pads of Kennedy Space Center. A jetty constructed of giant boulders adds to the landscape; a walkway that crosses it provides access to a largely deserted stretch of beach. There's a picnic area and campsites, too. Shops offer area souvenirs. ✉ *400 E. Jetty Rd., Cape Canaveral*, ☎ *407/783–7111*. 🎟 *$1 per car.* ⊙ *Daily 6 AM–9 PM.*

Dining

$$ ✗ **Lloyd's.** This Port Canaveral family-oriented dining spot sits snugly alongside the port's working docks, a venue that provides diners a spectacular view of coming-and-going cruise ships, net-draped shrimp boats, fishing pelicans, and—the topper—a drop-dead perfect vista for shuttle launches. The extensive menu brags that diners can not only see their catch come off the boat, they can order "the fish-of-the-hour." A large, airy upstairs bar with darts and a pool table offers elevator access, and a rooftop deck is home to live music on weekends. ⊠ *610 Glen Cheek Dr.,* ☎ *407/784–8899. AE, D, MC, V.*

Fishing

Cape Marina (⊠ 800 Scallop Dr., Port Canaveral, ☎ 407/783–8410), **Miss Cape Canaveral** (⊠ 630 Glen Cheek Dr., Port Canaveral, ☎ 407/783–5274), and **Pelican Princess** (⊠ 655 Glen Cheek Dr., Port Canaveral, ☎ 407/784–3473) are among the reliable charter companies for deep-sea fishing.

Titusville

This small oceanfront community is home to Kennedy Space Center, the nerve center of the U.S. space program. Here you'll find several attractions that are devoted to the history of space exploration.

Sights to See

Spaceport USA. This attraction just southeast of Titusville is one of Central Florida's most popular attractions. Many of Spaceport USA's attractions are free, including parking, where sections of the lot are named after the space shuttles. Within the facility is the outdoor **Rocket Garden,** its lawns bristling with rockets, a museum filled with spacecraft that have explored the last frontier, and several short films. There's also a full-scale replica of a space shuttle, the Explorer, where you can explore the payload bay, cockpit, and crew quarters. Kids love the space playground with a ⅕-scale Space Shuttle/Space Station gym.

The most moving exhibit is the **Astronauts Memorial,** a tribute to those who have died while in pursuit of space exploration. Dedicated in May, 1991, the memorial was financed mostly by Floridians, who purchased *Challenger* license plates. The 42.5-foot-high by 50-foot-wide "Space Mirror" tracks the movement of the sun throughout the day, using reflected sunlight to brilliantly illuminate the names of the 16 fallen astronauts that are carved into the monument's 70,400-pound polished granite surface.

To get the most out of a visit to Spaceport USA, you should take at least one of the two bus tours offered. These are the only way to see much of Kennedy Space Center up close. The **Red Tour** passes by some of NASA's office and assembly buildings, including current launch facilities and the space shuttle launching and landing sites. The **Blue Tour** goes to Cape Canaveral Air Force Station, where early launch pads and unmanned rockets illuminate the beginnings of the space program. Security concerns mandate that many sights be viewed through a tour bus window. However, live and recorded narrations are provided during both tours, and there are historical exhibits at camera stops. Be advised that due to launch schedules, not all sights may be included in the tours.

Three IMAX films are shown in the only back-to-back twin **IMAX theater complex** in the world. Projected onto a 5½-story screen, **The Dream Is Alive,** an awesome 40-minute film shot mostly by the astronauts, takes you from astronaut training and a thundering shuttle launch to an astronaut's-eye view of life aboard the shuttle while in space. **Destiny in Space** presents first-time views of the shuttle orbiting the Earth and thrilling flyovers of Mars and Venus. These two films are shown every 45 minutes in the IMAX I Theater. **The Blue Planet**— an environmental look at the Earth seen from 200 miles high—is shown three times a day in the IMAX II Theater. On Kennedy Space Center grounds, tune your car radio to AM 1320 for attraction information. ⊠ *Kennedy Space Center,* ☎ *407/452–2121.* ▨ *Bus tours*

$7, IMAX film $4. ☉ *Daily 9* AM*–dark, last tour 2 hours before dark, IMAX films daily 10–5:40; closed certain launch dates, so call ahead.*

United States Astronaut Hall of Fame. Here you can enter the world of virtual reality, thanks to an interactive display where you can lose your breath because of the 3-G pull of a mock G-force trainer. For a quiet interlude, view videotapes of historic moments in the space program. This is also home to **U.S. Space Camp,** which offers young people a hands-on learning environment that budding astronauts will love. ⊠ *S.R. 405,* ☎ *407/269–6100.* ☜ *$7.95.* ☉ *Daily 9–5, later in summer; closed Dec. 25.*

Valiant Air Command Warbird Air Museum. Aviation buffs won't want to miss this one. The museum is filled with aviation memorabilia from both world wars, Korea, and Vietnam, as well as extensive displays of vintage military flying gear and uniforms. ⊠ *6600 Tico Rd.,* ☎ *407/268–1941.* ☜ *$6.* ☉ *Daily 10–6; closed Thanksgiving, Dec. 25, and Jan. 1.*

Beaches

Canaveral National Seashore. The 57,000-acre Canaveral National Seashore—30 miles north of Cocoa Beach on U.S. A1A—is home to more than 250 species of birds and animals. The area is unspoiled and hilly with dunes, and the strand itself is sprinkled with seashells. Surf and lagoon fishing is available, and a hiking trail leads to the top of an Indian shell midden at Turtle Mound. There's a visitor center on U.S. A1A. Weekends are busy and parts of the park are closed before launches, sometimes as much as two weeks in advance, so call ahead. ⊠ *Titusville,* ☎ *904/428–3384.*

Playalinda Beach. Part of the national seashore, this is the longest stretch of undeveloped coast on Florida's Atlantic Seaboard. It is remote, with pristine sands; hundreds of giant sea turtles come ashore here from May to August to lay their eggs, and the extreme northern area is favored by nude sun worshippers. However, a law against nude sunbathing was enacted in 1995 and is enforced with various degrees of regularity. Eight parking lots anchor the beach at mile intervals. There are no lifeguards, but park rangers patrol. Take bug repellant in case of horseflies. To get here, follow U.S. 1 north into Titusville to Route 406 (I–95 Exit 80), follow Route 406 east across the Indian River, then Route 402 east for 12 more miles. Do visit the **Merritt Island Wildlife Refuge** (☎ *407/861–0667),* which you'll pass on this stretch, to see wildlife and rivers of grass up close, along nature trails. The refuge is open weekdays 8–4:30 and Saturday 9–5. ⊠ *Titusville,* ☎ *407/267–1110.*

Dining and Lodging

$$ ✕ **Flamingos.** Located in the Radisson Resort at the Port hotel—and close to the cruise-ship piers—this spot has earned high kudos from foodies for its Floridian-inspired spin on Continental specialties. The decor is haute Caribbean: beige walls, paintings of flamingos, wicker trim, bouquets of red jasmine flowers, and finger bowls. Florida-Gulf red snapper topped with crabmeat and orange hollandaise, and the shrimp with caper-seafood stuffing are two favored entrées. Try, if you dare, the Ultimate chocolate sensation—a chocolate mocha-meringue debauch, complete with white chocolate, chocolate mousse, warm fruit, and crème de cacao. ⊠ *8701 Astronaut Blvd.,* ☎ *407/784–0000. AE, D, MC, V.*

$$$ 🏨 **Radisson Resort at the Port.** This elegant resort directly across the street from Port Canaveral is the closest beach-area resort to Walt Disney World. Though it's not on the ocean, the hotel provides compli-

mentary transportation to Ron Jon's Surf Shop and the cruise ship terminals at Port Canaveral. Rooms have a Caribbean motif, with wicker appointments, hand-painted wallpaper, coffee machines, hair dryers, and ceiling fans; they come with one king-size or two double beds and have TVs with cable and HBO. The pool is lavish, in the best central Florida fashion, tropically landscaped and complete with a cascading 95-foot mountain waterfall. Facilities are equally abundant, as you'd expect of a resort of this caliber. ⊠ *8701 Astronaut Blvd., 32920,* ☎ *407/784–0000 or 800/333–3333,* ℻ *407/784–3737. 200 rooms. Restaurant, 2 pools, whirlpool, 2 tennis courts, health club, playground, laundry, business services, convention center, airport shuttle. AE, D, DC, MC, V.*

COCOA BEACH AREA A TO Z

Arriving and Departing

By Car

The Beeline Expressway (Rte. 528) is accessible from either I–4 or the Florida Turnpike. Tolls for the trip add up to $2.45 for a car. If you take the Beeline directly to the coast, you will end up in Port Canaveral, about 20 miles north of Cocoa Beach. The coast is about 90 minutes from WDW, 60 minutes from Orlando.

S.R. 520, which is reached from the Beeline—exit just past mile marker 30—is a slightly less direct, but more scenic route to Cocoa Beach. Continuing east on 520 will take you through the town of Cocoa and on into Cocoa Beach. 520 will take you right to A1A, the beach's main artery. In Cocoa Beach, A1A is known as Atlantic Avenue.

S.R. 50, known in Orlando as Colonial Drive, is also a straight shot to the coast. You'll have to get through some traffic, but once on the outskirts of Orlando, it's smooth sailing. S.R. 50 literally dead-ends at A1A in Titusville, just north of the access road to Spaceport U.S.A. If you're going to the Spaceport for the day, S.R. 50 is actually a more direct route than the Beeline.

By Plane

The nearest major airport is **Orlando International Airport** (☎ 407/825–2352) about a one-hour ride. The **Cocoa Beach Shuttle** (☎ 407/784–3831 or 800/633–0427) provides transportation to and from the airport. Reservations are required.

American Eagle, Continental, Delta, and U.S. Air provide some service to **Melbourne International Airport,** approximately a half-hour ride from Cocoa. The **Melbourne Airport Shuttle** (☎ 407/724-1600) ferries arriving and departing passengers.

Getting Around

By Bus

Space Coast Area Transit (☎ 407/633–1878) is the provider of local bus service. Fare is $1 adults, 50¢ for senior citizens, people with disabilities, or students with valid I.D. Route 9 runs between Merritt Square Mall and all major points along the beaches between Port Canaveral and Cocoa Beach.

By Car

The Space Coast is very easy to navigate. On the beach, the main thoroughfare is A1A, known as Atlantic Avenue in Cocoa Beach, and by other names in other beach towns. The area around the intersection of A1A and S.R. 520 tends to be congested at almost all hours. In general, however, traffic here is much lighter than in other towns along the coast. The principal route on the "mainland" is U.S. 1. To get back to Orlando, take either the Beeline (S.R. 528) or S.R. 520.

Contacts and Resources

Car Rentals
If you are driving from Orlando International Airport, all major car rental companies are located in the main terminal on level 1. Several car rental companies also have offices on the Space Coast. Call these numbers for the location nearest to where you'll be staying: **Avis** (☎ 800/331–2112), **Budget** (☎ 800/527–0700), **Hertz** (☎ 800/654–3131).

Emergencies
Dial 911 for **police, fire,** or **ambulance.**

Equipment Rentals
Rent surfboards, bodyboards, and beach bikes at **Ron Jon's Beach Outpost** (⊠ 199 E. Cocoa Beach Causeway, Cocoa Beach, ☎ 407/868–7588) located at the end of S.R. 520.

Guided Tours
AIRBOAT TOURS
Lone Cabbage Fish Camp. Airboat rides on the St. Johns river are offered here. Reservations are essential. ⊠ 8199 Rte. 520, Cocoa, ☎ 407/632–4199. ☎ $10.10, nighttime ride $20. No credit cards.

CARRIAGE RIDES
Cocoa Village Carriages. 20-minutes guided tours of Old Cocoa Village take passengers around the restored historic district. ☎ 407/631–2416. ☎ $20 for 2 passengers and on Sat.; $30 for 3 riders or more. ☉ Thurs.–Sat 6–10, Sat. 10–1.

Hospital
Cape Canaveral Hospital. There is a 24-hour emergency room. ⊠ 701 W. Cocoa Beach Causeway (Rte. 520), Cocoa Beach, ☎ 407/799–7111.

Visitor Information
Both the **Cocoa Beach Area Chamber of Commerce** (⊠ 400 Fortenberry Rd., Merritt Island 32952, ☎ 407/459–2200 or 800/572–4636) and the **Space Coast Office of Tourism** (⊠ 2725 St. Johns St., Melbourne 32940, ☎ 407/633–2110 or 800/USA–1969) provide general information as well as dates for rocket launches.

11 Portrait of Walt Disney World®

THE MOUSE AND THE DYNAMO

ICOULDN'T SLEEP the night before I went to Walt Disney World. A Floridian for more than 20 years, living two hours away by car, I had always patriotically avoided even going near the place. My family went. My neighbors went. (One of them, a 75-year-old man, has gone every year for 15 years to see what's new.) For my part, however, it depressed me that the Egyptians gave us the Pyramids, the Greeks the Parthenon, the French the Cathedral of Chartres, and our cultural contribution was . . . a celluloid mouse.

Indeed, the morning I drove to Orlando I felt I was making the sort of pilgrimage people used to make to Mont-Saint-Michel or Jerusalem. "You know, he almost put it in St. Louis," I said to my sister as we drove south on Route 19 through Ocala National Forest. "But Adolph Busch, the beer baron, stood up at a dinner they gave for Disney and said anyone who built a theme park and did not sell beer inside was crazy. So, on the plane back to California, Disney said, 'Forget about St. Louis.'" Why? "Because, he had no intention of selling beer. He disliked the odor of beer on hot days in amusement parks—like the parks in southern California he used to take his daughter to in the '30s and '40s."

I could have told her more. After reading Richard Schickel's *Disney Version,* John Taylor's *Storming the Magic Kingdom,* and an article by John McAleenan in the Orlando *Sentinel* about the actual building of Disney World, I was bursting with tidbits like that: The fact that Disney went ahead in 1954 with the building of Disneyland was chiefly because he could promote it on his weekly television show; that amusement parks were dying in the '50s, and the manufacturers of rides refused to build Disney the new ones he had in mind; that on the day Disney World opened, the people who built it actually wondered if anyone would come; that Disney himself had come up against ob-

stacles throughout his career, and ended up one of the most tenacious, determined, and resilient men in the history of American business. In fact, I was more fascinated by Disney's career (with these low points that people seem to have forgotten) than by his amusement parks. But I didn't mention any of this. I dropped my sister off in Apopka, a small town 10 miles from Orlando, and continued on alone to Orlando.

Walt Disney World is not in Orlando exactly but sits 20 miles southwest of downtown. It lies on both sides of a busy highway called I–4, on 28,000 acres of what used to be pinewoods, cattle pastures, and swampland, between two cities in two counties: Orlando, in Orange County, and Kissimmee, in Osceola County. Actually, Disney World exists in a world of its own—a separate entity, both physically and legally. Bill Donegan, an Orange County commissioner, likes to compare it to the Vatican.

THE REASON THERE'S A LOT OF space between Disney World and the two cities it lies between is that Walt Disney wanted it that way. When Disney decided to put his second theme park in Florida, he wanted enough land around it to form a buffer against the sort of commercial crud that had marched up Harbor Boulevard in Anaheim to the very edge of Disneyland, and to enable him to build his own hotels to house the guests who were staying outside Disneyland. So, where Disneyland sits on 180 acres, Disney World occupies 28,000—roughly the area of Boston. ("If he had it his way," says Joe Fowler, an ex-admiral who helped construct Disney World, "we would have bought 50,000 acres.")

In the mid-'60s, big parcels were easy to find in central Florida; it was still mostly rural. In his first flight over the unbroken pinewoods in 1965, Disney saw an island

---

This essay has been excerpted and adapted from an article that originally appeared in the August 1990 issue of Wigwag *magazine.*

in the middle of a lake down below and, imagining the fun he could have with it, said, "This is great. Buy it." (It later became Discovery Island, a bird sanctuary and zoological park.) He bought the land—for about $180 an acre—without letting the real estate agent and lawyer who handled the transaction know his identity. The publisher of the Orlando *Sentinel* learned the truth only by agreeing to keep it a secret; if the news got out, the deal was off. He kept the secret. In those days, everybody wanted growth. Forty-eight hours after the news that 28,000 acres had been acquired by Disney, land adjacent to his went up to $80,000 an acre. Anyone who studies Walt Disney's remarkable career will discover this: He was a sharp businessman.

BUT HE WAS NOT—and this is what's so strange, driving down I-4 in the middle of this boom—always the success we see today. His pedigree was one of failure. His father, one of 11 children born in Ontario and raised in Kansas, went south to Florida as a young man to grow citrus. (He met Walt's mother, a schoolteacher on vacation, there.) A freeze wiped out his grove, and he went north to Chicago, where he got work as a carpenter on the Columbian Exposition of 1893. For the next 10 years he worked as a small contractor. "My mother used to go out on a construction job and hammer and saw planks with the men," said Walt, who was born in Chicago in 1901, the youngest of four sons. His first name was that of the Congregational minister who christened him; his second, Elias, that of his father. When he was five, his father moved again, acquiring a farm near Marceline, Missouri. Four years later, the failure of the farm forced Walt's father to auction off the livestock and move once more, to Kansas City. There Walt worked a predawn newspaper route, in blizzards so bitter they gave him nightmares as an adult. He also took art classes. Right after the armistice in 1918, he went to France, where he sold fake German helmets as souvenirs to American G.I.s and painted the Croix de Guerre on their jackets for 10 francs apiece (his first paying art job). Back home, a job waited for him in a Chicago jelly factory his father had bought.

But he returned instead to Kansas City to get newspaper work, and ended up starting an animation business. It was not a success at first. Business was so poor, in fact, he had to tell his one big customer (a dentist who wanted an educational film for kids) that he couldn't meet him to discuss the project because he had no shoes: His only pair was being fixed. In 1923, at the age of 21, he gave up, like his father—but this time Disney went west, to Hollywood.

Each venture he pursued came, after some small success, to a dead end. When the banks lent him money—after the success of *Snow White and the Seven Dwarfs*— to build a studio, they insisted it be constructed so that if it failed, it could be converted into a hospital (which is why the hallways are wide enough for a bed to be rolled down the middle). In 1939, *Snow White* won an Academy Award (a big statue for Snow White, seven tiny ones for the dwarfs). In 1940, *Pinocchio* was such a bomb that bankers cut off credit to his company. But each time he reached a dead end, he came up with something. Mickey Mouse was invented near bankruptcy, on a train to Los Angeles from New York, where Disney had just learned that his Eastern distributor had lured his best people away. He started making nature movies only because his feature-length animation-film career petered out in 1959 with *Sleeping Beauty* (another flop). He survived because he plowed whatever profits he did make into his own company (Walt Disney Productions), lived modestly in a town where other studio heads aped the English aristocracy, always drove a hard bargain (on actors, the saying went: "Disney gets you on the way up or the way down"), and never surrendered the rights to a single one of his films or to the merchandising connected with them. This strategy made him one of the few moguls to survive into the '60s with his studio intact.

Intact and insular: The Disney organization was always a family enterprise. All four brothers ended up living in Los Angeles—they played croquet together at Roy's house on summer Sundays—but the company consisted of only Walt and Roy. Roy handled the finances. Walt was the creative half, though Richard Schickel says he could barely draw the images for which his studio became famous; another man, Ub Iwerks, was responsible for much of the animation that has burned itself into the national consciousness.

In 1953, Disney alienated Roy by forming a private company called Retlaw (Walter spelled backward) to control the merchandising rights to the name Walt Disney. Because the name Walt Disney was on just about everything connected to the studio, and Retlaw's income went to Walt and his two daughters, Roy was furious. The feud went on for nearly a decade, during most of which they refused to speak to each other. The feud ended up dividing the company into "Walt men" (marketing, studio, theme parks) and "Roy men" (finance, legal, administrative), and the schism lasted long after the brothers' deaths—Walt's in 1966 and Roy's in 1971.

While the brothers were living, however, even their feud couldn't alter the united front the Disney company presented to outsiders. Not only did Walt retain the rights to every film he made (something other studios surrendered, especially when TV came along) and control the merchandise associated with his characters, but he also formed a company to distribute the movies. Yet even this was not enough. When the banks cut off his line of credit in 1940, Disney was forced to issue stock to raise enough money to complete *Fantasia*, and issuing stock meant the Disney company was no longer his. Eventually, the stock would be bought by pension funds, institutional investors, and tycoons like Sid Bass, Irwin Jacobs, and Ivan Boesky. Disney did not live to see the struggle that ended with raiders almost dismembering the company. He did live, however, to see his studio finally hit it big with *Mary Poppins* (for a time, the sixth biggest-grossing movie ever) and, before that, to realize another of the many ideas everyone told him was crazy: Disneyland.

BY THE TIME DISNEY CAME TO Orlando, looking for a place to build a second theme park, he had become a shrewd and canny businessman, and he had also been burned. He had learned the importance of controlling his product. Disney World was his second child, and he meant to avoid all the mistakes he'd made with the first. Those mistakes—the reason Disney World is 20 miles from downtown Orlando on its own

tract of 28,000 acres—all involved the same thing: letting others have control. When he was building Disneyland, for instance, a local utility group appealed to his belief in private enterprise and persuaded him to let the company supply him with electricity. (Disney was such a staunch Republican that when L.B.J. decorated him with a medal in 1964, he wore a Goldwater button on his lapel.) Then one day he went down to the park and was horrified to see high-tension wires converging on his domain. The company refused to bury them unless he paid for it. (He did.) When security guards from another outside firm failed to show the right attitude toward his guests (never "customers"), Disney fired them, hired his own, and sent every Disney employee (actually, people who work at Disney World and Disneyland are never called employees but, rather, "cast members") to the University of Disneyland, in Anaheim, to make sure they remained friendly, no matter how tired they were. What Disney wanted was to do things his way.

Florida let him. After he'd obtained everything he could through private means, he got the rest of what he wanted through the Florida legislature: control over the land. The bill Florida passed in 1967 to welcome Disney is called the Reedy Creek Improvement District Act. What the act did was set up a special taxing region called the Reedy Creek Improvement District (after a small stream on the property), which was authorized to provide its own pest and flood control, waste-removal systems, fire protection, and building codes. The last provision was especially important to Disney. The Disney company says it asked for the Reedy legislation to remove from Orange and Osceola counties the burden of supplying an infrastructure, and allow Disney to build its own state-of-the-art structures. But according to an Orange County official, Disney really wanted Reedy Creek so it could avoid the lengthy process of obtaining building permits from the county. This is how Disney continues to beat its competitors to the punch. Its Disney-MGM Studios, for instance, opened months before Universal's theme park, 15 miles to the north, even though Universal broke ground a year before Disney did. Disney has always been faster than people thought possible. When the construction firm originally hired to build Disney World said it would not be able to finish on time, Disney fired them and hired its own team, headed by a former general who'd overseen the Normandy invasion and a former admiral—both graduates of M.I.T.—and met the deadline by working 24-hour shifts.

Indeed, Reedy Creek is not only immune to local building codes and permits, it is also free of having to pay impact fees; the impact fee on the average house built in Orange County today is $4,400. The fee for a Disney hotel with 7,000 rooms, Bill Donegan figures, would come to more than $18 million.

ON THE OTHER HAND, Reedy Creek contributes a lot of money to the local county governments. Besides levying taxes within its boundaries (Disney paying for Disney), it pays property taxes to Orange and Osceola counties as well. To date, Disney has paid $181 million in taxes to Orange County alone, half of which has been allocated to its schools. So, despite comparisons to the Vatican, Reedy Creek is not quite independent. And while there may be other special taxing districts, none of them are as famous, rich, or spectacularly successful as Reedy Creek.

In fact, the very success of Disney World has become its particular problem. Disney likes to point out that the phenomenal growth that has quadrupled the population of Orlando since 1960 would have occurred with or without Disney. One of the reasons Walt Disney chose the Orlando area was that growth was forecast. Disney is proud of the fact that it's the area's largest employer (more than 31,500 jobs). It also points out that the average visitor to central Florida spends only 4 of 13 days at Disney World. And yet—because of Disney World's hotel-building boom (Orlando already has more hotel rooms than Manhattan, but the area's occupancy rate is 81%, which is very high); its addition of a third theme park (the Disney-MGM Studios); its water parks (Typhoon Lagoon, River Country), campgrounds, and nightclubs; and its avowed intention to make Disney World the center of convention business in the Southeast—it appears to folks beneath the castle that Disney wants

to create a resort so all-inclusive that a guest never needs to leave it for anything but the plane home. This makes perfect sense for Disney, but it makes everyone around Disney World, particularly the hotels and attractions that live on Disney's spillover, nervous.

All this growth raises the question of who should pay for Disney World's astonishing success. The obvious problem is Orange County traffic. Because Disney does not have to pay impact fees, Orange County persuaded it in 1988 to chip in $1.3 million to improve the roads that feed into the highway leading to the Magic Kingdom (the infamous I-4); in exchange, Orange County made a matching grant and promised not to sue Reedy Creek for the next seven years. This was called the Interlocal Agreement. Bill Donegan, who says he'd have signed the original Reedy Creek Improvement District Act, voted no on the Interlocal Agreement. "It's a matter of balance. Quality of life," he says. "Disney-bashing is now a way of life."

That noted, most visitors still feel a thrill when they realize that they are finally coming to, yes, Walt Disney World! The first signs of Disney World are two huge hotels, looming above the highway, from whose pediments two gigantic swans, two gigantic dolphins, and several gigantic seashells look down like Ozymandias on the passing scene. Even before learning that they are the work of Michael Graves (Disney has hired some very fancy architects for its hotels), I thought, "Now, this is fun."

It's even more fun to get off I-4 and turn up a winding road into Disney's green domain (containing not only theme parks, hotels, campgrounds, lakes, and 7,200 acres of wilderness preserve but also a tiny village where Disney employees live). The road curves through dense woods to a sort of turnpike toll station (where you get a $4 parking ticket), ending in one of three immense parking lots (one for each park), where a cheerful Disney employee—I mean, cast member—directs you to a parking space. Then you get into a long train of what look like linked golf carts and are taken to the entrance of whichever park you're visiting: Epcot, the Magic Kingdom, or the Disney-MGM Studios.

Of the three theme parks in Disney World—the Magic Kingdom, opened in 1971, Epcot Center in 1982, and the Disney-MGM Studios in 1989—the newest is the smallest. Its parking lot holds 4,500 cars, while Epcot Center and the Magic Kingdom each have parking spaces for 12,000. (This is why the Disney-MGM Studios parking lot closed as early as 8:30 AM recently—when it fills up, the doors close.) The moment you enter Disney World you have the sensation that you're in the hands of invisible engineers. The experience is always fluid. The long lines do keep moving, and every line has a sign beside it saying how long the wait is.

WHAT YOU WAIT IN LINE for varies from park to park. The Studios are a re-creation of a Hollywood back lot, including directors who ask you if you want to be in their movie. Epcot consists of corporate showcases clustered near the entrance and a chain of 11 national pavilions ringing a lagoon. The pavilions are clever pastiches of indigenous landmarks (the Eiffel Tower, a Japanese teahouse, a Moroccan Casbah), most of which contain shops, restaurants, and theaters where films about each country are shown. The films are free; the shops and restaurants are not, and the feeling that you are in the hands of expert people-movers is surpassed only by the feeling that an awful lot of money is changing hands rapidly.

A cynical friend had warned me that Epcot Center is basically a big shopping mall, but it's really more than that. For one thing, it's full of performers, and the performers at all three parks are as important an element of the experience as the physical plant itself; acrobats, singers, comedians, and storytellers are constantly assembling, dispersing, and reappearing as you walk from one attraction to the next. The Magic Kingdom, in fact, has a famous subterranean system of corridors so that the cowboys, for instance, don't have to walk through the audience to stage their gunfights. Nor, for that matter, do the people who supply the restaurants; Disney didn't want his guests seeing Coke being delivered. The Magic Kingdom is, after all, supposed to be an illusion.

It's also curiously small, and smallness is part of the strategy—to make it toylike. Frontierland blends imperceptibly into Fantasyland, which is just around the corner from Tomorrowland, which leads you to Main Street, U.S.A., at the end of which is Cinderella Castle, where Cruella De Vil is singing a torch song on the castle steps while cowboys are having a shootout in Frontierland, a Mississippi steamboat is coming round the bend of a tiny river, and a brass band is playing near the Liberty Oak. The Magic Kingdom is the most intimate, shopworn, and emotionally charged of the three theme parks. Though they share the same cleanliness and the same extraordinary cleverness—Disney World, like God, is in the details—the Magic Kingdom is the most Disney of the parks. Only twice was the illusion shattered, when I noticed very small things: a broken door handle on the monorail; an attendant telling a man that his daughters weren't allowed to stand on the railing to watch Cruella De Vil—odd moments when reality intruded for just a second.

Mostly, though, the illusion holds as you walk around. And you walk around a lot. Indeed, the paradox of Disney World is that once you arrive, the chief cause of Orlando's troubles with Disney—the traffic that has filled county roads to the brim— completely vanishes. In Disney World you go by foot, monorail, or boat. (There are lots of lakes here; water was an important part of Disney's dream. Ironically, the big lake he admired from the air proved, on close inspection, to have brown water, which, the Disney people feared, visitors would think was dirty. So they drained the lake, dug up the muck, replaced it with sand, and filled it back up again.) You walk in and continue to walk—all day, into the night. "Do people faint?" I asked someone the second day of my visit. "No," she said, "but they do get sunburnt."

The sun here is so strong that just before opening, the Magic Kingdom had to be repainted because the colors that created the desired mood in Anaheim were all wrong in Orlando's clear glare. In Disney's original plan Epcot lay beneath a glass dome to keep out excess heat and humidity, but the dome never materialized. So, entering Epcot, I was out under the big, blue Florida sky in a large park of broad lawns, impeccable flower beds, architectural fantasies, and fountains—a sort of permanent World's Fair. Epcot, actually, is an acronym that stands for Experimental Prototype Community of Tomorrow. Disney, who thought of his parks as always changing, always improving—who got pleasure from knowing that the trees he planted would get bigger and more beautiful—wrote: "Epcot . . . will never cease to be a living blueprint of the future, where people actually live a life they can't find anywhere else in the world today." Besides a dome, it was to have had schools, churches, offices, apartments, stores, parks, golf courses, marinas, a monorail, a vacuum-tube trash-disposal system, a central computer controlling everything from streetlights to hotel reservations, and petless residents who behaved—as visitors to Disneyland were expected to—"properly." But Epcot has turned out to be what Star Wars was for Reagan: only a dream.

In a small theater off the town square of the Magic Kingdom, you used to be able to see a film about Disney, narrated by Walt himself. In it was a sketch of his proposal for Epcot. Set in a flat plain surrounded by the glowing circles of what might be monorails, its skyscrapers rise into the sky exactly as we thought they would, back in the '50s, in cities of the future. The reality could hardly be more ironic. Epcot has pinewoods, manicured flower beds, and perfectly circulating lakes and streams; Orlando provides the skyscrapers—off in the distance, on a broad, flat plain. It's a prototype of the problems that plague all Florida cities in the last decade of the century: where to put the cars, how to provide housing for the poor, how to control sprawl. (Bill Donegan says that after he voiced his complaints about all this at an urban affairs conference at Harvard, an official from Cleveland told him he envied Orlando's problems.) These are the problems of every place that is not an amusement park.

For that, to my astonishment when I finally got there, is all Disney World really is: an amusement park. A very nice amusement park. *Very* well done, but still, for all the brouhaha—the symbolism that politicians, intellectuals, and commentators find irresistible; the staggering financial success; the brilliant engineering and problem solving—just an amusement park. (In fact, there were so many English accents the day I went that I felt I was at

Brighton. England surpassed Canada in 1989 as the country that sent the most visitors, followed by Germany, Brazil, and Mexico.) It's a place to spend the day walking from one exhibit to another, buying postcards and souvenirs, eating ice cream, watching movies about France or China in circular theaters surrounded by giant screens, looking at masses of other people (strangely self-edited, as if Disney had chosen them, too), strolling past small children (and adults) being photographed with Pluto. ("How does he breathe?" I asked the attendant. "The way a dog breathes," he answered. "I mean the person inside," I said. "That's not a person," he explained. "That's Pluto.")

I**T'S A PLACE WHERE** litter is picked up immediately if anyone is so disreputable as to drop something on the ground, and where, standing on a Venetian bridge watching a crowd watch a juggler in the street by the Doge's Palace, I tapped on the balustrade and wondered, What is all this made of? (Fiberglass.) It's a place where you see kids in crazy hats (my favorite: the Donald Duck baseball cap, with a brim that quacks when squeezed) and where you'll overhear a boy standing next to you in line suddenly gasp, "Quick! Run! There's my parents!" It's—this came as a shock—a very big amusement park.

And yet it's not really just an amusement park—we all know that. The phrase Walt Disney concocted is "themed entertainment experience," which is actually a much more accurate description. There are no bumper cars here. This is a three-dimensional representation of the art world Disney created, and its appeal is subconscious and finally irresistible. (Emperor Hirohito of Japan used to wear, on informal occasions, a Mickey Mouse watch.) Schickel says that Disney removed the "secrets and silences" from childhood—subjected us all to the same sentimental kitsch. And it's true that Disney has a hold on childhood; one mother I know complained that a trip to Disney World seems to have become an American child's *right*. The Disney company knows this. The reason that Disney releases its classic animation features every seven years is that seven years is time enough for a new crop of children to grow up. And one of the factors in Disney's revival after the doldrums and confusion following Walt's death was the simple desire of a new generation of parents to take their kids to the Disney productions *they* had seen as children. Some product! Disney deals in family, childhood, nature, fairy tales, and the sort of timeless America that a lot of people feel vanished with *Son of Flubber*. (Until the mid-'70s, women were discouraged from wearing halter tops in Disneyland, and alcoholic drinks have been served here only recently, after dark, at large corporate parties.) The cleanliness, the sexlessness of Disney's world, is part of its appeal. The joke around the company—when Disney was alive, in fact—was that Walt himself could never have worked at Disneyland. He had a mustache, liked a stiff drink at the end of the day, and swore. To this day, cast members are forbidden to have facial hair.

DURING THE UNCERTAIN years following Disney's death, when company executives still felt him looking over their shoulders, everyone was aware that while the country itself had changed, Disney had to remain true to itself or lose its identity altogether. Faced with the fact that a hit movie for kids was now *Porky's*, Walt's son-in-law, Ron Miller, launched a new company in 1983—Touchstone Pictures—to enable Disney to keep up with the changing times without surrendering its special place in the American mind. (Even so, its first picture was *Splash*. Today there are some far less Disneyesque films on the market.) Everyone realized that Disney stood, ineluctably, for certain things. Things that give you goose bumps. The Disney company is so closely identified with a certain American gentility that when Saul Steinberg, the Wall Street investor, held a meeting of his staff in 1984 to consider a buyout of the company (with the backing of Michael Milken, the one-time junk-bond king), he was warned that news of a Jewish raider acquiring Disney and selling off the pieces might produce an anti-Semitic backlash. The raid proceeded anyway, and fending it off caused a shakeup in the Disney organization that not only reunited the two sides of the feuding family but also resulted in the

hiring of Michael Eisner and the late Frank Wells as chairman and president. The rest, as they say, is history. On January 29, 1987, Snow White and the Seven Dwarfs paraded onto the floor of the New York Stock Exchange to dramatize Disney's highest-ever first-quarter earnings.

Each year, the current president of Walt Disney Attractions gives Orange and Osceola counties a "State of Our World" address, outlining what Disney is considering over the next 5 or 10 years. There is still a lot of the 28,000 acres to be developed. Some of it is bog, but even so, what remains can't be covered with theme parks alone. Disney is thinking about a major new shopping mall, an office development, and in 10 years, perhaps, another park. ("No one really knows what Disney is thinking," one local official says.) In the meantime, its neighbors try to deal with their own future.

The feeling in the surrounding area seems often to be one of paranoia—that Disney is smarter, faster, and bigger than anyone else, and it is trying to duplicate in Reedy Creek anything a tourist might leave the Disney grounds to find. Reedy Creek comptroller Ray Maxwell scoffs at this idea. "There is plenty for everyone," he says. Indeed, he points out, Orlando makes so much money selling to Disney World itself that even if tourists *were* shuttled directly from the airport to Disney World and back, it would mean just as much business for Orange County, with none of the wear and tear. As far as the roads go, he says that most of the highways around Disney World are funded by the federal and state governments, not by the county. When Orange County refused to improve Route 535, a road Disney employees use to get to work, the state repaved it, believing that the public would benefit from improving the access of Disney's employees to their workplace. The geographical boundaries of Reedy Creek are easy to ascertain—they're fixed with a surveyor's exactitude—but the political boundaries are not.

To a commissioner like Donegan, Disney World is an arrogant city-state escaping its fair share of the costs of growth around Orlando. To Ray Maxwell, this is sheer jealousy: Disney is the reason for the incredible prosperity. (The assessed value of Osceola County was $500 million in 1974 and $5 *billion* in 1990.) The growth of Orlando, he says, is no greater than the growth in other parts of the state. The infrastructure Disney built when it arrived in Reedy Creek was infrastructure Orange and Osceola counties could not have provided themselves.

But the squabbles between Disney and central Florida are over something less tangible than money: culture. Disney executives were amazed when they came here to buy land in 1965 and one of the largest property owners sold them 7,500 acres on a handshake (a handshake he did not renege on when he learned the identity of his buyer). That was the way things were done in Florida in those days; the property owner only wanted permission to graze his cattle on the land till Disney opened. Florida—central Florida, certainly—was then a culture of ranchers, farmers, sleepy county courthouses, and timber companies. Now Disney sells an estimated 30 million tickets a year (the company no longer gives out attendance figures, because they affect the price of its stock), and people come here from all over America, and the world, to spend vacation time. (Summer, Christmas, and spring break are the busiest times; Monday is the busiest day, when people begin their vacations with fresh energy.) These people have caused change. Change would have come to Orlando anyway, no doubt, but Disney World has become its embodiment. A friend who has lived in Orlando since 1946 explains it this way: "Disney put us on the map. But I'm not sure I want to be on the map."

I **KNOW JUST WHAT HE MEANS.** At the same time, having finally come here, I'm impressed. Disney World is so well run and so well thought out—so technologically and environmentally sophisticated—that after I'd been here awhile I began to think the problem was with Orange County, not Reedy Creek: that maybe Disney should run Orlando, too. (A thought that also occurred to Ray Bradbury, who was so dazzled by Disneyland, he asked Walt Disney to run for mayor of Los Angeles. Disney thought it over, then replied, "Why should I run for mayor when I'm already king?") But as smart and innovative as the Disney operation is, it's not going to run Orlando or Kissimmee. It's a corporation run for the benefit of its stockholders—a testament to the ability of private enterprise. Here is everything technology, expertise, and energy can bring to bear on a large piece of property surrounded by the chaos of millions of people in pursuit of money, retirement, power, and golf.

That is why I lingered in the Magic Kingdom longer than I thought I would—mesmerized in particular by the town square—and finally went upstairs in City Hall to ask a Disney publicist, Pam Parks, about Disney's relationship with the real world.

"Disney-bashing waxes and wanes," she said, smiling. "I would be astonished if the local politicians supported Disney without reservation." Feeling that I was not going to get any more out of her about the political nuances of the situation, I inquired about a story I'd heard outside the gates: that Walt Disney, lover of technology and the future, believed in cryogenics (freezing the dead so that if a cure for what killed them is developed years from now they can be thawed out and brought back to life). "I must ask you a crazy question," I said. "Is Disney frozen?"

"His nephew Roy was here with his daughter a while ago," Parks replied, "and that's one of the things *he* said: 'Can you believe people actually think he's freeze-dried and lying in the castle?' "

"In the castle!" I said. The idea was immediately appealing: Disney up in one of the turrets with Cinderella, frozen in a futuristic fridge. This park, as Richard Schickel points out, is so much the ultimate expression of one man's ideas and taste that a frozen Disney would not be entirely out of place. I went downstairs and sat on a bench beneath the portico of City Hall to examine my Mickey Mouse hat (a yarmulke with two ears sticking out; you can have your name embroidered on the back, for free), write postcards (Snow White and Dopey), and watch the Whitmanesque spectacle of all these healthy, well-built families walking in tasteful, all-cotton sports clothes. (Shirts and shoes must be worn at all times, but there are no fat people in too-tight shorts.) I sat there for a long time, strangely happy. It was spellbinding: a sort of *Volkfest,* a huge swarm of European and American families—the people who came here to escape Europe, settled Australia, and would like to go next to the moon, no doubt, or Mars.

To be honest, I'd expected something different. Fear, loathing, a clammy dread—all combined to produce what I call red-alert insomnia: the sensation that someone is pouring battery acid through your brain. I'd even reread *The Education of Henry Adams* before coming, to prepare myself for a cultural epiphany, if not apocalypse. I reread *The Education* because, after seeing the Chicago Exposition of 1893—the one Walt's father helped put up—and the Paris Exposition of 1900, Adams titled a chapter in his autobiography "The Dynamo and the Virgin." The Dynamo was the symbol of the new, modern, industrial state—the one we've been living in since 1900. The Virgin was the symbol of Eve, the feminine principle, the presiding spirit of his beloved Middle Ages. Had Adams been alive to see Disney World, he would have had to rename his chapter "The Mouse and the Virgin." But Disney World wasn't exactly apocalyptic, now that I was here to see for myself. It was just a very nice amusement park that families can come to together. (So important to family life, the family vacation.) It was also more old-fashioned than new. The future wasn't what impressed me here. The space rides and deep-sea laboratory seemed sort of corny, what might excite a 10-year-old. It was what I was looking at now that cast a spell: the past. Specifically, this charming replica of a square in some midwestern town at the beginning of the century—not far from Marceline, Mis-

souri, perhaps. (Every brick, shingle, and gas lamp on Main Street, U.S.A., Disney had explained, is only five-eighths of its true size. "This cost more," he said, "but made the street a toy, and the imagination can play more freely with a toy. Besides, people like to think their world is somehow more grown-up than Papa's was." Shrewd man!)

The lights came on and twinkled in the trees. The stores were jammed. The recorded waltzes played, while poor Pluto—whoever was inside it—continued to stand in the garden to one side of City Hall, hugging small children, who sometimes beamed and sometimes panicked at his embrace. It was a set for *The Music Man.* It was the whole sentimental dream of Victorian life, of the American Midwest, that deepened and deepened its spell, there in the central Florida dusk. And its final irony is that this place, this wholly artificial town square, provided before my eyes the street life—the human interaction, the mingling—that our car-cities of the present have completely erased from contemporary existence. One gets in a car or flies in a plane many miles to come here to find the *gemütlichkeit* that cars and planes have obliterated. Disney World, which specializes in the past (Main Street, steamboats, cowboys, castle) and the future (Voyage to Mars, George Lucas, lasers, Tomorrowland), leaves the present to Orange County. Which is why I sat there, wondering how I was going to get back to the parking lot, get in the car, and drive home.

—Andrew Holleran

DISNEY: FURTHER READING

STILL THE MOST PERCEPTIVE book on Disney is *The Disney Version,* by Richard Schickel (Simon & Schuster, 1985). Disney's art is featured in *Disneyland: The Inside Story,* by Randy Bright (Harry N. Abrams), and a comprehensive history of the great Disney animation tradition is provided in *Disney Animation: The Illusion of Life,* by Frank Thomas and Ollie Johnston (Abbeville, 1981). For a good read about Disney and other animators, look for *Of Mice and Magic* (NAL Dutton, 1987), by Leonard Maltin. *Walt Disney: An American Original* (Pocket Books, 1980), by Bob Thomas, is full of anecdotes about the development of WDW, and Marc Elliot's *Walt Disney: Hollywood's Dark Prince* (Birch Lane Press, 1993) is a controversial look at the life of WDW's creator.

INDEX

NOTES

NOTES

NOTES

NOTES

The only guide to explore a Disney World® you've never seen before:

The one for grown-ups.

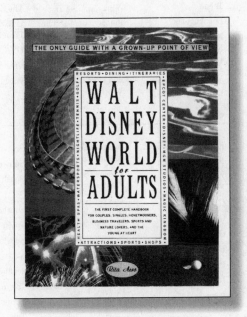

THE ONLY GUIDE WITH A GROWN-UP POINT OF VIEW

RESORTS • DINING • ITINERARIES

HEALTH SPAS • WATERSPORTS • NIGHTLIFE • TENNIS • GOLF

EPCOT CENTER • DISNEY-MGM STUDIOS • MAGIC KINGDOM

WALT DISNEY WORLD *for* ADULTS

THE FIRST COMPLETE HANDBOOK FOR COUPLES, SINGLES, HONEYMOONERS, BUSINESS TRAVELERS, SPORTS AND NATURE LOVERS, AND THE YOUNG AT HEART

• ATTRACTIONS • SPORTS • SHOPS •

Rita Aero

0-679-02490-5 $14.00 ($18.50 Can)

This is the only guide written specifically for the millions of adults who visit Walt Disney World® each year <u>without</u> kids. Upscale, sophisticated, packed full of facts and maps, *Walt Disney World® for Adults* provides up-to-date information on hotels, restaurants, sports facilities, and health clubs, as well as unique itineraries for adults. With *Walt Disney World® for Adults* in hand, you'll get the most out of one of the world's most fascinating, most complex playgrounds.

At bookstores everywhere, or call **1-800-533-6478.**

Fodor's

Fodor's Travel Publications

Available at bookstores everywhere, or call 1–800–533–6478, 24 hours a day.

Gold Guides

U.S.

Alaska

Arizona

Boston

California

Cape Cod, Martha's Vineyard, Nantucket

The Carolinas & the Georgia Coast

Chicago

Colorado

Florida

Hawai'i

Las Vegas, Reno, Tahoe

Los Angeles

Maine, Vermont, New Hampshire

Maui & Lāna'i

Miami & the Keys

New England

New Orleans

New York City

Pacific North Coast

Philadelphia & the Pennsylvania Dutch Country

The Rockies

San Diego

San Francisco

Santa Fe, Taos, Albuquerque

Seattle & Vancouver

The South

U.S. & British Virgin Islands

USA

Virginia & Maryland

Washington, D.C.

Foreign

Australia

Austria

The Bahamas

Belize & Guatemala

Bermuda

Canada

Cancún, Cozumel, Yucatán Peninsula

Caribbean

China

Costa Rica

Cuba

The Czech Republic & Slovakia

Eastern & Central Europe

Europe

Florence, Tuscany & Umbria

France

Germany

Great Britain

Greece

Hong Kong

India

Ireland

Israel

Italy

Japan

London

Madrid & Barcelona

Mexico

Montréal & Québec City

Moscow, St. Petersburg, Kiev

The Netherlands, Belgium & Luxembourg

New Zealand

Norway

Nova Scotia, New Brunswick, Prince Edward Island

Paris

Portugal

Provence & the Riviera

Scandinavia

Scotland

Singapore

South Africa

South America

Southeast Asia

Spain

Sweden

Switzerland

Thailand

Tokyo

Toronto

Turkey

Vienna & the Danube

Fodor's Special-Interest Guides

Caribbean Ports of Call

The Complete Guide to America's National Parks

Family Adventures

Gay Guide to the USA

Halliday's New England Food Explorer

Halliday's New Orleans Food Explorer

Healthy Escapes

Kodak Guide to Shooting Great Travel Pictures

Net Travel

Nights to Imagine

Rock & Roll Traveler USA

Sunday in New York

Sunday in San Francisco

Walt Disney World, Universal Studios and Orlando

Walt Disney World for Adults

Where Should We Take the Kids? California

Where Should We Take the Kids? Northeast

Worldwide Cruises and Ports of Call

Special Series

Affordables
Caribbean
Europe
Florida
France
Germany
Great Britain
Italy
London
Paris

Fodor's Bed & Breakfasts and Country Inns
America
California
The Mid-Atlantic
New England
The Pacific Northwest
The South
The Southwest
The Upper Great Lakes

The Berkeley Guides
California
Central America
Eastern Europe
Europe
France
Germany & Austria
Great Britain & Ireland
Italy
London
Mexico
New York City
Pacific Northwest & Alaska
Paris
San Francisco

Compass American Guides
Arizona
Canada
Chicago
Colorado
Hawaii
Idaho
Hollywood
Las Vegas

Maine
Manhattan
Montana
New Mexico
New Orleans
Oregon
San Francisco
Santa Fe
South Carolina
South Dakota
Southwest
Texas
Utah
Virginia
Washington
Wine Country
Wisconsin
Wyoming

Fodor's Citypacks
Atlanta
Hong Kong
London
New York City
Paris
Rome
San Francisco
Washington, D.C.

Fodor's Español
California
Caribe Occidental
Caribe Oriental
Gran Bretaña
Londres
Mexico
Nueva York
Paris

Fodor's Exploring Guides
Australia
Boston & New England
Britain
California
Caribbean
China
Egypt
Florence & Tuscany
Florida

France
Germany
Ireland
Israel
Italy
Japan
London
Mexico
Moscow & St. Petersburg
New York City
Paris
Prague
Provence
Rome
San Francisco
Scotland
Singapore & Malaysia
Spain
Thailand
Turkey
Venice

Fodor's Flashmaps
Boston
New York
San Francisco
Washington, D.C.

Fodor's Pocket Guides
Acapulco
Atlanta
Barbados
Jamaica
London
New York City
Paris
Prague
Puerto Rico
Rome
San Francisco
Washington, D.C.

Mobil Travel Guides
America's Best Hotels & Restaurants
California & the West
Frequent Traveler's Guide to Major Cities
Great Lakes
Mid-Atlantic

Northeast
Northwest & Great Plains
Southeast
Southwest & South Central

Rivages Guides
Bed and Breakfasts of Character and Charm in France
Hotels and Country Inns of Character and Charm in France
Hotels and Country Inns of Character and Charm in Italy
Hotels and Country Inns of Character and Charm in Paris
Hotels and Country Inns of Character and Charm in Portugal
Hotels and Country Inns of Character and Charm in Spain

Short Escapes
Britain
France
New England
Near New York City

Fodor's Sports
Golf Digest's Best Places to Play
Skiing USA
USA Today The Complete Four Sport Stadium Guide

Fodor's Vacation Planners
Great American Learning Vacations
Great American Sports & Adventure Vacations
Great American Vacations
Great American Vacations for Travelers with Disabilities
National Parks and Seashores of the East
National Parks of the West

CNN✈

Airport Network

Your
Window
To The
World
While You're
On The
Road

Keep in touch when you're traveling. Before you take off, tune in to CNN Airport Network. Now available in major airports across America, CNN Airport Network provides nonstop news, sports, business, weather and lifestyle programming. Both domestic and international. All piloted by the top-flight global resources of CNN. All up-to-the minute reporting. And just for travelers, CNN Airport Network features two daily Fodor's specials. "Travel Fact" provides enlightening, useful travel trivia, while "What's Happening" covers upcoming events in major cities worldwide. So why be bored waiting to board? TIME FLIES WHEN YOU'RE WATCHING THE WORLD THROUGH THE WINDOW OF CNN AIRPORT NETWORK!

Escape to ancient cities and

journey to   *exotic islands with*

CNN Travel Guide, a wealth of valuable advice. Host

Valerie Voss will take you to

all of your favorite destinations,

including those off the beaten

path. Tune-in to your passport to the world.

CNN TRAVEL GUIDE

SATURDAY 12:30 PMᴇᴛ   SUNDAY 4:30 PMᴇᴛ

WHEREVER YOU TRAVEL, *H*ELP IS NEVER FAR AWAY.

From planning your trip to providing travel assistance along the way, American Express® Travel Service Offices are always there to help.

Disney

American Express Travel Service
Epcot Center
Walt Disney World Resort
Lake Buena Vista
407/827-7500

American Express Travel Service
2 West Church Street, Suite 1
Sun Bank Center
Orlando
407/843-0004

Travel

http://www.americanexpress.com/travel

For the office nearest you, call 1-800-YES-AMEX.

Wet 'n Wild®

$3 OFF

Present this coupon and save $3.00 off the regular all-day adult or child admission price. Coupon good for up to six people. Not to be used in conjunction with any other discounted offer or afternoon pricing.

Expires 12/31/97

Wet'n Wild®

$3 OFF

Present this coupon and save $3.00 off the regular all-day adult or child admission price. Coupon good for up to six people. Not to be used in conjunction with any other discounted offer or afternoon pricing.

Expires 12/31/97

It's a Whole New Deal!

Moscow On Ice Live!
Star-studded ice show with elaborate sets, stunning costumes, dazzling lighting and music! **New Varieté Internationale**

Highly acclaimed European acrobatic acts! **Reptile Discovery** Entertaining and informative new show featuring "Banana Boy," a 14-foot albino python.

CYPRESS GARDENS.
WINTER HAVEN, FLORIDA
Florida's First Theme Park • Est. 1936

Located off U.S. 27, 22 miles south of I-4 halfway between Orlando & Tampa. For more information call: **800-282-2123**.

$3²⁵ OFF
Adult/Child
ADMISSIONS

Not valid with other discounts or on purchase of multi-visit passes or special ticket events. Limit six guests per coupon.

Expires 12/31/97. #819

Two Great Ways to Save!

For all of 1997, each single day, adult ticket purchaser may bring in one child (age 6 - 12) FREE.

New Lower **Senior Rates!**

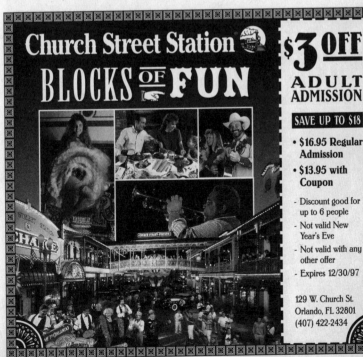

Church Street Station
BLOCKS OF FUN

$3 OFF
ADULT ADMISSION

SAVE UP TO $18

- **$16.95 Regular Admission**
- **$13.95 with Coupon**

- Discount good for up to 6 people
- Not valid New Year's Eve
- Not valid with any other offer
- Expires 12/30/97

129 W. Church St. Orlando, FL 32801 (407) 422-2434

5370A/5371C

$3⁰⁰ OFF

All-Day Studio Pass
Regular admission price $38.50 (plus tax)

RIDE THE MOVIES!

Universal Studios Florida®, the only place on earth where you can Ride The Movies®. Guests can thrill to Back To The Future®...The Ride™, Kongfrontation®, Earthquake®, E.T.®, A Day In The Park With Barney™ and TERMINATOR 2: 3-D BATTLE ACROSS TIME™!

20% OFF

Food and beverages purchased for your party (up to six) at Studio Stars Restaurant or Finnegan's Pub after 4pm.

Present this coupon to your server when ordering. Tax and gratuity not included. This coupon has no cash value and is not valid with any other specials or discounts including happy hour pricing. Valid through 12/31/97.

$3⁰⁰ OFF

**All-Day
Studio Pass**

$3.00 discount valid through 12/31/97. Coupon valid for up to 6 people and must be presented at the time of purchase. This offer has no cash value and is not valid with any other special discounts. Subject to change without notice. Parking Fee not included.

6183920001990

DINE HOLLYWOOD-STYLE

Be a part of the scene at the Studio Stars Restaurant (across from Ghostbusters®) or drop into Finnegan's Pub for Irish spirits, ales and entertainment. Your 20% discount is good for a party of six after 4pm! Remember to present this coupon when ordering.

Cannot be used in conjunction with any other promotion - including happy hour pricing.